CW00661661

SOCIAL SECURITY LEGI
SUPPLEMENT 202(

General Editor
Nick Wikeley, M.A. (Cantab)

Commentary by
Ian Hooker, LL.B.
Formerly Lecturer in Law, University of Nottingham
Formerly Chairman, Social Security Appeal Tribunals

John Mesher, B.A., B.C.L. (Oxon), LL.M. (Yale)
Retired Judge of the Upper Tribunal

Edward Mitchell, LL.B.
Judge of the Upper Tribunal

Richard Poynter B.C.L., M.A. (Oxon)
Judge of the Upper Tribunal

Mark Rowland, LL.B.
Retired Judge of the Upper Tribunal

Christopher Ward, M.A. (Cantab)
Judge of the Upper Tribunal

Nick Wikeley, M.A. (Cantab)
Judge of the Upper Tribunal,
Emeritus Professor of Law, University of Southampton

Consultant Editor
Child Poverty Action Group

SWEET & MAXWELL  THOMSON REUTERS

Published in 2021 by Thomson Reuters,
trading as Sweet & Maxwell.
Registered in England & Wales. Company No. 1679046.
Registered office 5 Canada Square, Canary Wharf, London E14 5AQ.

Typeset by Wright and Round Ltd., Gloucester
Printed and bound by CPI Group (UK) Ltd, Croydon, CR0 4YY

For further information on our products and services,
visit www.sweetandmaxwell.co.uk

No natural forests were destroyed to make this product.
Only farmed timber was used and re-planted.

A CIP catalogue record for this book is
available from the British Library

Print ISBN: 978–0–41–408712–5
Ebook ISBN 978–0–414–08714–9
Print and Ebook ISBN: 978–0–414–08713–2

Crown copyright material is reproduced with the permission
of the Controller of HMSO and the Queen's Printer for
Scotland.
All rights reserved. No part of this publication may
be reproduced or transmitted in any form or by any means,
or stored in any retrieval system of any nature without prior
written permission, except for permitted fair dealing under the
Copyright, Designs and Patents Act 1988, or in accordance
with the terms of a licence issued by the Copyright Licensing
Agency in respect of photocopying and/or reprographic
reproduction. Application for permission for other use
of copyright material including permission to reproduce
extracts in other published works shall be made to the publishers.
Full acknowledgement of author, publisher and source must
be given.
Material is contained in this publication for which publishing
permission has been sought, and for which copyright is
acknowledged. Permission to reproduce such material
cannot be granted by the publishers and application
must be made to the copyright holder.

Thomson Reuters, the Thomson Reuters Logo and
Sweet & Maxwell® are trademarks of Thomson Reuters.

Commentators have asserted their moral rights under
the Copyright, Designs and Patents Act 1988 to be identified
as the authors of the commentary in this Volume.

© 2021 Thomson Reuters

PREFACE

This is the Supplement to the 2020/21 edition of the five-volume work, *Social Security Legislation*, which was published in September 2020. Part I of this Supplement contains new legislation, presented in the same format as in the main volumes. Parts II, III, IV, V and VI contain the standard updating material—a separate Part for each volume of the main work–which amends the legislative text and key aspects of the commentary, drawing attention to important recent case law, so as to be up to date as at January 1, 2021 (we have selected a slightly later effective date than usual for the Supplement for obvious Brexit-related reasons). Finally, Part VII gives some notice of changes forthcoming between January 2021 and the date to which the main work (2021/22 edition) will be up to date (mid-April 2021) along with the April 2021 benefit rates.

The many updating changes in this Supplement include both the text and analysis of the key Brexit-related provisions on social security, namely those in the Immigration and Social Security Co-ordination (EU Withdrawal) Act 2020, the European Union (Future Relationship) Act 2020, the Protocol on Social Security Co-ordination and the Citizens' Rights (Application Deadline and Temporary Protection) (EU Exit) Regulations 2020, as well as significant amendments to the European Union (Withdrawal) Act 2018. The text also covers further case law developments both from the Court of Justice of the European Union and domestic courts and tribunals impacting on the right to reside. As ever, there are important developments in the Upper Tribunal jurisprudence relating to the descriptors for both personal independence payment (PIP) and employment and support allowance (ESA) (appeals for these benefits together form the great bulk of social security cases heard by the First-tier Tribunal (Social Entitlement Chamber)). We also include Coronavirus-related amendments to both substantive statutory provisions governing a wide range of social security benefits (including statutory sick pay) and procedural rules for appeals. Other new legislation includes the Childcare Act 2016 and associated secondary legislation, now brought within the jurisdiction of the Social Entitlement Chamber, and significant changes to devolved social security provision in Scotland including Carer's Assistance (Young Carer Grants) and Scottish Child Payments.

As always, we welcome comments from those who use this Supplement. Please address these to the General Editor, Nick Wikeley, c/o School of Law, The University of Southampton, Highfield, Southampton SO17 1BJ (njw@soton.ac.uk).

Ian Hooker
John Mesher
Edward Mitchell
Richard Poynter

Mark Rowland
Christopher Ward
Nick Wikeley

January 11, 2021

CONTENTS

USING THE UPDATING MATERIAL IN THIS SUPPLEMENT

The amendments and updating material contained in Parts II-VI of this Supplement are keyed in to the page numbers of the relevant main volume of *Social Security Legislation 2020/2021*. Where there have been a significant number of changes to a provision, the whole section, subsection, paragraph or regulation, as amended will tend to be reproduced. Other changes may be noted by an instruction to insert or substitute new material or to delete part of the existing text. The date the change takes effect is also noted. Where explanation is needed of the change, or there is updating relating to existing annotations but no change to the legislation, you will also find commentary in this Supplement. The updating material explains new statutory material, takes on board Upper Tribunal or court decisions, or gives prominence to points which now seem to warrant more detailed attention.

For the most part any relevant new legislation since the main volumes were published is contained in Part I, while amendments to existing legislative provisions are contained in Parts II-VI respectively, together with commentary on new case law. This Supplement amends the text of the main volumes of *Social Security Legislation 2020/21* to be up to date as at January 1, 2021.

Nick Wikeley
General Editor

PAGES OF MAIN VOLUMES AFFECTED BY MATERIAL IN THIS SUPPLEMENT

Pages of Main Volumes Affected by Material in this Supplement

Pages of Main Volumes Affected by Material in this Supplement

Pages of Main Volumes Affected by Material in this Supplement

Pages of Main Volumes Affected by Material in this Supplement

Pages of Main Volumes Affected by Material in this Supplement

TABLE OF ABBREVIATIONS USED IN THIS SERIES

1975 Act	Social Security Act 1975
1977 Act	Marriage (Scotland) Act 1977
1979 Act	Pneumoconiosis (Workers' Compensation) Act 1979
1986 Act	Social Security Act 1986
1996 Act	Employment Rights Act 1996
1998 Act	Social Security Act 1998
2002 Act	Tax Credits Act 2002
2004 Act	Gender Recognition Act 2004
2006 Act	Armed Forces Act 2006
2008 Act	Child Maintenance and Other Payments Act 2008
2013 Act	Marriage (Same Sex Couples) Act 2013
2014 Act	Marriage and Civil Partnership (Scotland) Act 2014
2018 Act	Social Security (Scotland) Act 2018
A1P1	Art.1 of Protocol 1 to the European Convention on Human Rights
AA	Attendance Allowance
AA 1992	Attendance Allowance Act 1992
AAC	Administrative Appeals Chamber
AACR	Administrative Appeals Chamber Reports
A.C.	Law Reports, Appeal Cases
A.C.D.	Administrative Court Digest
Admin	Administrative Court
Admin L.R.	Administrative Law Reports
Administration Act	Social Security Administration Act 1992
Administration Regulations	Statutory Paternity Pay and Statutory Adoption Pay (Administration) Regulations 2002
AIP	assessed income period
All E.R.	All England Reports
All E.R. (E.C.)	All England Reports (European Cases)
AMA	Adjudicating Medical Authorities
AO	Adjudication Officer
AOG	*Adjudication Officers Guide*
art.	article
Art.	Article
ASD	Autistic Spectrum Disorder

ASPP	Additional Statutory Paternity Pay
A.T.C.	Annotated Tax Cases
Attendance Allowance Regulations	Social Security (Attendance Allowance) Regulations 1991
AWT	All Work Test
BA	Benefits Agency
Benefits Act	Social Security Contributions and Benefits Act 1992
B.H.R.C.	Butterworths Human Rights Cases
B.L.G.R.	Butterworths Local Government Reports
Blue Books	*The Law Relating to Social Security*, Vols 1–11
B.P.I.R.	Bankruptcy and Personal Insolvency Reports
B.T.C.	British Tax Cases
BTEC	Business and Technology Education Council
B.V.C.	British Value Added Tax Reporter
B.W.C.C.	Butterworths Workmen's Compensation Cases
c.	chapter
C	Commissioner's decision
C&BA 1992	Social Security Contributions and Benefits Act 1992
CAA 2001	Capital Allowances Act 2001
CAB	Citizens Advice Bureau
CAO	Chief Adjudication Officer
CB	Child Benefit
CBA 1975	Child Benefit Act 1975
CBJSA	Contribution-Based Jobseeker's Allowance
C.C.L. Rep.	Community Care Law Reports
CCM	HMRC *New Tax Credits Claimant Compliance Manual*
C.E.C.	European Community Cases
CERA	cortical evoked response audiogram
CESA	Contribution-based Employment and Support Allowance
CFS	chronic fatigue syndrome
Ch.	Chancery Division Law Reports; Chapter
Charter	Charter of Fundamental Rights of the European Union
Citizenship Directive	Directive 2004/38/EC of the European Parliament and of the Council of April 29, 2004
CJEC	Court of Justice of the European Communities

CJEU	Court of Justice of the European Union
Claims and Payments Regulations	Social Security (Claims and Payments) Regulations 1987
Claims and Payments Regulations 1979	Social Security (Claims and Payments) Regulations 1979
Claims and Payments Regulations 2013	Universal Credit, Personal Independence Payment, Jobseeker's Allowance and Employment and Support Allowance (Claims and Payments) Regulations 2013
CM	Case Manager
CMA	Chief Medical Adviser
CMEC	Child Maintenance and Enforcement Commission
C.M.L.R.	Common Market Law Reports
C.O.D.	Crown Office Digest
COLL	*Collective Investment Schemes Sourcebook*
Community, The	European Community
Computation of Earnings Regulations	Social Security Benefit (Computation of Earnings) Regulations 1978
Computation of Earnings Regulations 1996	Social Security Benefit (Computation of Earnings) Regulations 1996
Consequential Provisions Act	Social Security (Consequential Provisions) Act 1992
Contributions and Benefits Act	Social Security Contributions and Benefits Act 1992
Contributions Regulations	Social Security (Contributions) Regulations 2001
COPD	chronic obstructive pulmonary disease
CP	Carer Premium; Chamber President
CPAG	Child Poverty Action Group
CPR	Civil Procedure Rules
Cr. App. R.	Criminal Appeal Reports
CRCA 2005	Commissioners for Revenue and Customs Act 2005
Credits Regulations 1974	Social Security (Credits) Regulations 1974
Credits Regulations 1975	Social Security (Credits) Regulations 1975
Crim. L.R.	Criminal Law Review
CRU	Compensation Recovery Unit
CSA 1995	Children (Scotland) Act 1995
CSIH	Inner House of the Court of Session (Scotland)
CSM	Child Support Maintenance
CS(NI)O 1995	Child Support (Northern Ireland) Order 1995
CSOH	Outer House of the Court of Session (Scotland)

CSPSSA 2000	Child Support, Pensions and Social Security Act 2000
CTA	Common Travel Area
CTA 2009	Corporation Tax Act 2009
CTA 2010	Corporation Tax Act 2010
CTB	Council Tax Benefit
CTC	Child Tax Credit
CTC Regulations	Child Tax Credit Regulations 2002
CTF	child trust fund
CTS	Carpal Tunnel Syndrome
DAC	Directive 2011/16/ EU (Directive on administrative co-operation in the field of taxation)
DAT	Disability Appeal Tribunal
dB	decibels
DCA	Department for Constitutional Affairs
DCP	Disabled Child Premium
Decisions and Appeals Regulations 1999	Social Security Contributions (Decisions and Appeals) Regulations 1999
Dependency Regulations	Social Security Benefit (Dependency) Regulations 1977
DfEE	Department for Education and Employment
DHSS	Department of Health and Social Security
Disability Living Allowance Regulations	Social Security (Disability Living Allowance) Regulations
DIY	do it yourself
DLA	Disability Living Allowance
DLA Regs 1991	Social Security (Disability Living Allowance) Regulations 1991
DLAAB	Disability Living Allowance Advisory Board
DLADWAA 1991	Disability Living Allowance and Disability Working Allowance Act 1991
DM	Decision Maker
DMA	Decision-making and Appeals
DMG	*Decision Makers' Guide*
DMP	Delegated Medical Practitioner
DP	Disability Premium
DPT	diffuse pleural thickening
DPTC	Disabled Person's Tax Credit
DRO	Debt Relief Order
DSD	Department for Social Development (Northern Ireland)
DSM IV; DSM-5	Diagnostic and Statistical Manual of Mental Disorders of the American Psychiatric Association

Table of Abbreviations used in this Series

DSS	Department of Social Security
DTI	Department of Trade and Industry
DWA	Disability Working Allowance
DWP	Department for Work and Pensions
DWPMS	Department for Work and Pensions Medical Service
EAA	Extrinsic Allergic Alveolitis
EAT	Employment Appeal Tribunal
EC	European Community
ECHR	European Convention on Human Rights
ECJ	European Court of Justice
E.C.R.	European Court Reports
ECSC	European Coal and Steel Community
ECSMA	European Convention on Social and Medical Assistance
EEA	European Economic Area
EEA EFTA Separation Agreement	Agreement on arrangements between Iceland, the Principality of Liechtenstein, the Kingdom of Norway and the United Kingdom of Great Britain and Northern Ireland following the withdrawal of the United Kingdom from the European Union, the EEA Agreement and other agreements applicable between the United Kingdom and the EEA EFTA States by virtue of the United Kingdom's membership of the European Union
EEA Regulations 2016	Immigration (European Economic Area) Regulations 2016
EEC	European Economic Community
EESSI	Electronic Exchange of Social Security Information
E.G.	Estates Gazette
E.G.L.R.	Estates Gazette Law Reports
EHC plan	education, health and care plan
EHIC	European Health Insurance Card
EHRC	European Human Rights Commission
E.H.R.R.	European Human Rights Reports
EL	employers' liability
E.L.R	Education Law Reports
EMA	Education Maintenance Allowance
EMP	Examining Medical Practitioner
Employment and Support Allowance Regulations	Employment and Support Allowance Regulations 2008
EPS	extended period of sickness
Eq. L.R.	Equality Law Reports
ERA	evoked response audiometry

Table of Abbreviations used in this Series

ERA scheme	Employment, Retention and Advancement scheme
ES	Employment Service
ESA	Employment and Support Allowance
ESA Regs 2013	Employment and Support Allowance Regulations 2013
ESA Regulations	Employment and Support Allowance Regulations 2008
ESA WCAt	Employment and Support Allowance Work Capability Assessment
ESC	employer supported childcare
ESE Scheme	Employment, Skills and Enterprise Scheme
ESE Regulations	Jobseeker's Allowance (Employment, Skills and Enterprise Scheme) Regulations 2011
ESES Regulations	Jobseeker's Allowance (Employment, Skills and Enterprise Scheme) Regulations 2011
ETA 1973	Employment and Training Act 1973
ETA(NI) 1950	Employment and Training Act (Northern Ireland) 1950
ETS	European Treaty Series
EU	European Union
Eu.L.R.	European Law Reports
EWCA Civ	Civil Division of the Court of Appeal (England and Wales)
EWHC Admin	Administrative Court, part of the High Court (England and Wales)
FA 1993	Finance Act 1993
FA 1996	Finance Act 1996
FA 2004	Finance Act 2004
Fam. Law	Family Law
FAS	Financial Assistance Scheme
F.C.R.	Family Court Reporter
FEV	forced expiratory volume
FIS	Family Income Supplement
FISMA 2000	Financial Services and Markets Act 2000
F.L.R.	Family Law Reports
FME	further medical evidence
F(No.2)A 2005	Finance (No.2) Act 2005
FOTRA	Free of Tax to Residents Abroad
FRAA	flat rate accrual amount
FRS Act 2004	Fire and Rescue Services Act 2004
FSCS	Financial Services Compensation Scheme
FTT	First-tier Tribunal

Table of Abbreviations used in this Series

General Benefit Regulations 1982	Social Security (General Benefit) Regulations 1982
General Regulations	Statutory Shared Parental Pay (General) Regulations 2014
GMCA	Greater Manchester Combined Authority
GMFRA	Greater Manchester Fire and Rescue Authority
GMP	Guaranteed Minimum Pension
GMWDA	Greater Manchester Waste Disposal Authority
GNVQ	General National Vocational Qualification
GP	General Practitioner
GRA	Gender Recognition Act 2004
GRB	Graduated Retirement Benefit
GRP	Graduated Retirement Pension
HB	Housing Benefit
HB (WSP) R (NI) 2017	Housing Benefit (Welfare Social Payment) Regulations (Northern Ireland) 2017
HBRB	Housing Benefit Review Board
HCA	Homes and Communities Agency
HCD	House of Commons Debates
HCP	healthcare professional
HCV	Hepatitis C virus
Health Service Act	National Health Service Act 2006
Health Service (Wales) Act	National Health Service (Wales) Act 2006
HIV	Human Immunodeficiency Virus
HL	House of Lords
H.L.R.	Housing Law Reports
HMIT	Her Majesty's Inspector of Taxes
HMRC	Her Majesty's Revenue and Customs
HMSO	Her Majesty's Stationery Office
Hospital In-Patients Regulations 1975	Social Security (Hospital In-Patients) Regulations 1975
HP	Health Professional
HPP	Higher Pensioner Premium
HRA 1998	Human Rights Act 1998
H.R.L.R.	Human Rights Law Reports
HRP	Home Responsibilities Protection
HSE	Health and Safety Executive
IAC	Immigration and Asylum Chamber
IAP	Intensive Activity Period
IB	Incapacity Benefit
IB PCA	Incapacity Benefit Personal Capability Assessment

Table of Abbreviations used in this Series

IB Regs	Social Security (Incapacity Benefit) Regulations 1994
IB Regulations	Social Security (Incapacity Benefit) Regulations 1994
IB/IS/SDA	Incapacity Benefits Regime
IBJSA	Income-Based Jobseeker's Allowance
IBS	Irritable Bowel Syndrome
ICA	Invalid Care Allowance
I.C.R.	Industrial Cases Reports
ICTA 1988	Income and Corporation Taxes Act 1988
IFW Regulations	Incapacity for Work (General) Regulations 1995
IH	Inner House of the Court of Session
I.I.	Industrial Injuries
IIAC	Industrial Injuries Advisory Council
IIDB	Industrial Injuries Disablement Benefit
ILO	International Labour Organization
Imm. A.R.	Immigration Appeal Reports
Incapacity for Work Regulations	Social Security (Incapacity for Work) (General) Regulations 1995
Income Support General Regulations	Income Support (General) Regulations 1987
IND	Immigration and Nationality Directorate of the Home Office
I.N.L.R.	Immigration and Nationality Law Reports
I.O.	Insurance Officer
IPPR	Institute of Public Policy Research
IRESA	Income-Related Employment and Support Allowance
I.R.L.R.	Industrial Relations Law Reports
IS	Income Support
IS Regs	Income Support Regulations
IS Regulations	Income Support (General) Regulations 1987
ISA	Individual Savings Account
ISBN	International Standard Book Number
ITA 2007	Income Tax Act 2007
ITEPA 2003	Income Tax, Earnings and Pensions Act 2003
I.T.L. Rep.	International Tax Law Reports
I.T.R.	Industrial Tribunals Reports
ITS	Independent Tribunal Service
ITTOIA 2005	Income Tax (Trading and Other Income) Act 2005
IVB	Invalidity Benefit

Table of Abbreviations used in this Series

IW (General) Regs	Social Security (Incapacity for Work) (General) Regulations 1995
IW (Transitional) Regs	Incapacity for Work (Transitional) Regulations
Jobseeker's Allowance Regulations	Jobseeker's Allowance Regulations 1996
Jobseeker's Regulations 1996	Jobseeker's Allowance Regulations 1996
JSA	Jobseeker's Allowance
JSA 1995	Jobseekers Act 1995
JSA (NI) Regulations	Jobseeker's Allowance (Northern Ireland) Regulations 1996
JSA (Transitional) Regulations	Jobseeker's Allowance (Transitional) Regulations 1996
JSA Regs 1996	Jobseeker's Allowance Regulations 1996
JSA Regs 2013	Jobseeker's Allowance Regulations 2013
JS(NI)O 1995	Jobseekers (Northern Ireland) Order 1995
J.S.S.L.	Journal of Social Security Law
J.S.W.L.	Journal of Social Welfare Law
K.B.	Law Reports, King's Bench
L.& T.R.	Landlord and Tenant Reports
LCW	limited capability for work
LCWA	Limited Capability for Work Assessment
LCWRA	limited capability for work-related activity
LDEDC Act 2009	Local Democracy, Economic Development and Construction Act 2009
LEA	local education authority
LEL	Lower Earnings Limit
LET	low earnings threshold
L.G. Rev.	Local Government Review
L.G.L.R.	Local Government Reports
L.J.R.	Law Journal Reports
LRP	liable relative payment
L.S.G.	Law Society Gazette
Luxembourg Court	Court of Justice of the European Union (also referred to as CJEC and ECJ)
MA	Maternity Allowance
MAF	Medical Assessment Framework
Maternity Allowance Regulations	Social Security (Maternity Allowance) Regulations 1987
MDC	Mayoral development corporation
ME	myalgic encephalomyelitis
Medical Evidence Regulations	Social Security (Medical Evidence) Regulations 1976
MEN	Mandatory Employment Notification
Mesher and Wood	*Income Support, the Social Fund and Family Credit: the Legislation* (1996)

M.H.L.R.	Mental Health Law Reports
MHP	mental health problems
MIF	minimum income floor
MIG	minimum income guarantee
Migration Regulations	Employment and Support Allowance (Transitional Provisions, Housing Benefit and Council Tax Benefit (Existing Awards) (No.2) Regulations 2010
MP	Member of Parliament
MRSA	methicillin-resistant Staphylococcus aureus
MS	Medical Services
MWA Regulations	Jobseeker's Allowance (Mandatory Work Activity Scheme) Regulations 2011
MWAS Regulations	Jobseeker's Allowance (Mandatory Work Activity Scheme) Regulations 2011
NCB	National Coal Board
NDPD	Notes on the Diagnosis of Prescribed Diseases
NHS	National Health Service
NI	National Insurance
N.I..	Northern Ireland Law Reports
NICA	Northern Ireland Court of Appeal
NICom	Northern Ireland Commissioner
NICs	National Insurance Contributions
NINO	National Insurance Number
NIRS 2	National Insurance Recording System
N.L.J.	New Law Journal
NMC	Nursing and Midwifery Council
Northern Ireland Contributions and Benefits Act	Social Security Contributions and Benefits (Northern Ireland) Act 1992
N.P.C.	New Property Cases
NRCGT	non-resident capital gains tax
NTC Manual	Clerical procedures manual on tax credits
NUM	National Union of Mineworkers
NUS	National Union of Students
OCD	obsessive compulsive disorder
Ogus, Barendt and Wikeley	A. Ogus, E. Barendt and N. Wikeley, *The Law of Social Security* (1995)
Old Cases Act	Industrial Injuries and Diseases (Old Cases) Act 1975
OPB	One Parent Benefit
O.P.L.R.	Occupational Pensions Law Reports
OPSSAT	Office of the President of Social Security Appeal Tribunals

Overlapping Benefits Regulations	Social Security (Overlapping Benefits) Regulations 1975
P	retirement pension case
P. & C.R.	Property and Compensation Reports
para.	paragraph
Pay Regulations	Statutory Paternity Pay and Statutory Adoption Pay (General) Regulations 2002; Statutory Shared Parental Pay (General) Regulations 2014
PAYE	Pay As You Earn
PC	Privy Council
PCA	Personal Capability Assessment
PCC	Police and Crime Commissioner
PD	Practice Direction; prescribed disease
Pens. L.R.	Pensions Law Reports
Pensions Act	Pension Schemes Act 1993
PEP	Personal Equity Plan
Persons Abroad Regulations	Social Security Benefit (Persons Abroad) Regulations 1975
Persons Residing Together Regulations	Social Security Benefit (Persons Residing Together) Regulations 1977
PIE	Period of Interruption of Employment
PILON	pay in lieu of notice
Pilot Scheme Regulations	Universal Credit (Work-Related Requirements) In Work Pilot Scheme and Amendment Regulations 2015
PIP	Personal Independence Payment
P.I.Q.R.	Personal Injuries and Quantum Reports
Polygamous Marriages Regulations	Social Security and Family Allowances (Polygamous Marriages) Regulations 1975
PPF	Pension Protection Fund
Prescribed Diseases Regulations	Social Security (Industrial Injuries) (Prescribed Diseases) Regulations 1985
PSCS	Pension Service Computer System
Pt	Part
PTA	pure tone audiometry
P.T.S.R.	Public and Third Sector Law Reports
PTWR 2000	Part-time Workers (Prevention of Less Favourable Treatment) Regulations 2000
PVS	private and voluntary sectors
Q.B.	Queen's Bench Law Reports
QBD	Queen's Bench Division
QCS Board	Quality Contract Scheme Board
QEF	qualifying earnings factor
QYP	qualifying young person
r.	rule

Table of Abbreviations used in this Series

R	Reported Decision
R.C.	Rules of the Court of Session
REA	Reduced Earnings Allowance
Reciprocal Agreement with Ireland	Convention on Social Security between the Government of the United Kingdom and Northern Ireland and the Government of Ireland
reg.	regulation
RIPA	Regulation of Investigatory Powers Act 2000
RMO	Responsible Medical Officer
rr.	rules
RR	reference rate
RSI	repetitive strain injury
RTI	Real Time Information
R.V.R.	Rating & Valuation Reporter
s.	section
S	Scottish Decision
SAP	Statutory Adoption Pay
SAPOE Regulations	Jobseeker's Allowance (Schemes for Assisting Persons to Obtain Employment) Regulations 2013
SAWS	Seasonal Agricultural Work Scheme
SAYE	Save As You Earn
SB	Supplementary Benefit
SBAT	Supplementary Benefit Appeal Tribunal
SBC	Supplementary Benefits Commission
S.C.	Session Cases
S.C. (H.L.)	Session Cases (House of Lords)
S.C. (P.C.)	Session Cases (Privy Council)
S.C.C.R.	Scottish Criminal Case Reports
S.C.L.R.	Scottish Civil Law Reports
Sch.	Schedule
SDA	Severe Disablement Allowance
SDP	Severe Disability Premium
SEC	Social Entitlement Chamber
SEN	special educational needs
SERPS	State Earnings Related Pension Scheme
ShPP	statutory shared parental pay
ShPP Regulations	Statutory Shared Parental Pay (General) Regulations 2014
SI	Statutory Instrument
SIP	Share Incentive Plan
S.J.	Solicitors Journal

S.J.L.B.	Solicitors Journal Law Brief
SLAN	statement like an award notice
S.L.T.	Scots Law Times
SMP	Statutory Maternity Pay
SMP (General) Regulations 1986	Statutory Maternity Pay (General) Regulations 1986
Social Security Directive	Council Directive 79/7/EEC of 19 December 1978 on the progressive implementation of the principle of equal treatment for men and women in matters of social security
SPC	State Pension Credit
SPC Regulations	State Pension Credit Regulations 2002
SPCA 2002	State Pension Credit Act 2002
SPL Regulations	Shared Parental Leave Regulations 2014
SPP	Statutory Paternity Pay
ss.	sections
SS (No.2) A 1980	Social Security (No.2) Act 1980
SSA 1975	Social Security Act 1975
SSA 1977	Social Security Act 1977
SSA 1978	Social Security Act 1978
SSA 1979	Social Security Act 1979
SSA 1981	Social Security Act 1981
SSA 1986	Social Security Act 1986
SSA 1988	Social Security Act 1988
SSA 1989	Social Security Act 1989
SSA 1990	Social Security Act 1990
SSA 1998	Social Security Act 1998
SSAA 1992	Social Security Administration Act 1992
SSAC	Social Security Advisory Committee
SSAT	Social Security Appeal Tribunal
SSCBA 1992	Social Security Contributions and Benefits Act 1992
SSCB(NI)A 1992	Social Security Contributions and Benefits (Northern Ireland) Act 1992
SSCPA 1992	Social Security (Consequential Provisions) Act 1992
SSD	Secretary of State for Defence
SSHBA 1982	Social Security and Housing Benefits Act 1982
SSHD	Secretary of State for the Home Department
SSI	Scottish Statutory Instrument
SS(MP)A 1977	Social Security (Miscellaneous Provisions) Act 1977
SSP	Statutory Sick Pay

SSP (General) Regulations	Statutory Sick Pay (General) Regulations 1982
SSPA 1975	Social Security Pensions Act 1975
SSPP	statutory shared parental pay
SSWP	Secretary of State for Work and Pensions
State Pension Credit Regulations	State Pension Credit Regulations 2002
S.T.C.	Simon's Tax Cases
S.T.C. (S.C.D.)	Simon's Tax Cases: Special Commissioners' Decisions
S.T.I.	Simon's Tax Intelligence
STIB	Short-Term Incapacity Benefit
subpara.	subparagraph
subs.	subsection
Swiss Citizens' Rights Agreement	Agreement between the United Kingdom of Great Britain and Northern Ireland and the Swiss Confederation on citizens' rights following the withdrawal of the United Kingdom from the European Union and the Free Movement of Persons Agreement
T	Tribunal of Commissioners' Decision
T.C.	Tax Cases
TCA 1999	Tax Credits Act 1999
TCA 2002	Tax Credits Act 2002
TCC	Technology and Construction Court
TCEA 2007	Tribunals, Courts and Enforcement Act 2007
TCGA 1992	Taxation of Chargeable Gains Act 2002
TCTM	*Tax Credits Technical Manual*
TEC	Treaty Establishing the European Community
TENS	transcutaneous electrical nerve stimulation
TEU	Treaty on European Union
TFC	tax-free childcare
TFEU	Treaty on the Functioning of the European Union
TIOPA 2010	Taxation (International and Other Provisions) Act 2010
TMA 1970	Taxes Management Act 1970
T.R.	Taxation Reports
Transfer of Functions Act	Social Security Contributions (Transfer of Functions etc.) Act 1999
Tribunal Procedure Rules	Tribunal Procedure (First-tier Tribunal)(Social Entitlement Chamber) Rules 2008
UB	Unemployment Benefit
UC	Universal Credit

UC Regs 2013	Universal Credit Regulations 2013
UCITS	Undertakings for Collective Investments in Transferable Securities
UKAIT	UK Asylum and Immigration Tribunal
UKBA	UK Border Agency of the Home Office
UKCC	United Kingdom Central Council for Nursing, Midwifery and Health Visiting
UKFTT	United Kingdom First-tier Tribunal Tax Chamber
UKHL	United Kingdom House of Lords
U.K.H.R.R.	United Kingdom Human Rights Reports
UKSC	United Kingdom Supreme Court
UKUT	United Kingdom Upper Tribunal
UN	United Nations
Universal Credit Regulations	Universal Credit Regulations 2013
URL	uniform resource locator
USI Regs	Social Security (Unemployment, Sickness and Invalidity Benefit) Regulations 1983
USI Regulations	Social Security (Unemployment, Sickness and Invalidity Benefit) Regulations 1983
UT	Upper Tribunal
VAT	Value Added Tax
VCM	vinyl chloride monomer
Vol.	Volume
VWF	Vibration White Finger
W	Welsh Decision
WCA	Work Capability Assessment
WCAt	limited capability for work assessment
WFHRAt	Work-Focused Health-Related Assessment
WFI	work-focused interview
WFTC	Working Families Tax Credit
Wikeley, Annotations	N. Wikeley, "Annotations to Jobseekers Act 1995 (c.18)" in *Current Law Statutes Annotated* (1995)
Wikeley, Ogus and Barendt	Wikeley, Ogus and Barendt, *The Law of Social Security* (2002)
Withdrawal Agreement	Agreement on the Withdrawal of the United Kingdom of Great Britain and Northern Ireland from the European Union and the European Atomic Energy Community 2019
W.L.R.	Weekly Law Reports
WLUK	Westlaw UK
Workmen's Compensation Acts	Workmen's Compensation Acts 1925 to 1945
WP	Widow's Pension

WPS	War Pensions Scheme
WRA 2007	Welfare Reform Act 2007
WRA 2009	Welfare Reform Act 2009
WRA 2012	Welfare Reform Act 2012
W-RA Regulations	Employment and Support Allowance (Work-Related Activity) Regulations 2011
WRAAt	Work-Related Activity Assessment
WRPA 1999	Welfare Reform and Pensions Act 1999
WRP(NI)O 1999	Welfare Reform and Pensions (Northern Ireland) Order 1999
WRWA 2016	Welfare Reform and Work Act 2016
WSP (LCP) R (NI) 2016	Welfare Supplementary Payment (Loss of Carer Payments) Regulations (Northern Ireland) 2016
WSP (LDRP) R (NI) 2016	Welfare Supplementary Payment (Loss of Disability-Related Premiums) Regulations (Northern Ireland) 2016
WSPR (NI) 2016	Welfare Supplementary Payment Regulations (Northern Ireland) 2016
WTC	Working Tax Credit
WTC Regulations	Working Tax Credit (Entitlement and Maximum Rate) Regulations 2002

TABLE OF CASES

Table of Cases

TABLE OF COMMISSIONERS' DECISIONS

TABLE OF EUROPEAN LEGISLATION

TABLE OF STATUTES

TABLE OF STATUTORY INSTRUMENTS

1

PART I

NEW LEGISLATION

NEW STATUTES

Childcare Act 2016

(2016 ch 5)

An Act to make provision about free childcare for young children of working parents and about the publication of information about childcare and related matters by local authorities in England.

[16th March 2016]

ARRANGEMENT OF SECTIONS

GENERAL NOTE

There is a patchwork of Government support for childcare. The Childcare   **1.001** Payments Act 2014 (covered in Vol 4 of this series) established Tax-Free Childcare (TFC), a scheme assisting towards the cost of childcare for working families. Roll-out of the TFC scheme was completed in February 2018. Typically the scheme operates through an online account which claimants can pay into to cover the cost of childcare for qualifying children with a registered provider. TFC is a UK wide scheme covering England, Scotland, Wales and Northern Ireland. In addition, a separate Government scheme provides for free childcare, as extended by the Childcare Act 2016. These free childcare arrangements are different for each of the four nations of the UK. For example, in England all three and four year olds can get 570 hours of free early education or childcare per year (around 15 hours a week over 38 weeks). In addition, families in paid work may be able to claim 30 hours a week childcare. In particular, s.1 of the Childcare Act 2016 places a duty on the Secretary of State to secure the availability of 30 hours of free childcare for qualifying children of working parents. In addition, Government support also takes the form of the childcare

3

element in working tax credit and universal credit and childcare vouchers for employer supported childcare.

Although claims for the TFC scheme under the 2014 Act and for free childcare under the 2016 Act are made through the same online process, the appellate arrangements differed at the outset. The First-tier Tribunal (Social Entitlement Chamber) has had jurisdiction to decide appeals relating to appealable decisions within the meaning of s.56(3) of the Childcare Payments Act 2014 since October 1, 2015 (see art.6(ea) of the First-tier Tribunal and Upper Tribunal (Chambers) Order 2010 (SI 2010/2655) as inserted by art.2(3) of the First-tier Tribunal and Upper Tribunal (Chambers) (Amendment) Order 2015 (SI 2015/1563)). However, appeals under the 2016 Act initially went to the Tax Chamber (see art.7 of the 2010 Order). They were only brought within the jurisdiction of the Social Entitlement Chamber with effect from March 6, 2020—see art.6(eb) of the 2010 Order as amended by art.2(2) of the First-tier Tribunal and Upper Tribunal (Chambers) (Amendment) Order 2020 (SI 2020/137). For arrangements in Wales, see the Childcare Funding (Wales) Act 2019, s.6 of which provides for regulations to be made that provide for appeals to the First-tier Tribunal.

Availability of free childcare

Duty to secure 30 hours free childcare available for working parents

1.002   **1.**—(1) The Secretary of State must secure that childcare is available free of charge for qualifying children of working parents for, or for a period equivalent to, 30 hours in each of 38 weeks in any year.

(2) "Qualifying child of working parents" means a young child—

(a) who is under compulsory school age,

(b) who is in England,

(c) who is of a description specified in regulations made by the Secretary of State,

(d) in respect of whom any conditions relating to a parent of the child, or a partner of a parent of the child, which are specified in such regulations, are met, and

(e) in respect of whom a declaration has been made, in accordance with such regulations, to the effect that the requirements of paragraphs (a) to (d) are satisfied.

(3) The conditions mentioned in subsection (2)(d) may, in particular, relate to the paid work undertaken by a parent or partner.

(4) For the purposes of subsections (2) and (3), the Secretary of State may by regulations—

(a) make provision about when a person is, or is not, to be regarded as another person's partner;

(b) make provision as to what is, or is not, paid work;

(c) specify circumstances in which a person is, or is not, to be regarded as in such work;

(d) make provision about—

(i) the form of a declaration and the manner in which it is to be made;

(ii) the conditions to be met by the person making a declaration;

(iii) the period for which a declaration has effect.

(5) For the purposes of assisting the Secretary of State in the discharge of the duty imposed by subsection (1), the Commissioners for Her Majesty's Revenue and Customs may carry out functions in connection with the making of determinations as to whether a child is a qualifying child of working parents.

(6) In determining, for the purposes of subsection (1), the amount of childcare that is available—

(a) account is to be taken of any childcare available under the duty imposed by section 7(1) of the Childcare Act 2006 (duty of English local authorities to secure early years provision free of charge in accordance with regulations), but

(b) no account is to be taken of childcare available otherwise than by virtue of that duty or the duty imposed by subsection (1).

(7) The Secretary of State must set out in regulations when a year begins for the purposes of determining in relation to a child whether the duty in subsection (1) has been discharged.

(8) The Secretary of State may by regulations make provision about the circumstances in which a child is, or is not, in England for the purposes of this section.

(9) In this section—

"childcare" has the meaning given by section 18 of the Childcare Act 2006;

"parent", in relation to a child, includes any individual who—

(a) has parental responsibility for the child, or

(b) has care of the child;

"parental responsibility" has the same meaning as in the Children Act 1989;

"young child": a child is a "young child" during the period—

(a) beginning with the child's birth, and

(b) ending immediately before the 1 September next following the date on which the child attains the age of 5.

Discharging the section 1(1) duty

2.—The Secretary of State may make regulations for the purpose of discharging the duty imposed by section 1(1) ("extended entitlement regulations").   1.003

(2) Extended entitlement regulations may (amongst other things)—

(a) require an English local authority to secure that childcare of such a description as may be specified is made available free of charge for children in their area who are qualifying children of working parents;

(b) make provision about how much childcare is to be so made available for each child, and about the times at which, and periods over which, that childcare is to be made available;

(c) make provision about the terms of any arrangements made between English local authorities and providers or arrangers of childcare for the purposes of meeting any requirement imposed under paragraph (a) or (b);

(d) impose obligations or confer powers on the Commissioners for Her Majesty's Revenue and Customs;

(e) make provision requiring information or documents to be provided by a person to the Secretary of State, the Commissioners for Her Majesty's Revenue and Customs or an English local authority;

(f) make provision for the purpose of enabling any person to check whether a child is a qualifying child of working parents;

(g) for that purpose, make provision about the disclosure of information held by a Minister of the Crown, the Commissioners for Her Majesty's Revenue and Customs or an English local authority;

(h) create criminal offences in connection with the onward disclosure of information obtained under paragraph (g) where that information relates to a particular person and is not disclosed in a way authorised by or specified in the regulations;

(i) make provision for reviews of, or appeals to the First-tier Tribunal against, determinations relating to a child's eligibility for childcare under section 1;

(j) make provision for a person specified in the regulations to impose financial penalties on persons in connection with—

   (i) false or misleading information provided, or statements made or provided, in connection with a determination of a child's eligibility for childcare under section 1, or

   (ii) dishonest conduct in connection with the process of making such a determination;

(k) require English local authorities, when discharging their duties under the regulations, to have regard to any guidance given from time to time by the Secretary of State.

(3) Extended entitlement regulations which impose a duty, or confer a power, on the Commissioners for Her Majesty's Revenue and Customs, or authorise disclosure of information held by the Commissioners, may only be made with the consent of the Treasury.

(4) In relation to a criminal offence created by virtue of subsection (2)(h), extended entitlement regulations may not provide for a penalty of imprisonment on conviction on indictment greater than imprisonment for a term not exceeding two years (whether or not accompanied by a fine).

(5) If provision is made by virtue of subsection (2)(j)—

(a) the maximum amount of any penalty that may be specified in, or determined in accordance with, the regulations is £3,000;

(b) the regulations must include provision enabling a person on whom a financial penalty is imposed—

   (i) to require a review of the imposition of the penalty or its amount by the person who imposed the penalty;

   (ii) to appeal against the imposition of the penalty or its amount to the First-tier Tribunal.

(6) The Secretary of State may by regulations substitute a different amount for the amount for the time being specified in subsection (5)(a).

(7) In section 15 of the Childcare Act 2006 (powers of Secretary of State to secure proper performance of English local authorities' powers and duties under Part 1 of that Act) references to Part 1 of that Act are to be read as including a reference to section 1 and this section.

(8) In this section—

"childcare" has the meaning given by section 18 of the Childcare Act 2006;

"English local authority" means—

    (a) a county council in England;

    (b) a metropolitan district council;

    (c) a non-metropolitan district council for an area for which there is no county council;

    (d) a London borough council;

    (e) the Common Council of the City of London (in their capacity as a local authority);

    (f) the Council of the Isles of Scilly;

"parent" has the same meaning as in section 1;

"qualifying child of working parents" has the meaning given by section 1(2).

Sections 1 and 2: consequential amendments

3.—(1) In section 99 of the Childcare Act 2006 (provision of information about young children: England), in subsection (1), omit the "and" at the end of paragraph (aa) and after paragraph (b) insert ", and   1.004

(c) any other person who provides early years provision for the purposes of section 1(1) of the Childcare Act 2016 (Secretary of State's duty to secure 30 hours free childcare available for working parents),".

(2) In Chapter 4 of Part 2 of the School Standards and Framework Act 1998 (financing of maintained schools)—

    (a) in section 45A (determination of specified budgets of local authority), after subsection (4B) insert—

        "(4C) For the purposes of this Part, a duty imposed on a local authority in England under section 2 of the Childcare Act 2016 (duties in connection with Secretary of State's duty to secure 30 hours free childcare for working parents) is also to be treated as an education function of the authority.";

    (b) in section 47ZA (free of charge early years provision outside a maintained school: budgetary framework: England), in subsection (3), for paragraph (a) (but not the "and" after it) substitute—

        "(a) for the purpose of the discharge of—

            (i) the authority's duty under section 7 of the Childcare Act 2006, or

            (ii) a duty imposed on the authority under section 2 of the Childcare Act 2016,".

Supplementary provision about regulations under sections 1 and 2

1.005   **4.**—(1) In this section "regulations" means regulations under section 1 or 2.

(2) Regulations may—

(a) confer a discretion on any person;

(b) make different provision for different purposes;

(c) make consequential, incidental, supplemental, transitional or saving provision;

(d) amend, repeal or revoke any provision made by or under an Act (whenever passed or made).

(3) Regulations are to be made by statutory instrument.

(4) A statutory instrument containing (whether alone or with other provision) regulations mentioned in subsection (5) may not be made unless a draft of the instrument has been laid before and approved by a resolution of each House of Parliament.

(5) The regulations referred to in subsection (4) are—

(a) the first regulations made under section 1;

(b) the first regulations made under section 2(1);

(c) any regulations under section 2(6);

(d) any other regulations that amend or repeal provision made by an Act.

(6) Any other statutory instrument containing regulations is subject to annulment in pursuance of a resolution of either House of Parliament.

Publication of information

Duty to publish information about childcare and related matters

1.006   **5.** In section 12 of the Childcare Act 2006 (duty to provide information, advice and assistance), after subsection (6) insert—

"(6A) Regulations may require each English local authority to publish information which is of a prescribed description and relates to any of the matters mentioned in paragraphs (a) to (c) of subsection (2).

(6B) Regulations under subsection (6A) may require information to be published—

(a) at prescribed intervals;

(b) in a prescribed manner.

(6C) Subsection (3) applies in relation to information prescribed under subsection (6A) as it applies in relation to information prescribed under subsection (2)."

General

Extent

1.007   **6.** This Act extends to England and Wales only.

Commencement

7.—(1) The following provisions come into force on the day on which   **1.008**
this Act is passed—

(a) section 1(5);

(b) section 6;

(c) this section;

(d) section 8.

(2) The remaining provisions of this Act come into force on such day
or days as may be appointed by regulations made by the Secretary of
State.

(3) Regulations under subsection (2) may appoint different days for
different purposes or different areas.

(4) The Secretary of State may by regulations make transitional or
saving provision in connection with the coming into force of any provision of this Act.

(5) Regulations under this section are to be made by statutory
instrument.

Short title

8. This Act may be cited as the Childcare Act 2016.   **1.009**

Social Security (Scotland) Act 2018

(2018 ASP 9)

SECTIONS REPRODUCED

PART 2

GIVING OF ASSISTANCE BY SCOTTISH MINISTERS

CHAPTER 2

TYPES OF ASSISTANCE TO BE GIVEN

PART 3

SUPPLEMENTING ASSISTANCE UNDER OTHER ENACTMENTS

PART 7

FINAL PROVISIONS

PART 2

GIVING OF ASSISTANCE BY SCOTTISH MINISTERS

CHAPTER 2

TYPES OF ASSISTANCE TO BE GIVEN

Carer's assistance

28.—(1) Carer's assistance is assistance (which may or may not take the form of money) given by the Scottish Ministers under section 24 to an individual who provides, or has provided, care to another individual who has a disability.

(2) The Scottish Ministers are to make regulations prescribing—

(a) the eligibility rules that are to be applied to determine whether an individual is entitled to carer's assistance, and

(b) what carer's assistance an individual who is entitled to it is to be given.

(3) Schedule 2 makes provision about the exercise of the power conferred by subsection (2).

1.010

GENERAL NOTE

This section and Schedule 2, below, came into force on October 14, 2019) see reg.3 of the Social Security (Scotland) Act 2018 (Commencement No.5, Revocation and Saving Provision) Regulations 2019 (SSI 2019/269)). This material was included in the Supplement for 2019/20 but was not brought forward into Volume I for 2020/21. It is repeated here in its updated form for convenience.

1.011

Winter heating assistance

30.—(1) Winter heating assistance is assistance (which may or may not take the form of money) given by the Scottish Ministers under section 24 to an individual to meet, or help towards meeting, the individual's heating costs during the winter months.

(2) The Scottish Ministers are to make regulations prescribing—

(a) the eligibility rules that are to be applied to determine whether an individual is entitled to winter heating assistance, and

(b) what winter heating assistance an individual who is entitled to it is to be given.

(3) Schedule 4 makes provision about the exercise of the power conferred by subsection (2).

1.012

GENERAL NOTE

This section came into force on September 1, 2020 (see the Social Security (Scotland) Act 2018 (Commencement No.7) Regulations 2020 (SSI 2020/127), reg.2. The power conferred by s.2 has been exercised to make the Winter Heating Assistance for Children and Young People (Scotland) Regulations 2020 (SSI 2020/352): see below.

1.012.1

Disability assistance

1.013   **31.**— (1) Disability assistance is assistance (which may or may not take the form of money) given by the Scottish Ministers under section 24 to an individual on account of the individual having—

(a) a disability arising from a physical or mental impairment, or

(b) a terminal illness.

(2) The Scottish Ministers are to make regulations prescribing—

(a) the eligibility rules that are to be applied to determine whether an individual is entitled to disability assistance, and

(b) what disability assistance an individual who is entitled to it is to be given.

(3) Schedule 5 makes provision about the exercise of the power conferred by subsection (2).

Short-term assistance

1.014   **36.**—(1) Short-term assistance is assistance (which may or may not take the form of money) given by the Scottish Ministers under section 24 to an individual on a short-term basis.

(2) The Scottish Ministers are to make regulations prescribing—

(a) the eligibility rules that are to be applied to determine whether an individual is entitled to short-term assistance, and

(b) what short-term assistance an individual who is entitled to it is to be given.

(3) Schedule 10 makes provision about the exercise of the power conferred by subsection (2).

GENERAL NOTE

1.014.1   This section came into force on October 8, 2020 (see the Social Security (Scotland) Act 2018 (Commencement No.8) Regulations (SSI 2020/295), reg.2(b)). No regulations have yet been made under this section.

PART 3

SUPPLEMENTING ASSISTANCE UNDER OTHER ENACTMENTS

Top up of reserved benefits

Power to provide for top up

1.015   **79.** (1) The Scottish Ministers may by regulations provide for financial assistance to be given to an individual who—

(a) is entitled to a reserved benefit, and

(b) appears to the Scottish Ministers to require financial assistance (in addition to any amount the individual receives by way of reserved benefit) for the purpose, or one of the purposes, for which the benefit is being provided.

(2) The power conferred by subsection (1) includes the power to make provision about—
  (a) determining entitlement (including specifying further eligibility rules that are to be used to determine whether an individual is entitled to the assistance),
  (b) the amount of assistance,
  (c) applications for assistance,
  (d) obtaining information,
  (e) appeals,
  (f) assistance given in error.
(3) In this section and section 80, "reserved benefit" means a benefit which is to any extent a reserved matter within the meaning of schedule 5 of the Scotland Act 1998.

Restrictions on power

80.— (1) Regulations under section 79 may not provide for financial assistance to be given to meet or help to meet housing costs.   1.016
(2) Regulations under section 79 may not provide for financial assistance to be given where the need for the assistance arises solely from reduction, non-payability or suspension of a reserved benefit as a result of an individual's conduct (for example, non-compliance with work-related requirements relating to the benefit).
(3) But subsection (2) does not prevent assistance from being given where the need for the assistance in question—
  (a) also arises from some exceptional event or exceptional circumstances, and
  (b) is immediate.

Carer's allowance: temporary provision

Carer's Allowance Supplement

81.—(1) The Scottish Ministers must make a payment (a "carer's   1.017
allowance supplement") to qualifying individuals in respect of each of the following periods of each financial year—
  (a) 1 April to 30 September, and
  (b) 1 October to 31 March.
[²(1A) A qualifying individual is an individual to whom subsection (2) or (2A) applies.]
(2) [²This subsection applies to] an individual who, on the qualifying date, was—
  (a) in receipt of a carer's allowance under section 70 of the Social Security Contributions and Benefits Act 1992, and
  (b) resident in Scotland.
[²(2A) This subsection applies to an individual whom the Scottish Ministers have determined in accordance with Part 2 of the Carer's Allowance Supplement and Young Carers Grants (Residence Requirements and Procedural Provisions) (EU Exit) (Scotland) Regulations 2020 (SSI 2020/475)—

(a) met the eligibility conditions in subsection (9) on the qualifying date (where the qualifying date is before IP completion day),

(b) met the eligibility conditions in subsection (11) on the qualifying date (where the qualifying date is after IP completion day and the individual has rights arising from a relevant EU regulation), or

(c) met the eligibility conditions in subsection (13) on the qualifying date (where the qualifying date is after IP completion day and the individual has rights arising from the UK-Ireland convention mentioned in that subsection).]

(3) The qualifying date is a date determined by the Scottish Ministers falling within the period to which the payment relates.

(4) The amount of a carer's allowance supplement is to be calculated according to the following formula [¹ (but see also subsection (4A))]—

$$(JSA - CA) \times 26$$

where—

JSA is whichever is the higher of—

(a) the weekly amount specified in regulation 79(1)(c) of the Job-seeker's Allowance Regulations 1996 (SI 1996/207) as it has effect on the qualifying date, and

(b) that amount as it would have effect on the qualifying date if it were adjusted for inflation in accordance with subsection (5), and CA is the weekly rate of carer's allowance specified in Part 3 of schedule 4 of the Social Security Contributions and Benefits Act 1992 as it has effect in Scotland on the qualifying date.

[¹ (4A) The amount of a carer's allowance supplement in respect of the period of 1 April 2020 to 30 September 2020 is £230.10 greater than that calculated according to the formula in subsection (4).]

(5) The Scottish Ministers must, before the start of each new tax year, beginning with the first new tax year beginning after this section comes into force—

(a) calculate what the weekly amount specified in regulation 79(1)(c) of the Jobseeker's Allowance Regulations 1996 ("the JSA Regulations") would be if it were adjusted for inflation,

(b) publish a statement explaining how they have calculated inflation for this purpose.

(6) In calculating the amount for the purpose of subsection (5)(a), the Scottish Ministers may take account of any change in the weekly amount specified in regulation 79(1)(c) of the JSA Regulations since this section came into force.

(7) For the purposes of subsection (5), a tax year means a period beginning with 6 April in one year and ending with 5 April in the next.

(8) The Scottish Ministers may by regulations modify this section so as to modify who is a qualifying individual for the purposes of this section.

[²(9) An individual met the eligibility conditions referred to in subsection (2A)(a) on a given date if, on that date, the individual—

(a) was in receipt of a carer's allowance under section 70 of the Social Security Contributions and Benefits Act 1992,

(b) was an individual—

    (i) to whom a relevant EU Regulation applied, and

    (ii) in respect of whom the United Kingdom was competent for payment of sickness benefits in cash for the purposes of Chapter 1 of Title III of the Regulation in question,

(c) was resident in—

    (i) Switzerland, or

    (ii) an EEA State other than the United Kingdom, and

(d) had a genuine and sufficient link to Scotland.

(10) The reference in subsection (9)(d) to an individual's link to Scotland being sufficient is to it being sufficiently close that if the individual were not entitled to the carer's allowance supplement this section—

(a) would be incompatible with EU law, or

(b) would have been incompatible with EU law immediately before IP completion day.

(11) An individual met the eligibility conditions referred to in subsection (2A)(b) on a given date if, on that date, the individual—

(a) was in receipt of a carer's allowance under section 70 of the Social Security Contributions and Benefits Act 1992,

(b) was an individual—

    (i) to whom the rules set out in a relevant EU regulation applied by virtue of—

        (A) Title III of Part 2 of the EU withdrawal agreement,

        (B) Part 3 or Article 23(4) of the Swiss citizens' rights agreement (as defined in section 39(1) of the European Union (Withdrawal Agreement) Act 2020),

        (C) Title III of the EEA EFTA separation agreement (as defined in that section), or

        (D) the agreement constituted by the exchange of letters set out in the schedule of the Family Allowances, National Insurance and Industrial Injuries (Gibraltar) Order 1974 (SI 1974/555) between the United Kingdom and Gibraltar, and

    (ii) in respect of whom the United Kingdom is, as a result, competent for payment of sickness benefits in cash,

(c) was resident in—

    (i) Switzerland,

    (ii) an EEA State, or

    (iii) Gibraltar, and

(d) had a genuine and sufficient link to Scotland.

(12) The reference in paragraph (d) of subsection (11) to an individual's link to Scotland being sufficient is to it being sufficiently close that if the individual were not entitled to the carer's allowance supplement this section would be incompatible with the applicable agreement mentioned in paragraph (b)(i) of that subsection.

(13) An individual met the eligibility conditions referred to in subsection (2A)(c) on a given date if, on that date, the individual—

   (a) was in receipt of a carer's allowance under section 70 of the Social Security Contributions and Benefits Act 1992,

   (b) was an individual—

      (i) to whom the convention on social security between the Government of the United Kingdom of Great Britain and Northern Ireland and the Government of Ireland signed at Dublin on 1 February 2019, as modified from time to time in accordance with any provision of it, applied, and

      (ii) in respect of whom the United Kingdom is, as a result, competent for payment of long term care benefits,

   (c) was resident in Ireland, and

   (d) had a genuine and sufficient link to Scotland.

(14) The reference in paragraph (d) of subsection (13) to an individual's link to Scotland being sufficient is to it being sufficiently close that if the individual were not entitled to the carer's allowance supplement, this section would be incompatible with the convention mentioned in paragraph (b) of that subsection.

(15) In this section—

"EEA State" means—

   (a) a member State of the European Union, or

   (b) any other State that is a party to the agreement on the European Economic Area signed at Oporto on 2 May 1992, together with the Protocol adjusting that Agreement signed at Brussels on 17 March 1993, as modified or supplemented from time to time,

"EU law" has the meaning given by subsection (9) of section 126 of the Scotland Act 1998, or if that subsection has been repealed, the meaning given by that subsection immediately before its repeal,

"relevant EU Regulation" means—

   (a) one of the following Regulations—

      (i) Council Regulation (EC) No 1408/71 of 14 June 1971 on the application of social security schemes to employed persons, to self-employed persons and to members of their families moving within the Community,

      (ii) Regulation (EC) No 883/2004 of the European Parliament and of the Council of 29 April 2004 on the coordination of social security systems, or

   (b) in relation to an individual to whom the exchange of letters mentioned in subsection (11)(b)(i)(D) applies, a Regulation mentioned in paragraph (a) as it forms part of domestic law by virtue of section 3 of the European Union (Withdrawal) Act 2018.]

AMENDMENTS

   1. Coronavirus (Scotland) (No.2) Act 2020 (asp 10) s.16(1) sch.1 para.6(2) (May 27, 2020)

   2. Carer's Allowance Supplement and Young Carer Grants (Residence Requirements and Procedural Provisions) (EU Exit) (Scotland) Regulations 2020 (SSI 2020/475) Sch.1 paras 1-5 (December 24, 2020).

16

GENERAL NOTE

The amendments noted above are temporary. They were originally to expire   **1.018**
on September 30, 2020 but have been extended to March 31, 2021 and may be
further extended to September 2021. (See Coronavirus (Scotland) (No.2) Act
2020 s.9).

Power to repeal temporary provision

82.—The Scottish Ministers may by regulations—   **1.019**
(a) repeal section 81 and revoke any regulations made under it, and
(b) repeal this section.

PART 7

FINAL PROVISIONS

Ancillary provision

95. The Scottish Ministers may by regulations make any incidental,   **1.020**
supplementary, consequential, transitional, transitory or saving provision they consider appropriate for the purposes of, or in connection with,
or for giving full effect to this Act or any provision made under it.

SCHEDULE 2

(introduced by section 28)

CARER'S ASSISTANCE REGULATIONS

PART 1

ELIGIBILITY

CHAPTER 1

ELIGIBILITY IS TO DEPEND ON BEING OR HAVING BEEN A CARER

1. (1) The regulations must be framed so that (subject to any provision   **1.021**
of the kind described in paragraph 2) an individual's eligibility in respect
of a given period depends on the individual having provided regular and
substantial care during that period to another individual to whom a
disability benefit is normally payable.
(2) The regulations—

17

(a) are to set out the circumstances in which an individual is to be regarded as having provided regular and substantial care to another individual during a period, and

(b) may, in particular, do so by reference to whether or not the number of hours of care provided during the period exceeds (or is deemed to exceed) a threshold specified in the regulations.

(3) In sub-paragraph (1), "disability benefit" has the meaning given in the interpretation provision in Section F1 of Part 2 of schedule 5 of the Scotland Act 1998.

2. (1) The regulations may be framed so that, despite the criterion described in paragraph 1(1) not being fulfilled in relation to a given period, an individual may nevertheless be eligible in respect of that period.

(2) Where the regulations allow an individual to be eligible in respect of a period in relation to which the criterion described in paragraph 1(1) is not fulfilled, they must be framed so that the individual's eligibility depends on the individual—

(a) having at some time provided care to another individual who has a disability, and

(b) as a result of doing so, having received—
(i) carer's assistance,
(ii) carer's allowance, or
(iii) invalid care allowance.

(3) In sub-paragraph (2)(b), "carer's allowance" and "invalid care allowance" both mean an allowance payable under section 70 of the Social Security Contributions and Benefits Act 1992.

CHAPTER 2

FURTHER CRITERIA

Carer's other activities

1.022   **3.** The regulations may make an individual's eligibility depend on—
(a) whether or not the individual is in—
(i) employment, or
(ii) education,
(b) the length of time the individual spends over a given period in—
(i) employment, or
(ii) education.

Multiple carers

4. The regulations may make an individual's eligibility depend on being the individual (or one of the individuals) selected through a process set out in the regulations in a case where more than one individual would otherwise be eligible as a result of providing care to the same cared-for person during a given period.

Residence and presence

5. The regulations may make an individual's eligibility depend on either or both—
(a) the individual, and
(b) the cared-for person,
being resident and present in a particular place.

Age

6. The regulations may make an individual's eligibility depend on the age of either or both—
(a) the individual, and
(b) the cared-for person.

Financial circumstances

7. The regulations may make an individual's eligibility depend on the individual's financial circumstances.

Receipt of, or eligibility for, other types of State assistance

8. The regulations may make an individual's eligibility depend on the individual—
(a) being, or not being, in receipt of another type of assistance (whether under this Act or another enactment),
(b) being, or not being, eligible or entitled to receive such assistance.

Application within specified period

9. The regulations may provide that an individual ceases to be eligible in respect of a given period unless, by a deadline specified in the regulations—
(a) the individual has applied for carer's assistance in respect of the period, or
(b) the Scottish Ministers have become required to make a determination of the individual's entitlement to carer's assistance in respect of the period by regulations under section 52.

PART 2

ASSISTANCE TO BE GIVEN

Meeting liabilities

10. The regulations may provide for the carer's assistance that is to be 1.023 given to an individual to be given (in whole or in part) by way of—

(a) payment to another person in order to meet, or contribute towards meeting, any liability the individual has to that person,

(b) deduction from any liability the individual has to the Scottish Ministers under section 63.

Restriction on giving assistance in a form other than money

11.—(1) The regulations may allow carer's assistance to be given to an individual in a form other than money only if the individual (or a person acting on the individual's behalf) has agreed to the assistance being given in that form.

(2) If the regulations include provision of the kind mentioned in sub-paragraph (1), they must allow an individual (or a person acting on the individual's behalf) to withdraw agreement to being given carer's assistance in a form other than money at any time.

(3) Despite sub-paragraph (1), the regulations may provide for carer's assistance to be given (in whole or in part) by way of deduction, at a reasonable level, from any liability the individual has to the Scottish Ministers under section 63 if the individual has unreasonably refused to agree to the assistance being given in that form.

(4) For the purpose of sub-paragraph (3), "reasonable level" means a level that is reasonable having regard to the financial circumstances of the individual.

PART 3

FINAL PROVISIONS

Generality of enabling power unaffected

12. Nothing in this schedule, apart from the following provisions, is to be taken to limit what may be prescribed in the regulations—

(a) Chapter 1 of Part 1,

(b) paragraph 11 in Part 2.

Interpretation

13. In this schedule—

"cared-for person" means the individual by providing care to whom the individual whose eligibility is in question has fulfilled the criterion described in paragraph 1(1) or 2(2),

"eligibility" means eligibility for carer's assistance and "eligible" means eligible for carer's assistance,

"the regulations" means regulations under section 28(2).

SCHEDULE 4

(introduced by section 30)

WINTER HEATING ASSISTANCE REGULATIONS

PART 1

ELIGIBILITY

Residence and presence

1. The regulations may make an individual's eligibility depend on the   1.024
individual being resident and present in a particular place.

Age

2. The regulations may make an individual's eligibility depend on the
age of either or both—
   (a) the individual, and
   (b) anyone who lives with the individual.

Financial circumstances

3. Subject to paragraph 4, the regulations may not make an individual's eligibility depend on the financial circumstances of either or
both—
   (a) the individual, and
   (b) anyone who lives with the individual.

Receipt of, or eligibility for, other types of State assistance

4. The regulations may make an individual's eligibility depend on
either or both the individual and anyone who lives with the individual—
   (a) being, or not being, in receipt of another type of assistance
       (whether under this Act or another enactment),
   (b) being, or not being, eligible or entitled to receive such assistance.

Application within specified period

5. The regulations may provide that an individual ceases to be eligible
in respect of a given period unless, by a deadline specified in the regulations—
   (a) the individual has applied for winter heating assistance in respect
       of the period, or
   (b) the Scottish Ministers have become required to make a determination of the individual's entitlement to winter heating assistance
       in respect of the period by regulations under section 52.

. . .

SCHEDULE 5

DISABILITY ASSISTANCE REGULATIONS

(introduced by section 31)

PART 1

ELIGIBILITY

CHAPTER 1

ELIGIBILITY IS TO DEPEND ON HAVING, OR HAVING HAD, A DISABILITY

1.025   **1.**—(1) The regulations must be framed so that (subject to any provision of the kind described in paragraph 2) an individual's eligibility in respect of a given period depends on the individual having, during that period—

    (a) a physical or mental impairment that—

        (i) has a significant and not short-term adverse effect on the individual's ability to carry out normal day-to-day activities, or

        (ii) otherwise gives rise to a significant and not short-term need, or

    (b) a terminal illness.

(2) The regulations must provide that an individual is to be regarded as having a terminal illness for the purpose of determining entitlement to disability assistance if, having had regard to the guidance mentioned in sub-paragraph (3), it is the clinical judgement of a registered medical practitioner that the individual has a progressive disease that can reasonably be expected to cause the individual's death.

(3) The Chief Medical Officer of the Scottish Administration is—

    (a) following consultation with registered medical practitioners, to prepare and from time to time revise, and

    (b) to make publicly available by such means as the Chief Medical Officer considers appropriate,

guidance that sets out when a progressive disease can reasonably be expected to cause an individual's death for the purpose of determining entitlement to disability assistance.

   2. (1) The regulations may be framed so that, despite the criterion described in paragraph 1(1) not being fulfilled in respect of a given period, an individual may nevertheless be eligible in respect of that period.

(2) Where the regulations allow an individual to be eligible in respect of a period in relation to which the criterion described in paragraph 1(1)

is not fulfilled, they must be framed so that the individual's eligibility depends on the individual having had, during some other period, a physical or mental impairment of the kind described in paragraph 1(1)(a).

CHAPTER 2

FURTHER CRITERIA

Nature and extent of disability and needs

3. The regulations may make an individual's eligibility depend on the nature and extent of—
(a) the individual's impairment,
(b) the needs of the individual in consequence of the impairment.

Residence and presence

4. The regulations may make an individual's eligibility depend on the individual being resident and present in a particular place.

Age

5. The regulations may make an individual's eligibility depend on the individual's age.

Financial circumstances

6. Subject to paragraph 7, the regulations may not make an individual's eligibility depend on the financial circumstances of either or both—
(a) the individual, and
(b) anyone who lives with the individual.

Receipt of, or eligibility for, other types of State assistance

7. The regulations may make an individual's eligibility depend on the individual—
(a) being, or not being, in receipt of another type of assistance (whether under this Act or another enactment),
(b) being, or not being, eligible or entitled to receive such assistance.

Application within specified period

8. The regulations may provide that an individual ceases to be eligible in respect of a given period unless, by a deadline specified in the regulations—
(a) the individual has applied for disability assistance in respect of the period, or

(b) the Scottish Ministers have become required to make a determination of the individual's entitlement to disability assistance in respect of the period by regulations under section 52.

CHAPTER 3

SPECIAL RULES FOR TERMINAL ILLNESS CASES

No minimum period

9. The regulations may not make the eligibility of an individual who has a terminal illness depend on the individual having had the illness for any length of time.

No requirement for assessment

10. The regulations may not make the eligibility of an individual who has a terminal illness depend on the individual producing any evidence of that fact beyond a diagnosis by a registered medical practitioner.

Eligibility from date of application

11. The regulations must be framed so that an individual who applies for disability assistance on the basis of having a terminal illness, and does have a terminal illness, is eligible, at the latest, from the day the application is made.

Entitlement to maximum amount

12. The regulations must be framed so that an individual who is eligible by reason of having a terminal illness is entitled to the maximum amount of the assistance that the individual is eligible for.

PART 2

ASSISTANCE TO BE GIVEN

CHAPTER 1

VALUE

Nature and extent of disability

1.026　　**13.** The regulations may make the value of the disability assistance that is to be given to an individual depend on the nature and extent of—

24

(a) the individual's impairment,

(b) the needs of the individual in consequence of the impairment.

Age

14. The regulations may make the value of the disability assistance that is to be given to an individual depend on the individual's age.

CHAPTER 2

FORM

Meeting liabilities

15. The regulations may provide for the disability assistance that is to be given to an individual to be given (in whole or in part) by way of—

(a) payment to another person in order to meet, or contribute towards meeting, any liability the individual has to that person,

(b) deduction from any liability the individual has to the Scottish Ministers under section 63.

Payment to someone else

16. The regulations may provide that, if the Scottish Ministers consider it appropriate in the circumstances, the disability assistance that is to be given to an individual may be given (in whole or in part) by way of payment to another person who is to use the payment to benefit the individual entitled to the assistance.

Restriction on giving assistance in a form other than money

17. (1) The regulations may allow disability assistance to be given to an individual in a form other than money only if the individual (or a person acting on the individual's behalf) has agreed to the assistance being given in that form.

(2) If the regulations include provision of the kind mentioned in sub-paragraph (1), they must allow an individual (or a person acting on the individual's behalf) to withdraw agreement to being given disability assistance in a form other than money at any time.

(3) Despite sub-paragraph (1), the regulations may provide for disability assistance to be given (in whole or in part) by way of deduction, at a reasonable level, from any liability the individual has to the Scottish Ministers under section 63 if the individual has unreasonably refused to agree to the assistance being given in that form.

(4) For the purpose of sub-paragraph (3), "reasonable level" means a level that is reasonable having regard to the financial circumstances of the individual.

Restriction on lump sums

18. The regulations may not provide for the disability assistance that is to be given to an individual to be given by way of a lump-sum payment where the individual's entitlement arises on account of the individual having, or having had—

  (a) pneumoconiosis,
  (b) byssinosis,
  (c) diffuse mesothelioma,
  (d) bilateral diffuse pleural thickening, or
  (e) primary carcinoma of the lung where there is accompanying evidence of—
      (i) asbestosis,
      (ii) bilateral diffuse pleural thickening, or
      (iii) both.

PART 3

FINAL PROVISIONS

Generality of enabling power unaffected

19. Nothing in this schedule, apart from the following provisions, is to be taken to limit what may be prescribed in the regulations—

  (a) Chapter 1 of Part 1,
  (b) paragraph 6 in Chapter 2 of Part 1,
  (c) Chapter 3 of Part 1,
  (d) paragraphs 17 and 18 in Chapter 2 of Part 2.

Interpretation

20. In this schedule—
"eligibility" means eligibility for disability assistance and "eligible" means eligible for disability assistance,
"the regulations" means regulations under section 31(2).

SCHEDULE 10

(introduced by section 36)

SHORT-TERM ASSISTANCE REGULATIONS

PART 1

ELIGIBILITY

Entitlement to other assistance being reviewed

1.027   **1.** (1) The regulations must be framed so that an individual is eligible for short-term assistance if—

(a) the individual is, or was, entitled to a particular type of assistance (other than short-term assistance) under a determination made on the basis that the individual has ongoing entitlement,

(b) that determination has been superseded by a determination under section 37 with the result that the individual—

    (i) is no longer entitled to the type of assistance in question, or

    (ii) is entitled to less assistance of the type in question,

(c) the individual's entitlement to the type of assistance in question is under review, and

(d) any further eligibility rules prescribed in the regulations are satisfied in the individual's case.

(2) An individual's entitlement to a particular type of assistance is under review within the meaning of sub-paragraph (1)(c) if—

(a) the individual has, under section 41, requested a re-determination of the individual's entitlement to the type of assistance in question and—

    (i) the Scottish Ministers have yet to make a determination of the individual's entitlement under section 43, and

    (ii) the individual has not, since requesting the re-determination, made an appeal to the First-tier Tribunal against a determination of the individual's entitlement, or

(b) the individual has, under section 46, appealed to the First-tier Tribunal against a determination of the individual's entitlement to the type of assistance in question and the First-tier Tribunal has yet to make a decision under section 49, or

(c) the First-tier Tribunal is considering, under section 48(1)(b), whether to give permission for the individual to bring an appeal against a determination of the individual's entitlement to the type of assistance in question.

PART 2

ASSISTANCE TO BE GIVEN

Value and form of assistance where entitlement to other assistance under review

2.—(1) This paragraph applies to any case in which an individual is eligible for short-term assistance by virtue of provision made in accordance with paragraph 1(1).

(2) In this paragraph, "the superseded determination" means the determination that has been superseded with one of the results mentioned in paragraph 1(1)(b), as a consequence of which the individual in question is eligible for short-term assistance.

(3) In relation to a case to which this paragraph applies, the regulations must provide for the value of the short-term assistance given to an individual in respect of any period to be equal to—

1.028

V1 – V2

where—
V1 is the value of the assistance that the individual would have been given in respect of the period under the superseded determination had it not been superseded, and

V2 is the value of the assistance that the individual is to be given in respect of the period under what is, at the time the individual becomes eligible for short-term assistance in respect of the period, the most recent determination of the individual's entitlement to the type of assistance to which the superseded determination relates.

(4) In relation to a case to which this paragraph applies, the regulations must provide for the rules regarding the form in which short-term assistance is given to an individual to be the same as the rules governing the form in which the type of assistance to which the superseded determination relates may be given.

PART 3

FINAL PROVISIONS

Generality of enabling power unaffected

1.029   **3.** Nothing in this schedule is to be taken to preclude the regulations from providing for an individual to be eligible for short-term assistance in circumstances other than those described in paragraph 1.

Interpretation

4. In this schedule, "the regulations" means regulations under section 36(2).

Immigration and Social Security Coordination (EU Withdrawal) Act 2020

(2020 c.20)

Power to modify retained direct EU legislation relating to social security co-ordination

6. (1) An appropriate authority may by regulations modify the retained direct EU legislation mentioned in subsection (2).   1.030

(2) The retained direct EU legislation is—

(a) Regulation (EC) No 883/2004 of the European Parliament and of the Council on the co-ordination of social security systems;

(b) Regulation (EC) No 987/2009 of the European Parliament and of the Council laying down the procedure for implementing Regulation (EC) No 883/2004;

(c) Regulation (EEC) No 1408/71 on the application of social security schemes to employed persons, to self-employed persons and to members of their families moving within the Community;

(d) Regulation (EEC) No 574/72 fixing the procedure for implementing Regulation (EEC) No 1408/71;

(e) Regulation (EC) No 859/2003 extending Regulation (EEC) No 1408/71 to nationals of non-EU Member Countries.

(3) The power to make regulations under subsection (1) includes power—

(a) to make different provision for different categories of person to whom they apply (and the categories may be defined by reference to a person's date of arrival in the United Kingdom, their immigration status, their nationality or otherwise);

(b) otherwise to make different provision for different purposes;

(c) to make supplementary, incidental, consequential, transitional, transitory or saving provision;

(d) to provide for a person to exercise a discretion in dealing with any matter.

(4) The power to make provision mentioned in subsection (3)(c) includes power to modify—

(a) any provision made by primary legislation passed before, or in the same Session as, this Act;

(b) any provision made under primary legislation before, or in the same Session as, this Act is passed;

(c) retained direct EU legislation which is not mentioned in subsection (2).

(5) EU-derived rights, powers, liabilities, obligations, restrictions, remedies and procedures cease to be recognised and available in domestic law so far as they are inconsistent with, or are otherwise capable of affecting the interpretation, application or operation of, provision made by regulations under this section.

(6) "EU-derived rights, powers, liabilities, obligations, restrictions, remedies and procedures" means any rights, powers, liabilities, obligations, restrictions, remedies and procedures which continue to be recognised and available in domestic law by virtue of section 4 of the European Union (Withdrawal) Act 2018 (including as they are modified by domestic law from time to time).

(7) In this section, "appropriate authority" means—

(a) the Secretary of State or the Treasury,

(b) a Northern Ireland department, or

(c) a Minister of the Crown acting jointly with a Northern Ireland department.

(8) Schedule 2 contains further provision about the power to make regulations under this section.

(9) Schedule 3 contains provision about the making of regulations under this section.

GENERAL NOTE

1.031   Regulations made under the power conferred by this section are the Social Security Co-ordination (Revocation of Retained Direct EU Legislation and Related Amendments) (EU Exit) Regulations 2020 (SI 2020/1508), discussed below in the General Notes to the various EU instruments concerned.

SCHEDULE 2

FURTHER PROVISION ABOUT THE SCOPE OF THE POWER UNDER SECTION 6

GENERAL NOTE

1.032   The Schedule contains detailed provisions relating to procedure where the interests of the legislature in Scotland or Northern Ireland are involved under the respective devolution settlements. It is not reproduced here to save space.

SCHEDULE 3

REGULATIONS UNDER SECTION 6

PART 1

STATUTORY INSTRUMENTS

1.033   **1.** Any power to make regulations under section 6—

(a) so far as exercisable by the Secretary of State or the Treasury, or by a Minister of the Crown acting jointly with a Northern Ireland department, is exercisable by statutory instrument, and

(b) so far as exercisable by a Northern Ireland department (other than when acting jointly with a Minister of the Crown), is exercisable by statutory rule for the purposes of the Statutory Rules (Northern Ireland) Order 1979 (SI 1979/1573 (NI 12)) (and not by statutory instrument).

PART 2

SCRUTINY OF REGULATIONS UNDER SECTION 6

Scrutiny where sole exercise

2. (1) A statutory instrument containing regulations of the Secretary of State or the Treasury under section 6 may not be made unless a draft of the instrument has been laid before, and approved by a resolution of, each House of Parliament.　　1.034

(2) Regulations of a Northern Ireland department under section 6 may not be made unless a draft of the regulations has been laid before, and approved by a resolution of, the Northern Ireland Assembly.

(3) This paragraph does not apply to regulations to which paragraph 3 applies (Minister of the Crown and a Northern Ireland department acting jointly).

Scrutiny where joint exercise

3. Regulations under section 6 of a Minister of the Crown acting jointly with a Northern Ireland department may not be made unless—
    (a) a draft of the statutory instrument containing those regulations has been laid before, and approved by a resolution of, each House of Parliament, and
    (b) a draft of the regulations has been laid before, and approved by a resolution of, the Northern Ireland Assembly.

Combination of instruments

4. (1) Sub-paragraph (2) applies to a statutory instrument containing regulations under section 6 which is subject to a procedure before Parliament for the approval of the instrument in draft before it is made.

(2) The statutory instrument may also include regulations under another Act which are made by statutory instrument which is subject to a procedure before Parliament that provides for the annulment of the instrument after it has been made.

(3) Where regulations are included as mentioned in sub-paragraph (2), the procedure applicable to the statutory instrument—
    (a) is the procedure mentioned in sub-paragraph (1), and
    (b) is not the procedure mentioned in sub-paragraph (2).

(4) Sub-paragraphs (1) to (3) apply in relation to a statutory rule as they apply in relation to a statutory instrument but as if—

(a) the references to Parliament were references to the Northern Ireland Assembly, and

(b) the reference to another Act in sub-paragraph (2) included Northern Ireland legislation.

(5) Sub-paragraphs (1) to (3) apply in relation to a statutory instrument containing regulations under section 6 which is subject to a procedure before the Northern Ireland Assembly as well as a procedure before Parliament as they apply to a statutory instrument containing regulations under section 6 which is subject to a procedure before Parliament but as if the references to Parliament were references to Parliament and the Northern Ireland Assembly.

(6) This paragraph does not prevent the inclusion of other regulations in a statutory instrument or statutory rule which contains regulations under section 6 (and, accordingly, references in this Schedule to an instrument containing regulations are to be read as references to an instrument containing (whether alone or with other provision) regulations).

The European Union (Future Relationship) Act 2020

(2020 c.29)

Social security co-ordination

26. (1) The following provisions of the Trade and Cooperation Agree- 1.035
ment, in its English language version, form part of domestic law on and
after the relevant day—

  (a) the SSC Protocol;

  (b) Title I of Heading 4 of Part 2 (Trade);

  (c) Articles COMPROV.17 and FINPROV.2, so far as applying to the
     SSC Protocol.

(2) Any enactment has effect on and after the relevant day with such
modifications as—

  (a) are required in consequence of subsection (1) or otherwise for the
     purposes of implementing the provisions mentioned in that sub-
     section, and

  (b) are capable of being ascertained from those provisions or other-
     wise from the Trade and Cooperation Agreement.

(3) Subsections (1) and (2)—

  (a) are subject to any equivalent or other provision—

    (i) which (whether before, on or after the relevant day) is made
      by or under this Act or any other enactment or otherwise
      forms part of domestic law, and

    (ii) which is for the purposes of (or has the effect of) implement-
      ing to any extent the Trade and Cooperation Agreement or
      any other future relationship agreement, and

  (b) do not limit the scope of any power which is capable of being
     exercised to make any such provision.

(4) The references to the Trade and Cooperation Agreement in—

  (a) subsections (1) and (2), and

  (b) the definition of "the SSC Protocol" in subsection (5),

are (except as provided in that definition) references to the agreement as
it has effect on the relevant day.

(5) In this section—

"domestic law" means—

  (a) in subsection (1), the law of England and Wales, Scotland and
     Northern Ireland, and

  (b) in subsection (3)(a)(i), the law of England and Wales, Scotland
     or Northern Ireland;

"relevant day", in relation to any provision mentioned in subsection
(1) or any aspect of it, means—

  (a) so far as the provision or aspect concerned is provisionally
     applied before it comes into force, the time and day from which
     the provisional application applies, and

  (b) so far as the provision or aspect concerned is not provisionally
     applied before it comes into force, the time and day when it
     comes into force;

"the SSC Protocol" means the Protocol on Social Security Coordination contained in the Trade and Cooperation Agreement, as that protocol is modified or supplemented from time to time in accordance with Article SSC.11(6), Article SSC.11(8) or Article SSC.68 of that protocol;

and references to the purposes of (or having the effect of) implementing an agreement (or any provision of an agreement) include references to the purposes of (or having the effect of) making provision consequential on any such implementation.

PROTOCOL ON SOCIAL SECURITY COORDINATION

GENERAL NOTE

1.036   The Protocol, which forms part of the EU-UK Trade and Co-operation Agreement concluded on December 24, 2020, derives its force in domestic law from s.26 of the European Union (Future Relationship) Act 2020 (above). While that section incorporates the Protocol into domestic law, its sweeping approach leaves open, at least for now, a number of questions concerning the enforceability of individual provisions.

The late emergence of the Protocol, along with the rest of the Trade and Co-operation Agreement, and its proximity to the copy date for the present volume, means that the Protocol's text below is based on a version published on www.gov.uk which indicates that "This document has been agreed between the European Union and the United Kingdom and is provided for information only. No rights may be derived from it until the date of application. The numbering of the articles is provisional."

Those who are within scope of the Citizens' Rights part of the Withdrawal Agreement will wish to explore its provisions in relation to social security co-ordination. It presently appears that the two schemes exist in parallel. While the Citizens' Rights provisions directly apply (in modified form) Regulation 883/2004 and its implementing Regulation 987/2009, the Protocol frequently draws on concepts and techniques from those Regulations, decisions on which will continue to be influential via the provisions of the European Union (Withdrawal) Act 2018.

TITLE I: GENERAL PROVISIONS

Article SSC.1: Definitions

1.037   For the purposes of this Protocol, the following definitions apply:
(a)   "activity as an employed person" means any activity or equivalent situation treated as such for the purposes of the social security legislation of the State in which such activity or equivalent situation exists;
(b)   "activity as a self-employed person" means any activity or equivalent situation treated as such for the purposes of the social

security legislation of the State in which such activity or equivalent situation exists;

(c)   "assisted conception services" means any medical, surgical or obstetric services provided for the purpose of assisting a person to carry a child;

(d)   "benefits in kind" means:

(i) for the purposes of Chapter 1 [Sickness, maternity and equivalent paternity benefits] of Title III, benefits in kind provided for under the legislation of a State which are intended to supply, make available, pay directly or reimburse the cost of medical care and products and services ancillary to that care;

(ii) for the purposes of Chapter 2 [Accidents at work and occupational diseases] of Title III, all benefits in kind relating to accidents at work and occupational diseases as defined in point (i) and provided for under the States' accidents at work and occupational diseases schemes;

(e)   "child-raising period" refers to any period which is credited under the pension legislation of a State or which provides a supplement to a pension explicitly for the reason that a person has raised a child, irrespective of the method used to calculate those periods and whether they accrue during the time of child-raising or are acknowledged retroactively;

(f)   "civil servant" means a person considered to be such or treated as such by the State to which the administration employing them is subject;

(g)   "competent authority" means, in respect of each State, the Minister, Ministers or other equivalent authority responsible for social security schemes throughout or in any part of the State in question;

(h)   "competent institution" means:

(i) the institution with which the person concerned is insured at the time of the application for benefit; or

(ii) the institution from which the person concerned is or would be entitled to benefits if that person or a member or members of their family resided in the State in which the institution is situated; or

(iii) the institution designated by the competent authority of the State concerned; or

(iv) in the case of a scheme relating to an employer's obligations in respect of the benefits set out in Article SSC.3(1) [Matters covered], either the employer or the insurer involved or, in default thereof, the body or authority designated by the competent authority of the State concerned;

(i)   "competent State" means the State in which the competent institution is situated;

(j)   "death grant" means any one-off payment in the event of death, excluding the lump-sum benefits referred to in point (w);

(k) "family benefit" means all benefits in kind or in cash intended to meet family expenses;

(l) "frontier worker" means any person pursuing an activity as an employed or self-employed person in a State and who resides in another State to which that person returns as a rule daily or at least once a week;

(m) "home base" means the place from where the crew member normally starts and ends a duty period or a series of duty periods, and where, under normal conditions, the operator/airline is not responsible for the accommodation of the crew member concerned;

(n) "institution" means, in respect of each State, the body or authority responsible for applying all or part of the legislation;

(o) "institution of the place of residence" and "institution of the place of stay" mean, respectively, the institution which is competent to provide benefits in the place where the person concerned resides and the institution which is competent to provide benefits in the place where the person concerned is staying, in accordance with the legislation administered by that institution or, where no such institution exists, the institution designated by the competent authority of the State concerned;

(p) "insured person", in relation to the social security branches covered by Chapters 1 [Sickness, maternity and equivalent paternity benefits] and 3 [Death grants] of Title III [Special provisions concerning the various categories of benefits], means any person satisfying the conditions required under the legislation of the State competent under Title II [Determination of the legislation applicable] in order to have the right to benefits, taking into account the provisions of this Protocol;

(q) "legislation" means, in respect of each State, laws, regulations and other statutory provisions and all other implementing measures relating to the social security branches covered by Article SSC.3(1) [Matters covered], but excludes contractual provisions other than those which serve to implement an insurance obligation arising from the laws and regulations referred to in this point or which have been the subject of a decision by the public authorities which makes them obligatory or extends their scope, provided that the State concerned makes a declaration to that effect, notified to the Specialised Committee on Social Security Coordination. The European Union shall publish such a declaration in the Official Journal of the European Union;

(r) "long-term care benefit" means a benefit in kind or in cash the purpose of which is to address the care needs of a person who, on account of impairment, requires considerable assistance, including but not limited to assistance from another person or persons to carry out essential activities of daily living for an extended period of time in order to support their personal autonomy; this includes benefits granted for the same purpose to a person providing such assistance;

(s) "member of the family" means:

(i) (A) any person defined or recognised as a member of the family or designated as a member of the household by the legislation under which benefits are provided;

(B) with regard to benefits in kind pursuant to Title III [Special provisions concerning the various categories of benefits], Chapter 1 [Sickness, maternity and equivalent paternity benefits], any person defined or recognised as a member of the family or designated as a member of the household by the legislation of the State in which that person resides;

(ii) if the legislation of a State which is applicable under sub-paragraph 1 does not make a distinction between the members of the family and other persons to whom it is applicable, the spouse, minor children, and dependent children who have reached the age of majority shall be considered members of the family;

(iii) if, under the legislation which is applicable under subparagraphs (1) and (2), a person is considered a member of the family or member of the household only if that person lives in the same household as the insured person or pensioner, this condition shall be considered satisfied if the person in question is mainly dependent on the insured person or pensioner;

(t) "period of employment" or "period of self-employment" mean periods so defined or recognised by the legislation under which they were completed, and all periods treated as such, where they are regarded by that legislation as equivalent to periods of employment or to periods of self-employment;

(u) "period of insurance" means periods of contribution, employment or self-employment as defined or recognised as periods of insurance by the legislation under which they were completed or considered as completed, and all periods treated as such, where they are regarded by that legislation as equivalent to periods of insurance;

(v) "period of residence" means periods so defined or recognised by the legislation under which they were completed or considered as completed;

(w) "pension" covers not only pensions but also lump-sum benefits which can be substituted for them and payments in the form of reimbursement of contributions and, subject to the provisions of Title III [Special provisions concerning the various categories of benefits], revaluation increases or supplementary allowances;

(x) "pre-retirement benefit" means all cash benefits, other than an unemployment benefit or an early old-age benefit, provided from a specified age to workers who have reduced, ceased or suspended their remunerative activities until the age at which they qualify for an old-age pension or an early retirement pension, the receipt of which is not conditional upon the person concerned being available to the employment services of the competent State; "early old-age benefit" means a benefit provided before the normal pension entitlement age is reached and which either continues to be provided once the said age is reached or is replaced by another old-age benefit;

(y) "refugee" has the meaning assigned to it in Article 1 of the Convention relating to the Status of Refugees, signed in Geneva on 28 July 1951;

(z) "registered office or place of business" means the registered office or place of business where the essential decisions of the undertaking are adopted and where the functions of its central administration are carried out;

(aa) "residence" means the place where a person habitually resides;

(bb) "special non-contributory cash benefits" means those non-contributory cash benefits which: (i) are intended to provide either: (A) supplementary, substitute or ancillary cover against the risks covered by the branches of social security referred to in Article SSC.3(1) [Matters covered], and which guarantee the persons concerned a minimum subsistence income having regard to the economic and social situation in the State concerned; or (B) solely specific protection for the disabled, closely linked to the said person's social environment in the State concerned, and (ii) where the financing exclusively derives from compulsory taxation intended to cover general public expenditure and the conditions for providing and for calculating the benefits are not dependent on any contribution in respect of the beneficiary. However, benefits provided to supplement a contributory benefit shall not be considered to be contributory benefits for this reason alone;

(cc) "special scheme for civil servants" means any social security scheme which is different from the general social security scheme applicable to employed persons in the State concerned and to which all, or certain categories of, civil servants are directly subject;

(dd) "stateless person" has the meaning assigned to it in Article 1 of the Convention relating to the Status of Stateless Persons, signed in New York on 28 September 1954;

(ee) "stay" means temporary residence.

Article SSC.2: Persons covered

1.038   This Protocol shall apply to persons, including stateless persons and refugees, who are or have been subject to the legislation of one or more States, as well as to the members of their families and their survivors.

Article SSC.3: Matters covered

1.039   1. This Protocol shall apply to the following branches of social security:

(a) sickness benefits;
(b) maternity and equivalent paternity benefits;
(c) invalidity benefits;
(d) old-age benefits;
(e) survivors' benefits;

(f) benefits in respect of accidents at work and occupational diseases;

(g) death grants;

(h) unemployment benefits;

(i) pre-retirement benefits.

2. Unless otherwise provided for in Annex SSC-6 [Special provisions for the application of the legislation of the Member States and of the United Kingdom], this Protocol shall apply to general and special social security schemes, whether contributory or non-contributory, and to schemes relating to the obligations of an employer or ship-owner.

3. The provisions of Title III [Special provisions concerning the various categories of benefits] shall not, however, affect the legislative provisions of any State concerning a ship-owner's obligations.

4. This Protocol shall not apply to:

(a) special non-contributory cash benefits listed in Part 1 [Special non-contributory cash benefits] of Annex SSC-1 [Certain benefits in cash to which the Protocol shall not apply];

(b) social and medical assistance;

(c) benefits in relation to which a State assumes the liability for damages to persons and provides for compensation, such as those for victims of war and military action or their consequences; victims of crime, assassination or terrorist acts; victims of damage occasioned by agents of the State in the course of their duties; or victims who have suffered a disadvantage for political or religious reasons or for reasons of descent;

(d) long-term care benefits which are listed in Part 2 [Long-term care benefits] of Annex SSC-1 [Certain benefits in cash to which this Protocol shall not apply];

(e) assisted conception services;

(f) payments which are connected to a branch of social security listed in paragraph (1) and which are:

   (i) paid to meet expenses for heating in cold weather; and

   (ii) listed in Part 3 [Payments which are connected to a branch of social security listed in Article SSC.3(1) [Matters covered] and which are paid to meet expenses for heating in cold weather (point (f) of Article SSC.3(4) [Matters covered]] of Annex SSC-1 [Certain benefits in cash to which this Protocol shall not apply]);

(g) family benefits.

Article SSC.4: Non-discrimination between Member States

1. Social security coordination arrangements established in this Protocol shall be based on the principle of non-discrimination between the Member States of the Union. 1.040

2. This article is without prejudice to any arrangements made between the United Kingdom and Ireland concerning the Common Travel Area.

Article SSC.5: Equality of treatment

1. Unless otherwise provided for in this Protocol, as regards the branches of social security covered by Article SSC.3(1) [Matters covered], persons to whom this Protocol applies shall enjoy the same benefits and be subject to the same obligations under the legislation of any State as the nationals thereof.

2. This provision does not apply to the matters referred to in Article SSC.3(4) [Matters covered].

Article SSC.6 : Equal treatment of benefits, income, facts or events

1.041   Unless otherwise provided for in this Protocol, the States shall ensure the application of the principle of equal treatment of benefits, income, facts or events in the following manner:

(a) where, under the legislation of the competent State, the receipt of social security benefits and other income has certain legal effects, the relevant provisions of that legislation shall also apply to the receipt of equivalent benefits acquired under the legislation of another State or to income acquired in another State;

(b) where, under the legislation of the competent State, legal effects are attributed to the occurrence of certain facts or events, that State shall take account of like facts or events that have occurred in any other State as though they had taken place in its own territory.

Article SSC.7: Aggregation of periods

1.042   Unless otherwise provided for in this Protocol, the competent institution of a State shall, to the extent necessary, take into account periods of insurance, employment, self-employment or residence completed under the legislation of any other State as though they were periods completed under the legislation which it applies, where its legislation makes conditional upon the completion of periods of insurance, employment, self-employment or residence:

(a) the acquisition, retention, duration or recovery of the right to benefits;

(b) the coverage by legislation; or

(c) the access to or the exemption from compulsory, optional continued or voluntary insurance.

Article SSC.8: Waiving of residence rules

1.043   The States shall ensure the application of the principle of exportability of cash benefits in accordance with paragraphs (a) and (b):

(a) Cash benefits payable under the legislation of a State or under this Protocol shall not be subject to any reduction, amendment, suspension, withdrawal or confiscation on account of the fact that the beneficiary or the members of their family reside in a State other than that in which the institution responsible for providing benefits is situated.

(b) Point (a) does not apply to the cash benefits covered by points (c) and (h) of Article SSC.3(1) [Matters covered].

Article SSC.9: Preventing of overlapping of benefits

Unless otherwise provided, this Protocol shall neither confer nor maintain the right to several benefits of the same kind for one and the same period of compulsory insurance. 1.044

TITLE II: DETERMINATION OF THE LEGISLATION APPLICABLE

Article SSC.10: General rules

1. Persons to whom this Protocol applies shall be subject to the legislation of a single State only. Such legislation shall be determined in accordance with this Title. 1.045

2. For the purposes of this Title, persons receiving cash benefits because or as a consequence of their activity as an employed or self-employed person shall be considered to be pursuing the said activity. This shall not apply to invalidity, old-age or survivors' pensions or to pensions in respect of accidents at work or occupational diseases or to sickness benefits in cash covering treatment for an unlimited period.

3. Subject to Articles SSC.12 [Pursuit of activities in two or more States] and SSC.13 [Voluntary insurance or optional continued insurance]:

(a) a person pursuing an activity as an employed or self-employed person in a State shall be subject to the legislation of that State;

(b) a civil servant shall be subject to the legislation of the State to which the administration employing them is subject;

(c) any other person to whom points (a) and (b) do not apply shall be subject to the legislation of the State of residence, without prejudice to other provisions of this Protocol guaranteeing them benefits under the legislation of one or more other States.

4. For the purposes of this Title, an activity as an employed or self-employed person normally pursued on board a vessel at sea flying the flag of a State shall be deemed to be an activity pursued in the said State. However, a person employed on board a vessel flying the flag of a State and remunerated for such activity by an undertaking or a person whose registered office or place of business is in another State shall be subject to the legislation of the latter State if that person resides in that State. The undertaking or person paying the remuneration shall be considered as the employer for the purposes of the said legislation.

5. An activity as a flight crew or cabin crew member performing air passenger or freight services shall be deemed to be an activity pursued in the State where the home base is located.

Article SSC.11: Detached workers

1. By way of derogation from Article SSC.10(3) [General rules] and as a transitional measure in relation to the situation that existed before the 1.046

entry into force of this Agreement, the following rules as regards the applicable legislation shall apply between the Member States listed in Category A of Annex SSC-8 [Transitional provisions regarding the application of Article SSC.11] and the United Kingdom:

(a) a person who pursues an activity as an employed person in a State for an employer which normally carries out its activities there and who is sent by that employer to another State to perform work on that employer's behalf shall continue to be subject to the legislation of the first State, provided that:

(i) the duration of such work does not exceed 24 months; and

(ii) that person is not sent to replace another detached worker.

(b) a person who normally pursues an activity as a self-employed person in a State who goes to pursue a similar activity in another State shall continue to be subject to the legislation of the first State, provided that the anticipated duration of such activity does not exceed 24 months.

2. By the date of entry into force of this Agreement, the Union shall notify the United Kingdom which of the following categories each Member State falls under:

(a) Category A: The Member State has notified the Union that it wishes to derogate from Article SSC.10 [General rules] in accordance with this article;

(b) Category B: The Member State has notified the Union that it does not wish to derogate from Article SSC.10 [General rules]; or

(c) Category C: The Member State has not indicated whether it wishes to derogate from Article SSC.10 [General rules] or not.

3. The document referred to in paragraph 2 shall become the content of Annex SSC-8 [Transitional provisions regarding the application of Article SSC.11] on the date of entry into force of this Agreement.

4. For Member States which are listed in Category A on the date of entry into force of this Agreement, points (a) and (b) of paragraph 1 shall apply.

5. For Member States which are listed in Category C on the date of entry into force of this Agreement, points (a) and (b) of paragraph 1 shall apply as though that Member State was listed in Category A for one month after the date of entry into force of this Agreement. The Specialised Committee on Social Security Coordination shall move a Member State from Category C to Category A if the Union notifies the Specialised Committee on Social Security Coordination that that Member State wishes to be so moved.

6. A month after the date of entry into force of this Agreement, Categories B and C will cease to exist. The Parties shall publish an updated Annex SSC-8 [Transitional provisions regarding the application of Article SSC.11] as soon as possible thereafter. For the purpose of paragraph 1, Annex [SSC-8] [Transitional provisions regarding the application of Article SSC.11] will be considered as containing only Category A Member States as from the date of that publication.

7. Where a person is in a situation referred to in paragraph 1 involving a Category C Member State before the publication of an updated Annex

SSC-8 [Transitional provisions regarding the application of Article SSC.11] in accordance with paragraph 6, paragraph 1 shall continue to apply to that person for the duration of their activities under paragraph 1.

8. The Union shall notify the Specialised Committee on Social Security Coordination if a Member State wishes to be removed from Category A of Annex SSC-8 [Transitional provisions regarding the application of Article SSC.11] and the Specialised Committee on Social Security Coordination shall, at the request of the Union remove that Member State from Category A of Annex SSC-8. The Parties shall publish an updated Annex SSC-8 [Transitional provisions regarding the application of Article SSC.11], which shall apply as from the first day of the second month following the receipt of the request by the Specialised Committee on Social Security Coordination.

9. Where a person is in a situation referred to in paragraph 1 before the publication of an updated Annex SSC-8 [Transitional provisions regarding the application of Article SSC.11] in accordance with paragraph 8, paragraph 1 shall continue to apply to that person for the duration of that person's activities under paragraph 1.

Article SSC.12: Pursuit of activities in two or more States

1. A person who normally pursues an activity as an employed person in one or more Member States as well as the United Kingdom shall be subject to: 1.047

  (a) the legislation of the State of residence if that person pursues a substantial part of their activity in that State; or

  (b) if that person does not pursue a substantial part of their activity in the State of residence:

    (i) the legislation of the State in which the registered office or place of business of the undertaking or employer is situated if that person is employed by one undertaking or employer; or

    (ii) the legislation of the State in which the registered office or place of business of the undertakings or employers is situated if that person is employed by two or more undertakings or employers which have their registered office or place of business in only one State; or

    (iii) the legislation of the State in which the registered office or place of business of the undertaking or employer is situated other than the State of residence if that person is employed by two or more undertakings or employers, which have their registered office or place of business in a Member State and the United Kingdom, one of which is the State of residence; or

    (iv) the legislation of the State of residence if that person is employed by two or more undertakings or employers, at least two of which have their registered office or place of business in different States other than the State of residence.

2. A person who normally pursues an activity as a self-employed person in one or more Member States as well as the United Kingdom shall be subject to:

(a) the legislation of the State of residence if that person pursues a substantial part of their activity in that State; or

(b) the legislation of the State in which the centre of interest of their activities is situated, if that person does not reside in one of the States in which that person pursues a substantial part of their activity.

3. A person who normally pursues an activity as an employed person and an activity as a self-employed person in two or more States shall be subject to the legislation of the State in which that person pursues an activity as an employed person or, if that person pursues such an activity in two or more States, to the legislation determined in accordance with paragraph 1.

4. A person who is employed as a civil servant by a State and who pursues an activity as an employed person or as a self-employed person in one or more other States shall be subject to the legislation of the State to which the administration employing that person is subject.

5. A person who normally pursues an activity as an employed person in two or more Member States (and not in the United Kingdom) shall be subject to the legislation of the United Kingdom if that person does not pursue a substantial part of that activity in the State of residence and that person:

(a) is employed by one or more undertakings or employers, all of which have their registered office or place of business in the United Kingdom;

(b) resides in a Member State and is employed by two or more undertakings or employers, all of which have their registered office or place of business in the United Kingdom and the Member State of residence;

(c) resides in the United Kingdom and is employed by two or more undertakings or employers, at least two of which have their registered office or place of business in different Member States; or

(d) resides in the United Kingdom and is employed by one or more undertakings or employers, none of which have a registered office or place of business in another State.

6. A person who normally pursues an activity as a self-employed person in two or more Member States (and not in the United Kingdom), without pursuing a substantial part of that activity in the State of residence, shall be subject to the legislation of the United Kingdom if the centre of interest of their activity is situated in the United Kingdom.

7. Paragraph 6 shall not apply in the case of a person who normally pursues an activity as an employed person and as a self-employed person in two or more Member States.

8. Persons referred to in paragraphs 1 to 6 shall be treated, for the purposes of the legislation determined in accordance with these provisions, as though they were pursuing all their activities as employed or self-employed persons and were receiving all their income in the State concerned.

Article SSC.13: Voluntary insurance or optional continued insurance

1. Articles SSC.10 [General rules] and SSC.12 [Pursuit of activities in two or more States] shall not apply to voluntary insurance or to optional continued insurance unless, in respect of one of the branches referred to in Article SSC.3 [Matters covered], only a voluntary scheme of insurance exists in a State.   **1.048**

2. Where, by virtue of the legislation of a State, the person concerned is subject to compulsory insurance in that State, that person may not be subject to a voluntary insurance scheme or an optional continued insurance scheme in another State. In all other cases in which, for a given branch, there is a choice between several voluntary insurance schemes or optional continued insurance schemes, the person concerned shall join only the scheme of their choice.

3. However, in respect of invalidity, old-age and survivors' benefits, the person concerned may join the voluntary or optional continued insurance scheme of a State, even if that person is compulsorily subject to the legislation of another State, provided that that person has been subject, at some stage in his or her career, to the legislation of the first State because or as a consequence of an activity as an employed or self-employed person and if such overlapping is explicitly or implicitly allowed under the legislation of the first State.

4. Where the legislation of a State makes admission to voluntary insurance or optional continued insurance conditional upon residence in that State or upon previous activity as an employed or self-employed person, Article SSC.6(b) [Equal treatment of benefits, income, facts or events] shall apply only to persons who have been subject, at some earlier stage, to the legislation of that State on the basis of an activity as an employed or self-employed person.

Article SSC.14: Obligations of the employer

1. An employer who has its registered office or place of business outside the competent State shall fulfil all the obligations laid down by the legislation applicable to its employees, notably the obligation to pay the contributions provided for by that legislation, as if it had its registered office or place of business in the competent State.   **1.049**

2. An employer who does not have a place of business in the State whose legislation is applicable and the employee may agree that the latter may fulfil the employer's obligations on its behalf as regards the payment of contributions without prejudice to the employer's underlying obligations. The employer shall send notice of such an arrangement to the competent institution of that State.

TITLE III: SPECIAL PROVISIONS CONCERNING THE VARIOUS
CATEGORIES OF BENEFITS

CHAPTER 1: SICKNESS, MATERNITY AND EQUIVALENT PATERNITY
BENEFITS

SECTION 1: INSURED PERSONS AND MEMBERS OF THEIR FAMILIES
EXCEPT PENSIONERS AND MEMBERS OF THEIR FAMILIES

Article SSC.15: Residence in a State other than the competent State

1.050   An insured person or members of their family who reside in a State other than the competent State shall receive in the State of residence benefits in kind provided, on behalf of the competent institution, by the institution of the place of residence, in accordance with the provisions of the legislation it applies, as though that person were insured under the said legislation.

Article SSC.16: Stay in the competent State when residence is in another State—special rules for the members of the families of frontier workers

1.051   1. Unless otherwise provided for by paragraph 2, the insured person and the members of their family referred to in Article SSC.15 [Residence in a State other than the competent State] shall also be entitled to benefits in kind while staying in the competent State. The benefits in kind shall be provided by the competent institution and at its own expense, in accordance with the provisions of the legislation it applies, as though the persons concerned resided in that State.

2. The members of the family of a frontier worker shall be entitled to benefits in kind during their stay in the competent State. Where the competent State is listed in Annex SSC-2 [Restriction of rights to benefits in kind for members of the family of a frontier worker] however, the members of the family of a frontier worker who reside in the same State as the frontier worker shall be entitled to benefits in kind in the competent State only under the conditions laid down in Article SSC.17(1) [Stay outside the competent State].

Article SSC.17: Stay outside the competent State

1.052   1. Unless otherwise provided for by paragraph 2, an insured person and the members of their family staying in a State other than the competent State shall be entitled to benefits in kind, provided on behalf of the competent institution by the institution of the place of stay in accordance with its legislation, as though the person were insured under that legislation, where:

(a) the benefits in kind become necessary on medical grounds during their stay, in the opinion of the provider of the benefits in kind,

taking into account the nature of the benefits and the expected length of the stay;
(b) the person did not travel to that State with the purpose of receiving the benefits in kind, unless the person is a passenger or member of the crew on a vessel or aircraft travelling to that State and the benefits in kind became necessary on medical grounds during the voyage or flight; and
(c) a valid entitlement document is presented in accordance with Article SSCI.22(1) [Stay in a State other than the competent State] of Annex SSC-7 [Implementing Part].

2. Appendix SSCI-2 [Entitlement document] lists benefits in kind which, in order to be provided during a stay in another State, require for practical reasons a prior agreement between the person concerned and the institution providing the care.

Article SSC.18: Travel with the purpose of receiving benefits in kind—authorisation to receive appropriate treatment outside the State of residence

1. Unless otherwise provided for by this Protocol, an insured person   1.053
travelling to another State with the purpose of receiving benefits in kind during the stay shall seek authorisation from the competent institution.

2. An insured person who is authorised by the competent institution to go to another State with the purpose of receiving the treatment appropriate to their condition shall receive the benefits in kind provided, on behalf of the competent institution, by the institution of the place of stay, in accordance with the provisions of the legislation it applies, as though that person were insured under the said legislation. The authorisation shall be accorded where the treatment in question is among the benefits provided for by the legislation in the State where the person concerned resides and where that person cannot be given such treatment within a time limit which is medically justifiable, taking into account their current state of health and the probable course of their illness.

3. Paragraphs 1 and 2 shall apply *mutatis mutandis* to the members of the family of an insured person.

4. If the members of the family of an insured person reside in a State other than the State in which the insured person resides, and this State has opted for reimbursement on the basis of fixed amounts, the cost of the benefits in kind referred to in paragraph 2 shall be borne by the institution of the place of residence of the members of the family. In this case, for the purposes of paragraph 1, the institution of the place of residence of the members of the family shall be considered to be the competent institution.

Article SSC.19: Cash benefits

1. An insured person and members of their family residing or staying   1.054
in a State other than the competent State shall be entitled to cash benefits provided by the competent institution in accordance with the legislation it applies. By agreement between the competent institution

and the institution of the place of residence or stay, such benefits may, however, be provided by the institution of the place of residence or stay at the expense of the competent institution in accordance with the legislation of the competent State.

2. The competent institution of a State whose legislation stipulates that the calculation of cash benefits shall be based on average income or on an average contribution basis shall determine such average income or average contribution basis exclusively by reference to the incomes confirmed as having been paid, or contribution bases applied, during the periods completed under the said legislation.

3. The competent institution of a State whose legislation provides that the calculation of cash benefits shall be based on standard income shall take into account exclusively the standard income or, where appropriate, the average of standard incomes for the periods completed under the said legislation.

4. Paragraphs 2 and 3 shall apply *mutatis mutandis* to cases where the legislation applied by the competent institution lays down a specific reference period which corresponds in the case in question either wholly or partly to the periods which the person concerned has completed under the legislation of one or more other States.

Article SSC.20: Pension claimants

1.055   1. An insured person who, on making a claim for a pension, or during the investigation thereof, ceases to be entitled to benefits in kind under the legislation of the State last competent, shall remain entitled to benefits in kind under the legislation of the State in which that person resides, provided that the pension claimant satisfies the insurance conditions of the legislation of the State referred to in paragraph 2. The right to benefits in kind in the State of residence shall also apply to the members of the family of the pension claimant.

2. The benefits in kind shall be chargeable to the institution of the State which, in the event of a pension being awarded, would become competent under Articles SSC.21 [Right to benefits in kind under the legislation of the State of residence] to SSC.23 [Pensions under the legislation of one or more States other than the State of residence, where there is a right to benefits in kind in the latter State]

SECTION 2: SPECIAL PROVISIONS FOR PENSIONERS AND MEMBERS OF THEIR FAMILIES

Article SSC.21: Right to benefits in kind under the legislation of the State of residence

1.056   A person who receives a pension or pensions under the legislation of two or more States, of which one is the State of residence, and who is entitled to benefits in kind under the legislation of that State, shall, with the members of their family, receive such benefits in kind from and at the expense of the institution of the place of residence, as though that person were a pensioner whose pension was payable solely under the legislation of that State.

Article SSC.22: No right to benefits in kind under the legislation of the State of residence

1. A person who: 1.057
   (a) resides in a State;
   (b) receives a pension or pensions under the legislation of one or more States; and
   (c) is not entitled to benefits in kind under the legislation of the State of residence,

shall nevertheless receive such benefits for themselves and the members of their family, insofar as the pensioner would be entitled to them under the legislation of the State competent in respect of their pension or at least one of the States competent, if that person resided in that State. The benefits in kind shall be provided at the expense of the institution referred to in paragraph 2 by the institution of the place of residence, as though the person concerned were entitled to a pension and entitled to benefits in kind under the legislation of that State.

2. In the cases covered by paragraph 1, the cost of the benefits in kind shall be borne by the institution as determined in accordance with the following rules:
   (a) where the pensioner is treated as if he or she were entitled to benefits in kind under the legislation of one State, the cost of those benefits shall be borne by the competent institution of that State;
   (b) where the pensioner is treated as if he or she were entitled to benefits in kind under the legislation of two or more States, the cost of those benefits shall be borne by the competent institution of the State to whose legislation the person has been subject for the longest period of time;
   (c) if the application of the rule in subparagraph (b) would result in several States being responsible for the cost of those benefits, the cost shall be borne by the competent institution of the State to whose legislation the pensioner was last subject.

Article SSC.23: Pensions under the legislation of one or more States other than the State of residence, where there is a right to benefits in kind in the latter State

Where a person receiving a pension or pensions under the legislation 1.058 of one or more States resides in a State under whose legislation the right to receive benefits in kind is not subject to conditions of insurance, or conditions of activity as an employed or self-employed person, and that person does not receive a pension from the State of residence, the cost of benefits in kind provided to them and to members of their family shall be borne by the institution of one of the States competent in respect of their pensions determined in accordance with Article SSC.22(2) [No right to benefits in kind under the legislation of the State of residence], to the

extent that the person and the members of their family would be entitled
to such benefits if that person resided in that State.

Article SSC.24: Residence of members of the family in a State other than the one in which the pensioner resides

1.059 Where a person:
  (a) receives a pension or pensions under the legislation of one or more
      States; and
  (b) resides in a State other than the one in which members of his or
      her family reside,
those members of that person's family shall be entitled to receive benefits
in kind from the institution of the place of their residence in accordance
with the legislation it applies insofar as the pensioner is entitled to
benefits in kind under the legislation of a State. The costs shall be borne
by the competent institution responsible for the costs of the benefits in
kind provided to the pensioner in their State of residence.

Article SSC.25: Stay of the pensioner or the members of their family in a State other than the State of residence—stay in the competent State—authorisation for appropriate treatment outside the State of residence

1. Article SSC.17 [Stay outside the competent State] shall apply
mutatis mutandis to:
  (a) a person receiving a pension or pensions under the legislation of
      one or more States and who is entitled to benefits in kind under
      the legislation of one of the States which provide their pen-
      sion(s);
  (b) the members of their family, who are staying in a State other than
      the one in which they reside.
2. Article SSC.16(1) [Stay in the competent State when residence is in
another State—special rules for the members of the families of frontier
workers] shall apply *mutatis mutandis* to the persons described in paragraph 1 when they stay in the State in which is situated the competent
institution responsible for the cost of the benefits in kind provided to the
pensioner in his or her State of residence and that State has opted for this
and is listed in Annex SSC-3 [More rights for pensioners returning to
the competent State].
3. Article SSC.18 [Travel with the purpose of receiving benefits in
kind—authorisation to receive appropriate treatment outside the State of
residence] shall apply *mutatis mutandis* to a pensioner or members of his
or her family who are staying in a State other than the one in which they
reside with the purpose of receiving in that State the treatment appropriate to their condition.
4. Unless otherwise provided for by paragraph 5, the cost of the
benefits in kind referred to in paragraphs 1 to 3 shall be borne by the
competent institution responsible for the cost of benefits in kind provided to the pensioner in their State of residence.
5. The cost of the benefits in kind referred to in paragraph 3 shall be
borne by the institution of the place of residence of the pensioner or of

the members of their family, if these persons reside in a State which has opted for reimbursement on the basis of fixed amounts. In these cases, for the purposes of paragraph 3, the institution of the place of residence of the pensioner or of the members of their family shall be considered to be the competent institution.

Article SSC.26: Cash benefits for pensioners

1. Cash benefits shall be paid to a person receiving a pension or pensions under the legislation of one or more States by the competent institution of the State in which is situated the competent institution responsible for the cost of benefits in kind provided to the pensioner in their State of residence. Article SSC.19 [Cash benefits] shall apply *mutatis mutandis*.   1.060

2. Paragraph 1 shall also apply to the members of a pensioner's family.

Article SSC.27: Contributions by pensioners

1. The institution of a State which is responsible under the legislation it applies for making deductions in respect of contributions for sickness, maternity and equivalent paternity benefits, may request and recover such deductions, calculated in accordance with the legislation it applies, only to the extent that the cost of the benefits pursuant to Articles SSC.21 [Right to benefits in kind under the legislation of the State of residence] to SSC.24 [Residence of members of the family in a State other than the one in which the pensioner resides] is to be borne by an institution of that State.   1.061

2. Where, in the cases referred to in Article SSC.23 [Pensions under the legislation of one or more States other than the State of residence, where there is a right to benefits in kind in the latter State], the acquisition of sickness, maternity and equivalent paternity benefits is subject to the payment of contributions or similar payments under the legislation of a State in which the pensioner concerned resides, these contributions shall not be payable by virtue of such residence.

SECTION 3: COMMON PROVISIONS

Article SSC.28: General provisions

Articles SSC.21 [Right to benefits in kind under the legislation of the State of residence] to SSC.27 [Contributions by pensioners] shall not apply to a pensioner or the members of their family who are entitled to benefits under the legislation of a State on the basis of an activity as an employed or self-employed person. In such a case, the person concerned shall be subject, for the purposes of this Chapter, to Articles SSC.15 [Residence in a State other than the competent State] to SSC.19 [Cash benefits].   1.062

Article SSC.29: Prioritising of the right to benefits in kind—special rule for the right of members of the family to benefits in the State of residence

1.063   1. Unless otherwise provided for by paragraph 2, where a member of the family has an independent right to benefits in kind based on the legislation of a State or on this Chapter such right shall take priority over a derivative right to benefits in kind for members of the family.

2. Unless otherwise provided for by paragraph 3, where the independent right in the State of residence exists directly and solely on the basis of the residence of the person concerned in that State, a derivative right to benefits in kind shall take priority over the independent right.

3. Notwithstanding paragraphs 1 and 2, benefits in kind shall be provided to the members of the family of an insured person at the expense of the competent institution in the State in which they reside, where:

(a) those members of the family reside in a State under whose legislation the right to benefits in kind is not subject to conditions of insurance or activity as an employed or self-employed person; and

(b) the spouse or the person caring for the children of the insured person pursues an activity as an employed or self-employed person in that State, or receives a pension from that State on the basis of an activity as an employed or self-employed person.

Article SSC.30: Reimbursements between institutions

1.064   1. The benefits in kind provided by the institution of a State on behalf of the institution of another State under this Chapter shall give rise to full reimbursement.

2. The reimbursements referred to in paragraph 1 shall be determined and effected in accordance with the arrangements set out in Annex SSC-7 [Implementing Part], either on production of proof of actual expenditure, or on the basis of fixed amounts for States whose legal or administrative structures are such that the use of reimbursement on the basis of actual expenditure is not appropriate.

3. The States, and their competent authorities, may provide for other methods of reimbursement or waive all reimbursement between the institutions coming under their jurisdiction.

CHAPTER 2: BENEFITS IN RESPECT OF ACCIDENTS AT WORK AND OCCUPATIONAL DISEASES

Article SSC.31: Right to benefits in kind and in cash

1.065   1. Without prejudice to any more favourable provisions in paragraphs 2 and 3 of this Article, Articles SSC.15 [Residence in a State other than the competent State], SSC.16(1) [Stay in the competent State when residence is in another State—special rules for the members of the families of frontier workers], SSC.17(1) [Stay outside the competent State] and 18(1) [Travel with the purpose of receiving benefits in kind —authorisation to receive appropriate treatment outside the State of residence] shall also apply to benefits relating to accidents at work or occupational diseases.

2. A person who has sustained an accident at work or has contracted an occupational disease and who resides or stays in a State other than the competent State shall be entitled to the special benefits in kind of the scheme covering accidents at work and occupational diseases provided, on behalf of the competent institution, by the institution of the place of residence or stay in accordance with the legislation which it applies, as though that person were insured under that legislation.

3. The competent institution may not refuse to grant the authorisation provided for in Article SSC.18(1) [Travel with the purpose of receiving benefits in kind—authorisation to receive appropriate treatment outside the State of residence] to a person who has sustained an accident at work or who has contracted an occupational disease and is entitled to benefits chargeable to that institution, where the treatment appropriate to his or her condition cannot be given in the State in which that person resides within a time limit which is medically justifiable, taking into account that person's current state of health and the probable course of the illness.

4. Article SSC.19 [Cash benefits] also applies to benefits falling within this Chapter.

Article SSC.32: Costs of transport

1. The competent institution of a State whose legislation provides for meeting the costs of transporting a person who has sustained an accident at work or is suffering from an occupational disease, either to their place of residence or to a hospital, shall meet such costs to the corresponding place in the State where the person resides, provided that that institution gives prior authorisation for such transport, duly taking into account the reasons justifying it. Such authorisation shall not be required in the case of a frontier worker. **1.066**

2. The competent institution of a State whose legislation provides for meeting the costs of transporting the body of a person killed in an accident at work to the place of burial shall, in accordance with the legislation it applies, meet such costs to the corresponding place in the State where the person was residing at the time of the accident.

Article SSC.33: Benefits for an occupational disease where the person suffering from such a disease has been exposed to the same risk in several States

When a person who has contracted an occupational disease has, under the legislation of two or more States, pursued an activity which by its nature is likely to cause the said disease, the benefits that that person or his or her survivors may claim shall be provided exclusively under the legislation of the last of those States whose conditions are satisfied. **1.067**

Article SSC.34: Aggravation of an occupational disease

1.068   In the event of aggravation of an occupational disease for which a person suffering from such a disease has received or is receiving benefits under the legislation of a State, the following rules shall apply:

(a) if the person concerned, while in receipt of benefits, has not pursued, under the legislation of another State, an activity as an employed or self-employed person likely to cause or aggravate the disease in question, the competent institution of the first State shall bear the cost of the benefits under the provisions of the legislation which it applies, taking into account the aggravation;

(b) if the person concerned, while in receipt of benefits, has pursued such an activity under the legislation of another State, the competent institution of the first State shall bear the cost of the benefits under the legislation it applies without taking the aggravation into account. The competent institution of the second State shall grant a supplement to the person concerned, the amount of which shall be equal to the difference between the amount of benefits due after the aggravation and the amount which would have been due prior to the aggravation under the legislation it applies, if the disease in question had occurred under the legislation of that State;

(c) the rules concerning reduction, suspension or withdrawal laid down by the legislation of a State shall not be invoked against persons receiving benefits provided by institutions of two States in accordance with point (b).

Article SSC.35: Rules for taking into account the special features of certain legislation

1.069   1. If there is no insurance against accidents at work or occupational diseases in the State in which the person concerned resides or stays, or if such insurance exists but there is no institution responsible for providing benefits in kind, those benefits shall be provided by the institution of the place of residence or stay responsible for providing benefits in kind in the event of sickness.

2. If there is no insurance against accidents at work or occupational diseases in the competent State, the provisions of this Chapter concerning benefits in kind shall nevertheless be applied to a person who is entitled to those benefits in the event of sickness, maternity or equivalent paternity under the legislation of that State if that person sustains an accident at work or suffers from an occupational disease during a residence or stay in another State. Costs shall be borne by the institution that is competent for the benefits in kind under the legislation of the competent State.

3. Article SSC.6 [Equal treatment of benefits, income, facts or events] shall apply to the competent institution in a State as regards the equivalence of accidents at work and occupational diseases which either have occurred or have been confirmed subsequently under the legislation of another State when assessing the degree of incapacity, the right to benefits or the amount thereof, on condition that:

(a) no compensation is due in respect of an accident at work or an occupational disease which had occurred or had been confirmed previously under the legislation it applies; and

(b) no compensation is due in respect of an accident at work or an occupational disease which had occurred or had been confirmed subsequently, under the legislation of the other State under which the accident at work or the occupational disease had occurred or been confirmed.

Article SSC.36: Reimbursements between institutions

1. Article SSC.30 [Reimbursements between institutions] shall also apply to benefits falling within this Chapter, and reimbursement shall be made on the basis of actual costs.   1.070

2. The States, or their competent authorities, may provide for other methods of reimbursement or waive all reimbursement between the institutions under their jurisdiction.

CHAPTER 3: DEATH GRANTS

Article SSC.37: Right to grants where death occurs in, or where the person entitled resides in, a State other than the competent one

1. When an insured person or a member of their family dies in a State other than the competent State, the death shall be deemed to have occurred in the competent State.   1.071

2. The competent institution shall be obliged to provide death grants payable under the legislation it applies, even if the person entitled resides in a State other than the competent State.

3. Paragraphs 1 and 2 shall also apply when the death is the result of an accident at work or an occupational disease.

Article SSC.38: Provision of benefits in the event of the death of a pensioner

1. In the event of the death of a pensioner who was entitled to a pension under the legislation of one State, or to pensions under the legislations of two or more States, when that pensioner was residing in a State other than that of the institution responsible for the cost of benefits in kind provided under Articles SSC.22 [No right to benefits in kind under the legislation of the State of residence] and SSC.23 [Pensions under the legislation of one or more States other than the State of residence, where there is a right to benefits in kind in the latter State], the death grants payable under the legislation administered by that institution shall be provided at its own expense as though the pensioner had been residing at the time of their death in the State in which that institution is situated.   1.072

2. Paragraph 1 shall apply *mutatis mutandis* to the members of the family of a pensioner.

CHAPTER 4: INVALIDITY BENEFITS

Article SSC.39: Calculation of invalidity benefits

1.073   Without prejudice to Article SSC.7 [Aggregation of periods], where, under the legislation of the State competent under Title II [Determination of the legislation applicable] of this Protocol, the amount of invalidity benefits is dependent on the duration of the periods of insurance, employment, self- employment or residence, the competent State is not required to take into account any such periods completed under the legislation of another State for the purposes of calculating the amount of invalidity benefit payable.

Article SSC.40: Special provisions on aggregation of periods

1.074   The competent institution of a State whose legislation makes the acquisition, retention or recovery of the right to benefits conditional upon the completion of periods of insurance or residence shall, where necessary, apply Article SSC.46 [Special provisions on aggregation of periods] *mutatis mutandis.*

Article SSC.41: Aggravation of invalidity

1.075   In the case of aggravation of an invalidity for which a person is receiving benefits under the legislation of a State in accordance with this Protocol, the benefit shall continue to be provided in accordance with this Chapter, taking the aggravation into account.

Article SSC.42: Conversion of invalidity benefits into old-age benefits

1.076   1. Where provided for in the legislation of the State paying invalidity benefit in accordance with this Protocol, invalidity benefits shall be converted into old-age benefits under the conditions laid down by the legislation under which they are provided and in accordance with Chapter 5 [Old-age and survivors' pensions].

2. Where a person receiving invalidity benefits can establish a claim to old-age benefits under the legislation of one or more other States, in accordance with Article SSC.45 [General provisions], any institution which is responsible for providing invalidity benefits under the legislation of a State shall continue to provide such a person with the invalidity benefits to which he or she is entitled under the legislation it applies until paragraph 1 becomes applicable in respect of that institution, or otherwise for as long as the person concerned satisfies the conditions for such benefits.

Article SSC.43: Special provisions for civil servants

1.077   Articles SSC.7 [Aggregation of periods], SSC.39 [Calculation of invalidity benefits], SSC.41 [Aggravation of invalidity], SSC.42 [Conversion of invalidity benefits into old-age benefits] and paragraphs 2 and 3 of Article SSC.55 [Special provisions for civil servants] shall apply *mutatis mutandis* to persons covered by a special scheme for civil servants.

CHAPTER 5: OLD-AGE AND SURVIVORS' PENSIONS

Article SSC.44: Taking into account child-raising periods

1. Where, under the legislation of the State which is competent under   1.078
Title II [Determination of the legislation applicable], no child-raising
period is taken into account, the institution of the State whose legislation, according to Title II [Determination of the legislation applicable],
was applicable to the person concerned on the grounds that he or she
was pursuing an activity as an employed or self-employed person at the
date when, under that legislation, the child-raising period started to be
taken into account for the child concerned, shall remain responsible for
taking into account that period as a child-raising period under its own
legislation, as if such child-raising took place in its own territory.

2. Paragraph 1 shall not apply if the person concerned is, or becomes,
subject to the legislation of another State due to the pursuit of an
employed or self-employed activity.

Article SSC.45: General provisions

1. All the competent institutions shall determine entitlement to bene-   1.079
fit, under all the legislations of the States to which the person concerned
has been subject, when a request for award has been submitted, unless
the person concerned expressly requests deferment of the award of old-
age benefits under the legislation of one or more States.

2. If at a given moment the person concerned does not satisfy, or no
longer satisfies, the conditions laid down by all the legislations of the
States to which that person has been subject, the institutions applying
legislation the conditions of which have been satisfied shall not take into
account, when performing the calculation in accordance with points (a)
or (b) of Article SSC.47(1) [Award of benefits], the periods completed
under the legislations the conditions of which have not been satisfied, or
are no longer satisfied, where this gives rise to a lower amount of benefit.

3. Paragraph 2 shall apply *mutatis mutandis* when the person concerned has expressly requested deferment of the award of old-age benefits.

4. A new calculation shall be performed automatically as and when the
conditions to be fulfilled under the other legislations are satisfied or
when a person requests the award of an old-age benefit deferred in
accordance with paragraph 1, unless the periods completed under the
other legislations have already been taken into account by virtue of
paragraphs 2 or 3.

Article SSC.46: Special provisions on aggregation of periods

1. Where the legislation of a State makes the granting of certain   1.080
benefits conditional upon the periods of insurance having been completed only in a specific activity as an employed or self-employed person
or in an occupation which is subject to a special scheme for employed or

self-employed persons, the competent institution of that State shall take into account periods completed under the legislation of other States only if completed under a corresponding scheme or, failing that, in the same occupation, or where appropriate, in the same activity as an employed or self-employed person.

If, account having been taken of the periods thus completed, the person concerned does not satisfy the conditions for receipt of the benefits of a special scheme, these periods shall be taken into account for the purposes of providing the benefits of the general scheme or, failing that, of the scheme applicable to manual or clerical workers, as the case may be, provided that the person concerned had been affiliated to one or other of those schemes.

2. The periods of insurance completed under a special scheme of a State shall be taken into account for the purposes of providing the benefits of the general scheme or, failing that, of the scheme applicable to manual or clerical workers, as the case may be, of another State, provided that the person concerned had been affiliated to one or other of those schemes, even if those periods have already been taken into account in the latter State under a special scheme.

3. Where the legislation or specific scheme of a State makes the acquisition, retention or recovery of the right to benefits conditional upon the person concerned being insured at the time of the materialisation of the risk, this condition shall be regarded as having been satisfied if that person has been previously insured under the legislation or specific scheme of that State and is, at the time of the materialisation of the risk, insured under the legislation of another State for the same risk or, failing that, if a benefit is due under the legislation of another State for the same risk. The latter condition shall, however, be deemed to be fulfilled in the cases referred to in Article SSC.52 [Periods of insurance or residence of less than one year].

Article SSC.47: Award of benefits

1.081   1. The competent institution shall calculate the amount of the benefit that would be due:
- (a) under the legislation it applies, only where the conditions for entitlement to benefits have been satisfied exclusively under national law (independent benefit);
- (b) by calculating a theoretical amount and subsequently an actual amount (pro rata benefit), as follows:
  - (i) the theoretical amount of the benefit is equal to the benefit which the person concerned could claim if all the periods of insurance or of residence which have been completed under the legislations of the other States had been completed under the legislation it applies on the date of the award of the benefit. If, under this legislation, the amount does not depend on the duration of the periods completed, that amount shall be regarded as being the theoretical amount;
  - (ii) the competent institution shall then establish the actual amount of the pro rata benefit by applying to the theoretical

amount the ratio between the duration of the periods completed before materialisation of the risk under the legislation it applies and the total duration of the periods completed before materialisation of the risk under the legislations of all the States concerned.

2. Where appropriate, the competent institution shall apply, to the amount calculated in accordance with points (a) and (b) of paragraph 1, all the rules relating to reduction, suspension or withdrawal, under the legislation it applies, within the limits provided for by Articles SSC.48 [Rules to prevent overlapping] to SSC.50 [Overlapping of benefits of a different kind].

3. The person concerned shall be entitled to receive from the competent institution of each State the higher of the amounts calculated in accordance with points (a) and (b) of paragraph 1.

4. Where the calculation pursuant to point (a) of paragraph 1 in one State invariably results in the independent benefit being equal to or higher than the pro rata benefit, calculated in accordance with point (b) of paragraph 1, the competent institution shall waive the pro rata calculation, provided that:

(a) such a situation is set out in Part 1 of Annex SSC-4 [Cases in which the pro rata calculation shall be waived or shall not apply].

(b) no legislation containing rules against overlapping, as referred to in Articles SSC.49 [Overlapping of benefits of the same kind] and SSC.50 [Overlapping of benefits of a different kind], is applicable unless the conditions laid down in Article SSC.50(2) [Overlapping of benefits of a different kind], are fulfilled; and

(c) Article SSC.52 [Periods of insurance or residence of less than one year] is not applicable in relation to periods completed under the legislation of another State in the specific circumstances of the case.

5. Notwithstanding the provisions of paragraphs 1, 2 and 3, the pro rata calculation shall not apply to schemes providing benefits in respect of which periods of time are of no relevance to the calculation, subject to such schemes being listed in part 2 of Annex SSC-4 [Cases in which the pro rata calculation shall be waived or shall not apply]. In such cases, the person concerned shall be entitled to the benefit calculated in accordance with the legislation of the State concerned.

Article SSC.48: Rules to prevent overlapping

1. Any overlapping of old-age and survivors' benefits calculated or provided on the basis of periods of insurance or residence completed by the same person shall be considered to be overlapping of benefits of the same kind. 1.082

2. Overlapping of benefits which cannot be considered to be of the same kind within the meaning of paragraph 1 shall be considered to be overlapping of benefits of a different kind.

3. The following provisions shall be applicable for the purposes of rules to prevent overlapping laid down by the legislation of a State in the

case of overlapping of a benefit in respect of old-age or survivors with a benefit of the same kind or a benefit of a different kind or with other income:

(a) the competent institution shall take into account the benefits or incomes acquired in another State only where the legislation it applies provides for benefits or income acquired abroad to be taken into account;

(b) the competent institution shall take into account the amount of benefits to be paid by another State before deduction of tax, social security contributions and other individual levies or deductions, unless the legislation it applies provides for the application of rules to prevent overlapping after such deductions, under the conditions and the procedures laid down in Annex SSC-7 [Implementing Part];

(c) the competent institution shall not take into account the amount of benefits acquired under the legislation of another State on the basis of voluntary insurance or continued optional insurance;

(d) if a single State applies rules to prevent overlapping because the person concerned receives benefits of the same or of a different kind under the legislation of other States or income acquired in other States, the benefit due may be reduced solely by the amount of such benefits or such income.

Article SSC.49: Overlapping of benefits of the same kind

1.083   1. Where benefits of the same kind due under the legislation of two or more States overlap, the rules to prevent overlapping laid down by the legislation of a State shall not be applicable to a pro rata benefit.

2. The rules to prevent overlapping shall apply to an independent benefit only if the benefit concerned is:

(a) a benefit the amount of which does not depend on the duration of periods of insurance or residence; or

(b) a benefit the amount of which is determined on the basis of a credited period deemed to have been completed between the date on which the risk materialised and a later date, overlapping with:

(i) a benefit of the same type, except where an agreement has been concluded between two or more States to avoid the same credited period being taken into account more than once; or

(ii) a benefit referred to in point (a).

The benefits and agreements referred to in points (a) and (b) are listed in Annex SSC-5 [Benefits and agreements which allow the application of Article SSC.49 [Overlapping of benefits of the same kind]].

Article SSC.50: Overlapping of benefits of a different kind

1.084   1. If the receipt of benefits of a different kind or other income requires the application of the rules to prevent overlapping provided for by the legislation of the States concerned regarding:

(a) two or more independent benefits, the competent institutions shall divide the amounts of the benefit or benefits or other income, as they have been taken into account, by the number of benefits subject to the said rules;

   however, the application of this subparagraph cannot deprive the person concerned of their status as a pensioner for the purposes of the other chapters of this Title under the conditions and the procedures laid down in Annex SSC-7 [Implementing Part];

(b) one or more pro rata benefits, the competent institutions shall take into account the benefit or benefits or other income and all the elements stipulated for applying the rules to prevent overlapping as a function of the ratio between the periods of insurance or residence established for the calculation referred to in point (b)(ii) of Article SSC.47(1) [Award of benefits];

(c) one or more independent benefits and one or more pro rata benefits, the competent institutions shall apply *mutatis mutandis* point (a) as regards independent benefits and point (b) as regards pro rata benefits.

2. The competent institution shall not apply the division stipulated in respect of independent benefits, if the legislation it applies provides for account to be taken of benefits of a different kind or other income and all other elements for calculating part of their amount determined as a function of the ratio between periods of insurance or residence referred to in point (b)(ii) of Article SSC.47(1) [Award of benefits].

3. Paragraphs 1 and 2 shall apply *mutatis mutandis* where the legislation of one or more States provides that a right to a benefit cannot be acquired in the case where the person concerned is in receipt of a benefit of a different kind, payable under the legislation of another State, or of other income.

Article SSC.51: Additional provisions for the calculation of benefits

For the calculation of the theoretical and pro rata amounts referred to in point (b) of Article SSC.47(1) [Award of benefits], the following rules shall apply: 1.085

(a) where the total length of the periods of insurance or residence completed before the risk materialised under the legislations of all the States concerned is longer than the maximum period required by the legislation of one of these States for receipt of full benefit, the competent institution of that State shall take into account this maximum period instead of the total length of the periods completed; this method of calculation shall not result in the imposition on that institution of the cost of a benefit greater than the full benefit provided for by the legislation it applies. This provision shall not apply to benefits the amount of which does not depend on the length of insurance;

(b) the procedure for taking into account overlapping periods is laid down in Annex SSC-7 [Implementing Part];

(c) if the legislation of a State provides that the benefits are to be calculated on the basis of incomes, contributions, bases of contributions, increases, earnings, other amounts or a combination of more than one of them (average, proportional, fixed or credited), the competent institution shall:
   (i) determine the basis for calculation of the benefits in accordance only with periods of insurance completed under the legislation it applies;
   (ii) use, in order to determine the amount to be calculated in accordance with the periods of insurance or residence completed under the legislation of the other States, the same elements determined or recorded for the periods of insurance completed under the legislation it applies;
where necessary in accordance with the procedures laid down in Annex SSC-6 [Special provisions for the application of the legislation of the Member States and of the United Kingdom] for the State concerned;

(d) in the event that point (c) is not applicable because the legislation of a State provides for the benefit to be calculated on the basis of elements other than periods of insurance or residence which are not linked to time, the competent institution shall take into account, in respect of each period of insurance or residence completed under the legislation of any other State, the amount of the capital accrued, the capital which is considered as having been accrued or any other element for the calculation under the legislation it administers divided by the corresponding units of periods in the pension scheme concerned.

2. The provisions of the legislation of a State concerning the revalorisation of the elements taken into account for the calculation of benefits shall apply, as appropriate, to the elements to be taken into account by the competent institution of that State, in accordance with paragraph 1, in respect of the periods of insurance or residence completed under the legislation of other States.

Article SSC.52: Periods of insurance or residence of less than one year

1.086   1. Notwithstanding point (b) of Article SSC.47(1) [Award of benefits], the institution of a State shall not be required to provide benefits in respect of periods completed under the legislation it applies which are taken into account when the risk materialises, if:
(a) the duration of the said periods is less than one year, and
(b) taking only these periods into account no right to benefit is acquired under that legislation.

For the purposes of this Article, 'periods' shall mean all periods of insurance, employment, self-employment or residence which either qualify for, or directly increase, the benefit concerned.

2. The competent institution of each of the States concerned shall take into account the periods referred to in paragraph 1, for the purposes of point (b)(i) of Article SSC.47(1) [Award of benefits].

3. If the effect of applying paragraph 1 would be to relieve all the institutions of the States concerned of their obligations, benefits shall be provided exclusively under the legislation of the last of those States whose conditions are satisfied, as if all the periods of insurance and residence completed and taken into account in accordance with Articles SSC.7 [Aggregation of periods] and SSC.46(1) and (2) [Special provisions on aggregation of periods] had been completed under the legislation of that State.

4. This Article shall not apply to schemes listed in Part 2 [Cases in which Article 47(5) applies] of Annex SSC-4 [Cases in which the pro rata calculation shall be waived or shall not apply].

Article SSC.53: Award of a supplement

1. A recipient of benefits to whom this Chapter applies may not, in the State of residence and under whose legislation a benefit is payable to them, be provided with a benefit which is less than the minimum benefit fixed by that legislation for a period of insurance or residence equal to all the periods taken into account for the payment in accordance with this Chapter.   1.087

2. The competent institution of that State shall pay them throughout the period of their residence in its territory a supplement equal to the difference between the total of the benefits due under this Chapter and the amount of the minimum benefit.

Article SSC.54: Recalculation and revaluation of benefits

1. If the method for determining benefits or the rules for calculating benefits are altered under the legislation of a State, or if the personal situation of the person concerned undergoes a relevant change which, under that legislation, would lead to an adjustment of the amount of the benefit, a recalculation shall be carried out in accordance with Article SSC.47 [Award of benefits].   1.088

2. On the other hand, if, by reason of an increase in the cost of living or changes in the level of income or other grounds for adjustment, the benefits of the State concerned are altered by a percentage or fixed amount, such percentage or fixed amount shall be applied directly to the benefits determined in accordance with Article SSC.47 [Award of benefits], without the need for a recalculation.

Article SSC.55: Special provisions for civil servants

1. Articles SSC.7 [Aggregation of periods], SSC.45 [General provisions], SSC.46(3) [Special provisions on aggregation of periods] and SSC.47 [Award of benefits] to SSC.54 [Recalculation and revaluation of benefits] shall apply *mutatis mutandis* to persons covered by a special scheme for civil servants.   1.089

2. However, if the legislation of a competent State makes the acquisition, liquidation, retention or recovery of the right to benefits under a special scheme for civil servants subject to the condition that all periods of insurance be completed under one or more special schemes for civil servants in that State, or be regarded by the legislation of that State as

equivalent to such periods, the competent institution of that State shall take into account only the periods which can be recognised under the legislation it applies.

If, account having been taken of the periods thus completed, the person concerned does not satisfy the conditions for the receipt of these benefits, these periods shall be taken into account for the award of benefits under the general scheme or, failing that, the scheme applicable to manual or clerical workers, as the case may be.

3. Where, under the legislation of a State, benefits under a special scheme for civil servants are calculated on the basis of the last salary or salaries received during a reference period, the competent institution of that State shall take into account, for the purposes of the calculation, only those salaries, duly revalued, which were received during the period or periods for which the person concerned was subject to that legislation.

CHAPTER 6: UNEMPLOYMENT BENEFITS

Article SSC.56: Special provisions on aggregation of periods of insurance, employment or self-employment

1.090   1. The competent institution of a State whose legislation makes the acquisition, retention, recovery or duration of the right to benefits conditional upon the completion of either periods of insurance, employment or self-employment shall, to the extent necessary, take into account periods of insurance, employment or self-employment completed under the legislation of any other State as though they were completed under the legislation it applies.

However, when the applicable legislation makes the right to benefits conditional on the completion of periods of insurance, the periods of employment or self-employment completed under the legislation of another State shall not be taken into account unless such periods would have been considered to be periods of insurance had they been completed in accordance with the applicable legislation.

2. The application of paragraph 1 of this Article shall be conditional on the person concerned having the most recently completed, in accordance with the legislation under which the benefits are claimed:

(a) periods of insurance, if that legislation requires periods of insurance,
(b) periods of employment, if that legislation requires periods of employment, or
(c) periods of self-employment, if that legislation requires periods of self-employment.

Article SSC.57: Calculation of unemployment benefits

1.091   1. Where the calculation of unemployment benefits is based on the amount of the previous salary or professional income of the person concerned, the competent State shall take into account the salary or professional income received by the person concerned based exclusively on their last activity as an employed or self-employed person under the legislation of the competent State.

2. Where the legislation applied by the competent State provides for a specific reference period for the determination of the salary or professional income used to calculate the amount of benefit, and the person concerned was subject to the legislation of another State for all or part of that reference period, the competent State shall only take into account the salary or professional income received during their last activity as an employed or self-employed person under that legislation.

CHAPTER 7: PRE-RETIREMENT BENEFITS

Article SSC.58: Benefits

When the applicable legislation makes the right to pre-retirement benefits conditional on the completion of periods of insurance, of employment or of self-employment, Article SSC.7 [Aggregation of periods] shall not apply.

1.092

TITLE IV: MISCELLANEOUS PROVISIONS

Article SSC.59: Cooperation

1. The competent authorities of the States shall notify the Specialised Committee on Social Security Coordination of any changes to their legislation as regards the branches of social security covered by Article SSC.3 [Matters covered] which are relevant to or may affect the implementation of this Protocol.

1.093

2. Unless this Protocol requires such information to be notified to the Specialised Committee on Social Security Coordination, the competent authorities of the States shall communicate to each other measures taken to implement this Protocol that are not notified under paragraph 1 and that are relevant for the implementation of the Protocol.

3. For the purposes of this Protocol, the authorities and institutions of the Member States and of the United Kingdom shall lend one another their good offices and act as though implementing their own legislation. The administrative assistance given by the said authorities and institutions shall, as a rule, be free of charge. However, the Specialised Committee on Social Security Coordination shall establish the nature of reimbursable expenses and the limits above which their reimbursement is due.

4. The authorities and institutions of the States may, for the purposes of this Protocol, communicate directly with one another and with the persons involved or their representatives.

5. The institutions and persons covered by this Protocol shall have a duty of mutual information and cooperation to ensure the correct implementation of this Protocol.

The institutions, in accordance with the principle of good administration, shall respond to all queries within a reasonable period of time and shall in this connection provide the persons concerned with any information required for exercising the rights conferred on them by this Protocol.

The persons concerned must inform the institutions of the competent State and of the State of residence as soon as possible of any change in their personal or family situation which affects their right to benefits under this Protocol.

6. Failure to respect the obligation of information referred to in the third subparagraph of paragraph 5 may result in the application of proportionate measures in accordance with national law. Nevertheless, these measures shall be equivalent to those applicable to similar situations under domestic law and shall not make it impossible or excessively difficult in practice for claimants to exercise the rights conferred on them by this Protocol.

7. In the event of difficulties in the interpretation or application of this Protocol which could jeopardise the rights of a person covered by it, the institution of the competent State or of the State of residence of the person concerned, shall contact the institution(s) of the State(s) concerned. If a solution cannot be found within a reasonable period, a Party may request to hold consultations in the framework of the Specialised Committee on Social Security Coordination.

8. The authorities, institutions and tribunals of one State may not reject applications or other documents submitted to them on the grounds that they are written in an official language of the Union, including in English.

Article SSC.60: Data processing

1.094   1. The States shall progressively use new technologies for the exchange, access and processing of the data required to apply this Protocol.

2. Each State shall be responsible for managing its own part of the data-processing services.

3. An electronic document sent or issued by an institution in conformity with the Protocol and Annex SSC-7 [Implementing Part] may not be rejected by any authority or institution of another State on the grounds that it was received by electronic means, once the receiving institution has declared that it can receive electronic documents. Reproduction and recording of such documents shall be presumed to be a correct and accurate reproduction of the original document or representation of the information it relates to, unless there is proof to the contrary.

4. An electronic document shall be considered valid if the computer system on which the document is recorded contains the safeguards necessary in order to prevent any alteration, disclosure or unauthorised access to the recording. It shall at any time be possible to reproduce the recorded information in an immediately readable form.

Article SSC.61: Exemptions

1. Any exemption from or reduction of taxes, stamp duty, notarial or registration fees provided for under the legislation of one State in respect of certificates or documents required to be produced in application of the legislation of that State shall be extended to similar certificates or documents required to be produced in application of the legislation of another State or of this Protocol. 1.095

2. All statements, documents and certificates of any kind whatsoever required to be produced in application of this Protocol shall be exempt from authentication by diplomatic or consular authorities.

Article SSC.62: Claims, declarations or appeals

Any claim, declaration or appeal which should have been submitted, in application of the legislation of one State, within a specified period to an authority, institution or tribunal of that State shall be admissible if it is submitted within the same period to a corresponding authority, institution or tribunal of another State. In such a case, the authority, institution or tribunal receiving the claim, declaration or appeal shall forward it without delay to the competent authority, institution or tribunal of the former State either directly or through the competent authorities of the States concerned. The date on which such claims, declarations or appeals were submitted to the authority, institution or tribunal of the second State shall be considered as the date of their submission to the competent authority, institution or tribunal. 1.096

Article SSC.63: Medical examinations

1. Medical examinations provided for by the legislation of one State may be carried out, at the request of the competent institution, in the territory of another State, by the institution of the place of stay or residence of the person entitled to benefits, under the conditions laid down in Annex SSC-7 [Implementing Part] or agreed between the competent authorities of the States concerned. 1.097

2. Medical examinations carried out under the conditions laid down in paragraph 1 shall be considered as having been carried out in the territory of the competent State.

Article SSC.64: Collection of contributions and recovery of benefits

1. Collection of contributions due to an institution of one State and recovery of benefits provided by the institution of one State but not due, may be effected in another State in accordance with the procedures and with the guarantees and privileges applicable to the collection of contributions due to the corresponding institution of the latter and the recovery of benefits provided by it but not due. 1.098

2. Enforceable decisions of the judicial and administrative authorities relating to the collection of contributions, interest and any other charges or to the recovery of benefits provided but not due under the legislation of one State shall be recognised and enforced at the request of the

competent institution in another State within the limits and in accordance with the procedures laid down by the legislation and any other procedures applicable to similar decisions of the latter. Such decisions shall be declared enforceable in that State insofar as the legislation and any other procedures of that State so require.

3. Claims of an institution of one State shall in enforcement, bankruptcy or settlement proceedings in another State enjoy the same privileges as the legislation that the latter accords to claims of the same kind.

4. The procedure for implementing this Article, including costs reimbursement, shall be governed by Annex SSC-7 [Implementing Part] or, where necessary and as a complementary measure, by means of agreements between the States.

Article SSC.65: Rights of institutions

1.099   1. If a person receives benefits under the legislation of a State in respect of an injury resulting from events occurring in another State, any rights of the institution responsible for providing benefits against a third party liable to provide compensation for the injury shall be governed by the following rules:

(a) where the institution responsible for providing benefits is, under the legislation it applies, subrogated to the rights which the beneficiary has against the third party, such subrogation shall be recognised by each State;

(b) where the institution responsible for providing benefits has a direct right against the third party, each State shall recognise such rights.

2. If a person receives benefits under the legislation of one State in respect of an injury resulting from events occurring in another State, the provisions of the said legislation which determine the cases in which the civil liability of employers or of their employees is to be excluded shall apply with regard to the said person or to the competent institution.

Paragraph 1 shall also apply to any rights of the institution responsible for providing benefits against employers or their employees in cases where their liability is not excluded.

3. Where, in accordance with Articles SSC.30(3) [Reimbursements between institutions] or 36(2) [Reimbursements between institutions], two or more States or their competent authorities have concluded an agreement to waive reimbursement between institutions under their jurisdiction, or, where reimbursement does not depend on the amount of benefits actually provided, any rights arising against a liable third party shall be governed by the following rules:

(a) where the institution of the State of residence or stay grants benefits to a person in respect of an injury sustained in its territory, that institution, in accordance with the provisions of the legislation it applies, shall exercise the right to subrogation or direct action against the third party liable to provide compensation for the injury;

(b) for the application of (a):

(i) the person receiving benefits shall be deemed to be insured with the institution of the place of residence or stay, and

(ii) that institution shall be deemed to be the institution responsible for providing benefits;

(c) paragraphs 1 and 2 shall remain applicable in respect of any benefits not covered by the waiver agreement or a reimbursement which does not depend on the amount of benefits actually provided.

Article SSC.66: Implementation of legislation

Special provisions for implementing the legislation of a certain State   1.100
are referred to in Annex SSC-6 [Special provisions for the application of the legislation of the Member States and of the United Kingdom].

TITLE V: FINAL PROVISIONS

Article SSC.67: Protection of individual rights

1. The Parties shall ensure in accordance with their domestic legal   1.101
orders that the provisions of the Protocol on Social Security Coordination have the force of law, either directly or through domestic legislation giving effect to these provisions, so that legal or natural persons can invoke the said provisions before domestic courts, tribunals and administrative authorities.

2. The Parties shall ensure the means for legal and natural persons to effectively protect their rights under this Protocol, such as the possibility to address complaints to administrative bodies or to bring legal action before a competent court or tribunal in an appropriate judicial procedure, in order to seek an adequate and timely remedy.

Article SSC.68: Amendments

The Specialised Committee on Social Security Coordination may   1.102
amend the Annexes and Appendices to this Protocol.

Article SSC.69: Termination of this Protocol

Without prejudice to Article FINPROV.8 [Termination], each Party   1.103
may at any moment terminate this Protocol, by written notification through diplomatic channels. In that event, this Protocol shall cease to be in force on the first day of the ninth month following the date of notification.

Article SSC.70: Sunset clause

1. This Protocol shall cease to apply fifteen years after the entry into   1.104
force of this Agreement.

2. Not less than 12 months before this Protocol ceases to apply in accordance with paragraph 1, either Party shall notify the other Party of

its wish to enter into negotiations with a view to concluding an updated Protocol.

Article SSC.71: Post-termination arrangements

1.105   When this Protocol ceases to apply pursuant to Article SSC.69 [Termination of this Protocol], Article SSC.70 [Sunset clause] or Article FINPROV.8 [Termination], the rights of insured persons regarding entitlements which are based on periods completed or facts or events that occurred before this Protocol ceases to apply shall be retained. The Partnership Council may lay down additional arrangements setting out appropriate consequential and transitional arrangements in good time before this Protocol ceases to apply.

ANNEX SSC-1: CERTAIN BENEFITS IN CASH TO WHICH THE PROTOCOL SHALL NOT APPLY

1.106   Part 1: Special non-contributory cash benefits (point (a) for Article SSC.3(4) [Matters covered])

(i) UNITED KINGDOM

(a) State Pension Credit (State Pension Credit Act 2002 and State Pension Credit Act (Northern Ireland) 2002)
(b) Income-based allowances for jobseekers (Jobseekers Act 1995 and Jobseekers (Northern Ireland) Order 1995)
(c) Disability Living Allowance, mobility component (Social Security Contributions and Benefits Act 1992 and Social Security Contributions and Benefits (Northern Ireland) Act 1992)
(d) Personal Independence Payment, mobility component (Welfare Reform Act 2012 (Part 4) and Welfare Reform (Northern Ireland) Order 2015 (Part 5))
(e) Employment and Support Allowance Income-related (Welfare Reform Act 2007 and Welfare Reform Act (Northern Ireland) 2007)
(f) Best Start Foods payment (Welfare Foods (Best Start Foods) (Scotland) Regulations 2019 (SSI 2019/193))
(g) Best Start Grants (pregnancy and baby grant, early learning grant, school-age grant) (The Early Years Assistance (Best Start Grants) (Scotland) Regulations 2018 (SSI 2018/370))
(h) Funeral Support Payment (Funeral Expense Assistance (Scotland) Regulations 2019 (SSI 2019/292)).

(ii) MEMBER STATES

1.107   AUSTRIA

Compensatory supplement (Federal Act of 9 September 1955 on General Social Insurance — ASVG, Federal Act of 11 October 1978 on Social insurance for persons engaged in trade and commerce — GSVG and Federal Act of 11 October 1978 on Social insurance for farmers — BSVG).

BELGIUM

(a) Income replacement allowance (Law of 27 February 1987)
(b) Guaranteed income for elderly persons (Law of 22 March 2001).

BULGARIA

Social Pension for old age (Article 89 of the Social Insurance Code).

CYPRUS

(a) Social Pension (Social Pension Law of 1995 (Law 25(I)/95), as amended)
(b) Severe motor disability allowance (Council of Ministers' Decisions Nos 38210 of 16 October 1992, 41370 of 1 August 1994, 46183 of 11 June 1997 and 53675 of 16 May 2001)
(c) Special grant to blind persons (Special Grants Law of 1996 (Law 77(I)/96), as amended).

CZECH REPUBLIC

Social allowance (State Social Support Act No 117/1995 Sb.).

DENMARK

Accommodation expenses for pensioners (Law on individual accommodation assistance, consolidated by Law No 204 of 29 March 1995).

ESTONIA

(a) Disabled adult allowance (Social Benefits for Disabled Persons Act 1.108 of 27 January 1999)
(b) State unemployment allowance (Labour Market Services and Support Act of 29 September 2005).

FINLAND

(a) Housing allowance for pensioners (Act concerning the Housing Allowance for pensioners, 571/2007)
(b) Labour market support (Act on Unemployment Benefits 1290/2002) (c) Special assistance for immigrants (Act on Special Assistance for Immigrants, 1192/2002).

FRANCE

(a) Supplementary allowances of:
(i) the Special Invalidity Fund; and
(ii) the Old Age Solidarity Fund in respect of acquired rights
(Law of 30 June 1956, codified in Book VIII of the Social Security Code);
(b) Disabled adults' allowance (Law of 30 June 1975, codified in Book VIII of the Social Security Code)

71

(c) Special allowance (Law of 10 July 1952, codified in Book VIII of the Social Security Code) in respect of acquired rights

(d) Old-age solidarity allowance (ordinance of 24 June 2004, codified in Book VIII of the Social Security Code) as of 1 January 2006.

GERMANY

(a) Basic subsistence income for the elderly and for persons with reduced earning capacity under Chapter 4 of Book XII of the Social Code

(b) Benefits to cover subsistence costs under the basic provision for jobseekers unless, with respect to these benefits, the eligibility requirements for a temporary supplement following receipt of unemployment benefit (Article 24(1) of Book II of the Social Code) are fulfilled.

GREECE

Special benefits for the elderly (Law 1296/82).

HUNGARY

1.109   (a) Invalidity annuity (Decree No 83/1987 (XII 27) of the Council of Ministers on Invalidity Annuity)

(b) Non-contributory old age allowance (Act III of 1993 on Social Administration and Social Benefits)

(c) Transport allowance (Government Decree No 164/1995 (XII 27) on Transport Allowances for Persons with Severe Physical Handicap).

IRELAND

(a) Jobseekers' allowance (Social Welfare Consolidation Act 2005, Part 3, Chapter 2)

(b) State pension (non-contributory) (Social Welfare Consolidation Act 2005, Part 3, Chapter 4)

(c) Widow's (non-contributory) pension and widower's (non-contributory) pension (Social Welfare Consolidation Act 2005, Part 3, Chapter 6)

(d) Disability allowance (Social Welfare Consolidation Act 2005, Part 3, Chapter 10)

(e) Mobility allowance (Health Act 1970, Section 61)

(f) Blind pension (Social Welfare Consolidation Act 2005, Part 3, Chapter 5).

ITALY

(a) Social pensions for persons without means (Law No 153 of 30 April 1969)

(b) Pensions and allowances for the civilian disabled or invalids (Laws No 118 of 30 March 1971, No 18 of 11 February 1980 and No 508 of 23 November 1988)

(c) Pensions and allowances for the deaf and dumb (Laws No 381 of 26 May 1970 and No 508 of 23 November 1988)

(d) Pensions and allowances for the civilian blind (Laws No 382 of 27 May 1970 and No 508 of 23 November 1988)

(e) Benefits supplementing the minimum pensions (Laws No 218 of 4 April 1952, No 638 of 11 November 1983 and No 407 of 29 December 1990)

(f) Benefits supplementing disability allowances (Law No 222 of 12 June 1984)

(g) Social allowance (Law No 335 of 8 August 1995)

(h) Social increase (Article 1(1) and (12) of Law No 544 of 29 December 1988 and successive amendments).

LATVIA

(a) State Social Security Benefit (Law on State Social Benefits of 1 January 2003) 1.110

(b) Allowance for the compensation of transportation expenses for disabled persons with restricted mobility (Law on State Social Benefits of 1 January 2003).

LITHUANIA

(a) Social assistance pension (Law of 2005 on State Social Assistance Benefits, Article 5)

(b) Relief compensation (Law of 2005 on State Social Assistance Benefits, Article 15)

(c) Transport compensation for the disabled who have mobility problems (Law of 2000 on Transport Compensation, Article 7).

LUXEMBOURG

Income for the seriously disabled (Article 1(2), Law of 12 September 2003), with the exception of persons recognised as being disabled workers and employed on the mainstream labour market or in a sheltered environment.

MALTA

(a) Supplementary allowance (Section 73 of the Social Security Act (Cap. 318) 1987)

(b) Age pension (Social Security Act (Cap. 318) 1987).

NETHERLANDS

(a) Work and Employment Support for Disabled Young Persons Act of 24 April 1997 (Wet Wajong)

(b) Supplementary Benefits Act of 6 November 1986 (TW).

POLAND

Social pension (Act of 27 June 2003 on social pensions).

PORTUGAL

(a) Non-contributory State old-age and invalidity pension (Decree-Law No 464/80 of 13 October 1980) 1.111

(b) Non-contributory widowhood pension (Regulatory Decree No 52/81 of 11 November 1981)

(c) Solidarity supplement for the elderly (Decree—Law No 232/2005 of 29 December 2005, amended by Decree—Law No 236/2006 of 11 December 2006).

SLOVAKIA

(a) Adjustment awarded before 1 January 2004 to pensions constituting the sole source of income

(b) Social pension which has been awarded before 1 January 2004.

SLOVENIA

(a) State pension (Pension and Disability Insurance Act of 23 December 1999)

(b) Income support for pensioners (Pension and Disability Insurance Act of 23 December 1999)

(c) Maintenance allowance (Pension and Disability Insurance Act of 23 December 1999).

SPAIN

(a) Minimum income guarantee (Law No 13/82 of 7 April 1982)

(b) Cash benefits to assist the elderly and invalids unable to work (Royal Decree No 2620/81 of 24 July 1981):

(i) Non-contributory invalidity and retirement pensions as provided for in Article 38(1) of the Consolidated Text of the General Law on Social Security, approved by Royal Legislative Decree No 1/1994 of 20 June 1994; and

(ii) the benefits which supplement the above pensions, as provided for in the legislation of the Comunidades Autonómas, where such supplements guarantee a minimum subsistence income having regard to the economic and social situation in the Comunidades Autonómas concerned;

(c) Allowances to promote mobility and to compensate for transport costs (Law No 13/1982 of 7 April 1982).

SWEDEN

(a) Housing supplements for persons receiving a pension (Law 2001:761);

(b) Financial support for the elderly (Law 2001:853).

Part 2: Long-term care benefits (point (d) of Article SSC.3(4) [Matters covered] of the Protocol)

(i) UNITED KINGDOM

1.112   (a) Attendance Allowance (Social Security Contributions and Benefits Act 1992, Social Security (Attendance Allowance) Regulations 1991, Social Security Contributions and Benefits (Northern Ireland) Act 1992 and Social Security (Attendance Allowance) Regulations (Northern Ireland) 1992)

(b) Carer's Allowance (Social Security Contributions and Benefits Act 1992, The Social Security (Invalid Care Allowance) Regulations 1976, Social Security Contributions and Benefits (Northern Ireland) Act 1992) and The Social Security (Invalid Care Allowance) Regulations 1976 (Northern Ireland)

(c) Disability Living Allowance, care component (Social Security Contributions and Benefits Act 1992, Social Security (Disability Living Allowance) Regulations 1991, Social Security Contributions and Benefits (Northern Ireland) Act 1992 and Social Security (Disability Living Allowance) Regulations (Northern Ireland) 1992)

(d) Personal Independence Payment, daily living component (Welfare Reform Act 2012 (Part 4), Social Security (Personal Independence Payment) Regulations 2013, The Personal Independence Payment (Transitional Provisions) Regulations 2013, Personal Independence Payment (Transitional Provisions) (Amendment) Regulations 2019, Welfare Reform (Northern Ireland) Order 2015 (Part 5), The Personal Independence Payment Regulations (Northern Ireland) 2016, The Personal Independence Payment (Transitional Provisions) Regulations (Northern Ireland) 2016 and Personal Independence Payment (Transitional Provisions) (Amendment) Regulations (Northern Ireland) 2019)

(e) Carer's Allowance Supplement (The Social Security (Scotland) Act 2018)

(f) Young Carer's Grant (The Carer's Assistance (Young Carer Grants) (Scotland) Regulations 2020 (as amended)).

(ii) MEMBER STATES

AUSTRIA

(a) Federal Long-term care allowance Act (Bundespflegegeldgesetz, 1.113 BPGG), original version BGBl. No.110/1993, last amendment BGBl- I No.100/2016

(b) Regulation on the staging of the Federal long-term care allowance (Einstufungsverordnung zum Bundespflegegeldgesetz (EinstV)):

(c) Regulation of the Federal minister for Labour, Social affairs and Consumer protection on needs assessments of care for children and young people in accordance with the Federal Nursing Care Act. (Bundespflegegeldgesetz , Kinder-EinstV)

(d) Numerous applicable statutory bases, e.g. Agreement between the Federal Government and the Länder on joint measures for persons in need of care. Social Assistance Acts and Disability Acts of the Länder

(e) Care Fund Law (Pflegefondsgesetz, PFG), Original version: Official Journal (BGBI. I) No.57/2011

(f) Care Services Statistics Ordinance 2012 (Pflegedienstleistungs-statistik-Verordnung 2012)

(g) Support for the 24-hour care: Federal Long-term care allowance Act (Bundespflegegeldgesetz,BPGG):

(h) Guidelines for the support of the 24-hour care (§ 21b of the Federal Long-term care allowance Act (Bundespflegegeldgesetz))

(i) Guidelines for granting benefits to support caring family members (§ 21a of the Federal Longterm care allowance Act (Bundespflege-geldgesetz))

(j) Care recourse interdiction

(k) Federal Act on a specific supplement due to the abolition of access to funds when housing people in inpatient care facilities

(l) Federal Act on a specific supplement due to the abolition of access to funds when housing people in inpatient care facilities for 2019 and 2020, BGBl. I No 95/2019.

BELGIUM

(a) Health Care and Sickness Benefit Compulsory Insurance Act (Loi relative à l'assurance obligatoire soins de santé et indemnités/Wet betreffende de verplichte verzekering voor geneeskundige verzorging en uitkeringen), coordinated on 14 July 1994

(b) Act of 27 February 1987 on allowances for persons with disabilities (Loi relative aux allocations aux personnes handicapées/Wet betreffende de tegemoetkomingen aan gehandicapten)

(c) Flemish social protection (Vlaamse sociale bescherming): Decree of the Flemish Parliament of 18 May 2018 on the organisation of Flemish social protection (Decreet houdende Vlaamse sociale bescherming/) and Orders of the Flemish government of 30 November 2018

(d) Walloon Code for Social Action and Health (Code wallon de l'Action sociale et de la Santé), decretal part. Part 1, book IIIter, instituted by Decree of 8 November 2018

(e) Walloon Regulatory Code for Social Action and Health, part I/1 instituted by Walloon Government Decree of 21 December 2018

(f) Decree of 13 December 2018 on offers to elderly or dependent persons as well as on palliative care (Dekret über die Angebote für Senioren und Personen mit Unterstützungsbedarf sowie über die Palliativpflege)

(g) Decree of 4th June 2007 on psychiatric nursing homes (Dekret über die psychiatrischen Pflegewohnheime)

(h) Government Decree of 20 June 2017 on mobility aids (Erlass über die Mobilitätshilfen)

(i) Decree of 13 December 2016 on the establishment of a German Community Office for selfdetermined life (Dekret zur Schaffung einer Dienststelle der Deutschsprachigen Gemeinschaft für selbstbestimmtes Leben)

(j) Royal Decree of 5th March 1990 on the allowance for assistance to the elderly (Arrêté royal du 5 mars 1990 relatif à l'allocation pour l'aide aux personnes âgées)

(k) Government Decree of 19 December 2019 on transitional arrangements relating to the procedure for obtaining a prior authorization or an approval for the coverage or the sharing of costs of long-term rehabilitation abroad (Erlass der Regierung zur übergansweisen Regelung des Verfahrens zur Erlangung einer Vorabgeehmigung oder Zustimmung zwecks Kostenübernahme oder Kostenbeteiligung für eine Langzeitrehabilitation im Ausland)

(l) Order of 21 December 2018 on Brussels health insurance bodies in the field of health care and assistance to people (Ordonnance du 21 décembre 2018 relative aux organismes assureurs bruxellois dans le domaine des soins de santé et de l'aide aux personnes)

(m) Cooperation between federated entities:

(n) Cooperation agreement of 31 December 2018 between the Flemish Community, the Walloon Region, the French Community Commission, the Joint Community Commission and the German-speaking Community concerning mobility aids

(o) Cooperation agreement of 31 December 2018 between the Flemish Community, the Walloon Region, the French Community, the Joint Community Commission, the French Community Commission and the German-speaking Community concerning the financing of care when using care institutions located outside the limits of the federated entity.

BULGARIA

(a) Social Insurance Code (Кодекс за социално осигуряване)1999   1.114
title amended 2003

(b) Law on Social Assistance (Закон за социално подпомагане), 1998

(c) Regulation on the Implementation of the Law on Social Assistance (Правилник за прилагане на Закона за социално подпомагане), 1998

(d) Law on Integration of People with Disabilities 2019 (Закон за хората с увреждания), 2019

(e) Personal Assistance Act 2019 (Закон за личната помощ) 2019 which will enter into force on 1st September 2019

(f) Regulation on the Implementation of the Law on Integration of People with Disabilities (Правилник за прилагане на Закона за интеграция на хората с увреждания), 2004

(g) Ordinance on the medical expertise (Наредба за медицинската експертиза) 2010

(h) Tariff of the Fees for Social Services Financed by the State Budget (ТариФа за таксите за социални услуги, Финансирани от държавния бюджет), 2003.

CROATIA

(a) Social Welfare Act (Zakon o socijalnoj skrbi) of 2013, OJ No.157/13, 152/14, 99/15, 52/16, 16/17, 130/17 and 98/19)

(b) Foster Families Act (Zakon o udomiteljstvu) OJ No.90/11 and 78/12, as amended

(c) Ordinance on minimum requirements for delivery of social services (Pravilnik o minimalnim uvjetima za pruanje socijalnih usluga) of 2014, OJ no 40/14 and 66/15

(d) Ordinance on participation and method of payment of beneficiaries in the maintenance costs of accommodation outside the family (Pravilnik o sudjelovanju i načinu plaćanja korisnika I drugih obveznika uzdržavanja u troškovima smještaja izvan vlastite obitelji) of 1998, OJ No.112/98 and 05/02, as amended

(e) Ordinance on the content and manner of keeping records of individuals who are professionally engaged in social services delivery as a profession (Pravilnik o sadržaju I načinu vođenja evidencije fizičkih osoba koje profesionalno pružaju socijalne usluge) of 2015, OJ No.66/15.

CYPRUS

(a) Social Welfare Services (Υπηρεσίες Κοινωικής Ευημερίας):

(b) The Guaranteed Minimum Income and in General the Social Benefits (Emergency Needs and Care Needs) Regulations and Decrees as they are amended or superseded. Homes for the Elderly and Disabled Persons Laws (Οι περί Στεγών για Ηλικιωμένους και Αναπήρους Νόμοι) of 1991 - 2011.[L. 222/91 and L. 65(I)/2011]

(c) Adult Day-Care Centres Laws (Οι περί Κέντρων Ενηλίκων Νόμοί)(L. 38(I)/1997 and L.64(I)/2011).

(d) State Aid Scheme, under the Regulation 360/2012 for the provision of services of general economic interest (De minimis) [Σχέδιο Κρατικών Ενισχύσεων Ήσσονος Σημασίας, βαση του Κανονισμού 360/2012 για την παροχή υπηρεσιών γενικού οικονομικού συμφέροντος]

(e) Welfare Benefits Administration Service (Υπηρεσία Διαχείρισης Επιδομάτων Πρόνοιας)

(f) The Guaranteed Minimum Income and generally for Welfare Benefits Law of 2014 as it is amended or superseded

(g) The Guaranteed Minimum Income and generally for Welfare Benefits Regulations and Decrees as they are amended or superseded.

CZECH REPUBLIC

1.115 (a) Act. No.108/2006 on social services (Zákon o sociálních službách)

(b) Act No.372/2011 on Health Services (Zákon o zdravotních službách)

(c) Act No.48/1997 on Public Health Insurance (Zákon o veřejném zdravotním pojištění).

DENMARK

(a) Consolidated Act No 988 of 17 August 2017 on Social Services (om social service)

(b) Consolidated Act No 119 of 1 February 2019 on Social Housing (om almene boliger).

ESTONIA

Social Welfare Act (Sotsiaalhoolekande seadus) 2016.

FINLAND

(a) Services and Assistance for the Disabled Act (Laki vammaisuuden perusteella järjestettävistä palveluista ja tukitoimista) of 3 April 1987

(b) Act on Supporting the Functional Capacity of the Ageing Population and on Social and Health Care Services for Older People (Laki ikääntyneen väestön toimintakyvyn tukemisesta sekä iäkkäiden sosiaali- ja terveyspalveluista) of 28 December 2012

(c) Social Welfare Act (Sosiaalihuoltolaki) of 30 December 2014

(d) Health Care Act (Terveydenhuoltolaki) of 30 December 2010

(e) Primary Health Care Act (Kansanterveyslaki) of 28 January 1972

(f) Act on Informal Care Support (Laki omaishoidon tuesta) of 2 December 2005 (g) Family Care Act (Perhehoitolaki) of 20 March 2015.

FRANCE

(a) Supplement for a third party (majoration pour tierce personne, MTP):

(b) Articles L. 341-4 and L. 355-1 of the Social Security Code (Code de la sécurité sociale)

(c) Supplementary benefit for recourse to a third party (prestation complémentaire pour recours à tierce personne): Article L. 434-2 of the Social Security Code

(d) Special education supplement for a disabled child (complément d'allocation d'éducation de l'enfant handicapé): Article L. 541-1 of the Social Security Code

(e) Disability compensation allowance (prestation de compensation du handicap, PCH): Articles L. 245-1 to L. 245-14 of the Social action and Family Code (Code de l'action sociale et des familles).

(f) Allowance for loss of autonomy (allocation personnalisée d'autonomie, APA): Articles L. 232-1 to L. 232-28 of the Social action and Family Code (Code de l'action sociale et des familles).

GERMANY

(a) Long-term care insurance (Pflegeversicherung):   1.116

(b) Social long-term care insurance for persons insured under statutory sickness insurance and private compulsory long-term care insurance for persons insured under private sickness insurance: Social Code Sozialgesetzbuch, Book XI (SGB XI), last amended by Article 2 of the Act of 21 December 2019 (BGBl. I p. 2913).

GREECE

(a) Law No.1140/1981, as amended

(b) Legislative Decree No.162/73 and Joint Ministerial Decision No.Π4β/5814/1997

(c) Ministerial Decision No.Π1γ/ΑΓΠ/οικ.14963 of 9 October 2001

(d) Law No.4025/2011

(e) Law No.4109/2013

(f) Law No.4199/2013 art. 127

(g) Law No.4368/2016 art. 334

(h) Law No.4483/2017 art. 153

(i) Law No.498/1-11-2018, art. 28, 30 and 31, for the "Unified Health Benefits Regulation" of the National Service Provider Organization Health (EOPYY).

HUNGARY

(a)Long-term care services providing personal social care (social services):

(b) Act III of 1993 on Social Administration and Social Assistance (törvény a szociális igazgatásról és szociális ellátásokról) supplemented by Government and Ministerial decrees.

IRELAND

(a) Health Act 1970 (No.1 of 1970)

(b) Nursing Homes Support Scheme Act 2009 (No.15 of 2009)

(c) Social Welfare Consolidation Act 2005:

(d) Constant Attendance Allowance

(e) Carer's Benefit

(f) Carer's Allowance This document has been agreed between the European Union and the United Kingdom and is provided for information only. No rights may be derived from it until the date of application. The numbering of the articles is provisional. 1174 24.12.2020

(g) Carer's Support Grant

(h) Domiciliary Care Allowance.

ITALY

1.117   (a) Law No.118 of 30 March 1971 on civilian invalidity benefits (Legge 30 Marzo 1971, n. 118 - Conversione in Legge del D.L. 30 gennaio 1971, n. 5 e nuove norme in favore dei mutilati ed invalidi civili)

(b) Law No.18 of 11 February 1980 on Constant attendance allowance (Legge 11 Febbraio 1980, n. 18 - Indennità di accompagnamento agli invalidi civili totalmente inabili)

(c) Law No.104 of 5 February 1992, Article 33 (Framework law on disability) (Legge 5 Febbraio 1992, n. 104 - Legge-quadro per l'assistenza, l'integrazione sociale e i diritti delle persone handicappate)

(d) Legislative Decree No.112 of 31 March 1998 on the transfer of legislative tasks and administrative competences from the State to the Regions and local entities (Decreto Legislativo 31 Marzo 1998, n. 112 - Conferimento di funzioni e compiti amministrativi dello Stato alle regioni ed agli enti locali, in attuazione del capo I della Legge 15 Marzo 1997, n. 59)

(e) Regulation (CE) 883/04.on social security coordination of the European Parliament and Council (Regolamento (CE) 883 del 29 aprile 2004 del Parlamento Europeo e del Consiglio, relativo al coordinamento dei sistemi di sicurezza sociale - SNCB—art 70 and Annex X)

(f) Law No.183 of 4 November 2010, Article 24, modifying the rules regarding the permits for the assistance to disabled persons in difficult situations (Legge n. 183 del 4 Novembre 2010, art. 24 - Modifiche alla disciplina in materia di permessi per l'assistenza a portatori di handicap in situazione di gravità)

(g) Law No.147 of 27 December 2013 containing provisions for drawing up the annual and pluriannual budget of the State—Stability Law 2014 (Disposizioni per la formazione del bilancio annuale e pluriennale dello Stato - Legge di stabilità 2014).

LATVIA

(a) Law on Social Services and Social Assistance (Sociālo pakalpojumu un sociālās palīdzības likums) 31/10/2002

(b) Medical Treatment Law (Ārstniecības likums) 12/06/1997

(c) Law on Patient Rights (Pacientu tiesību likums) 30/12/2009

(d) Regulations of the Cabinet of Ministers No.555 on Health care organisation and payment procedure (Ministru kabineta 2018. gada 28.augusta noteikumi Nr.555 "Veselības aprūpes pakalpojumu organizēšanas un samaksas kārtība") 28/08/2018

(e) Regulations of the Cabinet of Ministers No.275 on Procedures for Payment of Social Care and Social Rehabilitation Services and the Procedures for Covering Service Costs from a Local Government Budget (Ministru kabineta 2003.gada 27.maija noteikumi Nr.275 „Sociālās aprūpes un sociālās rehabilitācijas pakalpojumu samaksas kārtība un kārtība, kādā pakalpojuma izmaksas tiek segtas no pašvaldības budžeta") 27/05/2003

(f) Regulations of the Cabinet of Ministers No.138 on Receiving of Social Services and Social Assistance (Ministru kabineta 2019.gada 2.aprīļa noteikumi Nr 138 "Noteiku mi par sociālo pakalpojumu un sociālās palīdzības saņemšanu") 02/04/2019.

LITHUANIA

(a) Law on Target compensations (Tikslinių kompensacijų įastatymas) of 29 June 2016 (No.XII-2507)

(b) Law on Social Services (Socialinių paslaugų įstatymas) of 19 January 2006 (No.X-493)

(c) Law on Health Insurance (Sveikatos draudimo įstatymas) of 21 May 1996 (No I-1343)

(d) Law on Healthcare system (Sveikatos sistemos įstatymas) of 19 July 1994 (No I-552)

(e) Law on Health Care Institutions (Sveikatos priežiūros įstaigų įstatymas) of 6 June 1996 (No.I1367).

LUXEMBOURG

Law of 19 June 1998 introducing the dependency insurance, amended by the Law of 23 December 2005 and the Law of 29 August 2017. 1.118

MALTA

(a) Social Security Act (Att dwar is-Sigurta' Socjali) (Cap. 318)

(b) Subsidiary Legislation 318.19: State-Owned Institutions and Hostels Rates Regulations (Regolamenti dwar it-Trasferiment ta' Fondi għal Hostels Statali Indikati)

(c) Subsidiary Legislation 318.17: Transfer of Funds (Government Financed Beds) Regulations (Regolamenti dwar it-Trasferiment ta' Fondi għal Sodod Iffinanzjati mill-Gvern)

(d) Subsidiary Legislation 318.13: State Financed Residential Services Rates Regulations (Regolamenti dwar Rati għal Servizzi Residenzjali Finanzjali mill-Istat).

THE NETHERLANDS

Long term care act (Wet langdurige zorg (WLZ)), Law of 3 December 2014.

POLAND

(a) Law on Health Care Services financed from Public Means (Ustawa o świadczeniach opieki zdrowotnej finansowanych ze środków publicznych) of 27 August 2004

(b) Law on Social Assistance (Ustawa o pomocy społecznej) of 12 March 2004

(c) Law on Family Benefits (Ustawa o świadczeniach rodzinnych) of 28 November 2003

(d) Law on Social Pension (Ustawa o rencie socjalnej) of 27 June 2003

(e) Law on Social Insurance Fund Pensions (Ustawa o emeryturach i rentach z Funduszu Ubezpieczeń Społecznych) of 17 December 1998

(f) Law on Vocational and Social Rehabilitation and Employment of Disabled Persons (Ustawa o rehabilitacji zawodowej i społecznej oraz zatrudnianiu osób niepełnosprawnych) of 27 August 1997

(g) Law on support for pregnant women and their families "For life" (Ustawa o wsparciu kobiet w ciąży i rodzin "Zażyciem") of 4 November 2016

(h) Law on supplementary benefit for persons unable to live independently (Ustawa o świadczeniu uzupełniającym dla osób niezdolnych do samodzielnej egzystencji) of 31 July 2019

PORTUGAL

1.119   (a) Social insurance and guaranteeing sufficient resources:

(b) Statutory Decree 265/99 of 14 July 1999 on the long-term care supplement (complemento por dependência), as amended on several occasions

(c) Act 90/2009 of 31 August 2009 on the special protection system in case of disability (regime especial de proteção na invalidez), re-published in consolidated version by Statutory Decree 246/2015 of 20 October 2015, amended

(d) Social security system and National Health Service:

(e) Statutory Decree 101/06 of 6 June 2006 on the National network of integrated continuing care (rede de cuidados continuados integrados), re-published in a consolidated version in Statutory Decree 136/2015 of 28 July 2015

(f) Decree-Law n° 8/2010 of 28 January 2010, amended and republished by Decree-Law n° 22/2011 of 10 February 2011 on the creation of units and teams for integrated continuous care in mental health (unidades e equipas de cuidados continuados integrados de saúde mental)

(g) Decree n° 343/.2015 of 12 October 2015 on standards governing hospital and ambulatory paediatric care as well as the discharge management teams and the paediatric care teams within the framework of the national network of long-term integrated care (condições de instalação e funcionamento das unidades de internamento de cuidados integrados pediátricos e de ambulatório pediátricas, bem como as condições a que devem obedecer as equipas de gestão de altas e as equipas de cuidados continuados integrados destinadas a cuidados pediátricos da Rede Nacional de Cuidados Continuados Integrados)

(h) Law n° 6/2009 of 6 September on the status of informal carer (Estatuto do cuidador informal).

ROMANIA

(a) Law 17 of 6 March 2000 on Social Assistance of Senior Persons (Legea privind asistenta sociala a persoanelor varstnice), with subsequent amendments

(b) Law 448 of 6 December 2006 on Protection and Promotion of the Rights of Persons with Disability (Legea privind protectia si promovarea drepturilor persoanelor cu handicap), with subsequent amendments

(c) Social Assistance Law (Legea asistentei sociale) No.292 of 20 December 2011.

SLOVAKIA

(a) Law on Social Services (Zákon o sociálnych službách) No.448/2008

(b) Law on Financial Benefits for Compensation of Disabled Persons (Zákon o peňažných príspevkoch na kompenzáciu ťažkého zdravotného postihnutia) No.447/2008

(c) Law on Health Care and Services Related to Health Care (Zákon o zdravotnej starostlivosti a službách súvisiacich s poskytovaním zdravotnej starostlivosti) No.576/2004

(d) Law on Health Care Providers, Medical Workers and Professional Medical Associations (Zákon o poskytovateľóoch zdravotnej starostlivosti, zdravotníckych pracovníkoch a stavovských organizáciách v zdravotníctve) No.578/2004

(e) Law on Subsistence Minimum (Zákon o životnom minime) No.601/2003

(f) Law on Family (Zákon o rodine) No.36/2005

(g) Law on Social and legal protection of children and social guardianship (Zákon o sociálno-právnej ochrane detí a sociálnej kuratele) No.305/2005

(h) Law on Social Work (Zákon o sociálnej práci) No.219/2014.

SLOVENIA

1.120   No specific law related to long-term care. Long-term care benefits are included in the following acts:

(a) Pension and Disability Insurance Act (Zakon o pokojninskem in invalidskem zavarovanju) (Official Gazette of the Republic of Slovenia, No.96/2012, and subsequent amendments)

(b) Financial Social Assistance Act (Zakon o socialno vartsvenih prejemkih) (Official Gazette of the Republic of Slovenia, No.61/2010, and subsequent amendments)

(c) Exercise of Rights to Public Funds Act (Zakon o uveljavljanju pravic iz javnih sredstev) (Official Gazette of the Republic of Slovenia, No.62/2010, and subsequent amendments)

(d) Social Protection Act (Zakon o socialnem varstvu) (Official Gazette of the Republic of Slovenia, No.3/2004—official consolidated text, and subsequent amendments)

(e) Parental Care and Family Benefits Act (Zakon o starševskem varstvu in družinskih prejemkih) (Official Gazette of the Republic of Slovenia, No.110/2006—official consolidated text, and subsequent amendments)

(f) Mentally and Physically Handicapped Persons Act (Zakon o drubenem varstvu duševno in telesno prizadetih oseb) (Official Gazette of the Republic of Slovenia, No.41/83, and subsequent amendments)

(g) Health Care and Health Insurance Act (Zakon o zdravstvenem varstvu in zdravstvenem zavarovanju) (Official Gazette of the Republic of Slovenia, No.72/2006—official consolidated text, and subsequent amendments)

(h) War Veterans Act (Zakon o vojnih veteranih) (Official Gazette of the Republic of Slovenia, no 59/06 official consolidated text, and subsequent amendments)

(i) War Disability Act (Zakon o vojnih invalidih) (Official Gazette of the Republic of Slovenia, no 63/59 official consolidated text, and subsequent amendments)

(j) Fiscal Balance Act (Zakon za uravnoteženje javnih finance (ZUJF)) (Official Gazette of the Republic of Slovenia, No.40/2012, and subsequent amendments)

(k) Act Regulating Adjustments of Transfers to Individuals and Households in the Republic of Slovenia (Zakon o usklajevanju transferjev posameznikom in gospodinjstvom v Republiki Sloveniji) (Official Gazette of the Republic of Slovenia, No.114/2006—official consolidated text, and subsequent amendments).

SPAIN

(a) Law No.39/2006 on the Promotion of Personal Autonomy and Assistance to persons in situations of dependence of 14 December 2006, as amended
(b) Social Security General Act (Ley General de la Seguridad Social) approved by Legislative Royal Decree No.8/2015 of 30 October 2015
(c) Ministerial Order of 15 April 1969
(d) Royal Decree No.1300/95 of 21 July 1995, as amended
(e) Royal Decree No.1647/97 of 31 October 1997, as amended.

SWEDEN

(a) Social Services Act (Socialtjänstlagen (2001:453)) of 2001
(b) The Health Care Act (Hälso- och sjukvårdslag (2017:30)) of 2017.

Part 3: Payments which are connected to a branch of social security listed in Article SSC.3(1) [Matters covered] of the Protocol and which are paid to meet expenses for heating in cold weather (point (f) of Article SSC.3(4)[Matters covered] of the Protocol).

(i) UNITED KINGDOM   1.121

Winter Fuel Payment (Social Security Contributions and Benefits Act 1992, Social Fund Winter Fuel Payment Regulations 2000, Social Security Contributions and Benefits (Northern Ireland) Act 1992 and Social Fund Winter Fuel Payment Regulations (Northern Ireland) 2000).

(iii) MEMBER STATES

DENMARK

(a) Act on Social and state pensions, LBK No.983 of 23/09/2019
(b) Regulations on social and state pensions, BEK No.1602 of 27/12/2019.

ANNEX SSC-2: RESTRICTION OF RIGHTS TO BENEFITS IN KIND FOR MEMBERS OF THE FAMILY OF A FRONTIER WORKER

(referred to in Article SSC.16(2)[Stay in the competent State when   1.122
residence is in another State—special rules for the members of the
families of frontier workers])

CROATIA
DENMARK
IRELAND
FINLAND
SWEDEN
UNITED KINGDOM

ANNEX SSC-3: MORE RIGHTS FOR PENSIONERS RETURNING TO THE COMPETENT STATE

1.123   (Article SSC.25(2)[Stay of the pensioner or the members of their family in a State other than the State of residence—stay in the competent State—authorisation for appropriate treatment outside the State of residence])

AUSTRIA
BELGIUM
BULGARIA
CYPRUS
CZECH REPUBLIC
FRANCE
GERMANY
GREECE
HUNGARY
LUXEMBOURG
THE NETHERLANDS
POLAND
SLOVENIA
SPAIN
SWEDEN

ANNEX SSC-4: CASES IN WHICH THE PRO RATA CALCULATION SHALL BE WAIVED OR SHALL NOT APPLY

(Articles SSC.47(4) and 47(5) [Award of benefits])

PART 1: CASES IN WHICH THE PRO RATA CALCULATION SHALL BE WAIVED PURSUANT TO ARTICLE SSC.47(4) [AWARD OF BENEFITS]

1.124   AUSTRIA

(a) All applications for benefits under the Federal Act of 9 September 1955 on General Social Insurance—ASVG, the Federal Act of 11 October 1978 on social insurance for self-employed persons engaged in trade and commerce—GSVG, the Federal Act of 11 October 1978 on social insurance for self-employed farmers—BSVG and the Federal Act of 30 November 1978 on social insurance for the self-employed in the liberal professions (FSVG);

(b) All applications for survivors' pensions based on a pension account pursuant to the General Pensions Act (APG) of 18 November 2004, with the exception of cases under Part 2;

(c) All applications for survivors' pensions of the Austrian Provincial Chambers of Physicians (Landesärztekammer) based on basic provision (basic and any supplementary benefit, or basic pension);

(d) All applications for survivors' support from the pension fund of the Austrian Chamber of Veterinary Surgeons;

(e) All applications for benefits from widows and orphans pensions according to the statutes of the welfare institutions of the Austrian bar associations, Part A;

(f) All applications for benefits under the Notary Insurance Act of 3 February 1972—NVG 1972.

CYPRUS

All applications for old age, widow's and widower's pensions.

DENMARK

All applications for pensions referred to in the law on social pensions, except for pensions mentioned in [Annex SSC-5] [Benefits And Agreements Which Allow The Application Of Article SSC.49 [Overlapping of benefits of the same kind]]

IRELAND

All applications for state pension (transition), state pension (contributory), widow's (contributory) pension and widower's (contributory) pension.

LATVIA

(a) All applications for survivor's pensions (Law on State pensions of 1 January 1996; Law on State funded pensions of 1 July 2001).

LITHUANIA

All applications for State social insurance survivor's pensions calculated on the basis of the basic amount of survivor's pension (Law on State Social Insurance Pensions). 1.125

NETHERLANDS

All applications for old-age pensions under the law on general old-age insurance (AOW).

POLAND

All applications for old-age under the defined benefits scheme and survivors' pensions, except for the cases where the totalised periods of insurance completed under the legislation of more than one country are equal to or longer than 20 years for women and 25 years for men but the national periods of insurance are inferior to these limits (and not less than 15 years for women and 20 years for men), and the calculation is made under Articles 27 and 28 of the Act of 17 December 1998 (O.J. 2015, item 748).

PORTUGAL

All applications for old-age and survivors' pension claims, except for the cases where the totalised periods of insurance completed under the legislation of more than one country are equal to or longer than 21 calendar years but the national periods of insurance are equal or inferior to 20 years, and the calculation is made under Articles 32 and 33 of Decree-Law No 187/2007 of 10 May 2007.

SLOVAKIA

1.126   (a) All applications for survivors' pension (widow's pension, widower's and orphan's pension) calculated according to the legislation in force before 1 January 2004, the amount of which is derived from a pension formerly paid to the deceased;

(b) All applications for pensions calculated pursuant to Act No 461/2003 Coll. on social security as amended.

SWEDEN

(a) Applications for an old-age pension in the form of a guaranteed pension (Chapters 66 and 67 of the Social Insurance Code).

(b) Applications for an old-age pension in the form of a supplementary pension (Chapter 63 of the Social Insurance Code).

UNITED KINGDOM

All applications for retirement pension, state pension pursuant to Part 1 of the Pensions Act 2014, widows' and bereavement benefits, with the exception of those for which during a tax year beginning on or after 6 April 1975:

(i) the party concerned had completed periods of insurance, employment or residence under the legislation of the United Kingdom and a Member State; and one (or more) of the tax years was not considered a qualifying year within the meaning of the legislation of the United Kingdom;

(ii) the periods of insurance completed under the legislation in force in the United Kingdom for the periods prior to 5 July 1948 would be taken into account for the purposes of point (b) of Article SSC.47(1) of the Protocol by application of the periods of insurance, employment or residence under the legislation of a Member State.

All applications for additional pension pursuant to the Social Security Contributions and Benefits Act 1992, section 44, and the Social Security Contributions and Benefits (Northern Ireland) Act 1992, section 44.

PART 2: CASES IN WHICH ARTICLE SSC.47(5) [AWARD OF BENEFITS] APPLIES

AUSTRIA

(a) Old-age pensions and survivor's pensions derived thereof based on a pension account pursuant to the General Pensions Act (APG) of 18 November 2004;   1.127

(b) Compulsory allowances under Article 41 of the Federal Law of 28 December 2001, BGBl I Nr. 154 on the general salary fund of Austrian pharmacists (Pharmazeutische Gehaltskasse für Österreich);

(c) Retirement and early retirement pensions of the Austrian Provincial Chambers of Physicians based on basic provision (basic and any supplementary benefit, or basic pension), and all pension benefits of the Austrian Provincial Chambers of Physicians based on additional provision (additional or individual pension);

(d) Old-age support from the pension fund of the Austrian Chamber of Veterinary Surgeons;

(e) Benefits according to the statutes of the welfare institutions of the Austrian bar associations, Parts A and B, with the exception of applications for benefits from widows' and orphans' pensions according to the statutes of the welfare institutions of the Austrian bar associations, Part A;

(f) Benefits by the welfare institutions of the Federal Chamber of Architects and Consulting Engineers under the Austrian Civil Engineers' Chamber Act (Ziviltechnikerkammergesetz) 1993 and the statutes of the welfare institutions, with the exception of benefits on grounds of survivors' benefits deriving from the last-named benefits;

(g) Benefits according to the statute of the welfare institution of the Federal Chamber of Professional Accountants and Tax Advisors under the Austrian Professional Accountants and Tax Advisors' Act (Wirtschaftstreuhandberufsgesetz).

BULGARIA

Old age pensions from the Supplementary Compulsory Pension Insurance, under Part II, Title II, of the Social Insurance Code.

CROATIA

Pensions from the compulsory insurance scheme based on the individual capitalised savings according to the Compulsory and Voluntary Pension Funds Act (OG 49/99, as amended) and the Act on Pension Insurance Companies and Payment of Pensions Based on Individual Capitalised Savings (OG 106/99, as amended), except in the cases provided by Articles 47 and 48 of the Compulsory and Voluntary Pension Funds Act and survivor's pension).

CZECH REPUBLIC

Pensions paid from the Second Pillar scheme established by Act No 426/2011 Coll., on pension savings.   1.128

DENMARK

(a) Personal pensions;

(b) Benefits in the event of death (accrued based on contributions to Arbejdsmarkedets Tillægspension related to the time before 1 January 2002);

(c) Benefits in the event of death (accrued based on contributions to Arbejdsmarkedets Tillægspension related to the time after 1 January 2002) referred to in the Consolidated Act on Labour Market Supplementary Pension (Arbejdsmarkedets Tillægspension) 942:2009.

ESTONIA

Mandatory funded old-age pension scheme.

FRANCE

Basic or supplementary schemes in which old-age benefits are calculated on the basis of retirement points.

HUNGARY

Pension benefits based on membership of private pension funds.

LATVIA

Old-age pensions (Law on State pensions of 1 January 1996; Law on State funded pensions of 1 July 2001).

POLAND

Old-age pensions under the defined contribution scheme.

PORTUGAL

1.129 Supplementary pensions granted pursuant to Decree-Law No 26/2008 of 22 February 2008 (public capitalisation scheme). SLOVAKIA Mandatory old-age pension saving.

SLOVENIA

Pension from compulsory supplementary pension insurance.

SWEDEN

Old-age pension in the form of an income pension and a premium pension (Chapters 62 and 64 of the Social Insurance Code).

UNITED KINGDOM

Graduated retirement benefits paid pursuant to the National Insurance Act 1965, sections 36 and 37, and the National Insurance Act (Northern Ireland) 1966, sections 35 and 36.

ANNEX SSC-5: BENEFITS AND AGREEMENTS WHICH ALLOW THE APPLICATION OF ARTICLE SSC.49

[Overlapping of benefits of the same kind]

I. Benefits referred to in point (a) of Article SSC.49(2) [Overlapping of benefits of the same kind] of the Protocol, the amount of which is independent of the length of periods of insurance or residence completed   1.130

DENMARK

The full Danish national old-age pension acquired after 10 years' residence by persons who will have been awarded a pension by 1 October 1989

FINLAND

National pensions and spouse's pensions determined according to the transitional rules and awarded prior to the 1 of January 1994 (Act on Enforcement of the National Pensions Act, 569/2007)

The additional amount of child's pension when calculating independent benefit according to the National Pension Act (the National Pension Act, 568/2007)

FRANCE

Widower's or widow's invalidity pension under the general social security system or under the agricultural workers scheme where it is calculated on the basis of the deceased spouse's invalidity pension settled in accordance with point (a) of Article SSC.47(1) [Award of benefits].

GREECE

Benefits under Law No 4169/1961 relating to the agricultural insurance scheme (OGA)

NETHERLANDS

General Surviving Relatives Act of 21 December 1995 (ANW)   1.131

The Work and Income according to Labour Capacity Act of 10 November 2005 (WIA)

SPAIN

Survivors' pensions granted under the general and special schemes, with the exception of the Special Scheme for Civil Servants

SWEDEN

Income-related sickness compensation and income-related activity compensation (Chapter 34 of the Social Insurance Code)

91

Guaranteed pension and guaranteed compensation which replaced the full state pensions provided under the legislation on the state pension which applied before 1 January 1993, and the full state pension awarded under the transitional rules of the legislation applying from that date

II. Benefits referred to in point (b) of Article SSC.49(2) [Overlapping of benefits of the same kind] of the Protocol, the amount of which is determined by reference to a credited period deemed to have been completed between the date on which the risk materialised and a later date

FINLAND

Employment pensions for which account is taken of future periods according to the national legislation

GERMANY

Survivors' pensions, for which account is taken of a supplementary period
Old-age pensions, for which account is taken of a supplementary period already acquired

ITALY

Italian pensions for total incapacity for work (inabilità)

LATVIA

1.132   Survivors' pension calculated on the basis of assumed insurance periods (Article 23(8) of the Law on State Pensions of 1 January 1996)

LITHUANIA

(a) State social insurance work incapacity pensions, paid under the Law on State Social Insurance Pensions
(b) State social insurance survivors' and orphans' pensions, calculated on the basis of the work incapacity pension of the deceased under the Law on State Social Insurance Pensions

LUXEMBOURG

Survivors' pensions

SLOVAKIA

Slovak survivors' pension derived from the invalidity pension.

SPAIN

The pensions for retirement under the Special Scheme for Civil Servants due under Title I of the consolidated text of the Law on State Pensioners if at the time of materialisation of the risk the beneficiary was an active civil servant or treated as such; death and survivors' (widows'/

widowers', orphans' and parents') pensions due under Title I of the consolidated text of the Law on State Pensioners if at the time of death the civil servant was active or treated as such

SWEDEN

Sickness compensation and activity compensation in the form of guarantee compensation (Chapter 35 of the Social Insurance Code)

Survivors' pension calculated on the basis of credited insurance periods (Chapters 76-85 of the Social Insurance Code)

III. Agreements referred to in point (b)(i) of Article SSC.49(2) [Overlapping of benefits of the same kind] of the Protocol intended to prevent the same credited period being taken into account two or more times:

The Social Security Agreement of 28 April 1997 between the Republic of Finland and the Federal Republic of Germany

The Social Security Agreement of 10 November 2000 between the Republic of Finland and the Grand Duchy of Luxembourg

Nordic Convention on social security of 18 August 2003.

ANNEX SSC-6: SPECIAL PROVISIONS FOR THE APPLICATION OF THE LEGISLATION OF THE MEMBER STATES AND OF THE UNITED KINGDOM

(Articles SSC.3(2)[Matters covered], SSC.51(1)[Additional provisions for the calculation of benefits] and SSC.66 [Implementation of legislation])

AUSTRIA

1. For the purpose of acquiring periods in the pension insurance, attendance at a school or comparable educational establishment in another State shall be regarded as equivalent to attendance at a school or educational establishment pursuant to Articles 227(1)(1) and 228(1)(3) of the Allgemeines Sozialversicherungsgesetz (ASVG) (General Social Security Act), Article 116(7) of the Gewerbliches Sozialversicherungsgesetz (GSVG) (Federal Act on Social Insurance for Persons engaged in Trade and Commerce) and Article 107(7) of the Bauern-Sozialversicherungsgesetz (BSVG) (Social Security Act for Farmers), when the person concerned was subject at some time to Austrian legislation on the grounds that he pursued an activity as an employed or self-employed person, and the special contributions provided for under Article 227(3) of the ASVG, Article 116(9) of the GSVG and Article 107(9) of the BSGV for the purchase of such periods of education, are paid. 1.133

2. For the calculation of the pro rata benefit referred to in point (b) of Article SSC.47(1) [Award of benefits], special increments for contributions for supplementary insurance and the miners' supplementary benefit under Austrian legislation shall be disregarded. In those cases the pro

rata benefit calculated without those contributions shall, if appropriate, be increased by unreduced special increments for contributions for supplementary insurance and the miners' supplementary benefit.

3. Where pursuant to Article SSC.7 [Aggregation of periods] of the Protocol substitute periods under an Austrian pension insurance scheme have been completed but cannot form a basis for calculation pursuant to Articles 238 and 239 of the ASVG, Articles 122 and 123 of the GSVG and Articles 113 and 114 of the BSVG, the calculation basis for periods of childcare pursuant to Article 239 of the ASVG, Article 123 of the GSVG and Article 114 of the BSVG shall be used.

BULGARIA

Article 33(1) of the Bulgarian Health Insurance Act applies to all persons for whom Bulgaria is the competent Member State under Chapter 1 [Sickness, maternity and equivalent paternity benefits] of Title III [Special provisions concerning the various categories of benefits] of the Protocol.

CYPRUS

For the purpose of applying the provisions of Articles SSC.7 [Aggregation of periods], SSC.46 [Special provisions on aggregation of periods] and SSC.56 [Special provisions on aggregation of periods of insurance, employment or self-employment], for any period commencing on or after 6 October 1980, a week of insurance under the legislation of the Republic of Cyprus is determined by dividing the total insurable earnings for the relevant period by the weekly amount of the basic insurable earnings applicable in the relevant contribution year, provided that the number of weeks so determined shall not exceed the number of calendar weeks in the relevant period.

CZECH REPUBLIC

For the purposes of defining members of the family in accordance with point (s) of Article SSC.1 [Definitions] of the Protocol, 'spouse' includes registered partners as defined in the Czech act No.115/2006 Coll., on registered partnership.

DENMARK

1.134   1. (a) For the purpose of calculating the pension under the 'lov om social pension' (Social Pension Act), periods of activity as an employed or self-employed person completed under Danish legislation by a frontier worker or a worker who has gone to Denmark to do work of a seasonal nature are regarded as periods of residence completed in Denmark by the surviving spouse in so far as, during those periods, the surviving spouse was linked to the abovementioned worker by marriage without separation from bed and board or de facto separation on grounds of incompatibility, and provided that, during those periods, the spouse resided in the territory of another State. For the purposes of this point, 'work of a seasonal nature' means work which, being dependent on the succession of the seasons, automatically recurs each year.

(b) For the purpose of calculating the pension under the 'lov om social pension' (Social Pension Act), periods of activity as an employed or self-employed person completed under Danish legislation before 1 January 1984 by a person to whom point (a) does not apply shall be regarded as periods of residence completed in Denmark by the surviving spouse, in so far as, during those periods, the surviving spouse was linked to that person by marriage without separation from bed and board or de facto separation on grounds of incompatibility, and provided that, during those periods, the spouse resided in the territory of another State.

(c) Periods to be taken into account under points (a) and (b) shall not be taken into consideration if they coincide with the periods taken into account for the calculation of the pension due to the person concerned under the legislation on compulsory insurance of another State, or with the periods during which the person concerned received a pension under such legislation. Those periods shall, however, be taken into consideration if the annual amount of the said pension is less than half the basic amount of the social pension.

2. (a) Notwithstanding the provisions of Article SSC.7 [Aggregation of periods] of the Protocol, persons who have not been gainfully employed in one or more States are entitled to a Danish social pension only if they have been, or have previously been, permanent residents of Denmark for at least 3 years, subject to the age limits prescribed by Danish legislation. Subject to Article SSC.5 [Equality of treatment] of the Protocol, Article SSC.8 [Waiving of residence rules] of the Protocol does not apply to a Danish social pension to which entitlement has been acquired by such persons. (b) The provisions referred to in point (a) do not apply to Danish social pension entitlement for the members of the family of persons who are or have been gainfully employed in Denmark, or for students or the members of their families.

3. The temporary benefit for unemployed persons who have been admitted to the ledighedsydelse (flexible job' scheme) (Law No 455 of 10 June 1997) is covered by Chapter 6 [Unemployment Benefits] of Title III [Special provisions concerning the various categories of benefits] of the Protocol.

4. Where the beneficiary of a Danish social pension is also entitled to a survivor's pension from another State, those pensions for the implementation of Danish legislation shall be regarded as benefits of the same kind within the meaning of Article SSC.48(1) [Rules to prevent overlapping], subject to the condition, however, that the person whose periods of insurance or of residence serve as the basis for the calculation of the survivor's pension had also acquired a right to a Danish social pension.

ESTONIA

For the purpose of calculating parental benefits, periods of employment in States other than Estonia shall be considered to be based on the same average amount of Social Tax as paid during the periods of employment in Estonia with which they are aggregated. If during the reference year the person has been employed only in other States, the calculation of the benefit shall be considered to be based on the average Social Tax paid in Estonia between the reference year and the maternity leave.

FINLAND

1. For the purposes of determining entitlement and of calculating the amount of the Finnish national pension under Articles SSC.47 [Award of benefits] to 49 [Overlapping of benefits of the same kind], pensions acquired under the legislation of another State are treated in the same way as pensions acquired under Finnish legislation.

2. When applying point (b)(i) of Article SSC.47(1) [Award of benefits] for the purpose of calculating earnings for the credited period under Finnish legislation on earnings-related pensions, where an individual has pension insurance periods based on activity as an employed or self-employed person in another State for part of the reference period under Finnish legislation, the earnings for the credited period shall be equivalent to the sum of earnings obtained during the part of the reference period in Finland, divided by the number of months for which there were insurance periods in Finland during the reference period.

FRANCE

1.135   1. For persons receiving benefits in kind in France pursuant to Articles SSC.15 [Residence in a State other than the competent State], SSC.24 [Residence of members of the family in a State other than the one in which the pensioner resides] of the Protocol who are resident in the French departments of Haut-Rhin, Bas-Rhin or Moselle, benefits in kind provided on behalf of the institution of another State which is responsible for bearing their cost include benefits provided by both the general sickness insurance scheme and the obligatory supplementary local sickness insurance scheme of Alsace-Moselle.

2. French legislation applicable to a person engaged, or formerly engaged, in an activity as an employed or self-employed person for the application of Chapter 5 [Old-age and survivors' pensions] of Title III [Special provisions concerning the various categories of benefits] includes both the basic old-age insurance scheme(s) and the supplementary retirement scheme(s) to which the person concerned was subject.

GERMANY

1. Notwithstanding point (a) of Article SSC.6 [Equal treatment of benefits, income, facts or events] of the Protocol and Article 5(4) point 1 of the Sozialgesetzbuch VI (Volume VI of the Social Code), a person who receives a full old-age pension under the legislation of another State may request to be compulsorily insured under the German pension insurance scheme.

2. Notwithstanding point (a) of Article SSC.6 [Equal treatment of benefits, income, facts or events] of the Protocol and Article 7 of the Sozialgesetzbuch VI (Volume VI of the Social Code), a person who is

compulsorily insured in another State, or receives an old-age pension under the legislation of another State may join the voluntary insurance scheme in Germany.

3. For the purpose of granting cash benefits under §47(1) of SGB V, §47(1) of SGB VII and §200(2) of the Reichsversicherungsordnung to insured persons who live in another State, German insurance schemes calculate net pay, which is used to assess benefits, as if the insured person lived in Germany, unless the insured person requests an assessment on the basis of the net pay which he actually receives.

4. Nationals of other States whose place of residence or usual abode is outside Germany and who fulfil the general conditions of the German pension insurance scheme may pay voluntary contributions only if they had been voluntarily or compulsorily insured in the German pension insurance scheme at some time previously; this also applies to stateless persons and refugees whose place of residence or usual abode is in another State.

5. The pauschale Anrechnungszeit (fixed credit period) pursuant to Article 253 of the Sozialgesetzbuch VI (Volume VI of the Social Code) shall be determined exclusively with reference to German periods.

6. In cases where the German pension legislation, in force on 31 December 1991, is applicable for the recalculation of a pension, only the German legislation applies for the purposes of crediting German Ersatz-zeiten (substitute periods).

7. The German legislation on accidents at work and occupational diseases to be compensated for under the law governing foreign pensions and on benefits for insurance periods which can be credited under the law governing foreign pensions in the territories named in paragraph 1(2)(3) of the Act on affairs of displaced persons and refugees (Bundes-vertriebenengesetz) continues to apply within the scope of application of the Protocol, notwithstanding the provisions of paragraph 2 of the Act on foreign pensions (Fremdrentengesetz).

8. For the calculation of the theoretical amount referred to in point (b)(i) of Article SSC.47(1) [Award of benefits], in pension schemes for liberal professions, the competent institution shall take as a basis, in respect of each of the years of insurance completed under the legislation of any other State, the average annual pension entitlement acquired during the period of membership of the competent institution through the payment of contributions.

GREECE

1. Law No 1469/84 concerning voluntary affiliation to the pension insurance scheme for Greek nationals and foreign nationals of Greek origin is applicable to nationals of other States, stateless persons and refugees, where the persons concerned, regardless of their place of residence or stay, have at some time in the past been compulsorily or voluntarily affiliated to the Greek pension insurance scheme. 1.137

2. Notwithstanding point (a) of Article SSC.6 [Equal treatment of benefits, income, facts or events] of the Protocol and Article 34 of Law 1140/1981, a person who receives a pension in respect of accidents at

work or occupational diseases under the legislation of another State may request to be compulsorily insured under the legislation applied by OGA, to the extent that they pursue an activity falling within the scope of that legislation.

IRELAND

1. Notwithstanding Articles SSC.19(2) [Cash benefits] and SSC.57 [Calculation of unemployment benefits], for the purposes of calculating the prescribed reckonable weekly earnings of an insured person for the grant of sickness or unemployment benefit under Irish legislation, an amount equal to the average weekly wage of employed persons in the relevant prescribed year shall be credited to that insured person in respect of each week of activity as an employed person under the legislation of another State during that prescribed year.

MALTA

Special provisions for civil servants

(a) Solely for the purposes of the application of Articles SSC.43 [Special provisions for civil servants] and SSC.55 [Special provisions for civil servants] of the Protocol, persons employed under the Malta Armed Forces Act (Chapter 220 of the Laws of Malta), the Police Act (Chapter 164 of the Laws of Malta) and the Prisons Act (Chapter 260 of the Laws of Malta) shall be treated as civil servants;

(b) Pensions payable under the above Acts and under the Pensions Ordinance (Chapter 93 of the Laws of Malta) shall, solely for the purposes of point (cc) of Article SSC.1 [Definitions] of the Protocol, be considered as 'special schemes for civil servants'.

NETHERLANDS

1.138   1. Health care insurance

(a) As regards entitlement to benefits in kind under Dutch legislation, persons entitled to benefits in kind for the purpose of the implementation of Chapters 1 [Sickness, maternity and equivalent paternity benefits] and 2 [Benefits in respect of accidents at work and occupational diseases] of Title III of the Protocol shall mean:

(i) persons who, under Article 2 of the Zorgverzekeringswet (Health Care Insurance Act), are obliged to take out insurance under a health care insurer; and

(ii) in so far as they are not already included under point (i), members of the family of active military personnel who are living in another State and persons who are resident in another State and who, under the Protocol, are entitled to health care in their state of residence, the costs being borne by the Netherlands.

(b) The persons referred to in point 1(a)(i) must, in accordance with the provisions of the Zorgverzekeringswet (Health Care Insurance Act), take out insurance with a health care insurer, and the persons referred to in point 1(a)(ii) must register with the College voor zorgverzekeringen (Health Care Insurance Board);

(c) The provisions of the Zorgverzekeringswet (Health Care Insurance Act) and the Algemene Wet Bijzondere Ziektekosten (General Act on Exceptional Medical Expenses) concerning liability for the payment of contributions shall apply to the persons referred to in point (a) and the members of their families. In respect of members of the family, the contributions shall be levied on the person from whom the right to health care is derived with the exception of the members of the family of military personnel living in another State, who shall be levied directly;

(d) The provisions of the Zorgverzekeringswet (Health Care Insurance Act) concerning late insurance shall apply *mutatis mutandis* in the event of late registration with the College voor zorgverzekeringen (Health Care Insurance Board) in respect of the persons referred to in point (a)(ii).;

(e) Persons entitled to benefits in kind by virtue of the legislation of a State other than the Netherlands who reside in the Netherlands or stay temporarily in the Netherlands shall be entitled to benefits in kind in accordance with the policy offered to insured persons in the Netherlands by the institution of the place of residence or the place of stay, taking into account Article 11(1), (2) and (3) and Article 19(1) of the Zorgverzekeringswet (Health Care Insurance Act), as well as to benefits in kind provided for by the Algemene Wet Bijzondere Ziektekosten (General Act on Exceptional Medical Expenses);

(f) For the purposes of Articles SSC.21 [Right to benefits in kind under the legislation of the State of residence] to SSC.27 [Contributions by pensioners] of the Protocol, the following benefits (in addition to pensions covered by Chapters 4 [Invalidity benefits] and 5 [Old-age and survivors' pensions] of Title III [Special provisions concerning the various categories of benefits] of the Protocol shall be treated as pensions due under Dutch legislation:

— pensions awarded under the Law of 6 January 1966 on pensions for civil servants and their survivors (Algemene burgerlijke pensioenwet) (Netherlands Civil Service Pensions Act),
— pensions awarded under the Law of 6 October 1966 on pensions for military personnel and their survivors (Algemene militaire pensioenwet) (Military Pensions Act),
— benefits for incapacity for work awarded under the Law of 7 June 1972 on benefits for incapacity for work for military personnel (Wetarbeidsongeschiktheidsvoorziening militairen) (Military Personnel Incapacity for Work Act),
— pensions awarded under the Law of 15 February 1967 on: pensions for employees of the NV Nederlandse Spoorwegen (Dutch Railway Company) and their survivors (Spoorwegpensioenwet) (Railway Pensions Act),
— pensions awarded under the Reglement Dienstvoorwaarden Nederlandse Spoorwegen (governing conditions of employment of the Netherlands Railway Company),
— benefits awarded to retired persons before reaching the pensionable age of 65 years under a pension designed to provide income

for former employed persons in their old age, or benefits provided in the event of premature exit from the labour market under a scheme set up by the state or by an industrial agreement for persons aged 55 or over,
— benefits awarded to military personnel and civil servants under a scheme applicable in the event of redundancy, superannuation and early retirement.

(g) For the purposes of Article SSC.16(1) [Stay in the competent State when residence is in another State—special rules for the members of the families of frontier workers] of the Protocol, the persons referred to in point (a)(ii) of this paragraph who stay temporarily in the Netherlands shall be entitled to benefits in kind in accordance with the policy offered to insured persons in the Netherlands by the institution of the place of stay, taking into account Article 11(1), (2) and (3) and Article 19(1) of the Zorgverzekeringswet (Health Care Insurance Act), as well as to benefits in kind provided for by the Algemene Wet Bijzondere Ziektekosten (General Act on Exceptional Medical Expenses).

2. Application of the Algemene Ouderdomswet (AOW) (General Old Age Pensions Act)

1.139 (a) The reduction referred to in Article 13(1) of the AOW (General Old Age Pensions Act) shall not be applied for calendar years before 1 January 1957 during which a recipient not satisfying the conditions for having such years treated as periods of insurance:

— resided in the Netherlands between the ages of 15 and 65,
— while residing in another State, worked in the Netherlands for an employer established in the Netherlands, or
— worked in another State during periods regarded as periods of insurance under the Dutch social security system.

By way of derogation from Article 7 of the AOW, anyone who resided or worked in the Netherlands in accordance with the above conditions only prior to 1 January 1957 shall also be regarded as being entitled to a pension.

(b) The reduction referred to in Article 13(1) of the AOW shall not apply to calendar years prior to 2 August 1989 during which a person, between the ages of 15 and 65, who is or was married was not insured under the above legislation, while being resident in the territory of a State other than the Netherlands, if these calendar years coincide with periods of insurance completed by the person's spouse under the above legislation or with calendar years to be taken into account under point (a) of this paragraph, provided that the couple's marriage subsisted during that time.

By way of derogation from Article 7 of the AOW, such a person shall be regarded as being entitled to a pension.

(c) The reduction referred to in Article 13(2) of the AOW shall not apply to calendar years before 1 January 1957 during which a pensioner's spouse who fails to satisfy the conditions for having such years treated as periods of insurance:

— resided in the Netherlands between the ages of 15 and 65, or
— while residing in another State, worked in the Netherlands for an employer established in the Netherlands, or
— worked in another State during periods regarded as periods of insurance under the Netherlands social security system.

(d) The reduction referred to in Article 13(2) of the AOW shall not apply to calendar years prior to 2 August 1989 during which a pensioner's spouse resident in a State other than the Netherlands, between the ages of 15 and 65, was not insured under the AOW, if those calendar years coincide with periods of insurance completed by the pensioner under that legislation or with calendar years to be taken into account under point (a) of this paragraph, provided that the couple's marriage subsisted during that time.

(e) Points 2(a), 2(b), 2(c) and 2(d) shall not apply to periods which coincide with:

— periods which may be taken into account for calculating pension rights under the old-age insurance legislation of a State other than the Netherlands, or
— periods for which the person concerned has drawn an old-age pension under such legislation.

Periods of voluntary insurance under the system of another State shall not be taken into account for the purposes of this point.

(f) Points 2(a), 2(b), 2(c) and 2(d) shall apply only if the person concerned has resided in one or more States for 6 years after the age of 59 and only for such time as that person is resident in one of those States.

(g) By way of derogation from Chapter IV of the AOW, anyone resident in a State other than the Netherlands whose spouse is covered by compulsory insurance under that legislation shall be authorised to take out voluntary insurance under that legislation for periods during which the spouse is compulsorily insured.

This authorisation shall not cease where the spouse's compulsory insurance is terminated as a result of their death and where the survivor receives only a pension under the Algemene nabestaandenwet (General Surviving Relatives Act).

In any event, the authorisation in respect of voluntary insurance ceases on the date on which the person reaches the age of 65.

The contribution to be paid for voluntary insurance shall be set in accordance with the provisions relating to the determination of the contribution for voluntary insurance under the AOW. However, if the voluntary insurance follows on from a period of insurance as referred to in point 2(b), the contribution shall be set in accordance with the provisions relating to the determination of the contribution for compulsory insurance under the AOW, with the income to be taken into account being deemed to have been received in the Netherlands.

(h) The authorisation referred to in point 2(g) shall not be granted to anyone insured under another State's legislation on pensions or survivors' benefits;

(i) Anyone wishing to take out voluntary insurance under point 2(g) shall be required to apply for it to the Social Insurance Bank (Sociale Verzekeringsbank) not later than 1 year after the date on which the conditions for participation are fulfilled.

3. Application of the Algemene nabestaandenwet (ANW) (General Surviving Relatives Act)

1.140   (a) Where the surviving spouse is entitled to a survivor's pension under the ANW (General Surviving Relatives Act) pursuant to Article SSC.46(3) [Special provisions on aggregation of periods] of the Protocol, that pension shall be calculated in accordance with point (1)(b) of Article SSC.47 [Award of benefits] of the Protocol.

For the application of these provisions, periods of insurance prior to 1 October 1959 shall also be regarded as periods of insurance completed under Dutch legislation if during those periods the insured person, after the age of 15:

— resided in the Netherlands, or
— while resident in another State, worked in the Netherlands for an employer established in the Netherlands, or
— worked in another State during periods regarded as periods of insurance under the Dutch social security system.

(b) Account shall not be taken of the periods to be taken into consideration under point 3(a) which coincide with periods of compulsory insurance completed under the legislation of another State in respect of survivor's pensions;   (c) For the purposes of point (b) of Article SSC.47(1) [Award of benefits] of the Protocol, only periods of insurance completed under Dutch legislation after the age of 15 shall be taken into account as periods of insurance;

(d) By way of derogation from Article 63a(1) of the ANW, a person resident in a State other than the Netherlands whose spouse is compulsorily insured under the ANW shall be authorised to take out voluntary insurance under the ANW provided that such insurance has already begun by the date of application of the Protocol, but only for periods during which the spouse is compulsorily insured;

That authorisation shall cease as from the date of termination of the spouse's compulsory insurance under the ANW, unless the spouse's compulsory insurance is terminated as a result of their death and where the survivor only receives a pension under the ANW.

In any event, the authorisation in respect of voluntary insurance ceases on the date on which the person reaches the age of 65.

The contribution to be paid for voluntary insurance shall be set in accordance with the provisions relating to the determination of contributions for voluntary insurance under the ANW. However, if the voluntary insurance follows on from a period of insurance as referred to in point 2(b), the contribution shall be set in accordance with the provisions relating to the determination of contributions for compulsory insurance under the ANW, with the income to be taken into account being deemed to have been received in the Netherlands.

4. Application of Dutch legislation relating to incapacity for work

In calculating benefits under either the WAO, WIA or the WAZ, the Netherlands institutions shall take account of:

— periods of paid employment, and periods treated as such, completed in the Netherlands before 1 July 1967,
— periods of insurance completed under the WAO,
— periods of insurance completed by the person concerned, after the age of 15, under the Algemene Arbeidsongeschiktheidswet (General Act on Incapacity for Work), in so far as they do not coincide with the periods of insurance completed under the WAO,
— periods of insurance completed under the WAZ,
— periods of insurance completed under the WIA.

SPAIN

1. For the purpose of implementing point (1)(b) of Article SSC.47(1) [Award of benefits] of the Protocol, the years which the worker lacks to reach the pensionable or compulsory retirement age as stipulated under Article 31(4) of the consolidated version of the Ley de Clases Pasivas del Estado (Law on State Pensioners) shall be taken into account as actual years of service to the State only if at the time of the event in respect of which death pensions are due, the beneficiary was covered by Spain's special scheme for civil servants or was performing an activity assimilated under the scheme, or if, at the time of the event in respect of which the pensions are due, the beneficiary was performing an activity that would have required the person concerned to be included under the State's special scheme for civil servants, the armed forces or the judiciary, had the activity been performed in Spain. 1.141

2. (a) Under point (1)(c) of Article SSC.51 [Additional provisions for the calculation of benefits], the calculation of the theoretical Spanish benefit shall be carried out on the basis of the actual contributions of the person during the years immediately preceding payment of the last contribution to Spanish social security. Where, in the calculation of the basic amount for the pension, periods of insurance or residence under the legislation of other States have to be taken into account, the contribution basis in Spain which is closest in time to the reference periods shall be used for those periods, taking into account the development of the retail price index.

(b) The amount of the pension obtained shall be increased by the amount of the increases and revaluations calculated for each subsequent year for pensions of the same nature.

3. Periods completed in other States which must be calculated in the special scheme for civil servants, the armed forces and the judicial administration, will be treated in the same way, for the purposes of Article SSC.51 [Additional provisions for the calculation of benefits], as the periods closest in time covered as a civil servant in Spain.

4. The additional amounts based on age referred to in the Second Transitional Provision of the General Law on Social Security shall be applicable to all beneficiaries under the Protocol who have contributions to their name under the Spanish legislation prior to 1 January 1967; it shall not be possible, by application of Article SSC.6 [Equal treatment of

benefits, income, facts or events] of the Protocol, to treat periods of insurance credited in another State prior to 1 January 1967 as being the same as contributions paid in Spain, solely for the purposes of the Protocol. The date corresponding to 1 January 1967 shall be 1 August 1970 for the Special Scheme for Seafarers and 1 April 1969 for the Special Social Security Scheme for Coal Mining.

SWEDEN

1. The provisions of the Protocol on the aggregation of insurance periods and periods of residence shall not apply to the transitional provisions in the Swedish legislation on entitlement to guarantee pension for persons born in or before 1937 who have been resident in Sweden for a specified period before applying for a pension (Act 2000:798).

2. For the purpose of calculating income for notional income-related sickness compensation and income-related activity compensation in accordance with Chapter 8 of the Lag (1962:381) om allmän försäkring (the National Insurance Act), the following shall apply:

(a) where the insured person, during the reference period, has also been subject to the legislation of one or more other States on account of activity as an employed or self-employed person, income in the State(s) concerned shall be deemed to be equivalent to the insured person's average gross income in Sweden during the part of the reference period in Sweden, calculated by dividing the earnings in Sweden by the number of years over which those earnings accrued;

3. (a) For the purpose of calculating notional pension assets for income-based survivor's pension (Act 2000:461), if the requirement in Swedish legislation for pension entitlement in respect of at least three out of the 5 calendar years immediately preceding the insured person's death (reference period) is not met, account shall also be taken of insurance periods completed in other States as if they had been completed in Sweden. Insurance periods in other States shall be regarded as based on the average Swedish pension base. If the person concerned has only 1 year in Sweden with a pension base, each insurance period in another State shall be regarded as constituting the same amount.

(b) For the purpose of calculating notional pension credits for widows' pensions relating to deaths on or after 1 January 2003, if the requirement in Swedish legislation for pension credits in respect of at least two out of the 4 years immediately preceding the insured person's death (reference period) is not met and insurance periods were completed in another State during the reference period, those years shall be regarded as being based on the same pension credits as the Swedish year.

UNITED KINGDOM

1.142   1. Where, in accordance with United Kingdom legislation, a person may be entitled to a retirement pension if:

(a) the contributions of a former spouse are taken into account as if they were that person's own contributions; or

(b) the relevant contribution conditions are satisfied by that person's spouse or former spouse, then provided, in each case, that the spouse or former spouse is or had been exercising an activity as an employed or self-employed person, and had been subject to the legislation of two or more States, the provisions of Chapter 5 [Old-age and survivors' pensions] of Title III [Special provisions concerning the various categories of benefits] of the Protocol shall apply in order to determine entitlement under United Kingdom legislation. In that case, references in Chapter 5 [Old-age and survivors' pensions] of Title III [Special provisions concerning the various categories of benefits] of the Protocol to 'periods of insurance' shall be construed as references to periods of insurance completed by:

(i) a spouse or former spouse where a claim is made by:
— a married woman, or
— a person whose marriage has terminated otherwise than by the death of the spouse; or
(ii) a former spouse, where a claim is made by:
— a widower who immediately before pensionable age is not entitled to a widowed parent's allowance, or
— a widow who immediately before pensionable age is not entitled to a widowed mother's allowance, widowed parent's allowance or widow's pension, or who is only entitled to an age-related widow's pension calculated pursuant to point (b) of Article SSC.47(1) [Award of benefits] of the Protocol, and for this purpose 'age related widow's pension' means a widow's pension payable at a reduced rate in accordance with section 39(4) of the Social Security Contributions and Benefits Act 1992.

2. For the purposes of applying Article SSC.8 [Waiving of residence rules] of the Protocol in the case of old-age or survivors' cash benefits, pensions for accidents at work or occupational diseases and death grants, any beneficiary under United Kingdom legislation who is staying in the territory of another State shall, during that stay, be considered as if they resided in the territory of that other State.

3. (1) For the purpose of calculating an earnings factor in order to determine entitlement to benefits under United Kingdom legislation, for each week of activity as an employed person under the legislation of a Member State, and which commenced during the relevant income tax year within the meaning of United Kingdom legislation, the person concerned shall be deemed to have paid contributions as an employed earner, or have earnings on which contributions have been paid, on the basis of earnings equivalent to two-thirds of that year's upper earnings limit.

(2) For the purposes of point (b) of Article SSC.47(1) [Award of benefits] of the Protocol, where:

(a) in any income tax year starting on or after 6 April 1975, a person carrying out activity as an employed person has completed periods of insurance, employment or residence exclusively in a Member State, and the application of point (1) of this paragraph results in that year being counted as a qualifying year within the meaning of United Kingdom legislation for the purposes of point (b)(i) of Article SSC.47(1) [Award of benefits] of the Protocol, they shall be deemed to have been insured for 52 weeks in that year in that Member State;

(b) any income tax year starting on or after 6 April 1975 does not count as a qualifying year within the meaning of United Kingdom legislation for the purposes of point (b)(i) of Article SSC.47(1) [Award of benefits] of the Protocol, any periods of insurance, employment or residence completed in that year shall be disregarded.

(3) For the purpose of converting an earnings factor into periods of insurance, the earnings factor achieved in the relevant income tax year within the meaning of United Kingdom legislation shall be divided by that year's lower earnings limit. The result shall be expressed as a whole number, any remaining fraction being ignored. The figure so calculated shall be treated as representing the number of weeks of insurance completed under United Kingdom legislation during that year, provided that such figure shall not exceed the number of weeks during which in that year the person was subject to that legislation.

ANNEX SSC-7: IMPLEMENTING PART

TITLE I: GENERAL PROVISIONS

CHAPTER 1

Article SSCI.1: Definitions

1.143   1. For the purposes of this Annex, the definitions set out in Article SSC.1 [Definitions] apply.

2. In addition to the definitions referred to in paragraph 1:
 (a) "access point" means an entity providing:
  (i) an electronic contact point;
  (ii) automatic routing based on the address; and
  (iii) intelligent routing based on software that enables automatic checking and routing (for example, an artificial intelligence application) or human intervention;
 (b) "liaison body" means any body designated by the competent authority of a State for one or more of the branches of social security referred to in Article SSC.3 [Matters covered] of the Protocol to respond to requests for information and assistance for the purposes of the application of the Protocol and of this Annex and which has to fulfil the tasks assigned to it under Title IV [Financial provisions] of this Annex;
 (c) "document" means a set of data, irrespective of the medium used, structured in such a way that it can be exchanged electronically and which must be communicated in order to enable the operation of the Protocol and this Annex;

(d) "Structured Electronic Document" means any structured document in a format designed for the electronic exchange of information between States;

(e) "transmission by electronic means" means the transmission of data using electronic equipment for the processing (including digital compression) of data and employing wires, radio transmission, optical technologies or any other electromagnetic means;

(f) "fraud" means any deliberate act or deliberate omission to act, carried out with the intention to either:

    (i) receive social security benefits, or enable another person to receive social security benefits, when the conditions of entitlement to such benefits under the law of the State(s) concerned or the Protocol are not met; or

    (ii) avoid paying social security contributions, or enable another person to avoid paying social security contributions, when such contributions are required under the law of the State(s) concerned or the Protocol.

CHAPTER 2: PROVISIONS CONCERNING COOPERATION AND EXCHANGES OF DATA

Article SSCI.2: Scope and rules for exchanges between institutions

1. For the purposes of this Annex, exchanges between authorities of the States and institutions and persons covered by the Protocol shall be based on the principles of public service, efficiency, active assistance, rapid delivery and accessibility, including e-accessibility, in particular for the disabled and the elderly.   1.144

2. The institutions shall without delay provide or exchange all data necessary for establishing and determining the rights and obligations of persons to whom the Protocol applies. Such data shall be transferred between the States directly by the institutions themselves or indirectly via the liaison bodies.

3. Where a person has mistakenly submitted information, documents or claims to an institution in the territory of a State other than that in which the institution designated, in accordance with this Annex, is situated, the information, documents or claims shall be resubmitted without delay by the former institution to the institution designated in accordance with this Annex, indicating the date on which they were initially submitted. That date shall be binding on the latter institution. The institutions of the States shall not, however, be held liable, or be deemed to have taken a decision by virtue of their failure to act as a result of the late transmission of information, documents or claims by States' institutions.

4. Where data are transferred indirectly via the liaison body of the State of destination, time limits for responding to claims shall start from

the date when that liaison body received the claim, as if it had been received by the institution in that State.

Article SSCI.3: Scope and rules for exchanges between the persons concerned and institutions

1.145   1. The States shall ensure that the necessary information is made available to the persons concerned in order to inform them of the provisions introduced by the Protocol and this Annex to enable them to assert their rights. They shall also provide for user-friendly services.

2. Persons to whom the Protocol applies shall be required to forward to the relevant institution the information, documents or supporting evidence necessary to establish their situation or that of their families, to establish or maintain their rights and obligations and to determine the applicable legislation and their obligations under it.

3. To the extent necessary for the application of the Protocol and this Annex, the relevant institutions shall forward the information and issue the documents to the persons concerned without delay and in all cases within any time limits specified under the legislation of the State in question.

The relevant institution shall notify the claimant residing or staying in another State of its decision directly or through the liaison body of the State of residence or stay. When refusing the benefits, it shall also indicate the reasons for refusal, the remedies and periods allowed for appeals. A copy of this decision shall be sent to other involved institutions.

Article SSCI.4: Forms, documents and methods of exchanging data

1.146   1. Subject to Article SSCI.75 [Interim provisions for forms and documents] and Appendix SSCI-2 [Entitlement document], the structure, content and format of forms and documents issued on behalf of the States for the purposes of implementing the Protocol shall be agreed by the Specialised Committee on Social Security Coordination.

2. The transmission of data between the institutions or the liaison bodies may, subject to the approval of the Specialised Committee on Social Security Coordination, be carried out via the Electronic Exchange of Social Security Information. To the extent the forms and documents referred to in paragraph 1 are exchanged via the Electronic Exchange of Social Security Information, they shall respect the rules applicable to that system.

3. Where the transmission of data between institutions or the liaison bodies is not carried out via the Electronic Exchange of Social Security Information, the relevant institutions and liaison bodies shall use the arrangements appropriate to each case, and favour the use of electronic means as far as possible.

4. In their communications with the persons concerned, the relevant institutions shall use the arrangements appropriate to each case, and favour the use of electronic means as far as possible.

Article SSCI.5: Legal value of documents and supporting evidence issued in another State

1. Documents issued by the institution of a State and showing the position of a person for the purposes of the application of the Protocol and this Annex, and supporting evidence on the basis of which the documents have been issued, shall be accepted by the institutions of the other States for as long as they have not been withdrawn or declared to be invalid by the State in which they were issued.   1.147

2. Where there is doubt about the validity of a document or the accuracy of the facts on which the particulars contained therein are based, the institution of the State that receives the document shall ask the issuing institution for the necessary clarification and, where appropriate, the withdrawal of that document. The issuing institution shall reconsider the grounds for issuing the document and, if necessary, withdraw it.

3. Pursuant to paragraph 2, where there is doubt about the information provided by the persons concerned, the validity of a document or supporting evidence or the accuracy of the facts on which the particulars contained therein are based, the institution of the place of stay or residence shall, insofar as this is possible, at the request of the competent institution, proceed to the necessary verification of this information or document.

4. Where no agreement is reached between the institutions concerned, the matter may be brought before the Specialised Committee on Social Security Coordination by the competent authorities no earlier than one month following the date on which the institution that received the document submitted its request. The Specialised Committee on Social Security Coordination shall endeavour to reconcile the points of view within six months of the date on which the matter was brought before it.

Article SSCI.6 : Provisional application of legislation and provisional granting of benefits

1. Unless otherwise provided for in this Annex, where there is a difference of views between the institutions or authorities of two or more States concerning the determination of the applicable legislation, the person concerned shall be made provisionally subject to the legislation of one of those States, the order of priority being determined as follows: 1.148

(a) the legislation of the State where the person actually pursues their employment or self-employment, if the employment or self-employment is pursued in only one State;

(b) the legislation of the State of residence if the person concerned pursues employment or selfemployment in two or more States and performs part of their activity or activities in the State of residence, or if the person concerned is neither employed nor self-employed;

(c) in all other cases, the legislation of the State the application of which was first requested if the person pursues an activity, or activities, in two or more States.

2. Where there is a difference of views between the institutions or authorities of two or more States about which institution should provide the benefits in cash or in kind, the person concerned who could claim benefits if there was no dispute shall be entitled, on a provisional basis, to the benefits provided for by the legislation applied by the institution of that person's place of residence or, if that person does not reside on the territory of one of the States concerned, to the benefits provided for by the legislation applied by the institution to which the request was first submitted.

3. Where no agreement is reached between the institutions or authorities concerned, the matter may be brought before the Specialised Committee on Social Security Coordination by a Party no earlier than one month after the date on which the difference of views, as referred to in paragraph 1 or 2 arose. The Specialised Committee on Social Security Coordination shall seek to reconcile the points of view within six months of the date on which the matter was brought before it.

4. Where it is established either that the applicable legislation is not that of the State of provisional membership, or the institution which granted the benefits on a provisional basis was not the competent institution, the institution identified as being competent shall be deemed retroactively to have been so, as if that difference of views had not existed, at the latest from either the date of provisional membership or of the first provisional granting of the benefits concerned.

5. If necessary, the institution identified as being competent and the institution which provisionally paid the cash benefits or provisionally received contributions shall settle the financial situation of the person concerned as regards contributions and cash benefits paid provisionally, where appropriate, in accordance with Title IV, Chapter 2 [Recovery of benefits provided but not due, recovery of provisional payments and contributions, offsetting and assistance with recovery], of this Annex.

Benefits in kind granted provisionally by an institution in accordance with paragraph 2 shall be reimbursed by the competent institution in accordance with Title IV [Financial provisions] of this Annex.

Article SSCI.7: Provisional calculation of benefits and contributions

1.149   1. Unless otherwise provided for in this Annex to the Protocol, where a person is eligible for a benefit, or is liable to pay a contribution in accordance with the Protocol, and the competent institution does not have all the information concerning the situation in another State which is necessary to calculate definitively the amount of that benefit or contribution, that institution shall, on request of the person concerned, award this benefit or calculate this contribution on a provisional basis, if such a calculation is possible on the basis of the information at the disposal of that institution.

2. The benefit or the contribution concerned shall be recalculated once all the necessary supporting evidence or documents are provided to the institution concerned.

110

CHAPTER 3: OTHER GENERAL PROVISIONS FOR THE APPLICATION OF
THE PROTOCOL

Article SSCI.8: Other procedures between authorities and institutions

1. Two or more States, or their competent authorities, may agree   1.150
procedures other than those provided for by this Annex, provided that
such procedures do not adversely affect the rights or obligations of the
persons concerned.

2. Any agreements concluded to this end shall be notified to the
Specialised Committee on Social Security Coordination and listed in the
Appendix SSCI-1 [Implementing provisions for bilateral agreements
remaining in force and new bilateral implementing agreements].

3. Provisions contained in implementing agreements concluded
between two or more States with the same purpose as, or which are
similar to, those referred to in paragraph 2, which are in force on the day
preceding the entry into force of this Agreement, shall continue to apply,
for the purposes of relations between those States, provided they are also
included in Appendix SSCI-1 [Implementing provisions for bilateral
agreements remaining in force and new bilateral implementing agree-
ments].

Article SSCI.9 : Prevention of overlapping of benefits

Notwithstanding other provisions in the Protocol, when benefits due   1.151
under the legislation of two or more States are mutually reduced, suspended or withdrawn, any amounts that would not be paid in the event
of strict application of the rules concerning reduction, suspension or
withdrawal laid down by the legislation of the State concerned shall be
divided by the number of benefits subjected to reduction, suspension or
withdrawal.

Article SSCI.10: Elements for determining residence

1. Where there is a difference of views between the institutions of two   1.152
or more States about the determination of the residence of a person to
whom the Protocol applies, these institutions shall establish by common
agreement the centre of interests of the person concerned, based on an
overall assessment of all available information relating to relevant facts,
which may include, as appropriate:
 (a) the duration and continuity of presence on the territory of the
     States concerned;
 (b) that person's situation, including:
     (i) the nature and the specific characteristics of any activity
         pursued, in particular the place where such activity is habit-
         ually pursued, the stability of the activity, and the duration of
         any work contract;
     (ii) that person's family status and family ties;
     (iii) the exercise of any non-remunerated activity;

(iv) in the case of students, the source of that student's income;
(v) that person's housing situation, in particular how permanent it is;
(vi) the State in which that person is deemed to reside for taxation purposes.

2. Where the consideration of the various criteria based on relevant facts as set out in paragraph 1 does not lead to agreement between the institutions concerned, the person's intention, as it appears from such facts and circumstances, especially the reasons that led the person to move, shall be considered to be decisive for establishing that person's actual place of residence.

3. The centre of interest of a student who goes to another State to pursue a full time course of study shall not be considered as being in the State of study for the entire duration of the course of study in that State, without prejudice to the possibility of rebutting this presumption.

4. Paragraph 3 shall apply *mutatis mutandis* to the family members of the student.

Article SSCI.11: Aggregation of periods

1.153 1. For the purposes of applying Article SSC.7 [Aggregation of periods] of the Protocol the competent institution shall contact the institutions of the States to whose legislation the person concerned has also been subject in order to determine all the periods completed under their legislation.

2. The respective periods of insurance, employment, self-employment or residence completed under the legislation of a State shall be added to those completed under the legislation of any other State, insofar as necessary for the purposes of applying Article SSC.7 [Aggregation of periods] of the Protocol, provided that these periods do not overlap.

3. Where a period of insurance or residence which is completed in accordance with compulsory insurance under the legislation of a State coincides with a period of insurance completed on the basis of voluntary insurance or continued optional insurance under the legislation of another State, only the period completed on the basis of compulsory insurance shall be taken into account.

4. Where a period of insurance or residence other than an equivalent period completed under the legislation of a State coincides with an equivalent period on the basis of the legislation of another State, only the period other than an equivalent period shall be taken into account.

5. Any period regarded as equivalent under the legislation of two or more States shall be taken into account only by the institution of the State to whose legislation the person concerned was last compulsorily subject before that period. In the event that the person concerned was not compulsorily subject to the legislation of a State before that period, the latter shall be taken into account by the institution of the State to whose legislation the person concerned was compulsorily subject for the first time after that period.

6. In the event that the time in which certain periods of insurance or residence were completed under the legislation of a State cannot be

determined precisely, it shall be presumed that these periods do not overlap with periods of insurance or residence completed under the legislation of another State, and account shall be taken thereof, where advantageous to the person concerned, insofar as they can reasonably be taken into consideration.

Article SSCI.12: Rules for conversion of periods

1. Where periods completed under the legislation of a State are expressed in units different from those provided for by the legislation of another State, the conversion needed for the purpose of aggregation under Article SSC.7 [Aggregation of periods] of the Protocol shall be carried out under the following rules: 1.154

   (a) the period to be used as the basis for the conversion shall be that communicated by the institution of the State under whose legislation the period was completed;
   (b) in the case of schemes where the periods are expressed in days the conversion from days to other units, and vice versa, as well as between different schemes based on days shall be calculated according to the following table:

Scheme based on	1 day corresponds to	1 week corresponds to	1 month corresponds to	1 quarter corresponds to	Maximum of days in one calendar year
5 days	9 hours	5 days	22 days	66 days	264 days
6 days	8 hours	6 days	26 days	78 days	312 days
7 days	6 hours	7 days	30 days	90 days	360 days

   (c) in the case of schemes where the periods are expressed in units other than days,
      (i) three months or 13 weeks shall be equivalent to one quarter, and vice versa;
      (ii) one year shall be equivalent to four quarters, 12 months or 52 weeks, and vice versa;
      (iii) for the conversion of weeks into months, and vice versa, weeks and months shall be converted into days in accordance with the conversion rules for the schemes based on six days in the table in point (b);
   (d) in the case of periods expressed in fractions, those figures shall be converted into the next smaller integer unit applying the rules laid down in points (b) and (c). Fractions of years shall be converted into months unless the scheme involved is based on quarters;
   (e) if the conversion under this paragraph results in a fraction of a unit, the next higher integer unit shall be taken as the result of the conversion under this paragraph.

2. The application of paragraph 1 shall not have the effect of producing, for the total sum of the periods completed during one calendar year, a total exceeding the number of days indicated in the last column in the table in point (b) paragraph 1, 52 weeks, 12 months or four quarters.

If the periods to be converted correspond to the maximum annual amount of periods under the legislation of the State in which they have been completed, the application of paragraph 1 shall not result within one calendar year in periods that are shorter than the possible maximum annual amount of periods provided under the legislation concerned.

3. The conversion shall be carried out either in one single operation covering all those periods which were communicated as an aggregate, or for each year, if the periods were communicated on a year-by-year basis.

4. Where an institution communicates periods expressed in days, it shall at the same time indicate whether the scheme it administers is based on five days, six days or seven days.

TITLE II: DETERMINATION OF THE LEGISLATION APPLICABLE

Article SSCI.13: Details relating to Articles SSC.11 [Detached workers] and SSC.12 [Pursuit of activities in two or more States] of the Protocol

1.155   1. For the purposes of the application of point (a) of Article SSC.11(1) [Detached workers], a 'person who pursues an activity as an employed person in a State for an employer which normally carries out its activities there and who is sent by that employer to another State' shall include a person who is recruited with a view to being sent to another State, provided that, immediately before the start of that person's employment, the person concerned is already subject to the legislation of the State in which their employer is established.

2. For the purposes of the application of point (a) of Article SSC.11(1) [Detached workers] of the Protocol, the words 'which normally carries out its activities there' shall refer to an employer that ordinarily performs substantial activities, other than purely internal management activities, in the territory of the State in which it is established, taking account of all criteria characterising the activities carried out by the undertaking in question. The relevant criteria must be suited to the specific characteristics of each employer and the real nature of the activities carried out.

3. For the purposes of the application of point (b) of Article SSC.11(1) [Detached workers],the words 'who normally pursues an activity as a self-employed person' shall refer to a person who habitually carries out substantial activities in the territory of the State in which that person is established. In particular, that person must have already pursued their activity for some time before the date when they wish to take advantage of the provisions of that Article and, during any period of temporary activity in another State, must continue to fulfil, in the State where they are established, the requirements for the pursuit of their activity in order to be able to pursue it on their return.

4. For the purposes of the application of point (b) of Article SSC.11(1) [Detached workers], the criterion for determining whether the activity that a self-employed person goes to pursue in another State

is 'similar' to the self-employed activity normally pursued shall be that of the actual nature of the activity, rather than of the designation of employed or self-employed activity that may be given to this activity by the other State.

5. For the purposes of the application of Article SSC.12(1) and (5) [Pursuit of activities in two or more States] of the Protocol, a person who 'normally pursues an activity as an employed person' in 'one or more Member States as well as the United Kingdom', or in 'two or more Member States' respectively, shall refer to a person who simultaneously, or in alternation, for the same undertaking or employer or for various undertakings or employers, exercises one or more separate activities in such States.

6. For the purposes of Article SSC.12(1) and (5) [Pursuit of activities in two or more States] of the Protocol, an employed flight crew or cabin crew member normally pursuing air passenger or freight services in two or more States shall be subject to the legislation of the State where the home base, as defined in Article SSC.1 [Definitions] of the Protocol, is located.

7. Marginal activities shall be disregarded for the purposes of determining the applicable legislation under Article SSC.12 [Pursuit of activities in two or more States] of the Protocol. Article SSCI.15 [Procedure for the application of Article SSC.12] of this Annex shall apply to all cases under this Article.

8. For the purposes of the application of Article SSC.12(2) and (6) [Pursuit of activities in two or more States] of the Protocol, a person who 'normally pursues an activity as a self-employed person' in 'one or more Member States as well as the United Kingdom', or in 'two or more Member States respectively', shall refer, in particular, to a person who simultaneously or in alternation pursues one or more separate self-employed activities, irrespective of the nature of those activities, in such States.

9. For the purposes of distinguishing the activities under paragraphs 5 and 8 from the situations described in Article SSC.11(1) [Detached workers] of the Protocol, the duration of the activity in one or more States (whether it is permanent or of an ad hoc or temporary nature) shall be decisive. For these purposes, an overall assessment shall be made of all the relevant facts including, in particular, in the case of an employed person, the place of work as defined in the employment contract.

10. For the purposes of the application of Article SSC.12(1) (2), (5) and (6) [Pursuit of activities in two or more States] of the Protocol, a 'substantial part of employed or self-employed activity' pursued in a State shall mean a quantitatively substantial part of all the activities of the employed or selfemployed person pursued there, without this necessarily being the major part of those activities.

11. To determine whether a substantial part of the activities is pursued in a State, the following indicative criteria shall be taken into account:
(a) in the case of an employed activity, the working time or the remuneration; and

(b) in the case of a self-employed activity, the turnover, working time, number of services rendered or income. In the framework of an overall assessment, a share of less than 25% in respect of the criteria mentioned above shall be an indicator that a substantial part of the activities is not being pursued in the relevant State.

12. For the purposes of the application of point (b) of Article SSC.12(2) [Pursuit of activities in two or more States] of the Protocol, the 'centre of interest' of the activities of a self-employed person shall be determined by taking account of all the aspects of that person's occupational activities, notably the place where the person's fixed and permanent place of business is located, the habitual nature or the duration of the activities pursued, the number of services rendered, and the intention of the person concerned as revealed by all the circumstances.

13. For the determination of the applicable legislation under paragraphs 10, 11 and 12, the institutions concerned shall take into account the situation projected for the following 12 calendar months.

14. If a person pursues his or her activity as an employed person in two or more States on behalf of an employer established outside the territory of the States, and if this person resides in a State without pursuing substantial activity there, they shall be subject to the legislation of the State of residence.

Article SSCI.14: Procedures for the application of Article SSC.10(3)(b) and Article SSC.10(4) [General rules] and Article SSC.11 [Detached workers] of the Protocol (on the provision of information to the institutions concerned)

1.156   1. Unless otherwise provided for by Article SSCI.15 [Procedure for the application of Article SSC.12] of this Annex, where a person pursues their activity outside the competent State, the employer or, in the case of a person who does not pursue an activity as an employed person, the person concerned shall inform the competent institution of the State whose legislation is applicable thereof, whenever possible in advance. That institution shall issue the attestation referred to in Article SSCI.16(2) [Provision of information to persons concerned and employers] of this Annex to the person concerned and shall without delay make information concerning the legislation applicable to that person, pursuant to point (b) of Article SSC.10(3) [General rules] or Article SSC.11 [Detached workers] of the Protocol, available to the institution designated by the competent authority of the State in which the activity is pursued.

2. An employer within the meaning of Article SSC.10(4) [General rules] of the Protocol who has an employee on board a vessel flying the flag of another State shall inform the competent institution of the State whose legislation is applicable thereof whenever possible in advance. That institution shall, without delay, make information concerning the legislation applicable to the person concerned, pursuant to Article SSC.10(4) [General rules] of the Protocol, available to the institution designated by the competent authority of the State whose flag, the vessel on which the employee is to perform the activity, is flying.

Article SSCI.15: Procedure for the application of Article SSC.12 [Pursuit of activities in two or more States] of the Protocol

1. A person who pursues activities in two or more States, or where   1.157
Article SSC.12(5) or (6) [Pursuit of activities in two or more States]
applies, shall inform the institution designated by the competent authority of the State of residence thereof.

2. The designated institution of the place of residence shall without
delay determine the legislation applicable to the person concerned,
having regard to Article SSC.12 [Pursuit of activities in two or more
States] of the Protocol and Article SSCI.13 [Details relating to Articles SSC.11 [Detached workers] and SSC.12 [Pursuit of activities in
two or more States] of this Annex. That initial determination shall be
provisional. The institution shall inform the designated institutions of
each State in which an activity is pursued of its provisional determination.

3. The provisional determination of the applicable legislation, as provided for in paragraph 2, shall become definitive within two months of
the institutions designated by the competent authorities of the State(s)
concerned being informed of it, in accordance with paragraph 2, unless
the legislation has already been definitively determined on the basis of
paragraph 4, or at least one of the institutions concerned informs the
institution designated by the competent authority of the State of residence by the end of this two-month period that it cannot yet accept the
determination or that it takes a different view on this.

4. Where uncertainty about the determination of the applicable legislation requires contacts between the institutions or authorities of two or
more States, at the request of one or more of the institutions designated
by the competent authorities of the State(s) concerned, or of the competent authorities themselves, the legislation applicable to the person concerned shall be determined by common agreement, having regard to
Article SSC.12 [Pursuit of activities in two or more States] of the
Protocol and the relevant provisions of Article SSCI.13 [Details relating
to Articles SSC.11 [Detached workers] and SSC.12 [Pursuit of activities
in two or more States]] of this Annex.

Where there is a difference of views between the institutions or competent authorities concerned, those bodies shall seek agreement in accordance with the conditions set out above and Article SSCI.6 [Provisional
application of legislation and provisional granting of benefits] of this
Annex shall apply.

5. The competent institution of the State whose legislation is determined to be applicable either provisionally or definitively shall without
delay inform the person concerned.

6. If the person concerned fails to provide the information referred to
in paragraph 1, this Article shall be applied at the initiative of the
institution designated by the competent authority of the State of residence as soon as it is appraised of that person's situation, possibly via
another institution concerned.

Article SSCI.16: Provision of information to persons concerned and employers

1.158   1. The competent institution of the State whose legislation becomes applicable pursuant to Title II [Determination of the legislation applicable] of the Protocol shall inform the person concerned and, where appropriate, their employer(s) of the obligations laid down in that legislation. It shall provide them with the necessary assistance to complete the formalities required by that legislation.

2. At the request of the person concerned or of the employer, the competent institution of the State whose legislation is applicable pursuant to Title II [Determination of the legislation applicable] of the Protocol shall provide an attestation that such legislation is applicable and shall indicate, where appropriate, until what date and under what conditions.

Article SSCI.17: Cooperation between institutions

1.159   1. The relevant institutions shall communicate to the competent institution of the State whose legislation is applicable to a person pursuant to Title II [Determination of the legislation applicable] of the Protocol the necessary information required to establish the date on which that legislation becomes applicable and the contributions which that person and his or her employer(s) are liable to pay under that legislation.

2. The competent institution of the State whose legislation becomes applicable to a person pursuant to Title II [Determination of the legislation applicable] of the Protocol shall make the information indicating the date on which the application of that legislation takes effect available to the institution designated by the competent authority of the State to whose legislation that person was last subject.

Article SSCI.18: Cooperation in case of doubts about the validity of issued documents concerning the applicable legislation

1.160   1. Where there is doubt about the validity of a document showing the position of the person for the purposes of the applicable legislation or the accuracy of the facts on which the document is based, the institution of the State that receives the document shall ask the issuing institution for the necessary clarification and, where appropriate, the withdrawal or rectification of that document. The requesting institution shall substantiate its request and provide the relevant supporting documentation that gave rise to the request.

2. When receiving such a request, the issuing institution shall reconsider the grounds for issuing the document and, where an error is detected, withdraw it or rectify it within 30 working days from the receipt of the request. The withdrawal or rectification shall have retroactive effect. However, in cases where there is a risk of disproportionate outcome, and in particular, of the loss of status as an insured person for the whole or part of the relevant period in the State(s) concerned, the States shall consider a more proportionate arrangement in such case. When the

available evidence permits the issuing institution to find that the applicant of the document has committed fraud, it shall withdraw or rectify the document without delay and with retroactive effect.

TITLE III: SPECIAL PROVISIONS CONCERNING THE VARIOUS
CATEGORIES OF BENEFITS

CHAPTER 1: SICKNESS, MATERNITY AND EQUIVALENT PATERNITY
BENEFITS

Article SSCI.19: General implementing provisions

1. The competent authorities or institutions shall ensure that any necessary information is made available to insured persons regarding the procedures and conditions for the granting of benefits in kind where such benefits are received in the territory of a State other than that of the competent institution.   1.161

2. Notwithstanding point (a) of Article SSC.6 [Equal treatment of benefits, income, facts or events] of the Protocol, a State may become responsible for the cost of benefits in accordance with Article SSC.20 [Pension claimants] of the Protocol only if, either the insured person has made a claim for a pension under the legislation of that State, or in accordance with Articles SSC.21 [Right to benefits in kind under the legislation of the State of residence] to SSC.27 [Contributions by pensioners] of the Protocol, they receive a pension under the legislation of that State.

Article SSCI.20: Regime applicable in the event of the existence of more than one regime in the State of residence or stay

If the legislation of the State of residence or stay comprises more than one scheme of sickness, maternity and paternity insurance for more than one category of insured persons, the provisions applicable under Articles SSC.15 [Residence in a State other than the competent State], SSC.17(1) [Stay outside the competent State], SSC.18 [Travel with the purpose of receiving benefits in kind—authorisation to receive appropriate treatment outside the State of residence], SSC.20 [Pension claimants], SSC.22 [No right to benefits in kind under the legislation of the State of residence] and SSC.24 [Residence of members of the family in a State other than the one in which the pensioner resides] of the Protocol shall be those of the legislation on the general scheme for employed persons.   1.162

Article SSCI.21: Residence in a State other than the competent State Procedure and scope of right

1. For the purposes of the application of Article SSC.15 [Residence in a State other than the competent State], of the Protocol, the insured person or members of that person's family shall be obliged to register   1.163

promptly with the institution of the place of residence. Their right to benefits in kind in the State of residence shall be certified by a document issued by the competent institution upon request of the insured person or upon request of the institution of the place of residence.

2. The document referred to in paragraph 1 shall remain valid until the competent institution informs the institution of the place of residence of its cancellation.

The institution of the place of residence shall inform the competent institution of any registration under paragraph 1 and of any change or cancellation of that registration.

3. This Article shall apply *mutatis mutandis* to the persons referred to in Articles SSC.20 [Pension claimants], SSC.22 [No right to benefits in kind under the legislation of the State of residence] and SSC.23 [Pensions under the legislation of one or more States other than the State of residence, where there is a right to benefits in kind in the latter State], SSC.24 [Residence of members of the family in a State other than the one in which the pensioner resides] of the Protocol.

Reimbursement

4. Where a person or the members of that person's family:

(a) have been issued with the document referred to in paragraph 1;

(b) have registered that document with the institution of the place of residence in accordance with paragraph 1; and

(c) a health fee has been paid by or on behalf of the person or members of their family to the State of residence as part of an application for a permit to enter, stay, work or reside in that State,

that person or members of that person's family may apply to the institution of the State of residence for reimbursement (in whole or part, as the case may be) of the health fee paid.

4. Where a claim is made in accordance with paragraph 1, the institution of the State of residence shall determine that claim within three calendar months, starting on the day the claim was received, and shall make any reimbursement in accordance with this Article.

5. Where the period of validity of the document referred to in paragraph 1 is less than the period of time in respect of which the health fee has been paid, the amount reimbursed shall not exceed that portion of the health fee which corresponds to the period for which the document had been issued.

6. Where the health fee was paid by another person on behalf of a person to whom this Article applies, reimbursement may be made to that other person.

Article SSCI.22: Stay in a State other than the competent State

Procedure and scope of right

1.164   1. For the purposes of the application of Article SSC.17 [Stay outside the competent State] of the Protocol, the insured person shall present to the health care provider in the State of stay an entitlement document issued by the competent institution indicating his entitlement to benefits in kind. If the insured person does not have such a document, the institution of the place of stay, upon request or if otherwise necessary, shall contact the competent institution in order to obtain one.

2. That document shall indicate that the insured person is entitled to benefits in kind under the conditions laid down in Article SSC.17 [Stay outside the competent State] of the Protocol on the same terms as those applicable to persons insured under the legislation of the State of stay, and shall satisfy the requirements in Appendix SSCI.2.

3. The benefits in kind referred to in Article SSC.17(1) [Stay outside the competent State] of the Protocol shall refer to the benefits in kind which are provided in the State of stay, in accordance with its legislation, and which become necessary on medical grounds with a view to preventing an insured person from being forced to return, before the end of the planned duration of stay, to the competent State to obtain the necessary treatment.

Procedure and arrangements for meeting the costs and providing reimbursement of benefits in kind

4. If the insured person has actually borne the costs of all or part of the benefits in kind provided within the framework of Article SSC.17 [Stay outside the competent State] of the Protocol and if the legislation applied by the institution of the place of stay enables reimbursement of those costs to an insured person, they may send an application for reimbursement to the institution of the place of stay. In that case, that institution shall reimburse directly to that person the amount of the costs corresponding to those benefits within the limits of and under the conditions of the reimbursement rates laid down in its legislation.

5. If the reimbursement of such costs has not been requested directly from the institution of the place of stay, the costs incurred shall be reimbursed to the person concerned by the competent institution in accordance with the reimbursement rates administered by the institution of the place of stay or the amounts which would have been subject to reimbursement to the institution of the place of stay, if Article SSCI.47 [Principles] of this Annex had applied in the case concerned.

The institution of the place of stay shall provide the competent institution, upon request, with all necessary information about these rates or amounts.

6. By way of derogation from paragraph 5, the competent institution may undertake the reimbursement of the costs incurred within the limits of and under the conditions of the reimbursement rates laid down in its legislation, provided that the insured person has agreed to this provision being applied to them.

7. If the legislation of the State of stay does not provide for reimbursement pursuant to paragraphs 4 and 5 in the case concerned, the competent institution may reimburse the costs within the limits of and under the conditions of the reimbursement rates laid down in its legislation, without the agreement of the insured person.

8. The reimbursement to the insured person shall not, in any event, exceed the amount of costs actually incurred by them.

9. In the case of substantial expenditure, the competent institution may pay the insured person an appropriate advance as soon as that person submits the application for reimbursement to it.

Family Members

10. Paragraphs 1 to 9 shall apply *mutatis mutandis* to the members of the family of the insured person.

Reimbursement for students

11. Where a person:
(a) holds a valid entitlement document referred to in Appendix SSCI-2 issued by the competent institution;
(b) has been accepted by a higher education institution in a State other than the competent State ("State of study") to pursue a full time course of study leading to a higher education qualification recognised by that State, including diplomas, certificates or doctoral degrees at a higher education institution, which may cover a preparatory course prior to such education, in accordance with national law, or compulsory training;
(c) does not exercise, or has not exercised, an activity as an employed or self-employed person in the State of study during the period to which the health fee relates; and
(d) a health fee has been paid by or on behalf of that person to the State of study as part of an application for a permit to enter, stay or reside for the purposes of pursuing a full time course of study in that State;

that person may apply to the institution of the State of study for reimbursement (in whole or part, as the case may be) of the health fee paid.

12. Where a claim is made in accordance with paragraph 11, the institution of the State of study shall process and settle that claim within a reasonable period but not later than six calendar months starting on the day the claim was received and make any reimbursement in accordance with this Article.

13. Where the period of validity of the entitlement document referred to in point (a) of paragraph 11 is less than the period of time in respect of which the health fee has been paid, the amount of the health fee reimbursed shall be the amount paid which corresponds to the period of validity of that document.

14. Where the health fee was paid by another person on behalf of a person to whom this Article applies, reimbursement may be made to that other person.

15. Paragraphs 11 to 14 shall apply *mutatis mutandis* to the members of the family of that person.

16. This Article shall enter into force 12 months after the date of entry into force of this Agreement.

17. A person who satisfied the conditions in paragraph 11 in the period between the entry into force of this Agreement and the date specified in paragraph 16 may, upon the entry into force of this Article,

make a claim for reimbursement under paragraph 11 in relation to that period.

18. By way of derogation from Article SSC.5(1) [Equality of treatment], charges may be imposed by the State of study in accordance with its national law in respect of benefits in kind that do not fulfil the criteria set out in point (a) of Article SSC.17(1) [Stay outside the competent State] and which are provided to a person in respect of whom reimbursement has been made during that person's stay for the period to which that reimbursement relates.

Article SSCI.23: Scheduled treatment

Authorisation procedure

1. For the purposes of the application of Article SSC.18(1) [Travel with the purpose of receiving benefits in kind—authorisation to receive appropriate treatment outside the State of residence] of the Protocol, the insured person shall present a document issued by the competent institution to the institution of the place of stay. For the purposes of this Article, the competent institution shall mean the institution which bears the cost of the scheduled treatment; in the cases referred to in Article SSC.18(4) [Travel with the purpose of receiving benefits in kind—authorisation to receive appropriate treatment outside the State of residence] and SSC.25(5) [Stay of the pensioner or the members of their family in a State other than the State of residence—stay in the competent State—authorisation for appropriate treatment outside the State of residence] of the Protocol, in which the benefits in kind provided in the State of residence are reimbursed on the basis of fixed amounts, the competent institution shall mean the institution of the place of residence.

1.165

2. If an insured person does not reside in the competent State, they shall request authorisation from the institution of the place of residence, which shall forward it to the competent institution without delay.

In that event, the institution of the place of residence shall certify in a statement whether the conditions set out in the second sentence of Article SSC.18(2) [Travel with the purpose of receiving benefits in kind—authorisation to receive appropriate treatment outside the State of residence] of the Protocol are met in the State of residence.

The competent institution may refuse to grant the requested authorisation only if, in accordance with the assessment of the institution of the place of residence, the conditions set out in the second sentence of Article SSC.18(2) [Travel with the purpose of receiving benefits in kind—authorisation to receive appropriate treatment outside the State of residence] of the Protocol are not met in the State of residence of the insured person, or if the same treatment can be provided in the competent State itself, within a time-limit which is medically justifiable, taking into account the current state of health and the probable course of illness of the person concerned.

The competent institution shall inform the institution of the place of residence of its decision.

In the absence of a reply within the deadlines set by its national legislation, the authorisation shall be considered to have been granted by the competent institution.

3. If an insured person who does not reside in the competent Party is in need of urgent vitally necessary treatment, and the authorisation cannot be refused in accordance with the second sentence of Article SSC.18(2) [Travel with the purpose of receiving benefits in kind—authorisation to receive appropriate treatment outside the State of residence] of the Protocol, the authorisation shall be granted by the institution of the place of residence on behalf of the competent institution, which shall be immediately informed by the institution of the place of residence.

The competent institution shall accept the findings and the treatment options of the doctors approved by the institution of the place of residence that issues the authorisation, concerning the need for urgent vitally necessary treatment.

4. At any time during the procedure granting the authorisation, the competent institution shall retain the right to have the insured person examined by a doctor of its own choice in the Party of stay or residence.

5. The institution of the place of stay shall, without prejudice to any decision regarding authorisation, inform the competent institution if it appears medically appropriate to supplement the treatment covered by the existing authorisation.

Meeting the cost of benefits in kind incurred by the insured person

6. Without prejudice to paragraph 7, Article SSCI.22(4) and (5) [Stay in a State other than the competent State] of this Annex shall apply *mutatis mutandis.*

7. If the insured person has actually borne all or part of the costs for the authorised medical treatment themselves and the costs which the competent institution is obliged to reimburse to the institution of the place of stay or to the insured person according to paragraph 6 (actual cost) are lower than the costs which it would have had to assume for the same treatment in the competent State (notional cost), the competent institution shall reimburse, upon request, the cost of treatment incurred by the insured person up to the amount by which the notional cost exceeds the actual cost. The reimbursed sum may not, however, exceed the costs actually incurred by the insured person and may take account of the amount which the insured person would have had to pay if the treatment had been delivered in the competent State.

Meeting the costs of travel and stay as part of scheduled treatment

8. Where the national legislation of the competent institution provides for the reimbursement of the costs of travel and stay which are inseparable from the treatment of the insured person, such costs for the person concerned and, if necessary, for a person who must accompany them, shall be assumed by this institution when an authorisation is granted in the case of treatment in another State.

Family members

9. Paragraphs 1 to 8 shall apply *mutatis mutandis* to the members of the family of the insured person.

Article SSCI.24: Cash benefits relating to incapacity for work in the event of stay or residence in a State other than the competent State

Procedure to be followed by the insured person

1. If the legislation of the competent State requires that the insured person presents a certificate in order to be entitled to cash benefits relating to incapacity for work pursuant to Article SSC.19(1) [Cash benefits] of the Protocol, the insured person shall ask the doctor of the State of residence who established that person's state of health to certify his or her incapacity for work and its probable duration.   1.166

2. The insured person shall send the certificate to the competent institution within the time limit laid down by the legislation of the competent State.

3. Where the doctors providing treatment in the State of residence do not issue certificates of incapacity for work, and where such certificates are required under the legislation of the competent State, the person concerned shall apply directly to the institution of the place of residence. That institution shall immediately arrange for a medical assessment of the person's incapacity for work and for the certificate referred to in paragraph 1 to be drawn up. The certificate shall be forwarded to the competent institution forthwith.

4. The forwarding of the document referred to in paragraphs 1, 2 and 3 shall not exempt the insured person from fulfilling the obligations provided for by the applicable legislation, in particular with regard to that person's employer. Where appropriate, the employer or the competent institution may call upon the employee to participate in activities designed to promote and assist his or her return to employment.

Procedure to be followed by the institution of the State of residence

5. At the request of the competent institution, the institution of the place of residence shall carry out any necessary administrative checks or medical examinations of the person concerned in accordance with the legislation applied by this latter institution. The report of the examining doctor concerning, in particular, the probable duration of the incapacity for work, shall be forwarded without delay by the institution of the place of residence to the competent institution.

Procedure to be followed by the competent institution

6. The competent institution shall reserve the right to have the insured person examined by a doctor of its choice.

7. Without prejudice to the second sentence of Article SSC.19(1) [Cash benefits] of the Protocol, the competent institution shall pay the cash benefits directly to the person concerned and shall, where necessary, inform the institution of the place of residence thereof.

125

8. For the purposes of the application of Article SSC.19(1) [Cash benefits] of the Protocol, the particulars of the certificate of incapacity for work of an insured person drawn up in another State on the basis of the medical findings of the examining doctor or institution shall have the same legal value as a certificate drawn up in the competent State.

9. If the competent institution refuses the cash benefits, it shall notify its decision to the insured person and at the same time to the institution of the place of residence.

Procedure in the event of a stay in a State other than the competent State

10. Paragraphs 1 to 9 shall apply *mutatis mutandis* when the insured person stays in a State other than the competent State.

Article SSCI.25: Contributions by pensioners

1.167   If a person receives a pension from more than one State, the amount of contributions deducted from all the pensions paid shall, under no circumstances, be greater than the amount deducted in respect of a person who receives the same amount of pension from the competent State.

Article SSCI.26: Special implementing measures

1.168   1. When a person or a group of persons are exempted upon request from compulsory sickness insurance and such persons are thus not covered by a sickness insurance scheme to which the Protocol applies, the institution of a State shall not, solely because of this exemption, become responsible for bearing the costs of benefits in kind or in cash provided to such persons or to a member of their family under Title III, Chapter I [Sickness, maternity and equivalent paternity benefits], of the Protocol.

2. When the persons referred to in paragraph 1 and the members of their families reside in a State where the right to receive benefits in kind is not subject to conditions of insurance, or of activity as an employed or self-employed person, they shall be liable to pay the full costs of benefits in kind provided in their State of residence.

CHAPTER 2: BENEFITS IN RESPECT OF ACCIDENTS AT WORK AND OCCUPATIONAL DISEASES

Article SSCI.27: Right to benefits in kind and in cash in the event of residence or stay in a State other than the competent State

1.169   1. For the purposes of the application of Article SSC.31 [Right to benefits in kind and in cash] of the Protocol, the procedures laid down in Articles SSCI.21 [Residence in a State other than the competent State] to SSCI.24 [Cash benefits relating to incapacity for work in the event of stay or residence in a State other than the competent State] of this Annex shall apply *mutatis mutandis*.

2. When providing special benefits in kind in connection with accidents at work and occupational diseases under the national legislation of the State of stay or residence, the institution of that State shall without delay inform the competent institution.

Article SSCI.28: Procedure in the event of an accident at work or occupational disease which occurs in a State other than the competent State

1. If an accident at work occurs or an occupational disease is diag-   1.170
nosed for the first time in a State other than the competent State, the declaration or notification of the accident at work or the occupational disease, where the declaration or notification exists under national legislation, shall be carried out in accordance with the legislation of the competent State, without prejudice, where appropriate, to any other applicable legal provisions in force in the State in which the accident at work occurred or in which the first medical diagnosis of the occupational disease was made, which remain applicable in such cases. The declaration or notification shall be addressed to the competent institution.

2. The institution of the State in the territory of which the accident at work occurred or in which the occupational disease was first diagnosed, shall notify the competent institution of medical certificates drawn up in the territory of that State.

3. Where, as a result of an accident while travelling to or from work which occurs in the territory of a State other than the competent State, an inquiry is necessary in the territory of the first State in order to determine any entitlement to relevant benefits, a person may be appointed for that purpose by the competent institution, which shall inform the authorities of that State. The institutions shall cooperate with each other in order to assess all relevant information and to consult the reports and any other documents relating to the accident.

4. Following treatment, a detailed report accompanied by medical certificates relating to the permanent consequences of the accident or disease, in particular the injured person's present state and the recovery or stabilisation of injuries, shall be sent upon request of the competent institution. The relevant fees shall be paid by the institution of the place of residence or of stay, where appropriate, at the rate applied by that institution to the charge of the competent institution.

5. At the request of the institution of the place of residence or stay, where appropriate, the competent institution shall notify it of the decision setting the date for the recovery or stabilisation of injuries and, where appropriate, the decision concerning the granting of a pension.

Article SSCI.29: Disputes concerning the occupational nature of the accident or disease

1. Where the competent institution disputes the application of the   1.171
legislation relating to accidents at work or occupational diseases under Article SSC.31(2) [Right to benefits in kind and in cash] of the Protocol,

it shall without delay inform the institution of the place of residence or stay which provided the benefits in kind, which will then be considered as sickness insurance benefits.

2. When a final decision has been taken on that subject, the competent institution shall, without delay, inform the institution of the place of residence or stay which provided the benefits in kind.

Where an accident at work or occupational disease is not established, benefits in kind shall continue to be provided as sickness benefits if the person concerned is entitled to them.

Where an accident at work or occupational disease is established, sickness benefits in kind provided to the person concerned shall be considered as accident at work or occupational disease benefits from the date on which the accident at work occurred or the occupational disease was first medically diagnosed.

3. The second subparagraph of Article SSCI.6(5) [Provisional application of legislation and provisional granting of benefits] of this Annex shall apply *mutatis mutandis.*

Article SSCI.30: Procedure in the event of exposure to the risk of an occupational disease in two or more States

1.172   1. In the case referred to in Article SSC.33 [Benefits for an occupational disease where the person suffering from such a disease has been exposed to the same risk in several States] of the Protocol, the declaration or notification of the occupational disease shall be sent to the competent institution for occupational diseases of the last State under the legislation of which the person concerned pursued an activity likely to cause that disease.

When the institution to which the declaration or notification was sent establishes that an activity likely to cause the occupational disease in question was last pursued under the legislation of another State, it shall send the declaration or notification and all accompanying certificates to the equivalent institution in that State.

2. Where the institution of the last State under the legislation of which the person concerned pursued an activity likely to cause the occupational disease in question establishes that the person concerned or his survivors do not meet the requirements of that legislation, inter alia, because the person concerned had never pursued in that State an activity which caused the occupational disease or because that State does not recognise the occupational nature of the disease, that institution shall forward without delay the declaration or notification and all accompanying certificates, including the findings and reports of medical examinations performed by the first institution to the institution of the previous State under the legislation of which the person concerned pursued an activity likely to cause the occupational disease in question.

3. Where appropriate, the institutions shall reiterate the procedure set out in paragraph 2 going back as far as the equivalent institution in the State under whose legislation the person concerned first pursued an activity likely to cause the occupational disease in question.

Article SSCI.31: Exchange of information between institutions and advance payments in the event of an appeal against rejection

1. In the event of an appeal against a decision to refuse benefits taken   1.173
by the institution of a State under the legislation of which the person
concerned pursued an activity likely to cause the occupational disease in
question, that institution shall inform the institution to which the declaration or notification was sent, in accordance with the procedure provided for in Article SSCI.30(2) [Procedure in the event of exposure to
the risk of an occupational disease in two or more States] of this Annex,
and shall subsequently inform it when a final decision is reached.

2. Where a person is entitled to benefits under the legislation applied
by the institution to which the declaration or notification was sent, that
institution shall make the advance payments, the amount of which shall
be determined, where appropriate, after consulting the institution which
made the decision against which the appeal was lodged, and in such a
way that overpayments are avoided. The latter institution shall reimburse
the advance payments made if, as a result of the appeal, it is obliged to
provide those benefits. That amount will then be deducted from the
benefits due to the person concerned, in accordance with the procedure
provided for in Articles SSCI.56 [Benefits received unduly] and 57
[Provisionally paid benefits in cash or contributions] of this Annex.

3. The second subparagraph of Article SSCI.6(5) [Provisional application of legislation and provisional granting of benefits] of this Annex
shall apply *mutatis mutandis*.

Article SSCI.32: Aggravation of an occupational disease

In the cases covered by Article SSC.34 [Aggravation of an occupa-   1.174
tional disease] of the Protocol, the claimant must provide the institution
in the State from which they are claiming entitlement to benefits with
details concerning benefits previously granted for the occupational disease in question. That institution may contact any other previously
competent institution in order to obtain the information it considers
necessary.

Article SSCI.33: Assessment of the degree of incapacity in the event of occupational accidents or diseases which occurred previously or subsequently

Where a previous or subsequent incapacity for work was caused by an   1.175
accident which occurred when the person concerned was subject to the
legislation of a State which makes no distinction according to the origin
of the incapacity to work, the competent institution or the body designated by the competent authority of the State in question shall:
(a) upon request by the competent institution of another State, pro-
    vide information concerning the degree of the previous or sub-
    sequent incapacity for work, and where possible, information
    making it possible to determine whether the incapacity is the
    result of an accident at work within the meaning of the legislation
    applied by the institution in the other State;

(b) take into account the degree of incapacity caused by these previous or subsequent cases when determining the right to benefits and the amount, in accordance with the applicable legislation.

Article SSCI.34: Submission and investigation of claims for pensions or supplementary allowances

1.176   In order to receive a pension or supplementary allowance under the legislation of a State, the person concerned or their survivors residing in the territory of another State shall submit, where appropriate, a claim either to the competent institution or to the institution of the place of residence, which shall send it to the competent institution.

The claim shall contain the information required under the legislation applied by the competent institution.

CHAPTER 3: DEATH GRANTS

Article SSCI.35: Claim for death grants

1.177   For the purposes of applying Articles SSC.37 [Right to grants where death occurs in a State other than the competent one] and SSC.38 [Provision of benefits in the event of the death of a pensioner] of the Protocol, the claim for death grants shall be sent either to the competent institution or to the institution of the claimant's place of residence, which shall send it to the competent institution.

The claim shall contain the information required under the legislation applied by the competent institution.

CHAPTER 4: INVALIDITY BENEFITS AND OLD-AGE AND SURVIVORS' PENSIONS

Article SSCI.36: Additional provisions for the calculation of the benefit

1.178   1. For the purposes of calculating the theoretical amount and the actual amount of the benefit in accordance with Article SSC.47(1)(b) [Award of benefits] of the Protocol, the rules provided for in Article SSCI.11(3), (4), (5) and (6) [Aggregation of periods] of the Annex shall apply.

2. Where periods of voluntary or optional continued insurance have not been taken into account under Article SSC.11(3)[Aggregation of periods] of this Annex , the institution of the State under whose legislation those periods were completed shall calculate the amount corresponding to those periods under the legislation it applies. The actual amount of the benefit, calculated in accordance with Article SSC.47(1)(b) [Award of benefits] of the Protocol, shall be increased by the amount corresponding to periods of voluntary or optional continued insurance.

3. The institution of each State shall calculate, under the legislation it applies, the amount due corresponding to periods of voluntary or optional continued insurance which, under Article SSC.48(3)(c) [Rules to prevent overlapping] of the Protocol, shall not be subject to the another State's rules relating to withdrawal, reduction or suspension.

Where the legislation applied by the competent institution does not allow it to determine this amount directly, on the grounds that that legislation allocates different values to insurance periods, a notional amount may be established. The Specialised Committee on Social Security Coordination shall lay down the detailed arrangements for the determination of that notional amount.

Article SSCI.37: Claims for benefits

[A.] Submission of claims for old-age and survivors' pensions   1.179

1. The claimant shall submit a claim to the institution of his place of residence or to the institution of the last State whose legislation was applicable. If the person concerned was not, at any time, subject to the legislation applied by the institution of the place of residence, that institution shall forward the claim to the institution of the last State whose legislation was applicable.

2. The date of submission of the claim shall apply in all the institutions concerned.

3. By way of derogation from paragraph 2, if the claimant does not, despite having been asked to do so, notify the fact that he or she has been employed or has resided in other States, the date on which the claimant completes his or her initial claim or submits a new claim for his or her missing periods of employment or/and residence in a State shall be considered as the date of submission of the claim to the institution applying the legislation in question, subject to more favourable provisions of that legislation.

GENERAL NOTE

The original text does not contain a sub-heading "B".

Article SSCI.38: Certificates and information to be submitted with the claim by the claimant

1. The claim shall be submitted by the claimant in accordance with the   1.180
provisions of the legislation applied by the institution referred to in Article SSCI.37(1) [Claims for benefits] of this Annex, and be accompanied by the supporting documents required by that legislation. In particular, the claimant shall supply all available relevant information and supporting documents relating to periods of insurance (institutions, identification numbers), employment (employers) or self-employment (nature and place of activity) and residence (addresses) which may have been completed under other legislation, as well as the length of those periods.

2. Where, in accordance with Article SSC.45(1) [General Provisions] of the Protocol, the claimant requests deferment of the award of old-age

benefits under the legislation of one or more States, the claimant shall state that in their claim and specify under which legislation the deferment is requested. In order to enable the claimant to exercise that right, the institutions concerned shall, upon the request of the claimant, notify them of all the information available to them so that he or she can assess the consequences of concurrent or successive awards of benefits which they might claim.

3. Should the claimant withdraw a claim for benefits provided for under the legislation of a particular State, that withdrawal shall not be considered as a concurrent withdrawal of claims for benefits under the legislation of another State.

Article SSCI.39: Investigation of claims by the institutions concerned

Contact institution

1.181   1. The institution to which the claim for benefits is submitted or forwarded in accordance with Article SSCI.37(1) [Claims for benefits] of this Annex to the Protocol shall be referred to hereinafter as the 'contact institution'. The institution of the place of residence shall not be referred to as the contact institution if the person concerned has not, at any time, been subject to the legislation which that institution applies.

In addition to investigating the claim for benefits under the legislation which it applies, this institution shall, in its capacity as contact institution, promote the exchange of data, the communication of decisions and the operations necessary for the investigation of the claim by the institutions concerned, and supply the claimant, upon request, with any information relevant to the aspects of the investigation which arise under the Protocol, and keep the claimant informed of its progress.

Investigation of claims for old-age and survivors pensions

2. The contact institution shall, without delay, send claims for benefits and all the documents which it has available and, where appropriate, the relevant documents supplied by the claimant to all the institutions in question so that they can all start the investigation of the claim concurrently. The contact institution shall notify the other institutions of periods of insurance or residence subject to its legislation. It shall also indicate which documents shall be submitted at a later date and supplement the claim as soon as possible.

3. Each of the institutions in question shall notify the contact institution and the other institutions in question, as soon as possible, of the periods of insurance or residence subject to their legislation.

4. Each of the institutions in question shall calculate the amount of benefits in accordance with Article SSC.47 [Award of benefits] of the Protocol and shall notify the contact institution and the other institutions concerned of its decision, of the amount of benefits due and of any information required for the purposes of Articles SSC.48 [Rules to prevent overlapping] to SSC.50 [Overlapping of benefits of a different kind] of the Protocol.

5. Should an institution establish, on the basis of the information referred to in paragraphs 2 and 3 of this Article, that Article SSC.52(2) or (3) [Periods of insurance or residence of less than one year] of the Protocol is applicable, it shall inform the contact institution and the other institutions concerned.

Article SSCI.40: Notification of decisions to the claimant

1. Each institution shall notify the claimant of the decision it has taken in accordance with the applicable legislation. Each decision shall specify the remedies and periods allowed for appeals. Once the contact institution has been notified of all decisions taken by each institution, it shall send the claimant and the other institutions concerned a summary of those decisions. A model summary shall be drawn up by the Specialised Committee on Social Security Coordination. The summary shall be sent to the claimant in the language of the institution or, at the request of the claimant, in any language of their choice, including English, recognised as an official language of the Union. 1.182

2. Where it appears to the claimant following receipt of the summary that his or her rights may have been adversely affected by the interaction of decisions taken by two or more institutions, the claimant shall have the right to a review of the decisions by the institutions concerned within the time limits laid down in the respective national legislation. The time limits shall commence on the date of receipt of the summary. The claimant shall be notified of the result of the review in writing.

Article SSCI.41: Determination of the degree of invalidity

Each institution shall, in accordance with its legislation, have the possibility of having the claimant examined by a medical doctor or other expert of its choice to determine the degree of invalidity. However, the institution of a State shall take into consideration documents, medical reports and administrative information collected by the institution of any other State as if they had been drawn up in its own territory. 1.183

Article SSCI.42: Provisional instalments and advance payment of a benefit

1. Notwithstanding Article SSCI.7 [Provisional calculation of benefits and contributions] of this Annex, any institution which establishes, while investigating a claim for benefits, that the claimant is entitled to an independent benefit under the applicable legislation, in accordance with point (a) of Article SSC.47(1) [Award of benefits], shall pay that benefit without delay. That payment shall be considered provisional if the amount might be affected by the result of the claim investigation procedure. 1.184

2. Whenever it is evident from the information available that the claimant is entitled to a payment from an institution under point (b) of Article SSC.47(1) [Award of benefits] of the Protocol, that institution shall make an advance payment, the amount of which shall be as close as possible to the amount which will probably be paid under point (b) of Article SSC.47(1) [Award of benefits] of the Protocol.

3. Each institution which is obliged to pay the provisional benefits or advance payment under paragraphs 1 or 2 shall inform the claimant without delay, specifically drawing the claimant's attention to the provisional nature of the measure and any rights of appeal in accordance with its legislation.

Article SSCI.43: New calculation of benefits

1.185   1. Where there is a new calculation of benefits in accordance with Article SSC.45(4) [General provisions] and 54(1) [Recalculation and revaluation of benefits] of the Protocol, Article SSCI.42 [Provisional instalments and advance payment of a benefit] of this Annex shall be applicable *mutatis mutandis.*

2. Where there is a new calculation, withdrawal or suspension of the benefit, the institution which took the decision shall inform the person concerned without delay and shall inform each of the institutions in respect of which the person concerned has an entitlement.

Article SSCI.44: Measures intended to accelerate the pension calculation process

1.186   1. In order to facilitate and accelerate the investigation of claims and the payment of benefits, the institutions to whose legislation a person has been subject shall:

(a) exchange with or make available to institutions of other States the elements for identifying persons who change from one applicable national legislation to another, and together ensure that those identification elements are retained and correspond, or, failing that, provide those persons with the means to access their identification elements directly;

(b) sufficiently in advance of the minimum age for commencing pension rights or before an age to be determined by national legislation, exchange with or make available to the person concerned and to institutions of other States information (periods completed or other important elements) on the pension entitlements of persons who have changed from one applicable legislation to another or, failing that, inform those persons of, or provide them with, the means of familiarising themselves with their prospective benefit entitlement.

2. For the purposes of applying paragraph 1, the Specialised Committee on Social Security Coordination shall determine the elements of information to be exchanged or made available and shall establish the appropriate procedures and mechanisms, taking account of the characteristics, administrative and technical organisation, and the technological means at the disposal of national pension schemes. The Specialised Committee on Social Security Coordination shall ensure the implementation of those pension schemes by organising a follow-up to the measures taken and their application.

3. For the purposes of applying paragraph 1, the institution in the first State where a person is allocated a Personal Identification Number

(PIN) for the purposes of social security administration should be provided with the information referred to in this Article.

Article SSCI.45: Coordination measures in the States

1. Without prejudice to Article SSC.46 [Special provisions on aggregation of periods] of the Protocol, where national legislation includes rules for determining the institution responsible or the scheme applicable or for designating periods of insurance to a specific scheme, those rules shall be applied, taking into account only periods of insurance completed under the legislation of the State concerned.

2. Where national legislation includes rules for the coordination of special schemes for civil servants and the general scheme for employed persons, those rules shall not be affected by the provisions of the Protocol and of this Annex.

1.187

CHAPTER 5: UNEMPLOYMENT BENEFITS

Article SSCI.46: Aggregation of periods and calculation of benefits

1. Article SSCI.11(1) [Aggregation of periods] of this Annex shall apply *mutatis mutandis* to Article SSC.56 [Special provisions on aggregation of periods of insurance, employment or self-employment] of the Protocol. Without prejudice to the underlying obligations of the institutions involved, the person concerned may submit to the competent institution a document issued by the institution of the State to whose legislation they were subject in respect of that person's last activity as an employed or self-employed person specifying the periods completed under that legislation.

2. For the purposes of applying Article SSC.57 [Calculation of unemployment benefits] of the Protocol, the competent institution of a State whose legislation provides that the calculation of benefits varies with the number of members of the family shall also take into account the members of the family of the person concerned residing in another State as if they resided in the competent State. This provision shall not apply where, in the State of residence of members of the family, another person is entitled to unemployment benefits calculated on the basis of the number of members of the family.

1.188

TITLE IV: FINANCIAL PROVISIONS

CHAPTER 1: REIMBURSEMENT OF THE COST OF BENEFITS IN APPLICATION OF ARTICLE SSC.30 [Reimbursements between institutions] AND ARTICLE SSC.36 [Reimbursements between institutions] OF THE PROTOCOL

Articles SSCI.47—SSCl.54 *omitted*

1.189

CHAPTER 2: RECOVERY OF BENEFITS PROVIDED BUT NOT DUE, RECOVERY OF PROVISIONAL PAYMENTS AND CONTRIBUTIONS, OFFSETTING AND ASSISTANCE WITH RECOVERY

Section 1 : Principles

Article SSCI.55 : Common provisions

1.190   For the purposes of applying Article SSC.64 [Collection of contributions and recovery of benefits] of the Protocol and within the framework defined therein, the recovery of claims shall, wherever possible, be by way of offsetting either between the institutions of the Member State concerned and of the United Kingdom, or vis-à-vis the natural or legal person concerned in accordance with Articles SSCI.56 [Benefits received unduly] to SSCI.58 [Costs relating to offsetting] of this Annex. If it is not possible to recover all or any of the claim via this offsetting procedure, the remainder of the amount due shall be recovered in accordance with Articles SSCI.59 [Definitions and common provisions] to SSCI.69 [Costs related to recovery] of this Annex.

Section 2: Offsetting

Article SSCI.56: Benefits received unduly

1.191   1. If the institution of a State has paid undue benefits to a person, that institution may, within the terms and limits laid down in the legislation it applies, request the institution of the State responsible for paying benefits to the person concerned to deduct the undue amount from arrears or on-going payments owed to the person concerned regardless of the social security branch under which the benefit is paid. The institution of the latter State shall deduct the amount concerned subject to the conditions and limits applying to this kind of offsetting procedure in accordance with the legislation it applies in the same way as if it had made the overpayments itself, and shall transfer the amount deducted to the institution that has paid undue benefits.

2. By way of derogation from paragraph 1, if, when awarding or reviewing benefits in respect of invalidity benefits, old-age and survivors' pensions pursuant to Chapter 3 [Death grants] and 4 [Invalidity benefits] of Title III [Special provisions concerning the various categories of benefits] of the Protocol, the institution of a State has paid to a person benefits of undue sum, that institution may request the institution of the State responsible for the payment of corresponding benefits to the person concerned to deduct the amount overpaid from the arrears payable to the person concerned. After the latter institution has informed the institution that has paid an undue sum of these arrears, the institution which has paid the undue sum shall within two months communicate the amount of the undue sum. If the institution which is due to pay arrears receives that communication within the deadline it shall transfer the amount deducted to the institution which has paid undue sums. If the

deadline expires, that institution shall without delay pay out the arrears to the person concerned.

3. If a person has received social welfare assistance in one State during a period in which they were entitled to benefits under the legislation of another State, the body which provided the assistance may, if it is legally entitled to reclaim the benefits due to the person concerned, request the institution of any other State responsible for paying benefits in favour of the person concerned to deduct the amount of assistance paid from the amounts which that State pays to the person concerned.

This provision shall apply *mutatis mutandis* to any family member of a person concerned who has received assistance in the territory of a State during a period in which the insured person was entitled to benefits under the legislation of another State in respect of that family member.

The institution of a State which has paid an undue amount of assistance shall send a statement of the amount due to the institution of the other State, which shall then deduct the amount, subject to the conditions and limits laid down for this kind of offsetting procedure in accordance with the legislation it applies, and transfer the amount without delay to the institution that has paid the undue amount.

Article SSCI.57: Provisionally paid benefits in cash or contributions

1. For the purposes of applying Article SSCI.6 [Provisional application of legislation and provisional granting of benefits] of this Annex, at the latest three months after the applicable legislation has been determined or the institution responsible for paying the benefits has been identified, the institution which provisionally paid the cash benefits shall draw up a statement of the amount provisionally paid and shall send it to the institution identified as being competent. 1.192

The institution identified as being competent for paying the benefits shall deduct the amount due in respect of the provisional payment from the arrears of the corresponding benefits it owes to the person concerned and shall without delay transfer the amount deducted to the institution which provisionally paid the cash benefits.

If the amount of provisionally paid benefits exceeds the amount of arrears, or if arrears do not exist, the institution identified as being competent shall deduct this amount from ongoing payments subject to the conditions and limits applying to this kind of offsetting procedure under the legislation it applies, and without delay transfer the amount deducted to the institution which provisionally paid the cash benefits.

2. The institution which has provisionally received contributions from a legal or natural person shall not reimburse the amounts in question to the person who paid them until it has ascertained from the institution identified as being competent the sums due to it under Article SSCI.6(4) [Provisional application of legislation and provisional granting of benefits] of this Annex.

Upon request of the institution identified as being competent, which shall be made at the latest three months after the applicable legislation has been determined, the institution that has provisionally received contributions shall transfer them to the institution identified as being competent for that period for the purpose of settling the situation concerning the contributions owed by the legal or natural person to it. The contributions transferred shall be retroactively deemed as having been paid to the institution identified as being competent.

If the amount of provisionally paid contributions exceeds the amount the legal or natural person owes to the institution identified as being competent, the institution which provisionally received contributions shall reimburse the amount in excess to the legal or natural person concerned.

Article SSCI.58: Costs related to offsetting

1.193   No costs are payable where the debt is recovered via the offsetting procedure provided for in Articles SSCI.56 [Benefits received unduly] and SSCI.57 [Provisionally paid benefits in cash or contributions] of this Annex.

Section 3: Recovery

Article SSCI.59: Definitions and common provisions

1.194   1. For the purposes of this Section:
— "claim" means all claims relating to contributions or to benefits paid or provided unduly, including interest, fines, administrative penalties and all other charges and costs connected with the claim in accordance with the legislation of the State making the claim;
— "applicant party" means, in respect of each State, any institution which makes a request for information, notification or recovery concerning a claim as defined above,
— "requested party" means, in respect of each State, any institution to which a request for information, notification or recovery can be made.

2. Requests and any related communications between the States shall, in general, be addressed via designated institutions.

3. Practical implementation measures, including, among others, those related to Article SSCI.4 [Forms, documents and methods of exchanging data] of this Annex, and to setting a minimum threshold for the amounts for which a request for recovery can be made, shall be taken by the Specialised Committee on Social Security Coordination.

Article SSCI.60: Requests for information

1.195   1. At the request of the applicant party, the requested party shall provide any information which would be useful to the applicant party in the recovery of its claim.

2. In order to obtain that information, the requested party shall make use of the powers provided for under the laws, regulations or administrative practices applying to the recovery of similar claims arising in its

own State. The request for information shall indicate the name, last known address, and any other relevant information relating to the identification of the legal or natural person concerned to whom the information to be provided relates and the nature and amount of the claim in respect of which the request is made.

3. The requested party shall not be obliged to supply information:

(a) which it would not be able to obtain for the purpose of recovering similar claims arising in its own territory;

(b) which would disclose any commercial, industrial or professional secrets; or

(c) the disclosure of which would be liable to prejudice the security of or be contrary to the public policy of a State.

4. The requested party shall inform the applicant party of the grounds for refusing a request for information.

Article SSCI.61: Notification

1. The requested party shall, at the request of the applicant party, and in accordance with the rules in force for the notification of similar instruments or decisions in its own territory, notify the addressee of all instruments and decisions, including those of a judicial nature, which come from the State of the applicant party and which relate to a claim or to its recovery.

2. The request for notification shall indicate the name, address and any other relevant information relating to the identification of the addressee concerned to which the applicant party normally has access, the nature and the subject of the instrument or decision to be notified and, if necessary the name, address and any other relevant information relating to the identification of the debtor and the claim to which the instrument or decision relates, and any other useful information.

3. The requested party shall without delay inform the applicant party of the action taken on its request for notification and, particularly, of the date on which the decision or instrument was forwarded to the addressee.

Article SSCI.62: Request for recovery

1. At the request of the applicant party, the requested party shall recover claims that are the subject of an instrument permitting enforcement issued by the applicant party to the extent permitted by and in accordance with the laws and administrative practices in force in the State of the requested party.

2. The applicant party may only make a request for recovery if:

(a) it also provides to the requested party an official or certified copy of the instrument permitting enforcement of the claim in the State of the applicant party, except in cases where Article SSCI.64(3) [Payment arrangements and deadline] of this Annex;

(b) the claim or instrument permitting its enforcement are not contested in its own State;

1.196

1.197

139

   (c) it has, in its own State, applied appropriate recovery procedures available to it on the basis of the instrument referred to in paragraph 1, and the measures taken will not result in the payment in full of the claim;

   (d) the period of limitation according to its own legislation has not expired.

3. The request for recovery shall indicate:

   (a) the name, address and any other relevant information relating to the identification of the natural or legal person concerned or to the identification of any third party holding that person's assets;

   (b) the name, address and any other relevant information relating to the identification of the applicant party

   (c) a reference to the instrument permitting its enforcement, issued in the State of the applicant party

   (e) the nature and amount of the claim, including the principal, interest, fines, administrative penalties and all other charges and costs due indicated in the currencies of the State(s) of the applicant and requested parties

   (e) the date of notification of the instrument to the addressee by the applicant party or by the requested party

   (f) the date from which and the period during which enforcement is possible under the laws in force in the State of the applicant party

   (g) any other relevant information.

4. The request for recovery shall also contain a declaration by the applicant party confirming that the conditions laid down in paragraph 2 have been fulfilled.

5. The applicant party shall forward to the requested party any relevant information relating to the matter which gave rise to the request for recovery, as soon as this comes to its knowledge.

Article SSCI.63: Instrument permitting enforcement of recovery

1.198   1. In accordance with Article SSC.64(2) [Collection of contributions and recovery of benefits] of the Protocol, the instrument permitting enforcement of the claim shall be directly recognised and treated automatically as an instrument permitting the enforcement of a claim of the State of the requested party

2. Notwithstanding paragraph 1, the instrument permitting enforcement of the claim may, where appropriate and in accordance with the provisions in force in the State of the requested party, be accepted as, recognised as, supplemented with, or replaced by an instrument authorising enforcement in the territory of that State.

Within three months of the date of receipt of the request for recovery, the State(s) shall endeavour to complete the acceptance, recognition, supplementing or replacement, except in cases where the third subparagraph of this paragraph applies. States may not refuse to complete these actions where the instrument permitting enforcement is properly drawn up. The requested party shall inform the applicant party of the grounds for exceeding the three-month period.

If any of these actions should give rise to a dispute in connection with the claim or the instrument permitting enforcement issued by the applicant party, Article SSCI.65 [Contestation concerning the claim or the instrument permitting enforcement of its recovery and contestation concerning enforcement measures] of this Annex shall apply.

Article SSCI.64: Payment arrangements and deadline

1. Claims shall be recovered in the currency of the State of the requested party. The entire amount of the claim that is recovered by the requested party shall be remitted by the requested party to the applicant party. 1.199

2. The requested party may, where the laws, regulations or administrative provisions in force in its own State so permit, and after consulting the applicant party, allow the debtor time to pay or authorise payment by instalment. Any interest charged by the requested party in respect of such extra time to pay shall also be remitted to the applicant party.

3. From the date on which the instrument permitting enforcement of the recovery of the claim has been directly recognised in accordance with Article SSCI.63(1) [Instrument permitting enforcement of recovery] of this Annex, or accepted, recognised, supplemented or replaced in accordance with Article SSCI.63(2) [Instrument permitting enforcement of recovery] of this Annex to the Protocol, interest shall be charged for late payment under the laws, regulations and administrative provisions in force in the State of the requested party and shall also be remitted to the applicant party.

Article SSCI.65: Contestation concerning the claim or the instrument permitting enforcement of its recovery and contestation concerning enforcement measures

1. If, in the course of the recovery procedure, the claim or the instrument permitting its enforcement issued in the State of the applicant party are contested by an interested party, the action shall be brought by this party before the appropriate authorities of the State of the applicant party, in accordance with the laws in force in that State. The applicant party shall without delay notify the requested party of this action. The interested party may also inform the requested party of the action. 1.200

2. As soon as the requested party has received the notification or information referred to in paragraph 1 either from the applicant party or from the interested party, it shall suspend the enforcement procedure pending the decision of the appropriate authority in the matter, unless the applicant party requests otherwise in accordance with the second subparagraph of this paragraph. Should the requested party deem it necessary, and without prejudice to Article SSCI.68 [Precautionary measures] of this Annex, it may take precautionary measures to guarantee recovery insofar as the laws or regulations in force in its own State allow such action for similar claims.

Notwithstanding the first subparagraph, the applicant party may, in accordance with the laws, regulations and administrative practices in force in its own State, request the requested party to recover a contested claim, insofar as the relevant laws, regulations and administrative practices in force in the requested party's State allow such action. If the result of the contestation is subsequently favourable to the debtor, the applicant party shall be liable for the reimbursement of any sums recovered, together with any compensation due, in accordance with the legislation in force in the requested party's State.

3. Where the contestation concerns enforcement measures taken in the State of the requested party, the action shall be brought before the appropriate authority of that State in accordance with its laws and regulations.

4. Where the appropriate authority before which the action is brought in accordance with paragraph 1 is a judicial or administrative tribunal, the decision of that tribunal, insofar as it is favourable to the applicant party and permits recovery of the claim in the State of the applicant party, shall constitute the 'instrument permitting enforcement' within the meaning of Articles SSCI.62 [Request for recovery] and SSCI.63 [Instrument permitting enforcement of recovery] of the Annex and the recovery of the claim shall proceed on the basis of that decision.

Article SSCI.66: Limits applying to assistance

1.201   1. The requested party shall not be obliged:
  (a) to grant the assistance provided for in Articles SSCI.62 [Request for recovery] to SSCI.65 [Contestation concerning the claim or the instrument permitting enforcement of its recovery and contestation concerning enforcement measures] of this Annex, if recovery of the claim would, because of the situation of the debtor, create serious economic or social difficulties in the State of the requested party, insofar as the laws, regulations or administrative practices in force in the State of the requested party allow such action for similar national claims;
  (b) to grant the assistance provided for in Articles SSCI.60 [Request for information] to SSCI.65 [Contestation concerning the claim or the instrument permitting enforcement of its recovery and contestation concerning enforcement measures] of this Annex, if the initial request under Articles SSCI.60 [Request for information] to SSCI.62 [Request for recovery] of this Annex applies to claims more than five years old, dating from the moment the instrument permitting the recovery was established in accordance with the laws, regulations or administrative practices in force in the State of the applicant party at the date of the request. However, if the claim or instrument is contested, the time limit begins from the moment that the State of the applicant party establishes that the claim or the enforcement order permitting recovery may no longer be contested.

2. The requested party shall inform the applicant party of the grounds for refusing a request for assistance.

Article SSCI.67: Periods of limitation

1. Questions concerning periods of limitation shall be governed as follows: 1.202
  (a) by the laws in force in the State of the applicant party, insofar as they concern the claim or the instrument permitting its enforcement; and
  (b) by the laws in force in the State of the requested party, insofar as they concern enforcement measures in the requested State.
Periods of limitation according to the laws in force in the State of the requested party shall start from the date of direct recognition or from the date of acceptance, recognition, supplementing or replacement in accordance with Article SSCI.63 [Instrument permitting enforcement of recovery] of this Annex.

2. Steps taken in the recovery of claims by the requested party in pursuance of a request for assistance, which, if they had been carried out by the applicant party, would have had the effect of suspending or interrupting the period of limitation according to the laws in force in the State of the applicant party, shall be deemed to have been taken in the latter, insofar as that effect is concerned.

Article SSCI.68: Precautionary measures

Upon reasoned request by the applicant party, the requested party   1.203
shall take precautionary measures to ensure recovery of a claim insofar as the laws and regulations in force in the State of the requested party so permit. For the purposes of implementing the first paragraph, the provisions and procedures laid down in Articles SSCI.62 [Request for recovery], SSCI.63 [Instrument permitting enforcement of recovery], SSCI.65 [Contestation concerning the claim or the instrument permitting enforcement of its recovery and contestation concerning enforcement measures] and SSCI.66 [Limits applying to assistance] of this Annex shall apply *mutatis mutandis*.

Article SSCI.69: Costs related to recovery

1. The requested party shall recover from the natural or legal person   1.204
concerned and retain any costs linked to recovery which it incurs, in accordance with the laws and regulations of the State of the requested party that apply to similar claims.

2. Mutual assistance afforded under this Section shall, as a rule, be free of charge. However, where recovery poses a specific problem or concerns a very large amount in costs, the applicant and the requested parties may agree on reimbursement arrangements specific to the cases in question.

The State of the applicant party shall remain liable to the State of the requested party for any costs and any losses incurred as a result of actions held to be unfounded, as far as either the substance of the claim or the validity of the instrument issued by the applicant party is concerned.

TITLE V: MISCELLANEOUS, TRANSITIONAL AND FINAL PROVISIONS

Article SSCI.70: Medical examination and administrative checks

1.205   1. Without prejudice to other provisions, where a recipient or a claimant of benefits, or a member of that person's family, is staying or residing within the territory of a State other than that in which the debtor institution is located, the medical examination shall be carried out, at the request of that institution, by the institution of the beneficiary's place of stay or residence in accordance with the procedures laid down by the legislation applied by that institution.

The debtor institution shall inform the institution of the place of stay or residence of any special requirements, if necessary, to be followed and points to be covered by the medical examination.

2. The institution of the place of stay or residence shall forward a report to the debtor institution that requested the medical examination. This institution shall be bound by the findings of the institution of the place of stay or residence.

The debtor institution shall reserve the right to have the beneficiary examined by a doctor of its choice. However, the beneficiary may be asked to return to the State of the debtor institution only if that beneficiary is able to make the journey without prejudice to that person's health and the cost of travel and accommodation is paid for by the debtor institution.

3. Where a recipient or a claimant of benefits, or a member of that person's family, is staying or residing in the territory of a State other than that in which the debtor institution is located, the administrative check shall, at the request of the debtor institution, be performed by the institution of the beneficiary's place of stay or residence.

Paragraph 2 shall also apply in this case.

4. As an exception to the principle of free-of-charge mutual administrative cooperation in Article SSC.59(3) [Cooperation] of the Protocol, the effective amount of the expenses of the checks referred to in paragraphs 1 to 3 shall be refunded to the institution which was requested to carry them out by the debtor institution which requested them.

Article SSCI.71: Notifications

1.206   1. The States shall notify the Specialised Committee on Social Security Coordination of the details of the bodies and entities defined in Article.SSC.1 [Definitions] of the Protocol and points (a) and (b) of Article SSCI.1(2) [Definitions] of this Annex, and of the institutions designated in accordance with this Annex.

2. The bodies specified in paragraph 1 shall be provided with an electronic identity in the form of an identification code and electronic address.

3. The Specialised Committee on Social Security Coordination shall establish the structure, content and detailed arrangements, including the

common format and model, for notification of the details specified in paragraph 1.

4. For the purposes of implementing the Protocol, the United Kingdom may take part in the Electronic Exchange of Social Security Information and bear the related costs.

5. The States shall be responsible for keeping the information specified in paragraph 1 up to date.

Article SSCI.72: Information

The Specialised Committee on Social Security Coordination shall prepare the information needed to ensure that the parties concerned are aware of their rights and the administrative formalities required in order to assert them. This information shall, where possible, be disseminated electronically via publication online on sites accessible to the public. The Specialised Committee on Social Security Coordination shall ensure that the information is regularly updated and monitor the quality of services provided to customers. 1.207

Article SSCI.73: Currency conversion

For the purposes of applying the Protocol and this Annex, the exchange rate between two currencies shall be the reference rate published by the financial institution designated for this purpose by the Specialised Committee on Social Security Coordination. The date to be taken into account for determining the exchange rate shall be fixed by the Specialised Committee on Social Security Coordination. 1.208

Article SSCI.74: Implementing provisions

The Specialised Committee on Social Security Coordination may adopt further guidance on the implementation of the Protocol and of this Annex. 1.209

Article SSCI.75: Interim provisions for forms and documents

1. For an interim period, the end date of which shall be agreed by the Specialised Committee on Social Security Coordination, all forms and documents issued by the competent institutions in the format used immediately before the Protocol comes into force shall be valid for the purposes of implementing the Protocol and, where appropriate, shall continue to be used for the exchange of information between competent institutions. All such forms and documents issued before and during that interim period shall be valid until their expiry or cancellation. 1.210

2. The forms and documents valid in accordance with paragraph 1 include:

(a) European Health Insurance Cards issued on behalf of the United Kingdom, which shall be valid entitlement documents for the purposes of Articles SSC.17 [Stay outside the competent State], SSC.25(1) [Stay of the pensioner or the members of their family in a State other than the State of residence—stay in the competent State—authorisation for appropriate treatment outside the State of residence] and SSCI.22 [Stay in a State other than the competent State] of this Annex; and

(b) Portable documents which certify a person's social security situation as required to give effect to the Protocol

APPENDIX SSCI-1: ADMINISTRATIVE ARRANGEMENTS BETWEEN TWO OR MORE STATES (REFERRED TO IN ARTICLE SSCI.8 OF THIS ANNEX)

BELGIUM — UNITED KINGDOM

1.211   The Exchange of Letters of 4 May and 14 June 1976 regarding Article 105(2) of Regulation (EEC) No 574/72 (waiving of reimbursement of the costs of administrative checks and medical examinations)

The Exchange of Letters of 18 January and 14 March 1977 regarding Article 36(3) of Regulation (EEC) No 1408/71 (arrangement for reimbursement or waiving of reimbursement of the costs of benefits in kind provided under the terms of Chapter 1 of Title III of Regulation (EEC) No 1408/71) as amended by the Exchange of Letters of 4 May and 23 July 1982 (agreement for reimbursement of costs incurred under Article 22(1)(a) of Regulation (EEC) No 1408/71)

DENMARK — UNITED KINGDOM

The Exchange of Letters of 30 March and 19 April 1977 as modified by an Exchange of Letters of 8 November 1989 and of 10 January 1990 on agreement of waiving of reimbursement of the costs of benefits in kind and administrative checks and medical examinations

ESTONIA — UNITED KINGDOM

The Arrangement finalised on 29 March 2006 between the Competent Authorities of the Republic of Estonia and of the United Kingdom under Article 36(3) and 63(3) of Regulation (EEC) No 1408/71 establishing other methods of reimbursement of the costs of benefits in kind provided under Regulation (EC) No 883/2004 by both countries with effect from 1 May 2004

FINLAND — UNITED KINGDOM

The Exchange of Letters 1 and 20 June 1995 concerning Article 36(3) and 63(3) of Regulation (EEC) No 1408/71 (reimbursement or waiving of reimbursement of the cost of benefits in kind) and Article 105(2) of Regulation (EEC) 574/72 (waiving of reimbursement of the cost of administrative checks and medical examinations)

FRANCE — UNITED KINGDOM

1.212   The Exchange of Letters of 25 March and 28 April 1997 regarding Article 105(2) of Regulation (EEC) No 574/72 (waiving of reimbursement of the costs of administrative checks and medical examinations)

The Agreement of 8 December 1998 on the specific methods of determining the amounts to be reimbursed for benefits in kind pursuant to Regulations (EEC) No 1408/71 and (EEC) No 574/72

HUNGARY — UNITED KINGDOM

The Arrangement finalised on 1 November 2005 between the Competent Authorities of the Republic of Hungary and of the United Kingdom under Article 35(3) and 41(2) of Regulation (EEC) No 883/2004 establishing other methods of reimbursement of the costs of benefits in kind provided under that Regulation by both countries with effect from 1 May 2004

IRELAND — UNITED KINGDOM

The Exchange of Letters of 9 July 1975 regarding Article 36(3) and 63(3) of Regulation (EEC) No 1408/71 (arrangement for reimbursement or waiving of reimbursement of the costs of benefits in kind provided under the terms of Chapter 1 or 4 of Title III of Regulation (EEC) No 1408/71) and Article 105(2) of Regulation (EEC) No 574/72 (waiving of reimbursement of the costs of administrative checks and medical examinations)

ITALY — UNITED KINGDOM

The Arrangement signed on 15 December 2005 between the Competent Authorities of the Italian Republic and of the United Kingdom under Article 36(3) and 63(3) of Regulation (EEC) No 1408/71 establishing other methods of reimbursement of the costs of benefits in kind provided under Regulation (EC) No 883/2004 by both countries with effect from 1 January 2005

LUXEMBOURG — UNITED KINGDOM

The Exchange of Letters of 18 December 1975 and 20 January 1976   **1.213**
regarding Article 105(2) of Regulation (EEC) No 574/72 (waiving of reimbursement of the costs entailed in administrative checks and medical examinations referred to in Article 105 of Regulation (EEC) No 574/72)

MALTA — UNITED KINGDOM

The Arrangement finalised on 17 January 2007 between the Competent Authorities of Malta and of the United Kingdom under Article 35(3) and 41(2) of Regulation (EEC) No 883/2004 establishing other methods of reimbursement of the costs of benefits in kind provided under that Regulation by both countries with effect from 1 May 2004

NETHERLANDS — UNITED KINGDOM

The second sentence of Article 3 of the Administrative Arrangement of 12 June 1956 on the implementation of the Convention of 11 August 1954.

PORTUGAL — UNITED KINGDOM

The Arrangement of 8 June 2004 establishing other methods of reimbursement of the costs of benefits in kind provided by both countries with effect from 1 January 2003

SPAIN — UNITED KINGDOM

The Agreement of 18 June 1999 on the reimbursement of costs for benefits in kind granted pursuant to the provisions of Regulations (EEC) No 1408/71 and (EEC) No 574/72

SWEDEN — UNITED KINGDOM

The Arrangement of 15 April 1997 concerning Article 36(3) and Article 63(3) of Regulation (EEC) No 1408/71 (reimbursement or waiving of reimbursement of the cost of benefits in kind) and Article 105(2) of Regulation (EEC) No 574/72 (waiving of refunds of the costs of administrative checks and medical examinations) This document has been agreed between the European Union and the United Kingdom and is provided for information only. No rights may be derived from it until the date of application. The numbering of the articles is provisional. 1243 24.12.2020

APPENDIX SSCI-2

1.214   ENTITLEMENT DOCUMENT (ARTICLES SSC.17 [STAY OUTSIDE THE COMPETENT STATE], SSC.25(1) [STAY OF THE PENSIONER OR THE MEMBERS OF THEIR FAMILY IN A STATE OTHER THAN THE STATE OF RESIDENCE—STAY IN THE COMPETENT STATE—AUTHORISATION FOR APPROPRIATE TREATMENT OUTSIDE THE STATE OF RESIDENCE] AND SSCI.22 [STAY IN A STATE OTHER THAN THE COMPETENT STATE]

1. Entitlement documents issued for the purposes of Articles SSC.17 [Stay outside the competent State] and SSC.25(1) [Stay of the pensioner or the members of their family in a State other than the State of residence—stay in the competent State—authorisation for appropriate treatment outside the State of residence] by the competent institutions of Member States shall comply with Decision No S2 of 12 June 2009 of the Administrative Commission concerning the technical specifications of the European Health Insurance Card.

2. Entitlement documents issued for the purposes of Articles SSC.17 [Stay outside the competent State] and SSC.25(1) [Stay of the pensioner or the members of their family in a State other than the State of residence—stay in the competent State—authorisation for appropriate treatment outside the State of residence] by the competent institutions of the United Kingdom shall contain the following data:

(a) surname and forename of the document holder;

(b) personal identification number of the document holder;

(c) date of birth of the document holder;

(d) expiry date of the document;

(e) the code "UK" in lieu of the ISO code of the United Kingdom;

(f) identification number and acronym of the United Kingdom institution issuing the document;

(g) logical number of the document;

(h) in the case of a provisional document, the date of issue and date of delivery of the document, and the signature and stamp of the United Kingdom institution.

3. The technical specifications of entitlement documents issued by the United Kingdom shall be notified without delay to the Specialised Committee on Social Security Coordination in order to facilitate the acceptance of the respective documents by institutions of the Member States providing the benefits in kind.

HEALTHCARE REQUIRING PRIOR AGREEMENT (ARTICLES SSC.17 [STAY OUTSIDE THE COMPETENT STATE] AND SSC.25(1) [STAY OF THE PENSIONER OR THE MEMBERS OF THEIR FAMILY IN A STATE OTHER THAN THE STATE OF RESIDENCE—STAY IN THE COMPETENT STATE— AUTHORISATION FOR APPROPRIATE TREATMENT OUTSIDE THE STATE OF RESIDENCE])

1. The benefits in kind to be provided under Articles SSC.17 [Stay outside the competent State] and SSC.25(1) [Stay of the pensioner or the members of their family in a State other than the State of residence—stay in the competent State—authorisation for appropriate treatment outside the State of residence] of the Protocol shall include benefits provided in conjunction with chronic or existing illnesses as well as in conjunction with pregnancy and childbirth.   1.215

2. Benefits in kind, including those in conjunction with chronic or existing illnesses or in conjunction with childbirth, are not covered by these provisions when the objective of the stay in another State is to receive these treatments.

3. Any vital medical treatment which is only accessible in a specialised medical unit or by specialised staff or equipment must be subject to a prior agreement between the insured person and the unit providing the treatment in order to ensure that the treatment is available during the insured person's stay in a State other than the competent State or the one of residence.

4. A non-exhaustive list of the treatments which fulfil these criteria is the following:

(a) kidney dialysis;

(b) oxygen therapy;

(c) special asthma treatment;

(d) echocardiography in case of chronic autoimmune diseases;

(e) chemotherapy.

APPENDIX SSCI-3: STATES CLAIMING THE
REIMBURSEMENT OF THE COST OF BENEFITS IN KIND
ON THE BASIS OF FIXED AMOUNTS (REFERRED TO IN
ARTICLE SSCI.48(1) [Identification of the State(s) concerned] OF
THIS ANNEX)

1.216   IRELAND
SPAIN
CYPRUS
PORTUGAL
SWEDEN
UNITED KINGDOM

*ANNEX SSC-8: TRANSITIONAL PROVISIONS REGARDING
THE APPLICATION OF ARTICLE SSC.11*

[Detached workers]

MEMBER STATES

(SI 2016/1257)

NEW REGULATIONS

The Childcare (Early Years Provision Free of Charge) (Extended Entitlement) Regulations 2016

(SI 2016/1257)

Made 19th December 2016
Coming into force in accordance with regulation 1

The Secretary of State for Education makes the following Regulations in exercise of the powers conferred by sections 1(2), (3), (4) and (7), 2(1), (2), (4) and (5) and 4(2) of the Childcare Act 2016.

In accordance with section 4(4) of that Act, a draft of this instrument was laid before and approved by a resolution of each House of Parliament.

In accordance with section 2(3) of that Act, these Regulations are made with the consent of the Treasury.

ARRANGEMENT OF REGULATIONS

CHAPTER 3

DECLARATION IN RESPECT OF A YOUNG CHILD

CHAPTER 4

DETERMINATIONS

PART 3

INFORMATION, REVIEWS, APPEALS AND PENALTIES

CHAPTER 1

INFORMATION

CHAPTER 2

REVIEWS AND APPEALS OF DETERMINATIONS

CHAPTER 3

PENALTIES

PART 4

LOCAL AUTHORITIES' DUTY TO SECURE EARLY YEARS PROVISION

PART 5

CONSEQUENTIAL AMENDMENTS

PART 1

PRELIMINARY

Citation and commencement

1.217   **1.**—(1) These Regulations may be cited as the Childcare (Early Years Provision Free of Charge) (Extended Entitlement) Regulations 2016.

(2) Parts 1, 2, 3 and 5 of these Regulations come into force 21 days after the day on which these Regulations are made.

(3) Part 4 of these Regulations comes into force on 1st September 2017.

Interpretation

1.218   **2.**—(1) In these Regulations—

"the Act" means the Childcare Act 2016;

"the Commissioners" means the Commissioners for Her Majesty's Revenue and Customs;

[²"coronavirus" means severe acute respiratory syndrome coronavirus 2 (SARS-CoV-2);

"critical worker" means a worker in a critical sector listed in the document entitled "Critical workers who can access schools or educational settings" in the version published by the Cabinet Office and the Department for Education on 16 June 2020;]

"declaration" means a declaration under section 1(2)(e) of the Act;

"early years childminder" has the meaning given by section 96(4) of the Childcare Act 2006;

"early years childminder agency" has the meaning given by section 98(1) of the Childcare Act 2006;

"early years provider" has the meaning given by section 96(3) of the Childcare Act 2006;

"early years provision" has the meaning given by section 96(2) of the Childcare Act 2006;

"early years provision inspection report" means a report under one of the following—

(a) section 162A of the Education Act 2002 as it had effect prior to the coming into force of section 169 of, and Schedule 2 to, the Education and Skills Act 2008 (whether by Her Majesty's Chief Inspector of Education, Children's Services and Skills or by a body approved by the Secretary of State for the purposes of section 162A of the Education Act 2002);

(b) section 5 of the Education Act 2005;

(c) section 50 of the Childcare Act 2006; or

(d) section 109 of the Education and Skills Act 2008;

[¹"foster parent" means—

(a) a local authority foster parent within the meaning of section 105(1) of the Children Act 1989;

(b) a local authority foster parent within the meaning of section 197 of the Social Services and Well-Being (Wales) Act 2014;

(c) a person approved as a foster carer within the meaning of regulation 2 of the Looked After Children (Scotland) Regulations 2009; or

(d) a foster parent within the meaning of Article 27(3) of the Children (Northern Ireland) Order 1995;]

"minimum weekly income" means—

(a) for a person—

    (i) not yet aged 25 years; or

    (ii) to whom the apprenticeship rate applies, as determined in accordance with regulation 5 of the National Minimum Wage Regulations 2015,

the amount a person would be paid for 16 hours of work a week at the hourly rate for a person in that person's circumstances as set out in regulation 4A of the National Minimum Wage Regulations 2015;

(b) for a person aged 25 years or older, the amount a person would be paid for 16 hours of work a week at the hourly rate set out in regulation 4 of the National Minimum Wage Regulations 2015;

"paid work" means work done for payment or in expectation of payment and does not include being engaged by a charitable or voluntary organisation, or as a volunteer, in circumstances in which the payment received by or due to be paid to the person is in respect of expenses;

[1"responsible local authority" means—

(a) the local authority looking after the child in accordance with section 22(1) of the Children Act 1989; or

(b) where the child is looked after by a local authority within the meaning of regulation 3(2)(b), (c) or (d), the local authority discharging its duty under regulation 33 to secure the early years provision;]

"the Tribunal" means the First-tier Tribunal.

(2) A person's age for the purposes of establishing that person's "minimum weekly income"—

(a) except in the circumstances in sub-paragraph (b), is that person's age when that person, or that person's partner, makes the declaration;

(b) under regulation 5 where that person is in paid work as a self-employed person and relies on regulation 5(1)(b)(ii) to meet the requirement of being in qualifying paid work, is that person's age at the start of the tax year in which the declaration made by that person or that person's partner falls.

AMENDMENTS

1. Childcare (Disqualification) and Childcare (Early Years Provision Free of Charge) (Extended Entitlement) (Amendment) Regulations 2018 (SI 2018/794) reg.14 (August 31, 2018).

2. Childcare (Early Years Provision Free of Charge) (Extended Entitlement) (Coronavirus) (Amendment) Regulations 2020 (SI 2020/712) reg.3 (July 31, 2020).

PART 2

A QUALIFYING CHILD OF WORKING PARENTS

CHAPTER 1

CONDITIONS RELATING TO A QUALIFYING CHILD OF WORKING PARENTS

Description of a qualifying child of working parents

1.219   **3.**—(1) For the purposes of section 1(2)(c) of the Act, a young child is of a specified description if the young child—

(a) has attained the age of three years or will attain the age of three years within 16 weeks beginning with the day on which the declaration was made in relation to that child; and

(b) is not looked after by a local authority.

(2) In this regulation, except for the categories of children in paragraph (3), "looked after by a local authority" has the meaning given by—

(a) section 22(1) of the Children Act 1989;

(b) section 74(1) of the Social Services and Well-being (Wales) Act 2014;

(c) section 17(6) of the Children (Scotland) Act 1995; or

(d) article 25 of the Children (Northern Ireland) Order 1995 (with the modification that for the reference to a local authority there is substituted a reference to an authority within the meaning of article 2 of that Order).

(3) A child is not looked after by a local authority for the purposes of this regulation—

(a) during any period which is in the nature of a short-term break or is one of a series of such breaks for the purposes of providing respite for the person with whom the child normally lives;

(b) during any period when the child is placed with or continues to live with a person under section 22C(2) of the Children Act 1989;

[¹(ba) during any period when the child is placed with a foster parent under section 22C(6)(a) or (b) of the Children Act 1989;

(bb) during any period when the child is placed with a foster parent under section 81(6)(a) or (b) of the Social Services and Well-Being (Wales) Act 2014;

(bc) during any period when the child is placed with a foster parent under section 80 of the Adoption and Children (Scotland) Act 2007;

(bd) during any period when the child is placed with a foster parent under Article 27(2)(a) of the Children (Northern Ireland) Order 1995;]

(c) during any period when the child is placed with or continues to live with a person under section 81(2) of the Social Services and Well-being (Wales) Act 2014;

(d) during any period when the child is placed with or continues to live with a person defined in regulation 8(1) or 10(2) of the Looked after Children (Scotland) Regulations 2009; and

(e) during any period when the child is placed with or continues to live with a person under article 27(2) of the Children (Northern Ireland) Order 1995 where that person falls within article 27(4)(a) of that Order.

AMENDMENT

1. Childcare (Disqualification) and Childcare (Early Years Provision Free of Charge) (Extended Entitlement) (Amendment) Regulations 2018 (SI 2018/794) reg.15 (August 31, 2018).

CHAPTER 2

CONDITIONS RELATING TO A PARENT, AND ANY PARTNER OF THE
PARENT, OF THE CHILD

Specified conditions relating to a parent, and any partner of the parent, of the child

4.—[¹(A1) This regulation does not apply in relation to a child falling within regulations 3(3)(ba) to (bd).]   1.220

(1) For the purposes of section 1(2)(d) of the Act, a parent of the child must meet the following three conditions.

(2) The first condition is that the main reason, or one of the main reasons, the parent of the child seeks the free childcare referred to in section 1(1) of the Act is to enable the parent, or any partner of the parent, to work.

(3) The condition in paragraph (2) is treated as being met in relation to a person to whom any of the cases in regulation 8(1)(a) to (m) or 9(1)(b) applies.

(4) The second condition is that the parent of the child is in qualifying paid work in accordance with this Chapter.

(5) The third condition is that the parent does not expect their adjusted net income to exceed £100,000 in the relevant tax year.

[²(5A) The condition in paragraph (5) is treated as being met by a parent if—

(a) the parent is a critical worker;

(b) the relevant tax year is the tax year starting with 6th April 2020 and ending with 5th April 2021;

(c) the parent expects the parent's adjusted net income to exceed £100,000 but not to exceed £150,000 in that tax year; and

(d) the parent expects all the parent's income that exceeds £100,000 to be mainly attributable to earnings from work undertaken directly or indirectly as a result of the incidence or transmission of coronavirus.]

(6) The condition in paragraph (5) is treated as not being met by a parent if—

(a) the parent has made, or expects to make, a claim under section 809B of the Income Tax Act 2007 (claim for remittance basis to apply) for the relevant tax year; or

(b) the parent expects section 809E of that Act (application of remittance basis in certain cases without claim) to apply to the parent for the relevant tax year.

(7) Where a parent of the child has a partner (see regulation 10), that partner must also meet the conditions in paragraphs (4) and (5).

(8) In this regulation—

"adjusted net income" has the meaning given by section 58 of the Income Tax Act 2007;

"the relevant tax year" means the tax year in which the declaration by the parent or the parent's partner is made.

AMENDMENTS

1. Childcare (Disqualification) and Childcare (Early Years Provision Free of Charge) (Extended Entitlement) (Amendment) Regulations 2018 (SI 2018/794) reg.16 (August 31, 2020).
2. Childcare (Early Years Provision Free of Charge) (Extended Entitlement) (Coronavirus) (Amendment) Regulations 2020 (SI 2020/712) reg.4 (July 31, 2020).

[¹ Specified conditions relating to the parent, and any partner of the parent, of the child—foster parents

1.221   **4A.**—(1) This regulation applies in relation to a child falling within regulations 3(3)(ba) to (bd).

(2) For the purposes of section 1(2) of the Act, a parent of the child must meet the following five conditions.

(3) The first condition is that the parent is a foster parent and has the child placed with them.

(4) The second condition is that the main reason, or one of the main reasons, the parent of the child seeks the free childcare referred to in section 1(1) of the Act is to enable the parent, or any partner of the parent, to work.

(5) The condition in paragraph (4) is treated as being met in relation to any person to whom any of the cases in regulation 8(1)(a) to (m) or 9(1)(b) applies.

(6) The third condition is that the parent of the child is in work.

(7) In paragraphs (4) and (6) "work" means—

(a) in relation to the parent and their partner, where the partner is also the child's foster parent, paid work outside their role as a foster parent; and

(b) in relation to the partner of the parent, where the partner is not the child's foster parent, qualifying paid work.

(8) For the purposes of this regulation the parent is also treated as being in work if—

(a) the person—
    (i) has accepted an offer to work on or before the date of the declaration made in accordance with regulation 13; and
    (ii) expects the work to start within 31 days of that date; or
(b) the person—
    (i) is absent from work on unpaid leave on the date of the declaration made in accordance with regulation 13; and
    (ii) expects to return to work within 31 days of that date.
(9) The fourth condition is that—
(a) the parent; and
(b) any partner of the parent, where the partner is also the child's foster parent,
has had confirmation from the responsible local authority that the responsible local authority is satisfied that taking up paid work outside their role as a foster parent is consistent with the child's care plan.
(10) The fifth condition is that the parent does not expect their adjusted net income to exceed £100,000 in the relevant tax year.
[² (10A) The condition in paragraph (10) is treated as being met by a parent if—
(a) the parent is a critical worker;
(b) the relevant tax year is the tax year starting with 6th April 2020 and ending with 5th April 2021;
(c) the parent expects the parent's adjusted net income to exceed £100,000 but not to exceed £150,000 in that tax year; and
(d) the parent expects all the parent's income that exceeds £100,000 to be mainly attributable to earnings from work undertaken directly or indirectly as a result of the incidence or transmission of coronavirus.]
(11) The condition in paragraph (10) is treated as not being met by any parent if—
(a) the parent has made, or expects to make, a claim under section 809B of the Income Tax Act 2007 (claim for remittance basis to apply) for the relevant tax year, or
(b) the parent expects section 809E of that Act (application of remittance basis in certain cases without claim) to apply to the parent for the relevant tax year.
(11) Where a parent of the child has a partner, that partner must also meet the condition in paragraphs (6) and (10).
(11) In this regulation—
"adjusted net income" has the meaning given by section 58 of the Income Tax Act 2007;
"care plan" means—
(a) the 'care plan' as defined by regulation 2 of the Care Planning, Placement and Case Review (England) Regulations 2010;
(b) the 'care and support plan' as defined by regulation 2 of the Care Planning, Placement and Case Review (Wales) Regulations 2015;
(c) the 'child's plan' prepared in accordance with regulation 5 of the Looked After Children (Scotland) Regulations 2009; or

(d) the written record of the arrangements for the child's care made under regulation 3 of the Arrangements for the Placement of Children (General) Regulations (Northern Ireland) 1996;
"the relevant tax year" means the tax year in which the declaration by the parent or the parent's partner is made.]

AMENDMENTS

1. Childcare (Disqualification) and Childcare (Early Years Provision Free of Charge) (Extended Entitlement) (Amendment) Regulations 2018 (SI 2018/794), reg.17 (August 31, 2018).
2. Childcare (Early Years Provision Free of Charge) (Extended Entitlement) (Coronavirus) (Amendment) Regulations 2020 (SI 2020/712), reg.5 (July 31, 2020).

The requirement to be in qualifying paid work

1.222   5.—(1) A person is in qualifying paid work if ['the person holds a national insurance number and]—
    (a) the person is in paid work as an employed person whose expected income from the work in the period specified in paragraph (4) is greater than or equal to the relevant threshold; or
    (b) the person is in paid work as a self-employed person and either—
        (i) the person's expected income from the work in the period specified in paragraph (4) is greater than or equal to the relevant threshold; or
        (ii) the person's expected income from the work in the period specified in paragraph (5) is greater than or equal to four times the relevant threshold.
[¹ (1A) The requirement in paragraph (1) to hold a national insurance number does not apply to a person who is resident and in paid work in another EEA state.]
(2) For the purposes of this regulation a person is to be treated as in paid work as an employed person if—
    (a) the person—
        (i) has accepted an offer of work on or before the date of the declaration that person or that person's partner makes; and
        (ii) expects the work to start within [¹31] days of that date; or
    (b) the person—
        (i) is absent from work on unpaid leave on the date of the declaration that person or that person's partner makes; and
        (ii) expects to return to work within [¹31] days of that date.
(3) A person's "expected income" is the income which the person has a reasonable expectation of receiving, calculated in accordance with regulation 6.
(4) The period specified in this paragraph is—
    (a) the period of 3 months beginning with the date of the declaration the person or the person's partner makes; or
    (b) if paragraph (2)(a) or (b) applies, the period of 3 months beginning with the day on which the work is expected to start or the person is expected to return to work.

(5) The period specified in this paragraph is, in relation to a declaration made by the person or the person's partner, the tax year in which the date of the declaration falls.

(6) In this regulation, "the relevant threshold" is the product of the calculation—

$$M \times W$$

where—

M is the minimum weekly income; and

W is the number of weeks in the period specified in paragraph (4).

AMENDMENTS

1. Childcare (Early Years Provision Free of Charge) (Extended Entitlement) (Amendment) Regulations 2017 (SI 2017/1160) reg.3(2) (January 1. 2018).

Calculation of expected income

6.—(1) An employed person's expected income comprises the amount   1.223
of earnings the person expects to receive from—

(a) any employment under a contract of service; and

(b) any office, including an elected office.

(2) In paragraph (1), "earnings" has the meaning given by section 62 of the Income Tax (Earnings and Pensions) Act 2003.

(3) A self-employed person's expected income comprises—

(a) the amount of receipts the person expects to derive from a trade, profession or vocation less the amount of expenses the person expects to incur wholly and exclusively for the purposes of the trade, profession or vocation; or

(b) if the person carries on a trade, profession or vocation in a business partnership, the share expected to be allocated to the person of the partnership's receipts less the share expected to be allocated to that person of the partnership's expenses incurred wholly and exclusively for the purposes of the trade, profession or vocation.

(4) In calculating a self-employed person's income, receipts and expenses of a capital nature are to be disregarded.

(5) A person's expected income may include income from a person's employment and self-employment taken together.

(6) For the purposes of paragraph (5) a person may not rely on the condition in regulation 5(1)(b)(ii).

Self-employed persons: start-up periods

7.—(1) Where a self-employed person makes a declaration within a   1.224
start-up period, that person does not have to meet the requirement in regulation 5(1)(b) for the purposes of—

(a) that declaration; and

(b) that person's subsequent three declarations.

(2) A "start-up period" is the period of 12 months following the commencement by the self-employed person of any trade, profession or vocation.

161

(3) A self-employed person cannot rely on a second or subsequent start-up period (in relation to the commencement by that person of a new trade profession or vocation) unless at least 48 months have passed since the end of the previous start-up period.

(4) In paragraph (3) "the previous start-up period" is the period during which the person did not have to meet the condition in regulation 5(1)(b) or the condition in regulation 9(1)(b) of the Childcare Payments (Eligibility) Regulations 2015.

Qualifying paid work [¹and work outside role as a foster parent]: time off in connection with sickness or parenting

1.225   **8.**—(1) This regulation applies for any period during which a person—

(a) is paid statutory sick pay under Part 11 of the Social Security Contributions and Benefits Act 1992 or Part 11 of the Social Security Contributions and Benefits (Northern Ireland) Act 1992;

(b) is paid maternity allowance under section 35 of the Social Security Contributions and Benefits Act 1992 or section 35 of the Social Security Contributions and Benefits (Northern Ireland) Act 1992;

(c) is paid statutory maternity pay under Part 12 of the Social Security Contributions and Benefits Act 1992 or Part 12 of the Social Security Contributions and Benefits (Northern Ireland) Act 1992;

(d) is absent from work during an ordinary maternity leave period under section 71 of the Employment Rights Act 1996 or article 103 of the Employment Rights (Northern Ireland) Order 1996;

(e) is absent from work during an additional maternity leave period under section 73 of the Employment Rights Act 1996 or article 105 of the Employment Rights (Northern Ireland) Order 1996;

(f) is paid statutory paternity pay under Part 12ZA of the Social Security Contributions and Benefits Act 1992 or Part 12ZA of the Social Security Contributions and Benefits (Northern Ireland) Act 1992;

(g) is absent from work during a paternity leave period under section 80A or 80B of the Employment Rights Act 1996 or article 112A or 112B of the Employment Rights (Northern Ireland) Order 1996;

(h) is paid statutory adoption pay under Part 12ZB of the Social Security Contributions and Benefits Act 1992 or Part 12ZB of the Social Security Contributions and Benefits (Northern Ireland) Act 1992;

(i) is paid statutory shared parental pay under Part 12ZC of the Social Security Contributions and Benefits Act 1992 or Part 12ZC of the Social Security Contributions and Benefits (Northern Ireland) Act 1992;

(j) is absent from work during an ordinary adoption leave period under section 75A of the Employment Rights Act 1996 or article

107A of the Employment Rights (Northern Ireland) Order 1996;

(k) is absent from work during an additional adoption leave period under section 75B of the Employment Rights Act 1996 or Article 107B of the Employment Rights (Northern Ireland) Order 1996;

(l) is absent from work during a period of shared parental leave under section 75E or 75G of the Employment Rights Act 1996 or articles 107E and 107G of the Employment Rights (Northern Ireland) Order 1996; [³ . . .]

(m) is absent from work during a statutory parental leave period under section 76 of the Employment Rights Act 1996 or article 108 of the Employment Rights (Northern Ireland) Order 1996;

[³ (n) is absent from work during a period of parental bereavement leave under section 80EA of the Employment Rights Act 1996; or

(o) is paid statutory parental bereavement pay under Part 12ZD of the Social Security Contribution and Benefits Act 1992].

[¹ (2) Subject to paragraphs (3) and (4) where the person falls within regulation 4, or is not a foster parent but falls within regulation 4A, the person is regarded for the purposes of these Regulations—

(i) as in paid work during the period in paragraph (1), and

(ii) as having, for each week of that period, expected income from that work equal to the minimum weekly income.

(2A) Subject to paragraphs (3) and (4) where the person is a foster parent within regulation 4A, the person is regarded as being in paid work outside their role as a foster parent.]

(3) Paragraph (2) does not apply unless, immediately before the start of the period in any sub-paragraph of paragraph (1), either—

(a) the person was in qualifying paid work; [¹ . . .]

[¹ (aa) the person was in paid work outside their role as a foster parent; or]

(b) this regulation applied to the person by virtue of a different sub-paragraph of paragraph (1).

(4) Where a child whose placement for adoption caused the period in paragraph (1)(h), (j), (k) or (l) to run is the child in respect of whom a declaration is made, paragraph (2) applies only for the final [²31] days before the person returns to work.

(5) This regulation applies to a self-employed person during any period for which paragraph (1) would have applied in that person's case but for the fact that the work performed in the week immediately before the period began, although done for payment or in expectation of payment, was not performed under a contract of service.

(6) This regulation applies to a resident of another EEA state who under the law of that state—

(a) receives payments which are substantially similar in character to the payments in paragraph (1)(a) to (c), (f), (h) or (i); or

(b) is absent from work in circumstances which are substantially similar in character to a period of absence described in paragraph (1)(d), (e), (g) or (j) to (m).

AMENDMENTS

1. Childcare (Disqualification) and Childcare (Early Years Provision Free of Charge) (Extended Entitlement) (Amendment) Regulations 2018 (SI 2018/794) reg.18 (August 31, 2018).
2. Childcare (Early Years Provision Free of Charge) (Extended Entitlement) (Amendment) Regulations 2017 (SI 2017/1160) reg.3(3) (January 1, 2020).
3. Parental Bereavement Leave and Pay (Consequential Amendments to Subordinate Legislation) Regulations 2020 (SI 2020/354) reg.40 (April 6, 2020).

Qualifying paid work [¹ and paid work outside role as a foster parent]: caring, incapacity for work or limited capability for work

1.226   **9.**—(1) This regulation applies for any period during which—

[¹ (a) a person ("P") has—

   (i) a partner who is in qualifying paid work, or

   (ii) a partner who is in paid work outside their role as a foster parent; and]

(b) P is—

   (i) paid or entitled to incapacity benefit under section 30A, 40 or 41 of the Social Security Contributions and Benefits Act 1992 or section 30A, 40 or 41 of the Social Security Contributions and Benefits (Northern Ireland) Act 1992;

   (ii) paid or entitled to severe disablement allowance under section 68 of the Social Security Contributions and Benefits Act 1992 or section 68 of the Social Security Contributions and Benefits (Northern Ireland) Act 1992 (as they have effect by virtue of article 4 of the Welfare Reform and Pensions Act 1999 (Commencement No. 9, and Transitional and Savings Provisions) Order 2000 and article 4 of the Welfare Reform and Pensions (1999 Order) (Commencement No. 6 and Transitional and Savings Provisions) Order (Northern Ireland) 2000);

   (iii) paid or entitled to long-term incapacity benefit under regulation 11(4) or 17(1) of the Social Security (Incapacity Benefit) (Transitional) Regulations 1995 or regulation 11(4) or 17(1) of the Social Security (Incapacity Benefit) (Transitional) Regulations (Northern Ireland) 1995;

   (iv) paid or entitled to carer's allowance under section 70 of the Social Security Contributions and Benefits Act 1992 or section 70 of the Social Security Contributions and Benefits (Northern Ireland) Act 1992;

   (v) paid or entitled to contributory employment and support allowance under Part 1 of the Welfare Reform Act 2007 as amended by Schedule 3 and Part 1 of Schedule 14 to the Welfare Reform Act 2012 or under section 1 of the Welfare Reform Act (Northern Ireland) 2007;

    (vi) entitled to national insurance credits on the grounds of incapacity for work or limited capability for work under regulation 8B of the Social Security (Credits) Regulations 1975 or regulation 8B of the Social Security (Credits) Regulations (Northern Ireland) 1975;

    (vii) paid or entitled to the carer element of universal credit under regulation 29 of the Universal Credit Regulations 2013 or regulation 30 of the Universal Credit Regulations (Northern Ireland) 2016; or

    (viii) determined as having limited capability for work and work-related activity in accordance with regulations 39 and 40 of the Universal Credit Regulations 2013 or regulations 40 and 41 of the Universal Credit Regulations (Northern Ireland) 2016.

[¹ (2) For the purposes of the Act—

(a) where P falls within regulation 4 or is not a foster parent and falls within regulation 4A, P is regarded as—

    (i) being in paid work during that period, and

    (ii) as having, for each week of that period, expected income from that work equal to the minimum weekly income;

(b) where P falls within regulation 4A, P is regarded as in paid work outside their role as a foster parent.]

(3) P's partner is not in qualifying paid work [¹or paid work outside their role as a foster parent] for the purposes of paragraph (1)(a) during any period when that partner is paid or entitled to a benefit or an allowance, or is entitled to a credit, described in paragraph (1)(b).

(4) This regulation applies to a self-employed person, or that person's partner, during any period for which paragraph (1) would have applied in that person's, or that person's partner's, case but for the fact that the work performed in the week immediately before the period began, although done for payment or in expectation of payment, was not performed under a contract of service.

(5) This regulation applies to a resident of another EEA state who under the law of that state is entitled to a benefit, allowance or credit which is substantially similar in character to a benefit, allowance or credit described in paragraph (1)(b).

Amendments

1. Childcare (Disqualification) and Childcare (Early Years Provision Free of Charge) (Extended Entitlement) (Amendment) Regulations 2018 (SI 2018/794) reg.19 (August 31, 2018).

Partner of a parent of the child

10.—(1) For the purposes of section 1(2) and (3) of the Act, a person   1.227 is to be regarded as another person's partner if they are both at least 16 years old and either—

(a) they are married to, or civil partners of, each other and are members of the same household; or

(b) they are not married to, or civil partners of, each other but are living together as a married couple or as civil partners.

(2) Where two people are parties to a polygamous marriage, they are not regarded as partners for the purposes of section 1(2) and (3) of the Act if—

    (a) one of them is party to an earlier marriage that still subsists; and

    (b) the other party to that earlier marriage is living in the same household.

(3) A person's partner who is temporarily absent from the person's household at the date of the declaration is not to be regarded as the person's partner for the purposes of section 1(2) and (3) of the Act if—

    (a) the absence exceeds, or is expected to exceed, 6 months; or

    (b) the absent person is a prisoner.

(4) In this regulation, "polygamous marriage" means a marriage during which a party to it is married to more than one person and which took place under the laws of a country which permits polygamy.

CHAPTER 3

DECLARATION IN RESPECT OF A YOUNG CHILD

Conditions to be met by the person making the declaration

1.228   **11.** The person who makes the declaration must—

    [¹ (a) be—

        (i) the parent with whom the young child in respect of whom the declaration is being made normally lives, or that parent's partner, or

        (ii) the foster parent with whom the young child in respect of whom the declaration is being made is placed;]

    (b) be in the United Kingdom (within the meaning provided in regulation 12) on the date of the declaration; and

    (c) where the young child in respect of whom the declaration is being made is a child in respect of whom an active childcare account under section 17(3) of the Childcare Payments Act 2014 is held, be the account-holder (within the meaning of section 15(10) of that Act) for that account.

AMENDMENT

    1. Childcare (Disqualification) and Childcare (Early Years Provision Free of Charge) (Extended Entitlement) (Amendment) Regulations 2018 (SI 2018/794), reg.20 (August 31, 2018).

Being in the United Kingdom

1.229   **12.**—(1) Subject to paragraph (2), the following persons are treated for the purposes of regulation 11 as being in the United Kingdom—

    (a) a person who is ordinarily resident in the United Kingdom;

(b) a resident of another EEA state who is in paid work in the United Kingdom;

(c) a person in the United Kingdom as a refugee within the definition in Article 1 of the Convention relating to the Status of Refugees done at Geneva on 28th July 1951, as extended by Article 1(2) of the Protocol relating to the Status of Refugees done at New York on 31st January 1967;

(d) a person in the United Kingdom who has been granted, or who is deemed to have been granted, leave outside the rules (the "Immigration Rules") made under section 3(2) of the Immigration Act 1971 where that leave is—

   (i) discretionary leave to enter or remain in the United Kingdom;

   (ii) leave to remain under the Destitution Domestic Violence concession; or

   (iii) leave deemed to have been granted by virtue of regulation 3 of the Displaced Persons (Temporary Protection) Regulations 2005;

(e) a person in the United Kingdom who has humanitarian protection granted under the Immigration Rules;

(f) a person in the United Kingdom who has been deported, expelled or otherwise removed by compulsion of law from another country to the United Kingdom, but is not a person subject to immigration control.

(2) But the following persons are treated for the purposes of regulation 11 as not being in the United Kingdom—

(a) a person in the United Kingdom who—

   (i) is resident in the United Kingdom but is taxed, by virtue of double taxation arrangements, as if they were not so resident; and

   (ii) is not a resident of another EEA state who is in paid work in the United Kingdom;

(b) a person who is subject to immigration control.

(3) In this regulation—

"double taxation arrangements" means arrangements that have effect under section 2(1) of the Taxation (International and Other Provisions) Act 2010 (giving effect to arrangements made in relation to other territories);

"person subject to immigration control" has the meaning in section 115(9) of the Immigration and Asylum Act 1999.

Declaration: form and content

13.—[¹(1) Where a declaration is being made in accordance with   1.230 regulation 11(a)(i), the declaration must—

(a) be in the form specified by the Commissioners;

(b) be made to the Commissioners in accordance with regulation 14; and

(c) include information specified by the Commissioners—

    (i) to identify the person making the declaration, and any partner of that person;

    (ii) to identify the young child in respect of whom the declaration is being made; and

    (iii) to determine whether the young child is a qualifying child of working parents.

(2) Where a declaration is being made in accordance with regulation 11(a)(ii), the declaration must be in the form specified by the responsible authority.]

AMENDMENT

1. Childcare (Disqualification) and Childcare (Early Years Provision Free of Charge) (Extended Entitlement) (Amendment) Regulations 2018 (SI 2018/794), reg.21 (August 31, 2018).

Electronic communications

1.231   **14.**—[¹ (1) A declaration made in accordance with regulation 13(1) must be made by electronic communications.]

(2) A declaration by electronic communications shall be treated for the purposes of the Act as having been made, and received by the Commissioners, on the date on which it is recorded on an official computer system.

(3) Paragraph (1) does not apply if the Commissioners are satisfied that the person making the declaration—

    (a) is prevented, by a court order, from sending information by electronic communications;

    (b) holds beliefs which are incompatible with the use of electronic communications;

    (c) is unable to send information by electronic communications by reason of—

        (i) age;

        (ii) disability;

        (iii) inability to operate a computer effectively in a manner that cannot be remedied by the use of assisted digital support; or

        (iv) living in a remote location so that it is not reasonably practicable to use electronic communications; or

    (d) is prevented, for a continuous period of at least 7 days, by a technical failure affecting the Commissioners, from making a declaration.

(4) Where paragraph (3) applies, the declaration must be made to the Commissioners in the manner specified by the Commissioners.

(5) In this regulation—

    (a) "assisted digital support" includes both advice and assistance on how to make a declaration by means of electronic communications and entering a person's information into an electronic communications service on that person's behalf;

    (b) "electronic communications" includes any communications by means of an electronic communications service;

(c) "electronic communications service" has the meaning given by section 32 of the Communications Act 2003;

(d) "official computer system" means a computer system maintained by or on behalf of the Commissioners to send, store or process information.

AMENDMENT

1. Childcare (Disqualification) and Childcare (Early Years Provision Free of Charge) (Extended Entitlement) (Amendment) Regulations 2018 (SI 2018/794), reg.22 (August 31, 2018).

Period of time for which the first declaration has effect

15.—(1) In this regulation—   1.232

(a) "declaration period" means the first declaration period or a subsequent declaration period;

(b) "first declaration period" means the period described in paragraph (2);

(c) "subsequent declaration period" means a period described in paragraph (3).

(2) The first declaration in respect of a young child has effect for a period of three months, subject to paragraphs (5), (6), (7) and (9), beginning with the day on which a determination that the criteria in section 1(2)(b), (c) and (d) of the Act are met in relation to the child is made by—

(a) the Commissioners under regulation 17 or 21(6)(c); [² . . .]

[² (ba)the responsible local authority under regulation 17A, or]

(b) the Tribunal under regulation 24(4).

(3) At the end of the first declaration period, a series of consecutive new periods begins, each of which:

(a) begins with the day after that on which the preceding period ends, subject to paragraph (4); and

(b) lasts for three months, subject to paragraph (7).

(4) Each declaration period begins on the same day of a month except as follows—

(a) if the first declaration period begins on the 31st day of a month, each subsequent declaration period begins on the last day of the month;

(b) if the first declaration period begins on the 30th day of a month, each subsequent declaration period begins on the 30th day of the month, except in February where it shall begin on the 28th day or, in a leap year, the 29th day;

(c) if the first declaration period begins on the 29th day of a month, each subsequent declaration period begins on the 29th day of the month, except in February when it is not a leap year, where it shall begin on the 28th day.

(5) Where the young child in respect of whom the declaration is being made is a child in respect of whom a childcare account under section 17(3) of the Childcare Payments Act 2014 is held, the Commissioners may vary the length of the first declaration period under this regulation

for the purpose of aligning the start of the next declaration period with the start of the next entitlement period under regulation 4 of the Childcare Payments Regulations 2015.

(6) Where a person who has already made a declaration in respect of a child makes a declaration in respect of a subsequent child, the Commissioners [²or responsible local authority] may vary the length of the first declaration period under this regulation in respect of the subsequent child for the purpose of aligning the start of the next declaration period with the start of the next declaration period in respect of the other child.

(7) Where a person who has already made a declaration in respect of a child becomes the partner of another person who has already made a declaration in respect of a child, the Commissioners [²or responsible local authority] may vary the length of any declaration period in respect of any child of the person, or partner, in respect of whom a declaration has been made for the purpose of aligning the start of the next declaration period for any of those children with that of another of those children.

[¹(7A) Where a person ("A") who has already made a declaration in respect of a child becomes the partner of a person who holds a childcare account under section 17(3) of the Childcare Payments Act 2014, the Commissioners may vary the length of a declaration period in respect of that child for the purposes of aligning the start of the declaration period in respect of that child with the start of the next entitlement period of A's partner under regulation 4 of the Childcare Payments Regulations 2015.]

(8) The maximum length of time by which the Commissioners [²or responsible local authority] may vary a declaration period under paragraphs (5) to [¹(7A)] is two months.

(9) In circumstances other than those described in paragraphs (5) to [¹(7A)], the Commissioners [²or responsible local authority] may vary the length of the first declaration period by a maximum of one month.

AMENDMENTS

1. Childcare (Early Years Provision Free of Charge) (Extended Entitlement) (Amendment) Regulations 2017 (SI 2017/1160) reg.3(4) (January 1, 2018).
2. Childcare (Disqualification) and Childcare (Early Years Provision Free of Charge) (Extended Entitlement) (Amendment) Regulations 2018 (SI 2018/794) reg.23 (August 31, 2018).

Reconfirming declaration

1.233   **16.**—(1) Where a person who has made a declaration in respect of a young child which has effect in relation to a declaration period ("the active declaration period") makes a further declaration in respect of the same child it is a "reconfirming declaration".

(2) Where a reconfirming declaration is made during the last 28 days of the active declaration period, the reconfirming declaration has effect for the duration of the subsequent declaration period.

(3) Where a reconfirming declaration is made after the end of the most recent active declaration period but before the last 28 days of any subsequent declaration period, the reconfirming declaration has effect from the day on which a subsequent determination that the criteria in section 1(2)(b), (c) and (d) of the Act are met in relation to the child is made by—

(a) the Commissioners under regulation 17 or 21(6)(c); [¹ . . .]

[¹ (ba)the responsible local authority under regulation 17A, or]

(b) the Tribunal under regulation 24(4),

until the end of the declaration period in which that determination is made.

(4) Where a reconfirming declaration is made during the last 28 days of any declaration period following the most recent active declaration period, the reconfirming declaration has effect from the day on which a subsequent determination that the criteria in section 1(2)(b), (c) and (d) of the Act are met in relation to the child is made by—

(a) the Commissioners under regulation 17 or 21(6)(c); [¹ . . .]

[¹ (ba)the responsible local authority under regulation 17A, or]

(b) the Tribunal under regulation 24(4),

until the end of the declaration period after the declaration period in which that determination is made.

(5) In this regulation, "declaration period" and "subsequent declaration period" have the meanings given in regulation 15(1).

AMENDMENTS

1. The Childcare (Disqualification) and Childcare (Early Years Provision Free of Charge) (Extended Entitlement) (Amendment) Regulations 2018 (SI 2018/794), reg.24 (August 31, 2018).

CHAPTER 4

DETERMINATIONS

Determination by the Commissioners

17.—(1) Where a person makes a declaration in accordance with   1.234
regulation 13 or a reconfirming declaration in accordance with regulation 16, the Commissioners must make a determination as to whether the criteria in section 1(2)(b), (c) and (d) of the Act are met in relation to the child in respect of whom the declaration is made.

(2) Where the Commissioners make a determination under paragraph (1) they must notify the person who makes the declaration of the determination.

(3) A notification under paragraph (2) is to be made by electronic communications unless paragraph (4) applies.

(4) Where a notification under paragraph (2) is to be made to a person to whom regulation 14(3) applies, the notification is to be made in writing other than by electronic communications.

(5) The person who makes the declaration is deemed to be notified under paragraph (2) on the date on which the notification is sent.

[Determination by the responsible local authority

1.235   **17A.** Where a person makes a declaration in accordance with regulation 13 or a reconfirming declaration in accordance with regulation 16, the responsible local authority must make a determination as to whether the criteria in section 1(2)(b) and (d) of the Act are met in relation to the child in respect of whom the declaration is made.]

AMENDMENT

> 1. Childcare (Disqualification) and Childcare (Early Years Provision Free of Charge) (Extended Entitlement) (Amendment) Regulations 2018 (SI 2018/794) reg.26 (August 31. 2018).

PART 3

INFORMATION, REVIEWS, APPEALS AND PENALTIES

[¹ Application to determinations made under regulation 17

1.236   **18ZA.** Regulations 18 to 32 apply in relation to determinations made by the Commissioners under regulation 17 only.]

AMENDMENT

> 1. The Childcare (Disqualification) and Childcare (Early Years Provision Free of Charge) (Extended Entitlement) (Amendment) Regulations 2018 (SI 2018/794) reg.27 (August 31, 2018).

CHAPTER 1

INFORMATION

Supply of information

1.237   **18.**—(1) Information to which paragraph (2) or (3) applies may be supplied to the Commissioners, or a person providing services to the Commissioners, for use for the purpose of determining whether the criteria in section 1(2)(b), (c) and (d) of the Act are met in relation to the child.

(2) This paragraph applies to information held for the purposes of functions relating to social security—

(a) by the Secretary of State; or

(b) by a person providing services to the Secretary of State, in connection with the provision of those services.

(3) This paragraph applies to information held for the purposes of functions relating to immigration control—

(a) by the Secretary of State, or

(b) by a person providing services to the Secretary of State, in connection with the provision of those services.

(4) Information to which paragraph (5) applies may be supplied for use for the purpose of verifying whether a child is a qualifying child of working parents—

(a) to the Secretary of State, or a person providing services to the Secretary of State;

(b) to an English local authority, or a person exercising functions relating to verifying whether a child is a qualifying child of working parents on behalf of an English local authority;

(5) This paragraph applies to information held regarding whether a particular young child is a qualifying child of working parents—

(a) by the Commissioners; or

(b) by a person providing services to the Commissioners, in connection with the provision of those services.

(6) Information received by virtue of paragraph (1) or (4) may be supplied to another person to whom it could have been supplied under that paragraph for use for the same purpose.

Unauthorised disclosure of information received under regulation 18

19.—(1) A person commits an offence if the person discloses any information—   1.238

(a) which the person received by virtue of paragraph (1) or (4) of regulation 18; and

(b) which relates to a particular person;

unless the information is disclosed in accordance with paragraph (2) of this regulation.

(2) Information is disclosed in accordance with this paragraph if it is disclosed in any of the following ways—

(a) in accordance with regulation 18(6);

(b) in the course of a duty that the person disclosing it has in connection with the exercise of functions relating to establishing whether a child is a qualifying child of working parents;

(c) in accordance with an enactment or an order of a court; or

(d) with written consent given by or on behalf of the person to whom the information relates.

(3) It is a defence for a person charged with an offence under paragraph (1) to prove that the person reasonably believed that the disclosure was lawful.

(4) A person guilty of an offence under paragraph (1) is liable—

(a) on conviction on indictment, to imprisonment for a term not exceeding two years, or a fine, or both;

(b) on summary conviction, to imprisonment for a term not exceeding 12 months, or a fine, or both.

(5) In relation to an offence committed before the commencement of section 154(1) of the Criminal Justice Act 2003, the reference in paragraph (4)(b) to 12 months is to be read as a reference to 6 months.

CHAPTER 2

REVIEWS AND APPEALS OF DETERMINATIONS

Rights to review and appeal a determination under regulation 17

1.239   **20.** Where a person is notified of a determination under regulation 17, the notification must include details of the person's right to apply for a review of the determination (in accordance with regulation 21) and to appeal against the determination (in accordance with regulation 23).

Reviewing a determination under regulation 17

1.240   **21.**—(1) A person who makes a declaration may apply for a review of a determination that the criteria in section 1(2)(b), (c) and (d) of the Act are not met in relation to the child.
    (2) The application must be made—
    (a) to the Commissioners; and
    (b) either—
        (i) within the period of 30 days beginning with the day on which the applicant was notified of the determination; or
        (ii) if the period for making the application has been extended under regulation 22, within the extended period.
    (3) The application must be made—
    (a) in writing by electronic communications, and paragraphs (2) to (5) of regulation 14 apply as if for "declaration" wherever it appears there were substituted "application"; and
    (b) in such form as may be specified by the Commissioners.
    (4) The application must—
    (a) contain sufficient information to identify the applicant and the determination; and
    (b) set out the reasons for seeking a review of the determination.
    (5) If an application for a review of a determination is made to the Commissioners in accordance with this regulation, the Commissioners must review the determination.
    (6) On a review under this regulation, the Commissioners may—
    (a) uphold the determination;
    (b) substitute for the determination a determination that the criteria in section 1(2)(b), (c) and (d) of the Act are not met in relation to the child for a different reason; or
    (c) substitute for the determination a determination that the criteria in section 1(2)(b), (c) and (d) of the Act are met in relation to the child.

(7) If the applicant makes any representations to the Commissioners at a stage which gives the Commissioners a reasonable opportunity to consider them, the Commissioners must take account of them when carrying out the review.

(8) Where—

(a) the Commissioners notify the applicant of further information or evidence which they may need for carrying out the review, and

(b) the information or evidence is not provided to them within the period of 15 days beginning with the day on which the notification was given,

the review may proceed without that information or evidence.

(9) The Commissioners must notify the applicant of the matters set out in paragraph (10) within—

(a) the period of 30 days beginning with the day on which the Commissioners received the application for the review;

(b) if the applicant has been given a notice under paragraph (8), the period of 45 days beginning with that day; or

(c) such other period as the applicant and the Commissioners may agree.

(10) The matters referred to in paragraph (9) are—

(a) the conclusion on the review and the reasons for the conclusion;

(b) if the conclusion is that the determination is upheld or is substituted for a determination that the criteria in section 1(2)(b), (c) and (d) of the Act are not met in relation to the child for a different reason, details of the person's right to appeal against that determination.

(11) If the Commissioners do not comply with paragraph (9), the review is to be treated as having concluded that the determination is upheld and the Commissioners must notify the applicant of that conclusion.

Extension of time limit for applications for review

22.—(1) A person who wishes to make an application for a review of a determination under regulation 21 may apply to the Commissioners for an extension of the period for making the application. **1.241**

(2) An application under this regulation—

(a) must be made before the end of the period of 6 months beginning with the day after the last day of the period mentioned in regulation 21(2)(b)(i) ("the standard period");

(b) in such form as may be specified by the Commissioners;

(c) must be made by electronic communications and paragraphs (2) to (5) of regulation 14 apply as if for "declaration" wherever it appears there were substituted " application "; and

(d) must set out the reasons for seeking the extension.

(3) The Commissioners may grant an extension under this regulation if they are satisfied that—

(a) due to special circumstances, it was not practicable for the person to make the application under regulation 21 within the standard period, and

(b) it is reasonable in all the circumstances to grant the extension.

(4) If an application under this regulation is refused, it may not be renewed.

Appealing a determination under regulation 17

1.242   **23.**—(1) A person who makes a declaration may appeal against a determination that the criteria in section 1(2)(b), (c) and (d) of the Act are not met in relation to the child in respect of whom the declaration is made.

(2) But a person may not appeal under paragraph (1) unless—

(a) the person has applied under regulation 21 for a review of the determination; and

(b) the period applicable under regulation 21(9) has expired.

(3) An appeal under this regulation is an appeal to the Tribunal.

Powers of tribunal: appeals against determinations

1.243   **24.**—(1) This regulation applies where a person is appealing to the Tribunal under regulation 23 against a determination.

(2) The Tribunal may—

(a) uphold the determination; or

(b) quash the determination.

(3) The Tribunal may act as mentioned in paragraph (2)(b) only to the extent that it is satisfied that the determination was wrong on one or more of the following grounds—

(a) that the determination was based on an error of fact;

(b) that the determination was wrong in law.

(4) If the Tribunal quashes the determination, it must substitute its own determination for that of the Commissioners.

CHAPTER 3

PENALTIES

Penalties for inaccurate declarations

1.244   **25.**—(1) A person is liable to a penalty under this regulation if—

(a) the person makes a declaration that contains a material inaccuracy; and

(b) the inaccuracy is due to a failure by the person to take reasonable care.

(2) The amount of a penalty under this regulation may not exceed £300.

Penalties for providing false or misleading information or statements

26.—(1) A person making a declaration, or that person's partner, is   1.245
liable to a penalty under this regulation if the person provides false or
misleading information, or makes or provides false or misleading statements, as part of a declaration or at any of the other stages in the process
of the making of a determination under regulation 17 (including a review
under regulation 21) and—
  (a) the inaccuracy is due to a failure by the person providing the
      information or statements to take reasonable care;
  (b) the person knows of the inaccuracy at the time the information or
      statement is provided but does not inform the Commissioners at
      that time; or
  (c) the person later discovers the inaccuracy and fails to take reason-
      able steps to inform the Commissioners.
(2) The amount of a penalty under this regulation may not exceed
£500.

Penalties for dishonesty

27.—(1) A person making a declaration, or that person's partner, is   1.246
liable for a penalty under this regulation if—
  (a) the person does, or omits to do, any act as part of a declaration or
      at any of the other stages in the process of the making of a
      determination; and
  (b) the person's act or omission involves dishonesty.
(2) The amount of the penalty may not exceed £3,000.

Assessment and enforcement of penalties

28.—(1) Where a person becomes liable to a penalty under these   1.247
Regulations the Commissioners may assess the amount of the penalty.
(2) Where the Commissioners assess a penalty under paragraph (1)
they must—
  (a) notify the person of the imposition of that penalty; and
  (b) include in that notification details of the person's right to apply for
      a review of the decision (in accordance with regulation 29) and to
      appeal against the decision (in accordance with regulation 31).
(3) No penalty may be imposed under this regulation after—
  (a) the end of the period specified in paragraph (4); or
  (b) if earlier, the end of the period of 12 months beginning with the
      day on which the Commissioners first believed, or had reasonable
      grounds for believing, that the person was liable to the penalty.
(4) The period referred to in paragraph (3)(a) is—
  (a) the period of 4 years beginning with the day on which the person
      became liable to the penalty; or
  (b) in a case where the person became liable to the penalty as a result
      of the person's dishonesty, the period of 20 years beginning with
      that day.
(5) Where a person is notified of the imposition of a penalty under this
regulation, the penalty payable must be paid—

    (a) in a case where the person does not apply for a review of the penalty within the period specified in regulation 29, before the end of that period;

    (b) in a case where the person applies for a review of the penalty but does not give notice of an appeal against the penalty, before the end of the period in which notice of such an appeal could have been given;

    (c) in a case where notice of such an appeal has been given, on the day on which the appeal is determined or withdrawn.

(6) A penalty payable under these regulations is to be treated for the purposes of Part 6 of the Taxes Management Act 1970 (collection and recovery) as if it were tax charged in an assessment and due and payable.

Reviewing a penalty

1.248   **29.**—(1) Where a person has received notification under regulation 28(2) of the imposition of a penalty, that person may apply for a review of the imposition of the penalty or the assessment of the amount of the penalty or both.

(2) The application must be made—

    (a) to the Commissioners; and

    (b) either—

        (i) within the period of 30 days beginning with the day on which the applicant was notified of the decision; or

        (ii) if the period for making the application has been extended under regulation 30, within the extended period.

(3) The application must be made—

    (a) in writing by electronic communications and paragraphs (2) to (5) of regulation 14 apply as if for "declaration" wherever it appears there were substituted " application "; and

    (b) in such form as may be specified by the Commissioners.

(4) The application must—

    (a) contain sufficient information to identify the applicant and the decision; and

    (b) set out the reasons for seeking a review of the decision.

(5) If an application for a review of a decision is made to the Commissioners in accordance with this regulation, the Commissioners must review the decision.

(6) On a review under this regulation, the Commissioners may—

    (a) uphold the decision;

    (b) vary the decision; or

    (c) quash the decision.

(7) If the applicant makes any representations to the Commissioners at a stage which gives the Commissioners a reasonable opportunity to consider them, the Commissioners must take account of them when carrying out the review.

(8) Where—

    (a) the Commissioners notify the applicant of further information or evidence which they may need for carrying out the review, and

(b) the information or evidence is not provided to them within the period of 15 days beginning with the day on which the notice was given,

the review may proceed without that information or evidence.

(9) The Commissioners must notify the applicant of the matters set out in paragraph (10) within—

(a) the period of 30 days beginning with the day on which the Commissioners received the application for the review;

(b) if the applicant has been given a notice under paragraph (8), the period of 45 days beginning with that day; or

(c) such other period as the applicant and the Commissioners may agree.

(10) The matters referred to in paragraph (9) are—

(a) the conclusion on the review;

(b) the reasons for the conclusion;

(c) if the conclusion is that the decision is upheld or varied, details of the person's right to appeal against that decision.

(11) If the Commissioners do not comply with paragraph (9), the review is to be treated as having concluded that the decision is upheld and the Commissioners must notify the applicant of that conclusion.

Extension of time limit for applications for review

30.—(1) A person who wishes to make an application for a review under regulation 29 may apply to the Commissioners for an extension of the period for making the application.   1.249

(2) An application under this regulation must—

(a) be made before the end of the period of 6 months beginning with the day after the last day of the period mentioned in regulation 29(2)(b)(i) ("the standard period");

(b) be in such form as may be specified by the Commissioners;

(c) be made by electronic communications, and paragraphs (2) to (5) of regulation 14 apply as if for "declaration" wherever it appears there were substituted "application"; and

(d) set out the reasons for seeking the extension.

(3) The Commissioners may grant an extension under this regulation if they are satisfied that—

(a) due to special circumstances, it was not practicable for the person to make the application under regulation 29 within the standard period, and

(b) it is reasonable in all the circumstances to grant the extension.

(4) If an application under this regulation is refused, it may not be renewed.

Appealing against a penalty

31.—(1) Where a person has received notification under regulation 28(2) of the imposition of a penalty, that person may appeal against the imposition of the penalty or the assessment of the amount of the penalty or both.   1.250

(2) But a person may not appeal under paragraph (1) unless—

    (a) the person has applied under regulation 29 for a review of the decision; and

    (b) the period applicable under regulation 29(9) has expired.

    (3) An appeal under this regulation is an appeal to the Tribunal.

Powers of tribunal: appeals against penalties

1.251   **32.**—(1) This regulation applies where a person is appealing to the Tribunal under regulation 31 against a decision.

    (2) The Tribunal may—

    (a) uphold the penalty;

    (b) set aside the penalty; or

    (c) substitute for the penalty a penalty of an amount decided by the Tribunal.

    (3) If the Tribunal varies or quashes the decision, it must substitute its own decision for that of the Commissioners.

    (4) A decision of the Tribunal made by virtue of this regulation has the same effect as, and may be enforced in the same manner as, a decision of the Commissioners.

PART 4

LOCAL AUTHORITIES' DUTY TO SECURE EARLY YEARS PROVISION

Duty to secure early years provision free of charge

1.252   **33.** An English local authority must secure that the early years provision described in regulation 34 is available on the basis described in regulations 35 and 36 free of charge for each child in the authority's area who is a qualifying child of working parents.

Nature of early years provision

1.253   **34.**—(1) The early years provision referred to in regulation 33 is early years provision that is provided by an early years provider, other than an excluded provider, to whom section 40 of the Childcare Act 2006 (duty to implement Early Years Foundation Stage) applies.

    (2) In paragraph (1) an "excluded provider" is—

    (a) an independent school (other than an Academy within the meaning of section 1A of the Academies Act 2010) which does not meet the standards prescribed under section 157(1) of the Education Act 2002 in relation to the spiritual, moral, social and cultural development of pupils at the school;

    (b) an early years provider in relation to whom the local authority has reasonable grounds to believe—

        (i) does not actively promote the fundamental British values of democracy, the rule of law, individual liberty and mutual respect and tolerance of those with different faiths and beliefs; or

   (ii) promotes as evidence-based views or theories which are contrary to established scientific or historical evidence and explanations.

Availability of early years provision

35.—(1) The provision must be available for a period of 570 hours in any year and during no fewer than 38 weeks in any year.   1.254

(2) For the purposes of paragraph (1), and section 1(1) of the Act, the first year commences on the date specified in paragraph (3) applicable to the child in question, and subsequent years commence on the anniversary of that date.

(3) The date is—

(a) 1st April following the later of—
   (i) the date of a child's third birthday; and
   (ii) the date on which the determination in paragraph (4) in respect of that child is made,

where the later of those two dates is in the period 1st January to 31st March;

(b) 1st September following the later of—
   (i) the date of a child's third birthday; and
   (ii) the date on which the determination in paragraph (4) in respect of that child is made,

where the later of those two dates is in the period 1st April to 31st August;

(c) 1st January following the later of—
   (i) the date of a child's third birthday; and
   (ii) the date on which the determination in paragraph (4) in respect of that child is made,

where the later of those two dates is in the period 1st September to 31st December.

(4) For the purposes of paragraph (3), "the determination" is the first determination that the criteria in section 1(2)(b), (c) and (d) of the Act are met in relation to a child made by—

(a) the Commissioners under regulation 17 or 21(6)(c); or
(b) the Tribunal under regulation 24(4).

Requirement on local authority when discharging its duty under regulation 33

36.—(1) A local authority must discharge its duty under regulation 33   1.255
by making arrangements which secure that an early years provider chosen by a parent of the child provides the early years provision in cases where—

(a) the early years provider is willing to provide it, and
(b) the early years provider is willing to accept—
   (i) any terms as to the payments which would be made to the provider in respect of the provision, and
   (ii) any requirements which would be imposed by the local authority in accordance with regulation 38.

(2) In the case of early years provision other than by an early years childminder registered with an early years childminder agency, the requirement in paragraph (1) applies only if the provider is not the governing body of a maintained school, and—

(a) the overall effectiveness of the provision by the provider was awarded a grade of "satisfactory", or "requires improvement", or better, in the most recent early years provision inspection report published in respect of the provision; or

(b) an early years provision inspection report has not yet been published in respect of the provision.

(3) In the case of early years provision by an early years childminder registered with an early years childminder agency, the requirement in paragraph (1) applies only if—

(a) the childminder is registered with an agency which was awarded a grade of "effective" in the most recent early years childminder agency inspection report published in respect of the agency; or

(b) an early years childminder agency inspection report has not yet been published in respect of the agency.

(4) The requirement in paragraph (1) does not apply where—

(a) the local authority has reasonable grounds to believe that the person with whom the arrangements referred to in paragraph (1) are intended to be made is not able to satisfy a requirement imposed in respect of the early years provision; or

(b) in the case of early years provision by an early years childminder registered with an early years childminder agency, the early years childminder agency has notified the local authority that, in the reasonable opinion of the agency, the provision by the early years childminder registered with the agency is not of satisfactory quality.

(5) In this regulation "early years childminder agency inspection report" means a report under section 51E of the Childcare Act 2006.

Arrangements between local authorities and early years providers: termination

1.256   **37.** Arrangements made by the local authority for the purpose of complying with the requirement in regulation 36(1) must include provision allowing the local authority to terminate the arrangements if—

(a) in the case of early years provision of the description in regulation 36(2)(a), the overall effectiveness of the provision ceases to meet that description;

(b) in the case of early years provision of the description in regulation 36(2)(b), an early years provision inspection report is subsequently published in respect of the provision and the overall effectiveness of the provision by the provider is not awarded a grade of "satisfactory", or "requires improvement", or better;

(c) in the case of early years provision provided by a childminder registered with an early years childminder agency of the description in regulation 36(3)(a), the agency ceases to meet that description;

(d) in the case of early years provision provided by a childminder registered with an early years childminder agency of the description in regulation 36(3)(b), an early years childminder agency inspection report is published in respect of the agency and the agency is not awarded a grade of "effective";

(e) in the case of early years provision by an early years childminder registered with an early years childminder agency, the early years childminder agency has notified the local authority that, in the reasonable opinion of the agency, the provision by the early years childminder registered with the agency is not of satisfactory quality.

Arrangements between local authorities and early years providers: requirements

38.—(1) In making arrangements for the purposes of discharging its duty under regulation 33 with an early years provider (other than the governing body of a maintained school), or with an early years childminder agency, a local authority may impose on the person with whom the arrangements are made only requirements which— 1.257

(a) enable the local authority to comply with the requirement in regulation 36(1);

(b) enable the local authority to terminate the arrangements made pursuant to the requirement in regulation 36(1), in the circumstances prescribed in regulation 37;

(c) have as their purpose the satisfaction of any of the following objectives—

   (i) that the early years provision is provided free of charge;

   (ii) that the early years provision is provided in a pattern to suit the needs of the parents of the children for whom the early years provision is provided;

   (iii) that any financial assistance provided by a local authority under the arrangements is used properly and in accordance with the arrangements;

   (iv) the meeting of the needs of disabled children (within the meaning given by section 6 of the Equality Act 2010) and children with special educational needs (within the meaning given by section 20(1) of the Children and Families Act 2014) for whom the early years provision is provided;

   (v) the effective safeguarding and promotion of welfare of the children for whom the early years provision is provided;

   (vi) the active promotion of the fundamental British values of democracy, the rule of law, individual liberty and mutual respect and tolerance of those with different faiths and beliefs;

   (vii) that views or theories which are contrary to established scientific or historical evidence and explanations are not promoted as evidence-based in the early years provision;

   (viii) in circumstances where an early years provision inspection report awards a grade of less than "good" to the overall effectiveness of the early years provision, that the early years provider takes the measures identified in that report as necessary to improve the overall effectiveness of the early years provision, including, where applicable, participation in a training or other quality improvement programme; or

(d) are otherwise necessary for the effective administration of the arrangements.

(2) But a local authority may not impose requirements which—

(a) where the arrangements are made with an early years provider—

    (i) subject the quality of the early years provision to a quality assessment process by the local authority; or

    (ii) require the provider to attend any training or other quality improvement programme, other than any training or quality improvement programme identified in accordance with paragraph (1)(c)(viii);

(b) where the arrangements are made with an early years childminder agency, subject the quality of the services provided by the childminder agency to a quality assessment process by the local authority.

Having regard to guidance

1.258   **39.** In discharging its duty under regulation 33 a local authority must have regard to any guidance given from time to time by the Secretary of State.

PART 5

CONSEQUENTIAL AMENDMENTS

1.259   **40.–43.** [*Omitted*]

(SI 2019/1152)

The Universal Credit (Managed Migration Pilot and Miscellaneous Amendments) Regulations 2019

(SI 2019/1152)

Made: 18th July 2019

Laid before Parliament: 22nd July 2019

Coming into force in accordance with regulation 1

The Secretary of State for Work and Pensions makes the following Regulations in exercise of the powers conferred by sections 4(2) and 42(1), (2) and (3) of, and paragraph 4(1), (3)(a) and (4) of Schedule 1 to, and paragraph 1(1), 3(1)(a), 4(1), (2)(a), (c) and (d) and (3) and 6(a) of Schedule 6 to, the Welfare Reform Act 2012.

In accordance with section 173(1)(b) of the Social Security Administration Act 1992 the Social Security Advisory Committee has agreed that the proposals in respect of regulations 2 and 7, and certain proposals in respect of regulation 3(8), should not be referred to it. In accordance with section 172(1) of that Act, the Secretary of State has referred all other proposals in respect of these Regulations to the Social Security Advisory Committee.

In accordance with section 176(1) of the 1992 Act, in so far as these Regulations relate to housing benefit, the Secretary of State has consulted with organisations appearing to her to be representative of the authorities concerned in respect of the proposals for these Regulations.

ARRANGEMENT OF REGULATIONS

Citation and commencement

1.—(1) These Regulations may be cited as the Universal Credit (Managed Migration Pilot and Miscellaneous Amendments) Regulations 2019.

    1.260

(2) Regulations 2 and 3 and this regulation come into force on 24th July 2019.

(3) Regulations 4 and 5 come into force on 22nd July 2020.

(4) Regulation 6 comes into force on 23rd September 2020.

(5) Regulation 7 comes into force on 27th January 2021.

Managed migration pilot: limit on number of cases migrated

1.261   **2.** When the number of awards of universal credit made to persons to whom a notice has been issued under regulation 44 (migration notice) of the Universal Credit (Transitional Provisions) Regulations 2014 reaches 10,000, the Secretary of State must not issue further notices under that regulation.

Amendment of the Universal Credit (Transitional Provisions) Regulations 2014: managed migration (including provision for persons previously entitled to a severe disability premium)

1.262   **3.**—(1) The Universal Credit (Transitional Provisions) Regulations 2014 are amended as follows.

(2)-(8) *(Amendments incorporated into updating material in Part VI)*

Two week run-on of income support, income-based jobseeker's allowance and income-related employment and support allowance: amendment of the Universal Credit (Transitional Provisions) Regulations 2014

1.263   **4.**—(1) The Universal Credit (Transitional Provisions) Regulations 2014 are amended as follows.

(2)-(7) *(Amendments incorporated into updating material in Part VI)*

Two week run-on of income-based jobseeker's allowance and income-related employment and support allowance: day appointed for abolition

1.264   **5.**—(1) Subject to paragraph (2) where, in relation to any relevant claim for universal credit, an article ("the specified article") of any Order made under the powers in section 150(3) of the Welfare Reform Act 2012 provides for the coming into force of the amending provisions, the provision in that article for the day appointed is to be read as though the day appointed was the last day of the period of two weeks beginning with the day [¹ after the day] mentioned in that provision.

(2) For the purposes of paragraphs (6) and (7) of article 4 of the No. 9 Order (conversion to employment and support allowance of awards of incapacity benefit and severe disablement allowance), including as they apply for the purposes of any other Order made under section 150(3) of the Welfare Reform Act 2012, the day appointed by the specified article for the coming into force of the amending provisions shall be treated as though it was the day that applies apart from this regulation.

(3) In this regulation—

"amending provisions" has the meaning given by article 2(1) of the No. 9 Order;

"the No. 9 Order" means the Welfare Reform Act 2012 (Commencement No 9 and Transitional and Transitory Provision and Commencement No 8 and Savings and Transitional Provisions (Amendment) Order 2013;

"relevant claim for universal credit" means a claim for universal credit made on or after 22nd July 2020 including a claim where, under the article in question, the amending provisions come into force despite incorrect information having been given by the claimant, but excluding any claim that is treated as made by a couple in the circumstances referred to in regulation 9(8) (claims for universal credit by members of a couple) of the Universal Credit, Personal Independence Payment, Jobseeker's Allowance and Employment and Support Allowance (Claims and Payments) Regulations 2013.

AMENDMENT

1. Universal Credit (Managed Migration Pilot and Miscellaneous Amendments) (Amendment) Regulations 2020 (SI 2020/826) reg.2(2) (August 4, 2020).

12 month exemption from the minimum income floor for new claimants

6.—(1) In regulation 63(1) of the Universal Credit Regulations 2013 (start-up period) for sub-paragraph (a) substitute— **1.265**

"(a) regulation 62 (minimum income floor) has not previously applied to the claimant in relation to the trade, profession or vocation which is currently the claimant's main employment (whether in relation to the current award or a previous award); and".

(2) Regulation 59 (minimum income floor not to apply for first 12 months) of the Universal Credit (Transitional Provisions) Regulations 2014 is revoked.

Abolition of restriction on claims by persons entitled to a severe disability premium

7. Regulation 4A (restriction on claims for universal credit by persons entitled to a severe disability premium) of the Universal Credit (Transitional Provisions) Regulations 2014 is revoked. **1.266**

GENERAL NOTE

Note this regulation is not scheduled to come into force until January 27, 2021 (see reg.1(5)).

The Victims' Payments Regulations 2020

SI 2020/103

In force: February 24, 2020 and May 29, 2020

The Secretary of State, Northern Ireland Office, makes these Regulations in exercise of the powers conferred by sections 10 and 11 of the Northern Ireland (Executive Formation etc) Act 2019.
The Secretary of State has had regard to advice given by the Commission for Victims and Survivors for Northern Ireland in accordance with section 10(10) of that Act.

Part 1

Preliminary

Citation and commencement and extent

1.267 **1.**—(1) These Regulations may be cited as the Victims' Payments Regulations 2020.

(2) The following provisions come into force on the 24th February 2020—

(a) regulation 1;

(b) regulation 3;

(c) Schedule 1;

(d) paragraph 4(1) of Schedule 2, and regulation 15(8) so far as it relates to that paragraph;

(e) paragraphs 1, 4 and 5 of Schedule 3, and regulation 53 so far as it relates to that paragraph.

(3) The remaining provisions of these Regulations come into force on 29th May 2020.

(4) Except as provided by paragraphs (5) to (7), these Regulations extend to Northern Ireland only.

(5) Regulations 1, 2, 26, 28, 29 and 31 extend to England and Wales, Scotland and Northern Ireland.

(6) The amendments made by paragraph 2 of Schedule 3 extend to England and Wales only.

(7) Any other amendment made by these Regulations has the same extent as the provision it amends.

Disregard of payments and lump sums for certain purposes

1.268 **26.**—(1) A payment of victims' payments or a lump sum is to be disregarded—

(a) from the calculation of a person's income or capital when determining entitlement to a relevant social security benefit;

(b) for the purposes of an assessment of a person's ability to pay under regulations made under Article 36(6) or 99(5) (cost of providing residential accommodation) of the Health and Personal Social Services (Northern Ireland) Order 1972;

(c) for the purposes of determining whether a person should repay (either fully or in part) an award of criminal injuries compensation where the application for that award was determined before these Regulations come into force.

(2) In paragraph (1)—

"criminal injuries compensation" means compensation under a scheme established under the Criminal Injuries Compensation Act 1995 or the Criminal Injuries Compensation (Northern Ireland) Order 2002;

"relevant social security benefit" means any of the following—

(a) employment and support allowance under—
   (i) Part 1 of the Welfare Reform Act 2007 as it has effect apart from the amendments made by Schedule 3, and Part 1 of Schedule 14, to the Welfare Reform Act 2012 (to remove references to an income-related allowance);
   (ii) Part 1 of the Welfare Reform Act (Northern Ireland) 2007 as it has effect apart from the amendments made by Schedule 3, and Part 5 of Schedule 12, to the Welfare Reform Order (Northern Ireland) 2015 (to remove references to an income related allowance);

(b) housing benefit under—
   (i) Part 7 of the Social Security Contributions and Benefits Act 1992, or
   (ii) Part 7 of the Social Security Contributions and Benefits (Northern Ireland) Act 1992;

(c) income support under—
   (i) Part 7 of the Social Security Contributions and Benefits Act 1992, or
   (ii) Part 7 of the Social Security Contributions and Benefits (Northern Ireland) Act 1992;

(d) jobseeker's allowance under—
   (i) the Jobseekers Act 1995 as it has effect apart from the amendments made by Part 1 of Schedule 14 to the Welfare Reform Act 2012 (to remove references to an income-based allowance);
   (ii) the Jobseekers (Northern Ireland) Order 1995 as it has effect apart from the amendments made by Part 1 of Schedule 12 to the Welfare Reform Order (Northern Ireland) 2015 (to remove references to an income-based allowance);

(e) state pension credit under—
   (i) section 1 of the State Pension Credit Act 2002, or
   (ii) section 1 of the State Pension Credit Act (Northern Ireland) 2002;

(f) universal credit under—
   (i) Part 1 of the Welfare Reform Act 2012, or
   (ii) Part 2 of the Welfare Reform (Northern Ireland) Order 2015.

The Universal Credit (Coronavirus) (Self-employed Claimants and Reclaims) (Amendment) Regulations 2020

SI 2020/522

In force: May 21, 2020

The Secretary of State makes the following Regulations in exercise of powers conferred by sections 1(1) and 189(1), (4) and (6) of the Social Security Administration Act 1992 and section 42(1) to (3) of, and paragraph 4(1) and (6) of Schedule 1 to, the Welfare Reform Act 2012.

In accordance with section 173(1)(a) of the Social Security Administration Act 1992, it appears to the Secretary of State that by reason of the urgency of this matter it is inexpedient to refer the proposals in respect of these Regulations to the Social Security Advisory Committee.

Citation and commencement

1.269 **1.** These Regulations may be cited as the Universal Credit (Coronavirus) (Self-employed Claimants and Reclaims) (Amendment) Regulations 2020 and come into force on 21st May 2020.

Treatment of payments to self-employed universal credit claimants

1.270 **2.**—(1) For the purposes of regulation 57 (self-employed earnings) of the Universal Credit Regulations 2013—

(a) a payment under the Self-employment Income Support Scheme is to be treated as a receipt at step 1 of the calculation of self-employed earnings in the assessment period in which the claimant receives that payment; and

(b) no deduction may be made at step 1 of that calculation in respect of expenses comprising the salary or wages paid to an employee in so far as those expenses are covered by a payment under the Coronavirus Job Retention Scheme.

(2) For the purposes of section 5 (financial conditions) and section 8 (calculation of awards) of the Welfare Reform Act 2012, any payment made to a claimant carrying on a trade, profession or vocation—

(a) in relation to a furloughed employee under the Coronavirus Job Retention Scheme; or

(b) by way of a grant or loan to meet the expenses or losses of the trade, profession or vocation in relation to the outbreak of coronavirus disease,

is to be disregarded in the calculation of the claimant's capital for a period of 12 months from the date on which it is received.

(3) In this regulation—

"the Coronavirus Job Retention Scheme" means the scheme (as it has effect from time to time) that is the subject of the direction given by the Treasury on 15th April 2020 under section 76 of the Coronavirus Act 2020;

"the Self-employment Income Support Scheme" means the scheme (as it has effect from time to time) that is the subject of the

direction given by the Treasury on 30th April 2020 under that
section of that Act;

"coronavirus disease" has the meaning given in section 1 of the
Coronavirus Act 2020.

GENERAL NOTE

The prospective effect of this provision, and of the new reg.32A of the Claims
and Payments Regulations 2013 inserted by reg.3, was discussed in the notes to
reg.57 of and para.7 of Sch.10 to the Universal Credit Regulations in the
2020/21 edition of Vol.V.

The definition of "the Coronavirus Job Retention Scheme" covers the later
extensions to the scheme, because the later Treasury directions operate by way
of modification of that signed on April 15, 2020. See the directions signed on
June 25 and November 12, 2020, with the announcement of December 17, 2020
on the extension to cover April 2021 and the direction signed on January 25,
2021. The same principle works for the definition of "the Self-employed Income
Support Scheme.

Amendment of the UC etc. Claims and Payments Regulations

3. [*amendment incorporated into the updating material to in Part VI of this*   1.271
Supplement].

The Citizens' Rights (Application Deadline and Temporary Protection) (EU Exit) Regulations 2020

(SI 2020/1209)

In force: December 31, 2020 at 11.00 pm

The Secretary of State makes the following Regulations in exercise of the powers conferred by section 7(1) and (4) of, and paragraph 12 of Schedule 4 to, the European Union (Withdrawal Agreement) Act 2020.

These are the first regulations to be made under paragraphs (b), (c), (d), (e), (f) and (g) of section 7(1) of that Act. In accordance with paragraph 1(1) of Schedule 4 to that Act, a draft of these Regulations was laid before and approved by a resolution of each House of Parliament.

ARRANGEMENT OF REGULATIONS

PART 1

PRELIMINARY

PART 2

DEADLINE FOR APPLICATIONS

PART 3

SAVING OF THE EEA REGULATIONS 2016 ETC. DURING THE GRACE PERIOD AND WHILST APPLICATIONS ARE FINALLY DETERMINED

GENERAL NOTE

1.272   The Immigration (European Economic Area) Regulations 2016 were revoked on December 31, 2020 at 11.00 pm by s.1 of, and para.2(2) of Sch.1 to, the

Immigration and Social Security Co-ordination (EU Withdrawal) Act 2020 (see also reg.4(c) of SI 2020/1279). Despite that revocation, these regulations preserve (and, in some cases, modify) specified provisions in those Regulations during the "grace period" (see reg.3) during which it remains possible to apply for residence status under the EU Scheme and thereafter until an application has been finally determined. The grace period will expire at the end of June 30, 2021 (see the definition of "application deadline" in reg.2).

Importantly for this work, reg.4(4) provides that the provisions specified in reg.11—which include the provisions establishing the right to reside test for the means-tested social security benefits, tax credits and child benefit—continue to govern claims for those benefits by those applying for residence status "as if any reference to the EEA Regulations 2016 or any provision of those Regulations are to the Regulations or provision of the Regulations as continued in effect and modified by regulations 5 to 10". The effect is that applicants under the EU scheme will be treated, pending the final determination of that application, as having a right to reside for social security purposes if they would have had such a right had the 2016 Regulations had not been revoked.

These Regulations apply to those who have yet to make an application under the EU settlement scheme, or who have made an application which has not been finally determined: see the definition of "relevant person" in reg.3(6). There is therefore no overlap between these Regulations and Sch.4 to the Immigration and Social Security Co-ordination (EU Withdrawal) Act 2020 (Consequential, Saving, Transitional and Transitory Provisions) (EU Exit) Regulations 2020 (SI 2020/1309) (see below) which only apply to those who have been granted pre-settled status under that scheme.

PART 1

PRELIMINARY

Citation, commencement and interpretation

1.—(1) These Regulations may be cited as the Citizens' Rights (Application Deadline and Temporary Protection) (EU Exit) Regulations 2020 and come into force on IP completion day.   1.273

(2) In these Regulations—
"the EEA Regulations 2016" mean the Immigration (European Economic Area) Regulations 2016;
"application deadline" has the meaning given in regulation 2.

PART 2

DEADLINE FOR APPLICATIONS

Deadline for applications

2. The end of 30 June 2021 is the deadline for submission of an application for residence status ("application deadline") that applies for the purposes of the following provisions—   1.274

(a) the first sub-paragraph of Article 18(1)(b) of the withdrawal agreement;

(b) the first sub-paragraph of Article 17(1)(b) of the EEA EFTA separation agreement, and

(c) the first sentence of Article 16(1)(b) of the Swiss citizens' rights agreement.

PART 3

SAVING OF THE EEA REGULATIONS 2016 ETC. DURING THE GRACE
PERIOD AND WHILST APPLICATIONS ARE FINALLY DETERMINED

Grace period

1.275   **3.**—(1) This regulation has effect if the EEA Regulations 2016 are revoked on IP completion day (with or without savings).

(2) The provisions of the EEA Regulations 2016 specified in regulations 5 to 10 continue to have effect (despite the revocation of those Regulations) with the modifications specified in those regulations in relation to a relevant person during the grace period.

(3) The provisions specified in regulation 11 apply in relation to a relevant person during the grace period as if any reference to the EEA Regulations 2016 or any provision of those Regulations are to the Regulations or provision of the Regulations as continued in effect and modified by regulations 5 to 10.

(4) The enactments specified in regulation 12 apply in relation to a relevant person during the grace period with the modifications specified in that regulation.

(5) For the purposes of this regulation—

(a) the grace period is the period beginning immediately after IP completion day and ending with the application deadline;

(b) a person is to be treated as residing in the United Kingdom at any time which would be taken into account for the purposes of calculating periods when the person was continuously resident for the purposes of the EEA Regulations 2016 (see regulation 3);

(c) a person who does not have the right to reside in the United Kingdom permanently is to be treated as having such a right if the person had a right of permanent residence in the United Kingdom under those Regulations (see regulation 15) and who, immediately before IP completion day, has been absent from the United Kingdom for a continuous period of 5 years or less (disregarding any period of absence before the person acquired the right of permanent residence).

(6) In this regulation—

"EEA document" means—

(a) an EEA family permit issued under regulation 12 of the EEA Regulations 2016;

(b) a registration certificate issued under regulation 17 of those Regulations, or (c) a residence card issued under regulation 18 of those Regulations;

"family member"—

(a) has the same meaning as in paragraph (1) of regulation 7 of the EEA Regulations 2016 (read with paragraph (2) of that regulation) as those Regulations had effect immediately before IP completion day, and

(b) includes an extended family member within the meaning of regulation 8 of those Regulations as they had effect immediately before IP completion day if that person—

    (i) immediately before IP completion day satisfied the condition in regulation 8(5) of those Regulations (durable partner), or

    (ii) holds a valid EEA document (regardless of whether that document was issued before or after IP completion day);

"relevant family member", in relation to a person ("P"), means a family member who—

(a) was a family member of P immediately before IP completion day;

(b) is P's child and—

    (i) the child's other parent is a relevant person or has leave to enter or remain in the United Kingdom by virtue of residence scheme immigration rules;

    (ii) the child's other parent is a British citizen;

    (iii) P has sole or joint rights of custody of the child in the circumstances set out in the last point of Article 10(1)(e)(iii) of the withdrawal agreement or the last point of Article 9(1)(e)(iii) of the EEA EFTA separation agreement, or

    (iv) P falls within Article 10(1)(e)(iii) of the Swiss citizens' rights agreement (children of beneficiaries of that agreement);

(c) becomes a family member of P after IP completion day by virtue of being issued with an EEA document (see paragraph (b)(ii) of the definition of "family member"), or

(d) is the spouse or civil partner of P and P is a national of Switzerland;

"relevant person" means a person who does not have (and who has not, during the grace period, had) leave to enter or remain in the United Kingdom by virtue of residence scheme immigration rules and who—

(a) immediately before IP completion day—

    (i) was lawfully resident in the United Kingdom by virtue of the EEA Regulations 2016, or

    (ii) had a right of permanent residence in the United Kingdom under those Regulations (see regulation 15), or

(b) is not a person who falls within sub-paragraph (a) but is a relevant family member of a person who immediately before IP completion day—

    (aa) was lawfully resident in the United Kingdom by virtue of the EEA Regulations 2016, or

    (bb) had a right of permanent residence in the United Kingdom under those Regulations (see regulation 15).

Applications which have not been finally determined by the application deadline

1.276   **4.**—(1) This regulation has effect if the EEA Regulations 2016 are revoked on IP completion day (with or without savings).

(2) This regulation applies to a person ("the applicant") who—

(a) has made an in-time application (see paragraph (6)), and

(b) immediately before IP completion day—

    (i) was lawfully resident in the United Kingdom by virtue of the EEA Regulations 2016, or

    (ii) had a right of permanent residence in the United Kingdom under those Regulations (see regulation 15).

(3) The provisions of the EEA Regulations 2016 specified in regulations 5 to 10 continue to have effect (despite the revocation of those Regulations) with the modifications specified in those regulations in relation to the applicant during the relevant period.

(4) The provisions specified in regulation 11 apply in relation to the applicant during the relevant period as if any reference to the EEA Regulations 2016 or any provision of those Regulations are to the Regulations or provision of the Regulations as continued in effect and modified by regulations 5 to 10.

(5) The enactments specified in regulation 12 apply in relation to the applicant during the relevant period with the modifications specified in that regulation.

(6) For the purposes of this regulation—

(a) an in-time application is an application for leave to enter or remain in the United Kingdom by virtue of residence scheme immigration rules which—

    (i) is valid under residence scheme immigration rules;

    (ii) is made on or before the application deadline, and

    (iii) has not been withdrawn;

(b) the relevant period begins immediately after the application deadline and ends—

    (i) if the applicant is, by virtue of the in-time application, granted leave to enter or remain in the United Kingdom, on the day on which that leave is granted;

    (ii) if a decision is taken not to grant any leave to enter or remain in the United Kingdom in response to the applicant's application and the applicant does not appeal against that decision, on the first day on which the applicant is no longer entitled to appeal against that decision (ignoring any possibility of an appeal out of time with permission);

(iii) if a decision is taken not to grant any leave to enter or remain in the United Kingdom in response to the applicant's application and the applicant brings an appeal against that decision, on the day on which that appeal is finally determined, withdrawn or abandoned, or lapses under paragraph 3 of Schedule 1 to the Immigration (Citizens' Rights Appeals) (EU Exit) Regulations 2020;

(c) a person is to be treated as residing in the United Kingdom at any time which would be taken into account for the purposes of calculating periods when the person was continuously resident for the purposes of the EEA Regulations 2016 (see regulation 3);

(d) a person who does not have the right to reside in the United Kingdom permanently is to be treated as having such a right if the person had a right of permanent residence in the United Kingdom under those Regulations (see regulation 15) and who, immediately before IP completion day, has been absent from the United Kingdom for a continuous period of 5 years or less (disregarding any period of absence before the person acquired the right of permanent residence).

(7) For the purposes of paragraph (6)(b)(iii)—

(a) an appeal is not finally determined while (as the case may be)—

(i) an application for permission to appeal under section 11 or 13 of the Tribunals, Courts and Enforcement Act 2007 could be made or is awaiting determination;

(ii) permission to appeal under either of those sections has been granted and the appeal is awaiting determination;

(iii) an appeal has been remitted under section 12 or 14 of that Act and is awaiting determination;

(iv) any of the following applications could be made—

(aa) an application for leave to appeal under section 7 of the applied 1997 Act;

(bb) an application for a certificate under section 7B of the applied 1997 Act;

(cc) an application for permission to appeal under section 7C of the applied 1997 Act, or

(v) leave to appeal under section 7, or permission to appeal under section 7C, of the applied 1997 Act has been granted and the appeal is awaiting determination;

(b) an appeal is to be treated as abandoned if the appellant is granted leave to enter or remain in the United Kingdom by virtue of residence scheme immigration rules;

(c) an appeal is not to be treated as abandoned solely because the appellant leaves the United Kingdom.

(8) For the purposes of paragraph (7), "the applied 1997 Act" means the Special Immigration Appeals Commission Act 1997 as it applies for the purposes of the Immigration (Citizens' Rights Appeals) (EU Exit) Regulations 2020 by virtue of Part 2 of Schedule 1 to those Regulations.

Provisions relating to definitions etc.

1.277   **5.** The following provisions of Part 1 of the EEA Regulations 2016 (provisions relating to definitions etc.) with the modifications set out below are specified for the purposes of regulations 3 and 4—

    (a) regulation 2 (general interpretation) with the modifications that—

        (i) all instances of the words "or any other right conferred by the EU Treaties"—

            (aa) in so far as they relate to things done on or after exit day but before IP completion day, were a reference to a right conferred by the EU Treaties so far as they were applicable to and in the United Kingdom by virtue of Part 4 of the EU withdrawal agreement;

            (bb) in so far as they relate to things done on or after IP completion day, were omitted;

        (ii) all instances of the words "or the EU Treaties"—

            (aa) in so far as they relate to things done after exit day but before IP completion day, were a reference to the EU Treaties so far as they were applicable to and in the United Kingdom by virtue of Part 4 of the EU withdrawal agreement;

            (bb) in so far as they relate to things done on or after IP completion day, were omitted;

        (iii) in paragraph (b) of the definition of "EEA decision", ", a registration certificate, residence card, derivative residence card, document certifying permanent residence or permanent residence card" were omitted;

        (iv) in the definition of "EEA State", so far as relevant to things done after exit day, ", other than the United Kingdom" were omitted;

    (b) regulation 3 (continuity of residence);

    (c) regulation 4 ("worker", "self-employed person", "self-sufficient person" and "student") with the modification that, in paragraph (1)(b), for "in accordance with" there were substituted "within the meaning of";

    (d) regulation 5 ("worker or self-employed person who has ceased activity");

    (e) regulation 6 ("qualified person") with the modifications that—

        (i) in paragraph (4C), "and having a genuine chance of being engaged" were omitted;

        (ii) in paragraph (6), after "employment and" there were inserted ", when determining whether the person is a jobseeker,";

        (iii) in paragraph (7), after "continuing to seek employment and" there were inserted ", where that person is a jobseeker,";

    (f) regulation 7 ("family member");

    (g) regulation 8 ("extended family member") with the modification that paragraph (8)(c) were omitted;

(h) regulation 9 (family members and extended family members of British citizens) with the modifications that—

    (i) in paragraph (1), at the end there were inserted "and BC is to be treated as satisfying any requirement to be a qualified person";

    (ii) sub-paragraph (a) of paragraph (3) were omitted;

    (iii) paragraph (7) were omitted;

(i) regulation 9A (dual national: national of an EEA State who acquires British citizenship);

(j) regulation 10 ("family member who has retained the right of residence") with the modification that, in paragraph (5)(a), "the initiation of proceedings for" were omitted.

Provisions relating to residence rights

6. The following provisions of Parts 2 and 3 of the EEA Regulations 2016 (provisions relating to residence rights and residence documentation) with the modifications set out below are specified for the purposes of regulations 3 and 4—   1.278

(a) regulation 11 (right of admission to the United Kingdom) with the modifications that—

    (i) sub-paragraph (a) of paragraph (2) were omitted;

    (ii) in paragraph (3), for ", a permanent residence card or a qualifying EEA State residence card" there were substituted "or a permanent residence card";

    (iii) paragraph (4) were omitted;

(b) regulation 12 (issue of EEA family permit) with the modification that in paragraph (4), before sub-paragraph (a), there were inserted—

    "(aa) the extended family member satisfies the condition in paragraph (5) of regulation 8;";

(c) regulation 13 (initial right of residence) with the modification that in paragraph (4), after "26(3) (misuse of right to reside)", there were inserted ", 27A (decisions taken on conducive grounds)";

(d) regulation 14 (extended right of residence) with the modification that in paragraph (4), after "26(3)", there were inserted ", 27A";

(e) regulation 15 (right of permanent residence) with the modification that in paragraph (4), after "26(3)", there were inserted ", 27A";

(f) regulation 16 (derivative right to reside) with the modifications that—

    (i) in paragraph (5)(c), for "another" there were substituted "an";

    (ii) in paragraph (12), after "26(3)", there were inserted ", 27A";

(g) regulation 21 (procedure for applications for documentation under this Part and regulation 12) with the modifications that—

    (i) in paragraph (1) and in paragraph (4A), "documentation under this Part, or for" were omitted;

(ii) in paragraph (2), "this Part or" and ", as the case may be, as well as that required by paragraph (5)," were omitted;
(iii) paragraphs (3), (5) and (6) were omitted;
(h) regulation 22 (verification of a right of residence) with the modifications that—
    (i) in paragraph (1)(b), the words "or documentation issued under Part 3" were omitted;
    (ii) in paragraph (2)(a), the words "or documentation under this Part" were omitted.

Provisions relating to powers of refusal of admission and removal etc.

1.279   **7.** [*Omitted*]

Provisions relating to procedures in relation to EEA decisions

1.280   **8.** [*Omitted*]

Provisions relating to appeals

1.281   **9.** [*Omitted*]

Miscellaneous provisions

1.282   **10.** The following provisions of Part 7 of the EEA Regulations 2016 (miscellaneous provisions) with the modifications set out below are specified for the purposes of regulations 3 and 4—
(a) regulation 43 (effect on other legislation);
(b) regulation 45 (revocations, savings, transitory and transitional provisions and consequential modifications) (except in so far as it relates to Part 1 of Schedule 4);
(c) Schedule 3 (effect on other legislation) with the modification that in paragraph 3, "a qualifying EEA State residence card," were omitted;
(d) Part 2 of Schedule 4 (savings and modifications);
(e) Schedule 6 (transitional provisions) with the modification that in paragraph 4(1), paragraphs (b) to (f) were omitted;
(f) Schedule 7 (consequential modifications).

Entitlement to benefits and public services

1.283   **11.** The provisions specified in this regulation are—
(a) regulation 21AA (special cases: supplemental—persons from abroad) of the Income Support (General) Regulations 1987;
(b) [*Omitted*]
(c) regulation 85A (special cases: supplemental—persons from abroad) of the Jobseeker's Allowance Regulations 1996;
(d) [*Omitted*]
(e) regulation 2 (persons not in Great Britain) of the State Pension Credit Regulations 2002;

(f)   regulation 3 (circumstances in which a person is treated as not being in the United Kingdom) of the Tax Credits (Residence) Regulations 2003;

(g)   [*Omitted*]

[¹ (ga) regulation 7 (funeral payments: entitlement) of the Social Fund Maternity and Funeral Expenses (General) Regulations 2005;

(gb)   [*Omitted*];]

(h)-(n) [*Omitted*]

(o)   regulation 70 (special cases: supplemental—persons from abroad) of the Employment and Support Allowance Regulations 2008;

(p)   [*Omitted*]

(q)-(s) [*Omitted*]

(t)   regulations 2 (interpretation) and 9 (persons treated as not being in Great Britain) of the Universal Credit Regulations 2013;

(u)-(y) [*Omitted*]

AMENDMENT

1. Immigration and Social Security Co-ordination (EU Withdrawal) Act 2020 (Consequential, Saving, Transitional and Transitory Provisions) (EU Exit) Regulations 2020 (SI 2020/1309) reg.49 (December 31, 2020 at 11.00 pm).

Modification of other enactments

12.—(1) The following enactments with the modifications set out below are specified for the purposes of regulations 3 and 4—   1.284

(a)-(f) [*Omitted*]

(g)   section 7(1) of the Immigration Act 1988 (persons exercising Community rights and nationals of member States)(c), as it had effect immediately before IP completion day, with the modification that "of an enforceable EU right or" were omitted;

(h)   section 10 of the Immigration and Asylum Act 1999 (removal of persons unlawfully in the United Kingdom), as it had effect immediately before IP completion day, with the modification that in subsection (5) "of an enforceable EU right or" were omitted;

(i)   section 115 of that Act (exclusion from benefits), as it had effect immediately before IP completion day;

(j)-(p) [*Omitted*]

(q)   Part 2 of the Schedule to the Social Security (Immigration and Asylum) Consequential Amendments Regulations 2000 (persons not excluded from certain benefits under section 115 of the Immigration and Asylum Act 1999), as it had effect immediately before IP completion day;

(r)-(w) [*Omitted*]

(2) Any reference in another enactment to a person who, under the Immigration Act 1971, requires leave to enter or remain in the United

Kingdom (including section 13 of the Asylum and Immigration Act 1996) is to be read in light of paragraph (1)(g) above (application with modification of section 7 of the Immigration Act 1988).

Evidencing status

1.285   **13.** Where any question arises as to whether a person is or was lawfully resident in the United Kingdom at a particular point in time by virtue of the EEA Regulations 2016 (including as continued in effect and modified by these Regulations) for the purposes of these Regulations, it is for the individual in question to prove that they were.

(SI 2020/1309)

The Immigration and Social Security Co-ordination (EU Withdrawal) Act 2020 (Consequential, Saving, Transitional and Transitory Provisions) (EU Exit) Regulations 2020

(SI 2020/1309)

In force: December 31, 2020 at 11.00 pm

The Secretary of State makes the following Regulations in exercise of the power conferred by sections 5 and 8(5) of the Immigration and Social Security Co-ordination (EU Withdrawal) Act 2020.

ARRANGEMENT OF REGULATIONS

PART 1

INTRODUCTION

PART 2

IMMIGRATION

PART 3

ACCESS TO BENEFITS AND SERVICES

PART 4

NATIONALITY

PART 5

SAVING PROVISION IN CONNECTION WITH THE EC ASSOCIATION AGREEMENT WITH TURKEY

203

PART 6

SAVING PROVISION IN CONNECTION WITH THE IMMIGRATION
(EUROPEANECONOMIC AREA) REGULATIONS 2016

82. [*Omitted*]

PART 7

SAVING PROVISION IN RELATION TO ACCESS TO BENEFITS AND SERVICES

83. Saving provision in relation to access to benefits and services

PART 8

TRANSITIONAL AND FURTHER SAVING PROVISION

84. [*Omitted*]
SCHEDULES 1-3—[*Omitted*]
SCHEDULE 4—Saving provision in relation to access to benefits and services
SCHEDULE 5—[*Omitted*]

GENERAL NOTE

1.286   Parts 2-4 of these regulations make consequential amendments to various
provisions in primary and secondary legislation following the UK's withdrawal
from the EU and the coming into force of the Immigration and Social Security
Co-ordination (EU Withdrawal) Act 2020. Where those amendments relate to
provisions that are reproduced in the main volumes, they have been taken into
account in the Noter-up.

For certain specified purposes, Parts 5-7 save—often with modifications—provisions that were repealed by the 2020 Act. It is important to note that the
provisions that are saved (and the modifications that are made) differ according
to the purpose for which they are being saved (and modified). For the purposes
of entitled to means-tested social security benefits, tax credits and child benefit,
the relevant savings and modifications are set out in Sch.4.

Paragraph 4 of that Schedule saves and modifies parts of the Immigration
(European Economic Area) Regulations 2016 (which were otherwise revoked on
December 31, 2020 at 11.00 pm by s.1 of, and para.2(2) of Sch.1 to, the
Immigration and Social Security Co-ordination (EU Withdrawal) Act 2020 and
reg.4(c) of SI 2020/1279), for the purposes of the provisions of social security
law listed in para.3.

Note that those savings apply where the claimant is a "member of the post-
transition period group": see paras 1(b) and (2) of Sch.4. In plain English, the
members of that group are those who have pre-settled status under the EU
settlement scheme. There is therefore no overlap between these Regulations and
the Citizens' Rights (Application Deadline and Temporary Protection) (EU
Exit) Regulations 2020 (SI 2020/1209) (see above), which apply to those who
have not made an application under that scheme or who have made an application that has yet to be finally determined.

PART 1

INTRODUCTION

Citation, commencement and extent

1.—(1) These Regulations may be cited as the Immigration and Social   1.287
Security Co-ordination (EU Withdrawal) Act 2020 (Consequential,
Saving, Transitional and Transitory Provisions) (EU Exit) Regulations
2020.

(2) These Regulations come into force at the time and on the date
when paragraph 2(2) of, Schedule 1 to, the 2020 Act comes into force
for all purposes except for—

(a)-(c) [*Omitted*].

(3) Any provision of these Regulations which amends, repeals or
revokes an enactment has the same extent as the enactment amended,
repealed or revoked (ignoring extent by virtue of an Order in Council
under any of the Immigration Acts).

(4) Any saving, transitional or transitory provision in these Regulations has the same extent within the United Kingdom as the provision to
which it relates.

Interpretation—General

2. In these Regulations—   1.288
"the 2020 Act" means the Immigration and Social Security Co-or-
    dination (EU Withdrawal) Act 2020;
"commencement day" means the time at and date on which the
    Immigration (European Economic Area) Regulations 2016 are
    revoked for all purposes.

PART 7

SAVING PROVISION IN CONNECTION WITH ACCESS TO BENEFITS AND
SERVICES

Saving provision in connection with access to benefits and services

83. Schedule 4 has effect.   1.289

Regulation 83

SCHEDULE 4

Saving provision in relation to access to benefits and services
1. In this Schedule—   1.290
(a) "EEA Regulations 2016" means the Immigration (European Economic Area) Reg-
    ulations 2016 as they had effect immediately before they were revoked;

(b) "member of the post-transition period group" means a person who has limited leave to enter, or remain in, the United Kingdom granted by virtue of residence scheme immigration rules within the meaning given by section 17 of the European Union (Withdrawal Agreement) Act 2020.

2. For the purposes of the provisions specified in paragraph 3 the provisions of the EEA Regulations 2016 specified in paragraph 4 continue to have effect in relation to a person who is a member of the post-transition period group, with the specified modifications, despite the revocation of those Regulations by the 2020 Act.

3. The provisions specified in this paragraph are—

(a) regulation 21AA (special cases: supplemental—persons from abroad) of the Income Support (General) Regulations 1987;

(b) [*Omitted*]

(c) regulation 85A (special cases: supplemental—persons from abroad) of the Jobseeker's Allowance Regulations 1996;

(d)-(e) [*Omitted*];

(f) regulation 2 (persons not in Great Britain) of the State Pension Credit Regulations 2002;

(g) [*Omitted*];

(h) regulation 3 (circumstances in which a person is treated as not being in the United Kingdom) of the Tax Credits (Residence) Regulations 2003;

(i) regulation 7 (funeral payments: entitlement) of the Social Fund Maternity and Funeral Expenses (General) Regulations 2005;

(j)-(n) [*Omitted*];

(o) regulations 23 (circumstances in which person treated as not being in Great Britain) and 27 (circumstances in which person treated as not being in Northern Ireland) of the Child Benefit (General) Regulations 2006;

(p)-(q) [*Omitted*]

(r) regulation 70 (special cases: supplemental—persons from abroad) of the Employment and Support Allowance Regulations 2008;

(s)-(v) [*Omitted*]

(w) regulations 2 (interpretation) and 9 (persons treated as not being in Great Britain) of the Universal Credit Regulations 2013;

(x)-(bb) [*Omitted*]

4. The following provisions of the EEA Regulations 2016 are, with the modifications provided for, specified for the purposes of paragraph 2—

(a) regulation 2 (general interpretation) with the following modifications—

    (i) as if all instances of the words "or any other right conferred by the EU Treaties"—

        (aa) in so far as they relate to things done on or after exit day but before commencement day, were a reference to a right conferred by the EU Treaties so far as they were applicable to and in the United Kingdom by virtue of Part 4 of the EU withdrawal agreement;

        (bb) in so far as they relate to things done on or after commencement day, were omitted;

    (ii) as if all instances of the words "or the EU Treaties"—

        (aa) in so far as they relate to things done on or after exit day but before commencement day, were a reference to the EU Treaties so far as they were applicable to and in the United Kingdom by virtue of Part 4 of the EU withdrawal agreement;

        (bb) in so far as they relate to things done on or after commencement day, were omitted;

    (iii) as if, at the end of the definition of "deportation order", there were inserted "or under section 5(1) of the Immigration Act 1971";

    (iv) as if, in the definition of "EEA State", the words ", other than the United Kingdom" were omitted;

    (v) as if, at the end of the definition of "exclusion order", there were inserted "or directions issued by the Secretary of State for a person not to be given entry to the United Kingdom on the grounds that the person's exclusion is conducive to the public good";

(b) regulation 3 (continuity of residence) with the modification that, at the end of paragraph (3)(c), there were inserted "or the Immigration Acts";

(c) regulation 4 ("worker", "self-employed person", "self-sufficient person" and "student") with the modification that, in paragraph (1)(b), "in accordance with" there were substituted "within the meaning of";

(d) regulation 5 ("worker or self-employed person who has ceased activity");

(e) regulation 6 ("qualified person") with the following modifications—

    (i) in paragraph (4C), "and having a genuine chance of being engaged" were omitted;

    (ii) in paragraph (6), after "employment and" there were inserted ", when determining whether the person is a jobseeker,";

    (iii) in paragraph (7), after "continuing to seek employment and" there were inserted ", where that person is a jobseeker";

(f) regulation 7 ("family member");

(g) regulation 8 ("extended family member") with the modification that paragraph (8) were omitted;

(h) regulation 9 (family members and extended family members of British citizens) with the following modifications—

    (i) in paragraph (1), at the end there were inserted "and BC is to be treated as satisfying any requirement to be a qualified person";

    (ii) sub-paragraph (a) of paragraph (3) were omitted;

    (iii) paragraph (7) were omitted;

(i) regulation 9A (dual national: national of an EEA State who acquires British citizenship);

(j) regulation 10 ("family member who has retained the right of residence") with the following modifications—

    (i) in paragraph (2)(b), in so far as it applies to residence in the United Kingdom after commencement day, for "in accordance with these Regulations" there were substituted "lawfully";

    (ii) in paragraph (5)(a), "the initiation of proceedings for" were omitted;

(k) regulation 13 (initial right of residence) with the modification that in paragraph (4), for the words from "where the Secretary of State" to "as the case may be,", there were substituted "if that person is subject to a deportation order or exclusion order unless that order";

(l) regulation 14 (extended right of residence) with the modification that in paragraph (4), for the words from "where the Secretary of State" to "as the case may be,", there were substituted "if that person is subject to a deportation order or exclusion order unless that order";

(m) regulation 15 (right of permanent residence) with the following modifications—

    (i) in so far as it applies to residence in the United Kingdom after commencement day, as if the EEA Regulations 2016 (with the modifications set out in this paragraph) had been in force at all relevant times and as if for the words "in accordance with these Regulations" in each place they occur there were substituted "lawfully";

    (ii) in paragraph (4), for the words from "where the Secretary of State" to "as the case may be,", there were substituted "if that person is subject to a deportation order or exclusion order unless that order";

(n) regulation 16 (derivative right to reside) with the following modifications—

    (i) in paragraph (5)(c), for "another" there were substituted "an";

    (ii) in paragraph (12), for the words from "where the Secretary of State" to "or 31(1), unless that decision" there were substituted "if that person is subject to a deportation order or exclusion order unless that order".

Continued application of section 7(1) of the Immigration Act 1988 for purposes of housing legislation

5-7. [*Omitted*]

1.291

The European Union (Withdrawal) Act 2018 (Relevant Court) (Retained EU Case Law) Regulations 2020

(SI 2020/1525)

In force: 31 December 2020

The Secretary of State makes these Regulations in exercise of the powers conferred by section 6(5A)(a), (b) and (c) and (5B)(a) of the European Union (Withdrawal) Act 2018.

In accordance with section 6(5C) of that Act, the Secretary of State has carried out the necessary consultations.

In accordance with paragraph 9A of Schedule 7 to that Act, a draft of this instrument has been laid before, and approved by a resolution of, each House of Parliament.

ARRANGEMENT OF REGULATIONS

1. Citation and commencement
2. Interpretation
3. Relevant courts
4. Extent to which a relevant court is not bound by retained EU case law
5. Test to be applied

Citation and commencement

1.292   **1.** These Regulations may be cited as the European Union (Withdrawal) Act 2018 (Relevant Court) (Retained EU Case Law) Regulations 2020 and come into force on IP completion day.

Interpretation

1.293   **2.** In these Regulations—
"the 2018 Act" means the European Union (Withdrawal) Act 2018;
"post-transition case law" means any principles laid down by, and any decisions of, a court or tribunal in the United Kingdom, as they have effect on or after IP completion day.

Relevant courts

1.294   **3.** For the purposes of section 6 of the 2018 Act, each of the following is a relevant court—
(a)   *omitted,*
(b)   the Court of Appeal in England and Wales,
(c)   the Inner House of the Court of Session,
(d)–(f) *omitted,* and
(g)   the Court of Appeal in Northern Ireland.

Extent to which a relevant court is not bound by retained EU case law

1.295   **4.** (1) A relevant court is not bound by any retained EU case law except as provided in paragraph (2).

208

(2) A relevant court is bound by retained EU case law so far as there is post-transition case law which modifies or applies that retained EU case law and which is binding on the relevant court.

Test to be applied

5. In deciding whether to depart from any retained EU case law by virtue of section 6(4)(ba) of the 2018 Act and these Regulations, a relevant court must apply the same test as the Supreme Court would apply in deciding whether to depart from the case law of the Supreme Court.

1.296

NEW SCOTTISH STATUTORY INSTRUMENTS

The Carer's Assistance (Young Carer Grants) (Scotland) Regulations 2019

(SSI 2019/324)

In force: October 21, 2019

The Scottish Ministers make the following Regulations in exercise of the powers conferred by sections 28, 41(4)(a), 43(5) and 52 of the Social Security (Scotland) Act 2018 and all other powers enabling them to do so.

In accordance with section 96(2) of that Act, a draft of this instrument has been laid before and approved by resolution of the Scottish Parliament.

In accordance with section 97(2) of that Act, the Scottish Ministers have consulted the Scottish Commission on Social Security.

REGULATIONS REPRODUCED

1. Citation and Commencement
2. Interpretation
3. Overview
4. Making of applications
5. Conditions relating to the care being provided
6. Conditions relating to the person or persons being cared for
7. Further eligibility conditions
8. Conditions relating to residence
9. Periods for redetermination requests
10. Multiple applications involving care of the same person
11. Determination following backdated award of assistance
12. Amount and form of young carer grants

GENERAL NOTE

1.297   These regulations establish a scheme under s.28 of the Social Security (Scotland) Act 2018 for making grants to 16-18 year-olds who are acting as carers for disabled people.

PART 1

INTRODUCTORY AND INTERPRETATION

Citation and commencement

1. These Regulations may be cited as the Carer's Assistance (Young Carer Grants) (Scotland) Regulations 2019 and come into force on the first Monday after the day on which they are made.

1.298

Interpretation

2. In these Regulations—

"applicant" means a person who has applied for a young carer grant,

"determination" means a determination of an individual's entitlement under section 37 of the Social Security (Scotland) Act 2018,

"the qualifying period" means the period of 13 weeks described in regulation 5(1),

"young carer grant" means the grant provided for by these Regulations.

1.299

PART 2

ELIGIBILITY

Overview

3.—(1) A person who applies for a young carer grant is entitled to receive it if that person meets the conditions prescribed in these Regulations.

1.300

(2) Regulation 4 provides for the making of applications, including providing conditions related to the age of the applicant.

(3) Regulation 5 provides conditions relating to the care being provided and regulation 6 provides conditions relating to the person or persons being cared for.

(4) Regulation 7 provides further conditions relating to receipt of assistance and the status of the applicant.

(5) Regulation 8 provides conditions relating to the applicant's residence.

(6) Part 3 provides timescales for some procedural matters, including situations that involve multiple applications relating to care of the same person, and provides for when the Scottish Ministers must determine that an individual is entitled to a young carer grant without an application.

(7) Regulation 12 makes provision about the assistance that an applicant is entitled to receive.

Making of applications

1.301   4.—(1) A person is entitled to a young carer grant if, on the day their application for that assistance is made, they are aged at least 16 and are under the age of 19.

(2) In a non-leap year, the birthday of a person born on 29 February is to be taken to be 28 February.

[¹(3) An application is to be treated as made—

(a) in a case where paragraph (7) applies, on the day after the end of the 13 week period to which the application relates,

(b) in any other case, on the day it is received by the Scottish Ministers.]

(4) In a case where, by virtue of a regulation 11, a determination is to be, or has been, made without an application, references in these Regulations to the day the application is made are to be read in accordance with paragraph (3) of that regulation.

(5) For the avoidance of doubt, a thing that purports to be an application is not an application unless it is—

(a) made in the form, and

(b) accompanied by the evidence,

required by the Scottish Ministers under section 38(1) of the Social Security (Scotland) Act 2018.

(6) For the purposes of determining assistance, the period of an application is the period of 13 weeks ending with the day before the day of the application for a grant and an application in respect of any other period of 13 weeks is to be regarded as an application for a different period, despite any overlap between the two periods.

[¹(7) This paragraph applies where—

(a) an application for a young carer grant is made on or after the day on which the Carer's Allowance Supplement and Young Carer Grants (Residence Requirements and Procedural Provisions) (EU Exit) (Scotland) Regulations 2020 came into force,

(b) the application relates to a period of 13 weeks beginning after 21 October 2019 and ending before the day mentioned in sub-paragraph (a), and

(c) it appears to the Scottish Ministers that the applicant would be likely to have been entitled to a young carer grant on making an application on the day after the end of that 13 week period were it not for the requirement in regulation 8(3)(a) of these Regulations to have previously been properly paid a young carer grant, as it had effect immediately before the date on which the Carer's Allowance Supplement and Young Carer Grants (Residence Requirements and Procedural Provisions) (EU Exit) (Scotland) Regulations 2020 came into force.]

AMENDMENTS

1. Carer's Allowance Supplement and Young Carer Grants (Residence Requirements and Procedural Provisions) (EU Exit) (Scotland) Regulations 2020 (SSI 2020/475) reg.11(2) (December 24, 2020).

Conditions relating to the care being provided

5.—(1) To qualify for a young carer grant the applicant must have 1.302
provided care, over the period of 13 weeks ending with the day before the
day on which their application for a grant is made ("the qualifying
period")—

(a) to a person or persons described in regulation 6,

(b) for the number of hours, and in the number of weeks, described
   in paragraph (2),

(c) as described in paragraph (3), and

(d) which was not provided in the manner described in paragraph
   (4).

(2) The care must have been provided—

(a) for at least 208 hours during the qualifying period, and

(b) in at least 10 weeks during that period.

(3) The care provided must involve activity that promotes the physical,
mental or emotional well-being of the person being cared for.

(4) The care must not have been provided by the applicant—

(a) under or by virtue of a contract, unless the contract is of a kind
   specified by regulations under section 1(3)(a) of the Carers (Scotland) Act 2016 as not to be regarded as a contract for the purposes
   of that Act, or

(b) as voluntary work.

Conditions relating to the person or persons being cared for

6.—(1) To qualify for a young carer grant the person or persons being 1.303
cared for must, throughout the qualifying period and on the day the
application for assistance is made, each be a person to whom a qualifying
disability benefit is normally payable.

(2) An applicant may combine hours caring for up to three persons
during the qualifying period.

(3) In paragraph (1), "qualifying disability benefit" means a disability
benefit, or where applicable a component of a disability benefit, which is
of a type, and being paid at a rate, that would entitle a person who cares
for the recipient of that benefit and who meets the relevant qualifying
conditions to—

(a) carer's assistance, payable under section 28 of the Social Security
   (Scotland) Act 2018, or

(b) carer's allowance, payable under section 70 of the Social Security
   Contributions and Benefits Act 1992) or section 70 of the Social
   Security Contributions and Benefits (Northern Ireland) Act
   1992.

Further eligibility conditions

7.—(1) An applicant is not entitled to a young carer grant if, on the 1.304
day their application is made, the applicant is in receipt of a benefit
named in regulation 6(3)(a) or (b) in respect of any of the persons being
cared for.

(2) An applicant is not entitled to a young carer grant if they have
applied for a benefit named in regulation 6(3)(a) or (b) in respect of a

period that includes the day their application is made, unless it has already been determined that the applicant is ineligible for that benefit in respect of that day.

[¹(3) An applicant is not entitled to a young carer grant if they have previously received a young carer grant, unless—

(a) the day their application is made is at least one year after the day of the application in respect of which that grant was paid, or

(b) in a case where regulation 4(7) applies, the day their application is made is at least one year either before or after the application in respect of which the grant was paid.]

[¹ (4) Paragraph (5) applies if—

(a) any other person has been paid a young carer grant in respect of care of any of the persons being cared for in an application for a young carer grant, and

(b) either—

   (i) that grant was paid as a result of an application made during the year immediately preceding the day the applicant makes his or her application, or

   (ii) in a case where regulation 4(7) applies, that grant was paid as a result of an application made during the year immediately preceding or following the day the applicant makes his or her application.]

(5) The applicant is not entitled to a young carer grant unless—

(a) the other person who was paid a young carer grant has died, or

(b) the Scottish Ministers have concluded that a young carer grant should not have been paid to the other person.

(6) If an applicant has already received three young carer grants, they are not entitled to a further young carer grant.

(7) An applicant is not entitled to a young carer grant if, on the day their application is made, they are subject to immigration control within the meaning of section 115(9) of the Immigration and Asylum Act 1999, unless the applicant falls within a category or description of persons specified in Part 2 of the schedule of the Social Security (Immigration and Asylum) Consequential Amendments Regulations 2000 (persons not excluded under section 115 of the Immigration and Asylum Act 1999 from entitlement to various social security benefits).

[¹(7) In paragraph (5)(a), in a case where regulation 4(7) applies, the reference to the other person who was paid a young carer grant having died is to be read as a reference to that other person having died before the day on which the applicant's application was made.]

AMENDMENTS

   1. Carer's Allowance Supplement and Young Carer Grants (Residence Requirements and Procedural Provisions) (EU Exit) (Scotland) Regulations 2020 (SSI 2020/475) reg.11(3) (December 24, 2020).

Conditions relating to residence

1.305   **8.**—(1) Subject to paragraphs (2) and (3), to qualify for a young carer grant the applicant must, on the day their application is made for that assistance, be—

(a) habitually resident in the United Kingdom, the Channel Islands, the Isle of Man, the European Economic Area or Switzerland, and

(b) ordinarily resident in Scotland.

(2) Paragraph (1)(a) does not apply to the following persons (if they meet the condition in paragraph (1)(b) of being ordinarily resident in Scotland)—

(a) a refugee within the definition in Article 1 of the Convention relating to the status of refugees done at Geneva on 28 July 1951, as extended by article 1(2) of the Protocol relating to the status of refugees done at New York on 31 January 1967,

(b) a person who has been granted, or who is deemed to have been granted, leave outside the rules made under section 3(2) of the Immigration Act 1971, where that leave is—

   (i) discretionary leave to enter or remain in the United Kingdom,

   (ii) leave to remain under the destitution domestic violence concession, or

   (iii) leave deemed to have been granted by virtue of regulation 3 of the Displaced Persons (Temporary Protection) Regulations 2005,

(c) a person who has humanitarian protection granted under the rules made under section 3(2) of the Immigration Act 1971, or

(d) a person who—

   (i) is not subject to immigration control within the meaning of section 115(9) of the Immigration and Asylum Act 1999, and

   (ii) is in the United Kingdom as a result of deportation, expulsion or other removal by compulsion of law from another country to the United Kingdom.

[¹(3) An applicant who is not ordinarily resident in the United Kingdom does not have to meet the condition in paragraph (1)(b) (and therefore is entitled to a young carer grant) if—

(a) they satisfy the conditions in paragraph (4) on the day on which the application is made, if the application is made before IP completion day,

(b) they satisfy the conditions in paragraph (5) on the day the application is made, if the application is made after IP completion day and the individual has rights arising from a relevant EU regulation, or

(c) they satisfy the conditions in paragraph (6) on the day the application is made, if the application is made after IP completion day and the individual has rights arising from the UK-Ireland convention mentioned in that paragraph.

(4) The conditions referred to in paragraph (3)(a) are that the applicant must—

(a) be an individual—

   (i) to whom a relevant EU Regulation applies, and

(ii) in respect of whom the United Kingdom is competent for payment of sickness benefits in cash for the purposes of Chapter 1 of Title III of the Regulation in question,

(b) be resident in—
    (i) Switzerland, or
    (ii) an EEA State other than the United Kingdom,

(c) have a genuine and sufficient link to Scotland, and

(d) meet the other conditions prescribed in these Regulations.

(5) The conditions referred to in paragraph (3)(b) are that the applicant must—

(a) be an individual—
    (i) to whom the rules set out in a relevant EU regulation apply by virtue of—
        (aa) Title III of Part 2 of the EU withdrawal agreement,
        (bb) Part 3 or Article 23(4) of the Swiss citizens' rights agreement (as defined in section 39(1) of the European Union (Withdrawal Agreement) Act 2020),
        (cc) Title III of the EEA EFTA separation agreement (as defined in that section), or
        (dd) the agreement constituted by the exchange of letters set out in the schedule of the Family Allowances, National Insurance and Industrial Injuries (Gibraltar) Order 1974, and
    (ii) in respect of whom the United Kingdom is, as a result, competent for payment of sickness benefits in cash,

(b) be resident in—
    (i) Switzerland,
    (ii) an EEA state, or
    (iii) Gibraltar,

(c) have a genuine and sufficient link to Scotland, and

(d) meet the other conditions prescribed in these Regulations.

(6) The conditions referred to in paragraph (3)(c) are that the applicant must—

(a) be an individual—
    (i) to whom the convention on Social Security between the Government of the United Kingdom of Great Britain and Northern Ireland and the Government of Ireland signed at Dublin on 1 February 2019, as modified from time to time in accordance with any provision of it, applies, and
    (ii) in respect of whom the United Kingdom is, as a result, competent for payment of long term care benefits,

(b) be resident in Ireland,

(c) have a genuine and sufficient link to Scotland, and

(d) meet the other conditions prescribed in these Regulations.

(7) The reference in paragraph (4)(c) to an individual's link to Scotland being sufficient is to it being sufficiently close that if the individual were not entitled to a young carer grant paragraph (4)—

(a) would be incompatible with EU law, or

(b) would have been incompatible with EU law immediately preceding IP completion day.

(8) The reference in paragraph (5)(c) to an individual's link to Scotland being sufficient is to it being sufficiently close that if the individual where not entitled to a young carer grant, paragraph (5) would be incompatible with the applicable agreement referred to in that paragraph.

(9) The reference in paragraph (6)(c) to an individual's link to Scotland being sufficient is to its being sufficiently close that if the individual were not entitled to a young carer grant, paragraph (6) would be incompatible with the convention mentioned in that paragraph.

(10) In this regulation—

"EEA State" means—

(a) any member state of the European Union or

(b) any other state that is party to the agreement on the European Economic Area signed at Oporto on 2 May 1992, together with the Protocol adjusting that Agreement signed at Brussels on 17 March 1993, as modified or supplemented from time to time,

"EU law" has the meaning given by subsection (9) of section 126 of the Scotland Act 1998 or, if that subsection has been repealed, the meaning given by that subsection immediately before its repeal,

"relevant EU Regulation" means—

(a) one of the following Regulations—

(i) Council Regulation (EC) No 1408/71 of 14 June 1971 on the application of social security schemes to employed persons, to self-employed persons and to members of their families moving within the Community,

(ii) Regulation (EC) No 883/2004 of the European Parliament and of the Council of 29 April 2004 on the coordination of social security systems, or

(b) in relation to an individual to whom the exchange of letters mentioned in paragraph (5)(a)(i)(dd) applies, a Regulation mentioned in paragraph (a) as it forms part of domestic law by virtue of section 3 of the European Union (Withdrawal) Act 2018.]

AMENDMENTS

1. Carer's Allowance Supplement and Young Carer Grants (Residence Requirements and Procedural Provisions) (EU Exit) (Scotland) Regulations 2020 (SSI 2020/475) reg.11(4) (December 24, 2020).

PART 3

PROCEDURAL MATTERS

Periods for redetermination requests

9.—(1) The period for requesting a re-determination of entitlement to a young carer grant, under section 41 of the Social Security (Scotland) Act 2018, is 31 days beginning with the day that the applicant is 1.306

informed, in accordance with section 40 of that Act, of the right to make the request.

(2) The period allowed for re-determination (within the meaning of section 43 of that Act) is 16 working days beginning with—

(a) the day that the request for a re-determination is received by the Scottish Ministers, or

(b) where the request for a re-determination is received by the Scottish Ministers later than the period prescribed by paragraph (1), the day on which the Scottish Ministers, or on appeal the First-tier Tribunal for Scotland, decide that the applicant has a good reason for not requesting the re-determination sooner.

(3) For the purpose of paragraph (2), a "working day" is a day other than—

(a) a Saturday,

(b) a Sunday, or

(c) a bank holiday in Scotland under the Banking and Financial Dealings Act 1971.

Multiple applications involving care of the same person

1.307 **10.**—(1) Paragraphs (2) and (3) apply where two or more applicants state that they are caring for the same person.

(2) The Scottish Ministers must determine which (if any) of the applicants is to be entitled to receive a young carer grant.

(3) Where the applications were made at different times, the Scottish Ministers must determine the application made first before determining any other application.

Determination following backdated award of assistance

1.308 **11.**—(1) The Scottish Ministers are to make a determination of an individual's entitlement to a young carer grant without receiving an application where—

(a) an application has previously been made for a young carer grant ("the application"),

(b) the determination made in respect of the application was that the applicant was not entitled to a young carer grant,

(c) the only reason for the applicant not being entitled to a young carer grant was that a person being cared for was not in receipt of a qualifying disability benefit as required by regulation 6 throughout the qualifying period for the application and on the day of the application,

(d) the Scottish Ministers establish that—

(i) an award of a qualifying disability benefit has been made to the person being cared for that is a backdated award,

(ii) had that award been made before the day of the application, a determination that the individual is entitled to a young carer grant would have been made instead, and

(e) no other person has received a young carer grant since the day of the application, in respect of care of the person being cared for.

(2) In making a determination required by paragraph (1) the Scottish Ministers are to use—

(a) the information provided in the application that led to the original determination, and

(b) any other information they have obtained in connection with that application.

(3) Where a determination is to be, or has been, made without an application by virtue of this regulation, references in these Regulations to the day the application is made are to be read as references to the day the application that led to the original determination was made.

(4) In this regulation a "backdated award" means an award of assistance for a day, or a period that begins on a day, that falls before the day the decision to make that award was taken.

PART 4

ASSISTANCE TO BE GIVEN

Amount and form of young carer grants

12.—(1) [¹Subject to paragraph (1A), a young carer grant] is to be   1.309
given as a payment of £300.

[¹ (1A) Where the application for a young carer grant relates to a qualifying period which ended before the date on which the Carer's Allowance Supplement and Young Carer Grants (Residence Requirements and Procedural Provisions) (EU Exit) (Scotland) Regulations 2020 came into force, the amount of young carer grant to be given is the amount specified in paragraph (1) as it had effect on the day on which the application was made.]

(2) A young carer grant is to be given as money (subject to paragraph (3)).

(3) If—

(a) the Scottish Ministers offer to give an applicant some or all of the value of a young carer grant in a form other than money, and

(b) the applicant agrees to be given the grant in that form,

the grant is to be given in that form, unless the applicant withdraws agreement before the grant is given.

AMENDMENTS

1. Carer's Allowance Supplement and Young Carer Grants (Residence Requirements and Procedural Provisions) (EU Exit) (Scotland) Regulations 2020 (SSI 2020/475) reg.11(5) (December 24, 2020).

GENERAL NOTE

The young carer grant is paid as an annual payment. Until April 1,   1.310
2020 it was paid at the rate provided in this regulation. From that date it has been the sum of £305.10. This increase was made in accordance with the duty to have regard to the rate of inflation provided for in s. 77 (now s.86A) of the Social Security (Scotland) Act 2018.

The Carer's Allowance (Coronavirus) (Breaks in Care) (Scotland) Regulations 2020

(SSI 2020/117, as amended)

Made: 1st April 2020

Laid before the Scottish Parliament: 2nd April 2020

Coming into force: 3rd April 2020

The Scottish Ministers make the following Regulations in exercise of the powers conferred by sections 70(8) and 175(1) and (3) of the Social Security Contributions and Benefits Act 1992 and all other powers enabling them to do so.

Citation, commencement and interpretation

1.311   **1.**—(1) These Regulations may be cited as the Carer's Allowance (Coronavirus) (Breaks in Care) (Scotland) Regulations 2020 and come into force on 3 April 2020.

(2) In these Regulations—

"carer's allowance" means the allowance paid under section 70 of the Social Security Contributions and Benefits Act 1992 (invalid care allowance),

"coronavirus" means severe acute respiratory syndrome coronavirus 2 (SARS-CoV-2),

"isolation" in relation to a person means separation of that person from any other person in such manner as to prevent infection or contamination with coronavirus, and

"severely disabled person" has the meaning given in section 70(2) of the Social Security Contributions and Benefits Act 1992.

Entitlement to carer's allowance while unable to care as a result of coronavirus

1.312   **2.**—(1) This regulation applies where a person in receipt of carer's allowance ("A") is temporarily unable to care for the severely disabled person ("B") in respect of whom the carer's allowance is paid by reason of isolation due to, or infection with, coronavirus of either A or B.

(2) Regulation 4(2) of the Social Security (Invalid Care Allowance) Regulations 1976 (circumstances in which persons are or are not to be treated as engaged or regularly and substantially engaged in caring for severely disabled persons) is to be read as if the words from "and" at the end of sub-paragraph (a) to the end of sub-paragraph (b) were omitted.

Expiry

1.313   **3.** Regulation 2 ceases to have effect [¹on 12 May 2021 at 2359 hours].

220

AMENDMENT

1. Carer's Allowance (Coronavirus) (Breaks in Care) (Scotland) Amendment Regulations 2020 (SSI 2020/350 reg.2(2) (December 3, 2020).

[¹Continued disregard of breaks in care related to coronavirus

4.—(1) This regulation applies where a person who is in receipt of carer's allowance ("A") on or after 13 May 2021 temporarily ceases to care for the severely disabled person ("B") in respect of whom the carer's allowance is paid.

1.314

(2) For the purposes of regulation 4(2)(b) of the Social Security (Invalid Care Allowance) Regulations 1976, there is to be disregarded any week in which A did not meet the requirements of regulation 4(1) of those Regulations in respect of care for B where—

(a) the break in A's care for B occurred between 3 April 2020 and 13 May 2021, and

(b) the break in care arose because of isolation due to, or infection with, coronavirus of either A or B.]

AMENDMENT

1. Carer's Allowance (Coronavirus) (Breaks in Care) (Scotland) Amendment Regulations 2020 (SSI 2020/350 reg.2(3) (December 3, 2020).

The Scottish Child Payment Regulations 2020

(SSI 2020/351)

Made: 3rd November 2020

Coming into force: 9th November 2020

The Scottish Ministers make the following Regulations in exercise of the powers conferred by sections 79 and 95 of the Social Security (Scotland) Act 2018 and all other powers enabling them to do so.

In accordance with section 96(2) of that Act, a draft of these Regulations has been laid before and approved by resolution of the Scottish Parliament.

In accordance with section 97(2) of that Act, the Scottish Ministers have informed the Scottish Commission on Social Security of their proposals, notified the Scottish Parliament that they have done so and made their proposals publicly available by such means as they consider appropriate.

ARRANGEMENT OF REGULATIONS

PART 1

INTRODUCTION

PART 2

INTERPRETATION *General*

Expressions about time and timing

Expressions about inter-personal relationships

PART 1

INTRODUCTION

Citation

1. These Regulations may be cited as the Scottish Child Payment   1.315
Regulations 2020.

Commencement

2. These Regulations come into force on the first Monday after the day   1.316
on which they are made.

Overview

1.317   **3.**—(1) Part 2 makes provision about the interpretation of these Regulations.

(2) Part 3 makes provision about eligibility and the assistance that is to be given to eligible individuals in connection with having responsibility for a child (referred to in these Regulations as a "Scottish child payment").

(3) Part 4 makes transitory provision.

(4) The schedule makes provision about matters of procedure for applying for, and determining entitlement to, a Scottish child payment.

PART 2

INTERPRETATION

General

References to the 2018 Act

1.318   **4.** In these Regulations "the 2018 Act" means the Social Security (Scotland) Act 2018.

Expressions about time and timing

When an application is to be treated as made

1.319   **5.** A reference to the day on which an application is made means the day on which an application is received by the Scottish Ministers or, as the context may require, the day on which the application is treated as having been made by virtue of regulation 25 or the schedule.

Meaning of "working day"

1.320   **6.** A "working day" means a day other than—
(a) a Saturday,
(b) a Sunday, or
(c) a day which is a bank holiday in Scotland under the Banking and Financial Dealings Act 1971.

Calculation of the age of a child born on 29 February

1.321   **7.** When calculating the age of a child born on 29 February for the purposes of these Regulations, in a non-leap year the birthday of the child is to be taken to be 28 February.

Meaning of "week"

8. A "week" means a period of 7 days. 1.322

Expressions about inter-personal relationships

Meaning of being responsible for a child

9. An individual is to be regarded as responsible for a child on a day 1.323 only if at least one or more of the following statements is true—
(a) the child is a dependant of the individual on that day,
(b) the child is a dependant of the individual's partner on that day.

Meaning of "partner"

10. A person ("A") is the partner of another person ("B") on a day 1.324 only if, on that day, A and B would be regarded as a couple for the purposes of Part 1 of the Welfare Reform Act 2012 (see section 39 of that Act).

Meaning of "kinship carer"

11. A person is a kinship carer for a child on a day if— 1.325
(a) the person is a qualifying person in relation to the child within the meaning of section 72(2) of the Children and Young People (Scotland) Act 2014, and
(b) on that day, the child lives with the person (exclusively or predominantly) under the terms of—
  (i) a kinship care order as defined in section 72(1) of the Children and Young People (Scotland) Act 2014, or
  (ii) an agreement between the person, the person's partner or both of them and—
    (aa) a local authority by which the child is looked after within the meaning of section 17(6) of the Children (Scotland) Act 1995,
    (bb) a local authority in England or Wales by which the child is looked after within the meaning of section 105(4) of the Children Act 1989, or
    (cc) an authority in Northern Ireland by which the child is looked after within the meaning of article 25 of the Children (Northern Ireland) Order 1995.

Meaning of "dependant"

12.—(1) A child is to be regarded as a dependant of a person on a day 1.326 only if—
(a) paragraph (2) applies, or
(b) on that day the person is a kinship carer for the child.
(2) This paragraph applies if—
(a) the person has been awarded—
  (i) child tax credit, child benefit or state pension credit for the day in question (or for a period that includes that day), or

(ii) universal credit for an assessment period that includes the day in question, and

(b) the child is recognised to be a child for whom the person has responsibility in terms of that award of assistance.

(3) It is immaterial for the purpose of this regulation that the award of assistance to that person referred to in paragraph (2) does not include any amount in respect of the child due to a rule that restricts the number of dependants in respect of whom the person can be given that type of assistance.

Expressions about social security assistance

Meaning of determination of entitlement to a Scottish child payment

1.327   **13.**—(1) Unless the context otherwise requires, references in these Regulations to a determination of an individual's entitlement to a Scottish child payment are to a determination made—

(a) by the Scottish Ministers—
    (i) under paragraph 3 of the schedule, or
    (ii) (following a request for a re-determination) under paragraph 16 of the schedule,

(b) by the First-Tier Tribunal for Scotland—
    (i) under paragraph 22 of the schedule in an appeal against a determination made by the Scottish Ministers, or
    (ii) (subsequent to such an appeal) under its Tribunals Act powers,

(c) by the Upper Tribunal for Scotland under its Tribunals Act powers (subsequent to an appeal against, or following a review of, a decision of the First-tier Tribunal).

(2) In this regulation, "Tribunals Act powers" means powers under Part 6 (review or appeal of decisions) of the Tribunals (Scotland) Act 2014.

(3) A determination of an individual's entitlement to a Scottish child payment consists of—

(a) a decision about whether or not the eligibility rules specified in regulation 18 are satisfied in the individual's case,

(b) if those rules are satisfied, a decision (taken in accordance with these Regulations) about what assistance the individual is entitled to be given, and

(c) if the determination is to be made on the basis that the individual has ongoing entitlement to a Scottish child payment, a decision about what assistance the determination is to entitle the individual to be given in the future.

Meaning of references to specified kinds of assistance

1.328   **14.** For the purposes of these Regulations, references to a kind of assistance specified in this regulation are to—

(a) child tax credit under the Tax Credits Act 2002,
(b) income-based jobseeker's allowance under the Jobseekers Act 1995,
(c) income-related employment and support allowance under Part 1 of the Welfare Reform Act 2007,
(d) income support under Part VII of the Social Security Contributions and Benefits Act 1992,
(e) state pension credit under the State Pension Credit Act 2002,
(f) universal credit under Part 1 of the Welfare Reform Act 2012,
(g) working tax credit under the Tax Credits Act 2002.

Meaning of references to assistance being awarded

15.—(1) An individual is not to be regarded as having been awarded 1.329 a kind of assistance specified in regulation 14 for a day or a period if the award was made in error (whether or not induced by the individual).

(2) For the avoidance of doubt, an individual is to be regarded as having been awarded assistance for a day or period even if the sum awarded is reduced to £0 as a result of a sanction.

Meaning of "assessment period" in relation to universal credit

16. "Assessment period" means a period in respect of which universal 1.330 credit may be payable to the individual in question in accordance with section 7 of the Welfare Reform Act 2012.

PART 3

ELIGIBILITY AND ASSISTANCE TO BE GIVEN

Duty to give assistance

17. The Scottish Ministers must give an individual whatever assistance 1.331 the individual is entitled to be given under a determination of the individual's entitlement to a Scottish child payment.

Eligibility for a Scottish child payment

18. An individual is eligible for a Scottish child payment in respect of 1.332 a child if—
(a) the individual has made an application for the payment (or an application is treated as having been made by the individual by virtue of a provision in the schedule requiring the Scottish Ministers to make a determination without application in the individual's case),
(b) the child is under 6 years of age on the day the application is made,

    (c) no other individual has received, or is due to receive, a Scottish child payment in respect of the child and the period that the payment will cover (other than in circumstances where paragraph 10(1)(b) of the schedule applies),

    (d) the individual is ordinarily resident in Scotland on the day the application is made,

    (e) the individual is responsible for the child on the day the application is made, and

    (f) the individual has been awarded, for the day the application is made (or for a period or universal credit assessment period which includes that day), assistance of a kind specified in regulation 14.

Ongoing entitlement

1.333   **19.**—(1) A determination of an individual's entitlement to a Scottish child payment in respect of a child and a week may be made on the basis that the individual has an ongoing entitlement to a Scottish child payment.

(2) A determination of ongoing entitlement is made on the basis that the individual will continue to be entitled to a Scottish child payment in respect of that child in each subsequent week until—

    (a) the week following any week in which the individual ceases to have responsibility for the child,

    (b) the week following that in which the child attains the age of 6 years,

    (c) the week following any week in which the individual ceases to be ordinarily resident in Scotland,

    (d) any week in which no award of assistance of a kind specified in regulation 14 is made to the individual for any day in that week.

Value and form of a Scottish child payment

1.334   **20.**—(1) The value of a Scottish child payment in respect of a child is £10 per week.

(2) A Scottish child payment may only be given as money, except as provided for by paragraph (3).

(3) Where an individual has a liability to the Scottish Ministers under section 63 of the 2018 Act (liability for assistance given in error), or under paragraph 29 of the schedule of these Regulations, the individual's Scottish child payment may be given (in whole or in part) by way of deduction, at a reasonable level, from that liability either—

    (a) with the agreement of the individual, or

    (b) without the individual's agreement, where the individual has unreasonably refused to agree to the assistance being given in that form.

(4) For the purpose of sub-paragraph (3), "reasonable level" means a level that is reasonable having regard to the financial circumstances of the individual.

Time of payment

21.—(1) Following a determination that an individual is entitled to a   1.335
Scottish child payment, the payment is to be given in accordance with
paragraph (2).

(2) Payments are to be made in respect of periods of 4 weeks, in
arrears, so that—
  (a) the first payment is made in the last week of the period of 4 weeks
      beginning with the day on which the application is made (the
      individual's first payment period), and
  (b) subsequent payments are made in the last week of each successive
      period of 4 weeks in which the individual continues to be entitled
      to a Scottish child payment for at least one week by virtue of
      regulation 19.

Individual's right to stop receiving assistance

22.—(1) An individual may request that the Scottish Ministers cancel   1.336
a determination of the individual's entitlement to assistance.

(2) On being requested to do so under paragraph (1), the Scottish
Ministers must cancel a determination—
  (a) with immediate effect, or
  (b) with effect from a later date specified in the request.

(3) An individual is not entitled, and is not to become entitled, to be
given assistance by a determination after it has been cancelled.

(4) A request under paragraph (1) must be made in such form as the
Scottish Ministers require.

(5) The Scottish Ministers must publicise any requirements for the
time being set under paragraph (4).

Later determination supersedes earlier

23.—(1) The latest determination of an individual's entitlement to a   1.337
Scottish child payment in respect of a given period or event supersedes
any earlier determination insofar as it deals with the individual's entitlement to a Scottish child payment in respect of the same period or
event.

(2) Accordingly the individual is not entitled, and is not to become
entitled, to be given a Scottish child payment in respect of that period or
event by the earlier determination insofar as it has been superseded.

PART 4

TRANSITORY PROVISION

Definitions—initial period

24.—(1) Regulations 25, 26, and 27 apply in respect of the initial   1.338
application period and the initial payment period.

(2) For the purposes of this Part—

(a) the "initial application period" means the period beginning with the day on which these Regulations come into force and ending on the day which falls 14 weeks after that day, and

(b) the "initial payment period" means the period beginning with the day immediately after the end of the initial application period and ending on the day which falls 4 weeks after that day.

When an application is treated as made—initial period

1.339   **25.** Any application for a Scottish child payment which is received by the Scottish Ministers during the initial application period is to be treated for the purposes of these Regulations as having been made on the day immediately after the expiry of that period.

Time of payment—initial period

1.340   **26.** Where an individual's first payment period (see regulation 21(2)(a)) would fall wholly or partly in the initial payment period, regulation 21(2) does not apply and instead—

(a) the first payment to the individual is to be made in arrears on such date within the initial payment period as the Scottish Ministers consider appropriate,

(b) subsequent payments to the individual are to be made in the last week of each successive period of 4 weeks in which the individual continues to be entitled to a Scottish child payment for at least one week by virtue of regulation 19.

Duty to notify—initial period

1.341   **27.**—(1) The Scottish Ministers may place a duty to notify them about a change in circumstances on a person to whom sub-paragraph (3) or (4) applies.

(2) The Scottish Ministers place a duty under paragraph (1) by informing the person—

(a) of the changes in circumstances which the person has a duty to notify them about,

(b) of the way in which the person is to notify them, and

(c) that failing to notify them about a change in any of those circumstances in that way, so that an individual's entitlement to a Scottish child payment is determined on the basis of information that is false or misleading, may be an offence under section 72 of the 2018 Act.

(3) This sub-paragraph applies to an individual in respect of whom an application for a Scottish child payment is made during the initial application period.

(4) This sub-paragraph applies to a person acting on behalf of an individual to whom sub-paragraph (3) applies in relation to any application for a Scottish child payment during the initial period.

SCHEDULE

PROCEDURAL MATTERS

PART 1

APPLICATIONS AND DETERMINATION OF APPLICATIONS

Requirement for applications

1.—(1) Except as provided for by Part 2 of this schedule, an individual is not entitled to 1.342
a Scottish child payment unless an application is made to the Scottish Ministers.

(2) If, before making a determination on the basis of an application, the Scottish
Ministers consider that the applicant—

(a) would not be eligible for the Scottish child payment applied for if the application
were treated as made on the day they received it, and

(b) would be eligible for the Scottish child payment applied for if the application were
treated as made on a day falling within the period of 14 days beginning with the day
they received it,

the Scottish Ministers may choose the day within that 14 day period on which the
application is to be treated as made.

(3) For the avoidance of doubt, an application for assistance must be—

(a) made in such form, and

(b) accompanied by such evidence,

as the Scottish Ministers require.

(4) If the Scottish Ministers reject something purporting to be an application for a
Scottish child payment, they must inform the individual concerned of—

(a) the decision to do that,

(b) the reasons for it, and

(c) the individual's right to appeal under paragraph 23(1).

Withdrawal of application

2.—(1) An individual who has made an application for a Scottish child payment may 1.343
request that the Scottish Ministers disregard it.

(2) If an individual requests that an application be disregarded—

(a) the Scottish Ministers are not to make a determination of the individual's entitlement to a Scottish child payment on the basis of the application, and

(b) accordingly, their duty to do so under paragraph 3 ceases to apply.

(3) A request under sub-paragraph (1) must be made in such form as the Scottish
Ministers require.

(4) The Scottish Ministers must publicise any requirements for the time being set under
sub-paragraph (3).

Duty to make a determination of entitlement

3. The Scottish Ministers must make a determination of an individual's entitlement to 1.344
a Scottish child payment—

(a) on receiving an application for a Scottish child payment from the individual, or

(b) when required to do so by Part 2 of this schedule.

Notice of determination

4.—(1) Having made a determination under paragraph 3 of an individual's entitlement 1.345
to a Scottish child payment, the Scottish Ministers must inform the individual—

(a) of the determination,

(b) of the reasons for it,

(c) of the individual's right under paragraph 14 to request that the Scottish Ministers
re-determine the individual's entitlement to the payment, and

(d) that the individual will have the right under paragraph 19 to appeal to the First-tier
Tribunal against the determination should the Scottish Ministers fail to deal with a
request for a re-determination in the period allowed for re-determination.

(2) The Scottish Ministers must fulfil their duty under sub-paragraph (1) in a way that
leaves the individual with a record of the information which the individual can show to, or
otherwise share with, others.

Multiple determinations involving the same child

1.346   5.—(1) Where the Scottish Ministers are required by paragraph 3 to make a determination of the entitlement of two or more individuals for a Scottish child payment in respect of the same child and the same period, the determination must be made in accordance with sub-paragraphs (2) to (4).

(2) For the avoidance of doubt, the Scottish Ministers must—

(a) make a determination of each individual's entitlement, notwithstanding that another individual may have previously been properly awarded a Scottish child payment in respect of the child (and continue to receive that payment), and

(b) in so doing, determine which (if any) of the individuals is to be entitled to a Scottish child payment in respect of the child.

(3) Where the Scottish Ministers decide that two or more individuals are eligible for a Scottish child payment in respect of the child and the period (see regulations 18 and 19), they must apply the rules in sub-paragraph (4) to determine which of the individuals is to be entitled to the payment.

(4) The rules are that—

(a) where only one individual has been awarded child tax credit, state pension credit or universal credit for the day, or assessment period that includes the day, in question (and the child is recognised to be a child for whom the individual has responsibility in terms of that award of assistance), that individual is entitled to the payment,

(b) where none of the individuals have been awarded assistance as described in sub-paragraph (4)(a), and only one individual has been awarded child benefit for the day in question (and the child is recognised to be a child for whom the individual has responsibility in terms of that award of assistance), that individual is entitled to the payment,

(c) where the individuals are kinship carers for the child, and none of them have been awarded any kind of assistance as described in sub-paragraph (4)(a) or (4)(b), the individual whose determination is to be made first is entitled to the payment,

(d) where one individual has been awarded child benefit for the day in question, and another individual is a kinship carer for the child, the individual who is the kinship carer for the child is entitled to the payment.

(5) For the purposes of sub-paragraph (4), the Scottish Ministers must determine the entitlement of the individual whose entitlement first fell to be determined in accordance with paragraph 3 (whether on receipt of an application from the individual or by virtue of Part 2 of this schedule) before making any other determination.

PART 2

DETERMINATION WITHOUT APPLICATION

Determination following official error resulting in underpayment

1.347   6.—(1) The Scottish Ministers are to make a determination of an individual's entitlement to a Scottish child payment (without receiving an application) where—

(a) they have previously made a determination of the individual's entitlement to the payment ("the original determination"),

(b) they establish that due to an official error the original determination was incorrect resulting in the individual—

(i) not being given a Scottish child payment to which the individual was entitled, or

(ii) being given a lower award than that to which the individual was entitled,

(c) the Scottish Ministers are not considering a request for a re-determination of the individual's entitlement to the Scottish child payment, and

(d) the individual has not appealed to the First-tier Tribunal for Scotland against the Scottish Ministers' determination of the individual's entitlement to the Scottish child payment.

(2) In making a determination required by sub-paragraph (1) the Scottish Ministers are to use—

(a) the information provided in the application that led to the original determination, and

(b) any other information they have obtained in connection with that application.

232

(3) Where a determination is to be, or has been, made without an application by virtue of this paragraph, references in these Regulations to the day the application is made are to be read as references to the day the application that led to the original determination was made.

(4) In this paragraph, "official error" means an error made by someone acting on behalf of the Scottish Ministers or on behalf of a Minister of the Crown that was not materially contributed to by anyone not so acting.

Determination following error resulting in overpayment

7.—(1) The Scottish Ministers are to make a determination of an individual's entitlement to a Scottish child payment (without receiving an application) where—

1.348

   (a) they have previously made a determination of the individual's entitlement to the payment ("the original determination"),

   (b) they establish that due to an error the original determination was incorrect resulting in the individual—

      (i) being given a Scottish child payment to which they were not entitled, or

      (ii) being given a higher award than that to which they were entitled,

   (c) the Scottish Ministers are not considering a request for a re-determination of the individual's entitlement to the Scottish child payment, and

   (d) the individual has not made an appeal (to the First-tier Tribunal for Scotland or Upper Tribunal) against the Scottish Ministers' determination of the individual's entitlement to the Scottish child payment, that has not yet been determined.

(2) In making a determination required by sub-paragraph (1) the Scottish Ministers are to use—

   (a) the information provided in the application that led to the original determination,

   (b) any other information they have obtained in connection with that application, and

   (c) any other information available to them that is relevant to their consideration of whether the individual is entitled to a Scottish child payment.

(3) Where a determination is to be, or has been, made without an application by virtue of this paragraph, references in these Regulations to the day the application is made are to be read as references to the day the application that led to the original determination was made.

(4) In this paragraph, references to an "error" are to—

   (a) an error in the performance of a function conferred by virtue of these Regulations, including a decision under regulation 13 being made—

      (i) wrongly, or

      (ii) correctly but on the basis of—

         (aa) incorrect information, or

         (bb) an assumption which proves to be wrong,

   (b) a new decision under regulation 13 not being made after an assumption on the basis of which an earlier decision was made has proved to be wrong.

Determination following backdated award of assistance

8.—(1) The Scottish Ministers are to make a determination of an individual's entitlement to a Scottish child payment (without receiving an application) where the circumstances in sub-paragraphs (2) to (5) apply.

1.349

(2) A determination has previously been made that the individual is not entitled to the payment in connection with the child ("the original determination").

(3) The Scottish Ministers establish that a backdated award of assistance of a kind specified in—

   (a) regulation 12(2)(a) is made in circumstances in which regulation 12(2)(b) applies, or

   (b) regulation 14 is made.

(4) The award referred to in sub-paragraph (3) ("the backdated award") is backdated to a day, or a period that begins on a day, that falls no later than the day on which the original determination was made.

(5) Had the backdated award been made before the original determination, a determination that the individual is entitled to a Scottish child payment would have been made instead.

(6) For the purposes of this paragraph, an award is backdated if it relates to a day, or a period that begins on a day, that falls before the day the decision to make the award was taken.

1.350   **9.**—(1) In making a determination required by paragraph 8 the Scottish Ministers are to use—

    (a) the information provided in the application that led to the original determination, and

    (b) any other information they have obtained in connection with that application.

(2) Where a determination is to be, or has been, made without an application by virtue of paragraph 8, references in these Regulations to the day the application is made are to be read as references to the day the application that led to the original determination was made.

Determination following change of circumstances etc.

1.351   **10.**—(1) The Scottish Ministers are to make a determination of an individual's entitlement to a Scottish child payment in respect of a child (without receiving an application) where an individual has ongoing entitlement to a Scottish child payment (see regulation 19) and they—

    (a) consider that a change in circumstances is likely to mean that an individual is no longer entitled to such a payment,

    (b) wish to make an award of a Scottish child payment in relation to that child to a different individual following a determination that that other individual is to be entitled to the payment in respect of the child (see paragraph 5).

(2) Where—

    (a) sub-paragraph (1)(a) applies, references in these Regulations to the day on which the application is made are to be read as references to the day on which the change in circumstances occurred or, if that is not known, the day on which the Scottish Ministers became aware of the change in circumstances,

    (b) sub-paragraph (1)(b) applies, references in these Regulations to the day on which the application is made are to be read as references to the day on which the Scottish Ministers determine the entitlement of the other person referred to in that sub-paragraph.

(3) In sub-paragraph (1)(a), "a change in circumstances" means a change in the circumstances of the individual in relation to any of the matters listed in regulation 18.

Determination following award of a Scottish child payment in respect of another child

1.352   **11.**—(1) The Scottish Ministers are to make a determination of an individual's entitlement to a Scottish child payment in respect of a child (without receiving an application) where—

    (a) the individual has been properly awarded a Scottish child payment in respect of another child and has an ongoing entitlement to that payment (see regulation 19),

    (b) the individual notifies the Scottish Ministers that the individual has responsibility for the child (see regulation 9), and

    (c) it appears to the Scottish Ministers that, unless there is a change in circumstances, the individual is likely to be entitled to a Scottish child payment in respect of the child.

(2) In making a determination required by sub-paragraph (1), the Scottish Ministers may use such of the information they have obtained in connection with the award referred to in sub-paragraph (1)(a) as appears to them to be relevant.

(3) Where a determination is to be made by virtue of this paragraph, references in these Regulations to the day the application is made are to be read as references to—

    (a) the day on which notification is given under sub-paragraph (1)(b), or

    (b) such earlier day not more than 4 weeks before that day on which the child was recognised to be a child for whom the individual has responsibility in terms of an award of assistance mentioned in regulation 12(2)(a).

Determination following cessation of award of a Scottish child payment

1.353   **12.**—(1) The Scottish Ministers are to make a determination of an individual's entitlement to a Scottish child payment in respect of a child (without receiving an application) where the circumstances in sub-paragraphs (2) to (5) apply.

(2) The individual has previously been properly awarded a Scottish child payment in respect of a child.

(3) A determination has subsequently been made that the individual is no longer entitled to the Scottish child payment in respect of that child due to a change of circumstances relating to the matters listed in—

(a) regulation 18(e) (where the individual ceased to have responsibility for the child), or

(b) regulation 18(f) (where no award of assistance of a kind specified in regulation 14 was made to the individual for any day in a relevant week).

(4) It appears to the Scottish Ministers that, due to a change in the individual's circumstances in relation to the matters referred to in sub-paragraph (3), the individual is likely to once again be entitled to a Scottish child payment in respect of the child.

(5) Not more than 12 weeks have passed since the determination referred to in sub-paragraph (3).

(6) Where a determination is to be made by virtue of this paragraph, references in these Regulations to the day the application is made are to be read as references to the day on which the change in circumstances occurred or, if that is not known, the day on which the Scottish Ministers became aware of the change in circumstances.

Determination to effect a deduction decision

13.—(1) The Scottish Ministers are to make a determination of an individual's entitlement to a Scottish child payment (without receiving an application) where the circumstances in sub-paragraphs (2) and (3) apply.   1.354

(2) This sub-paragraph applies where—

(a) regulation 20 allows a Scottish child payment to be given to the individual by way of deduction, or

(b) a Scottish child payment is being given to the individual by way of deduction, and the Scottish Ministers consider that may no longer be appropriate.

(3) This sub-paragraph applies where the Scottish Ministers have decided to—

(a) vary the amount of Scottish child payment to be given by way of deduction (including introducing a deduction, where the full amount of Scottish child payment was previously given as money),

(b) vary any period for which the individual's Scottish child payment is to be given by way of deduction that may have been specified in a previous determination of the individual's entitlement, or

(c) cease making deductions, and instead give the individual's Scottish child payment in the form of money.

(4) The Scottish Ministers are to make a determination (without receiving an applica-
tion) where an individual who is receiving a Scottish child payment by way of deduction under a previous determination of entitlement notifies the Scottish Ministers that the individual—

(a) withdraws their agreement to their Scottish child payment being given by way of deduction,

(b) wishes the Scottish Ministers to increase the amount of their Scottish child payment that is given by way of deduction,

(c) wishes the Scottish Ministers to decrease the amount of their Scottish child payment that is given by way of deduction (including ceasing the deduction), or

(d) wishes the Scottish Ministers to amend the length of any period referred to in sub-paragraph (3)(b).

(5) Where a determination is made in pursuance of sub-paragraph (1) or (4), references in these Regulations to the day on which the application is made are to be read as references to the day on which the determination is made.

PART 3

RE-DETERMINATION OF ENTITLEMENT

Right to request re-determination and periods allowed

14.—(1) An individual may request that the Scottish Ministers re-determine the individual's entitlement to a Scottish child payment, after being informed (in accordance with   1.355
paragraph 4(1)) of a determination by the Ministers of the individual's entitlement to such a payment.

(2) Unless sub-paragraph (3) applies, a request for re-determination is valid only if it is made before the end of the period of 31 days beginning with the day that the individual is informed (in accordance with paragraph 4(1)) of the right to make the request.

(3) A request for re-determination is valid if it is made after that period has ended, but before the end of the day that falls one year after the day on which the individual is informed (in accordance with paragraph 4(1)) of the determination, if the individual has a good reason for not requesting a re-determination sooner (see paragraph 15).

(4) A request for re-determination is valid only if it is made in such form as the Scottish Ministers require.

(5) If the Scottish Ministers decide that something purporting to be a request for a re-determination does not satisfy the condition in sub-paragraph (4), they must inform the individual concerned of—

(a) the decision,

(b) the reasons for it, and

(c) the individual's right to appeal under paragraph 23.

Late request for re-determination

1.356   **15.**—(1) It is for the Scottish Ministers, or on appeal under paragraph 23 the First-tier Tribunal for Scotland, to decide whether, for the purpose of paragraph 14(3), an individual has a good reason for not requesting a re-determination sooner.

(2) Where the Scottish Ministers have made a decision under sub-paragraph (1), they must inform the individual concerned—

(a) of the decision, and

(b) if the decision is that the individual has no good reason for not requesting a re-determination sooner, of—

(i) the reasons for the decision, and

(ii) the individual's right to appeal under paragraph 23.

Duty to re-determine and period allowed

1.357   **16.**—(1) On receiving a valid request under paragraph 14 to re-determine an individual's entitlement to a Scottish child payment, the Scottish Ministers are to make a determination of the individual's entitlement to that payment.

(2) The Scottish Ministers must aim to make that determination within the period of 16 working days beginning with—

(a) the day that the request for a re-determination is received by the Scottish Ministers, or

(b) in the case of a request for a re-determination to which paragraph 14(3) applies (late requests), the day on which it is decided by the Scottish Ministers or (as the case may be) the First-tier Tribunal for Scotland that the individual has a good reason for not requesting a re-determination sooner.

(3) If the Scottish Ministers fail to make the determination within that period—

(a) their duty to make the determination ends (but they may still make it), and

(b) paragraph 18 applies.

Notice of re-determination

1.358   **17.**—(1) Having made a determination under paragraph 16(1) of an individual's entitlement to a Scottish child payment, the Scottish Ministers must—

(a) inform the individual—

(i) of the determination,

(ii) of the reasons for it,

(iii) of the individual's right under paragraph 19 to appeal to the First-tier Tribunal against the determination, and

(b) provide the individual with a form that the individual can complete and submit to the Scottish Ministers in order to bring an appeal against the determination.

(2) The Scottish Ministers must fulfil their duty under sub-paragraph (1)(a) in a way that leaves the individual with a record of the information which the individual can show to, or otherwise share with, others.

Notice where re-determination not made timeously

1.359   **18.**—(1) Where the Scottish Ministers fail to make a determination under paragraph 16 within the period allowed by paragraph 16(2), the Scottish Ministers must—

(a) inform the individual—

(i) that the individual's request for a re-determination has not been dealt with within the period allowed, and

(ii) that the individual therefore has the right to appeal to the First-tier Tribunal against the determination under paragraph 3 which prompted the request for a re-determination, and

(b) provide the individual with a form that the individual can complete and submit to the Scottish Ministers in order to bring an appeal against the determination.

(2) The Scottish Ministers must fulfil their duty under sub-paragraph (1)(a) in a way that leaves the individual with a record of the information which the individual can show to, or otherwise share with, others.

PART 4

APPEALS

Right to appeal to the First-tier Tribunal against determination

19.—(1) An individual may appeal to the First-tier Tribunal for Scotland—   **1.360**

(a) against a determination under paragraph 16 of the individual's entitlement to a Scottish child payment, or

(b) in a case where sub-paragraph (2) applies, against the determination under paragraph 3 referred to in that sub-paragraph.

(2) This sub-paragraph applies where—

(a) having been informed of a determination under paragraph 3 of the individual's entitlement to a Scottish child payment, the individual has made a request for a re-determination under paragraph 14, and

(b) the Scottish Ministers have failed to make a determination under paragraph 16 in consequence of that request within the period of 16 working days described in paragraph 16(2).

Initiating an appeal

20.—(1) To bring an appeal against a determination, an individual must submit to the   **1.361**
Scottish Ministers the form provided under paragraph 17(1)(b) or (as the case may be) paragraph 18(1)(b) in relation to the determination.

(2) On receiving a form submitted under sub-paragraph (1), the Scottish Ministers must send—

(a) the form, and

(b) the information held by them that they used to make the determination in question,

to the First-tier Tribunal.

(3) Having complied with sub-paragraph (2), the Scottish Ministers must inform the individual to whom the determination in question relates that they have done so.

(4) In this paragraph, references to a form include a copy of a form.

(5) For the avoidance of doubt, the form that the Scottish Ministers provide under paragraph 17 and 18 need not be a physical form.

Deadline for appealing

21.—(1) An appeal under paragraph 19—   **1.362**

(a) may be brought without the First-tier Tribunal's permission if an appeal application is made within the period of 31 days beginning with the day the relevant event occurred,

(b) may be brought only with the First-tier Tribunal's permission if an appeal application is made after the period mentioned in sub-paragraph (1)(a),

(c) may not be brought if an appeal application has not been made within the period of one year beginning with the day the relevant event occurred.

(2) In sub-paragraph (1)—

(a) "the relevant event" means—

(i) in the case of an appeal against a determination under paragraph 16(1), the individual to whom the determination relates being informed of it in accordance with paragraph 17(1),

(ii) in the case of an appeal against a determination under paragraph 3 the individual to whom the determination relates being informed (in accordance with paragraph 18(1)) that the individual has the right to appeal against it,

(b) an appeal application is made when a form, that relates to the determination in question and has been completed to the extent that Scottish Tribunal Rules require, is received by the Scottish Ministers having been submitted in accordance with paragraph 20(1).

(3) The First-tier Tribunal may give permission under sub-paragraph (1)(b) for an appeal to be brought only if it is satisfied that there is a good reason for the application not having been made sooner.

First-tier Tribunal's power to determine entitlement

1.363   **22.** In an appeal under paragraph 19 against a determination of an individual's entitlement to a Scottish child payment, the First-tier Tribunal may—

(a) uphold the determination, or

(b) make its own determination of the individual's entitlement to a Scottish child payment.

Appeal to First-tier Tribunal against process decisions

1.364   **23.**—(1) An individual may appeal to the First-tier Tribunal for Scotland against a decision by the Scottish Ministers—

(a) to reject something purporting to be an application for assistance (see paragraph 1)),

(b) that something purporting to be a request for a re-determination does not satisfy the condition in paragraph 14(4),

(c) that an individual has no good reason for not requesting a re-determination sooner (see paragraph 15).

(2) An appeal under this paragraph—

(a) may be brought without the First-tier Tribunal's permission within the period of 31 days beginning with the day the individual was informed of the decision in accordance with these Regulations,

(b) may be brought only with the First-tier Tribunal's permission after the period mentioned in sub-paragraph (2)(a),

(c) may not be brought after the end of the period of one year beginning with the day the individual was informed of the decision in accordance with these Regulations.

(3) The First-tier Tribunal may give permission under sub-paragraph (2)(b) for an appeal to be made only if it is satisfied that there is a good reason for the appeal not having been made sooner.

(4) A decision by the First-tier Tribunal about—

(a) the outcome of an appeal under this paragraph, or

(b) whether to give permission under sub-paragraph (2)(b) for an appeal to be brought, is final.

(5) Accordingly (and without prejudice to the generality of sub-paragraph (4)), any such decision by the First-tier Tribunal may be neither—

(a) reviewed under section 43 of the Tribunals (Scotland) Act 2014(**19**), nor

(b) appealed against under section 46 of that Act.

Presumption for purposes of paragraphs 4, 14, 15, 17, 18 and 20

1.365   **24.**—(1) Sub-paragraph (2) applies in relation to the references in paragraphs 4, 14, 15, 17, 18, and 20 to an individual being informed of something by the Scottish Ministers in accordance with these Regulations.

(2) Where, in order to fulfil their duty to inform an individual of something, the Scottish Ministers send information—

(a) through the postal service to the last known address the Scottish Ministers have for the individual, or

(b) by email to the email address most recently provided to the Scottish Ministers by the individual for the purposes of these Regulations,

the individual is to be taken to have received the information 48 hours after it is sent by the Scottish Ministers unless the contrary is shown.

PART 5

FURTHER PROVISION ABOUT DETERMINING ENTITLEMENT

Obtaining information to make determination

25.—(1) Where the Scottish Ministers are determining an individual's entitlement to a Scottish child payment, and require further information in order to satisfy themselves about any matter material to the making of the determination, they may request that the individual provide them with the information within such period as they specify.   **1.366**

(2) If the individual fails to provide information requested under sub-paragraph (1) within the specified period the Scottish Ministers may, without further consideration, proceed to make the determination on the basis that the individual does not satisfy the eligibility rules in regulation 18, or (as the case may be) that the individual has no continuing entitlement under regulation 19.

Duty to notify change of circumstances

26.—(1) The Scottish Ministers may place a duty to notify them about a change in circumstances on a person to whom sub-paragraph (3) or (4) applies.   **1.367**

(2) The Scottish Ministers place a duty under sub-paragraph (1) on a person by informing the person—

(a) of the changes in circumstances which the person has a duty to notify them about,

(b) of the way in which the person is to notify them, and

(c) that failing to notify them about a change in any of those circumstances in that way may be an offence under section 72 of the 2018 Act.

(3) This sub-paragraph applies to an individual who is to be given a Scottish child payment under a determination made on the basis that the individual has ongoing entitlement to a Scottish child payment.

(4) This sub-paragraph applies to a person acting on behalf of an individual to whom sub-paragraph (3) applies in relation to any application for a Scottish child payment or the determination of the individual's entitlement.

Lifting of duty to notify change of circumstances

27.—(1) A duty to notify the Scottish Ministers about a change of circumstances placed on a person under regulation 27 or paragraph 26 ceases to apply when—   **1.368**

(a) it is lifted under sub-paragraph (2), or

(b) it stops being the case that a change in any of the circumstances to which the duty relates can affect someone's entitlement to be given a Scottish child payment.

(2) The Scottish Ministers may lift a duty placed on a person under regulation 27 or paragraph 26 by informing the person that the duty is lifted.

(3) Under sub-paragraph (2), the Scottish Ministers may lift a duty as it relates to some or all of the changes in circumstances which the person has a duty to notify them about.

Right to support

28.—(1) The Scottish Ministers must comply with an individual's wish to have another person ("a supporter") present during any discussion relating to the individual's entitlement to a Scottish child payment, unless the wish is unreasonable.   **1.369**

(2) The Scottish Ministers' duty under sub-paragraph (1) includes ensuring that any person acting on their behalf complies with such a wish, unless the wish is unreasonable.

(3) The role of a supporter is to support the individual in question during the discussion, and includes making representations on the individual's behalf.

(4) Nothing in this paragraph is to be read as requiring the Scottish Ministers to provide or pay for a supporter.

PART 6

RECOVERY OF VALUE OF ASSISTANCE

Liability for assistance given in error

29.—(1) An individual is liable to pay the Scottish Ministers the value of any assistance that was given to the individual due to an error (but see paragraph 30).   **1.370**

(2) For the avoidance of doubt, the individual's liability under sub-paragraph (1) is limited to the difference in value between—

(a) the assistance that was given, and

(b) the assistance (if any) that would have been given had the error not been made.

(3) If the assistance was given in a form other than money, its value for the purposes of this paragraph is what giving it cost the Scottish Ministers (excluding any administration costs).

(4) In this paragraph and paragraph 30, references to an error are to—

(a) an error in the performance of a function conferred by virtue of these Regulations, including a decision under regulation 13 being made—

(i) wrongly, or

(ii) correctly but on the basis of—

(aa) incorrect information, or

(bb) an assumption which proves to be wrong.

(b) a new decision under regulation 13 not being made after an assumption on the basis of which an earlier decision was made has proved to be wrong.

Exclusion from liability

1.371   **30.**—(1) An individual has no liability under paragraph 29(1) in respect of assistance given due to an error if the error is neither—

(a) the individual's fault, nor

(b) the kind of error that an individual could reasonably be expected to notice.

(2) For the purpose of this paragraph, an error is an individual's fault if it is caused or contributed to by the individual—

(a) providing false or misleading information,

(b) failing to notify the Scottish Ministers about a change in circumstances in breach of a duty to do so under regulation 27 or paragraph 26, or

(c) causing another person to do either of those things.

(3) In considering whether an error is of a kind that an individual could reasonably be expected to notice, the following are amongst the matters to which regard is to be had—

(a) the extent to which the value of the assistance given in error exceeds the value of the assistance that would have been given (if any) had the error not been made,

(b) whether any information given to the individual by the Scottish Ministers prior to, or immediately after, the assistance being given would have alerted a reasonable person to the fact that a decision had been, or was to be, made on the basis of incorrect information or a wrong assumption.

(4) In—

(a) sub-paragraph (2)(a), the reference to providing information includes making a statement,

(b) sub-paragraph (3)(b), the reference to information given to the individual by the Scottish Ministers does not include information explaining why the Ministers consider the assistance to have been given in error.

Consideration for debtor's circumstances

1.372   **31.**—(1) This paragraph applies to decisions of the Scottish Ministers about—

(a) whether to seek to recover money owed under paragraph 29, and

(b) the method by which money owed under that paragraph is to be recovered.

(2) In making a decision to which this paragraph applies, the Scottish Ministers must have regard to the financial circumstances of the individual who owes the money (so far as those circumstances are known to the Ministers).

Exclusion of other rights of recovery

1.373   **32.**—(1) An individual given assistance in error has no non-statutory obligation based on redress or unjustified enrichment to pay the value of that assistance to the Scottish Ministers.

(2) In sub-paragraph (1)—

(a) "non-statutory obligation" means an obligation that arises from a rule of law rather than an enactment,

(b) the reference to assistance being given in error is to be construed in accordance with paragraph 29(4).

Liability where assistance given for period after death

33.—(1) An individual's estate is liable to pay the Scottish Ministers the value of any assistance that was given to the individual under regulation 17 in respect of a period after the individual's death.   1.374

(2) For the avoidance of doubt, assistance may be regarded as having been given to an individual for the purposes of this paragraph despite being given after the individual's death.

PART 7

CORONAVIRUS—RELAXATION OF DEADLINES

Re-determination and appeal deadlines

34.—(1) A request for a re-determination is valid, despite being made after the expiry of the period described in sub-paragraph (3) of paragraph 14, if the person deciding whether the individual has a good reason for not requesting a re-determination sooner decides that the individual has a good reason that is related to coronavirus.   1.375

(2) An appeal may be brought under paragraph 19, despite the appeal application being made after the expiry of the period described in sub-paragraph (1)(c) of paragraph 21, if the First-tier Tribunal gives permission for the appeal to be brought under sub-paragraph (1)(b) of that paragraph on the basis of being satisfied that the good reason for the application not being made sooner is related to coronavirus.

(3) Any provision of Scottish Tribunal Rules that would (but for this sub-paragraph) have the effect of precluding an appeal being brought by virtue of sub-paragraph (2) is to be disregarded to the extent that it would have that effect.

(4) In this paragraph, "coronavirus" has the meaning given by section 1 of the Coronavirus (Scotland) Act 2020.

Timing of applications for Scottish child payment

35.—(1) Sub-paragraph (2) applies where these Regulations make an individual's eligibility for a Scottish child payment depend (in any way) on an application being made by a particular time.   1.376

(2) The person determining an individual's entitlement to the assistance may treat the individual's application as having been made by that time if satisfied that the reason for its not being made sooner is related to coronavirus.

(3) For the avoidance of doubt, the provisions of these Regulations that make a child's age at the time an application is made material to the determination of an individual's entitlement to a Scottish child payment are to be understood to make the individual's eligibility depend on the application being made by a particular time (namely the time at which the child ceases to be the specified age or fall within the specified age bracket).

(4) In this paragraph, "coronavirus" has the meaning given by section 1 of the Coronavirus (Scotland) Act 2020.

The Winter Heating Assistance for Children and Young People (Scotland) Regulations 2020

(SSI 2020/352)

Made: 3rd November 2020

Coming into force: 9th November 2020

The Scottish Ministers make the following Regulations in exercise of the powers conferred by sections 30(2), 41(4)(a), 43(5) and 52 of the Social Security (Scotland) Act 2018 and all other powers enabling them to do so.

In accordance with section 96(2) of that Act, a draft of this instrument has been laid before and approved by resolution of the Scottish Parliament.

In accordance with section 97(2) of that Act, the Scottish Ministers have informed the Scottish Commission on Social Security of their proposals, notified the Scottish Parliament that they have done so and made their proposals publicly available by such means as they consider appropriate.

The powers to make these Regulations are exercised together by virtue of section 33(2) of the Interpretation and Legislative Reform (Scotland) Act 2010. These Regulations are subject to the affirmative procedure by virtue of section 33(3) of that Act.

ARRANGEMENT OF REGULATIONS

Citation and commencement

1.377 **1.** These Regulations may be cited as the Winter Heating Assistance for Children and Young People (Scotland) Regulations 2020 and they come into force on 9 November 2020.

Interpretation

1.378 **2.** In these Regulations—
"the 2018 Act" means the Social Security (Scotland) Act 2018,
"backdated award" means an award of assistance for a day, or period that begins on a day, that falls before the day the decision to make an award is taken,

"child" means a person who has not yet reached the age of 16 years,

"child winter heating assistance" means winter heating assistance to which a child or young person is entitled,

"determination" means a determination of entitlement within the meaning of section 25 of the 2018 Act,

"Disability Living Allowance" means a disability living allowance under section 71 of the Social Security Contributions and Benefits Act 1992,

"qualifying week" means the week running from the third Monday in September in any year, and

"young person" means a person who is aged 16, 17 or 18.

Overview

3.—(1) Regulation 4 provides for eligibility rules for determining entitlement to child winter heating assistance.   1.379

(2) Regulations 5 to 9 make provision about matters of procedure for determining entitlement to child winter heating assistance.

(3) Regulations 10 and 11 make provision about the child winter heating assistance that is to be given to individuals who are eligible for assistance.

Eligibility rules for child winter heating assistance

4.—(1) An individual is entitled to be paid child winter heating assistance in respect of a qualifying week if, in respect of any day within the qualifying week the individual is—   1.380

(a) a child or young person,

(b) entitled to receive payment of the highest rate of the care component of Disability Living Allowance, and

(c) either—

    (i) resident in Scotland, or

    (ii) habitually resident in an EEA state listed in the schedule and has a genuine and sufficient link to Scotland.

(2) For the purposes of the rule in paragraph (1)(b), an individual is to be treated as being entitled to receive payment even if, throughout the qualifying week, regulation 9 (persons in care homes) of the Social Security (Disability Living Allowance) Regulations 1991 applies to the individual.

Determination of entitlement to child winter heating assistance without application

5. The Scottish Ministers must, without receiving an application, make a determination of an individual's entitlement to child winter heating assistance under section 30 of the 2018 Act by the end of December in any year where it appears to the Scottish Ministers from information available to them that the individual is likely to meet the eligibility rules in regulation 4(1)(a), (b) and (c)(i).   1.381

Determination following official error—underpayments

1.382   **6.**—(1) The Scottish Ministers must make a determination of an individual's entitlement to child winter heating assistance without receiving an application where—

    (a) they have previously made a determination of the individual's entitlement to winter heating assistance, and

    (b) they establish that, due to official error, that determination was incorrect resulting in the individual not being given an award of winter heating assistance to which they were entitled.

(2) In this regulation, "official error" means an error made by the Scottish Ministers or a Minister of the Crown that was not materially contributed to by anyone else.

Determination following official error—overpayments

1.383   **7.**—(1) The Scottish Ministers must make a determination of an individual's entitlement to winter heating assistance without receiving an application where—

    (a) they have previously made a determination of the individual's entitlement to winter heating assistance, and

    (b) they establish that, due to official error, that determination was incorrect resulting in the individual being given an award of winter heating assistance to which they were not entitled.

(2) In this regulation, "official error" means an error made by the Scottish Ministers or a Minister of the Crown that was—

    (a) not materially contributed to by anyone else, or

    (b) made on the basis of—

        (i) incorrect information, or

        (ii) an assumption which proves to be wrong.

Determination following backdated award of assistance

1.384   **8.** The Scottish Ministers must make a determination of an individual's entitlement to child winter heating assistance without receiving an application where—

    (a) a determination has previously been made that the individual is not entitled to child winter heating assistance, and

    (b) the Scottish Ministers establish that—

        (i) following an appeal, an award of the highest rate of the care component of Disability Living Allowance is made that is a backdated award, and

        (ii) had that award been made before the original determination, a determination that the individual is entitled to child winter heating assistance would have been made instead.

Periods for re-determination requests

1.385   **9.**—(1) The period for requesting a re-determination of entitlement to child winter heating assistance under section 41 of the 2018 Act is 42 days beginning with the day that the individual is informed, in accordance with section 40 of that Act, of the right to make the request.

(2) In relation to determining entitlement to child winter heating assistance, the period allowed for re-determination (within the meaning of section 43 of that Act) is 16 working days beginning with—

(a) the day that the request for a re-determination is received by the Scottish Ministers, or

(b) where the request for a re-determination is received by the Scottish Ministers later than the period prescribed by paragraph (1), the day on which the Scottish Ministers, or, on appeal, the First-tier Tribunal for Scotland, decide that the individual has a good reason for not requesting the re-determination sooner.

(3) For the purpose of paragraph (2), a "working day" is a day other than—

(a) a Saturday,

(b) a Sunday, or

(c) a bank holiday in Scotland under the Banking and Financial Dealings Act 1971.

Value and form of child winter heating assistance

10.—(1) The value of child winter heating assistance is £200.   1.386

(2) Child winter heating assistance is to be given in the form of money in a single payment.

Making payments

11.—(1) Where child winter heating assistance is payable in respect of   1.387
a young person, the Scottish Ministers may, where they consider it appropriate, make the payment to another person to be used for the benefit of the young person.

(2) Where the Scottish Ministers consider, for any reason, that it is no longer appropriate for a particular person who falls within paragraph (1) to continue to receive the payment, they may cease making payment to that person and pay it instead to the young person or another person.

Regulation 4

SCHEDULE

Republic of Austria   1.388
Kingdom of Belgium
Republic of Bulgaria
Republic of Croatia
Czech Republic
Kingdom of Denmark
Republic of Estonia
Republic of Finland
Federal Republic of Germany
Republic of Hungary
Republic of Iceland
Republic of Ireland
Republic of Italy
Republic of Latvia
Principality of Liechtenstein
Republic of Lithuania
Grand Duchy of Luxembourg

Kingdom of the Netherlands
Kingdom of Norway
Republic of Poland
Republic of Romania
Slovak Republic
Republic of Slovenia
Kingdom of Sweden
Swiss Confederation

The Carer's Allowance Supplement and Young Carer Grants (Residence Requirements and Procedural Provisions) (EU Exit) (Scotland) Regulations 2020

(SSI 2020/475)

Made 23rd December 2020

Coming into force 24th December 2020

The Scottish Ministers make the following Regulations in exercise of the powers conferred by sections 28(2), 81(8) and 95 of the Social Security (Scotland) Act 2018 ("the 2018 Act"), section 2(2) of the European Communities Act 1972, section 13 of the European Union (Withdrawal Agreement) Act 2020 and all other powers enabling them to do so.

In accordance with section 97(2) of the 2018 Act, the Scottish Ministers have informed the Scottish Commission on Social Security ("the Commission") of their proposals, notified the Scottish Parliament that they have done so and made their proposals publicly available by such means as they consider appropriate.

The Scottish Ministers have laid a response to the Commission's report on the proposals for the regulations in accordance with section 97(9)(a) of the 2018 Act.

In accordance with section 96(2) of the 2018 Act and paragraphs 2 and 2A of schedule 2 of the European Communities Act 1972, a draft of this instrument has been laid before and approved by resolution of the Scottish Parliament.

ARRANGEMENT OF REGULATIONS

PART 1

INTRODUCTORY

PART 2

CARER'S ALLOWANCE SUPPLEMENT FOR INDIVIDUALS RESIDENT OUTSIDE SCOTLAND

PART 3

YOUNG CARER GRANTS

PART 1

INTRODUCTORY

Citation and commencement

1.389   **1.** These Regulations may be cited as the Carer's Allowance Supplement and Young Carer Grants (Residence Requirements and Procedural Provisions) (EU Exit) (Scotland) Regulations 2020 and come into force on the day after the day on which they are made.

Interpretation

1.390   **2.** In these Regulations—
"qualifying date" means a date determined by the Scottish Ministers in accordance with section 81(3) of the 2018 Act,
"the 2018 Act" means the Social Security (Scotland) Act 2018.

PART 2

CARER'S ALLOWANCE SUPPLEMENT FOR INDIVIDUALS RESIDENT OUTSIDE SCOTLAND

Amendment of the Social Security (Scotland) Act 2018

1.391   **3.** Section 81 of the 2018 Act is modified in accordance with schedule 1.

Meaning of determination of entitlement to a carer's allowance supplement

1.392   **4.**—(1) References in these Regulations to a determination of an individual's entitlement to a carer's allowance supplement for the purposes of section 81(2A) of the 2018 Act are references to a determination made—
    (a) by the Scottish Ministers—
        (i) under regulation 5, or

(ii) (following a request for a re-determination) under paragraph 6 of schedule 2 of these Regulations,

(b) by the First-tier Tribunal for Scotland—
(i) under paragraph 12 of schedule 2 of these Regulations in an appeal against a determination made by the Scottish Ministers, or
(ii) (subsequent to such an appeal) under its Tribunals Act powers,

(c) by the Upper Tribunal for Scotland under its Tribunals Act powers (subsequent to an appeal against, or a review of, a decision of the First-tier Tribunal),

(d) by the Court of Session under its Tribunals Act powers (in an appeal against a decision of the Upper Tribunal), or

(e) by the Supreme Court of the United Kingdom—
(i) in an appeal under section 40 of the Court of Session Act 1988 against a decision of the Court of Session, or
(ii) on a reference made by the Court of Session under schedule 6 of the Scotland Act 1998.

(2) In this regulation—

"determination" means—
(a) a decision about whether the individual meets the conditions in section 81(9), (11) or (13) of the 2018 Act,
(b) if those conditions are satisfied, a decision about what assistance by way of carer's allowance supplement the individual is entitled to be given,
(c) decision about whether the individual's application for a carer's allowance supplement is possibly premature,

"Tribunals Act powers" means the powers under Part 6 (review or appeal of decisions) of the Tribunals (Scotland) Act 2014.

Determination of entitlement to a carer's allowance supplement for individuals resident outside Scotland

5.—(1) The Scottish Ministers are to make a determination of an individual's entitlement to a carer's allowance supplement for the purposes of section 81(2A) of the 2018 Act—   **1.393**
(a) on receiving an application from the individual, or
(b) when required to do so by regulation 7, 8 or 9, without receiving an application.

(2) A determination may be made under paragraph (1) in respect of any qualifying date before or after the coming into force of these Regulations.

(3) Paragraph (4) applies where there is a subsequent determination of an individual's entitlement to a carer's allowance supplement in respect of a qualifying date.

(4) Where this paragraph applies—
(a) the latest determination supersedes any earlier determination insofar as it deals with the individual's entitlement to a carer's allowance supplement in respect of the same qualifying date, and

(b) the individual is not entitled, and is not to become entitled, to a carer's allowance supplement in respect of that qualifying date by the earlier determination.

Timing of applications for a determination of entitlement to a carer's allowance supplement for individuals resident outside Scotland

1.394   **6.** For the purposes of regulation 5, an individual may make an application on, or at any time after, the first qualifying date on which an individual considers themselves to have been a person to whom section 81(2A) of the 2018 Act applies.

Determination of entitlement to a carer's allowance supplement without application for individuals resident outside Scotland

1.395   **7.** The Scottish Ministers are to make a determination of an individual's entitlement to a carer's allowance supplement under regulation 5, without receiving an application, where—

(a) it appears to the Scottish Ministers from information available to them that the individual is likely to meet the conditions in section 81(9) or (as the case may be) section 81(11) or (13) of the 2018 Act in respect of one or more qualifying dates,

(b) the Scottish Ministers have previously made a determination that an individual does not meet the conditions in section 81(9) or (as the case may be) section 81(11) or (13) of the 2018 Act in respect of a qualifying date ("the original determination"), and—

   (i) the Scottish Ministers establish that the individual has received an award of carer's allowance under section 70 of the Social Security Contributions and Benefits Act 1992,

   (ii) the award referred to in sub-paragraph (i) is backdated to include the relevant qualifying date, and

   (iii) it appears to the Scottish Ministers that, had the backdated award been made before the original determination, it is likely that a determination that the individual met the conditions in section 81(9) or (as the case may be) section 81(11) or (13) of the 2018 Act would have been made instead,

(c) the individual received a payment of carer's allowance supplement in respect of the most recent qualifying date pursuant to a determination made by the Scottish Ministers under regulation 5.

Determination following official error - underpayments

1.396   **8.**—(1) The Scottish Ministers are to make a determination under regulation 5 without receiving an application where—

(a) they have previously made a determination under regulation 5 of the individual's entitlement to a carer's allowance supplement, and

(b) they establish that due to an official error that determination was incorrect resulting in the individual not being paid a carer's allowance supplement to which they were entitled.

(2) In this regulation, "official error" means an error made by someone acting on behalf of the Scottish Ministers or on behalf of a Minister of the Crown that was not materially contributed to by anyone not so acting.

Determination following error—overpayments

9.—(1) The Scottish Ministers are to make a determination under regulation 5 without receiving an application where— 1.397
  (a) they have previously made a determination under regulation 5 of the individual's entitlement to a carer's allowance supplement, and
  (b) they establish that due to an error that determination was incorrect resulting in the individual being paid a carer's allowance supplement to which they were not entitled.
(2) In this regulation, "error" means an error in the performance of a function conferred by these Regulations which leads to a determination being made—
  (a) wrongly, or
  (b) correctly but on the basis of incorrect information.

Procedure

10. Schedule 2 makes further provision about matters of procedure for applying for, and determining entitlement to, a carer's allowance supplement for the purposes of section 81(2A) of the 2018 Act. 1.398

PART 3

YOUNG CARER GRANTS

Amendment of eligibility conditions

11.—(Amendments incorporated into SSI 2020/324 above) 1.399

Regulation 3

SCHEDULE 1

Amendment of the Social Security (Scotland) Act 2018

(Amendments incorporated into 2018 Act above)

Regulation 10

SCHEDULE 2

Procedural Matters: Carer's Allowance Supplement

PART 1

APPLICATION AND DETERMINATION OF APPLICATIONS

Form of application

1.—(1) An application under regulation 5 must be— 1.400
  (a) made in such form, and

(b) accompanied by such evidence as the Scottish Ministers require.

(2) The Scottish Ministers must publicise any requirements for the time being set under sub-paragraph (1).

(3) Once—

(a) an individual has applied for a carer's allowance supplement in respect of a particular qualifying date, and

(b) the Scottish Ministers have made a determination of the individual's entitlement to a carer's allowance supplement in respect of that date,

the individual cannot make another application for carer's allowance supplement in respect of that qualifying date.

(4) Despite paragraph (3), an individual may make another application for a carer's allowance supplement in respect of that qualifying date if the latest determination of the individual's entitlement to assistance in respect of that date states that the individual may make another application.

(5) If the Scottish Ministers reject something purporting to be an application for a carer's allowance supplement they must inform the individual of—

(a) the decision to do that,

(b) the reasons for it, and

(c) the individual's right to appeal under paragraph 13.

Withdrawal of application

2.—(1) An individual who has made an application for a carer's allowance supplement under regulation 5 may request that the Scottish Ministers disregard it.

(2) If an individual requests that an application be disregarded—

(a) the Scottish Ministers are not to make a determination of entitlement on the basis of the application, and

(b) accordingly, their duty to do so under regulation 5 ceases to apply.

(3) A request under sub-paragraph (1) must be made in such form as the Scottish Ministers require.

(4) The Scottish Ministers must publicise any requirements for the time being set under sub-paragraph (3).

Notice of determination

3.—(1) Having made a determination under regulation 5 of an individual's entitlement to a carer's allowance supplement the Scottish Ministers must inform the individual—

(a) of the determination,

(b) of the reasons for it,

(c) of the individual's right under paragraph 4 to request that the Scottish Ministers re-determine the individual's entitlement to the payment, and

(d) that the individual will have the right under paragraph 9 to appeal to the First-tier Tribunal against the determination should the Scottish Ministers fail to deal with a request for a re-determination in the period allowed for re-determination.

(2) The Scottish Ministers must fulfil their duty under sub-paragraph (1) in a way that leaves the individual with a record of the information which the individual can show to, or otherwise share with, others.

PART 2

RE-DETERMINATION OF ENTITLEMENT

Right to request re-determination and periods allowed

1.401   **4.**—(1) An individual may request that the Scottish Ministers re-determine the individual's entitlement to a carer's allowance supplement after being informed (in accordance with paragraph 3) of a determination by the Scottish Ministers of the individual's entitlement to such a payment.

(2) Unless sub-paragraph (3) applies, a request for re-determination is valid only if it is made before the end of the period of 31 days beginning with the day that the individual is informed (in accordance with paragraph 3) of the right to make the request.

(3) A request for re-determination is valid if it is made after that period has ended, but before the end of the day that falls one year after the day on which the individual is informed (in accordance with paragraph 3) of the determination, if the individual has a good reason for not requesting a re-determination sooner (see paragraph 5).

(4) A request for re-determination is valid only if it is made in such form as the Scottish Ministers require.

(5) The Scottish Ministers must publicise any requirement for the time being set under sub-paragraph (4).

(6) If the Scottish Ministers decide that something purporting to be a request for a re-determination does not satisfy the condition in sub-paragraph (4), they must inform the individual concerned of—

(a) the decision,

(b) the reasons for it, and

(c) the individual's right to appeal under paragraph 13.

Late request for re-determination

5.—(1) It is for—

(a) the Scottish Ministers, or

(b) on appeal under paragraph 13 the First-tier Tribunal for Scotland,

to decide whether, for the purpose of paragraph 4(3), an individual has a good reason for not requesting a re-determination sooner.

(2) Where the Scottish Ministers have made a decision under sub-paragraph (1), they must inform the individual concerned—

(a) of the decision, and

(b) if the decision is that the individual has no good reason for not requesting a re-determination sooner, of—

(i) the reasons for the decision, and

(ii) the individual's right to appeal under paragraph 13.

Duty to re-determine and period allowed

6.—(1) On receiving a valid request under paragraph 4 to re-determine an individual's entitlement to a carer's allowance supplement the Scottish Ministers are to make a determination of the individual's entitlement to that payment.

(2) The Scottish Ministers must aim to make that determination within the period of 16 working days beginning with—

(a) the day that the request for a re-determination is received by the Scottish Ministers, or

(b) in the case of a request for a re-determination to which paragraph 4(3) applies (late requests), the day on which it is decided by the Scottish Ministers or (as the case may be) the First-tier Tribunal for Scotland that the individual has a good reason for not requesting a re-determination sooner.

(3) If the Scottish Ministers fail to make the determination within that period—

(a) their duty to make the determination ends (but they may still make it), and

(b) paragraph 8 applies.

(4) For the purpose of sub-paragraph (2), a "working day" is a day other than—

(a) a Saturday

(b) a Sunday, or

(c) a bank holiday in Scotland under the Banking and Financial Dealings Act 1971.

Notice of re-determination

7.—(1) Having made a determination under paragraph 6 of an individual's entitlement to a carers allowance supplement, the Scottish Ministers must—

(a) inform the individual—

(i) of the determination,

(ii) of the reasons for it,

(iii) of the individual's right to appeal to the First-tier Tribunal under regulation 9 against the determination, and

(b) provide the individual with a form that the individual can complete and submit to the Scottish Ministers in order to bring an appeal against the determination.

(2) The Scottish Ministers must fulfil their duty under sub-paragraph (1)(a) in a way that leaves the individual with a record of the information which the individual can show to, or otherwise share with, others.

Notice where re-determination not made timeously

8.—(1) Where the Scottish Ministers fail to make a determination under paragraph 6 within the period allowed by paragraph 6(2), the Scottish Ministers must—
(a) inform the individual—
    (i) that the individual's request for a re-determination has not been dealt with within the period allowed, and
    (ii) that the individual therefore has the right to appeal to the First-tier Tribunal against the determination under regulation 5 which prompted the request for a re-determination, and
(b) provide the individual with a form that the individual can complete and submit to the Scottish Ministers in order to bring an appeal against the determination.
(2) The Scottish Ministers must fulfil their duty under sub-paragraph (1)(a) in a way that leaves the individual with a record of the information which the individual can show to, or otherwise share with, others.

PART 3

APPEALS

Right to appeal to First-tier Tribunal against determination

1.402

9.—(1) An individual may appeal to the First-tier Tribunal for Scotland—
(a) against a determination under paragraph 6 of the individual's entitlement to a carer's allowance supplement, or
(b) in a case where sub-paragraph (2) applies, against the determination under regulation 5 referred to in that sub-paragraph.
(2) This sub-paragraph applies where—
(a) having been informed of a determination under regulation 5 of the individual's entitlement to a carer's allowance supplement, the individual has made a request for a re-determination under paragraph 4, and
(b) the Scottish Ministers have failed to make a determination under paragraph 6 in consequence of that request within the period described in paragraph 6(2).

Initiating an appeal

10.—(1) To bring an appeal against a determination, an individual must submit to the Scottish Ministers the form provided under paragraph 7(1)(b) or (as the case may be) paragraph 8(1)(b) in relation to the determination.
(2) On receiving a form submitted under sub-paragraph (1), the Scottish Ministers must send—
(a) the form, and
(b) the information held by them that they used to make the determination in question, to the First-tier Tribunal.
(3) Having complied with sub-paragraph (2), the Scottish Ministers must inform the individual to whom the determination in question relates that they have done so.
(4) In this paragraph, references to a form include a copy of a form.
(5) For the avoidance of doubt, the form that the Scottish Ministers provide under paragraph 7 or 8 need not be a physical form.

Deadline for appealing

11.—(1) An appeal under paragraph 9—
(a) may be brought without the First-tier Tribunal's permission if an appeal application is made within the period of 31 days beginning with the day the relevant event occurred,
(b) may be brought only with the First-tier Tribunal's permission if an appeal application is made after the period mentioned in sub-paragraph (1)(a),

(c) may not be brought if an appeal application has not been made within the period of one year beginning with the day the relevant event occurred.

(2) In sub-paragraph (1)—

(a) "the relevant event" means—

    (i) in the case of an appeal against a determination under paragraph 6, the individual to whom the determination relates being informed of it in accordance with paragraph 7(1),

    (ii) in the case of an appeal against a determination under regulation 5, the individual to whom the determination relates being informed (in accordance with paragraph 8(1)) that the individual has the right to appeal against it,

(b) an appeal application is made when a form, that relates to the determination in question and has been completed to the extent that Scottish Tribunal Rules require, is received by the Scottish Ministers having been submitted in accordance with paragraph 10(1).

(3) The First-tier Tribunal may give permission under sub-paragraph (1)(b) for an appeal to be brought only if it is satisfied that there is a good reason for the application not having been made sooner.

(4) In sub-paragraph (2)(b), "Scottish Tribunal Rules" has the meaning given by section 68(2) of the Tribunals (Scotland) Act 2014.

First-tier Tribunal's power to determine entitlement

12. In an appeal under paragraph 9 against a determination of an individual's entitlement to a carer's allowance supplement, the First-tier Tribunal may—

(a) uphold the determination, or

(b) make its own determination of the individual's entitlement to a carer's allowance supplement.

Appeal to First-tier Tribunal against process decisions

13.—(1) An individual may appeal to the First-tier Tribunal for Scotland against a decision by the Scottish Ministers—

(a) to reject something purporting to be an application for a carer's allowance supplement (see paragraph 1)),

(b) that something purporting to be a request for a re-determination does not satisfy the condition in paragraph 4(4),

(c) that an individual has no good reason for not requesting a re-determination sooner (see paragraph 5).

(2) An appeal under this paragraph—

(a) may be brought without the First-tier Tribunal's permission within the period of 31 days beginning with the day the individual was informed of the decision in accordance with these Regulations,

(b) may be brought only with the First-tier Tribunal's permission after the period mentioned in sub-paragraph (2)(a),

(c) may not be brought after the end of the period of one year beginning with the day the individual was informed of the decision in accordance with these Regulations.

(3) The First-tier Tribunal may give permission under sub-paragraph (2)(b) for an appeal to be made only if it is satisfied that there is a good reason for the appeal not having been made sooner.

(4) A decision by the First-tier Tribunal about—

(a) the outcome of an appeal under this paragraph, or

(b) whether to give permission under sub-paragraph (2)(b) for an appeal to be brought, is final.

(5) Accordingly (and without prejudice to the generality of sub-paragraph (4)), any such decision by the First-tier Tribunal may be neither—

(a) reviewed under section 43 of the Tribunals (Scotland) Act 2014, nor

(b) appealed against under section 46 of that Act.

Presumption for purposes of paragraphs 1, 3, 4, 5, 7, 8 and 10

14.—(1) Sub-paragraph (2) applies in relation to the references in paragraphs 1, 3, 4, 5, 7, 8, and 10 to an individual being informed of something by the Scottish Ministers in accordance with a provision of these Regulations.

(2) Where, in order to fulfil their duty to inform an individual of something, the Scottish Ministers send information—

(a) through the postal service to the last known address the Scottish Ministers have for the individual, or

(b) by email to the email address most recently provided to the Scottish Ministers by the individual for the purposes of these Regulations,

the individual is to be taken to have received the information 48 hours after it is sent by the Scottish Ministers unless the contrary is shown.

Amendment of the Social Security Appeals (Expenses and Allowances) (Scotland) Regulations 2018

15.—(1) The Social Security Appeals (Expenses and Allowances) (Scotland) Regulations 2018 are amended in accordance with paragraph (2).

(2) In regulation 3(1) (payment of expenses) for the words from "by" in the second place where it appears to "before" substitute "by the Social Security (Scotland) Act 2018, by regulations made under that Act or by the Carer's Allowance Supplement and Young Carer Grants (Residence Requirements and Procedural Provisions) (EU Exit) (Scotland) Regulations 2020, before".

PART 4

FURTHER PROVISION ABOUT DETERMINING ENTITLEMENT

Obtaining information to make a determination

1.403 **16.**—(1) When the Scottish Ministers are determining an individual's entitlement to a carer's allowance supplement for the purposes of section 81(2A) of the 2018 Act—

(a) they require further information in order to satisfy themselves about any matter material to the making of the determination, and

(b) they may request that the individual provide them with the information within such period as they specify.

(2) If the individual fails to provide the requested information by the end of the specified period, the Scottish Ministers may, without further consideration, proceed to make the determination on the basis that the individual does not satisfy the conditions in section 81(9) or (as the case may be) section 81(11) or (13) of the 2018 Act.

Duty to inform about possible eligibility

17.—(1) Paragraph (2) applies if, in the course of their making a determination of an individual's entitlement to a carer's allowance supplement under regulation 5, it appears to the Scottish Ministers that the individual may be entitled to a type of assistance described in Chapter 2 of Part 2 of the 2018 Act or to assistance provided for by regulations made under section 79 of that Act.

(2) The Scottish Ministers must—

(a) inform the individual that the individual may be eligible for the assistance, and

(b) either—

(i) provide the individual with information about how to apply for it, or

(ii) if regulations made under section 52 or 79 of the 2018 Act so allow, ask the individual whether they should proceed with making a determination of the individual's entitlement to the assistance without receiving an application.

(3) Paragraph (2)(b)(ii) does not preclude the Scottish Ministers from requesting further information under paragraph 16 for the purpose of determining the individual's entitlement to the assistance described in paragraph (1).

Appointment of a person to act on behalf of an individual

18. Section 58 or (as the case may be) section 85B of the 2018 Act applies in respect of the determination of an individual's entitlement to a carer's allowance supplement under regulation 5 as it does to a determination of entitlement to assistance under Part 2 or 3 of the 2018 Act.

PART 5

CORONAVIRUS—RELAXATION OF DEADLINES

Re-determination and appeal deadlines

19.—(1) A request for a re-determination is valid, despite being made after the expiry of the period described in paragraph 4(3), if the person deciding whether the individual has a good reason for not requesting a re-determination sooner decides that the individual has a good reason that is related to coronavirus.   **1.404**

(2) An appeal may be brought under paragraph 9 despite the appeal application being made after the expiry of the period described in paragraph 11(1)(c), if the First-tier Tribunal gives permission for the appeal to be brought under sub-paragraph (1)(b) of that paragraph on the basis of being satisfied that the good reason for the application not being made sooner is related to coronavirus.

(3) Any provision of Scottish Tribunal Rules that would (but for this sub-paragraph) have the effect of precluding an appeal being brought by virtue of sub-paragraph (2) is to be disregarded to the extent that it would have that effect.

(4) In this paragraph—

"coronavirus" has the meaning given by section 1 of the Coronavirus (Scotland) Act 2020,

"Scottish Tribunal Rules" has the meaning given by paragraph 11(4).

Social Security (Scotland) Act 2018 (Information-Sharing and Scottish Child Payment) (Consequential Provision and Modifications) Order 2020

(SSI 2020/482)

Made 30th April 2020

Laid before Parliament 6th May 2020

Coming into force in accordance with article 1(2)

The Secretary of State makes the following Order in exercise of the powers conferred by sections 104 and 113(2) and (5) of the Scotland Act 1998.

ARRANGEMENT OF ARTICLES

PART 1

INTRODUCTORY

Citation, commencement and extent

1.405   **1.**—(1) This Order may be cited as the Social Security (Scotland) Act 2018 (Information-Sharing and Scottish Child Payment) (Consequential Provision and Modifications) Order 2020.

(2) This Order comes into force immediately after the coming into force of the first Regulations made under section 79 of the Social Security (Scotland) Act 2018.

(3) Except as provided in paragraph (4), this Order extends to the whole of the United Kingdom.

(4) Each amendment made by this Order has the same extent as the provision being amended.

PART 2

INFORMATION-SHARING

Information-sharing

2.—(1) This paragraph applies to information which is held for the   1.406
purposes of any HMRC functions—

(a) by the Commissioners for Her Majesty's Revenue and Customs, or

(b) by a person providing services to them.

(2) Information to which paragraph (1) applies may be supplied to the Scottish Ministers, or to a person providing services to the Scottish Ministers, for use for the purposes of a relevant Scottish social security function.

(3) This paragraph applies to information which is held for the purposes of a relevant Scottish social security function by the Scottish Ministers or by a person providing services to the Scottish Ministers.

(4) Information to which paragraph (3) applies may be supplied—

(a) to the Commissioners for Her Majesty's Revenue and Customs, or

(b) to a person providing services to them,

for use for the purposes of HMRC functions.

(5) Information supplied under this article must not be supplied by the recipient of the information to any other person or body without—

(a) the authority of the Commissioners for Her Majesty's Revenue and Customs, in the case of information supplied under paragraph (2),

(b) the authority of the Scottish Ministers, in the case of information supplied under paragraph (4).

(6) Where information supplied under this article has been used for the purposes for which it was supplied, it is lawful for it to be used for any purposes for which information held for those purposes could be used.

(7) In this article—

"HMRC functions" means any function—

(a) for which the Commissioners for Her Majesty's Revenue and Customs are responsible by virtue of section 5 of the Commissioners for Revenue and Customs Act 2005,

(b) which relates to a matter listed in Schedule 1 to that Act,

(c) which is conferred by or under the Childcare Payments Act 2014, or

(d) which is conferred by or under section 2 of, or Schedule 2 to, the Savings (Government Contributions) Act 2017,

"relevant Scottish social security function" is any function of the Scottish Ministers under the Social Security (Scotland) Act 2018 and any regulations made under it.

(8) This article does not limit the circumstances in which information may be supplied apart from this article.

PART 3

DISREGARDS AND EXCEPTION IN RELATION TO SCOTTISH CHILD PAYMENT

Amendment of the Income Support (General) Regulations 1987

1.407   **3.** (Amendment incorporated into updating material in Part III)

Amendment of the Jobseeker's Allowance Regulations 1996

1.408   **4.** (Amendment incorporated into updating material in Part III)

Amendment of the State Pension Credit Regulations 2002

1.409   **5.** (Amendment incorporated into updating material in Part III)

Amendment of the Employment and Support Allowance Regulations 2008

1.410   **8.** (Amendment incorporated into updating material in Part II)

PART II

UPDATING MATERIAL
VOLUME I

NON MEANS TESTED BENEFITS AND EMPLOYMENT AND SUPPORT ALLOWANCE

Commentary by

Ian Hooker

John Mesher

Edward Mitchell

Richard Poynter

Christopher Ward

Nick Wikeley

p.28, *Social Security Contributions and Benefits Act 1992 s.1 (Outline of contributory system)*

In sub-section (5) for the words "and statutory shared parental pay" 2.001
there should be substituted "statutory shared parental pay and statutory
parental bereavement pay" (Parental Bereavement Leave and Pay Act
2018, s.1 and Schedule, para.9) (January 18, 2020).

p.32, *Social Security Contributions and Benefits Act 1992 s.4 (Payments treated as remuneration, and earnings)*

As a result of amendments made by the Parental Bereavement Leave 2.002
and Pay Act 2018, s.1 and Schedule, para.10 (January 18, 2020), the
closing words of s.4(1)(a) should read:

"(v) statutory adoption pay;
 (vi) statutory shared parental pay; or
 (vii) statutory parental bereavement pay; and".

p.33, *Social Security Contributions and Benefits Act*

The note at 1.46 should list, as the omitted sections, sections 2.003
4A-19.

p.63, *annotation to the Social Security Contributions and Benefits Act 1992 s.44 (Category A retirement pension)*

Section 44 is modified to the extent necessary to give effect to a 2.004
Convention on Social Security entered into on February 1, 2019, by the
Government of the United Kingdom and the Government of Ireland
(Article 2(1) of the Social Security (Ireland) Order 2019 (SI 2019/622).
The Convention seeks to maintain, following the UK's withdrawal from
the European Union, certain UK social security entitlements of citizens
of the Republic of Ireland. This includes mutual recognition of social
security contributions for the purposes of UK retirement pension. The
Convention took effect on December 31, 2020.

p.73, *amendment to the Social Security Contributions and Benefits Act 1992 s.48 (Use of former spouse's contributions)*

With effect from December 7, 2020, reg.38 of the Marriage and Civil 2.005
Partnership (Northern Ireland) (No. 2) Regulations 2020 (SI
2020/1143) amended s.48A by inserting the following words at the end
of s.48(5)(a):

"or Part 3 of of the Marriage and Civil Partnership (Northern Ireland)
(No 2) Regulations 2020 or Part 3 or 4 of the Marriage of Same Sex
Couples (Conversion of Civil Partnership) Regulations 2014."

p.74, *amendment to the Social Security Contributions and Benefits Act 1992 s.48 (Use of former spouse's contributions)*

2.006　With effect from December 7, 2020, reg.38 of the Marriage and Civil Partnership (Northern Ireland) (No.2) Regulations 2020 (SI 2020/1143) amended s.48 by inserting the following subsection after subsection (5):

"(6) For the purposes of this section, a marriage is not to be treated as having terminated by reason of its having been converted into a civil partnership under Part 3, 4 or 5 of the Marriage and Civil Partnership (Northern Ireland) (No 2) Regulations 2020."

p.75, *amendment to the Social Security Contributions and Benefits Act 1992 s.48A (Category B retirement pension for married person or civil partner)*

2.007　With effect from December 7, 2020, reg.38 of the Marriage and Civil Partnership (Northern Ireland) (No.2) Regulations 2020 (SI 2020/1143) amended s.48A by inserting the following subsections after subsection (6):

"(6A) For the purposes of subsection (5)(b), a person is not to be treated as having ceased to be in a civil partnership by reason of its having been converted into a marriage under—
  (a) Part 3 of the Marriage and Civil Partnership (Northern Ireland) (No 2) Regulations 2020, or
  (b) Part 3 or 4 of the Marriage of Same Sex Couples (Conversion of Civil Partnership) Regulations 2014 where the civil partnership is a convertible Northern Ireland civil partnership as defined by regulation 2 of those Regulations.

(6B) For the purposes of subsection (5)(b), a person is not to be treated as having ceased to be married by reason of the person's marriage having been converted into a civil partnership under Part 3, 4 or 5 of the Marriage and Civil Partnership (Northern Ireland) (No 2) Regulations 2020."

p.81, *annotation to the Social Security Contributions and Benefits Act 1992 s.48C (Category B retirement pension: general)*

2.008　Section 48C is modified to the extent necessary to give effect to a Convention on Social Security entered into on February 1, 2019, by the Government of the United Kingdom and the Government of Ireland (Article 2(1) of the Social Security (Ireland) Order 2019 (SI 2019/622). The Convention seeks to maintain, following the UK's withdrawal from the European Union, certain UK social security entitlements of citizens of the Republic of Ireland. This includes rules for mutual recognition of social security contributions for the purposes of UK retirement pension. The Convention took effect on December 31, 2020.

p.83, *annotation to the Social Security Contributions and Benefits Act 1992 s.51 (Category B retirement pension for widows, widowers and surviving civil partners who attained pensionable age before 6 April 2010)*

Section 51 is modified to the extent necessary to give effect to a **2.009** Convention on Social Security entered into on February 1, 2019, by the Government of the United Kingdom and the Government of Ireland (Article 2(1) of the Social Security (Ireland) Order 2019 (SI 2019/622). The Convention seeks to maintain, following the UK's withdrawal from the European Union, certain UK social security entitlements of citizens of the Republic of Ireland. This includes rules for mutual recognition of social security contributions for the purposes of UK retirement pension. The Convention took effect on December 31, 2020.

p.98, *annotation to the Social Security Contributions and Benefits Act 1992 s.62 (Graduated retirement benefit)*

A Convention on Social Security, entered into on February 1, 2019, **2.010** by the Government of the United Kingdom and the Government of Ireland (given effect in UK law by Article 2(1) of the Social Security (Ireland) Order 2019 (SI 2019/622)), generally seeks to maintain, following the UK's withdrawal from the European Union, certain UK social security entitlements of citizens of the Republic of Ireland. The Convention includes rules for mutual recognition of social security contributions for the purposes of UK pension benefits. However, these rules do not apply for the purposes of graduated retirement benefit payable by virtue of any graduated contributions paid before 6 April 1975 (article 29 of the Convention). The Convention took effect on December 31, 2020.

p.219, *annotation to the Social Security Contributions and Benefits Act 1992 s.103(1) (Disablement pension)*

On the question of whether there is a need for separate claims for **2.011** separate accidents or diseases, see the analysis by Judge Rowland in *MH v SSWP (II)* [2020] UKUT 297 (AAC) at paras 14-20. Judge Rowland expressly declined to decide "whether a claim for disablement pension made in respect of one prescribed disease may, before it is determined, be treated as having been made, additionally or alternatively, in respect of another prescribed disease without a further, formal, claim having been submitted" (see para.17). However, the Judge expressed the view that "in practice, it may therefore generally be necessary for the claimant to identify any prescribed disease that he or she wishes the Secretary of State to consider, but it does not follow that he or she must do so by way of a formal claim or that the Secretary of State may not act on her own initiative to, say, consider a similar prescribed disease to one in respect of which a formal claim has been made" (para.18). Judge Rowland was prepared to accept that "the Secretary of State is entitled, although perhaps not required, to issue a separate decision as regards entitlement to disablement pension in respect of each prescribed disease that she has considered" (para.19). Judge Rowland concluded as follows (para.71; see also para.20) that:

"where the Secretary of State has made a decision awarding or disallowing disablement pension in respect of a particular prescribed disease, the First-tier Tribunal can only consider that prescribed disease if the claimant has appealed against that decision or it can treat the claimant as having done so, which requires that the claimant had a right of appeal against that decision."

See also, following *CI/420/1994, ED v SSWP (II)*[2009] UKUT 206 (AAC) and *DD v SSWP (II)* [2020] UKUT 302 (AAC). In both cases the claimant had an existing award of disablement benefit; in those circumstances a 'claim' for a new prescribed disease was treated as an application for a supersession of the existing award rather than a fresh claim as such. Any new assessment was therefore effective from the date of notification of the request, and entitlement could not be backdated three months as with a new claim.

p.223, *annotation to the Social Security Contributions and Benefits Act 1992 s.103(1) (Disablement pension)*

2.012   On *R(I) 4/03*, see Judge Rowland's observation in *MH v SSWP (II)* [2020] UKUT 297 (AAC) at para.14:

" . . . it appears to be clear from *R(I) 4/03* at [31] to [35] that a separate claim in respect of a prescribed disease is possible, and presumably necessary, if there has been a previous award of disablement benefit in respect of either another prescribed disease or an industrial accident, but that it does not necessarily follow that there needs to be a separate claim for disablement pension in respect of each prescribed disease before any final decision awarding (or disallowing) disablement benefit has been made."

p.227, *annotation to the Social Security Contributions and Benefits Act 1992 s.108(1) (Benefit in respect of prescribed industrial diseases, etc)*

2.013   Judge Rowland explained as follows in *MH v SSWP (II)* [2020] UKUT 297 (AAC) at para.10:

"10. The combined effect of section 108(1) of the 1992 Act and regulation 2(a) of the 1985 Regulations is that, in respect of any particular disease or injury, three issues arise before further consideration can be given to a claimant's possible entitlement to disablement pension. It is necessary for a claimant to show (a) that he or she was employed in an occupation set out in the second column of Schedule 1 to the 1985 Regulations ("issue (a)", the "relevant occupation" issue), (b) that he or she is actually suffering from the particular disease or injury set out in column 1 of that Schedule ("issue (b)", the "diagnosis" issue) and (c) that he or she is suffering from the disease "due to the nature of that employment" ("issue (c)", the "causation" issue)."

p.233, *annotation to the Social Security Contributions and Benefits Act 1992 s.113 (General provisions as to disqualification and suspension— reciprocal agreements)*

Following the withdrawal of the United Kingdom from the European Union, a more nuanced consideration is now required than simply whether persons from abroad are assisted "by the European Union rules" and reference should be made to the "New legislation" section and to the updating material in relation to *Vol.III* and *Vol.V.*   2.013.1

p.236, *annotation to the Social Security Contributions and Benefits Act 1992 s.115(3) (Crown employment—Parts I to VI)*

See further *MH v SSWP (II)* [2020] UKUT 297 (AAC) at para.68.   2.014

p.245, *amendment to the Social Security Contributions and Benefits Act 1992 s.148 (Entitlement of Pensioners to Christmas Bonus)*

With effect from 11.00pm on December 30, 2020, reg. 2 of the Social Security (Amendment) (EU Exit) Regulations 2019 (SI 2019/128) amended s.148 by substituting "a" for "any other" in subsection (1)(b).   2.015

p.250, *Social Security Contributions and Benefits Act*

After the note relating to Part XIIZC, there should be the following note: 2.016

Part XIIZD

Statutory Parental Bereavement Pay

171ZZ6.-171ZZ15. *Omitted*
See Vol. IV: Tax Credits and HMRC-administered Social Security Benefits

p.327, *annotation to the Pensions Act 1995 s. 126 (Equalisation of pension age and of entitlement to certain benefits and increase in pensionable age)*

In *R. (on the application of Delve) v The Secretary of State for Work and Pensions* [2020] EWCA Civ 1199, the Court of Appeal rejected a challenge brought against the equalisation of state pension ages for men and women, as provided for by s.126 (as amended) and connected subordinate legislation, which involves raising the state pension age for women born after April 5, 1950. The case was brought by two women who, at the date of the Court's decision, had state pension ages of 66 in   2.017

common with any man or woman born between October 6, 1954 and April 5, 1960. The claimants' challenge had been rejected by the High Court (Divisional Court) and the case went on appeal to the Court of Appeal.

The first ground of challenge was that the claimants had been subjected to discrimination, contrary to Article 14 of the European Convention on Human Rights, taken with Article 1 of Protocol 1 to the Convention. Article 1 provides that every person is entitled to the peaceful enjoyment of her possessions, and that no one is to be deprived of her possessions except in the public interest and subject to conditions provided for by law and the general principles of international law. The claimants drew attention to the staggered equalisation of state pension age, which divides the female (and male) population into cohorts by reference to date of birth, and argued that they were subject to a difference of treatment as compared with the cohorts for older women namely for those born between 6 April 1950 and 5 October 1954 (pensionable age falling between 60 and 66) and for women born before 6 April 1950 pensionable age of 60). On the basis that the claimants had established a difference of treatment, the issue under Article 14 was whether the difference was justified. The Court of Appeal held that there was no basis for impugning the High Court's conclusion that the legislation which equalised (and then raised) state pension age was justified. The legislation was operating in a field of macro-economic policy where "the decision-making power of Parliament is very great". The evidence of the UK Government, accepted by the High Court, was that there had been an urgent economic need for pensions reform and that, in formulating pensions policy, the Government had recognised the difficulties that women still face in building up adequate pension entitlement. The Court of Appeal agreed with the High Court's assessment that the Government's decision to strike the balance it did between various age groups, as expressed in the framing of equalisation cohorts, could not be described as manifestly without reasonable foundation. It was not therefore discriminatory contrary to Article 14 of the Convention.

The Court of Appeal also rejected the claimants' argument that the equalisation legislation was indirectly discriminatory on the ground of sex. The claimants had relied on Article 4 of the Social Security Directive which prohibits discrimination on the ground of sex, directly or indirectly, regarding, amongst other things, calculation of benefits and conditions governing the duration and retention of entitlement to benefits. The Court, however, accepted the UK Government's argument that Article 7 of the Directive applied, which provides that the Directive is without prejudice to the right of Member States to exclude from the its scope "the determination of pensionable age for the purposes of granting old age and retirement benefits". In particular, the claimants' argument that Article 7 does not permit progressive adaptation towards equalisation as opposed to temporary retention of differential pension ages, was rejected.

Finally, the Court of Appeal rejected the claimants' challenges to the High Court's findings that the steps taken by the UK Government to notify the claimants of changes to their pension entitlements were neither inadequate nor unreasonable. The High Court's finding was properly supported by the evidence before it of various measures taken by the UK Government to publicise changes to state pension age.

p.338, *Gender Recognition Act 2004—General Note*

Following the review and consultation carried out by the Government on possible reform of the Act, in a written statement to Parliament (September 22, 2020), the Minister (Liz Truss MP) indicated the Government's view was that the balance struck by the Act was correct. 2.018

p.454, *annotation to Pensions Act 2014 s.2 (Entitlement to state pension at full or reduced rate)*

Section 2 is modified to the extent necessary to give effect to a Convention on Social Security entered into on February 1, 2019, by the Government of the United Kingdom and the Government of Ireland (art.2(1) of the Social Security (Ireland) Order 2019 (SI 2019/622). The Convention seeks to maintain, following the UK's departure from the European Union, certain UK social security entitlements of citizens of the Republic of Ireland. This includes rules for mutual recognition of social security contributions for the purposes of state pension under the 2014 Act. The Convention took effect on December 31, 2020. 2.019

p.479, *annotation to Pensions Act s.30 Bereavement Support Payment (General Note—Forfeiture)*

But where the claimant has been found to be unfit to plead so that he is not charged with any criminal offence, the forfeiture rule does not apply at all. See the decision of Judge Mitchell in *On a reference under the Forfeiture Act 1982 in respect of W (GRB)* [2020] UKUT 155 (AAC). 2.020

pp.489-490, *amendment to Schedule 6 to the Pensions Act 2014 (Reduced rate elections: effect on rate of section 4 pension)*

With effect from December 7, 2020, reg.47 of the Marriage and Civil Partnership (Northern Ireland) (No.2) Regulations 2020 (SI 2020/1143) amended Sch.6 by inserting the following sub-paragraph in para.4 of the Schedule and numbering the existing provision in para.4, sub-para.(1) 2.021

"(2) For the purposes of this paragraph—
  (a) a civil partnership is not to be treated as having come to an end by reason of its having been converted into a marriage under Part 3 of the Marriage and Civil Partnership (Northern Ireland) (No 2) Regulations 2020;
  (b) a civil partnership is not to be treated as having come to an end by reason of its having been converted into a marriage under Part 3 or 4 of the Marriage of Same Sex Couples (Conversion of Civil Partnership) Regulations 2014 where it is a convertible

Northern Ireland civil partnership as defined by regulation 2 of those Regulations.

(3) For the purposes of this paragraph, a marriage is not to be treated as having come to an end by reason of its having been converted into a civil partnership under Part 3, 4 or 5 of the Marriage and Civil Partnership (Northern Ireland) (No.2) Regulations 2020."

p.659, *Social Security Benefit (Persons Abroad) Regulations 1975 reg.10C (Modification of Parts II and III of the Act, etc)*

2.022   With effect from December 31, 2020, the following amendments are made by the Social Security (Amendment) (EU Exit) Regulations 2019 (SI 2019/128), reg.4 and Schedule (as applied by European Union (Withdrawal Agreement) Act 2020 Sch.5 para.1(1)):

(a) in paragraph (1), in the definition of "prescribed area", omit "(other than the United Kingdom)";

(b) in paragraph (2)—

(i) in sub-paragraph (a), for "or a member State (including the United Kingdom)" substitute ", a member State or the United Kingdom";

(ii) in sub-paragraph (b), omit "(other than the United Kingdom)".

p.660, *Social Security (Persons Abroad) Regulations 1975, reg.11 (Modification of the Act in relation to employment on the Continental Shelf)*

2.023   With effect from December 31, 2020, the following amendments are made by the Social Security (Amendment) (EU Exit) Regulations 2019 SI 2019/128, reg.4 and Schedule (as applied by European Union (Withdrawal Agreement) Act 2020 Sch.5 para.1(1)):

(a) in paragraph (1), in the definition of "prescribed area", omit "(other than the United Kingdom)";

(b) in paragraph (1A)(b)(iv), for "or a member State (including the United Kingdom)" substitute ", a member State or the United Kingdom";

(c) in paragraph (2A)(d), for "or a member State (including the United Kingdom)" substitute ", a member State or the United Kingdom";

(d) in paragraph (2B), omit "(other than the United Kingdom)".

p.697, *annotation to Social Security (Disability Living Allowance) Regulations 1991 (SI 1991/2890) reg.2 (Conditions as to residence and presence in United Kingdom)*

2.024   The validity of the amendments made to the past presence test in 2013 has been considered again in the UT by Judge Ward in *TS v SSWP (DLA); EK v SSWP (DLA)* [2020] UKUT 284 (AAC). He finds that the amending regulations were made in breach of the claimant's human rights and has disapplied those regulations. In reaching this conclusion Judge Ward finds that the claimant's position as a child returning to the

UK after a period spent abroad was a matter affecting their status; he reaches a contrary conclusion to that of Judge Jacobs in the case of *FM v SSWP (DLA)* [2017] UKUT 380 (AAC); [2019] AACR 8 because he finds that in the intervening time since that earlier decision was made the concept of status has been widened. He finds also that the difference in treatment between a child suffering from disablement, who has remained resident in this country, and one brought back from abroad (in one case from New Zealand, in the other from Australia) could not be justified by the reasons given for that difference in treatment by the Secretary of State. The reason given was to effect savings in the social security budget. While the judge accepted that cost-saving was a legitimate aim of the Government, he found that as carried out it was manifestly without reasonable justification. As the case had been argued on the basis that it was the 2013 amending regulations that breached the claimant's human rights and those regulations that could not be justified, Judge Ward held that it was open to him to disapply only the amending regulations thereby reinstating the earlier, less onerous, past presence test.

In addition, the judge considered whether it was competent for him to consider the validity of the past presence test in its amended form under the requirements of s.149 of the Equality Act 2010—the Public Sector Equality Duty. He finds, after a full consideration of earlier authorities, as had Judge Wright in *A-K v SSWP (DLA)* [2017] UKUT 420 (AAC), that the UT has no jurisdiction in relation to breaches of the PSED, but in view of the fact that his decision might be appealed further, he went on to examine whether, if he had such jurisdiction, he would have found there to have been such a breach. In his view there was. This was contrary to the conclusion reached by Judge Jacobs in the *FM* case, but Judge Ward was provided with a great deal of further evidence regarding the preparation of the 2013 amending regulations alongside the Personal Independence Regulations that were being made at the same time. From this, it had become clear that no Equality Assessment had been prepared for the amending regulations and even the draft assessment that had been prepared for the PIP regulations was never in fact completed and was never submitted to the Minister for consideration.

p.744, *annotation to Social Security (Disability Living Allowance) Regulations 1991 (SI 1991/2890) reg.12(6) (severely mentally impaired—severe behavioural problems)*

The correct approach to the conditions prescribed in para.(6) is 2.025 considered in *XTC v SSWP (DLA)* [2020] UKUT 342 (AAC). The claimant was a 10-year-old boy on the autistic spectrum who had been denied mobility component at the higher rate. It was accepted that he met the conditions in s.73(3)(a) of the Contributions and Benefits Act (both the day and the night conditions) and that he also satisfied para.(5) of reg.12 (arrested development etc. affecting intelligence and social functioning), but the FTT that heard his appeal did not accept that his behaviour satisfied the conditions of para.(6). The FTT heard evidence from the boy's father that he had played with his penis in public at the supermarket, at school and in front of a neighbour's child. The tribunal found that this did not amount to "extremely disruptive behaviour", did not involve a risk of physical injury or of damage, and did not require intervention to be made regularly. Judge Church, in the UT took the view that, applying the test of extremely disruptive behaviour as explained in earlier cases, this behaviour was so far "wholly out of the ordinary" and would be so disruptive that it could not be regarded as other than "extreme". He remitted the case on this and other grounds.

While it might have been open for the FTT to have found on the evidence before it that there was no risk of physical injury or damage, emphasis seems to have been put by the representative of the Secretary of State on the fact that the child was described by his parents as "not a violent or disruptive child". Judge Church points out that there is no need for the behaviour that might lead to injury or damage to be violent. Clearly that is the case when intervention is necessary to prevent accidental injury. It is likely also that the evidence given by his parents meant that he was not deliberately disruptive whereas, his behaviour might disrupt the activities of others, including his parents, whenever intervention was required.

Judge Church gives further guidance on the matter of the regularity with which intervention is required. It is necessary in his view for the tribunal to ascertain the number and frequency with which incidents occur that satisfy all three conditions prescribed by the paragraph and then to determine if intervention is required regularly according to the ordinary meaning of that word.

This case is interesting also because reference is made to the introduction of video evidence to the FTT hearing. The claimant's father had wished to do that in order to show how large and powerful his son was and how much he had to be restrained. The record of proceedings had no reference to this matter at all. Judge Church points out that such evidence was competent under the Tribunal Rules (as to which see Vol III of this work) and that the record should have shown that the request had been made (he accepted the father's evidence to that effect) and that it should have recorded reasons why the tribunal had decided not to receive such evidence if that were the case. Equally, had they decided to receive the evidence reasons should have been recorded for doing so.

p.781, *annotation to Social Security (Personal Independence Payment) Regulations (SI 2013/377) reg.3 (Evidence from earlier DLA claim)*

2.026   The need for an FTT to adjourn and call for evidence that formed the basis of an earlier award of DLA has been considered again in *BH v SSWP (PIP)* [2020] UKUT 338 (AAC) by Judge Hemingway. This was a case where the claimant had been awarded the highest rate of the care component and the higher rate of the mobility component for DLA but had scored no points on being transferred to PIP. The FTT that heard his appeal awarded five points for the daily living component and none for mobility and hence dismissed his appeal. They gave as their reasons for not adjourning to obtain the DLA evidence that such evidence would have been five years old and that, in any case, the claimant had not requested that the evidence be produced when that question had been put to him when he made his appeal. Judge Hemingway concluded (though narrowly) that, in the circumstances of this case, those reasons were not a sufficient explanation of the decision not to adjourn. He points out that the nature of the claimant's disability (arthritis in his back and legs) was unlikely to have improved which meant that the five-year-old evidence might still be relevant. Though the waiver of his opportunity to request the medical evidence might be taken into account it should not regarded as conclusive of whether the FTT should decide to adjourn; but nor did the judge think that the FTT had done that in this case.

Judge Hemingway observed too, that the decision on the DLA claim to award the higher rate for mobility must have meant that the DM then found him to be "virtually unable to walk", a conclusion that could have a direct correlation to the Descriptors to be applied for the mobility component of PIP. The FTT had said that they found the claimant's description of his condition both in writing and before the tribunal, to have been "exaggerated". Judge Hemingway thought that although this "came close", it did not succeed as a sufficient explanation of the inconsistency between the awards. It could have been that the FTT thought that the claimant's condition had improved (though, as he had said, that seems unlikely) or that the earlier award had been generous. The case was remitted for a rehearing.

p.798, *annotation to Personal Independence Payment Regulations 2013 (SI 2013/377) reg.11 (General Note—redetermination of entitlement and need for ground for revision or supersession)*

The GENERAL NOTE to this regulation should have added to it refer-   2.027
ence to *BD v SSWP* [2020] UKUT 178 (AAC), where Judge Jacobs has confirmed the approach adopted in the earlier decisions noted there. In addition, *DS v SSWP (PIP)* [2016] UKUT 538 (AAC) has been reported as [2017] AACR 19.

p.807, *amendment to the Social Security (Personal Independence Payment) Regulations 2013 (SI 2013/377) reg.27 (Revision and supersession of an award after the person has reached the relevant age)*

With effect from November 30, 2020, reg. 2(1) of the Social Security   2.028
(Personal Independence Payment) (Amendment) Regulations 2020 (SI 2020/1235) amended reg.27 as follows:

For paragraph (2) substitute—
    "(2) Where the original award includes an award of the mobility component and is superseded—
    (a) pursuant to regulation 23 of the Decisions and Appeals Regulations for a relevant change of circumstance which occurred after C reached the relevant age; or
    (b) pursuant to regulation 26(1)(a) of the Decisions and Appeals Regulations, where—

(i) the application for supersession was made by C after C reached the relevant age, or

(ii) the supersession proceedings were initiated by the Secretary of State after C reached the relevant age,

the restrictions in paragraph (3) apply in relation to the supersession.".

And after paragraph (2) insert—

"(2A) In paragraph (2), "the Decisions and Appeals Regulations" means the Universal Credit, Personal Independence Payment, Jobseeker's Allowance and Employment and Support Allowance (Decisions and Appeals) Regulations 2013.".

Note the amendments made by these regulations apply only to England and Wales. The same amendments, coming into force at the same time have been made in respect of Scotland by the Social Security (Personal Independence Payment) Amendment (Scotland) Regulations 2020 (SI 2020/340).

GENERAL NOTE

2.029   This amendment has the effect of extending the restrictions imposed by paragraph (3) of the regulation so that it applies not only following supersession for a change of circumstances that occurred after the claimant reached the relevant age, but also applies to a supersession made at the request of the claimant or following intervention by the Secretary of State (usually by the receipt of evidence from an HCP) and where the application for supersession began after the claimant reached the relevant age.

p.824, *annotation to Social Security (Personal Independence Payment) Regulations 2013 (SI 2013/377) Sch. 1 ("aided" and "aid or appliance")*

2.030   *CW v SSWP (PIP)* [2016] UKUT 197 (AAC) has been reported as [2016] AACR 44.

p.825, *annotation to Social Security (Personal Independence Payment) Regulations 2013 (SI 2013/377) Sch. 1 ("prompting")*

2.031   The reference to *CPIP/1534/2015* should read *MB v SSWP (PIP)* [2016] UKUT 250 (AAC).

p.830, *annotation to Social Security (Personal Independence Payment) Regulations 2013 (SI 2013/377) Sch.1 (Activity 1—preparing food)*

2.032   *CW v SSWP (PIP)* [2016] UKUT 197 (AAC) has been reported as [2016] AACR 44. The reference to *AM v SSWP* [2015] UKUT 215 (AAC) should read *SSWP v AM* [2015] UKUT 215 (AAC).

p.833, *annotation to Social Security (Personal Independence Payment) Regulations 2013 (SI 2013/377) Sch. 1 (Activity 2—Taking nutrition)*

2.033   The reference to *AI v SSWP (PIP)* [2016] UKUT 512 (AAC) should be to *SA v SSWP (PIP)* [2015] UKUT 512 (AAC).

p.834, *annotation to Social Security (Personal Independence Payment) Regulations 2013 (SI 2013/377) Sch. 1 (Activity 3—Manging therapy or monitoring health condition)*

The case of *CM v SSWP (PIP)* [2020] UKUT 259 (AAC) raises the question, but does not answer, whether a foot balm product used by diabetics (amongst others) to soften skin on their feet, should be regarded as "medication" or as "therapy". The question was not answered because, before Judge Perez, the claimant abandoned that part of his appeal. The point was not without significance because, in his case, were the product to be regarded as medication it would score one point under Descriptor 3b(ii), but if it were therapy it could score two points under Descriptor 3c and that would have made the difference, for him, between benefit at the standard rate and benefit at the enhanced rate. Judge Perez thought no criticism should attach to either the claimant or his advisers because they were faced with an argument and 199 pages of supporting evidence from the Secretary of State in favour of its being medication. But the point remains open now for decision at an FTT. **2.034**

p.835, *annotation to Social Security (Personal Independence Payment) Regulations 2013 (SI 2013/377) Sch.1 (Activity 3—Manging therapy or monitoring health condition)*

The reference to *IM v SSWP (PIP)* [2015] UKUT 680 (AAC) should be *to SSWP v IM (PIP)* [2015] UKUT 680 (AAC). **2.035**

pp.838-839, *annotation to Social Security (Personal Independence Payment) Regulations 2013 (SI 2013/377) Sch.1 (Activity 3—Manging therapy or monitoring health condition)*

PE v SSWP (PIP) [2015] UKUT 309 (AAC), cited on p.838, has been reported as [2016] AACR 10. The reference on p.839 to *IM v SSWP (PIP)* [2015] UKUT 680 (AAC) should be *to SSWP v IM (PIP)* [2015] UKUT 680 (AAC). **2.036**

p.839, *annotation to Social Security (Personal Independence Payment) Regulations 2013 (SI 2013/377) Sch. 1 (Activity 4—Washing and bathing)*

CW v SSWP (PIP) [2016] UKUT 197 (AAC) has been reported as [2016] AACR 44. **2.037**

p.840, *annotation to Social Security (Personal Independence Payment) Regulations 2013 (SI 2013/377) Sch. 1 (Activity 4—Washing and bathing—cochlear implants)*

Two cases heard together by Judge Perez, *KT and SH v SSWP (PIP)* [2020] UKUT 252 (AAC), both concern claimants who were required **2.038** to remove the cochlear implants with which they were fitted while they were using a shower or bath. Without those devices neither claimant could hear an alarm that would warn them of either a fire or a burglary in the house. In both cases the argument was put that this required the presence of another person in the home to warn them of danger and would qualify them for two points under Descriptor 4c (needs supervision to be able to wash or bathe). Alternatively, if the risk could be managed by a visual alarm that would qualify for the same score under Descriptor 4b (needs an aid or appliance to be able to wash or bathe). Counsel for the Secretary of State had agreed that, in both cases, applying the test established in *RJ v SSWP (PIP)* [2017] UKUT 105 (AAC) the FTT had made an error of law in applying the test of whether a claimant could accomplish a task "safely" when they failed to explain why, given the claimants' inability to hear an alarm, that the risk created could reasonably or sensibly be ignored. Subsequently, they agreed also, that it would not be washing or bathing to an acceptable standard if the claimant were required to do so with the bathroom door open, thereby making it more possible to hear the alarm or possibly to see signs of the danger.

Rather than remit the cases for rehearing, Judge Perez substituted a decision of her own. In deciding not to remit the judge was mindful of the fact that typical FTT hearings are scheduled to be completed in 60 to 90 minutes. In rehearing these cases counsel for the Secretary of State had argued that the FTT should consider statistical evidence as to the likelihood of fire occurring, or of burglary, together with, evidence of the extent of harm to be expected in either case. In the judge's view this would be too onerous a task to be undertaken in the allotted time, but, in any case, she also took the view that neither an FTT, nor herself in reaching the current decision, should have regard to such evidence because it would mean that the risk to be assessed would vary according to the area in which the claimant lived as well as to the type and construction of the premises. In her view the ability for a claimant to succeed should depend only upon factors that relate to the condition of the claimant themselves and not to other external factors. This was not to say that every claimant who was required to remove their hearing devices was entitled to succeed on a claim such as this; it would still be necessary for the claimant to show the extent of their hearing impairment, whether they needed to remove the aid when showering or bathing, whether without the aid they were unable to hear a normal warning device and, consequently, whether it was necessary for them to have an aid or appliance or supervision whilst they were showering or bathing.

Judge Perez had been presented with extensive statistical evidence to show that the risk of harm from fire occurring in domestic premises was slight. For the period covered by that evidence the risk of domestic fires at which fire services had attended was 1 in 270,000. Counsel had argued that this risk was *de minimis*, or at least so small that it could reasonably and sensibly be ignored. The judge disagreed. She refers to the case of *R(A)2/89* in which Commissioner Monroe had decided that, in the case of a claimant who was tetraplegic, the risk to him from a fire in the home was such that it could not reasonably be ignored even if it was remote. Using that test, which she found to be consistent with the views of the panel of three judges in the *RJ* case, she found that the risk to claimants in the present cases was such that it could not reasonably or sensibly be ignored. Judge Perez goes on to find that on the evidence submitted by both claimants each should be entitled to two points under Activity 4.

In this decision Judge Perez has held that entitlement should not depend upon the different views that might be taken by an FTT of the degree or the acceptability of risk from fire, except in so far as there might be differences in the degree of the claimant's hearing impairment and the need for them to remove their hearing devices and the consequent need for aid or supervision. In all other respects, the risk from fire should be treated as unacceptable so as to make the act of showering and bathing unsafe. Other means of washing were not raised in these cases. Nor was it necessary for the judge to decide on risks arising from burglary because counsel had conceded that if the risk of fire made the activity unsafe the claimant was entitled to succeed.

Note that in this case the judge finds specifically (in para.149) on evidence presented on behalf of the Secretary of State, that a person without hearing impairment would be able to hear a normal alarm whilst showering with the bathroom door shut. This is important because were that not so it could be argued, on the same basis as in *CW v SSWP (PIP)* [2016] UKUT 197 (AAC) that an inability to hear an alarm while in the shower was not a measure of disability for the purpose of claiming PIP (*cf.* sitting on a bed while putting on one's trousers).

p.842, *annotation to Social Security (Personal Independence Payment) Regulations (SI 2013/377) Sch. 1 (Activity 5—Managing toilet needs or incontinence)*

PE v SSWP (PIP) [2015] UKUT 309 (AAC) has been reported as 2.039
[2016] AACR 10.

p.846, *annotation to Social Security (Personal Independence Payment) Regulations (SI 2013/377) Sch.1 (Activity 7—Communicating verbally)*

PE v SSWP (PIP) [2015] UKUT 309 (AAC) has been reported as 2.040
[2016] AACR 10. The reference to *GJ v SSWP (PIP)* [2016] UKUT 8 (AAC) should be to *SSWP v GJ (PIP)* [2016] UKUT 8 (AAC).

p.852, *annotation to Social Security (Personal Independence Payment) Regulations (SI 2013/377) Sch.1 (Activity 9—Engaging with other people face to face)*

The reference to *AM v SSWP (PIP)* [215] UKUT 215 (AAC) at the 2.041
top of the page should be to *SSWP v AM (PIP)* [2015] UKUT 215 (AAC).

p.853, *annotation to Social Security (Personal Independence Payment) Regulations (SI 2013/377) Sch.1 (Activity 9—Engaging with other people face to face—relationship with reg.4(2A))*

2.042   The relationship between this Activity, in particular Descriptor 9d, and reg.4(2A) has been considered again in *JT v SSWP (PIP)* [2020] UKUT 186 (AAC). The claimant suffered from paranoid schizophrenia and although he had been well controlled for a number of years still had difficulty in meeting with other people because of anxiety and stress. In the FTT the claimant had been awarded 4 points under Descriptor 9c. He appealed on the ground that the FTT had not dealt adequately with his claim under Descriptor 9d. Evidence found by the FTT suggested that he met occasionally with people to whom he was known including some students and a neighbour, and that when accompanied by his mother he was able to attend his doctor's surgery, at the HCP interview and on two occasions at a FTT hearing, (though he did not attend at the hearing from which he was appealing). Judge Rowland deals at some length with the relationship between Activity 9 and reg.4(2A). He begins by reminding us that the provisions in reg.4(2A) were written originally to appear in the *Assessment Guide* but were moved by amending regulations that came into force at the same time as the main regulations. That may explain, he suggests, why they might have been written without the same attention to linguistic precision and may explain the ill-fit that there is sometimes between the regulation and the Activities. In the judge's view neither the words of reg.4(2A) nor those of Activity 9 can be read in a literal sense but must be approached in a way that gives reasonable effect to both. He rejects the possibility that the words might be read so that, having concluded that a claimant "cannot" form a relationship safely and satisfactorily but for a reason other than those specified in Descriptor 9d, he could then fail to score under any other part of Activity 9 because those Descriptors require that the claimant "can" form a relationship albeit with help or support. Activity 9d and reg 4(2A) must be read, he suggests, as if the word "cannot" means that the claimant is able to relate to others (either with or without support), but, if in doing so, he suffers overwhelming anxiety or endangerment then reg.4(2A) is not satisfied and at the same time the claimant "cannot" be said to be able to form a relationship.

> "29. For my part, it seems important to recognise that regulation 4(2A) does not impose absolute standards, save in regulation 4(2A)(d) in respect of which the definition of "reasonable time period" in regulation 4(4)(c) is more prescriptive. It is not entirely clear to me how appropriate regulation 4(2A)(d) is in the context of activity 9 but the point does not arise for specific determination on this appeal. As regards the other subparagraphs, there are elements of judgment involved and the reality of the position of the individual claimant concerned must, I suggest, be taken into account when considering what is safe, acceptable or reasonable. So too, must the terms of descriptor 9(d). Judge Mark suggested that that descriptor has to be taken to refer to "such engagement as [the claimant] may be capable

of" without suffering "overwhelming psychological distress" or exhibiting "behaviour which would result in a substantial risk of harm to the claimant or another person". However, if that is so for descriptor 9(d), it must also be true for descriptors 9(a), 9(b) and 9(c). Moreover, I do not consider that this would be to disapply regulation 4(2A), as Judge Ovey suggested; rather it would be to describe how regulation 4(2A) is to be applied in the context of this activity. (This is, I accept, only a semantic difference, as is my suggesting how regulation 4(2) generally applies to "cannot . . . " descriptors (see paragraph 21 above), in preference to Judge Ovey's view that it does not apply to such descriptors at all.)

30. One has to bear in mind that activity 9 was included in the Regulations before regulation 4(2A) and might perhaps have been drafted differently had it been otherwise. As I have already said, there is an element of "the chicken and the egg" about descriptor 9(d). This is particularly so when it is read with regulation 4(2A), and it is that that gives rise to the difficulties identified by Judge Mark. In my view, the provisions can only be reconciled if it is accepted that heads (i) and (ii) affect the way in which regulation 4(2A) applies."

Counsel for the Secretary of State had put to Judge Rowland that the decision of the three-judge panel in *MR v SSWP (PIP)* [2016] UKUT 531 (AAC); [2018] AACR 12 had said that the word "overwhelming" in Descriptor 9d. set a very high threshold and that being anxious, worried or emotional would not be enough to meet that standard. Judge Rowland says that a "very high threshold" is still a relative term and that the panel should not be regarded as having made a gloss on the statutory words. In *MR*, he suggests, the panel was merely explaining that, on the facts of two of the cases before them, the claimant had not met the required standard.

p.856, *annotation to Social Security (Personal Independence Payment) Regulations 2013 (SI 2013/377) Sch.1 (Mobility Component—planning and following a journey)*

The statement in the *PIP Assessment Guide* concerning the ability to use public transport and the meaning to be given to it, has been considered again by Judge Wikeley in *HO'H v SSWP (PIP)* [2020] UKUT 135 (AAC). The claimant was disabled because of a stroke. It appears that he was able to make some progress on foot, probably with the aid of a stick, but the history of his PIP awards left the extent of that ability unclear. However, the claimant contended that this disability made it impossible for him to walk to any bus stop or to any train station. He said, as well, that he would be unable to use a bus or train when he got there. There appeared to be no evidence as to why he might not be able to use the bus or train, but the case proceeded on the basis that it was accepted that he could not access either form of public transport. The claimant's argument was that he should, therefore, score at least another 10 points under Descriptor 1(d) to add to whatever score he had for Activity 2.

2.043

Judge Wikeley first reiterates the view that the *PIP Assessment Guide* is not a statement of what the law is but an expression of what the Secretary of State might have thought it to be. More importantly, however, he goes on to examine how that statement should be understood when read in the context of the *Guide*. While the decision of the three-judge panel in *MH v SSWP (PIP)* [2016] UKUT 531 (AAC) accepts that there may be interaction between mental and physical disabilities for both mobility Activities they accept that the primary distinction is that Activity 1 is concerned mainly with mental disabilities and Activity 2 with physical ones.

When read in the context of the *Guide* it then becomes clear that the ability to use public transport to make an unfamiliar journey was to be a way of measuring the claimant's cognitive, psychological or sensory capability. A physical inability to access, or even to use public transport, should therefore be relevant mainly when measuring Activity 2.

p.863, *annotation to Social Security (Personal Independence Payment) Regulations 2013 (SI 2013/377) Mobility—Activity 2—Moving around)*

2.044   It seems that it is not uncommon for FTT to be provided with evidence that a claimant has made a journey by air and are therefore invited to reach a conclusion on the basis of that information, about the claimant's ability to walk within the airport. In *LG v SSWP (PIP)* [2020] UKUT 343 (AAC) the claimant was reported to have made three such journeys to Egypt, each involving a change of aircraft in Turkey. There was evidence that she had a wheelchair and assistance each time at Manchester airport, but not at the other airports. Judge Hemingway allowed an appeal and directed a rehearing of the appeal. In doing so he refers to the earlier case of *JT v SSWP (DLA)* [2013] UKUT 221 (AAC) where, on similar evidence, Judge Wright had remitted the case because the FTT had failed to examine in sufficient detail exactly what walking had been involved and then to take account of pain or discomfort that the claimant might have experienced as well as to allow for the time taken and the need for any periods of rest. He noted also that the majority, if not all, of the walking involved would have been indoors whereas the test for DLA required also consideration of the claimant's ability to walk outdoors. While this last element does not arise in relation to PIP mobility Judge Hemingway thought that all the rest of the judge's reservations were equally applicable to a claim for PIP by reference to reg.4 and in particular reg.4(2A). A submission of behalf of the Secretary of State had accepted that the strictures set out in the earlier case were equally applicable to a claim for PIP. What is worth noting also, is that, in both cases, the judges include as a factor to be taken into account that a claimant may be motivated to make an exceptional effort, or to endure more pain, by the occasion of making such a journey and possibly the reason for which they are doing so.

p.979, *amendment to the Marriage and Civil Partnership (Scotland) Act 2014 and Civil Partnership Act 2014 (Consequential Provisions and Modifications) Order 2014 (SI 2014/3229)*

With effect from January 13, 2020, reg.52 of the Marriage (Same-sex   2.045
Couples) and Civil Partnership (Opposite-sex Couples) (Northern Ireland) Regulations 2019 (SI 2019/1514) amended art.3 of the 2014 Order (Extent) by inserting the following words at the end of para.(2):

"but see regulation 43(1) of the Marriage (Same-sex Couples) and Civil Partnership (Opposite-sex Couples) (Northern Ireland) Regulations 2019)"

p.984, *annotation to the State Pension Regulations 2015 (SI 2015/173)*

The 2015 Regulations are modified to the extent necessary to give   2.046
effect to a Convention on Social Security entered into on February 1, 2019, by the Government of the United Kingdom and the Government of Ireland (art.2(1) of the Social Security (Ireland) Order 2019 (SI 2019/622). The Convention seeks to maintain, following the UK's departure from the European Union, certain UK social security entitlements of citizens of the Republic of Ireland. This includes rules for mutual recognition of social security contributions for the purposes of the state pension provided for by the Pensions Act 2014 and the 2015 Regulations. The Convention took effect on December 31, 2020.

p.1036, *amendment to the Employment and Support Allowance Regulations 2008 (SI 2008/794) reg.2(1) (Interpretation)*

With effect from July 15, 2020, reg.7(2)(a) of the Social Security   2.046.1
(Income and Capital) (Miscellaneous Amendments) Regulations 2020 (SI 2020/618) inserted a new definition of "Grenfell Tower payment" immediately before the definition of "guaranteed income payment" as follows:

""Grenfell Tower payment" means a payment made to a person because that person was affected by the fire on 14th June 2017 at Grenfell Tower, or a payment to the personal representative of such a person—
  (a) from the £5 million fund announced on 16th June 2017 for the benefit of certain persons affected by the fire on 14th June 2017 at Grenfell Tower and known as the Grenfell Tower Residents' Discretionary Fund;
  (b) by the Royal Borough of Kensington and Chelsea; or
  (c) by a registered charity;"

p.1039, *amendment to the Employment and Support Allowance Regulations 2008 (SI 2008/794) reg.2(1) (Interpretation)*

With effect from July 15, 2020, reg.7(2)(a) of the Social Security   2.046.2
(Income and Capital) (Miscellaneous Amendments) Regulations 2020

(SI 2020/618) inserted a new definition of "the National Emergencies Trust" immediately after the definition of "mobility supplement" as follows:

""the National Emergencies Trust" means the registered charity of that name (number 1182809) established on 28th March 2019;"

p.1040, *amendment to the Employment and Support Allowance Regulations 2008 (SI 2008/794) reg.2(1) (Interpretation—"qualifying person")*

2.046.3   With effect from July 15, 2020, reg.7(2)(b) of the Social Security (Income and Capital) (Miscellaneous Amendments) Regulations 2020 (SI 2020/618) amended the definition of "qualifying person" by inserting the words "a Grenfell Tower payment has been made or" after the words "means a person in respect of whom" and inserting the words ", the National Emergencies Trust" after the words "the We Love Manchester Emergency Fund"."

pp.1114-1117, *annotation to the Employment and Support Allowance Regulations 2008 (SI 2008/794) reg.30 (Conditions for treating a claimant as having limited capability for work until a determination about limited capability for work has been made)*

2.047   *R. (on the application of Connor) v SSWP* [2020] EWHC 1999 holds that the requirement to undertake the mandatory reconsideration process before appealing is unlawful in its application to ESA claimants who meet the conditions for payment while an appeal is pending. Swift J concluded "that regulation 3ZA of the Decisions and Appeals Regulations is a disproportionate interference with the right of access to court, so far as it applies to claimants to ESA who, once an appeal is initiated, meet the conditions for payment pending appeal under regulation 30(3) of the ESA Regulations" (at [28]). Swift J explained his reasoning as follows (at [31]):

"when it comes to ESA claimants such as Mr Connor who, were an appeal to be in progress would meet the conditions for payment pending appeal under regulation 30(2) of the ESA Regulations, the requirement under regulation 3ZA is disproportionate having regard to the combined effect of (a) the period of time the benefits claimant will now need to wait before the right of appeal arises; and (b) the unexplained absence of any provision for payment of ESA during that period equivalent to the payment pending appeal arrangements that arise once an appeal has been started."

Swift J accordingly made "a declaration to the effect that regulation 3ZA of the Decisions and Appeals Regulations is unlawful insofar as it is applied to ESA claimants who would, if pursuing an appeal to the First-tier Tribunal, subject to compliance with the condition at regulation 30(2) of the ESA Regulations, be entitled to receive payment pending appeal pursuant to regulation 30(3)" (at [35]).

pp.1126-1130, *annotation to the Employment and Support Allowance Regulations 2008 (SI 2008/794) reg.35 (Certain claimants to be treated as having limited capability for work-related activity)*

In *RP v SSWP (ESA)* [2020] UKUT 148 Upper Tribunal Judge   2.048
Wright considered three main issues. The first was the progress the Secretary of State had made in providing a claimant's ESA 'adjudication history' with the appeal response to the FTT (paras 34-39). The second was the role of the 'Work Coach' in Jobcentre Plus in setting work-related activity for an individual claimant (paras 16-28). The third was the provision by the Secretary of State of the appellant's ESA 'action plan' to the First-tier Tribunal in an appeal where reg.35(2) was in issue (paras 29-33). It was held that the Secretary of State's appeals responses in ESA work capability appeals ought, where relevant, to include the claimant's ESA adjudication history and action plan since July 2018. Allowing the claimant's appeal, the Judge highlighted two main errors on the part of the FTT:

"14. First, the tribunal's lack of curiosity or concern about the mangled and adjudication history it was provided with in the Secretary of State's appeal response meant that it failed properly to appraise itself of the decision the appellant was seeking to have superseded and changed. . . .

15. Second, as is now rightly accepted by the Secretary of State, if the 'Work Coach' (or 'Job Coach', the titles appear to be used interchangeably) had advised the appellant to seek placement in the support group then that was plainly relevant evidence, and so the First-tier Tribunal's apparent lack of interest in this evidential area was a further material error of law. . . . "

The Secretary of State's failure to provide accurate lists of work-related activity in appeals which concerned the assessment of 'substantial risk' under reg.35(2) was revisited again in *MR v SSWP (ESA)* [2020] UKUT 210 (AAC). The FTT in that case, which had been provided with a list of 'soft skills' (e.g. setting an alarm clock, getting out of bed and leaving the house), had concluded that the claimant did not meet the terms of reg.35(2) as he could manage those 'soft skills'. However, on appeal to the Upper Tribunal, Judge Wright held that the FTT "was misled in so concluding because the 'soft skills' of work-related activities was a not a true reflection of the extent of the work-related activities claimants may have been expected to undertake in March 2017. Perhaps most critically (and worryingly), the list being of soft skills, it did not contain the more, or most, onerous forms of work-related activities." Judge Wright further explored in detail why it was that the Secretary of State's responses to such FTT appeals failed to comply with the relevant legal requirements. Having reviewed that sorry saga, Judge Wright concluded as follows:

"42. The 'soft skills' list, therefore, ought not in fact have appeared in any ESA work capability appeal after January 2018, and in any event was irrelevant as accurate lists of the most and least onerous types of available work-related activity even before that date. In consequence,

First-tier Tribunals will need to investigate with conspicuous care any work capability assessment appeals in which the 'soft skills' list is put forward as evidence of the available work-related activity."

pp.1169-1170, *amendment to the Employment And Support Allowance Regulations 2008 (2008/7954) reg.70 (Special cases: supplemental—persons from abroad)*

2.048.1   As a result of a series of further amendments, and from various dates as noted below, reg.70 has been amended so that it reads as follows:

Special cases: supplemental—persons from abroad

70.—(1) "Person from abroad" means, subject to the following provisions of this regulation, a claimant who is not habitually resident in the United Kingdom, the Channel Islands, the Isle of Man or the Republic of Ireland.

(2) A claimant must not be treated as habitually resident in the United Kingdom, the Channel Islands, the Isle of Man or the Republic of Ireland unless the claimant has a right to reside in (as the case may be) the United Kingdom, the Channel Islands, the Isle of Man or the Republic of Ireland other than a right to reside which falls within paragraph (3) or (3A).

(3) A right to reside falls within this paragraph if it is one which exists by virtue of, or in accordance with, one or more of the following

    (a)   regulation 13 of the Immigration (European Economic Area) Regulations 2016;

    (b)   regulation 14 of those Regulations, but only in a case where the right exists under that regulation because the claimant is—

        (i) a jobseeker for the purpose of the definition of "qualified person" in regulation 6(1) of those Regulations; or

        (ii) a family member (within the meaning of regulation 7 of those Regulations) of such a jobseeker; [10 or]

    (bb) regulation 16 of those Regulations, but only in a case where the right exists under that regulation because the claimant satisfies the criteria in paragraph (5) of that regulation [11; or]

[10 . . .] [11 (c) having arrived in the United Kingdom with an entry clearance that was granted under Appendix EU (Family Permit) to the immigration rules made under section 3(2) of that Act.]

[10 (d)   . . .]

[10 (e)   . . .]

    (3A) A right to reside falls within this paragraph if it exists by virtue of a claimant having been granted limited leave to enter, or remain in, the United Kingdom under the Immigration Act 1971 by virtue of—

    (a)   Appendix EU to the immigration rules made under section 3(2) of that Act; or

(b) being a person with a Zambrano right to reside as defined in Annex 1 of Appendix EU to the immigration rules made under section 3(2) of that Act.

[⁹(3B) Paragraph (3A)(a) does not apply to a person who—
(a) has a right to reside granted by virtue of being a family member of a relevant person of Northern Ireland; and
(b) would have a right to reside under the Immigration (European Economic Area) Regulations 2016 if the relevant person of Northern Ireland were an EEA national, provided that the right to reside does not fall within paragraph (3).]

(4) A claimant is not a person from abroad if the claimant is—
(za) a qualified person for the purposes of regulation 6 of the Immigration (European Economic Area) Regulations 2016 as a worker or a self-employed person;
(zb) a family member of a person referred to in sub-paragraph (za) [⁹ . . .];
(zc) a person who has a right to reside permanently in the United Kingdom by virtue of regulation 15(1)(c), (d) or (e) of those Regulations;
[⁹(zd) a family member of a relevant person of Northern Ireland, with a right to reside which falls within paragraph (3A)(a), provided that the relevant person of Northern Ireland falls within sub-paragraph (za), or would do so but for the fact that they are not an EEA national;]
[¹⁰(ze) a frontier worker within the meaning of regulation 3 of the Citizens' Rights (Frontier Workers) (EU Exit) Regulations 2020;
(zf) a family member of a person referred to in sub-paragraph (ze), who has been granted limited leave to enter, or remain in, the United Kingdom by virtue of Appendix EU to the immigration rules made under section 3(2) of the Immigration Act 1971;]
(g) a refugee within the definition in Article 1 of the Convention relating to the Status of Refugees done at Geneva on 28th July 1951, as extended by Article 1(2) of the Protocol relating to the Status of Refugees done at New York on 31st January 1967;
(h) a person who has been granted leave or who is deemed to have been granted leave outside the rules made under section 3(2) of the Immigration Act 1971 where that leave is—
(i) discretionary leave to enter or remain in the United Kingdom;
(ii) leave to remain under the Destitution Domestic Violence concession; or
(iii) leave deemed to have been granted by virtue of regulation 3 of the Displaced Persons (Temporary Protection) Regulations 2005;
(i) a person who has humanitarian protection granted under those rules; or
(j) a person who is not a person subject to immigration control within the meaning of section 115(9) of the Immigration and Asylum Act and who is in the United Kingdom as a result of

deportation, expulsion or other removal by compulsion of law
from another country to the United Kingdom;

[⁹ (5) In this regulation—

"EEA national" has the meaning given in regulation 2(1) of the
Immigration (European Economic Area) Regulations 2016;

"family member" has the meaning given in regulation 7(1)(a), (b) or
(c) of the Immigration (European Economic Area) Regulations
2016 except that regulation 7(4) of those Regulations does not
apply for the purposes of paragraphs (3B) and (4)(zd);

"relevant person of Northern Ireland" has the meaning given in Annex
1 of Appendix EU to the immigration rules made under section
3(2) of the Immigration Act 1971.]

[¹⁰ (6) References in this regulation to the Immigration (European
Economic Area) Regulations 2016 are to be read with Schedule 4 to
the Immigration and Social Security Co-ordination (EU Withdrawal)
Act 2020 (Consequential, Saving, Transitional and Transitory Provisions) Regulations 2020.]

AMENDMENTS

9. Social Security (Income-Related Benefits) (Persons of Northern Ireland
—Family Members) (Amendment) Regulations 2020 (SI 2020/683) reg.7
(August 24, 2020).
10. Immigration and Social Security Co-ordination (EU Withdrawal) Act
2020 (Consequential, Saving, Transitional and Transitory Provisions)
(EU Exit) Regulations 2020 (SI 2020/1309) reg.73 (December 31, 2020
at 11.00 pm).
11. Immigration (Citizens' Rights etc.) (EU Exit) Regulations 2020 (SI
2020/1372) reg 23 (December 31, 2020 immediately after 11.00 pm).

MODIFICATIONS

By reg.83 of and paras 2 and 3(r) of Sch.4 to SI 2020/1309, the provisions of
the Immigration (European Economic Area) Regulations 2016 that are specified
in para.(4) of that Schedule continue to have effect in relation to a "member of
the post-transition period group" (*i.e.*, to those who have "pre-settled status") as
if they had not been revoked, but subject to the modifications set out in para.(4):
see further the *Noter-up* to the 2016 Regulations below.

pp.1207-8, *amendments to the Employment and Support Allowance
Regulations 2008 (SI 2008/794) reg.107 (Notional income—income due to
be paid or income paid to or in respect of a third party)*

2.049   With effect from July 15, 2020, reg.7(3) of the Social Security
(Income and Capital) (Miscellaneous Amendments) Regulations 2020
(SI 2020/618) substituted "paragraph (5) or (5A)" for "paragraph (5)"
in paras (3) and (4) and inserted ", the National Emergencies Trust"
after "the We Love Manchester Emergency Fund" in para.(5)(a). It also
inserted the following after para.(5):

"(5A) Paragraphs (3) and (4) do not apply in respect of a payment of
income which is a Grenfell Tower payment."

There are new definitions of "Grenfell Tower Payment" and "the National Emergencies Trust" in reg.2(1).

p.1213, *amendment to the Employment and Support Allowance Regulations 2008 (SI 2008/794) reg.112(8) (Income treated as capital)*

With effect from July 15, 2020, reg.7(4) of the Social Security (Income and Capital) (Miscellaneous Amendments) Regulations 2020 (SI 2020/618) substituted the following for para.(8):

2.050

"(8) This paragraph applies to—
  (a) any payment which is made under or by the Macfarlane Trust, the Macfarlane (Special Payments) Trust, the Macfarlane (Special Payments) (No.2) Trust, the Fund, the Eileen Trust, MFET Limited, the Skipton Fund, the Caxton Foundation, the Scottish Infected Blood Support Scheme, an approved blood scheme, the London Emergencies Trust, the We Love Manchester Emergency Fund, the National Emergencies Trust or the Independent Living Fund (2006); or
  (b) any Grenfell Tower payment."

There are new definitions of "Grenfell Tower Payment" and "the National Emergencies Trust" in reg.2(1).

pp.1216-7, *amendments to the Employment and Support Allowance Regulations 2008 (SI 2008/794) reg.116 (Notional capital)*

With effect from July 15, 2020, reg.7(5) of the Social Security (Income and Capital) (Miscellaneous Amendments) Regulations 2020 (SI 2020/618) substituted "paragraph (5) or (5A)" for "paragraph (5)" in paras (3) and (4), inserted ", the National Emergencies Trust" after "the We Love Manchester Emergency Fund" in para.(5)(a) and inserted the following after para.(5):

2.051

"(5A) Paragraphs (3) and (4) do not apply in respect of a payment of capital which is a Grenfell Tower payment."

There are new definitions of "Grenfell Tower Payment" and "the National Emergencies Trust" in reg.2(1).

p.1233, *amendment to the Employment and Support Allowance Regulations 2008 (SI 2008/794) reg.131 (Students: interpretation)*

With effect from July 15, 2020, reg.7(6) of the Social Security (Income and Capital) (Miscellaneous Amendments) Regulations 2020 (SI 2020/618) substituted the following for the definition of "postgraduate master's degree loan":

2.052

""postgraduate loan" means a loan to a student undertaking a postgraduate master's degree course or a postgraduate doctoral degree course pursuant to regulations made under section 22 of the Teaching and Higher Education Act 1998;"

p.1236, *amendment to the Employment and Support Allowance Regulations 2008 (SI 2008/794) reg.132(3) (Calculation of grant income)*

2.053   With effect from July 15, 2020, reg.7(7) of the Social Security (Income and Capital) (Miscellaneous Amendments) Regulations 2020 (SI 2020/618) omitted the words "master's degree" in both places.

pp.1240-2, *amendments to the Employment and Support Allowance Regulations 2008 (SI 2008/794) reg.137(1), (4), (4A) and (5A) and heading (Treatment of student loans and postgraduate master's degree loans)*

2.054   With effect from July 15, 2020, reg.7(8) of the Social Security (Income and Capital) (Miscellaneous Amendments) Regulations 2020 (SI 2020/618) omitted the words "master's degree" in all places.

p.1245, *amendment to the Employment and Support Allowance Regulations 2008 (SI 2008/794) reg.141 (Further disregard of student's income)*

2.055   With effect from July 15, 2020, reg.7(9) of the Social Security (Income and Capital) (Miscellaneous Amendments) Regulations 2020 (SI 2020/618) omitted the words "master's degree".

p.1262, *modification of the Employment and Support Allowance Regulations 2008 (2008/794) reg.156 (Circumstances in which a person is to be treated as being or not being a member of the household)*

2.055.1   With effect from November 12, 2020, the final sentence under the heading, *Modification*, should read:

"By reg.6 of SI 2020/409, as amended by reg.2 of the Social Security (Coronavirus) (Prisoners) Amendment Regulations 2020 (SI 2020/1156), the modification will expire at the end of May 12, 2021."

p.1354, *modification of the Employment and Support Allowance Regulations 2008 (2008/794) Sch.5 (Special cases)*

2.055.2   With effect from November 12, 2020, the final sentence under the heading, *Modification*, should read:

"By reg.6 of SI 2020/409, as amended by reg.2 of the Social Security (Coronavirus) (Prisoners) Amendment Regulations 2020 (SI 2020/1156), the modification will expire at the end of May 12, 2021."

p.1367, *amendment to the Employment and Support Allowance Regulations 2008 (SI 2008/794) Sch.6, para.19 (Interpretation—definition of "qualifying person")*

2.055.3   With effect from July 15, 2020, reg.7(1) and (10) of the Social Security (Income and Capital) (Miscellaneous Amendments) Regulations

2020 (SI 2020/618) amended sub-para.(8)(b) of para.19 by inserting the words "any Grenfell Tower payment or" at the beginning, and the words ", the National Emergencies Trust" after the words "the We Love Manchester Emergency Fund".

p.1378, *amendment to the Employment and Support Allowance Regulations 2008 (SI 2008/794) Sch.8, para.22(2) (Sums to be disregarded in the calculation of income other than earnings: income in kind)*

With effect from July 15, 2020, reg.7(11)(a) of the Social Security (Income and Capital) (Miscellaneous Amendments) Regulations 2020 (SI 2020/618) inserted "is a Grenfell Tower payment or" after "income in kind" and ", the National Emergencies Trust" after "the We Love Manchester Emergency Fund". There are new definitions of "Grenfell Tower Payment" and "the National Emergencies Trust" in reg.2(1).

pp.1381-2, *amendments to the Employment and Support Allowance Regulations 2008 (SI 2008/794) Sch.8, para.41 (Sums to be disregarded in the calculation of income other than earnings: payments from certain funds)*

With effect from July 15, 2020, reg.7(11)(b) of the Social Security (Income and Capital) (Miscellaneous Amendments) Regulations 2020 (SI 2020/618) amended para.41 by inserting the words in square brackets in sub-paras (1) and (7) as set out below without footnotes for previous amendments and inserting a new sub-para.(1A) (the text of sub-paras (1) and (7) in the main volume omits some recent amendments):

"(1) Any payment made under or by the Macfarlane Trust, the Macfarlane (Special Payments) Trust, the Macfarlane (Special Payments) (No. 2) Trust ("the Trusts"), the Fund, the Eileen Trust, MFET Limited, the Skipton Fund, the Caxton Foundation, the Scottish Infected Blood Support Scheme, an approved blood scheme, the London Emergencies Trust, the We Love Manchester Emergency Fund[, the National Emergencies Trust] or the Independent Living Fund (2006).
[(1A) Any Grenfell Tower payment.]"

"(7) For the purposes of sub-paragraphs (2) to (6), any reference to the Trusts is to be construed as including a reference to the Fund, the Eileen Trust, MFET Limited, the Skipton Fund, the Caxton Foundation, the Scottish Infected Blood Support Scheme, an approved blood scheme, the London Emergencies Trust, the We Love Manchester Emergency Fund[, the National Emergencies Trust] and the London Bombings Relief Charitable Fund."

Regulation 7(11)(b) also inserted ", or from a Grenfell Tower payment," after "Trusts to which sub-paragraph (1) refers" in sub-paras (2)

2.056

2.057

and (3) and "or from a Grenfell Tower payment," after "Trusts to which sub-paragraph (1) refers," in sub-paras (4) and (5) and (without the closing comma) after "or deriving from any of the Trusts" in sub-para.(6).

p.1385, *amendment to the Employment and Support Allowance Regulations 2008 (SI 2008/794) Sch.8 (Sums to be disregarded in the calculation of income other than earnings)*

2.058   With effect from November 9, 2020, art.8(2) of the Social Security (Scotland) Act 2018 (Information-sharing and Scottish Child Payment) (Consequential Provision and Modifications) Order 2020 (SI 2020/482) inserted the following after para.71:

"**72.** Any Scottish child payment assistance given in accordance with [. . .] section 79 of the Social Security (Scotland) Act 2018."

The relevant regulations are the Scottish Child Payment Regulations 2020 (SSI 2020/351) (see Part I of this Supplement), which provide for a payment of £10 per week (paid four-weekly in arrears) to claimants in receipt of a UK income-related benefit who are responsible for a child under the age of six. Applications and initial payments cannot have effect before mid-February 2021. See para.11(1)(a) of Sch.9 for the disregard as capital of payments of arrears.

With effect from November 9, 2020, art.14(2) of the Social Security (Scotland) Act 2018 (Young Carer Grants, Short-Term Assistance and Winter Heating Assistance) (Consequential Provision and Modifications) Order 2020 (SI 2020/989) inserted the following after para.72:

"**73.** Any short-term assistance given in accordance with regulations made under section 36 of the Social Security (Scotland) Act 2018."

The introduction was planned for 2020 of payments to be made to claimants who have appealed against or requested redetermination of a determination to reduce or stop paying another form of assistance (initially in relation to the new child disability payments to replace DLA for the under-18s) under the 2018 Act. The plans have been deferred to summer 2021 for a pilot of the child disability payment and the autumn for a full roll-out. See para.11(1)(a) of Sch.9 for the disregard as capital of payments of arrears.

p.1388, *annotation to the Employment and Support Allowance Regulations 2008 (SI 2008/794) Sch.8 (Sums to be disregarded in the calculation of income other than earnings)*

2.059   With effect from May 29, 2020, reg.26(1)(a) of the Victims' Payments Regulations 2020 (SI 2020/103) (see Part I of this Supplement) provides that a victims' payment or a lump sum under those Regulations is to be disregarded as income.

p.1390, *amendment to the Employment and Support Allowance Regulations 2008 (SI 2008/794) Sch.9, para.11(1)(a) (Capital to be disregarded: payments of arrears of certain benefits etc.)*

With effect from November 9, 2020, art.8(3) of the Social Security 2.060 (Scotland) Act 2018 (Information-sharing and Scottish Child Payment) (Consequential Provision and Modifications) Order 2020 (SI 2020/482) substituted "8, 10, 11, 66 or 72 of Schedule 8" for "8, 10, 11 or 66 of Schedule 8".

With effect from November 9, 2020, art.14(3) of the Social Security (Scotland) Act 2018 (Young Carer Grants, Short-Term Assistance and Winter Heating Assistance) (Consequential Provision and Modifications) Order 2020 (SI 2020/989) substituted "8, 10, 11, 66, 72 or 73" for "8, 10, 11, 66 or 72".

pp.1392-3, *amendments to the Employment and Support Allowance Regulations 2008 (SI 2008/794) Sch.9, para.27 (Capital to be disregarded: payments from certain funds) and 31 (Capital to be disregarded: certain payments in kind)*

With effect from July 15, 2020, reg.7(12)(a) of the Social Security 2.061 (Income and Capital) (Miscellaneous Amendments) Regulations 2020 (SI 2020/618) inserted ", the National Emergencies Trust" after "We Love Manchester Emergency Fund" in sub-paras (1) and (7) of para.27. It inserted the following after sub-para.(1):

"(1A) Any Grenfell Tower payment or any payment made by the Child Migrants Trust (registered charity number 1171479) under the scheme for former British child migrants."

It inserted ", or from a Grenfell Tower payment," after "Trusts to which sub-paragraph (1) refers" in sub-paras (2) and (3) and "or from a Grenfell Tower payment," after "Trusts to which sub-paragraph (1) refers," in sub-paras (4) and (5) and (without the closing comma) after "or deriving from any of the Trusts" in sub-para.(6).

With effect from July 15, 2020, reg.7(12)(b) of the Social Security (Income and Capital) (Miscellaneous Amendments) Regulations 2020 (SI 2020/618) inserted "which is a Grenfell Tower payment or" after "Any payment in kind" in para.31.

There are new definitions of "Grenfell Tower Payment" and "the National Emergencies Trust" in reg.2(1).

p.1398, *amendment to the Employment and Support Allowance Regulations 2008 (SI 2008/794) Sch.9 (Capital to be disregarded)*

With effect from November 9, 2020, art.7 of the Social Security 2.062 (Scotland) Act 2018 (Young Carer Grants, Short-Term Assistance and Winter Heating Assistance) (Consequential Provision and Modifications) Order 2020 (SI 2020/989) inserted the following after para.64:

"**65.** Any assistance given in accordance with the Carer's Assistance (Young Carer Grants) (Scotland) Regulations 2019."

Under the specified regulations (SSI 2019/324), in operation from October 21, 2019, young carer grants of (from April 2020) £305.10, limited to one a year, are payable in Scotland to carers aged 16 to 18 who care for at least 16 hours a week over a 13-week period for a person who normally receives a disability benefit (see Part I of this Supplement). There appears to have been a gap during which grants were not disregarded as capital. No disregard as income has been introduced, but no doubt the grants are in their nature payments of capital.

With effect from the same date art.20 of the same Order inserted the following after para.65:

> "**66.** Any winter heating assistance given in accordance with regulations made under section 30 of the Social Security (Scotland) Act 2018."

The relevant regulations are the Winter Heating Assistance for Children and Young People (Scotland) Regulations 2020 (SSI 2020/352, in operation from November 9, 2020) (see Part I of this Supplement), which initially provide an automatic annual grant in November 2020 to a family of £200 for each child entitled to the highest rate of the care component of DLA in the week of September 21–27, 2020.

p.1400, *annotation to the Employment and Support Allowance Regulations 2008 (SI 2008/794) Sch.9 (Capital to be disregarded)*

2.063   With effect from May 29, 2020, reg.26(1)(a) of the Victims' Payments Regulations 2020 (SI 2020/103) (see Part I of this Supplement) provides that a victims' payment or a lump sum under those Regulations is to be disregarded as capital.

p.1566, *annotation to the Social Security (Industrial Injuries) (Prescribed Diseases) Regulations 1985 (SI 1985/967) Sch.1 P.D. A12 (Carpal tunnel syndrome)*

2.064   Dr Reed's evidence in *CI/3745/2006* was cited by Judge Poynter in *SM v SSWP (IIDB)* [2020] UKUT 287 (AAC) where the FTT had wrongly directed itself that "the ulnar nerve not the median nerve serves the ring finger. Carpal tunnel syndrome does not cause symptoms in the ring finger." In fact, as Judge Poynter observed, "the Median nerve also serves the lateral half of the ring finger (i.e., the side nearest the thumb)" (at para.7). Thus by "basing its decision in this appeal on the mistaken premise that the Median nerve does not supply the ring finger, the First-tier Tribunal failed to exercise its enabling role correctly. On the contrary, it hindered the proper presentation of the claimant's case by setting up an obstacle of which she was unaware and which had no basis in fact" (at para.47). Allowing the claimant's appeal and remitting the case for re-hearing, Judge Poynter summarised the position as follows:

> "4. The fact that only the Median nerve—and not the Ulnar or Radial nerves, the other two nerves that supply the hand—pass through the carpal tunnel is important. It means that if a claimant's neurological

symptoms in the hand do not follow the distribution of the Median nerve then, at least—and subject to what is said in paragraph 14 below—any loss of function in the hand is not caused solely by PD A12 and, at most, that the claimant does not suffer from that condition."

Paragraph 14 of the decision noted that there is some evidence that carpal tunnel syndrome can also produce symptoms in the hand as a whole.

PART III

UPDATING MATERIAL
VOLUME II

INCOME SUPPORT, JOBSEEKER'S ALLOWANCE, STATE PENSION CREDIT AND THE SOCIAL FUND

Commentary by

John Mesher

Richard Poynter

Nick Wikeley

p.33, *annotation to the old style Jobseekers Act 1995 s.1(2) (The jobseeker's allowance: conditions of entitlement—temporary coronavirus provisions)*

With effect from November 12, 2020, the new reg.10(2B) of the   3.001
Social Security (Coronavirus) (Further Measures) Regulations 2020 (SI
2020/371), as inserted by reg.2 of the Social Security (Coronavirus)
(Further Measures) (Amendment) and Miscellaneous Amendment Regulations 2020 (SI 2020/1201), made May 12, 2021 the date of expiry of
the effect of reg.8 of SI 2020/371. Note that the original date of expiry
of reg.8 was November 12, 2020, not (as suggested in error at one place
in the main volume) the last day of the period of three months beginning
on March 30, 2020.

p.222, *amendment to the Jobseekers (Back to Work Schemes) Act 2013*

With effect from October 3, 2020, art.2 of the Jobseekers (Back to   3.002
Work Schemes Act 2013) (Remedial) Order 2020 (SI 2020/1085)
inserted the following after s.1:

**"1A. Certain appeals against penalties under the 2011 Regula-
tions**

(1) This section applies where—

(a) the Secretary of State has made a decision imposing on a
claimant for jobseeker's allowance a penalty for failing to comply with the 2011 Regulations ("the penalty decision"), and

(b) the claimant lodged an appeal against the penalty decision
before 26 March 2013, and the appeal had not been finally
determined, abandoned or withdrawn before 26 March 2013.

(2) If the Secretary of State revises the penalty decision under
section 9 of the Social Security Act 1998, in making the revised
decision, the Secretary of State must disregard subsections (1) to (6)
of section 1 of this Act and subsection (12) of section 1 so far as it
relates to those subsections.

(3) Subsection (4) applies where a tribunal has decided the appeal
before this section comes into force.

(4) In a case where the tribunal decided to uphold the penalty
decision (in whole or in part), the Secretary of State must make a
decision superseding the tribunal's decision.

(5) In making a superseding decision under subsection (4), the
Secretary of State must disregard subsections (1) to (6) of section 1
and subsection (12) of section 1 so far as it relates to those subsections.

(6) Section 10(1)(b) of the Social Security Act 1998 (power of the
Secretary of State to supersede a tribunal decision) does not apply in
a case where subsection (4) applies.

(7) A superseding decision made under subsection (4) is to be
treated for all purposes as if it were a superseding decision made under
section 10 of the Social Security Act 1998.

(8) Subsection (9) applies where, after this section has come into force, a court or tribunal is considering—

(a)

the appeal mentioned in subsection (1)(b),

(b) an appeal against a revised decision made under section 9 of the Social Security Act 1998 by virtue of subsection (2), or

(c) an appeal against a superseding decision made under subsection (4).

(9) In considering the appeal, the court or tribunal must disregard subsections (1) to (6) of section 1 and subsection (12) of section 1 so far as it relates to those subsections.

(10) A revised decision made by virtue of subsection (2) and a superseding decision made under subsection (4) are to be treated as having effect from the date on which the penalty decision had effect (other than for the purposes of any rule as to the time allowed for bringing an appeal).

(11) In this section—

"the 2011 Regulations" has the same meaning as in section 1;

"court" means the Court of Appeal, the Court of Session or the Supreme Court;

"tribunal" means the First-tier Tribunal or the Upper Tribunal.

1B. Certain appeals against penalties under the Mandatory Work Activity Scheme Regulations

(1) This section applies where—

(a) the Secretary of State has made a decision imposing on a claimant for jobseeker's allowance a penalty for failing to comply with the Mandatory Work Activity Scheme Regulations ("the penalty decision"), and

(b) the claimant lodged an appeal against the penalty decision before 26 March 2013, and the appeal had not been finally determined, abandoned or withdrawn before 26 March 2013.

(2) If the Secretary of State revises the penalty decision under section 9 of the Social Security Act 1998, in making the revised decision, the Secretary of State must disregard subsections (7) to (9) of section 1 of this Act and subsection (12) of section 1 so far as it relates to those subsections.

(3) Subsection (4) applies where a tribunal has decided the appeal before this section comes into force.

(4) In a case where—

(a) the tribunal decided to uphold the penalty decision (in whole or in part), and

(b) the Secretary of State decides that subsection (7), (8) or (9) of section 1 or subsection (12) of section 1 so far as it relates to those subsections may be relevant to the tribunal's decision,

the Secretary of State must make a decision superseding the tribunal's decision.

(5) In making a superseding decision under subsection (4), the

Secretary of State must disregard subsections (7) to (9) of section 1 and subsection (12) of section 1 so far as it relates to those subsections.

(6) Section 10(1)(b) of the Social Security Act 1998 (power of the Secretary of State to supersede a tribunal decision) does not apply in a case where subsection (4) applies.

(7) A superseding decision made under subsection (4) is to be treated for all purposes as if it were a superseding decision made under section 10 of the Social Security Act 1998.

(8) Subsection (9) applies where, after this section has come into force, a court or tribunal is considering—

(a) the appeal mentioned in subsection (1)(b),

(b) an appeal against a revised decision made under section 9 of the Social Security Act 1998 by virtue of subsection (2), or

(c) an appeal against a superseding decision made under subsection (4).

(9) In considering the appeal, the court or tribunal must disregard subsections (7) to (9) of section 1 and subsection (12) of section 1 so far as it relates to those subsections.

(10) A revised decision made by virtue of subsection (2) and a superseding decision made under subsection (4) are to be treated as having effect from the date on which the penalty decision had effect (other than for the purposes of any rule as to the time allowed for bringing an appeal).

(11) In this section—

"the Mandatory Work Activity Scheme Regulations" has the same meaning as in section 1;

"court" has the same meaning as in section 1A; and

"tribunal" has the same meaning as in section 1A."

p.235, *amendment to the Income Support (General) Regulations 1987 (SI 1987/1967) reg.2 (Interpretation—definition of "Grenfell Tower payment")*

With effect from July 15, 2020, reg.2(1) and (2)(a) of the Social Security (Income and Capital) (Miscellaneous Amendments) Regulations 2020 (SI 2020/618) inserted a new definition of "Grenfell Tower payment") immediately before the definition of "a guaranteed income payment" as follows: 3.003

""Grenfell Tower payment" means a payment made to a person because that person was affected by the fire on 14th June 2017 at Grenfell Tower, or a payment to the personal representative of such a person—

(a) from the £5 million fund announced on 16th June 2017 for the benefit of certain persons affected by the fire on 14th June 2017 at Grenfell Tower and known as the Grenfell Tower Residents' Discretionary Fund;

(b) by the Royal Borough of Kensington and Chelsea; or

(c) by a registered charity"

p.236, *amendment to the Income Support (General) Regulations 1987 (SI 1987/1967) reg.2 (Interpretation—definition of "the National Emergencies Trust")*

3.004   With effect from July 15, 2020, reg.2(1) and (2)(a) of the Social Security (Income and Capital) (Miscellaneous Amendments) Regulations 2020 (SI 2020/618) inserted a new definition of "the National Emergencies Trust" immediately after the definition of "mobility supplement" as follows:

"""the National Emergencies Trust" means the registered charity of that name (number 1182809) established on 28th March 2019;"

p.238, *amendment to the Income Support (General) Regulations 1987 (SI 1987/1967) reg.2 (Interpretation—definition of "qualifying person")*

3.005   With effect from July 15, 2020, reg.2(1) and (2)(b) of the Social Security (Income and Capital) (Miscellaneous Amendments) Regulations 2020 (SI 2020/618) amended the definition of "qualifying person" to read as follows:

"""qualifying person" means a person in respect of whom [a Grenfell Tower payment has been made or] payment has been made from the Fund, the Eileen Trust, MFET Limited the Skipton Fund, the Caxton Foundation, the Scottish Infected Blood Support Scheme, an approved blood scheme, the London Emergencies Trust, the We Love Manchester Emergency Fund [, the National Emergencies Trust] or the London Bombings Relief Charitable Fund;"

pp.251-252, *commentary to the Income Support (General) Regulations 1987 (SI 1987/1967) reg.2(1) (Interpretation—"Couple"—Spouses and civil partners)*

3.006   In *SH v Department for Communities (IS)* [2020] NICom 30, Mr Commissioner Stockman emphasised (at para.70) that the "admirable signposts" (see the commentary on *Crake v SBC, Butterworth v SBC* on pp.251-253 of the Main Volume) only apply to unmarried couples:

"Technically, they cannot be the appropriate criteria to address in determining the only question that arises from regulation 2 of the IS Regulations, namely whether the applicant and A [who were married] were members of the same household. As that particular issue is addressed at point (a) of the criteria, there would be something oddly recursive in a consideration of that same issue in terms of the remaining criteria from (b) to (f). I consider that the issues from (b) to (f) are only of direct relevance in the present case if they shed particular light on issue (a)."

p.315, *modification of the Income Support Regulations 1987 (SI 1987/1967) reg.16 (Circumstances in which a person is to be treated as being or not being a member of the household)*

With effect from November 12, 2020, the final sentence under the heading, *Modification,* should read: 3.007

"By reg.6 of SI 2020/409, as amended by reg.2 of the Social Security (Coronavirus) (Prisoners) Amendment Regulations 2020 (SI 2020/1156), the modification will expire at the end of May 12, 2021."

p.329, *modification of the Income Support Regulations 1987 (SI 1987/1967) reg.21 (Special cases)*

With effect from November 12, 2020, the final sentence under the heading, *Modification,* should read: 3.008

"By reg.6 of SI 2020/409, as amended by reg.2 of the Social Security (Coronavirus) (Prisoners) Amendment Regulations 2020 (SI 2020/1156), the modification will expire at the end of May 12, 2021."

pp.333-334, *amendment to the Income Support (General) Regulations 1987 (SI 1987/1967) reg.21AA (Special cases: supplemental—persons from abroad)*

As a result of a series of further amendments, and from various dates as noted below, reg.21AA has been amended so that it reads as follows: 3.009

Special cases: supplemental—persons from abroad

    21AA.—(1) "Person from abroad" means, subject to the following provisions of this regulation, a claimant who is not habitually resident in the United Kingdom, the Channel Islands, the Isle of Man or the Republic of Ireland.

    (2) No claimant shall be treated as habitually resident in the United Kingdom, the Channel Islands, the Isle of Man or the Republic of Ireland unless he has a right to reside in (as the case may be) the United Kingdom, the Channel Islands, the Isle of Man or the Republic of Ireland other than a right to reside which falls within paragraph (3) or (3A).

    (3) A right to reside falls within this paragraph if it is one which exists by virtue of, or in accordance with, one or more of the following—

    (a) regulation 13 of the Immigration (European Economic area Regulations 2016;

    (b) regulation 14 of those Regulations, but only in a case where the right exists under that regulation because the claimant is—

      (i) a jobseeker for the purpose of the definition of "qualified person" in regulation 6(1) of those Regulations, or

      (ii) a family member (within the meaning of regulation 7 of those Regulations) of such a jobseeker; [¹⁴ or]

  (bb) regulation 16 of those Regulations, but only in a case where the right exists under that regulation because the claimant satisfies the criteria in paragraph (5) of that regulation;

[¹⁴ . . .] (c) Article 6 of Council Directive No. 2004/38/EC;

  (d) [¹⁴ . . .]

  (e) [¹⁴ . . .]

(3A) A right to reside falls within this paragraph if it exists by virtue of a claimant having been granted limited leave to enter, or remain in, the United Kingdom under the Immigration Act 1971 by virtue of—

  (a) Appendix EU to the immigration rules made under section 3(2) of that Act; [¹⁵ . . .]

  (b) being a person with a Zambrano right to reside as defined in Annex 1 of Appendix EU to the immigration rules made under section 3(2) of that Act [¹⁵; or

  (c) having arrived in the United Kingdom with an entry clearance that was granted under Appendix EU (Family Permit) to the immigration rules made under section 3(2) of that Act.]

[¹³(3B) Paragraph (3A)(a) does not apply to a person who—

  (a) has a right to reside granted by virtue of being a family member of a relevant person of Northern Ireland; and

  (b) would have a right to reside under the Immigration (European Economic Area) Regulations 2016 if the relevant person of Northern Ireland were an EEA national, provided that the right to reside does not fall within paragraph (3).]

(4) A claimant is not a person from abroad if he is—

  (za) a qualified person for the purposes of regulation 6 of the Immigration (European Economic Area) Regulations 2006 as a worker or a self-employed person;

  (zb) a family member of a person referred to in sub-paragraph (za) [¹³ . . .];

  (zc) a person who has a right to reside permanently in the United Kingdom by virtue of regulation 15(1)(c), (d) or (e) of those Regulations;

[¹³(zd) a family member of a relevant person of Northern Ireland, with a right to reside which falls within paragraph (3A)(a), provided that the relevant person of Northern Ireland falls within sub-paragraph (za), or would do so but for the fact that they are not an EEA national;]

[¹⁴(ze) a frontier worker within the meaning of regulation 3 of the Citizens' Rights (Frontier Workers) (EU Exit) Regulations 2020;

  (zf) a family member, of a person referred to in sub-paragraph (ze), who has been granted limited leave to enter, or remain in, the United Kingdom by virtue of Appendix EU to the immigration rules made under section 3(2) of the Immigration Act 1971;]

  (g) a refugee within the definition in Article 1 of the Convention relating to the Status of Refugees done at Geneva on 28th July

1951, as extended by Article 1(2) of the Protocol relating to the Status of Refugees done at New York on 31st January 1967;

(h) a person who has been granted leave or who is deemed to have been granted leave outside the rules made under section 3(2) of the Immigration Act 1971 where that leave is—

(i) discretionary leave to enter or remain in the United Kingdom;

(ii) leave to remain under the Destitution Domestic Violence concession; or

(iii) leave deemed to have been granted by virtue of regulation 3 of the Displaced Persons (Temporary Protection) Regulations 2005;

(hh) a person who has humanitarian protection granted under those rules; or

(i) a person who is not a person subject to immigration control within the meaning of section 115(9) of the Immigration and Asylum Act and who is in the United Kingdom as a result of his deportation, expulsion or other removal by compulsion of law from another country to the United Kingdom;

[¹³ (5) In this regulation—

"EEA national" has the meaning given in regulation 2(1) of the Immigration (European Economic Area) Regulations 2016;

"family member" has the meaning given in regulation 7(1)(a), (b) or (c) of the Immigration (European Economic Area) Regulations 2016 except that regulation 7(4) of those Regulations does not apply for the purposes of paragraphs (3B) and (4)(zd);

"relevant person of Northern Ireland" has the meaning given in Annex 1 of Appendix EU to the immigration rules made under section 3(2) of the Immigration Act 1971(11).]

[¹⁴ (6) In this regulation references to the Immigration (European Economic Area) Regulations 2016 are to be read with Schedule 4 to the Immigration and Social Security Co-ordination (EU Withdrawal) Act 2020 (Consequential, Saving, Transitional and Transitory Provisions) Regulations 2020.]

AMENDMENTS

13. Social Security (Income-Related Benefits) (Persons of Northern Ireland —Family Members) (Amendment) Regulations 2020 (SI 2020/683) reg.2 (August 24, 2020).

14. Immigration and Social Security Co-ordination (EU Withdrawal) Act 2020 (Consequential, Saving, Transitional and Transitory Provisions) (EU Exit) Regulations 2020 (SI 2020/1309) reg.53 (December 31, 2020 at 11.00 pm).

15. Immigration (Citizens' Rights etc.) (EU Exit) Regulations 2020 (SI 2020/1372) reg 8 (December 31, 2020 immediately after 11.00 pm).

MODIFICATIONS

By reg.83 of, and paras 2 and 3(a) of Sch.4 to, SI 2020/1309, the provisions of the Immigration (European Economic Area) Regulations 2016 that are specified in para.(4) of that Schedule continue to have effect in relation to a "member of the post-transition period group" (*i.e.*, to those who have "pre-settled status") as if they had not been revoked, but subject to the modifications set out in para.(4): see further the *Noter-up* to the 2016 Regulations below.

pp.397-399, *annotations to the Income Support Regulations 1987 (SI 1987/1967) reg.37 (Earnings of self-employed earners)*

3.010   A third tranche of SEISS payments in respect of the three months from November 2020 to January 2021 has been made available for application (see the Self-employed Income Support Scheme Grant Extension 3 Direction signed on November 21, 2020). The payment will meet 80% of qualifying trading profits, capped at £7,500 for the three months. The previous tranche in respect of the three months from August to October 2020 met only 70% of qualifying trading profits capped at £6,750 (see the Self-employed Income Support Scheme Extension Direction signed on July 1, 2020). A fourth tranche for the period from February to April 2021 has been announced. The existence of the further tranches would tend to strengthen the argument that the payments are income receipts, not capital receipts, for the self-employed, but the problem of how to attribute them under reg.30 remains.

The Coronavirus Job Retention Scheme has been extended to cover the period from November 2020 to the end of April 2021 with the level of reimbursement for hours not worked being 80% of usual salary (see the Coronavirus Act 2020 Functions of Her Majesty's Revenue and Customs (Coronavirus Job Retention Scheme) Direction signed on November 12, 2020 and the announcement of December 17, 2020 with the Direction signed on January 25, 2021). The previous extension, mentioned in the main volume, was authorised by the Direction signed on June 25, 2020.

pp.422-424, *amendments to the Income Support Regulations 1987 (SI 1987/1967) reg.42(4), (4ZA)(a) and (4ZB) (Notional income)*

3.011   With effect from July 15, 2020, reg.2(3) of the Social Security (Income and Capital) (Miscellaneous Amendments) Regulations 2020 (SI 2020/618) substituted "paragraph (4ZA) or (4ZB)" for "paragraph (4ZA)" in para.(4), inserted ", the National Emergencies Trust" after "the We Love Manchester Emergency Fund" in para.(4ZA) and inserted the following after para.(4ZA):

"(4ZB) Paragraph (4) shall not apply in respect of a payment of income which is a Grenfell Tower payment."

There are new definitions of "Grenfell Tower Payment" and "the National Emergencies Trust" in reg.2(1).

pp.442-443, *annotation to the Income Support Regulations 1987 (SI 1987/1967) reg.46 (Calculation of capital)*

3.012   *MS v DfC (JSA)* [2020] NICom 42 holds that where a tribunal is not satisfied by a claimant's assertion that they have disposed of money, so that the amount remains part of their actual capital, it is not necessary for the tribunal to make a positive finding of fact about where the money was held. Submissions to the contrary were based on a misreading of remarks in *DMcC v DSD (IS)* [2012] NICom 326.

p.460, *amendments to the Income Support Regulations 1987 (SI 1987/1967) reg.48(10) (Income treated as capital)*

With effect from July 15, 2020, reg.2(4) of the Social Security   3.013
(Income and Capital) (Miscellaneous Amendments) Regulations 2020
(SI 2020/618) inserted ", the National Emergencies Trust" after "the We Love Manchester Emergency Fund" in para.(10)(c) and inserted the following after para.10(a):

"(ab) which is a Grenfell Tower payment."

There are new definitions of "Grenfell Tower Payment" and "the National Emergencies Trust" in reg.2(1).

pp.469-70, *amendments to the Income Support Regulations 1987 (SI 1987/1967) reg.51(3), (3A)(a) and (3B) (Notional capital)*

With effect from July 15, 2020, reg.2(5) of the Social Security   3.014
(Income and Capital) (Miscellaneous Amendments) Regulations 2020
(SI 2020/618) substituted "paragraph (3A) or (3B)" for "paragraph (3A)" in para.(3), inserted ", the National Emergencies Trust" after "the We Love Manchester Emergency Fund" in para.(3A) and inserted the following after para.(3A):

"(3B) Paragraph (3) shall not apply in respect of a payment of capital which is a Grenfell Tower payment."

There are new definitions of "Grenfell Tower Payment" and "the National Emergencies Trust" in reg.2(1).

p.516, *amendment to the Income Support Regulations 1987 (SI 1987/1967) reg.61 (Students: interpretation)*

With effect from July 15, 2020, reg.2(6) of the Social Security   3.015
(Income and Capital) (Miscellaneous Amendments) Regulations 2020
(SI 2020/618) substituted the following for the definition of "post-graduate master's degree loan":

""postgraduate loan" means a loan to a student undertaking a post-graduate master's degree course or a postgraduate doctoral degree course pursuant to regulations made under section 22 of the Teaching and Higher Education Act 1998;"

p.530, *amendment to the Income Support Regulations 1987 (SI 1987/1967) reg.62(2A) (Calculation of grant income)*

With effect from July 15, 2020, reg.2(7) of the Social Security   3.016
(Income and Capital) (Miscellaneous Amendments) Regulations 2020
(SI 2020/618) omitted the words "master's degree" in both places.

pp.537-539, *amendments to the Income Support Regulations 1987 (SI 1987/1967) reg.66A(1), (3) and (4A) and heading (Treatment of student loans and postgraduate master's degree loans)*

3.017   With effect from July 15, 2020, reg.2(8) of the Social Security (Income and Capital) (Miscellaneous Amendments) Regulations 2020 (SI 2020/618) omitted the words "master's degree" in all places.

p.545, *amendment to the Income Support Regulations 1987 (SI 1987/1967) reg.67A (Further disregard of student's income)*

3.018   With effect from July 15, 2020, reg.2(9) of the Social Security (Income and Capital) (Miscellaneous Amendments) Regulations 2020 (SI 2020/618) omitted the words "master's degree".

p.608, *amendment to the Income Support (General) Regulations 1987 (SI 1987/1967) Sch.3, para.18 (Non-dependant deductions)*

3.019   With effect from July 15, 2020, reg.2(1) and (10) of the Social Security (Income and Capital) (Miscellaneous Amendments) Regulations 2020 (SI 2020/618) amended sub-para.(8)(b) of para.18 by inserting the words "any Grenfell Tower payment or" at the beginning, and the words ", the National Emergencies Trust" after the words "the We Love Manchester Emergency Fund".

p.646, *amendment to the Income Support Regulations 1987 (SI 1987/1967) Sch.9, para.21(2) (Sums to be disregarded in the calculation of income other than earnings: income in kind)*

3.020   With effect from July 15, 2020, reg.2(11)(a) of the Social Security (Income and Capital) (Miscellaneous Amendments) Regulations 2020 (SI 2020/618) inserted "is a Grenfell Tower payment or" after "income in kind" and ", the National Emergencies Trust" after "the We Love Manchester Emergency Fund". There are new definitions of "Grenfell Tower Payment" and "the National Emergencies Trust" in reg.2(1).

pp.650-651, *amendment to the Income Support Regulations 1987 (SI 1987/1967) Sch.9, para.39 (Sums to be disregarded in the calculation of income other than earnings: payments from certain funds)*

3.021   With effect from July 15, 2020, reg.2(11)(b) of the Social Security (Income and Capital) (Miscellaneous Amendments) Regulations 2020 (SI 2020/618) inserted ", the National Emergencies Trust" after "the We Love Manchester Emergency Fund" in sub-paras (1) and (7). It inserted the following after sub-para.(1):

"(1A) Any Grenfell Tower payment."

It inserted ", or from a Grenfell Tower payment," after "Trusts to which sub-paragraph (1) refers" in sub-paras (2) and (3) and "or from a Grenfell Tower payment," after "Trusts to which sub-paragraph (1) refers," in sub-paras (4) and (5) and (without the closing comma) after "or deriving from any of the Trusts" in sub-para.(6).

There are new definitions of "Grenfell Tower Payment" and "the National Emergencies Trust" in reg.2(1).

p.653, *amendment to the Income Support Regulations 1987 (SI 1987/1967) Sch.9 (Sums to be disregarded in the calculation of income other than earnings)*

With effect from November 9, 2020, art.3(2) of the Social Security   3.022
(Scotland) Act 2018 (Information-sharing and Scottish Child Payment) (Consequential Provision and Modifications) Order 2020 (SI 2020/482) inserted the following after para.83:

> "**84.** Any Scottish child payment assistance given in accordance with section 79 of the Social Security (Scotland) Act 2018."

The relevant regulations are the Scottish Child Payment Regulations 2020 (SSI 2020/351) (see Part I of this Supplement), which provide for a payment of £10 per week (paid four-weekly in arrears) to claimants in receipt of a UK income-related benefit who are responsible for a child under the age of six. Applications and initial payments cannot have effect before mid-February 2021. See para.7(1)(a) of Sch.10 for the disregard as capital of payments of arrears.

With effect from November 9, 2020, art.9(2) of the Social Security (Scotland) Act 2018 (Young Carer Grants, Short-Term Assistance and Winter Heating Assistance) (Consequential Provision and Modifications) Order 2020 (SI 2020/989) inserted the following after para.84:

> "**85.** Any short-term assistance given in accordance with regulations made under section 36 of the Social Security (Scotland) Act 2018."

The introduction was planned for 2020 of payments to be made to claimants who have appealed against or requested redetermination of a determination to reduce or stop paying another form of assistance (initially in relation to the new child disability payments to replace DLA for the under-18s) under the 2018 Act. The plans were deferred until summer 2021 for a pilot of the child disability payment and the autumn for a full roll-out. See para.7(1)(a) of Sch.10 for the disregard as capital of payments of arrears.

p.663, *annotations to the Income Support Regulations 1987 (SI 1987/1967) Sch.9 (Sums to be disregarded in the calculation of income other than earnings)*

Insert the following in the list of provisions after the entry for para.83:   3.023

    Para.84   Scottish child payments;
    Para.85   Scottish short-term assistance.

p.664, *annotations to the Income Support Regulations 1987 (SI 1987/1967) Sch.9 (Sums to be disregarded in the calculation of income other than earnings)*

With effect from May 29, 2020, reg.26(1)(a) of the Victims' Payments   3.024
Regulations 2020 (SI 2020/103) (see Part I of this Supplement) provides

that a victims' payment or a lump sum under those Regulations is to be disregarded as income.

The £500 payment, administered by local authorities, to be made to those in England entitled to a qualifying income-related benefit (including income support, income-related ESA and income-based JSA) who are required by NHS Test and Trace on or after September 28, 2020 (down to at least March 31, 2021) to self-isolate for 14 (or 10) days, are unable to work from home and will lose income from employment or self-employment as a result was said in the guidance on scheme eligibility not to affect entitlement to other benefits. The same was to apply to the discretionary payment available to those not entitled to a qualifying benefit. However, there has been no amendment to Sch.9 or its equivalents, or elsewhere, to disregard such payments (or payments under the very similar, but not identical, schemes available in Wales, Scotland and Northern Ireland) as income (in contrast to the position in universal credit: see the entry for pp.316–20 of Vol.V). The payments would appear to be in the nature of income because, with the eligibility condition that income will be lost, they constitute compensation for loss of the income that would otherwise have been received (see the notes to reg.23 in the main volume). Could a discretionary payment possibly be regarded as a voluntary payment not made or due to be made at regular intervals and so to be treated as capital under reg.48(9)?

The intention was also expressed that the £500 payments were not to be taken into account as capital. If the suggestion above is correct, they are not as such payments of capital. But there is nothing in the legislation to prevent any amount remaining out of the £500 at the end of the required days of self-isolation from counting as capital under the usual principles.

p.669, *annotation to the Income Support Regulations 1987 (SI 1987/1967) Sch.9, para.15 (Sums to be disregarded in the calculation of income other than earnings: charitable and voluntary payments etc made at regular intervals)*

3.025   *SM v SSWP (ESA)* [2020] UKUT 265 (AAC) has followed *LG v SSWP (ESA)* [2019] UKUT 220 (AAC), [2020] AACR 5 in finding that payments made by trustees under discretionary powers were voluntary and so fell within the equivalent ESA disregard. The decision also held that payments made by trustees of the claimant's parents' wills were not "made by a person for the maintenance of any member of his family or of his former partner or of his children", so as to fall within the exception in para.(2)(a). The payments made by the trustees were not to be regarded as having been made by the parents.

p.681, *amendment to the Income Support Regulations 1987 (SI 1987/1967) Sch.10, para.7(1)(a) (Capital to be disregarded: payments of arrears of certain benefits etc.)*

3.026   With effect from November 9, 2020, art.3(3) of the Social Security (Scotland) Act 2018 (Information-sharing and Scottish Child Payment)

(Consequential Provision and Modifications) Order 2020 (SI 2020/482) substituted "6, 8, 9, 76A or 84 of Schedule 9" for "6, 8, 9 or 76A of Schedule 9".

With effect from November 9, 2020, art.9(3) of the Social Security (Scotland) Act 2018 (Young Carer Grants, Short-Term Assistance and Winter Heating Assistance) (Consequential Provision and Modifications) Order 2020 (SI 2020/989) substituted "9, 76A, 84 or 85" for "9, 76A or 84".

p.684, *amendment to the Income Support Regulations 1987 (SI 1987/1967) Sch.10, para.22 (Capital to be disregarded: payments from certain funds)*

With effect from July 15, 2020, reg.2(12)(a) of the Social Security 3.027 (Income and Capital) (Miscellaneous Amendments) Regulations 2020 (SI 2020/618) inserted ", the National Emergencies Trust" after "the We Love Manchester Emergency Fund" in sub-paras (1) and (7) (an obvious error in the placing of the comma has been corrected). It inserted the following after sub-para.(1):

"(1A) Any Grenfell Tower payment or any payment made by the Child Migrants Trust (registered charity number 1171479) under the scheme for former British child migrants."

It inserted ", or from a Grenfell Tower payment," after "Trusts to which sub-paragraph (1) refers" in sub-paras (2) and (3) and "or from a Grenfell Tower payment," after "Trusts to which sub-paragraph (1) refers," in sub-paras (4) and (5) and (without the closing comma) after "or deriving from any of the Trusts" in sub-para.(6).

There are new definitions of "Grenfell Tower Payment" and "the National Emergencies Trust" in reg.2(1).

p.685, *amendment to the Income Support Regulations 1987 (SI 1987/1967) Sch.10, para.29 (Capital to be disregarded: certain payments in kind)*

With effect from July 15, 2020, reg.2(12)(b) of the Social Security 3.028 (Income and Capital) (Miscellaneous Amendments) Regulations 2020 (SI 2020/618) inserted "which is a Grenfell Tower payment or" after "Any payment in kind". There is a new definition of "Grenfell Tower Payment" in reg.2(1).

p.689, *amendment to the Income Support Regulations 1987 (SI 1987/1967) Sch.10 (Capital to be disregarded)*

With effect from November 9, 2020, art.2 of the Social Security 3.029 (Scotland) Act 2018 (Young Carer Grants, Short-Term Assistance and Winter Heating Assistance) (Consequential Provision and Modifications) Order 2020 (SI 2020/989) inserted the following after para.76:

"**77.** Any assistance given in accordance with the Carer's Assistance (Young Carer Grants) (Scotland) Regulations 2019."

Under the specified regulations (SSI 2019/324, in operation from October 21, 2019), young carer grants of (from April 2020) £305.10, limited to one a year, are payable in Scotland to carers aged 16 to 18 who care for at least 16 hours a week over a 13-week period for a person who normally receives a disability benefit (see Part I of this Supplement). There appears to have been a gap during which grants were not disregarded as capital. No disregard as income has been introduced, but no doubt the grants are in their nature payments of capital.

With effect from the same date art.15 of the same Order inserted the following after para.77:

"**78.** Any winter heating assistance given in accordance with regulations made under section 30 of the Social Security (Scotland) Act 2018."

The relevant regulations are the Winter Heating Assistance for Children and Young People (Scotland) Regulations 2020 (SSI 2020/352, in operation from November 9, 2020) (see Part I of this Supplement), which initially provide an automatic annual grant in November 2020 to a family of £200 for each child entitled to the highest rate of the care component of DLA in the week of September 21–27, 2020.

p.696, *annotation to the Income Support Regulations 1987 (SI 1987/1967) Sch.10 (Capital to be disregarded)*

3.030 Insert the following in the list of provisions after the entry for para. 76:

"*Para.77* Scottish young carer grants;
Para.78 Scottish winter heating assistance."

With effect from May 29, 2020, reg.26(1)(a) of the Victims' Payments Regulations 2020 (SI 2020/103) (see Part I of this Supplement) provides that a victims' payment or a lump sum under those Regulations is to be disregarded as capital.

p.698, *annotation to the Income Support Regulations 1987 (SI 1987/1967) Sch.10, para.3 (Capital to be disregarded: proceeds of sale of former home to be used for purchase of new home within 26 weeks or longer if reasonable)*

3.031 In *EAM v SSWP (UC)* [2020] UKUT 247 (AAC), Judge Poynter has declined to follow *R(IS) 7/01* and the other decisions referred to there as being inconsistent with the principle conclusively confirmed in *In re B (Children)* [2008] UKHL 35, [2009] A.C. 11 that there is only one civil standard of proof and that is proof that the fact in issue more probably occurred than not. His view was that to apply a test to the equivalent provision in para.13 of Sch.10 to the Universal Credit Regulations 2013 in terms of any kind of certainty was to place a higher burden on the claimant than the balance of probabilities. Although he agreed with the proposition in *R(IS) 7/01* that a mere genuine intention to use the sum to purchase a new home is not enough, he continued in para.33 that the phrase "is to be used for the purchase of premises" is about "what in all

310

the circumstances of the case (including the claimant's intentions) is likely to happen in practice." Then he said in para.34 that to the extent that the *R(IS) 7/01* test requires a claimant to prove any fact to any standard other than the balance of probabilities he declined to follow that decision.

There are at least two problems in applying *EAM* in the context of income support, income-related ESA and income-based JSA. One is that it was not necessary to the decision for the judge to reach a definite conclusion on the correctness of *R(IS) 7/01*. On the facts as found by the First-tier Tribunal, the remaining amount attributable to the proceeds of sale of the claimant's home (£37,000) was not enough to buy a new home for her and her partner, so that they would need a mortgage, which on the balance of probabilities they would be unable to secure because of the level of their indebtedness. Accordingly, although the tribunal had been inconsistent on the nature of the test and had seemed to apply a test of practical certainty in concluding that the sum was not to be disregarded, its decision was not set aside because the same result would have followed if Judge Poynter's suggested test had been used. That undermines the basis for not following a reported decision that might otherwise have existed if a First-tier Tribunal or the Secretary of State considered Judge Poynter's reasoning, especially as supported by House of Lords' authority, to be persuasive.

The second problem is that the judge's reasoning appears dubious. There is a slight uncertainty about whether the disagreement with *R(IS) 7/01* extends only to the burden of proving facts necessary to the application of the legislative test or whether it extends also to the burden of showing that that test is met in all the circumstances as established by findings of fact. On balance, the latter seems to be intended. But then the result in accordance with para.33 is that the test to be applied is whether it is more likely than not that the sum will be used for the purchase of premises. Such a test appears, as a matter of the ordinary use of language, to be significantly different from and less restrictive than the legislative test in terms of "is to be used". Arguably, Judge Poynter's approach conflates the nature of the burden of proving that the legislative test is met with the true meaning of that test.

Unless and until *EAM* is taken to the Court of Appeal or there is some further decision clarifying the issue (which may well take some years), tribunals may wish to hedge their bets by applying both approaches in the alternative, but only if properly satisfied that the outcome would be the same whichever was applied. If not so satisfied, a choice will have to be made as to whether the reasoning in *EAM* is sufficiently persuasive to be preferred to the approach approved in *R(IS) 7/01*.

p.829, *amendment to the Jobseeker's Allowance Regulations 1996 (SI 1996/207) reg.1(3) (Interpretation—definition of "Grenfell Tower payment")*

With effect from July 15, 2020, reg.3(1) and (2)(a) of the Social Security (Income and Capital) (Miscellaneous Amendments) Regulations 2020 (SI 2020/618) inserted a new definition of "Grenfell Tower **3.032** payment") immediately before the definition of "a guaranteed income payment" as follows:

""Grenfell Tower payment" means a payment made to a person because that person was affected by the fire on 14th June 2017 at Grenfell Tower, or a payment to the personal representative of such a person—

(a) from the £5 million fund announced on 16th June 2017 for the benefit of certain persons affected by the fire on 14th June 2017 at Grenfell Tower and known as the Grenfell Tower Residents' Discretionary Fund;

(b) by the Royal Borough of Kensington and Chelsea; or

(c) by a registered charity"

p.831, *amendment to the Jobseeker's Allowance Regulations 1996 (SI 1996/207) reg.1(3) (Interpretation—definition of "the National Emergencies Trust")*

3.033   With effect from July 15, 2020, reg.3(1) and (2)(a) of the Social Security (Income and Capital) (Miscellaneous Amendments) Regulations 2020 (SI 2020/618) inserted a new definition of "the National Emergencies Trust" immediately after the definition of "mobility supplement" as follows:

""the National Emergencies Trust" means the registered charity of that name (number 1182809) established on 28th March 2019;"

pp.832-833, *amendment to the Jobseeker's Allowance Regulations 1996 (SI 1996/207) reg.1(3) (Interpretation—definition of "qualifying person")*

3.034   With effect from July 15, 2020, reg.3(1) and (2)(b) of the Social Security (Income and Capital) (Miscellaneous Amendments) Regulations 2020 (SI 2020/618) amended the definition of "qualifying person" to read as follows:

""qualifying person" means a person in respect of whom [a Grenfell Tower payment has been made or] payment has been made from the Fund, the Eileen Trust, MFET Limited the Skipton Fund, the Caxton Foundation, the Scottish Infected Blood Support Scheme, an approved blood scheme, the London Emergencies Trust, the We Love Manchester Emergency Fund [, the National Emergencies Trust] or the London Bombings Relief Charitable Fund;"

p.886, *modifications and annotation to the Jobseeker's Allowance Regulations 1996 (SI 1996/207) reg.15(1)(b) (Circumstances in which a person is not be regarded as available: prisoners on temporary release)*

3.035   With effect from November 12, 2020, the period of operation of the modification to reg.15(1)(b) has been extended to May 12, 2021 by reg.2 of the Social Security (Coronavirus) (Prisoners) Amendment Regulations 2020 (SI 2020/1156). The absence of any modification in relation to the Prisons (Scotland) Act 1989 stems, not from the reason suggested in the main volume, but from the use of different legislation to authorise temporary release of prisoners in Scotland during the coronavirus outbreak.

p.912, *annotation to the Jobseeker's Allowance Regulations 1996 (SI 1996/207) reg.23 (Attendance)*

DC v SSWP (JSA) [2020] UKUT 257 (AAC) has decided the issue   3.036
of interpretation left open in *CS v SSWP (JSA)* [2015] UKUT 61 (AAC), holding that reg.23 allows the oral notification of the manner, time and place of an interview in the course of face to face contact. That was because of the use of the permissive "may" in the regulation and of the lack of any apparent reason for not accepting such notification if oral notification by telephone is accepted. But the tribunal had erred in upholding the decision that the claimant's entitlement to old style JSA terminated on the day of the interview that he had failed to participate in, because he had on the previous day posted a letter to the DWP saying that he would no longer attend for daily signing until he had been given formal notification of the purpose of that requirement. Thus, as accepted by the Secretary of State before the Upper Tribunal, the claimant had made contact with an employment officer within the period ending five working days after the day of the interview, so that entitlement could not cease under reg.25(1)(a). The claimant was, though, subject to a four-week sanction under s.19A(2)(a) of the old style Jobseekers Act 1995 and reg.69A because the judge found that he did not have good reason for failing to participate in the interview. A refusal to attend by way of ultimatum could not amount to good reason. That conclusion must have been reached on the basis that the claimant had been given a sufficient explanation of the purpose orally.

Judge West also noted, in explaining why permission to appeal had been refused on a point, that, although the work coach had apparently expressed the requirement as being to sign daily, the daily visit for evidence of daily jobsearch to be seen entailed an interview as well. The Secretary of State did not rely in the Upper Tribunal on any failure under reg.24(6) and (10) to provide a signed declaration, but that failure could not have led to the termination of entitlement under regs 25(1)(c) and 26(c) because the making of contact with an employment officer within the time limit prevented that result under reg.27. As explained in the notes to reg.27 in the main volume, despite the words of reg.27, there is no requirement for the claimant also to show a good reason for failing to provide the declaration. On the four-week sanction, the prohibition on a reduction in benefit in reg.23 cases (reg.70A(2)(b)) would have been excluded by reg.70A(3). The prohibition in reg.24 cases has no exceptions.

p.1005, *modification of the Jobseeker's Allowance Regulations 1996 (SI 1996/207) reg.78 (Circumstances in which a person is to be treated as being or not being a member of the household)*

With effect from November 12, 2020, the final sentence under the   3.037
heading, *Modification*, should read:

"By reg.6 of SI 2020/409, as amended by reg.2 of the Social Security (Coronavirus) (Prisoners) Amendment Regulations 2020 (SI 2020/1156), the modification will expire at the end of May 12, 2021."

p.1016, *modification of the Jobseeker's Allowance Regulations 1996 (SI 1996/207) reg.85 (Special cases)*

3.038   With effect from November 12, 2020, the final sentence under the heading, *Modification*, should read:

"By reg.6 of SI 2020/409, as amended by reg.2 of the Social Security (Coronavirus) (Prisoners) Amendment Regulations 2020 (SI 2020/1156), the modification will expire at the end of May 12, 2021."

pp.1016-1017, *amendment to the Jobseeker's Allowance Regulations 1996 (SI 1996/207) reg.85A (Special cases: supplemental—persons from abroad)*

3.039   As a result of a series of further amendments, and from various dates as noted below, reg.85A has been amended so that it reads as follows

Special cases: supplemental—persons from abroad
    85A.—(1) "Person from abroad" means, subject to the following provisions of this regulation, a claimant who is not habitually resident in the United Kingdom, the Channel Islands, the Isle of Man or the Republic of Ireland.
    (2) No claimant shall be treated as habitually resident in the United Kingdom, the Channel Islands, the Isle of Man or the Republic of Ireland unless—
    (a) subject to the exceptions in paragraph (2A), the claimant has been living in any of those places for the past three months; and
    (b) the claimant has a right to reside in any of those places, other than a right to reside which falls within paragraph (3) or (3A).
    (2A) The exceptions are where the claimant has at any time during the period referred to in paragraph (2)(a)—
    (a) paid either Class 1 or Class 2 contributions by virtue of regulation 114, 118, 146 or 147 of the Social Security (Contributions) Regulations 2001 or by virtue of an Order in Council having effect under section 179 of the Social Security Administration Act 1992; or
    (b) been a Crown servant posted to perform overseas the duties of a Crown servant; or
    (c) been a member of Her Majesty's forces posted to perform overseas the duties of a member of Her Majesty's forces.
    (3) A right to reside falls within this paragraph if it is one which exists by virtue of, or in accordance with, one or more of the following—

314

(a) regulation 13 of the Immigration (European Economic Area) Regulations 2016; [¹⁵ or]

(aa) regulation 16 of those Regulations, but only in a case where the right exists under that regulation because the claimant satisfies the criteria in paragraph (5) of that regulation;

(b) [¹⁵ ...]

(c) [¹⁵ ...]

(3A) A right to reside falls within this paragraph if it exists by virtue of a claimant having been granted limited leave to enter, or remain in, the United Kingdom under the Immigration Act 1971 by virtue of—

(a) Appendix EU to the immigration rules made under section 3(2) of that Act; [¹⁶ ...]

(b) being a person with a Zambrano right to reside as defined in Annex 1 of Appendix EU to the immigration rules made under section 3(2) of that Act [¹⁶; or

(c) having arrived in the United Kingdom with an entry clearance that was granted under Appendix EU (Family Permit) to the immigration rules made under section 3(2) of that Act.]

[¹⁴ (3B) Paragraph (3A)(a) does not apply to a person who—

(a) has a right to reside granted by virtue of being a family member of a relevant person of Northern Ireland; and

(b) would have a right to reside under the Immigration (European Economic Area) Regulations 2016 if the relevant person of Northern Ireland were an EEA national, provided that the right to reside does not fall within paragraph (3A).]

(4) A claimant is not a person from abroad if he is—

(za) a qualified person for the purposes of regulation 6 of the Immigration (European Economic Area) Regulations 2006 as a worker or a self-employed person;

(zb) a family member of a person referred to in subparagraph (za) [¹⁴ ...];

(zc) a person who has a right to reside permanently in the United Kingdom by virtue of regulation 15(1)(c), (d) or (e) of those Regulations;

[¹⁴(zd) a family member of a relevant person of Northern Ireland, with a right to reside which falls within paragraph (3A)(a), provided that the relevant person of Northern Ireland falls within sub-paragraph (za), or would do so but for the fact that they are not an EEA national;]

[¹⁵(ze) a frontier worker within the meaning of regulation 3 of the Citizens' Rights (Frontier Workers) (EU Exit) Regulations 2020;

(zf) a family member, of a person referred to in sub-paragraph (ze), who has been granted limited leave to enter, or remain in, the United Kingdom by virtue of Appendix EU to the immigration rules made under section 3(2) of the Immigration Act 1971;]

(g) a refugee within the definition in Article 1 of the Convention relating to the Status of Refugees done at Geneva on 28th July

1951, as extended by Article 1(2) of the Protocol relating to the Status of Refugees done at New York on 31st January 1967;

(h) a person who has been granted leave or who is deemed to have been granted leave outside the rules made under section 3(2) of the Immigration Act 1971 where that leave is—

    (i) discretionary leave to enter or remain in the United Kingdom;

    (ii) leave to remain under the Destitution Domestic Violence concession; or

    (iii) leave deemed to have been granted by virtue of regulation 3 of the Displaced Persons (Temporary Protection) Regulations 2005;

(hh) a person who has humanitarian protection granted under those rules; or

(i) a person who is not a person subject to immigration control within the meaning of section 115(9) of the Immigration and Asylum Act and who is in the United Kingdom as a result of his deportation, expulsion or other removal by compulsion of law from another country to the United Kingdom;

[¹⁴ (5) In this regulation—

"EEA national" has the meaning given in regulation 2(1) of the Immigration (European Economic Area) Regulations 2016;

"family member" has the meaning given in regulation 7(1)(a), (b) or (c) of the Immigration (European Economic Area) Regulations 2016 except that regulation 7(4) of those Regulations does not apply for the purposes of paragraphs (3B) and (4)(zd);

"relevant person of Northern Ireland" has the meaning given in Annex 1 of Appendix EU to the immigration rules made under section 3(2) of the Immigration Act 1971.]

[¹⁵ (6) In this regulation references to the Immigration (European Economic Area) Regulations 2016 are to be read with Schedule 4 to the Immigration and Social Security Co-ordination (EU Withdrawal) Act 2020 (Consequential, Saving, Transitional and Transitory Provisions) Regulations 2020.]

AMENDMENTS

14. Social Security (Income-Related Benefits) (Persons of Northern Ireland - Family Members) (Amendment) Regulations 2020 (SI 2020/683) reg.3 (August 24, 2020).

15. Immigration and Social Security Co-ordination (EU Withdrawal) Act 2020 (Consequential, Saving, Transitional and Transitory Provisions) (EU Exit) Regulations 2020 (SI 2020/1309) reg.55 (December 31, 2020 at 11.00 pm).

16. Immigration (Citizens' Rights etc.) (EU Exit) Regulations 2020 (SI 2020/1372) reg 10 (December 31, 2020 immediately after 11.00 pm).

MODIFICATIONS

By reg.83 of, and paras 2 and 3(c) of Sch.4 to, SI 2020/1309, the provisions of the Immigration (European Economic Area) Regulations 2016 that are specified in para.(4) of that Schedule continue to have effect in relation to a "member of the post-transition period group" (*i.e.*, to those who have "pre-settled status") as if they had not been revoked, but subject to the modifications set out in para.(4): see further the *Noter-up* to the 2016 Regulations below.

p.1056, *amendments to the Jobseeker's Allowance Regulations 1996 (SI 1996/207) reg.105(10A) (Notional income)*

With effect from July 15, 2020, reg.3(3) of the Social Security (Income and Capital) (Miscellaneous Amendments) Regulations 2020 (SI 2020/618) inserted ", the National Emergencies Trust" after "the We Love Manchester Emergency Fund" and inserted the following after sub-para.(a): **3.040**

"(ab) which is a Grenfell Tower payment;"

There are new definitions of "Grenfell Tower Payment" and "the National Emergencies Trust" in reg.1(3).

p.1064, *amendments to the Jobseeker's Allowance Regulations 1996 (SI 1996/207) reg.110(10) (Income treated as capital)*

With effect from July 15, 2020, reg.3(4) of the Social Security (Income and Capital) (Miscellaneous Amendments) Regulations 2020 (SI 2020/618) inserted ", the National Emergencies Trust" after "the We Love Manchester Emergency Fund" in para.(10)(c) and inserted the following after para.(10)(a): **3.041**

"(ab) which is a Grenfell Tower payment;"

There are new definitions of "Grenfell Tower Payment" and "the National Emergencies Trust" in reg.1(3).

pp.1067-1068, *amendments to the Jobseeker's Allowance Regulations 1996 (SI 1996/2077) reg.113 (Notional capital)*

With effect from July 15, 2020, reg.3(5) of the Social Security (Income and Capital) (Miscellaneous Amendments) Regulations 2020 (SI 2020/618) substituted "paragraph (3A) or (3B)" for "paragraph (3A)" in para.(3), inserted ", the National Emergencies Trust" after "the We Love Manchester Emergency Fund" in para.(3A) and inserted the following after para.(3A): **3.042**

"(3B) Paragraph (3) shall not apply in respect of a payment of capital which is a Grenfell Tower payment."

There are new definitions of "Grenfell Tower Payment" and "the National Emergencies Trust" in reg.1(3).

p.1084, *amendment to the Jobseeker's Allowance Regulations 1996 (SI 1996/207) reg.130 (Students: interpretation)*

With effect from July 15, 2020, reg.3(6) of the Social Security (Income and Capital) (Miscellaneous Amendments) Regulations 2020 **3.043**

(SI 2020/618) substituted the following for the definition of "post-graduate master's degree loan":

> ""postgraduate loan" means a loan to a student undertaking a post-graduate master's degree course or a postgraduate doctoral degree course pursuant to regulations made under section 22 of the Teaching and Higher Education Act 1998;"

p.1088, *amendment to the Jobseeker's Allowance Regulations 1996 (SI 1996/207) reg.131(3) (Calculation of grant income)*

3.044   With effect from July 15, 2020, reg.3(7) of the Social Security (Income and Capital) (Miscellaneous Amendments) Regulations 2020 (SI 2020/618) omitted the words "master's degree" in both places.

pp.1092-1094, *amendments to the Jobseeker's Allowance Regulations 1996 (SI 1996/207) reg.136(1), (3) and (4A) and heading (Treatment of student loans and postgraduate master's degree loans)*

3.045   With effect from July 15, 2020, reg.3(8) of the Social Security (Income and Capital) (Miscellaneous Amendments) Regulations 2020 (SI 2020/618) omitted the words "master's degree" in all places.

p.1097, *amendment to the Jobseeker's Allowance Regulations 1996 (SI 1996/207) reg.137A (Further disregard of student's income)*

3.046   With effect from July 15, 2020, reg.3(9) of the Social Security (Income and Capital) (Miscellaneous Amendments) Regulations 2020 (SI 2020/618) omitted the words "master's degree".

p.1163, *amendment to the Jobseeker's Allowance Regulations 1996 (SI 1996/207) Sch.2, para.17 (Non-dependant deductions)*

3.047   With effect from July 15, 2020, reg.2(1) and (10) of the Social Security (Income and Capital) (Miscellaneous Amendments) Regulations 2020 (SI 2020/618) amended sub-para.(8)(b) of para.17 by inserting the words "any Grenfell Tower payment or" at the beginning, and the words ", the National Emergencies Trust" after the words "the We Love Manchester Emergency Fund".

p.1190, *amendment to the Jobseeker's Allowance Regulations 1996 (SI 1996/207) Sch.7, para.22(2) (Sums to be disregarded in the calculation of income other than earnings: income in kind)*

3.048   With effect from July 15, 2020, reg.3(11)(a) of the Social Security (Income and Capital) (Miscellaneous Amendments) Regulations 2020 (SI 2020/618) inserted "is a Grenfell Tower payment or" after "income in kind" and ", the National Emergencies Trust" after "the We Love Manchester Emergency Fund". There are new definitions of "Grenfell Tower Payment" and "the National Emergencies Trust" in reg.1(3).

pp.1193–1194, *amendment to the Jobseeker's Allowance Regulations 1996 (SI 1996/207) Sch.7, para.41 (Sums to be disregarded in the calculation of income other than earnings: payments from certain funds)*

With effect from July 15, 2020, reg.3(11)(b) of the Social Security (Income and Capital) (Miscellaneous Amendments) Regulations 2020 (SI 2020/618) inserted ", the National Emergencies Trust" after "the We Love Manchester Emergency Fund" in sub-para. (1). It inserted the following after sub-para.(1): **3.049**

"(1A) Any Grenfell Tower payment."

It inserted ", or from a Grenfell Tower payment," after "Trusts to which sub-paragraph (1) refers" in sub-paras (2) and (3) and "or from a Grenfell Tower payment," after "Trusts to which sub-paragraph (1) refers," in sub-paras (4) and (5) and (without the closing comma) after "or deriving from any of the Trusts" in sub-para.(6). It inserted ", the National Emergencies Trust" after "MFET Limited" in sub-para.(7).

There are new definitions of "Grenfell Tower Payment" and "the National Emergencies Trust" in reg.1(3).

p.1197, *amendment to the Jobseeker's Allowance Regulations 1996 (SI 1996/207) Sch.7 (Sums to be disregarded in the calculation of income other than earnings)*

With effect from November 9, 2020, art.4(2) of the Social Security (Scotland) Act 2018 (Information-sharing and Scottish Child Payment) (Consequential Provision and Modifications) Order 2020 (SI 2020/482) inserted the following after para.79: **3.050**

"**80.** Any Scottish child payment assistance given in accordance with section 79 of the Social Security (Scotland) Act 2018."

The relevant regulations are the Scottish Child Payment Regulations 2020 (SSI 2020/351) (see Part I of this Supplement), which provide for a payment of £10 per week (paid four-weekly in arrears) to claimants in receipt of a UK income-related benefit who are responsible for a child under the age of six. Applications and initial payments cannot have effect before mid-February 2021. See para.12(1)(a) of Sch.8 for the disregard as capital of payments of arrears.

With effect from November 9, 2020, art.10(2) of the Social Security (Scotland) Act 2018 (Young Carer Grants, Short-Term Assistance and Winter Heating Assistance) (Consequential Provision and Modifications) Order 2020 (SI 2020/989) inserted the following after para.80:

"**81.** Any short-term assistance given in accordance with regulations made under section 36 of the Social Security (Scotland) Act 2018."

The introduction was planned for 2020 of payments to be made to claimants who have appealed against or requested redetermination of a determination to reduce or stop paying another form of assistance (initially in relation to the new child disability payments to replace DLA for the under-18s) under the 2018 Act. The plans were deferred until summer 2021 for a pilot of the child disability payment and the autumn for a full roll-out. See para.12(1)(a) of Sch.8 for the disregard as capital of payments of arrears.

p.1203, *annotation to the Jobseeker's Allowance Regulations 1996 (SI 1996/207) Sch.7 (Sums to be disregarded in the calculation of income other than earnings)*

3.051 With effect from May 29, 2020, reg.26(1)(a) of the Victims' Payments Regulations 2020 (SI 2020/103) (see Part I of this Supplement) provides that a victims' payment or a lump sum under those Regulations is to be disregarded as income.

p.1206, *amendment to the Jobseeker's Allowance Regulations 1996 (SI 1996/207) Sch.8, para.12(1)(a) (Capital to be disregarded: payments of arrears of certain benefits etc.)*

3.052 With effect from November 9, 2020, art.4(3) of the Social Security (Scotland) Act 2018 (Information-sharing and Scottish Child Payment) (Consequential Provision and Modifications) Order 2020 (SI 2020/482) substituted "7, 9, 10, 72A or 80 of Schedule 9" for "7, 9, 10 or 72A of Schedule 9".

With effect from November 9, 2020, art.10(3) of the Social Security (Scotland) Act 2018 (Young Carer Grants, Short-Term Assistance and Winter Heating Assistance) (Consequential Provision and Modifications) Order 2020 (SI 2020/989) substituted "10, 72A, 80 or 81" for "10, 72A or 80".

p.1208, *amendments to the Jobseeker's Allowance Regulations 1996 (SI 1996/207) Sch.8, para.22 (Capital to be disregarded: payments from certain funds)*

3.053 With effect from July 15, 2020, reg.3(12)(a) of the Social Security (Income and Capital) (Miscellaneous Amendments) Regulations 2020 (SI 2020/618) inserted ", the National Emergencies Trust" after "the London Bombings Relief Charitable Fund" in sub-para.(1). It inserted the following after sub-para.(1):

"(1A) Any Grenfell Tower payment or any payment made by the Child Migrants Trust (registered charity number 1171479) under the scheme for former British child migrants."

'It inserted ", or from a Grenfell Tower payment," after "Trusts to which sub-paragraph (1) refers" in sub-paras (2) and (3) and "or from a Grenfell Tower payment," after "Trusts to which sub-paragraph (1) refers," in sub-paras (4) and (5) and (without the closing comma) after "or deriving from any of the Trusts" in sub-para.(6)."

There are new definitions of "Grenfell Tower Payment" and "the National Emergencies Trust" in reg.1(3).

p.1209, *amendment to the Jobseeker's Allowance Regulations 1996 (SI 1996/207) Sch.8, para.31 (Capital to be disregarded: certain payments in kind)*

With effect from July 15, 2020, reg.3(12)(b) of the Social Security (Income and Capital) (Miscellaneous Amendments) Regulations 2020 (SI 2020/618) inserted "which is a Grenfell Tower payment or" after "Any payment in kind". There is a new definition of "Grenfell Tower Payment" in reg.1(3). **3.054**

p.1213, *amendment to the Jobseeker's Allowance Regulations 1996 (SI 1996/207) Sch.8 (Capital to be disregarded)*

With effect from November 9, 2020, art.3 of the Social Security (Scotland) Act 2018 (Young Carer Grants, Short-Term Assistance and Winter Heating Assistance) (Consequential Provision and Modifications) Order 2020 (SI 2020/989) inserted the following after para.69: **3.055**

"70. Any assistance given in accordance with the Carer's Assistance (Young Carer Grants) (Scotland) Regulations 2019."

Under the specified regulations (SSI 2019/324, in operation from October 21, 2019), young carer grants of (from April 2020) £305.10, limited to one a year, are payable in Scotland to carers aged 16 to 18 who care for at least 16 hours a week over a 13-week period for a person who normally receives a disability benefit (see Part I of this Supplement). There appears to have been a gap during which grants were not disregarded as capital. No disregard as income has been introduced, but no doubt the grants are in their nature payments of capital.

With effect from the same date art.16 of the same Order inserted the following after para.77:

"71. Any winter heating assistance given in accordance with regulations made under section 30 of the Social Security (Scotland) Act 2018."

The relevant regulations are the Winter Heating Assistance for Children and Young People (Scotland) Regulations 2020 (SSI 2020/352, in operation from November 9, 2020) (see Part I of this Supplement), which initially provide an automatic annual grant in November 2020 to a family of £200 for each child entitled to the highest rate of the care component of DLA in the week of September 21-27, 2020.

p.1216, *annotation to the Jobseeker's Allowance Regulations 1996 (SI 1996/207) Sch.8 (Capital to be disregarded)*

With effect from May 29, 2020, reg.26(1)(a) of the Victims' Payments Regulations 2020 (SI 2020/103) (see Part I of this Supplement) provides that a victims' payment or a lump sum under those Regulations is to be disregarded as capital. **3.056**

p.1242, *amendment to the State Pension Credit Regulations 2002 (SI 2002/1792) reg.1(2) (Interpretation)*

3.057 With effect from July 15, 2020, reg.4(2)(a) of the Social Security (Income and Capital) (Miscellaneous Amendments) Regulations 2020 (SI 2020/618) amended reg.1(2) by inserting after the definition of "The Graduated Retirement Benefit Regulations" the following new definition—

""Grenfell Tower payment" means a payment made to a person because that person was affected by the fire on 14th June 2017 at Grenfell Tower, or a payment to the personal representative of such a person—
  (a) from the £5 million fund announced on 16th June 2017 for the benefit of certain persons affected by the fire on 14th June 2017 at Grenfell Tower and known as the Grenfell Tower Residents' Discretionary Fund;
  (b) by the Royal Borough of Kensington and Chelsea; or
  (c) by a registered charity;".

p.1244, *amendment to the State Pension Credit Regulations 2002 (SI 2002/1792) reg.1(2) (Interpretation)*

3.058 With effect from July 15, 2020, reg.4(2)(a) of the Social Security (Income and Capital) (Miscellaneous Amendments) Regulations 2020 (SI 2020/618) amended reg.1(2) by inserting after the definition of "MFET Limited" the following new definition—

""the National Emergencies Trust" means the registered charity of that name (number 1182809) established on 28th March 2019;".

p.1245, *amendment to the State Pension Credit Regulations 2002 (SI 2002/1792) reg.1(2) (Interpretation)*

3.059 With effect from July 15, 2020, reg.4(2)(b) of the Social Security (Income and Capital) (Miscellaneous Amendments) Regulations 2020 (SI 2020/618) amended the definition of "qualifying person" in reg.1(2) by inserting "a Grenfell Tower payment has been made or" after "means a person in respect of whom" and by inserting ", the National Emergencies Trust" after "the We Love Manchester Emergency Fund".

p.1249, *annotation to the State Pension Credit Regulations 2002 (SI 2002/1792) reg.1(2) (Interpretation—"Prisoner")*

3.060 With effect from November 12, 2020, reg.2 of the Social Security (Coronavirus) (Prisoners) Amendment Regulations 2020 (SI 2020/1156) amended reg.6 of SI 2020/409 by substituting "14 months" for "eight months".

pp.1250–1251, *amendment to the State Pension Credit Regulations 2002 (SI 2002/1792) reg.2 (Persons not in Great Britain)*

With effect from December 31, 2020, reg.13 of the Immigration   3.061
(Citizens' Rights etc.) (EU Exit) Regulations 2020 (SI 2020/1372)
amended para.(3A) by omitting "or" at the end of sub-para.(a) and
inserting at the end of sub-para.(b) the following new sub-paragraph—

"; or
    (c) having arrived in the United Kingdom with an entry clearance
that was granted under Appendix EU (Family Permit) to the immigration rules made under section 3(2) of that Act.".

With effect from August 24, 2020, reg.4(2) of the Social Security
(Income-Related Benefits) (Persons of Northern Ireland—Family Members) (Amendment) Regulations 2020 (SI 2020/683) amended reg.2 by
inserting after para.(3A) the following new paragraph—

"(3B) Paragraph (3A)(a) does not apply to a person who—
    (a) has a right to reside granted by virtue of being a family member
of a relevant person of Northern Ireland; and
    (b) would have a right to reside under the Immigration (European
Economic Area) Regulations 2016 if the relevant person of
Northern Ireland were an EEA national, provided that the right
to reside does not fall within paragraph (3)."

The same amending regulations omitted the words "within the meaning of regulation 7(1)(a), (b) or (c) of those Regulations" in para.(4)(zb)
and inserted after para.(4)(zc) the following new sub-paragraph—

"(zd) a family member of a relevant person of Northern Ireland, with
a right to reside which falls within paragraph (3A)(a), provided that
the relevant person of Northern Ireland falls within sub-paragraph
(za), or would do so but for the fact that they are not an EEA
national;";

Finally, the same amending regulations inserted after para.(4) the
following new definitions provision—

"(5) In this regulation—
    "EEA national" has the meaning given in regulation 2(1) of the
Immigration (European Economic Area) Regulations 2016;
    "family member" has the meaning given in regulation 7(1)(a), (b) or
(c) of the Immigration (European Economic Area) Regulations
2016 except that regulation 7(4) of those Regulations does not
apply for the purposes of paragraphs (3B) and (4)(zd);
    "relevant person of Northern Ireland" has the meaning given in Annex
1 of Appendix EU to the immigration rules made under section 3(2)
of the Immigration Act 1971."

With effect from December 31, 2020, reg.59 of the Immigration and
Social Security Co-ordination (EU Withdrawal) Act 2020 (Consequential, Saving, Transitional and Transitory Provisions) (EU Exit) Regulations 2020 (SI 2020/1309) amended reg.2 by inserting "or" at the end of

para.(3)(b)(ii); by omitting paras (3)(c) to (e); and by inserting after para.(4)(zd) the following new sub-paragraphs—

"(ze) a frontier worker within the meaning of regulation 3 of the Citizens' Rights (Frontier Workers) (EU Exit) Regulations 2020;

(zf) a family member of a person referred to in sub-paragraph (ze), who has been granted limited leave to enter, or remain in, the United Kingdom by virtue of Appendix EU to the immigration rules made under section 3(2) of the Immigration Act 1971;".

The same amending regulations inserted after para.(5) the following new paragraph —

"(6) In this regulation references to the Immigration (European Economic Area) Regulations 2016 are to be read with Schedule 4 to the Immigration and Social Security Co-ordination (EU Withdrawal) Act 2020 (Consequential, Saving, Transitional and Transitory Provisions) Regulations 2020."

pp.1258-1259, *amendments to the State Pension Credit Regulations 2002 (SI 2002/1792) reg.5 (Persons treated as being or not being members of the same household)*

3.062   With effect from November 25, 2020, reg.2(2)(a) of the Universal Credit (Persons who have attained state pension credit qualifying age) (Amendment) Regulations 2020 (SI 2020/655) amended reg.5(2) by substituting "paragraphs (1) and (5)" for "paragraph (1)". Regulation 2(2)(b) of the same amending regulations then inserted after para.(2) the following new paragraphs—

"(3) Paragraph (5) applies where a claimant ("C"), who has attained the qualifying age, would otherwise not be entitled to either state pension credit or universal credit, because—
(a) but for that paragraph, C would be a member of the same household as a partner who has not attained the qualifying age and therefore a member of a mixed-age couple excluded from state pension credit by virtue of section 4(1A), and
(b) C is neither entitled to universal credit jointly with that partner, nor entitled to universal credit as a single person, in one of the cases set out in paragraph (4).
(4) The cases are where C is not entitled to universal credit because C has attained the qualifying age and—
(a) any of the following paragraphs of regulation 3 of the Universal Credit Regulations 2013 (couples) applies, and in the case of paragraph (ii) below, one of the following circumstances applies—
(i) paragraph (3) (treatment of certain couples—universal credit may only be claimed as a single person);
(ii) paragraph (4) (treatment of polygamous marriages), so that C is not entitled to universal credit because C may only claim universal credit either as one of two parties to a

polygamous marriage to be treated as a couple where the other party has also attained the qualifying age, or as a remaining party to such a marriage to be treated as single;

(iii) paragraph (6) (absence from the household—universal credit may only be claimed as a single person); or

(b) C lost joint entitlement to universal credit as part of a mixed-age couple due to one of the following changes of circumstances taking effect from a date (namely the first day of the universal credit assessment period in which the change occurred) that is earlier than when, but for paragraph (5), the same change would take effect for the purposes of state pension credit, those changes being where—

(i) C and their partner are no longer a couple; or

(ii) C is party to a marriage that is no longer polygamous and C's remaining spouse has attained the qualifying age.

(5) Where this paragraph applies—

(a) C and their partner, who are to be treated as a non-polygamous couple in accordance with sub-paragraph (a)(ii) of paragraph (4), or who are no longer parties to a polygamous marriage in accordance with sub-paragraph (b)(ii), are to be treated as members of the same household as each other but not of that of any party (or parties) with whom they are not part of a couple in accordance with those provisions; or

(b) C, who is to be treated as single in accordance with sub-paragraph (a)(i) to (iii) of paragraph (4), or is single in accordance with sub-paragraph (b)(i), is to be treated as though C is not a member of the same household as any party (or parties) with whom C is not part of a couple in accordance with those provisions,

where paragraph (4)(a) applies, with effect from the date on which the relevant paragraph of regulation 3 of the Universal Credit Regulations 2013 first applies to C, or, where paragraph (4)(b) applies, with effect from the date referred to in paragraph (4)(b) on which C lost entitlement to universal credit.

(6) In this regulation—

(a) in relation to universal credit entitlement, "assessment period" has the meaning prescribed by regulation 21 of the Universal Credit Regulations 2013;

(b) "mixed-age", in respect of a couple or a marriage, means where one member has attained the qualifying age and the other has not;

(c) the definition in sub-paragraph (b) includes a polygamous marriage where at least one party to the marriage has attained the qualifying age and at least one has not; and

(d) "polygamous marriage" means a marriage during which a party to it is married to more than one person and which took place under the laws of a country that permits polygamy.".

p.1275, *amendments to the State Pension Credit Regulations 2002 (SI 2002/1792) reg.15 (Income for the purposes of the Act)*

3.063   With effect from November 25, 2020, reg.2(3) of the Universal Credit (Persons who have attained state pension credit qualifying age) (Amendment) Regulations 2020 (SI 2020/655) amended reg.15 by inserting before sub-paragraph (1)(a) the following entry—

"(za) universal credit;".

p.1276, *amendments to the State Pension Credit Regulations 2002 (SI 2002/1792) reg.15 (Income for the purposes of the Act)*

3.064   With effect from November 9, 2020, art.5(2) of the Social Security (Scotland) Act 2018 (Information-Sharing and Scottish Child Payment) (Consequential Provision and Modifications) Order 2020 (SI 2020/482) amended reg.15(1) by inserting after sub-para.(rc) the following—

"(rd) any Scottish child payment assistance given in accordance with section 79 of the Social Security (Scotland) Act 2018."

With effect from November 9, 2020, art.4(2) of the Social Security (Scotland) Act 2018 (Young Carer Grants, Short-Term Assistance and Winter Heating Assistance) (Consequential Provision and Modifications) Order 2020 (SI 2020/989) amended reg.15(1) by inserting after sub-para.(rd) the following—

"(re) any assistance given in accordance with the Carer's Assistance (Young Carer Grants) (Scotland) Regulations 2019;".

p.1313, *amendment to the State Pension Credit Regulations 2002 (SI 2002/1792) Sch.II para.14(8) (Housing costs)*

3.065   With effect from July 15, 2020, reg.4(3) of the Social Security (Income and Capital) (Miscellaneous Amendments) Regulations 2020 (SI 2020/618) amended para.14(8) by inserting ", the National Emergencies Trust" after "the We Love Manchester Emergency Fund" in para.(b) and inserting after para.(b) the following new sub-paragraph—

"(ba) any Grenfell Tower payment;".

pp.1330-1331, *amendment to the State Pension Credit Regulations 2002 (SI 2002/1792) Sch.V para.15 (Income from capital)*

3.066   With effect from July 15, 2020, reg.4(4)(a) of the Social Security (Income and Capital) (Miscellaneous Amendments) Regulations 2020 (SI 2020/618) amended para.15 as follows:

(i) in para.(1), after "the We Love Manchester Emergency Fund" insert ", the National Emergencies Trust";

(ii) after para.(1), insert—

"(1A) Any Grenfell Tower payment or any payment made by the Child Migrants Trust (registered charity number 1171479) under the scheme for former British child migrants.";

   (iii) in sub-paras.(2) and (3), after "Trusts to which sub-paragraph (1) refers" insert ", or from a Grenfell Tower payment,";
   (iv) in sub-paras.(4) and (5), after "Trusts to which sub-paragraph (1) refers," insert "or from a Grenfell Tower payment,";
   (v) in sub-para.(6), after "or deriving from any of the Trusts" insert "or from a Grenfell Tower payment";
   (vi) in sub-para.(7), after "the We Love Manchester Emergency Fund" insert ", the National Emergencies Trust";

p.1332, *amendment to the State Pension Credit Regulations 2002 (SI 2002/1792) Sch.V para.20 (Income from capital)*

With effect from July 15, 2020, reg.4(4)(b) of the Social Security (Income and Capital) (Miscellaneous Amendments) Regulations 2020 (SI 2020/618) deleted "council tax." at the end of sub-para.(1)(f) of para.20 and substituted the following— **3.067**

"; council tax;
   (g) to rectify, or to compensate for, an error made by an officer of the Department for Work and Pensions which was not caused or materially contributed to by any person outside the Department and which prevented or delayed an assessment of the claimant's entitlement to contributory employment and support allowance.".

p.1332, *amendment to the State Pension Credit Regulations 2002 (SI 2002/1792) Sch.V para.20 (Income from capital)*

With effect from November 9, 2020, art.5(3) of the Social Security (Scotland) Act 2018 (Information-Sharing and Scottish Child Payment) (Consequential Provision and Modifications) Order 2020 (SI 2020/482) amended Part 1 of Sch.5 by inserting after para.20(2)(t) the following new sub-paragraph— **3.068**

"(u) any Scottish child payment assistance given in accordance with section 79 of the Social Security (Scotland) Act 2018."

With effect from November 9, 2020, art.4(3) of the Social Security (Scotland) Act 2018 (Young Carer Grants, Short-Term Assistance and Winter Heating Assistance) (Consequential Provision and Modifications) Order 2020 (SI 2020/989) amended Part 1 of Sch.5 by inserting after para.20(2)(u) the following new sub-paragraph—

"(v) any assistance given in accordance with the Carer's Assistance (Young Carer Grants) (Scotland) Regulations 2019.".

pp.1332-1333, *amendment to the State Pension Credit Regulations 2002 (SI 2002/1792) Sch.V para.20A (Income from capital)*

With effect from July 15, 2020, reg.4(4)(b) of the Social Security (Income and Capital) (Miscellaneous Amendments) Regulations 2020 (SI 2020/618) amended para.20A by substituting "relevant benefit, or to which paragraph 20(1)(g) applies, and which has been" for "relevant **3.069** benefit and has been" in para.(1); by inserting "or 9A" after "paragraph 9(2)" in sub-para.(2)(f); and by inserting after sub-para.(2)(j) the following—

"(k) regulations 10A to 10C of the Universal Credit (Transitional Provisions) Regulations 2014;".

p.1344, *amendment to the Social Fund Cold Weather Payments (General) Regulations 1988 (1998/1724) reg.1 (Interpretation—definition of "mean daily temperature")*

3.070   With effect from July 9, 2020, reg.3(1) and (2)(a) of the Social Fund and Social Security (Claims and Payments) (Amendment) Regulations 2020 (SI 2020/600) amended the definition of "mean daily temperature" in reg.1 by substituting the word "site" for the word "station".

p.1345, *amendment to the Social Fund Cold Weather Payments (General) Regulations 1988 (1998/1724) reg.1 (Interpretation—definition of "station")*

3.071   With effect from July 9, 2020, reg.3(1) and (2)(b) of the Social Fund and Social Security (Claims and Payments) (Amendment) Regulations 2020 (SI 2020/600) amended reg.1 by substituting the following definition of "site" for the definition of "station":

""site" means a site accredited by the Met Office in relation to which a period of cold weather may be forecasted or recorded for the purposes of these Regulations;"

pp.1350-1351, *amendment to the Social Fund Cold Weather Payments (General) Regulations 1988 (1998/1724) reg.2 (Prescribed circumstances)*

3.072   With effect from July 9, 2020, reg.3(1) and (3) of the Social Fund and Social Security (Claims and Payments) (Amendment) Regulations 2020 (SI 2020/600) amended reg.2(1), (1A), (1B), (2) and (7) by substituting the word "site" for the word "station" wherever the latter word occurred.

p.1353, *amendment to the Social Fund Cold Weather Payments (General) Regulations 1988 (1998/1724) reg.2A (Designation of primary and secondary stations)*

3.073   With effect from July 9, 2020, reg.3(1) and (4) of the Social Fund and Social Security (Claims and Payments) (Amendment) Regulations 2020 (SI 2020/600) amended the heading of reg.2A by substituting the word "sites" for the word "stations".

With effect from July 9, 2020, reg.3(1) and (5) of the Social Fund and Social Security (Claims and Payments) (Amendment) Regulations 2020 (SI 2020/600) amended reg.2A by substituting the word "site" for the word "station" in both places.

p.1354, *amendment to the Social Fund Cold Weather Payments (General) Regulations 1988 (1998/1724) reg.2C (Review and variation of designations)*

With effect from July 9, 2020, reg.3(1) and (6) of the Social Fund and Social Security (Claims and Payments) (Amendment) Regulations 2020 (SI 2020/600) amended para.(6) of reg.2C by substituting the word "site" for the word "station". 　3.074

p.1387, *amendment to the Social Fund Maternity and Funeral Expenses (General) Regulations 2005 (2005/3061) reg.7 (Funeral payments: entitlement)*

With effect from December 31, 2020 at 11.00 pm, reg.62 of the Immigration and Social Security Co-ordination (EU Withdrawal) Act 2020 (Consequential, Saving, Transitional and Transitory Provisions) (EU Exit) Regulations 2020 (SI 2020/1309) amended reg.7 by substituting the following for para.10: 　3.075

"(10) This paragraph applies where the responsible person or the responsible person's partner is—
  (a) a qualified person within the meaning of regulation 6(1)(b) (worker) or (c) (self-employed person) of the Immigration (European Economic Area) Regulations 2016 (the EEA Regulations);
  (b) a person who retains the status referred to in sub-paragraph (a) pursuant to regulation 6(2) or (4) of the EEA Regulations;
  (c) a person who is a family member of a person referred to in sub-paragraph (a) or (b) within the meaning of regulation 7(1) of the EEA Regulations; or
  (d) a person who has a right to reside permanently in the United Kingdom by virtue of regulation 15(1)(c), (d) or (e) of the EEA Regulations;
  (e) a person granted indefinite leave to enter, or remain in, the United Kingdom under the Immigration Act 1971 by virtue of Appendix EU to the immigration rules made under section 3(2) of that Act."

and by inserting a new para.(11) as follows:

"(11) References in this regulation to the Immigration (European Economic Area) Regulations 2016 are to be read with Schedule 4 to the Immigration and Social Security Co-ordination (EU Withdrawal) Act 2020 (Consequential, Saving, Transitional and Transitory Provisions) Regulations 2020."

p.1388, *modifications for the purpose of the Social Fund Maternity and Funeral Expenses (General) Regulations 2005 (2005/3061) reg.7 (Funeral payments: entitlement)*

Paras (10) and (11) of reg.7 refer to the Immigration (European Economic Area) Regulations 2016. Those Regulations were revoked 　3.076

with effect from December 31, 2020 at 11.00 pm by s.1 of, and para. 2(2) of Sch.1 to, the Immigration and Social Security Co-ordination (EU Withdrawal) Act 2020. However, by reg.83 of, and paras 2 and 3(i) of Sch.4 to, SI 2020/1309, the provisions of the 2016 Regulations that are specified in para.(4) of that Schedule continue to have effect in relation to a "member of the post-transition period group" (i.e., to those who have "pre-settled status") as if they had not been revoked, but subject to the modifications set out in para.(4): see further the Noter-up to the 2016 Regulations below.

pp.1399-1400, *amendment to the Social Fund Maternity and Funeral Expenses (General) Regulations 2005 (2005/3061) reg.9 (Amount of funeral payment)*

3.077   With effect from July 9, 2020, reg.2 of the Social Fund and Social Security (Claims and Payments) (Amendment) Regulations 2020 (SI 2020/600) amended para.(3)(a)(ii) of reg.9 by substituting the word "and" for the word "or" after the words "where the burial takes place,".

p.1422, *annotation to the new style Jobseekers Act 1995 s.1(2) (the jobseeker's allowance: conditions of entitlement—temporary coronavirus provisions)*

3.078   With effect from November 12, 2020, the new reg.10(2B) of the Social Security (Coronavirus) (Further Measures) Regulations 2020 (SI 2020/371), as inserted by reg.2 of the Social Security (Coronavirus) (Further Measures) (Amendment) and Miscellaneous Amendment Regulations 2020 (SI 2020/1201), made May 12, 2021 the date of expiry of the effect of reg.8 of SI 2020/371. Note that the original date of expiry of reg.8 was November 12, 2020, not (as stated in error at one place in the main volume) the last day of the period of three months beginning on March 30, 2020.

p.1439, *annotations to the new style Jobseekers Act 1995 s.6B (work-focused interview requirement)*

3.079   *JB v SSWP (UC)* [2018] UKUT 360 (AAC) was endorsed and applied in *KG v SSWP (UC)* [2020] UKUT 307 (AAC). Before the Upper Tribunal the Secretary of State accepted that the available evidence did not show that the claimant had been properly notified of the requirement to take part in the particular telephone interview with his work coach, so that no sanction could be applied under the equivalent of s.6K. The documents were ambiguous as to whether the interview was under the equivalent of s.6B or the equivalent of s.6G (connected requirements) and what issues the claimant was told were to be investigated, and left it unclear whether he had been adequately informed of the consequences of non-compliance.

p.1448, *annotations to the new style Jobseekers Act 1995 s.6F (imposition of work-related requirements)*

JB v SSWP (UC) [2018] UKUT 360 (AAC) (see the notes to ss.6A and 6B in the main volume) was endorsed and applied in *KG v SSWP (UC)* [2020] UKUT 307 (AAC). Before the Upper Tribunal the Secretary of State accepted that the available evidence did not show that the claimant had been properly notified of the requirement to take part in the particular telephone interview with his work coach, so that no sanction could be applied under the equivalent of s.6K. The documents were ambiguous whether the interview was under the equivalent of s.6B (work-focused interview requirement) or the equivalent of s.6G (connected requirements) and what issues the claimant was told were to be investigated, and left it unclear whether he had been adequately informed of the consequences of non-compliance. **3.080**

p.1449, *annotations to the new style Jobseekers Act 1995 s.6G (connected requirements)*

JB v SSWP (UC) [2018] UKUT 360 (AAC) (see the notes to ss.6A and 6B in the main volume) was endorsed and applied in *KG v SSWP (UC)* [2020] UKUT 307 (AAC). Before the Upper Tribunal the Secretary of State accepted that the available evidence did not show that the claimant had been properly notified of the requirement to take part in the particular telephone interview with his work coach, so that no sanction could be applied under the equivalent of s.6K. The documents were ambiguous whether the interview was under the equivalent of s.6B (work-focused interview requirement) or the equivalent of s.6G and what issues the claimant was told were to be investigated, and left it unclear whether he had been adequately informed of the consequences of non-compliance. **3.081**

p.1554, *annotation to the Jobseeker's Allowance Regulations 2013 (SI 2013/378) reg.46 (short periods of sickness—temporary coronavirus provisions)*

With effect from November 12, 2020, the new reg.10(2B) of the Social Security (Coronavirus) (Further Measures) Regulations 2020 (SI 2020/371), as inserted by reg.2 of the Social Security (Coronavirus) (Further Measures) (Amendment) and Miscellaneous Amendment Regulations 2020 (SI 2020/1201), made May 12, 2021 the date of expiry of the effect of reg.8 of SI 2020/371. **3.082**

p.1559, *annotation to the Jobseeker's Allowance Regulations 2013 (SI 2013/378) reg.46A (extended period of sickness—temporary coronavirus provisions)*

With effect from November 12, 2020, the new reg.10(2B) of the Social Security (Coronavirus) (Further Measures) Regulations 2020 (SI 2020/371), as inserted by reg.2 of the Social Security (Coronavirus) **3.083**

(Further Measures) (Amendment) and Miscellaneous Amendment Regulations 2020 (SI 2020/1201), made May 12, 2021 the date of expiry of the effect of reg.8 of SI 2020/371.

p.1607, *correction to the Early Years Assistance (Best Start Grants) (Scotland) Regulations 2018 (SSI 2018/370) Sch.2, para.3(4) (Exception to paragraph 1(b))*

3.083.1   The text of para.3(4) in the main volume should read:

"(4) [¹ Since the first grant recipient applied for a pregnancy and baby grant or a sure start maternity grant in respect of the child, or the date the decision referred to in sub-paragraph (3)(b) was taken], the applicant has not been—

(a) the partner of the first grant recipient;
(b) a dependant of the first grant recipient; or
(c) an individual, or the partner of an individual, for whom the first grant recipient is a dependant."

p.1607, *amendment to the Early Years Assistance (Best Start Grants) (Scotland) Regulations 2018 (SSI 2018/370) Sch.2, para.4 (Pregnancy and baby grant—Eligibility—Residence requirement)*

3.084   With effect from December 31, 2020 at 11.00 pm, reg.3(1) and (2) of the Social Security Co-ordination (EU Exit) (Scotland) (Amendments etc.) Regulations 2020 (SSI 2020/399) amended para.4(2) of Sch.2 to read as follows:

"(2) The condition referred to in sub-paragraph (1)(b) is met on any day that the individual is—

(a) habitually resident in the United Kingdom, the Channel Islands, [or the Isle of Man];
[(aa) a person who, or has a partner who, is habitually resident in the European Economic Area or Switzerland and—
  (i) is a qualified person within the meaning of regulation 6(1)(a) (jobseeker), (b) (worker), (c) (self-employed person), (d) (self-sufficient person) or (e) (student) of the Immigration (European Economic Area) Regulations 2016 (the EEA Regulations);
  (ii) retains the status referred to in sub-head (i) pursuant to regulation 6(2) or (4) of the EEA Regulations;
  (iii) is a family member of a person referred to in sub-head (i) or (ii) within the meaning of regulation 7(1) of the EEA Regulations;
  (iv) has a right to reside permanently in the United Kingdom by virtue of regulation 15(1) of the EEA Regulations; or
  (v) has been granted indefinite or limited leave to enter, or remain in, the United Kingdom under the Immigration Act 1971 by virtue of Appendix EU to the immigration rules made under section 3(2) of that Act.]

(b)   a refugee within the definition in Article 1 of the Convention relating to the status of refugees done at Geneva on 28th July 1951, as extended by article 1(2) of the Protocol relating to the status of refugees done at New York on 31st January 1967;

(c)   a person who has been granted, or who is deemed to have been granted, leave outside the rules made under section 3(2) of the Immigration Act 1971, where that leave is—

    (i)   discretionary leave to enter or remain in the United Kingdom;

    (ii) leave to remain under the destitution domestic violence concession; or

    (iii) leave deemed to have been granted by virtue of regulation 3 of the Displaced Persons (Temporary Protection) Regulations 2005;

(d)   a person who has humanitarian protection granted under the rules made under section 3(2) of the Immigration Act 1971; or

(e)   a person who—

    (i)   is not subject to immigration control within the meaning of section 115(9) of the Immigration and Asylum Act 1999; and

    (ii) is in the United Kingdom as a result of deportation, expulsion or other removal by compulsion of law from another country to the United Kingdom."

p.1609, *amendment to the Early Years Assistance (Best Start Grants) (Scotland) Regulations 2018 (SSI 2018/370) new Schedule 3 (Early Learning Grant)*

With effect from April 29, 2019, reg.6 of the Early Years Assistance **3.085** (Best Start Grants) (Scotland) Amendment (No. 2) Regulations 2019 (SSI 2019/157) inserted a new Schedule 3 as follows:

SCHEDULE 3   "Regulation 3(4)

EARLY LEARNING GRANT

PART 1

ELIGIBILITY

Eligibility
1. An individual is eligible for an early learning grant in respect of a child if—
(a) the individual's application for the grant is made on or after the day that the Early Years Assistance (Best Start Grants) (Scotland) Amendment (No. 2) Regulations 2019 are made (see regulation 4 in relation to when an application is to be treated as made),
(b) the individual's application for the grant is made in the period that—
  (i) begins on the child's 2nd birthday, and
  (ii) ends at the end of the day that falls 6 months after the child's 3rd birthday,
(c) no-one else has received, or is due to receive, an early learning grant in respect of the child (but see paragraph 2),

(d) on the day the application is made the individual satisfies the residence requirement set by paragraph 3,

(e) either the individual or the individual's partner is (or both of them are) responsible for the child on the day the application is made,

(f) at least one of these statements is true—

    (i) the individual or the individual's partner has (or both of them have) been awarded, for the day the application is made (or for a period which includes that day), assistance of a kind specified in regulation 11,

    (ii) the individual or the individual's partner has (or both of them have) been awarded universal credit for—

        (aa) the assessment period that includes the day the application is made, or

        (bb) the assessment period that ended immediately before the assessment period mentioned in sub-head (aa) started,

    (iii) on the day the application is made the individual is under 18 years of age,

    (iv) on the day the application is made the individual is—

        (aa) 18 or 19 years of age, and

        (bb) a dependant of another individual, and

(g) the child is not, on the day the application is made, living in a residential establishment as defined in section 202(1) of the Children's Hearings (Scotland) Act 2011.

Exception to paragraph 1(c)

2.—(1) For the purpose of determining the entitlement of the individual referred to in this paragraph as the applicant, the eligibility condition in paragraph 1(c) is to be ignored in the circumstance described by sub-paragraphs (2) to (6).

(2) An individual ("the first grant recipient") has been, or is due to be, given an early learning grant in respect of the child.

(3) Another individual ("the applicant") first came to be responsible for the child after—

(a) the first grant recipient applied for an early learning grant in respect of the child, or

(b) a determination of the first grant recipient's entitlement to an early learning grant

in respect of the child was made without an application (see Part 2 of schedule 1).

(4) The applicant has not been the partner of the first grant recipient at any time since the first grant recipient applied for an early learning grant in respect of the child.

(5) On the day the applicant applies, the child does not normally live with the first grant recipient.

(6) On the day the applicant applies, no-one other than the first grant recipient has been, or is due to be, given an early learning grant in respect of the child.

(7) In this paragraph, references to "the day the applicant applies" are to the day the applicant's application for an early learning grant in respect of the child is made.

Residence requirement

3.—(1) The residence requirement referred to in paragraph 1(d) is satisfied by an individual on a day if, on that day—

(a) the individual is ordinarily resident in Scotland, and

(b) in a case where neither the individual nor the individual's partner has been awarded assistance as mentioned in paragraph 1(f)(i) or (ii), the condition set by sub-paragraph (2) is also met.

(2) The condition referred to in sub-paragraph (1)(b) is met on any day that the individual is—

(a) habitually resident in the United Kingdom, the Channel Islands [¹ or the Isle of Man],

[¹ (aa) a person who, or has a partner who, is habitually resident in the European Economic Area or Switzerland and—

    (i) is a qualified person within the meaning of regulation 6(1)(a) (jobseeker), (b) (worker), (c) (self-employed person), (d) (self-sufficient person) or (e) (student) of the Immigration (European Economic Area) Regulations 2016 (the EEA Regulations);

(ii) retains the status referred to in sub-head (i) pursuant to regulation 6(2) or (4) of the EEA Regulations;

(iii) is a family member of a person referred to in sub-head (i) or (ii) within the meaning of regulation 7(1) of the EEA Regulations;

(iv) has a right to reside permanently in the United Kingdom by virtue of regulation 15(1) of the EEA Regulations; or

(v) has been granted indefinite or limited leave to enter, or remain in, the United Kingdom under the Immigration Act 1971 by virtue of Appendix EU to the immigration rules made under section 3(2) of that Act."]

(b) a refugee within the definition in Article 1 of the Convention relating to the status of refugees done at Geneva on 28 July 1951, as extended by article 1(2) of the Protocol relating to the status of refugees done at New York on 31 January 1967,

(c) a person who has been granted, or who is deemed to have been granted, leave outside the rules made under section 3(2) of the Immigration Act 1971(a), where that leave is—

(i) discretionary leave to enter or remain in the United Kingdom,

(ii) leave to remain under the destitution domestic violence concession, or

(iii) leave deemed to have been granted by virtue of regulation 3 of the Displaced Persons (Temporary Protection) Regulations 2005,

(d) a person who has humanitarian protection granted under the rules made under section 3(2) of the Immigration Act 1971,

(e) a person who—

(i) is not subject to immigration control within the meaning of section 115(9) of the Immigration and Asylum Act 1999, and

(ii) is in the United Kingdom as a result of deportation, expulsion or other removal by compulsion of law from another country to the United Kingdom.

PART 2

ASSISTANCE TO BE GIVEN

Value of grant

4. The value of an early learning grant is £250.

Form in which grant is given

5.—(1) Subject to sub-paragraph (2), an early learning grant is to be given as money.

(2) If—

(a) the Scottish Ministers offer to give an individual some or all of the value of an early learning grant in a form other than money, and

(b) the individual agrees to be given the grant in that form, the grant is to be given in that form, unless the individual withdraws agreement before the grant is given.".

AMENDMENT

1. Social Security Co-ordination (EU Exit) (Scotland) (Amendments etc.) Regulations 2020 (SSI 2020/399), reg.3(1) and (3) (December 31, 2020 at 11.00 pm).

p.1609, *amendment to the Early Years Assistance (Best Start Grants) (Scotland) Regulations 2018 (SSI 2018/370) new Schedule 4 (School age grant)*

With effect from June 3, 2019, reg.9 of the Early Years Assistance (Best Start Grants) (Scotland) Amendment (No. 2) Regulations 2019 (SSI 2019/157) inserted a new Schedule 4 as follows: **3.086**

"SCHEDULE 4 Regulation 3(5)

S<small>CHOOL-AGE GRANT</small>

P<small>ART</small> 1

E<small>LIGIBILITY</small>

Eligibility

1. An individual is eligible for a school-age grant in respect of a child if—
    (a) the individual's application for the grant is made on or after 3 June 2019 (see regulation 4 in relation to when an application is to be treated as made),
    (b) the individual's application for the grant is made within the period described in paragraph 2,
    (c) no-one else has received, or is due to receive, a school-age grant in respect of the child (but see paragraph 3),
    (d) on the day the application is made the individual satisfies the residence requirement set by paragraph 4,
    (e) either the individual or the individual's partner is (or both of them are) responsible for the child on the day the application is made,
    (f) at least one of these statements is true—
        (i) the individual or the individual's partner has (or both of them have) been awarded, for the day the application is made (or for a period which includes that day), assistance of a kind specified in regulation 11,
        (ii) the individual or the individual's partner has (or both of them have) been awarded universal credit for—
            (aa) the assessment period that includes the day the application is made, or
            (bb) the assessment period that ended immediately before the assessment period mentioned in sub-head (aa) started,
        (iii) on the day the application is made the individual is under 18 years of age,
        (iv) on the day the application is made the individual is—
            (aa) 18 or 19 years of age, and
            (bb) a dependant of another individual, and
    (g) the child is not, on the day the application is made, living in a residential establishment as defined in section 202(1) of the Children's Hearings (Scotland) Act 2011.

Period within which application must be made

2.—(1) The period referred to in paragraph 1(b)—
    (a) begins on 1 June in the relevant year, and
    (b) ends at the end of the last day of February in the following year.
    (2) In sub-paragraph (1), "the relevant year" means—
    (a) if the child's birthday is in January or February, the calendar year in which the child's 4th birthday falls,
    (b) otherwise, the calendar year in which the child's 5th birthday falls.

Exception to paragraph 1(c)

3.—(1) For the purpose of determining the entitlement of the individual referred to in this paragraph as the applicant, the eligibility condition in paragraph 1(c) is to be ignored in the circumstance described by sub-paragraphs (2) to (6).
    (2) An individual ("the first grant recipient") has been, or is due to be, given a school-age grant in respect of the child.
    (3) Another individual ("the applicant") first came to be responsible for the child after—
    (a) the first grant recipient applied for a school-age grant in respect of the child, or
    (b) a determination of the first grant recipient's entitlement to a school-age grant in respect of the child was made without an application (see Part 2 of schedule 1).
    (4) The applicant has not been the partner of the first grant recipient at any time since the first grant recipient applied for a school-age grant in respect of the child.
    (5) On the day the applicant applies, the child does not normally live with the first grant recipient.

(6) On the day the applicant applies, no-one other than the first grant recipient has been, or is due to be, given a school-age grant in respect of the child.

(7) In this paragraph, references to "the day the applicant applies" are to the day the applicant's application for a school-age grant in respect of the child is made.

Residence requirement

4.—(1) The residence requirement referred to in paragraph 1(d) is satisfied by an individual on a day if, on that day—

(a) the individual is ordinarily resident in Scotland, and

(b) in a case where neither the individual nor the individual's partner has been awarded assistance as mentioned in paragraph 1(f)(i) or (ii), the condition set by sub-paragraph (2) is also met.

(2) The condition referred to in sub-paragraph (1)(b) is met on any day that the individual is—

(a) habitually resident in the United Kingdom, the Channel Islands [¹ or the Isle of Man],

[¹ (aa) a person who, or has a partner who, is habitually resident in the European Economic Area or Switzerland and—

    (i) is a qualified person within the meaning of regulation 6(1)(a) (jobseeker), (b) (worker), (c) (self-employed person), (d) (self-sufficient person) or (e) (student) of the Immigration (European Economic Area) Regulations 2016 (the EEA Regulations);

    (ii) retains the status referred to in sub-head (i) pursuant to regulation 6(2) or (4) of the EEA Regulations;

    (iii) is a family member of a person referred to in sub-head (i) or (ii) within the meaning of regulation 7(1) of the EEA Regulations;

    (iv) has a right to reside permanently in the United Kingdom by virtue of regulation 15(1) of the EEA Regulations; or

    (v) has been granted indefinite or limited leave to enter, or remain in, the United Kingdom under the Immigration Act 1971 by virtue of Appendix EU to the immigration rules made under section 3(2) of that Act.]

(b) a refugee within the definition in Article 1 of the Convention relating to the status of refugees done at Geneva on 28 July 1951, as extended by article 1(2) of the Protocol relating to the status of refugees done at New York on 31 January 1967,

(c) a person who has been granted, or who is deemed to have been granted, leave outside the rules made under section 3(2) of the Immigration Act 1971, where that leave is—

    (i) discretionary leave to enter or remain in the United Kingdom,

    (ii) leave to remain under the destitution domestic violence concession, or

    (iii) leave deemed to have been granted by virtue of regulation 3 of the Displaced Persons (Temporary Protection) Regulations 2005,

(d) a person who has humanitarian protection granted under the rules made under section 3(2) of the Immigration Act 1971,

(e) a person who—

    (i) is not subject to immigration control within the meaning of section 115(9) of the Immigration and Asylum Act 1999, and

    (ii) is in the United Kingdom as a result of deportation, expulsion or other removal by compulsion of law from another country to the United Kingdom.

PART 2

ASSISTANCE TO BE GIVEN

Value of grant

5. The value of a school-age grant is £250.

Form in which grant is given

6.—(1) Subject to sub-paragraph (2), a school-age grant is to be given as money.

(2) If—

(a) the Scottish Ministers offer to give an individual some or all of the value of a school-age grant in a form other than money, and

(b) the individual agrees to be given the grant in that form, the grant is to be given in that form, unless the individual withdraws agreement before the grant is given.".

AMENDMENT

1. Social Security Co-ordination (EU Exit) (Scotland) (Amendments etc.) Regulations 2020 (SSI 2020/399), reg.3(1) and (4) (December 31, 2020 at 11.00 pm).

p.1614, *amendment to the Funeral Expense Assistance (Scotland) Regulations 2019 (SSI 2019/292) reg.9 (Residence conditions, place of funeral and status)*

3.087   With effect from December 31, 2020 at 11.00 pm, reg.5(1) and (2) of the Social Security Co-ordination (EU Exit) (Scotland) (Amendments etc.) Regulations 2020 (SSI 2020/399) substituted the following for reg.9(3):

"(3) This paragraph applies where the applicant is, or has a partner who is—

(a) a qualified person within the meaning of regulation 6(1)(b) (worker) or (c) (self-employed person) of the Immigration (European Economic Area) Regulations 2016 (the EEA Regulations);

(b) a person who retains the status referred to in sub-paragraph (a) pursuant to regulation 6(2) or (4) of the EEA Regulations;

(c) a person who is a family member of a person referred to in sub-paragraph (a) or (b) within the meaning of regulation 7(1) of the EEA Regulations;

(d) a person who has a right to reside permanently in the United Kingdom by virtue of regulation 15(1)(c), (d) or (e) of the EEA Regulations; or

(e) a person granted indefinite or limited leave to enter, or remain in, the United Kingdom under the Immigration Act 1971 by virtue of Appendix EU to the immigration rules made under section 3(2) of that Act."

p.1615, *amendment to the Funeral Expense Assistance (Scotland) Regulations 2019 (SSI 2019/292) reg.11 (Estate of deceased person)*

3.088   In relation to applications for funeral expense assistance made on or after April 1, 2020, reg.5(1) and (2) of the Funeral Expense Assistance and Young Carer Grants (Up-rating) (Miscellaneous Amendments) (Scotland) Regulations 2020 (SSI 2020/99) amended reg.11 by inserting the words "pre-paid funeral plan," immediately after the words "burial club,".

pp.1616-1617, *amendment to the Funeral Expense Assistance (Scotland) Regulations 2019 (SSI 2019/292) reg.13 (Amount of funeral expense assistance)*

In relation to applications for funeral expense assistance made on or   **3.089** after April 1, 2020, reg.5(1) and (3) of the Funeral Expense Assistance and Young Carer Grants (Up-rating) (Miscellaneous Amendments) (Scotland) Regulations 2020 (SSI 2020/99) amended reg.13 by (1) substituting the figure "£1000" for the figure "£700" in para.(1)(b); (2) substituting the figure "£20.35" for the figure "£20" in para.(4)(b); (3) substituting the figure "£122.05" for the figure "£120" in para.(6); and (4) substituting a new para.(6)(a) as follows:

"(a) has left in place a pre-paid funeral plan, and".

p.1617, *amendment to the Funeral Expense Assistance(Scotland) Regulations 2019 (SSI 2019/292) reg.14 (Deductions from an award of funeral expense assistance)*

In relation to applications for funeral expense assistance made on or   **3.090** after April 1, 2020, reg.5(1) and (4) of the Funeral Expense Assistance and Young Carer Grants (Up-rating) (Miscellaneous Amendments) (Scotland) Regulations 2020 (SSI 2020/99) amended reg.14 by omitting the words "pre-paid funeral plan," and "plan" in para.(1)(b).

PART IV

UPDATING MATERIAL
VOLUME III

ADMINISTRATION, ADJUDICATION AND
THE EUROPEAN DIMENSION

Commentary by

Mark Rowland

Christopher Ward

pp.6-7, *annotation to Forfeiture Act 1982 s.4(1)-(1H) (Upper Tribunal to decide whether rule applies to social security benefits)*

The forfeiture rule was disapplied (under s.2 of the Act) in *In re*   4.001
Challen, decd [2020] EWHC 1330 (Ch); [2020] 3 W.L.R. 440, where a woman had pleaded guilty to manslaughter on the grounds of diminished responsibility. She had beaten her husband to death with a hammer after she had endured his coercive control throughout a 40-year relationship. The judgment of the High Court includes a useful survey of the law.

In *SSWP v LK (RP)* [2019] UKUT 421 (AAC), it was found that the forfeiture rule did not apply at all. The claimant had shot her husband with his shotgun in 1992 but had said it was an accident. She had been acquitted of murder and, the judge inferred, manslaughter in 1993. She had been awarded a Category B retirement pension in 2007 without the forfeiture question being considered—and the forfeiture question would have arisen if she had claimed widow's benefit after her husband's death—but the case was referred to the Upper Tribunal for consideration under s.4 of the 1982 Act only in 2019. The reference was not accompanied by any evidence other than of the bare fact of the acquittal, but, by chance, the claimant was able to instruct the solicitor who had acted for her in the criminal trial and he remembered the case and was able to supply his recollection of the issues in it. The Upper Tribunal referred to *R(G) 2/90* (mentioned in the annotation to s.1 in the main work) and declined to go behind the acquittal, having decided not to carry out any further investigation of the case. The judge expressed some scepticism as to the Secretary of State's assertion that no further evidence could be found, but decided not to make further enquiries due both to the delay in making the reference and the unlikelihood of there being sufficiently cogent evidence to justify deciding the reference against the claimant. The judge also raised the question whether the reference should have been made at all in the absence of any evidence, but, having received submissions from the Secretary of State, was inclined to accept that a reference was mandatory in any case where there had been a prosecution in respect of a killing (because a prosecution implied that there had been evidence that the killing was unlawful and so raised a question to be determined under s.4), although he did not reach a concluded view on the issue. Clearly, any reference should have been made when a claim for widow's benefit or Category B retirement pension was first made.

p.74, *Social Security Administration Act 1992 s.71 (Failure to disclose)*

For important decisions by the Northern Ireland Social Security   4.002
Commissioners, with the benefit of unusually detailed evidence, on the extent to which *Hinchy* may be applicable given the move from paper-based to computerised systems in the period since 1993-98 (which *Hinchy* concerned), see *SK v Department for Communities (ESA)* [2020] NiCom 73 and *PMcL v Department for Communities (ESA)* [2020] NiCom 20.

p.81, *Social Security Administration Act 1992 s.71 (Causation)*

4.003 For important decisions by the Northern Ireland Social Security Commissioners, with the benefit of unusually detailed evidence, on the extent to which *Hinchy* may be applicable given the move from paper-based to computerised systems in the period since 1993-98 (which *Hinchy* concerned) and the impact on issues of causation, see *SK v Department for Communities (ESA)* [2020] NiCom 73 and *PMcL v Department for Communities (ESA)* [2020] NiCom 21.

pp.91-92, *Social Security Administration Act 1992 s.73 (Overlapping benefits—general)*

4.004 With effect from December 31, 2020, in subsection (5), substitute "member State" for "member State other than the United Kingdom" (Social Security (Amendment) (EU Exit) Regulations 2019 (SI 2019/128), reg.3(2) (as applied by European Union (Withdrawal Agreement) Act 2020 Sch.5 para.1(1)).

pp.92-93, *Social Security Administration Act 1992 s.74 (Income support and other payments)*

4.005 With effect from December 31, 2020, in subsection (2)(a), substitute "member State" for "member State other than the United Kingdom" (Social Security (Amendment) (EU Exit) Regulations 2019 (SI 2019/128), reg.3(3) (as applied by European Union (Withdrawal Agreement) Act 2020 Sch.5 para.1(1)).

p.101, *Social Security Administration Act 1992 s.80 (Child benefit—overlap with benefits under legislation of other member States)*

4.006 With effect from December 31, 2020, in the title of the section, omit the word "other"; and in the body of the section, substitute "member State" for "member State other than the United Kingdom" (Social Security (Amendment) (EU Exit) Regulations 2019 (SI 2019/128), reg.3(4) (as applied by European Union (Withdrawal Agreement) Act 2020 Sch.5 para.1(1)).

pp.154-155, *Social Security Administration Act 1992 s.179 (Reciprocal Agreements with countries outside the United Kingdom)*

4.007 With effect from December 16, 2020, the following amendments were made by the Social Security Co-ordination (Revocation of Retained Direct EU Legislation and Related Amendments) (EU Exit) Regulations 2020 (SI 2020/1508), reg.10 and Schedule:

In subsection (1)—
(a) in paragraph (a), after "United Kingdom" insert "or an international organisation";
(b) in paragraph (b), after "other government" insert "or international organisation".

In subsection (3)—
    (a) in paragraph (a)—
        (i) for "law of the country" substitute "law in force in the country";
        (ii) after "agreement is made" insert "or has effect";
    (b) in paragraph (b), for "law of that country" substitute "law in force in that country".

In subsection (4), after paragraph (aj) insert—

"(ak) to Regulation (EC) No 883/2004 of the European Parliament and of the Council of 29 April 2004 on the coordination of social security systems, as it forms part of domestic law by virtue of section 3 of the European Union (Withdrawal) Act 2018;

(al) to Regulation (EC) No 987/2009 of the European Parliament and of the Council of 16 September 2009 laying down the procedure for implementing Regulation (EC) No 883/2004, as it forms part of domestic law by virtue of section 3 of the European Union (Withdrawal) Act 2018;

(am) to Council Regulation (EEC) No 1408/71 of 14 June 1971 on the application of social security schemes to employed persons, to self-employed persons and to members of their families moving within the Community, as it forms part of domestic law by virtue of section 3 of the European Union (Withdrawal) Act 2018;

(an) to Council Regulation (EEC) No 574/72 of 21 March 1972 laying down the procedure for implementing Regulation (EEC) No 1408/71 on the application of social security schemes to employed persons, to self-employed persons and to members of their families moving within the Community, as it forms part of domestic law by virtue of section 3 of the European Union (Withdrawal) Act 2018;

(ao) to Council Regulation (EC) No 859/2003 of 14 May 2003 extending the provisions of Regulation (EEC) No 1408/71 and Regulation (EEC) No 574/72 to nationals of third countries who are not already covered by those provisions solely on the ground of their nationality, as it forms part of domestic law by virtue of section 3 of the European Union (Withdrawal) Act 2018.".

After subsection (5) insert—

"(6) In this section, "international organisation" means an organisation of which—
    (a) two or more sovereign powers are members, or
    (b) the governments of two or more sovereign powers are members.".

p.175, *annotation to Social Security (Recovery of Benefits) Act 1997*

In *R. (on the application of Aviva Insurance Ltd) v Secretary of State for Work and Pensions* [2020] EWHC 3118 (Admin), Henshaw J held that the Secretary of State's interpretation of provisions of the 1997 Act was incompatible with the European Convention on Human Rights because, combined with other developments in the law concerned with liability to pay compensation to those suffering from certain industrial diseases,   **4.008** they had the effect of requiring insurers under policies underwritten before the Act was enacted to pay to the Secretary of State amounts that did not correspond to any damage caused by their insured where either the insured was guilty of contributory negligence or the insured was only one of two or more employers liable for such damage and the insurer's contribution to the victim's exposure was limited.

In a second judgment (*R. (on the application of Aviva Insurance Limited) v Secretary of State for Work and Pensions* [2021] EWHC 30 (Admin)), Henshaw J held that the Act (particularly s.6) should be "read down" under s.3 of the Human Rights Act 1998 "so as to make a proportionate reduction in the liability to repay benefits under the Act of an insurer under a policy of insurance issued before 19 March 1997 [the date the Act received Royal Assent] indemnifying its insured for liability to pay damages for a disease (and the liability under the Act of any reinsurer in respect of such a policy), if and to the extent that the insured's liability to the person suffering from the disease:

    i. is (or was) for a proportion only of the damages otherwise due to the person suffering from the disease, by reason of the contributory negligence of that person; and/or

    ii. is (or was) for damages in respect of part only of a disease constituting a 'divisible' injury (in the sense that periods of exposure can be linked on a causal basis to the onset or severity of the disease because it is a dose—related disease, whose extent and severity is related to the quantity of fibres ingested) in respect of which the relevant State benefits were paid; and/or

    iii. would, but for section 3 of the Compensation Act 2006, have been for only a proportion of the damages attributable to a disease constituting an 'indivisible' injury."

This is to be done from the date when the illegality began, which in relation to heads (i) and (ii) was October 2, 2000 (when the Human Rights Act 1998 came into effect) and in relation to head (iii) was the end of 2002 (a reasonable time after the handing down of the decision in *Fairchild v Glenhaven Funeral Services Ltd* [2002] UKHL 22; [2003] 1 A.C. 32).

Issues arising on the insurers' substantial claim for compensation for their financial loss were transferred to the Chancery Division of the High Court.

Henshaw J gave both parties permission to appeal to the Court of Appeal.

pp.224-225, *annotation to Social Security Act 1998 s.8(1) (Decisions by Secretary of State)*

4.009   In *MH v SSWP (II)* [2020] UKUT 297 (AAC), the judge raised the question whether a claim for disablement pension made in respect of one prescribed industrial disease may, before it is determined, be treated as having been made, additionally or alternatively, in respect of another prescribed disease without a further, formal, claim having been submitted. In the event, he left that question open, but he accepted that the Secretary of State was entitled, although perhaps not required, to issue

346

a separate decision as regards entitlement to disablement pension in respect of each prescribed disease that she had considered.

In *NSP v Stoke-on-Trent CC (HB)* [2020] UKUT 311 (AAC), it was pointed out that any decision that there has been an overpayment that is recoverable from a claimant's landlord should also be addressed to a claimant, both because it may raise issues as to the claimant's entitlement (in respect of which the claimant will have a right of appeal) and also because the landlord is entitled to know whether the overpayment is also recoverable from the claimant (as is likely to be the case). Reference was made to *R(H) 6/06*.

pp.235-236, *annotation to Social Security Act 1998 s.10(1) (Decisions superseding earlier decision)*

Amendments made to the Jobseekers (Back to Work Schemes) Act 4.010
2013 by the Jobseekers (Back to Work Schemes) Act 2013 (Remedial) Order 2020 (SI 2020/1085) (see Part III above) have the effect of excluding s.10(1)(b) of the 1998 Act and substituting separate powers of supersession in respect of decisions of the First-tier Tribunal upholding, in appeals brought before 26 March 2013 but determined on or after that date, penalties imposed under the Jobseeker's Allowance (Employment, Skills and Enterprise Scheme) Regulations 2011 or the Jobseeker's Allowance (Mandatory Work Activity Scheme) Regulations 2011 that were unlawful in the light of *Secretary of State for Work and Pensions v Reilly* [2016] EWCA Civ 413; [2017] Q.B. 257; [2017] AACR 14. For the background, see pp. 212 to 217 and 1219 to 1222 of Volume II of the main work.

DD v SSWP (II) [2020] UKUT 302 (AAC) is a case indistinguishable from *ED v SSWP* [2009] UKUT 206 (AAC), mentioned in the main work. The distinction drawn between those cases and *R(I) 4/03* (also mentioned in the main work), is that *R(I) 4/03* concerned a new claim that a claimant had suffered an industrial injury, whereas, in the more recent cases, it had been accepted that the claimant had suffered an industrial injury or had contracted an industrial disease and it had been found that, after some years of not suffering any loss of faculty in respect of that injury or disease, the claimant was now suffering such a loss of faculty. In an industrial disease case, there may be a question whether a disease of the same type as one from which the claimant had previously suffered has been contracted afresh or whether the condition has merely lain dormant for a while, but that issue was not specifically raised in *DD*.

pp.241-264, *annotation to Social Security Act 1998 s.12 (Appeal to First-tier Tribunal)*

It was reiterated in *MM v SSWP (IS)* [2020] UKUT 220 (AAC) that 4.011
there can be no appeal unless the Secretary of State has made a decision. In that case, the claimant had brought an appeal because the Secretary of State had failed to give a decision. If the First-tier Tribunal thought there might be merit in such an argument, it could say so and seek

observations from the Secretary of State, but any formal judicial remedy would have to be sought by the claimant through judicial review proceedings in the High Court.

If a decision-maker was exercising a broad discretion but the relevant public authority had a published policy as to how the discretion should normally be exercised, the First-tier Tribunal should take that policy as its starting point and give reasons for departing from it (*Marshall v Waltham Forest LBC* [2020] UKUT 35 (LC); [2020] 1 W.L.R. 3187, a case where there was a detailed policy as to the level of penalties to be imposed under s.249A of the Housing Act 2004). Statements in that case and cases cited in it to the effect that the First-tier Tribunal and magistrates' courts exercising similar roles are not entitled to consider the lawfulness of a policy were *obiter dicta* and possibly open to doubt, given that it is well established that the First-tier Tribunal has the power to consider the lawfulness of subordinate legislation (see *Chief Adjudication Officer v Foster* [1993] A.C. 754 (also reported as *R(IS) 22/93*)).

SM v Livewell Southwest CIC [2020] UKUT 191 (AAC) (mentioned on p.254 of the main work) is now reported at [2020] 1 W.L.R. 5171. In *PA v HMRC (TC)* [2020] UKUT 324 (AAC), the judge disagreed with the reasoning in *AO v Shepway DC (HB)* [2013] UKUT 9 (AAC) (mentioned on p.254 of the main work) and held that the First-tier Tribunal was a "court" within section 1 of the Vexatious Actions (Scotland) Act 1898. In appealing to the First-tier Tribunal, the Appellant had "instituted" "legal proceedings" contrary to an order made under that provision, because he had not obtained the leave of a Lord Ordinary, and so the First-tier Tribunal had not had jurisdiction to consider his appeal and ought to have struck it out.

In *MH v SSWP (II)* [2020] UKUT 297 (AAC), the judge raised the question whether a claim for disablement pension made in respect of one prescribed industrial disease may, before it is determined, be treated as having been made, additionally or alternatively, in respect of another prescribed disease without a further, formal, claim having been submitted. In the event, he left that question open, but he accepted that the Secretary of State was entitled, although perhaps not required, to issue a separate decision as regards entitlement to disablement pension in respect of each prescribed disease that she had considered. At [20], he considered the implications that had for the First-tier Tribunal—

"20. It is unnecessary for me to decide whether this has the result that, on an appeal, the First-tier Tribunal is unable to consider a prescribed disease that has not been considered by the Secretary of State at all—it may be sufficient that the First-tier Tribunal ensure that the Secretary of State has had an opportunity to consider it and obtain her own medical advice—but it does have the result that there will often, perhaps usually, be a decision in respect of every prescribed disease that has been considered. Where the claimant has appealed against a decision in respect of one prescribed disease, the First-tier Tribunal can only treat the claimant as also having appealed against the decision in respect of another prescribed disease if the claimant had, either when bringing the first appeal or at a later stage during the course of the proceedings, a right of appeal against that other decision. That is because, subject to supersession, revision or an appeal, a decision of the Secretary of State is final (see s.17 of the Social Security Act 1998). There may in practice not be a right of appeal against a decision either because there has not been "mandatory reconsideration" (see reg.3ZA of the Social Security and Child Support (Decisions and Appeals) Regulation 1999 (SI 1999/991)) or because the absolute time limit for appealing has expired—i.e., the appeal is late and there is no adequate to extend the time for appealing (see rule 22(8)(b) of the Tribunal Procedure (First-tier Tribunal) (Social Entitlement Chamber) Rules 2008 (SI 2008/2685)). If there was, or is, a right of appeal that has not been expressly exercised, it will be for the First-tier Tribunal to decide, as a matter of judicial discretion, whether to waive procedural requirements and to treat the claimant as having brought an appeal."

pp.301-302, *annotation to Social Security Act 1998 s.39 (Interpretation etc. of Chapter II)*

In *MH v SSWP (II)* [2020] UKUT 297 (AAC), a health care pro- 4.012
fessional was required to advise the Secretary of State whether a disease suffered by the claimant had been caused by his exposure to chemical agents in the course of his employment. The judge said—

"53. . . . the lack of evidence in the documentation did not entitle the health care professional simply to say that the claimant had not proved his case, given that the Secretary of State had accepted that the claimant had been exposed to chemical agents known to cause the prescribed disease. It was, as I understand her role, her function to use her expertise to give her own opinion and, unless there was an adverse inference to be drawn from the lack of evidence, the lack of documentary evidence on that particular issue required her to obtain evidence either by taking a history from the claimant or examining him or obtaining (or suggesting that someone else obtain) the results of tests or the opinion of a specialist or whatever else might be required. This is because the Secretary of State's role, and therefore that of a health care professional upon whose advice the Secretary of State will rely and who in practice has the role formerly exercised by adjudicating medical authorities, is inquisitorial or at least investigatory (see *Kerr v Department for Social Development* [2004] UKHL 23; [2004] 1 W.L.R. 1372 (also reported as an appendix to *R1/04(SF)*) even if it is described as merely advisory."

pp.318-320, *annotation to Social Security Contributions (Transfer of Functions, etc.) Act 1999, s.8 (Decisions by officers of Board)*

Regulation 155A of the Social Security (Contributions) Regulations 4.012.1
2001 (SI 2001/1004) prescribes decisions to be taken by HMRC for the purposes of s.8(1)(m) of the 1999 Act. Such decisions include decisions relating to disputes as to the appropriate "earnings period" for calculating contributions and a variety of decisions relating to late applications

for refunds or repayments of overpaid contributions and the late payment of contributions, such as whether "the reason for the non-payment is the contributor's ignorance or error, and, if so, whether that ignorance or error was due to his failure to exercise due care and diligence" or whether an employer's failure to pay contributions was "neither with the consent or connivance of the primary contributor nor attributable to any negligence on the part of the [employee]". The consequence of such decisions may be that late-paid contributions should be treated as having been paid earlier than they were actually paid, so that entitlement to benefit can be derived from them. In *NJ v SSWP (RP)* [2021] UKUT 21 (AAC), the First-tier Tribunal was misled by an inadequate submission by the Secretary of State and consequently erred in failing to refer such a question to the Secretary of State, for onward reference to HMRC under reg.38A of the Social Security and Child Support (Decisions and Appeals) Regulations 1999 (see pp.723-724 of the main work).

p.406, *Amendment to the Social Security (Claims and Payments) Regulations 1987 (SI 1987/1968) reg.4ZC (Electronic claims for benefit)*

4.013   With effect from July 9, 2020, the words below were added at the end of paragraph (2) by the Social Fund and Social Security (Claims and Payments) (Amendment) Regulations 2020 (SI 2020/600) reg.4:

"(l)   a social fund funeral payment;
(m)   a social fund payment in respect of maternity expenses;
(n)   maternity allowance."

p.442, *Social Security (Claims and Payments) Regulations 1987 reg.13A (Advance award of disability living allowance)*

4.014   Erratum: the reference to *CDLA/3071/2005* should read *CDLA/3071/2008*. See also the review of the authorities on this regulation in *TS and EK v SSWP (DLA)* [2020] UKUT 284 (AAC) at paras 185-196.

p.484, *Amendments to the Social Security (Claims and Payments) Regulations 1987 (SI 1987/1968) reg.30 (Payments on death)*

4.015   With effect from July 9, 2020, paragraphs (c) and (d) were omitted from paragraph (4B) and the word "and" inserted at the end of paragraph (a) by the Social Fund and Social Security (Claims and Payments) (Amendment) Regulations 2020 (SI 2020/600) reg.4.

p.496, *Amendment to the Social Security (Claims and Payments) Regulations 1987 (SI 1987/1968) reg.32A (Information given electronically)*

4.016   With effect from July 9, 2020, the words below were added at the end of paragraph (2) by the Social Fund and Social Security (Claims and Payments) (Amendment) Regulations 2020 (SI 2020/600) reg.4:
"(l)   a social fund payment in respect of maternity expenses;
(m) maternity allowance."

p.552, *Amendment to the Social Security (Claims and Payments) Regulations 1987 (SI 1987/1968) Sch.9ZC (Electronic communication)*

With effect from July 9, 2020, the words below were added at the end 4.017 of paragraph 2(1) by the Social Fund and Social Security (Claims and Payments) (Amendment) Regulations 2020 (SI 2020/600) reg.4:
"(m) a social fund payment in respect of maternity expenses;
(n) maternity allowance."

p.572, *Time within which a claim for universal credit is to be made*

In *CP v SSWP (UC)* [2020] UKUT 309 (AAC) Judge Jacobs ruled 4.018 that, in circumstances where a housing benefit claimant has moved to a new local authority area, a notification from the new authority that housing benefit could no longer be claimed amounted to a 'notification of expiry of benefit' under regulation 26(3)(aa), thus enabling back-dating of the universal credit claim.

p.576, *Amendment to the Universal Credit, etc. (Claims and Payments) Regulations 2013 (SI 2013/380) (Reclaims of universal credit after nil award due to earnings)*

With effect from May 21, 2020, reg.3 of the Universal Credit (Coro- 4.019 navirus) (Self-employed Claimants and Reclaims) (Amendment) Regulations 2020 (SI 2020/522) adds the following:

"**32A.**—(1) This regulation applies where—
(a) a claim is made for universal credit, but no award is made because the condition in section 5(1)(b) or 5(2)(b) of the 2012 Act (condition that the claimant's income, or joint claimants' combined income is such that the amount payable would not be less than the prescribed minimum) is not met; or
(b) entitlement to an award of universal credit ceases because that condition is not met.
(2) The Secretary of State may, subject to any conditions the Secretary of State considers appropriate, treat the claimant (or joint claimants) as making a claim on the first day of each subsequent month, up to a maximum of 5, that would have been an assessment period if an award had been made or, as the case may be, if the award had continued."

p.578, *Amendment to the Universal Credit, etc. (Claims and Payments) Regulations 2013 (SI 2013/380) reg.38 (Evidence and information in connection with an award)*

With effect from July 13, 2020, reg.3 of the Universal Credit (Mis- 4.020 cellaneous Amendments) Regulations 2020 (SI 2020/611) makes the following amendments to reg.38:
in paragraph (1), for "apart from paragraph (7)" substitute "apart from paragraphs (7) and (9)"; and
after paragraph (8) insert—

"(9) A landlord, in a case where a claimant's award of universal credit includes an amount in respect of housing costs or where the award may be revised or superseded to include such an amount, must supply such information or evidence in connection with the award, or any question arising out of it, as the Secretary of State may require, and must do so within one month of being required to do so or such longer period as the Secretary of State considers reasonable."

p.579, *Amendment to the Universal Credit, etc. (Claims and Payments) Regulations 2013 (SI 2013/380) reg.40 (Information to be provided to rent officers)*

4.021 With effect from July 13, 2020, reg.3 of the Universal Credit (Miscellaneous Amendments) Regulations 2020 (SI 2020/611) substituted "regulations 37 and 38" for "regulation 37".

p.584, *Amendment to the Universal Credit, etc. (Claims and Payments) Regulations 2013 (SI 2013/380) reg.47 (Payment of universal credit)*

4.022 With effect from November 25, 2020, para. (7) is omitted from reg.47 by the Universal Credit (Persons who have attained state pension credit qualifying age) (Amendment) Regulations 2020 (SI 2020/655) reg.4.

p.598, *Amendments to the Social Security (Electronic Communications) Consolidation and Amendment Directions 2011*

4.023 With effect from October 20, 2020, the Social Security (Electronic Communications) (Amendment) (No.3) Directions 2020 inserted after sub-para.(j) in para. 1(2)

"(k) bereavement support payment."

With effect from August 13, 2020, amendments below were made to para.(2) by the Social Security (Electronic Communications) (Amendment) (No.2) Directions 2020. The further, square-bracketed, amendments were made by the Social Security (Electronic Communications) (Amendment) (No.3) Directions 2020 with effect from October 20, 2020.

At the end of paragraph (a) insert—

"(xiv) a social fund funeral payment;
  (xv) a social fund payment in respect of maternity expenses;
  (xvi) maternity allowance."

In paragraph (b), after "or state pension credit" insert—

", or a social fund funeral payment, or a social fund payment in respect of maternity expenses, or maternity allowance [or bereavement support payment]".

In sub-paragraph (c), after "state pension credit" insert—

", or a social fund funeral payment, or a social fund payment in respect of maternity expenses, or maternity allowance [or bereavement support payment].".

pp.665-666, *annotation to the Social Security and Child Support (Decisions and Appeals) Regulations 1999 reg.6(2) (Supersession of decisions)*

See the supplementary annotation to reg.26 of the Universal Credit, Personal Independence Payment, Jobseeker's Allowance and Employment and Support Allowance (Decisions and Appeals) Regulations 2013, below.   4.023.1

p.724, *annotation to the Social Security and Child Support (Decisions and Appeals) Regulations 1999 reg.38A*

See the supplementary annotation to s.8 of the Social Security Contributions (Transfer of Functions, etc.) Act 1999, above.   4.023.2

p.761, *annotation to the Universal Credit, Personal Independence Payment, Jobseeker's Allowance and Employment and Support Allowance (Decisions and Appeals) Regulations 2013 reg.23 (Changes of circumstances)*

See the supplementary annotation to reg.26, below.   4.023.3

pp.763-764, *annotation to the Universal Credit, Personal Independence Payment, Jobseeker's Allowance and Employment and Support Allowance (Decisions and Appeals) Regulations 2013 reg.26 (Medical evidence and limited capability for work etc.)*

The importance of distinguishing between a supersession on the ground of change of circumstances under reg.23 and supersession on the ground of the receipt of new medical evidence under reg.26 was stressed in *MH v SSWP (PIP)* [2020] UKUT 185 (AAC), where the claimant was apparently entitled to the enhanced rate of the mobility component of personal independence payment but had reached pensionable age before the Secretary of State superseded the award under reg.26 and substituted an award at the standard rate. The First-tier Tribunal dismissed the claimant's appeal on the ground that the restrictions on awards of the mobility component to those over pensionable age that are imposed by reg.27(2) of the Social Security (Personal Independence Payment) Regulations 2013 (see p.807 of Vol.1 of the main work) applied. However, those restrictions apply only where there has been a supersession under reg.23 based on a change of circumstances after the claimant reached pensionable age and, although the First-tier Tribunal could have substituted a supersession under reg.23, it failed to make any finding that there had been such a material change of circumstances. Furthermore, because it had wrongly understood the limitations imposed by reg.27(2) of the Personal Independence Payment Regulations to apply, it had not considered at all whether the claimant continued to satisfy the basic conditions for the enhanced rate of the mobility component.   4.023.4

p.789, *amendment to the Universal Credit, Personal Independence Payment, Jobseeker's Allowance and Employment and Support Allowance (Decisions and Appeals) Regulations 2013 Sch.1 (Effective dates for superseding decisions made on the ground of a change of circumstances)*

4.024 With effect from November 25, 2020, reg.5 of the Universal Credit (Persons who have attained state pension credit qualifying age) (Amendment) Regulations 2020 (SI 2020/655) amended Sch.1 by substituting for para.26—

> "**26.** Where, in any assessment period, a claimant reaches the qualifying age for state pension credit under the State Pension Credit Act 2002, where claiming as a single person or as a member of a couple to whom regulation 3(2)(a) of the Universal Credit Regulations applies, a superseding decision made in consequence of the person reaching that age takes effect on the first day of the assessment period following that in which the change of circumstances occurs or is expected to occur."

The explanatory note to the amending Regulations says that this amendment, with others, is intended "to provide a smooth transition" between universal credit and state pension credit and/or housing benefit. It has the effect that an award of universal credit may overlap to a small extent with the alternative benefits to which the claimant may become entitled upon reaching the qualifying age.

p.912, *Social Security (Payments on Account, Overpayments and Recovery) Regulations 1988, reg.8*

4.025 With effect from December 31, 2020, in paragraph (1)(g) omit the words "other than the United Kingdom" (Social Security (Amendment) (EU Exit) Regulations 2019 (SI 2019/128) reg.4 and Sch., para.5) (as applied by European Union (Withdrawal Agreement) Act 2020 Sch.5 para.1(1)). Schedule, para 5 further provides that the amendment "also has effect in relation to regulation 8 as that regulation relates to child benefit and guardian's allowance by virtue of the transitional provision in reg.44 (recovery of overpayments from awards of child benefit and guardian's allowance) of the Child Benefit and Guardian's Allowance (Administration) Regulations 2003.

p.958, *amendment to the Social Security (Recovery of Benefits) Regulations 1997 reg.2(2) (exempted trusts and payments)*

4.026 With effect from May 29, 2020, reg.27(1) of the Victims' Payments Regulations 2020 (SI 2020/103) amended reg.2(2) by inserting at the end—

> "(q) any payment of victims' payments, or of a lump sum, under the Victims' Payments Regulations 2020."

The 2020 Regulations provide for payments to be made to those injured in a "Troubles-related incident", which is defined in s.10(11) of the

Northern Ireland (Executive Formation etc) Act 2019 as "an incident involving an act of violence or force carried out in Ireland, the United Kingdom or anywhere in Europe for a reason related to the constitutional status of Northern Ireland or to political or sectarian hostility between people there".

p.972, *amendment to the Social Security (Recovery of Benefits) (Lump Sum Payments) Regulations 2008 reg.7(2) (exempted trusts and payments)*

With effect from May 29, 2020, reg.27(3) of the Victims' Payments Regulations 2020 (SI 2020/103) amended reg.7(2) by inserting at the end— 4.027

"(n) any payment of victims' payments, or of a lump sum, under the Victims' Payments Regulations 2020."

The 2020 Regulations provide for payments to be made to those injured in a "Troubles-related incident", which is defined in s.10(11) of the Northern Ireland (Executive Formation etc) Act 2019 as "an incident involving an act of violence or force carried out in Ireland, the United Kingdom or anywhere in Europe for a reason related to the constitutional status of Northern Ireland or to political or sectarian hostility between people there".

p.1061, *United Kingdom Withdrawal from the European Union*

On December 31, 2020, the "implementation period" in connection with the United Kingdom's withdrawal from the European Union came to an end. A consequence of that was that the operation of EU law, which had been in large measure preserved during that period by s.1A of the European Union (Withdrawal) Act 2018, ceased. The relevance of matters of EU law is now determined by domestic legislation. Sections 2 to 7C of the European Union (Withdrawal) Act 2018 make provision, important in structural terms, concerning the ongoing status of, and interpretation (ss.6 and 7C and see also Sch.1, para.5 and Sch.8, paras 1-2A) to be given to, various forms of EU law and domestic legislation associated with it. 4.028

In the social security context the impact of the more general provisions is likely to be secondary in many cases to the express provision made by Part 2 of the Withdrawal Agreement in respect of Citizens' Rights. Part 2 addresses the preservation of limited rights associated with the exercise of freedom of movement before the end of the implementation period and also social security co-ordination issues. The content of Part 2 does not mirror, but borrows substantially from, Directive 2004/38 (the Citizenship Directive) and follows Regulation 883/2004 and the implementing regulation, Regulation 987/2009. Caselaw on these provisions will remain relevant for a considerable time to come. Rights which under the Withdrawal Agreement are intended to be directly enforceable are given effect in domestic law by s.7A of the 2018 Act.

While (subject to transitional provisions) it is no longer generally possible for a UK court or tribunal to make a new reference to the Court of Justice of the European Union under art.267 TFEU, express provision is made by the Withdrawal Agreement for such references to be possible in relation to Part 2 for (broadly) an 8 year period.

It may be critical to determine whether or not a person falls within the scope of Part 2 of the Withdrawal Agreement, as for those who do not, the legal environment has significantly altered. Rights of free movement are abolished by the Immigration and Social Security Co-ordination (EU Withdrawal) Act 2020, with the intention that immigration from EU member States (other than Ireland, in respect of which the Common Travel Area assumes greater importance) will in future be governed by the Immigration Rules. Matters of social security co-ordination in such cases are intended to be addressed via the Protocol on Social Security Co-ordination which forms part of the Trade and Co-operation Agreement concluded between the European Union and the United Kingdom on December 24, 2020.

The UK Government's increasing reliance on domestic legislation included the creation of "EU settled status" under Appendix EU of the Immigration Rules, which took full effect from March 30, 2019. Such status was granted with a relatively light touch and those who were able to establish a continuous qualifying period of residence of five years and were granted settled status in consequence are able to rely on that status as a sufficient right to reside for benefit purposes following the Social Security (Income-related Benefits)(Updating and Amendment) (EU Exit) Regulations 2019 (SI 2019/872) and the Child Benefit and Child Tax Credit (Amendment) (EU Exit) Regulations 2019 (SI 2019/867). Both sets of Regulations have been in force since May 7, 2019 and are incorporated in the text in other volumes relating to the benefits concerned.

The position of those granted only "pre-settled" status (because they could not at the time demonstrate the five year period above) is more complex. Under the legislation as it stands relating to the various benefits, the right to reside conferred by a grant of pre-settled status was excluded from being a qualifying right to reside for benefit purposes, with the consequence that such people were required to establish a right to reside under the existing categories (i.e. as a worker, self-employed person, self-sufficient person etc.) However, on December 18, 2020 in *Fratila v SSWP* [2020] EWCA Civ 1741 the Court of Appeal held that that exclusion contravened established EU case law. There are likely to be those with pre-settled status whose benefit claims will have been refused on the basis of the domestic legislation, or who were deterred from applying because of it. On February 22, 2021 the Secretary of State was given permission to appeal against the Court of Appeal's decision. The implications of the decision, both up to the end of the implementation period, and indeed thereafter, remain to be worked out. For the Secretary of State's position, see ADM Memo 2/21 and DMG Memo 1/21.

Finally, mention should be made of the temporary provision made by The Citizens' Rights (Application Deadline and Temporary Protection) (EU Exit) Regulations 2020 (SI 2020/1209) (see the "New Legislation" section) which preserves the ability to rely on a modified form of the

Immigration (European Economic Area) Regulations 2016, in order to cater for those yet to make their application for settled status (in such cases the preservation is time-limited, to 30 June 2021) or whose applications are yet to be determined. See the commentary to the Immigration (European Economic Area) Regulations 2016 under *Vol. V,* below.

p.1062, *The Treaty of Lisbon (Changes in Terminology) Order 2011*

The Order remains in force, but its relevance is confined to the extent   4.029
to which the EU law to which it is ancillary remains relevant in the post-Brexit legislative structure.

pp.1066-1082, *Amendments to the European Union (Withdrawal) Act 2018*

GENERAL NOTE

The expiry of the "implementation period" on December 31, 2020 has resulted in significant changes to the text of this Act. Relevant provisions are included. Some material is repeated from the 2020 main volume, sometimes in modified form, in order to facilitate reading the legislation as in force from December 31, 2020. For the text during the implementation period, please refer to the main volume.

Repeal of the European Communities Act 1972

1. The European Communities Act 1972 is repealed on exit day.   4.031

GENERAL NOTE

This was, but is no longer, subject to s.1A, which preserved the effect of the 1972 Act in modified form during the implementation period ending on December 31, 2020 ("IP completion day").

Saving for ECA for implementation period

[¹1A. [² ...]   4.032
(5) Subsections (1) to (4) are repealed on IP completion day.
(6) In this Act—
"the implementation period" means the transition or implementation period provided for by Part 4 of the withdrawal agreement and beginning with exit day and ending on IP completion day;
"IP completion day" (and related expressions) have the same meaning as in the European Union (Withdrawal Agreement) Act 2020 (see section 39(1) to (5) of that Act);
"withdrawal agreement" has the same meaning as in that Act (see section 39(1) and (6) of that Act).
(7) In this Act—
(a) references to the European Communities Act 1972 are to be read, so far as the context permits or requires, as being or (as the case may be) including references to that Act as it continues to have effect by virtue of subsections (2) to (4) above, and

(b) references to any Part of the withdrawal agreement or the EEA EFTA separation agreement include references to any other provisions of that agreement so far as applying to that Part.]

AMENDMENTS

1. European Union (Withdrawal Agreement) Act 2020 s.1 (January 31, 2020).
2. European Union (Withdrawal) Act 2018 s.1A(5) (December 31, 2020).

DEFINITIONS

"domestic law": see s.20(1).
"exit day": see s.20(1).
"IP completion day" see the European Union (Withdrawal Agreement) Act 2020 s.39(1).
"Minister of the Crown": s.20(1).
"withdrawal agreement" means "the agreement between the United Kingdom and the EU under Article 50(2) of the Treaty on European Union which sets out the arrangements for the United Kingdom's withdrawal from the EU (as that agreement is modified from time to time in accordance with any provision of it)" (2020 Act, s.39(1)). Section 39(6) of the 2020 Act is not relevant to social security.

[¹**Saving for EU-derived domestic legislation for implementation period**

4.033   **1B.** [² . . .]
(6) Subsections (1) to (5) are repealed on IP completion day.
(7) In this Act 'EU-derived domestic legislation' means any enactment so far as—
(a) made under section 2(2) of, or paragraph 1A of Schedule 2 to, the European Communities Act 1972,
(b) passed or made, or operating, for a purpose mentioned in section 2(2)(a) or (b) of that Act,
(c) relating to—
  (i) anything which falls within paragraph (a) or (b), or
  (ii) any rights, powers, liabilities, obligations, restrictions, remedies or procedures which are recognised and available in domestic law by virtue of section 2(1) of the European Communities Act 1972, or
(d) relating otherwise to the EU or the EEA,
but does not include any enactment contained in the European Communities Act 1972 or any enactment contained in this Act or the European Union (Withdrawal Agreement) Act 2020 or in regulations made under this Act or the Act of 2020.]

AMENDMENTS

1. European Union (Withdrawal Agreement) Act 2020 s.1 (January 31, 2020).
2. European Union (Withdrawal) Act 2018 s.1B(6) (December 31, 2020).

DEFINITIONS

"domestic law": see s.20(1).
"the EEA": see s.20(1).
"enactment": see s.20(1).
"EU entity": see s.20(1).
"exit day": see s.20(1).
"withdrawal agreement": see s.1A(6).

Saving for EU-derived domestic legislation

2. (1) EU-derived domestic legislation, as it has effect in domestic law   4.034
immediately before [¹IP completion day], continues to have effect in
domestic law on and after [¹IP completion day].
[² . . .]
(3) This section is subject to section 5 and Schedule 1 (exceptions to
savings and incorporation) [³ and section 5A (savings and incorporation:
supplementary)]

AMENDMENTS

1. European Union (Withdrawal Agreement) Act 2020 s.25(1)(a) (December 31, 2020) (SI 2020/1622 reg.5(d)).
2. European Union (Withdrawal Agreement) Act 2020 s.25(1)(b) (December 31, 2020) (SI 2020/1622 reg.5(d)).
3. European Union (Withdrawal Agreement) Act 2020 s.25(1)(c) (December 31, 2020) (SI 2020/1622 reg.5(d)).

DEFINITIONS

"domestic law": see s.20(1).
"EU-derived domestic legislation": see s.1B(7).
"IP completion day": see the European Union (Withdrawal Agreement) Act
2020 s.39(1).

Incorporation of direct EU legislation

3. (1) Direct EU legislation, so far as operative immediately before   4.035
[¹IP completion day], forms part of domestic law on and after [¹IP
completion day].
(2) In this Act 'direct EU legislation' means—
(a) any EU regulation, EU decision or EU tertiary legislation, as it
    has effect in EU law immediately before [²IP completion day] and
    so far as—
    [³(ai) it is applicable to and in the United Kingdom by virtue of
    Part 4 of the withdrawal agreement,
    (bi) it neither has effect nor is to have effect by virtue of section
    7A or 7B,]
    (i) it is not an exempt EU instrument (for which see section
    20(1) and Schedule 6) [⁴and],
    [⁵ . . .]
    (iii) its effect is not reproduced in an enactment to which
    section 2(1) applies,
(b) any Annex to the EEA agreement, as it has effect in EU law
    immediately before [⁶IP completion day] and so far as—

[⁷(ai) it is applicable to and in the United Kingdom by virtue of Part 4 of the withdrawal agreement,

(bi) it neither has effect nor is to have effect by virtue of section 7A or 7B,]

(i) it refers to, or contains adaptations of, anything falling within paragraph (a), and

(ii) its effect is not reproduced in an enactment to which section 2(1) applies, or

(c) Protocol 1 to the EEA agreement (which contains horizontal adaptations that apply in relation to EU instruments referred to in the Annexes to that agreement), as it has effect in EU law immediately before [⁸IP completion day and so far as—]

[⁸(i) it is applicable to and in the United Kingdom by virtue of Part 4 of the withdrawal agreement, and

(ii) it neither has effect nor is to have effect by virtue of section 7A or 7B.]

(3) For the purposes of this Act, any direct EU legislation is operative immediately before [⁹IP completion day] if—

(a) in the case of anything which comes into force at a particular time and is stated to apply from a later time, it is in force and applies immediately before [⁹IP completion day],

(b) in the case of a decision which specifies to whom it is addressed, it has been notified to that person before [⁹IP completion day], and

(c) in any other case, it is in force immediately before [⁹IP completion day] .

(4) This section—

(a) brings into domestic law any direct EU legislation only in the form of the English language version of that legislation, and

(b) does not apply to any such legislation for which there is no such version,

but paragraph (a) does not affect the use of the other language versions of that legislation for the purposes of interpreting it.

(5) This section is subject to section 5 and Schedule 1 (exceptions to savings and incorporation) [¹⁰and section 5A (savings and incorporation: supplementary)].

AMENDMENTS

1. European Union (Withdrawal Agreement) Act 2020 s.25(2)(a) (December 31, 2020) (SI 2020/1622 reg.5(d)).
2. European Union (Withdrawal Agreement) Act 2020 s.25(2)(b)(i) (December 31, 2020) (SI 2020/1622 reg.5(d)).
3. European Union (Withdrawal Agreement) Act 2020 s.25(2)(b)(ii) (December 31, 2020) (SI 2020/1622 reg.5(d)).
4. European Union (Withdrawal Agreement) Act 2020 s.25(2)(b)(iii) (December 31, 2020) (SI 2020/1622 reg.5(d)).
5. European Union (Withdrawal Agreement) Act 2020 s.25(2)(b)(iv) (December 31, 2020) (SI 2020/1622 reg.5(d)).
6. European Union (Withdrawal Agreement) Act 2020 s.25(2)(c)(i) (December 31, 2020) (SI 2020/1622 reg.5(d)).

7. European Union (Withdrawal Agreement) Act 2020 s.25(2)(c)(ii) (December 31, 2020) (SI 2020/1622 reg.5(d)).
8. European Union (Withdrawal Agreement) Act 2020 s.25(2)(d) (December 31, 2020) (SI 2020/1622 reg.5(d)).
9. European Union (Withdrawal Agreement) Act 2020 s.25(2)(e) (December 31, 2020) (SI 2020/1622 reg.5(d)).
10. European Union (Withdrawal Agreement) Act 2020 s.25(2)(f) (December 31, 2020) (SI 2020/1622 reg.5(d)).

DEFINITIONS

"direct EU legislation": see s.3(2).
"domestic law": see s.20(1).
"EEA agreement": Schedule 1 to the Interpretation Act 1978.
"EU decision": see s.20(1).
"EU regulation": see s.20(1).
"EU tertiary legislation": see s.20(1).
"exempt EU instrument": see s.20(1).
"IP completion day": see the European Union (Withdrawal Agreement) Act 2020 s.39(1).
"withdrawal agreement": see s.1A(6).

Saving for rights etc. under section 2(1) of the ECA

4. (1) Any rights, powers, liabilities, obligations, restrictions, remedies   4.036
and procedures which, immediately before ['IP completion day] —
   (a) are recognised and available in domestic law by virtue of section
         2(1) of the European Communities Act 1972, and
   (b) are enforced, allowed and followed accordingly,
continue on and after ['IP completion day] to be recognised and available in domestic law (and to be enforced, allowed and followed accordingly).
   (2) Subsection (1) does not apply to any rights, powers, liabilities, obligations, restrictions, remedies or procedures so far as they—
   (a) form part of domestic law by virtue of section 3, [² . . .]
   [²(aa) are, or are to be, recognised and available in domestic law (and
         enforced, allowed and followed accordingly) by virtue of section
         7A or 7B, or]
   (b) arise under an EU directive (including as applied by the EEA
         agreement) and are not of a kind recognised by the European
         Court or any court or tribunal in the United Kingdom in a case
         decided before [³IP completion day] (whether or not as an
         essential part of the decision in the case).
   (3) This section is subject to section 5 and Schedule 1 (exceptions to savings and incorporation) [⁴and section 5A (savings and incorporation: supplementary)].

AMENDMENTS

1. European Union (Withdrawal Agreement) Act 2020 s.25(3)(a) (December 31, 2020) (SI 2020/1622 reg.5(d)).
2. European Union (Withdrawal Agreement) Act 2020 s.25(3)(b)(i) (December 31, 2020) (SI 2020/1622 reg.5(d)).

3. European Union (Withdrawal Agreement) Act 2020 s.25(3)(b)(ii) (December 31, 2020) (SI 2020/1622 reg.5(d)).
4. European Union (Withdrawal Agreement) Act 2020 s.25(3)(c) (December 31, 2020) (SI 2020/1622 reg.5(d)).

DEFINITIONS

"domestic law": see s.20(1).
"EEA agreement": see Schedule 1 to the Interpretation Act 1978.
"EU directive": see s.20(1).
"European Communities Act 1972": see Schedule 1 to the Interpretation Act 1978.
"European Court": see Schedule 1 to the Interpretation Act 1978.
"IP completion day": see the European Union (Withdrawal Agreement) Act 2020 s.39(1).

GENERAL NOTE

Under this section rights at December 31, 2020 under provisions of Directives which had direct effect are preserved, unless caught by to the carve-outs in subsections (2) and (3) or by express provision, such as that in Pt 3 of Sch.1 to the Immigration and Social Security Co-ordination (EU Withdrawal) Act 2020.

Exceptions to savings and incorporation

4.037   5. (1) The principle of the supremacy of EU law does not apply to any enactment or rule of law passed or made on or after [¹IP completion day].

(2) Accordingly, the principle of the supremacy of EU law continues to apply on or after [¹IP completion day] so far as relevant to the interpretation, disapplication or quashing of any enactment or rule of law passed or made before [¹IP completion day].

(3) Subsection (1) does not prevent the principle of the supremacy of EU law from applying to a modification made on or after [¹IP completion day] of any enactment or rule of law passed or made before [¹IP completion day] if the application of the principle is consistent with the intention of the modification.

(4) The Charter of Fundamental Rights is not part of domestic law on or after [¹IP completion day].

(5) Subsection (4) does not affect the retention in domestic law on or after [¹IP completion day] in accordance with this Act of any fundamental rights or principles which exist irrespective of the Charter (and references to the Charter in any case law are, so far as necessary for this purpose, to be read as if they were references to any corresponding retained fundamental rights or principles).

(6) Schedule 1 (which makes further provision about exceptions to savings and incorporation) has effect.

[¹(7) Subsections (1) to (6) and Schedule 1 are subject to relevant separation agreement law (for which see section 7C).]

AMENDMENTS

1. European Union (Withdrawal Agreement) Act 2020 s.25(4)(a) (December 31, 2020) (SI 2020/1622 reg.5(d)).

DEFINITIONS

"Charter of Fundamental Rights: see s.20(1).
"domestic law": see s.20(1).
"enactment": see s.20(1).
"IP completion day": see the European Union (Withdrawal Agreement) Act
2020 s.39(1).
"modification": see s.20(1) for "modify" and related expressions.

[¹Savings and incorporation: supplementary

5A. The fact that anything which continues to be, or forms part of,   4.038
domestic law on or after IP completion day by virtue of section 2, 3 or
4 has an effect immediately before IP completion day which is time
—limited by reference to the implementation period does not prevent it
from having an indefinite effect on and after IP completion day by virtue
of section 2, 3 or 4.]

AMENDMENT

1. European Union (Withdrawal Agreement) Act 2020 s.25(5)
   (December 31, 2020) (SI 2020/1622 reg.5(d)).

DEFINITIONS

"domestic law": see s.20(1).
"IP completion day": see the European Union (Withdrawal Agreement) Act
2020 s.39(1).
"implementation period": see s.1A(6).

Interpretation of retained EU law

6. (1) A court or tribunal—   4.039
(a) is not bound by any principles laid down, or any decisions made,
    on or after [¹IP completion day] by the European Court, and
(b) cannot refer any matter to the European Court on or after [¹IP
    completion day].
(2) Subject to this and subsections (3) to (6), a court or tribunal may
have regard to anything done on or after [¹IP completion day] by the
European Court, another EU entity or the EU so far as it is relevant to
any matter before the court or tribunal.
(3) Any question as to the validity, meaning or effect of any retained
EU law is to be decided, so far as that law is unmodified on or after [¹IP
completion day] and so far as they are relevant to it—
(a) in accordance with any retained case law and any retained general
    principles of EU law, and
(b) having regard (among other things) to the limits, immediately
    before [¹IP completion day], of EU competences.
(4) But—
(a)   the Supreme Court is not bound by any retained EU case
       law,
(b)   the High Court of Justiciary is not bound by any retained EU
       case law when—

      (i) sitting as a court of appeal otherwise than in relation to a compatibility issue (within the meaning given by section 288ZA(2) of the Criminal Procedure (Scotland) Act 1995) or a devolution issue (within the meaning given by paragraph 1 of Schedule 6 to the Scotland Act 1998), or

      (ii) sitting on a reference under section 123(1) of the Criminal Procedure (Scotland) Act 1995, [² . . .]

[²(ba) a relevant court or relevant tribunal is not bound by any retained EU case law so far as is provided for by regulations under subsection (5A), and]

(c) no court or tribunal is bound by any retained domestic case law that it would not otherwise be bound by.

(5) In deciding whether to depart from any retained EU case law [³ by virtue of subsection (4)(a) or (b)], the Supreme Court or the High Court of Justiciary must apply the same test as it would apply in deciding whether to depart from its own case law.

[⁴(5A) A Minister of the Crown may by regulations provide for—

(a) a court or tribunal to be a relevant court or (as the case may be) a relevant tribunal for the purposes of this section,

(b) the extent to which, or circumstances in which, a relevant court or relevant tribunal is not to be bound by retained EU case law,

(c) the test which a relevant court or relevant tribunal must apply in deciding whether to depart from any retained EU case law, or

(d) considerations which are to be relevant to—

      (i) the Supreme Court or the High Court of Justiciary in applying the test mentioned in subsection (5), or

      (ii) a relevant court or relevant tribunal in applying any test provided for by virtue of paragraph (c) above.

(5B) Regulations under subsection (5A) may (among other things) provide for—

(a) the High Court of Justiciary to be a relevant court when sitting otherwise than as mentioned in subsection (4)(b)(i) and (ii),

(b) the extent to which, or circumstances in which, a relevant court or relevant tribunal not being bound by retained EU case law includes (or does not include) that court or tribunal not being bound by retained domestic case law which relates to retained EU case law,

(c) other matters arising in relation to retained domestic case law which relates to retained EU case law (including by making provision of a kind which could be made in relation to retained EU case law), or

(d) the test mentioned in paragraph (c) of subsection (5A) or the considerations mentioned in paragraph (d) of that subsection to be determined (whether with or without the consent of a Minister of the Crown) by a person mentioned in subsection (5C)(a) to (e) or by more than one of those persons acting jointly.

(5C) Before making regulations under subsection (5A), a Minister of the Crown must consult—

(a) the President of the Supreme Court,

(b) the Lord Chief Justice of England and Wales,

(c) the Lord President of the Court of Session,

(d) the Lord Chief Justice of Northern Ireland,

(e) the Senior President of Tribunals, and

(f) such other persons as the Minister of the Crown considers appropriate.

(5D) No regulations may be made under subsection (5A) after IP completion day.]

(6) Subsection (3) does not prevent the validity, meaning or effect of any retained EU law which has been modified on or after [¹IP completion day] from being decided as provided for in that subsection if doing so is consistent with the intention of the modifications.

[⁵(6A) Subsections (1) to (6) are subject to relevant separation agreement law (for which see section 7C).]

(7) In this Act—

"retained case law" means—

(a) retained domestic case law, and

(b) retained EU case law;

"retained domestic case law" means any principles laid down by, and any decisions of, a court or tribunal in the United Kingdom, as they have effect immediately before [¹IP completion day] and so far as they—

(a) relate to anything to which section 2, 3 or 4 applies, and

(b) are not excluded by section 5 or Schedule 1,

(as those principles and decisions are modified by or under this Act or by other domestic law from time to time);

"retained EU case law" means any principles laid down by, and any decisions of, the European Court, as they have effect in EU law immediately before [¹IP completion day] and so far as they—

(a) relate to anything to which section 2, 3 or 4 applies, and

(b) are not excluded by section 5 or Schedule 1,

(as those principles and decisions are modified by or under this Act or by other domestic law from time to time);

"retained EU law" means anything which, on or after [¹IP completion day], continues to be, or forms part of, domestic law by virtue of section 2, 3 or 4 or subsection (3) or (6) above (as that body of law is added to or otherwise modified by or under this Act or by other domestic law from time to time);

"retained general principles of EU law" means the general principles of EU law, as they have effect in EU law immediately before [¹IP completion day] and so far as they—

(a) relate to anything to which section 2, 3 or 4 applies, and

(b) are not excluded by section 5 or Schedule 1,

(as those principles are modified by or under this Act or by other domestic law from time to time).

AMENDMENTS

1. European Union (Withdrawal Agreement) Act 2020 s.26(1)(a) (January 31, 2020 for limited purposes; December 31, 2020 otherwise) (SI 2020/1622 reg.5(e)).

2. European Union (Withdrawal Agreement) Act 2020 s.26(1)(b) (December 31, 2020) (SI 2020/1622 reg.5(e)).
3. European Union (Withdrawal Agreement) Act 2020 s.26(1)(c) (December 31, 2020) (SI 2020/1622 reg.5(e)).
4. European Union (Withdrawal Agreement) Act 2020 s.26(1)(d) (May 19, 2020) SI 2020/518, reg 2(l).
5. European Union (Withdrawal Agreement) Act 2020 s.26(1)(e) (December 31, 2020) (SI 2020/1622 reg.5(e)).

DEFINITIONS

In addition to the definitions set out in s.6(7), note the following:
"European Court": see Schedule 1 to the Interpretation Act 1978.
"EU entity": see s.20(1).
"the EU": see Schedule 1 to the Interpretation Act 1978.
"IP completion day": see the European Union (Withdrawal Agreement) Act 2020 s.39(1).
"Minister of the Crown": see s.20(1).
"tribunal": see s.20(1).
"unmodified": see s.20(1) for "modify" and related expressions.

GENERAL NOTE

Despite what s.6(1)(b) says, art.157 of the Withdrawal Agreement does allow references to be made to the CJEU in relation to the Citizens Rights provisions.

The regulations under s.6(5A) are the European Union (Withdrawal) Act 2018 (Relevant Court) (Retained EU Case Law) Regulations 2020 (SI 2020/1525) (above).

Status of retained EU law

4.040

7. (1) Anything which—
(a) was, immediately before exit day, primary legislation of a particular kind, subordinate legislation of a particular kind or another enactment of a particular kind, and
(b) continues to be domestic law on and after exit day by virtue of [¹section 1A(2) or 1B(2)],
continues to be domestic law as an enactment of the same kind.
[²(1A) Anything which—
(a) was, immediately before IP completion day, primary legislation of a particular kind, subordinate legislation of a particular kind or another enactment of a particular kind, and
(b) continues to be domestic law on and after IP completion day by virtue of section 2,
continues to be domestic law as an enactment of the same kind.]
(2) Retained direct principal EU legislation cannot be modified by any primary or subordinate legislation other than—
(a) an Act of Parliament,
(b) any other primary legislation (so far as it has the power to make such a modification), or
(c) any subordinate legislation so far as it is made under a power which permits such a modification by virtue of—

    (i) paragraph 3, 5(3)(a) or (4)(a), 8(3), 10(3)(a) or (4)(a), 11(2)(a) or 12(3) of Schedule 8,

    (ii) any other provision made by or under this Act,

    (iii) any provision made by or under an Act of Parliament passed before, and in the same Session as, this Act, or

    (iv) any provision made on or after the passing of this Act by or under primary legislation.

(3) Retained direct minor EU legislation cannot be modified by any primary or subordinate legislation other than—

(a) an Act of Parliament,

(b) any other primary legislation (so far as it has the power to make such a modification), or

(c) any subordinate legislation so far as it is made under a power which permits such a modification by virtue of—

    (i) paragraph 3, 5(2) or (4)(a), 8(3), 10(2) or (4)(a) or 12(3) of Schedule 8,

    (ii) any other provision made by or under this Act,

    (iii) any provision made by or under an Act of Parliament passed before, and in the same Session as, this Act, or

    (iv) any provision made on or after the passing of this Act by or under primary legislation.

(4) Anything which is retained EU law by virtue of section 4 cannot be modified by any primary or subordinate legislation other than—

(a) an Act of Parliament,

(b) any other primary legislation (so far as it has the power to make such a modification), or

(c) any subordinate legislation so far as it is made under a power which permits such a modification by virtue of—

    (i) paragraph 3, 5(3)(b) or (4)(b), 8(3), 10(3)(b) or (4)(b), 11(2)(b) or 12(3) of Schedule 8,

    (ii) any other provision made by or under this Act,

    (iii) any provision made by or under an Act of Parliament passed before, and in the same Session as, this Act, or

    (iv) any provision made on or after the passing of this Act by or under primary legislation.

(5) For other provisions about the status of retained EU law, see—

(a)   section 5(1) to (3) [³and (7)] (status of retained EU law in relation to other enactments or rules of law),

(b)   section 6 (status of retained case law and retained general principles of EU law),

[⁴(ba) section 7C (status of case law of European Court etc. in relation to retained EU law which is relevant separation agreement law),]

(c)   section 15(2) and Part 2 of Schedule 5 (status of retained EU law for the purposes of the rules of evidence),

(d)   paragraphs 13 to 16 of Schedule 8 (affirmative and enhanced scrutiny procedure for, and information about, instruments which amend or revoke subordinate legislation under section 2(2) of the European Communities Act 1972 including subordinate legislation implementing EU directives),

(e)   paragraphs 19 and 20 of that Schedule (status of certain
        retained direct EU legislation for the purposes of the Inter-
        pretation Act 1978), and
(f)   paragraph 30 of that Schedule (status of retained direct EU
        legislation for the purposes of the Human Rights Act 1998).
(6) In this Act—
"retained direct minor EU legislation" means any retained direct EU
    legislation which is not retained direct principal EU legislation;
"retained direct principal EU legislation" means—
        (a) any EU regulation so far as it—
             (i)   forms part of domestic law on and after [⁵IP comple-
                   tion day] by virtue of section 3, and
             (ii) was not EU tertiary legislation immediately before
                   [⁵IP completion day], or
        (b) any Annex to the EEA agreement so far as it—
             (i)   forms part of domestic law on and after [⁵IP comple-
                   tion day] by virtue of section 3, and
             (ii) refers to, or contains adaptations of, any EU regula-
                   tion so far as it falls within paragraph (a),
(as modified by or under this Act or by other domestic law from time to
time).

AMENDMENTS

    1. European Union (Withdrawal Agreement) Act 2020 Sch.5(2)
        para.40(2) (January 31, 2020).
    2. European Union (Withdrawal Agreement) Act 2020 Sch.5(2)
        para.40(3) (December 31, 2020) (SI 2020/1622 reg.5(j)).
    3. European Union (Withdrawal Agreement) Act 2020 Sch.5(2)
        para.40(4)(a) (December 31, 2020) (SI 2020/1622 reg.5(j)).
    4. European Union (Withdrawal Agreement) Act 2020 Sch.5(2)
        para.40(4)(b) (December 31, 2020) (SI 2020/1622 reg.5(j)).
    5. European Union (Withdrawal Agreement) Act 2020 Sch.5(2)
        para.40(5) (January 31, 2020).

DEFINITIONS

    "domestic law": see s.20(1).
    "EEA agreement": see Schedule 1 to the Interpretation Act 1978.
    "enactment": see s.20(1).
    "European Court": see Schedule 1 to the Interpretation Act 1978.
    "exit day": see s.20(1) to (5).
    "IP completion day": see.s.1A(6).
    "modify": see s.20(1).
    "primary legislation": see s.20(1).
    "retained case law": see s.6(7).
    "retained direct EU legislation": see s.20(1).
    "retained direct minor EU legislation": see s.7(6).
    "retained direct principal EU legislation": see s.7(6).
    "retained EU law": see s.6(7).
    "retained general principles of EU law": see s.6(7).
    "subordinate legislation": see s.20(1).

[¹General implementation of remainder of withdrawal agreement

7A. (1) Subsection (2) applies to—   4.041
  (a) all such rights, powers, liabilities, obligations and restrictions from time to time created or arising by or under the withdrawal agreement, and
  (b) all such remedies and procedures from time to time provided for by or under the withdrawal agreement,
as in accordance with the withdrawal agreement are without further enactment to be given legal effect or used in the United Kingdom.

(2) The rights, powers, liabilities, obligations, restrictions, remedies and procedures concerned are to be—
  (a) recognised and available in domestic law, and
  (b) enforced, allowed and followed accordingly.

(3) Every enactment (including an enactment contained in this Act) is to be read and has effect subject to subsection (2).

(4) This section does not apply in relation to Part 4 of the withdrawal agreement so far as section 2(1) of the European Communities Act 1972 applies in relation to that Part.

(5) See also (among other things)—
  (a) Part 3 of the European Union (Withdrawal Agreement) Act 2020 (further provision about citizens' rights),
  (b) *omitted*,
  (c) section 7C of this Act (interpretation of law relating to withdrawal agreement etc.),
  (d)–(f) *omitted*]

AMENDMENT

  1. European Union (Withdrawal Agreement) Act 2020 s.5 (January 31, 2020).

DEFINITIONS

  "domestic law": see s.20(1).
  "enactment": see s.20(1).
  "European Communities Act 1972": see s.1A(7)(a).
  "withdrawal agreement": see s.1A(6).

[¹General implementation of EEA EFTA and Swiss agreements

7B. (1) Subsection (2) applies to all such rights, powers, liabilities,   4.042
obligations, restrictions, remedies and procedures as—
  (a) would from time to time be created or arise, or (in the case of remedies or procedures) be provided for, by or under the EEA EFTA separation agreement or the Swiss citizens' rights agreement, and
  (b) would, in accordance with Article 4(1) of the withdrawal agreement, be required to be given legal effect or used in the United Kingdom without further enactment,
if that Article were to apply in relation to the EEA EFTA separation agreement and the Swiss citizens' rights agreement, those agreements

369

were part of EU law and the relevant EEA states and Switzerland were member States.

(2) The rights, powers, liabilities, obligations, restrictions, remedies and procedures concerned are to be—

    (a) recognised and available in domestic law, and

    (b) enforced, allowed and followed accordingly.

(3) Every enactment (other than section 7A but otherwise including an enactment contained in this Act) is to be read and has effect subject to subsection (2).

(4) See also (among other things)—

    (a) Part 3 of the European Union (Withdrawal Agreement) Act 2020 (further provision about citizens' rights),

    (b) section 7C of this Act (interpretation of law relating to the EEA EFTA separation agreement and the Swiss citizens' rights agreement etc.),

    (c) section 8B of this Act (power in connection with certain other separation issues), and

    (d) Part 1B of Schedule 2 to this Act (powers involving devolved authorities in connection with certain other separation issues).

(5) In this section 'the relevant EEA states' means Norway, Iceland and Liechtenstein.

(6) In this Act 'EEA EFTA separation agreement' and 'Swiss citizens' rights agreement' have the same meanings as in the European Union (Withdrawal Agreement) Act 2020 (see section 39(1) of that Act).]

AMENDMENT

    1. European Union (Withdrawal Agreement) Act 2020 s.5 (January 31, 2020).

DEFINITIONS

"devolved authority": see s.20(1).

"domestic law": see s.20(1).

"EEA EFTA separation agreement" means (as modified from time to time in accordance with any provision of it) the Agreement on arrangements between Iceland, the Principality of Liechtenstein, the Kingdom of Norway and the United Kingdom of Great Britain and Northern Ireland following the withdrawal of the United Kingdom from the European Union, the EEA Agreement and other agreements applicable between the United Kingdom and the EEA EFTA States by virtue of the United Kingdom's membership of the European Union": European Union (Withdrawal Agreement) Act 2020 s.39(1).

"enactment": see s.20(1).

"Swiss citizens' rights agreement" means (as modified from time to time in accordance with any provision of it) the Agreement signed at Bern on 25 February 2019 between the United Kingdom of Great Britain and Northern Ireland and the Swiss Confederation on citizens' rights following the withdrawal of the United Kingdom from—

    (a) the European Union, and

    (b) the free movement of persons agreement,

so far as the Agreement operates for the purposes of the case where 'specified date' for the purposes of that Agreement has the meaning given in Article 2(b)(ii) of that Agreement": European Union (Withdrawal Agreement) Act 2020 s.39(1).

The EEA EFTA separation agreement and Swiss citizens' rights agreement are not included in the main volume or in this updating volume. They may respectively be found at *https://www.gov.uk/government/news/eea–efta–separation–agreement* and *https://www.gov.uk/government/publications/swiss–citizens–rights–agreement–and–explainer* [both accessed December 27, 2020].

[¹**Interpretation of relevant separation agreement law**

7C. (1) Any question as to the validity, meaning or effect of any relevant separation agreement law is to be decided, so far as they are applicable—   4.043

(a) in accordance with the withdrawal agreement, the EEA EFTA separation agreement and the Swiss citizens' rights agreement, and

(b) having regard (among other things) to the desirability of ensuring that, where one of those agreements makes provision which corresponds to provision made by another of those agreements, the effect of relevant separation agreement law in relation to the matters dealt with by the corresponding provision in each agreement is consistent.

(2) See (among other things)—

(a) Article 4 of the withdrawal agreement (methods and principles relating to the effect, the implementation and the application of the agreement),

(b) Articles 158 and 160 of the withdrawal agreement (jurisdiction of the European Court in relation to Part 2 and certain provisions of Part 5 of the agreement),

(c) *omitted*,

(d) Article 4 of the EEA EFTA separation agreement (methods and principles relating to the effect, the implementation and the application of the agreement), and

(e) Article 4 of the Swiss citizens' rights agreement (methods and principles relating to the effect, the implementation and the application of the agreement).

(3) In this Act 'relevant separation agreement law' means—

(a) any of the following provisions or anything which is domestic law by virtue of any of them—

(i) section 7A, 7B, 8B or 8C or Part 1B or 1C of Schedule 2 or this section, or

(ii) Part 3, or section 20, of the European Union (Withdrawal Agreement) Act 2020 (citizens' rights and financial provision), or

(b) anything not falling within paragraph (a) so far as it is domestic law for the purposes of, or otherwise within the scope of—

(i) the withdrawal agreement (other than Part 4 of that agreement),

(ii) the EEA EFTA separation agreement, or

(iii) the Swiss citizens' rights agreement,

as that body of law is added to or otherwise modified by or under this Act or by other domestic law from time to time.]

AMENDMENT

1. European Union (Withdrawal Agreement) Act 2020 s.26(2) (January 31, 2020).

DEFINITIONS

"domestic law": see s.20(1).
"EEA EFTA separation agreement" and "Swiss citizens' rights agreement": see Definitions to s.7B.
"relevant separation agreement law": see s.7C(3).
"withdrawal agreement": see s.1A(6).

GENERAL NOTE

For the text of "the EEA EFTA separation agreement" and "Swiss citizens' rights agreement, see General Note to s.7B.

Dealing with deficiencies arising from withdrawal

4.044   **8.** (1) A Minister of the Crown may by regulations make such provision as the Minister considers appropriate to prevent, remedy or mitigate—

(a) any failure of retained EU law to operate effectively, or

(b) any other deficiency in retained EU law,

arising from the withdrawal of the United Kingdom from the EU.

(2) Deficiencies in retained EU law are where the Minister considers that retained EU law—

(a) contains anything which has no practical application in relation to the United Kingdom or any part of it or is otherwise redundant or substantially redundant,

(b) confers functions on, or in relation to, EU entities which no longer have functions in that respect under EU law in relation to the United Kingdom or any part of it,

(c) makes provision for, or in connection with, reciprocal arrangements between—

    (i) the United Kingdom or any part of it or a public authority in the United Kingdom, and

    (ii) the EU, an EU entity, a member State or a public authority in a member State,

which no longer exist or are no longer appropriate,

(d) makes provision for, or in connection with, other arrangements which —

    (i) involve the EU, an EU entity, a member State or a public authority in a member State, or

    (ii) are otherwise dependent upon the United Kingdom's membership of the EU [[1]or Part 4 of the withdrawal agreement],

and which no longer exist or are no longer appropriate,

(e) makes provision for, or in connection with, any reciprocal or other arrangements not falling within paragraph (c) or (d) which no longer exist, or are no longer appropriate, as a result of the United Kingdom ceasing to be a party to any of the EU Treaties [²or as a result of either the end of the implementation period or any other effect of the withdrawal agreement],

[³(ea) is not clear in its effect as a result of the operation of any provision of sections 2 to 6 or Schedule 1,]

(f)   does not contain any functions or restrictions which—

    (i) were in an EU directive and in force immediately before [⁴IP completion day] (including any power to make EU tertiary legislation), and

    (ii) it is appropriate to retain, or

(g)   contains EU references which are no longer appropriate.

(3) There is also a deficiency in retained EU law where the Minister considers that there is—

(a) anything in retained EU law which is of a similar kind to any deficiency which falls within subsection (2), or

(b) a deficiency in retained EU law of a kind described, or provided for, in regulations made by a Minister of the Crown.

(4) But retained EU law is not deficient merely because it does not contain any modification of EU law which is adopted or notified, comes into force or only applies on or after [⁵IP completion day].

(5) Regulations under subsection (1) may make any provision that could be made by an Act of Parliament.

(6) Regulations under subsection (1) may (among other things) provide for functions of EU entities or public authorities in member States (including making an instrument of a legislative character or providing funding) to be—

(a) exercisable instead by a public authority (whether or not established for the purpose) in the United Kingdom, or

(b) replaced, abolished or otherwise modified.

(7) But regulations under subsection (1) may not—

(a) impose or increase taxation or fees,

(b) make retrospective provision,

(c) create a relevant criminal offence,

(d) establish a public authority,

[⁶ . . .]

(f) amend, repeal or revoke the Human Rights Act 1998 or any subordinate legislation made under it, or

(g) amend or repeal the Scotland Act 1998, the Government of Wales Act 2006 or the Northern Ireland Act 1998 (unless the regulations are made by virtue of paragraph 21(b) of Schedule 7 to this Act or are amending or repealing any provision of those Acts which modifies another enactment).

(8) No regulations may be made under this section after the end of the period of two years beginning with [⁷IP completion day].

(9) [⁸The reference in subsection (1) to a failure or other deficiency arising from the withdrawal of the United Kingdom from the EU includes a reference to any failure or other deficiency arising from—

(a) any aspect of that withdrawal, including (among other things)—

    (i) the end of the implementation period, or

> (ii) any other effect of the withdrawal agreement, or
(b) that withdrawal, or any such aspect of it, taken together with the operation of any provision, or the interaction between any provisions, made by or under this Act [⁹or the European Union (Withdrawal Agreement) Act 2020].]

AMENDMENTS

1. European Union (Withdrawal Agreement) Act 2020 s.27(2)(a) (January 31, 2020).
2. European Union (Withdrawal Agreement) Act 2020 s.27(2)(b) (January 31, 2020).
3. European Union (Withdrawal Agreement) Act 2020 s.27(2)(c) (January 31, 2020).
4. European Union (Withdrawal Agreement) Act 2020 s.27(2)(d) (January 31, 2020).
5. European Union (Withdrawal Agreement) Act 2020 s.27(3) (January 31, 2020).
6. European Union (Withdrawal Agreement) Act 2020 s.27(4) (January 31, 2020).
7. European Union (Withdrawal Agreement) Act 2020 s.27(5) (January 31, 2020).
8. European Union (Withdrawal Agreement) Act 2020 s.27(6)(a) (January 31, 2020).
9. European Union (Withdrawal Agreement) Act 2020 s.27(6)(b) (January 31, 2020).

DEFINITIONS

"the EU": see Schedule 1 to the Interpretation Act 1978.
"EU directive": see s.20(1).
"EU entity": see s.20(1).
"EU references": see s.20(1).
"EU tertiary legislation": see s.20(1).
"EU Treaties": see Schedule 1 to the Interpretation Act 1978.
"implementation period": see s.1A(6).
"IP completion day": see s.1A(6).
"member State": see s.20(1) and Schedule 1 to the Interpretation Act 1978.
"Minister of the Crown": see s.20(1).
"modification": see, via "modify", s.20(1).
"public authority": see s.20(1).
"public authority in the United Kingdom": see s.20(8).
"retained EU law": see s.6(7).
"withdrawal agreement": see s.1A(6).

[¹**Supplementary power in connection with implementation period**

4.045   **8A.** (1) A Minister of the Crown may by regulations—
(a) provide for other modifications for the purposes of section 1B(3)(f)(i) (whether applying in all cases or particular cases or descriptions of case),

(b) provide for subsection (3) or (4) of section 1B not to apply to any
   extent in particular cases or descriptions of case,

(c) make different provision in particular cases or descriptions of case
   to that made by subsection (3) or (4) of that section,

(d) modify any enactment contained in this Act in consequence of any
   repeal made by section 1A(5) or 1B(6), or

(e) make such provision not falling within paragraph (a), (b), (c) or
   (d) as the Minister considers appropriate for any purpose of, or
   otherwise in connection with, Part 4 of the withdrawal agreement.

(2) The power to make regulations under subsection (1) may (among
other things) be exercised by modifying any provision made by or under
an enactment.

(3) In subsection (2) *'enactment'* does not include primary legislation
passed or made after IP completion day.

(4) No regulations may be made under subsection (1) after the end of
the period of two years beginning with IP completion day.]

AMENDMENT

1. European Union (Withdrawal Agreement) Act 2020 s.3 (January 23,
   2020).

DEFINITIONS

"enactment": see s.20(1).
"Minister of the Crown": see s.20(1).
"modifications"/"modifying": see s.20(1).
"withdrawal agreement": see s.1A(6).

GENERAL NOTE

Schedule 2 (not reproduced in the main volume or this volume) confers
powers to make regulations involving devolved authorities which correspond to
the powers conferred by ss.8 to 8C.

Interpretation

20. (1) In this Act—   4.046
"Charter of Fundamental Rights" means the Charter of Fundamental
   Rights of the European Union of 7 December 2000, as adapted at
   Strasbourg on 12 December 2007;
[1"Commons sitting day' means a day on which the House of Commons is sitting (and a day is only a day on which the House of
   Commons is sitting if the House begins to sit on that day);
"devolved authority" means—
   (a) the Scottish Ministers,
   (b) the Welsh Ministers, or
   (c) a Northern Ireland department;
"domestic law" means—

    (a) in [²sections 3, 7A and 7B], the law of England and Wales, Scotland and Northern Ireland, and

    (b) in any other case, the law of England and Wales, Scotland or Northern Ireland;

"the EEA" means the European Economic Area;

"enactment" means an enactment whenever passed or made and includes—

    (a) an enactment contained in any Order in Council, order, rules, regulations, scheme, warrant, byelaw or other instrument made under an Act,

    (b) an enactment contained in any Order in Council made in exercise of Her Majesty's Prerogative,

    (c) an enactment contained in, or in an instrument made under, an Act of the Scottish Parliament,

    (d) an enactment contained in, or in an instrument made under, a Measure or Act of the National Assembly for Wales,

    (e) an enactment contained in, or in an instrument made under, Northern Ireland legislation,

    (f) an enactment contained in any instrument made by a member of the Scottish Government, the Welsh Ministers, the First Minister for Wales, the Counsel General to the Welsh Government, a Northern Ireland Minister, the First Minister in Northern Ireland, the deputy First Minister in Northern Ireland or a Northern Ireland department in exercise of prerogative or other executive functions of Her Majesty which are exercisable by such a person on behalf of Her Majesty,

    (g) an enactment contained in, or in an instrument made under, a Measure of the Church Assembly or of the General Synod of the Church of England, and

    (h) except in [³sections 1B and 7] or where there is otherwise a contrary intention, any retained direct EU legislation;

"EU decision" means—

    (a) a decision within the meaning of Article 288 of the Treaty on the Functioning of the European Union, or

    (b) a decision under former Article 34(2)(c) of the Treaty on European Union;

"EU directive" means a directive within the meaning of Article 288 of the Treaty on the Functioning of the European Union;

"EU entity" means an EU institution or any office, body or agency of the EU;

"EU reference" means—

    (a) any reference to the EU, an EU entity or a member State,

    (b) any reference to an EU directive or any other EU law, or

    (c) any other reference which relates to the EU;

"EU regulation" means a regulation within the meaning of Article 288 of the Treaty on the Functioning of the European Union;

"EU tertiary legislation" means—
- (a) any provision made under—
    - (i) an EU regulation,
    - (ii) a decision within the meaning of Article 288 of the Treaty on the Functioning of the European Union, or
    - (iii) an EU directive,

    by virtue of Article 290 or 291(2) of the Treaty on the Functioning of the European Union or former Article 202 of the Treaty establishing the European Community, or
- (b) any measure adopted in accordance with former Article 34(2)(c) of the Treaty on European Union to implement decisions under former Article 34(2)(c),

but does not include any such provision or measure which is an EU directive;

"exempt EU instrument" means anything which is an exempt EU instrument by virtue of Schedule 6;

[[4]"exit day" means [[5]31 January 2020] at 11.00 p.m. (and see subsections (2) to (5));]

[[14]"future relationship agreement" has the same meaning as in the European Union (Future Relationship) Act 2020 (see section 37 of that Act);]

[[6]"Joint Committee" means the Joint Committee established by Article 164(1) of the withdrawal agreement;

"Lords sitting day" means a day on which the House of Lords is sitting (and a day is only a day on which the House of Lords is sitting if the House begins to sit on that day);]

"member State" (except in the definitions of 'direct EU legislation' and 'EU reference') does not include the United Kingdom;

"Minister of the Crown" has the same meaning as in the Ministers of the Crown Act 1975 and also includes the Commissioners for Her Majesty's Revenue and Customs;

"modify" includes amend, repeal or revoke (and related expressions are to be read accordingly);

"Northern Ireland devolved authority" means the First Minister and deputy First Minister in Northern Ireland acting jointly, a Northern Ireland Minister or a Northern Ireland department;

"primary legislation" means—
- (a) an Act of Parliament,
- (b) an Act of the Scottish Parliament,
- (c) a Measure or Act of the National Assembly for Wales, or
- (d) Northern Ireland legislation;

"public authority" means a public authority within the meaning of section 6 of the Human Rights Act 1998;

[[7]"ratify", whether in relation to the withdrawal agreement or otherwise, has the same meaning as it does for the purposes of Part 2 of the Constitutional Reform and Governance Act 2010 in relation to a treaty (see section 25 of that Act);]

"relevant criminal offence" means an offence for which an individual who has reached the age of 18 (or, in relation to Scotland or Northern Ireland, 21) is capable of being sentenced to imprisonment for a term of more than 2 years (ignoring any enactment prohibiting or restricting the imprisonment of individuals who have no previous convictions);

"retained direct EU legislation" means any direct EU legislation which forms part of domestic law by virtue of section 3 (as modified by or under this Act or by other domestic law from time to time, and including any instruments made under it on or after [8IP completion day]);

"retrospective provision", in relation to provision made by regulations, means provision taking effect from a date earlier than the date on which the regulations are made;

"subordinate legislation" means—

(a) any Order in Council, order, rules, regulations, scheme, warrant, byelaw or other instrument made under any Act, or

(b) any instrument made under an Act of the Scottish Parliament, Northern Ireland legislation or a Measure or Act of the National Assembly for Wales,

and (except in section 7 or Schedule 2 or where there is a contrary intention) includes any Order in Council, order, rules, regulations, scheme, warrant, byelaw or other instrument made on or after [9IP completion day] under any retained direct EU legislation;

"tribunal" means any tribunal in which legal proceedings may be brought;

'Wales' and 'Welsh zone' have the same meaning as in the Government of Wales Act 2006 (see section 158 of that Act)[10.]

[10 . . .]

[11(2) In this Act references to before, after or on exit day, or to beginning with exit day, are to be read as references to before, after or at 11.00 p.m. on [1231 January 2020] or (as the case may be) to beginning with 11.00 p.m. on that day.]]

(3)—(5) *omitted*

[12(5A) In this Act references to anything which continues to be domestic law by virtue of section 1B(2) include—

(a) references to anything to which section 1B(2) applies which continues to be domestic law on or after exit day (whether or not it would have done so irrespective of that provision), and

(b) references to anything which continues to be domestic law on or after exit day by virtue of section 1B(2) (as that body of law is added to or otherwise modified by or under this Act or by other domestic law from time to time).]

(6) In this Act references to anything which continues to be domestic law by virtue of section 2 include references to anything to which subsection (1) of that section applies which continues to be domestic law

on or after [¹³IP completion day] (whether or not it would have done so irrespective of that section).

(7) In this Act references to anything which is retained EU law by virtue of section 4 include references to any modifications, made by or under this Act or by other domestic law from time to time, of the rights, powers, liabilities, obligations, restrictions, remedies or procedures concerned.

(8) References in this Act (however expressed) to a public authority in the United Kingdom include references to a public authority in any part of the United Kingdom.

(9) References in this Act to former Article 34(2)(c) of the Treaty on European Union are references to that Article as it had effect at any time before the coming into force of the Treaty of Lisbon.

(10) *omitted*

AMENDMENTS

1. European Union (Withdrawal Agreement) Act 2020 Sch.5 para.44(2)(a) (January 23, 2020).
2. European Union (Withdrawal Agreement) Act 2020 Sch.5 para.44(2)(b) (January 31, 2020).
3. European Union (Withdrawal Agreement) Act 2020 Sch.5 para.44(2)(c) (January 31, 2020).
4. The European Union (Withdrawal) Act 2018 (Exit Day) (Amendment) (No.2) Regulations 2019 (SI 2019/859) reg.2(2) (April 11, 2019).
5. The European Union (Withdrawal) Act 2018 (Exit Day) (Amendment) (No.3) Regulations 2019 (SI 2019/1423) reg.2(2) (October 30, 2019).
6. European Union (Withdrawal Agreement) Act 2020 Sch.5 para.44(2)(d) (January 23, 2020).
7. European Union (Withdrawal Agreement) Act 2020 Sch.5 para.66 (January 23, 2020).
8. European Union (Withdrawal Agreement) Act 2020 Sch.5 para.44(2)(f) (January 31, 2020).
9. European Union (Withdrawal Agreement) Act 2020 Sch.5 para.44(2)(g) (January 31, 2020).
10. European Union (Withdrawal Agreement) Act 2020 Sch.5 para.44(2)(h) (January 31, 2020).
11. The subsection is shown as it stands, having previously been amended by SI 2019/718, reg.2(3), SI 2019/859, reg.2(3) and SI 2019/1423, reg.2(3), to which reference may be made for the tortuous legislative history.
12. European Union (Withdrawal Agreement) Act 2020 Sch.5 para.44(3) (January 23, 2020).
13. European Union (Withdrawal Agreement) Act 2020 Sch.5 para.44(4) (January 31, 2020).
14. European Union (Future Relationship) Act 2020 s.39 and Sch.6 para.6 (December 31, 2020).

Index of defined expressions

21. (1) In this Act, the expressions listed in the left-hand column have the meaning given by, or are to be interpreted in accordance with, the provisions listed in the right-hand column.

4.047

379

Expression	Provision
[¹Anything which continues to be domestic law by virtue of section 1B(2)	Section 20(5A)]
Anything which continues to be domestic law by virtue of section 2	Section 20(6)
Anything which is retained EU law by virtue of section 4	Section 20(7)
Article (in relation to the Treaty on European Union or the Treaty on the Functioning of the European Union)	Section 20(10)
Charter of Fundamental Rights	Section 20(1)
[²Commons sitting day	Section 20(1)]
Devolved authority	Section 20(1)
Direct EU legislation	Section 3(2)
Domestic law	Section 20(1)
The EEA	Section 20(1)
EEA agreement	Schedule 1 to the Interpretation Act 1978
[³EEA EFTA separation agreement	Section 7B(6)]
Enactment	Section 20(1)
The EU	Schedule 1 to the Interpretation Act 1978
EU decision	Section 20(1)
[⁴EU-derived domestic legislation	Section 1B(7)]
EU directive	Section 20(1)
EU entity	Section 20(1)
EU institution	Schedule 1 to the Interpretation Act 1978
EU instrument	Schedule 1 to the Interpretation Act 1978

Expression	Provision
Euratom Treaty	Schedule 1 to the Interpretation Act 1978
EU reference	Section 20(1)
EU regulation	Section 20(1)
[⁵European Communities Act 1972	Section 1A(7)(a)]
European Court	Schedule 1 to the Interpretation Act 1978
EU tertiary legislation	Section 20(1)
EU Treaties	Schedule 1 to the Interpretation Act 1978
Exempt EU instrument	Section 20(1)
Exit day (and related expressions)	Section 20(1) to (5)
[¹²"Future relationship agreement	Section 20(1)"]
[⁶Implementation period	Section 1A(6)
IP completion day (and related expressions)	Section 1A(6)
Joint Committee	Section 20(1)
Lords sitting day	Section 20(1)]
Member State	Section 20(1) and Schedule 1 to the Interpretation Act 1978
Minister of the Crown	Section 20(1)
Modify (and related expressions)	Section 20(1)
Northern Ireland devolved authority	Section 20(1)
Operative (in relation to direct EU legislation)	Section 3(3)
[⁷Part (of withdrawal agreement or EEA EFTA separation agreement)	Section 1A(7)(b)]
Primary legislation	Section 20(1)

Expression	Provision
Public authority	Section 20(1)
Public authority in the United Kingdom (however expressed)	Section 20(8)
[8Qualifying Northern Ireland goods	Section 8C(6)
Ratify	Section 20(1)]
Relevant criminal offence	Section 20(1) (and paragraph 44 of Schedule 8)
[9Relevant separation agreement law	Section 7C(3)]
Retained case law	Section 6(7)
Retained direct EU legislation	Section 20(1)
Retained direct minor EU legislation	Section 7(6)
Retained direct principal EU legislation	Section 7(6)
Retained domestic case law	Section 6(7)
Retained EU case law	Section 6(7)
Retained EU law	Section 6(7)
Retained general principles of EU law	Section 6(7)
Retrospective provision	Section 20(1)
Subordinate legislation	Section 20(1)
[10Swiss citizens' rights agreement	Section 7B(6)]
Tribunal	Section 20(1)
Wales	Section 20(1)
Welsh zone	Section 20(1)
Withdrawal agreement[11	Section 1A(6)]

(2) See paragraph 22 of Schedule 8 for amendments made by this Act to Schedule 1 to the Interpretation Act 1978.

AMENDMENTS

1. European Union (Withdrawal Agreement) Act 2020 s.42(7) (January 31, 2020).
2. European Union (Withdrawal Agreement) Act 2020 s.42(7), Sch.5 para. 45(b) (January 31, 2020).
3. European Union (Withdrawal Agreement) Act 2020 s.42(7), Sch.5 para. 45(c) (January 31, 2020).
4. European Union (Withdrawal Agreement) Act 2020 s.42(7), Sch.5 para. 45(d) (January 31, 2020).
5. European Union (Withdrawal Agreement) Act 2020 s.42(7), Sch.5 para. 45(e) (January 31, 2020).
6. European Union (Withdrawal Agreement) Act 2020 s.42(7), Sch.5 para. 45(f) (January 31, 2020).
7. European Union (Withdrawal Agreement) Act 2020 s.42(7), Sch.5 para. 45(g) (January 31, 2020).
8. European Union (Withdrawal Agreement) Act 2020 s.42(7), Sch.5 para. 45(h) (January 31, 2020).
9. European Union (Withdrawal Agreement) Act 2020 s.42(7), Sch.5 para. 45(i) (January 31, 2020).
10. European Union (Withdrawal Agreement) Act 2020 s.42(7), Sch.5 para. 45(j) (January 31, 2020).
11. European Union (Withdrawal Agreement) Act 2020 s.42(7), Sch.5 para. 45(k) (January 31, 2020).
12. European Union (Future Relationship) Act 2020 s.39 and Sch.6 para.7 (December 31, 2020).

Consequential and transitional provision

23. (1) A Minister of the Crown may by regulations make such   4.048
provision as the Minister considers appropriate in consequence of this
Act.

(2) The power to make regulations under subsection (1) may (among
other things) be exercised by modifying any provision made by or under
an enactment.

(3) In subsection (2) *'enactment'* does not include primary legislation
passed or made after [¹IP completion day].

(4) No regulations may be made under subsection (1) after the end of
the period of 10 years beginning with [²IP completion day].

(5) Parts 1 and 2 of Schedule 8 (which contain consequential provision) have effect.

(6) A Minister of the Crown may by regulations make such transitional,
transitory or saving provision as the Minister considers appropriate in
connection with the coming into force of any provision of this Act
(including its operation in connection with [³or IP completion day]).

(7) Parts 3 and 4 of Schedule 8 (which contain transitional, transitory
and saving provision) have effect.

(8) The enactments mentioned in Schedule 9 (which contains repeals
not made elsewhere in this Act) are repealed to the extent specified.

AMENDMENTS

1. European Union (Withdrawal Agreement) Act 2020 s.42(7), Sch.5 para. 46(2) (January 31, 2020).

2. European Union (Withdrawal Agreement) Act 2020 s.42(7), Sch.5 para. 46(3) (January 31, 2020).
3. European Union (Withdrawal Agreement) Act 2020 s.42(7), Sch.5 para. 46(4) (January 31, 2020).

DEFINITION

"Minister of the Crown": see s.20(1).

GENERAL NOTE

Selected paragraphs of Schedule 8 are included below. Schedule 9 is not reproduced in this volume or the main volume.

Extent

4.049   **24.** (1) Subject to subsections (2) and (3), this Act extends to England and Wales, Scotland and Northern Ireland.

(2) Any provision of this Act which amends or repeals an enactment has the same extent as the enactment amended or repealed.

(3) [*omitted*]

DEFINITION

"enactment": see s.20(1).

Commencement and short title

4.050   **25.** (1) The following provisions—

(a) sections 8 to 11 (including Schedule 2),
(b) paragraphs 4, 5, 21(2)(b), 48(b), 51(2)(c) and (d) and (4) of Schedule 3 (and section 12(8) and (12) so far as relating to those paragraphs),
(c) sections 13 and 14 (including Schedule 4),
(d) sections 16 to 18,
(e) sections 20 to 22 (including Schedules 6 and 7),
(f) section 23(1) to (4) and (6),
(g) paragraph 41(10), 43 and 44 of Schedule 8 (and section 23(7) so far as relating to those paragraphs),
(h) section 24, and
(i) this section,

come into force on the day on which this Act is passed.

(2), (3) [*omitted*]

(4) The provisions of this Act, so far as they are not brought into force by subsections (1) to (3), come into force on such day as a Minister of the Crown may by regulations appoint; and different days may be appointed for different purposes.

(5) This Act may be cited as the European Union (Withdrawal) Act 2018.

DEFINITION

"Minister of the Crown": see s.20(1).

GENERAL NOTE

The commencement of this Act was complex, reflecting its 2018 origins and the evolving political landscape which eventually resulted in the European Union (Withdrawal Agreement) Act 2020 which made very substantial amendments to the 2018 Act, some of them temporary in nature to provide for the implementation period between "exit day" and "IP completion day" and others with longer term effect from IP completion day.

The following commencement orders have been made in respect of the 2018 Act:

European Union (Withdrawal) Act 2018 (Commencement and Transitional Provisions) Regulations 2018/808

European Union (Withdrawal) Act 2018 (Commencement No.2) Regulations 2019/399

European Union (Withdrawal) Act 2018 (Commencement No.3) Regulations 2019/1077

European Union (Withdrawal) Act 2018 (Commencement No.4) Regulations 2019/1198

European Union (Withdrawal) Act 2018 (Commencement No.5, Transitional Provisions and Amendment) Regulations 2020/74

European Union (Withdrawal) Act 2018 and European Union (Withdrawal Agreement) Act 2020 (Commencement, Transitional and Savings Provisions) Regulations 2020/1622

and the following in respect of the 2020 Act:

European Union (Withdrawal Agreement) Act 2020 (Commencement No.1) Regulations 2020/75

European Union (Withdrawal Agreement) Act 2020 (Commencement No.2) Regulations 2020/317

European Union (Withdrawal Agreement) Act 2020 (Commencement No.3) Regulations 2020/518

European Union (Withdrawal) Act 2018 and European Union (Withdrawal Agreement) Act 2020 (Commencement, Transitional and Savings Provisions) Regulations 2020/1622

SCHEDULES

SCHEDULE 1

FURTHER PROVISION ABOUT EXCEPTIONS TO SAVINGS AND INCORPORATION

Challenges to validity of retained EU law

1. (1) There is no right in domestic law on or after ['IP completion day] to challenge any retained EU law on the basis that, immediately before ['IP completion day], an EU instrument was invalid.   **4.051**

(2) Sub-paragraph (1) does not apply so far as—

(a) the European Court has decided before ['IP completion day] that the instrument is invalid, or

(b) the challenge is of a kind described, or provided for, in regulations made by a Minister of the Crown.

(3) Regulations under sub-paragraph (2)(b) may (among other things) provide for a challenge which would otherwise have been against an EU institution to be against a public authority in the United Kingdom.

General principles of EU law

2. No general principle of EU law is part of domestic law on or after [²IP completion day] if it was not recognised as a general principle of EU law by the European Court in a

385

case decided before [²IP completion day] (whether or not as an essential part of the decision in the case).

3. (1) There is no right of action in domestic law on or after [³IP completion day] based on a failure to comply with any of the general principles of EU law.

(2) No court or tribunal or other public authority may, on or after [³IP completion day] —

(a) disapply or quash any enactment or other rule of law, or

(b) quash any conduct or otherwise decide that it is unlawful,

because it is incompatible with any of the general principles of EU law.

Rule in Francovich

4. There is no right in domestic law on or after [⁴IP completion day] to damages in accordance with the rule in *Francovich*.

Interpretation

5. (1) References in section 5 and this Schedule to the principle of the supremacy of EU law, the Charter of Fundamental Rights, any general principle of EU law or the rule in *Francovich* are to be read as references to that principle, Charter or rule so far as it would otherwise continue to be, or form part of, domestic law on or after [⁵IP completion day] [⁶by virtue of section 2, 3, 4 or 6(3) or (6) and otherwise in accordance with this Act].

(2) Accordingly (among other things) the references to the principle of the supremacy of EU law in section 5(2) and (3) do not include anything which would bring into domestic law any modification of EU law which is adopted or notified, comes into force or only applies on or after [⁵IP completion day].

AMENDMENTS

1. European Union (Withdrawal Agreement) Act 2020 s.25(6)(a) (January 31, 2020 for limited purposes; otherwise December 31, 2020) (SI 2020/1622 reg.3(k)).

2. European Union (Withdrawal Agreement) Act 2020 s.25(6)(a) (substitution came into force on January 31, 2020 but only takes effect on December 31, 2020 by SI 2020/1622 reg.3(k)).

3. European Union (Withdrawal Agreement) Act 2020 s.25(6)(a) (substitution came into force on January 31, 2020 but only takes effect on December 31, 2020 by SI 2020/1622 reg.3(k))

4. European Union (Withdrawal Agreement) Act 2020 s.25(6)(a) (substitution came into force on January 31, 2020 but only takes effect on December 31, 2020 by SI 2020/1622 reg.3(k)).

5. European Union (Withdrawal Agreement) Act 2020 c. 1 Pt 4 s.25(6)(a) (substitution came into force on January 31, 2020 but only takes effect on December 31, 2020 by SI 2020/1622 reg.3(k))

6. European Union (Withdrawal Agreement) Act 2020 Pt 4 s.25(6)(b) (December 31, 2020) (SI 2020/1622 reg.5(d)).

GENERAL NOTE

A limited exception to Sch.1, para.1 is provided by the Challenges to Validity of EU Instruments (EU Exit) Regulations 2019 (SI 2019/673).

SCHEDULE 5

PUBLICATION AND RULES OF EVIDENCE

Questions as to meaning of EU law

4.052 **3.** (1) Where it is necessary [¹in legal proceedings] to decide a question as to—

(a) the meaning or effect in EU law of any of the EU Treaties or any other treaty relating to the EU, or

(b) the validity, meaning or effect in EU law of any EU instrument,
the question is to be treated [² . . .] as a question of law.
(2) In this paragraph—
[³ . . .]
'treaty' includes—
  (a) any international agreement, and
  (b) any protocol or annex to a treaty or international agreement.

Power to make provision about judicial notice and admissibility

4. (1) A Minister of the Crown may by regulations—
  (a) make provision enabling or requiring judicial notice to be taken of a relevant matter,
    or
  (b) provide for the admissibility in any legal proceedings of specified evidence of—
     (i) a relevant matter, or
     (ii) instruments or documents issued by or in the custody of an EU entity.
(2) Regulations under sub-paragraph (1)(b) may provide that evidence is admissible only where specified conditions are met (for example, conditions as to certification of documents).
(3) Regulations under this paragraph may modify any provision made by or under an enactment.
(4) In sub-paragraph (3) 'enactment' does not include primary legislation passed or made after [⁴IP completion day].
(5) For the purposes of this paragraph each of the following is a "relevant matter"—
  (a) retained EU law,
  (b) EU law,
  (c) the EEA agreement, [⁵ . . .]
[⁵(ca) the EEA EFTA separation agreement,
  (cb) the Swiss citizens' rights agreement,
  (cc) the withdrawal agreement, and]
  (d) anything which is specified in the regulations and which relates to a matter mentioned in paragraph (a), (b) [⁶, (c), (ca), (cb) or (cc)].

AMENDMENTS

1. European Union (Withdrawal Agreement) Act 2020 Sch.5(2) para.48(3)(a)(i) (December 31, 2020) (SI 2020/1622 reg.5(j)).
2. European Union (Withdrawal Agreement) Act 2020 Sch.5(2) para.48(3)(a)(ii) (December 31, 2020) (SI 2020/1622 reg.5(j)).
3. European Union (Withdrawal Agreement) Act 2020 Sch.5(2) para.48(3)(b) (December 31, 2020) (SI 2020/1622 reg.5(j)).
4. European Union (Withdrawal Agreement) Act 2020 Sch.5(2) para.48(4)(a) (January 31, 2020).
5. European Union (Withdrawal Agreement) Act 2020 Sch.5(2) para.48(4)(b)(i) (January 31, 2020).
6. European Union (Withdrawal Agreement) Act 2020 Sch.5(2) para.48(4)(b)(ii) (January 31, 2020).

SCHEDULE 8

CONSEQUENTIAL, TRANSITIONAL, TRANSITORY AND SAVING PROVISION

1. (1) Any reference which, immediately before exit day—   **4.053**
  (a) exists in—
     (i) any enactment,
     (ii) any EU regulation, EU decision, EU tertiary legislation or provision of the EEA agreement which is to form part of domestic law by virtue of section 3, or
     (iii) any document relating to anything falling within sub-paragraph (i) or (ii), and

(b) is a reference to (as it has effect from time to time) any EU regulation, EU decision, EU tertiary legislation or provision of the EEA agreement which is to form part of domestic law by virtue of section 3,

is to be read, on or after exit day, as a reference to the EU regulation, EU decision, EU tertiary legislation or provision of the EEA agreement as it forms part of domestic law by virtue of section 3 and, unless the contrary intention appears, as modified by domestic law from time to time.

(2) Sub-paragraph (1) does not apply to any reference which forms part of a power to make, confirm or approve subordinate legislation so far as the power to make the subordinate legislation—

(a) continues to be part of domestic law by virtue of section 2, and

(b) is subject to a procedure before Parliament, the Scottish Parliament, the National Assembly for Wales or the Northern Ireland Assembly.

(3) Sub-paragraphs (1) and (2) are subject to any other provision made by or under this Act or any other enactment.

[¹**Existing ambulatory references to relevant separation agreement law**

1A. (1) Any reference which, immediately before IP completion day—

(a) exists in—

  (i) any enactment,

  (ii) any EU regulation, EU decision, EU tertiary legislation or provision of the EEA agreement which is to form part of domestic law by virtue of section 3, or

  (iii) any document relating to anything falling within sub-paragraph (i) or (ii), and

(b) is a reference to (as it has effect from time to time) any of the EU Treaties, any EU instrument or any other document of an EU entity,

is, if the treaty, instrument or document has effect on or after IP completion day by virtue of section 7A or 7B and so far as required for the purposes of relevant separation agreement law, to be read on or after that day as, or including, a reference to the treaty, instrument or document as it so has effect (including, so far as so required, as it has effect from time to time).

(2) In sub-paragraph (1) 'treaty' includes any international agreement (and any protocol or annex to a treaty or international agreement).

(3) Sub-paragraphs (1) and (2) are subject to any other provision made by or under this Act or any other enactment.]

2.(1) Any reference which—

(a) exists, immediately before exit day, in—

  (i) any enactment,

  (ii) any EU regulation, EU decision, EU tertiary legislation or provision of the EEA agreement which is to form part of domestic law by virtue of section 3, or

  (iii) any document relating to anything falling within sub-paragraph (i) or (ii),

(b) is not a reference to which paragraph 1(1) applies, and

(c) is, immediately before exit day, a reference to (as it has effect from time to time) any of the EU Treaties, any EU instrument or any other document of an EU entity,

is to be read, on or after exit day, as a reference to the EU Treaty, instrument or document as it has effect immediately before exit day.

(2) Sub-paragraph (1) does not apply to any reference which forms part of a power to make, confirm or approve subordinate legislation so far as the power to make the subordinate legislation—

(a) continues to be part of domestic law by virtue of section 2, and

(b) is subject to a procedure before Parliament, the Scottish Parliament, the National Assembly for Wales or the Northern Ireland Assembly.

(3) Sub-paragraphs (1) and (2) are subject to any other provision made by or under this Act or any other enactment.

[¹**2A.— Existing non-ambulatory references**

(1) Any reference which, immediately before IP completion day—

(a) exists in—

  (i) any enactment, or

(ii) any EU regulation, EU decision, EU tertiary legislation or provision of the EEA agreement which is to form part of domestic law by virtue of section 3, and

(b) is a reference to any of the EU Treaties, any EU instrument or any other document of an EU entity as it has effect at a particular time which is earlier than IP completion day,

is to be read, on or after IP completion day, in accordance with one or more of subparagraphs (2) to (4).

(2) If the treaty, instrument or document has effect by virtue of section 7A or 7B on or after IP completion day and so far as required for the purposes of relevant separation agreement law, the reference is to be read on or after that day as, or as including, a reference to the treaty, instrument or document as it so has effect (including, so far as so required, as it has effect from time to time).

(3) So far as—

(a) the reference is a reference to—

(i) any EU regulation, EU decision or EU tertiary legislation,

(ii) any provision of the EEA agreement, or

(iii) any part of anything falling within sub-paragraph (i) or (ii),

(b) what has been referred to ("the subject law") is to form part of domestic law by virtue of section 3 [. . . *omitted*]

(c) there has been no relevant modification of the subject law after the particular time and before IP completion day [. . . *omitted*],

the reference is to be read, on or after IP completion day, as a reference to the subject law as it forms part of domestic law by virtue of section 3 [. . . *omitted*]

(4) So far as the reference is not to be read in accordance with sub-paragraphs (2) and (3), the reference is to be read, on or after IP completion day, as a reference to the treaty, instrument or document as it had effect in EU law at the particular time.

(5) Sub-paragraph (3) does not determine whether, where the subject law is modified by domestic law on or after IP completion day, the reference is to be read as a reference to the subject law as modified; [. . . *omitted*].

(6) This paragraph is subject to any provision made by or under this Act or any other enactment.

(7) In this paragraph—

'relevant modification' means any modification in EU law which—

(a) is to form part of domestic law by virtue of section 3 [. . . *omitted*] and

(b) would, if the reference were to the subject law as modified, result in an alteration to the effect of the reference (ignoring any alteration which is irrelevant in the context concerned);

'the subject law' has the meaning given by sub-paragraph (3)(b);

'treaty' includes any international agreement (and any protocol or annex to a treaty or international agreement).]

Human Rights Act 1998

30. (1) This paragraph has effect for the purposes of the Human Rights Act 1998.

(2) Any retained direct principal EU legislation is to be treated as primary legislation.

(3) Any retained direct minor EU legislation is to be treated as primary legislation so far as it amends any primary legislation but otherwise is to be treated as subordinate legislation.

(4) In this paragraph 'amend', 'primary legislation' and 'subordinate legislation' have the same meaning as in the Human Rights Act 1998.

Continuation of existing acts etc.

[⁷**36A.** (1) Anything done—

(a) in connection with anything which continues to be domestic law by virtue ofsection 1A(2) or 1B(2), or

(b) for a purpose mentioned in section 2(2)(a) or (b) of the European Communities Act 1972 or otherwise related to the EU or the EEA,

if in force or effective immediately before exit day, continues to be in force or effective on and after exit day.

(2) Anything done—

(a) in connection with anything which continues to be domestic law by virtue of section 1A(2) or 1B(2), or

(b) for a purpose mentioned in section 2(2)(a) or (b) of theEuropean Communities Act 1972 or otherwise related to the EU or the EEA,

which, immediately before exit day, is in the process of being done continues to be done on and after exit day

(3) Sub-paragraphs (1) and (2) are subject to—

(a) sections 1 to 1B and the withdrawal of the United Kingdom from the EU,

(b) any provision made under section 23(6) of this Act or section 41(5) of the European Union (Withdrawal Agreement) Act 2020, and

(c) any other provision made by or under this Act, the European Union (Withdrawal Agreement) Act 2020 or any other enactment.

(4) References in this paragraph to anything done include references to anything omitted to be done.]

37. (1) Anything done—

(a) in connection with anything which continues to be, or forms part of, domestic law by virtue of section 2, 3, 4 or 6(3) or (6), or

(b) for a purpose mentioned in section 2(2)(a) or (b) of the European Communities Act 1972 or otherwise related to the EU or the EEA,

if in force or effective immediately before exit day, continues to be in force or effective on and after exit day.

(2) Anything done—

(a) in connection with anything which continues to be, or forms part of, domestic law by virtue of section 2, 3, 4 or 6(3) or (6), or

(b) for a purpose mentioned in section 2(2)(a) or (b) of the European Communities Act 1972 or otherwise related to the EU or the EEA,

which, immediately before exit day, is in the process of being done continues to be done on and after exit day.

(3) Sub-paragraphs (1) and (2) are subject to—

(a) section 1 and the withdrawal of the United Kingdom from the EU,

(b) sections 2 to 6 and Schedule 1,

(c) any provision made under section 23(6), and

(d) any other provision made by or under this Act or any other enactment.

(4) References in this paragraph to anything done include references to anything omitted to be done.

Retention of existing EU law

[²**37A.** The repeal of section 1A(1) to (4) by section 1A(5) and the repeal of section 1B(1) to (5) by section 1B(6) do not prevent an enactment to which section 2 applies from continuing to be read, on and after IP completion day and by virtue of section 2, in accordance with section 1B(3) or (4).]

38. Section 4(2)(b) does not apply in relation to any rights, powers, liabilities, obligations, restrictions, remedies or procedures so far as they are of a kind recognised by a court or tribunal in the United Kingdom in a case decided on or after [³IP completion day] but begun before [³IP completion day] (whether or not as an essential part of the decision in the case).

39. (1) Subject as follows and subject to [⁴relevant separation agreement law (for which see section 7C) and] any provision made by regulations under [⁵section 23(6) of this Act or section 41(5) of the European Union (Withdrawal Agreement) Act 2020 section 5(4) and paragraphs 1 to 4 of Schedule 1] apply in relation to anything occurring before [⁶IP completion day] (as well as anything occurring on or after [⁶IP completion day]).

(2) Section 5(4) and paragraphs 1 to 4 of Schedule 1 do not affect any decision of a court or tribunal made before [⁴IP completion day].

(3) Section 5(4) and paragraphs 3 and 4 of Schedule 1 do not apply in relation to any proceedings begun, but not finally decided, before a court or tribunal in the United Kingdom before [⁶IP completion day].

(4) Paragraphs 1 to 4 of Schedule 1 do not apply in relation to any conduct which occurred before [⁶IP completion day] which gives rise to any criminal liability.

(5) Paragraph 3 of Schedule 1 does not apply in relation to any proceedings begun within the period of three years beginning with [⁶IP completion day] so far as—

(a) the proceedings involve a challenge to anything which occurred before [⁵IP completion day], and

(b) the challenge is not for the disapplication or quashing of—

    (i) an Act of Parliament or a rule of law which is not an enactment, or

    (ii) any enactment, or anything else, not falling within sub-paragraph (i) which, as
a result of anything falling within that sub-paragraph, could not have been
different or which gives effect to, or enforces, anything falling within that sub-
paragraph.

(6) Paragraph 3(2) of Schedule 1 does not apply in relation to any decision of a court or
tribunal, or other public authority, on or after [⁶IP completion day] which is a necessary
consequence of any decision of a court or tribunal made before [⁶IP completion day] or
made on or after that day by virtue of this paragraph.

(7) Paragraph 4 of Schedule 1 does not apply in relation to any proceedings begun within
the period of two years beginning with [⁶IP completion day] so far as the proceedings relate
to anything which occurred before [⁶IP completion day].

AMENDMENTS

1. European Union Withdrawal (Consequential Modifications) (EU Exit)
   Regulations 2020 (SI 2020/1447) reg.3 (December 31, 2020).
2. European Union (Withdrawal Agreement) Act 2020 Sch.5(2) para.56(3)
   (December 31, 2020) (SI 2020/1622) reg.5(j).
3. European Union (Withdrawal Agreement) Act 2020 Sch.5(2) para.56(4)
   (December 31, 2020) (SI 2020/1622) reg.5(j).
4. European Union (Withdrawal Agreement) Act 2020 Sch.5(2) para.
   56(5)(b)(i) (December 31, 2020) (SI 2020/1622) reg.5(j).
5. European Union (Withdrawal Agreement) Act 2020 Sch.5(2) para.
   56(5)(b)(ii) (December 31, 2020) (SI 2020/1622) reg.5(j).
6. European Union (Withdrawal Agreement) Act 2020 Sch.5(2) para.
   56(5)(a) (December 31, 2020) (SI 2020/1622) reg.5(j).
7. European Union (Withdrawal Agreement) Act 2020 Sch.5(2) para.55(2)
   (January 31, 2020) (SI 2020/75) reg.4.

p.1082, *European Union (Withdrawal Agreement) Act 2020*

PART 3

CITIZENS' RIGHTS

RIGHTS IN RELATION TO ENTRY AND RESIDENCE

Rights related to residence: application deadline and temporary protection

7.—(1) A Minister of the Crown may by regulations make such   4.054
provision as the Minister considers appropriate for any of the following
purposes—

(a) specifying the deadline that applies for the purposes of—

391

(i) the first sub-paragraph of Article 18(1)(b) of the withdrawal agreement (deadline for the submission of applications for the new residence status described in Article 18(1));

(ii) the first sub-paragraph of Article 17(1)(b) of the EEA EFTA separation agreement (deadline for the submission of applications for the new residence status described in Article 17(1));

(iii) the first sentence of Article 16(1)(b) of the Swiss citizens' rights agreement (deadline for the submission of applications for the new residence status described in Article 16(1));

(b) implementing Article 18(2) of the withdrawal agreement (protection for Union citizens etc. in the period prior to the deadline for the submission of applications for the new residence status described in Article 18(1));

(c) implementing Article 17(2) of the EEA EFTA separation agreement (protection for EEA EFTA nationals etc. in the period prior to the deadline for the submission of applications for the new residence status described in Article 17(1));

(d) implementing Article 16(2) of the Swiss citizens' rights agreement (protection for Swiss nationals etc. in the period prior to the deadline for the submission of applications for the new residence status described in Article 16(1));

(e) implementing Article 18(3) of the withdrawal agreement (protection for Union citizens etc. pending a final decision on an application for the new residence status described in Article 18(1));

(f) implementing Article 17(3) of the EEA EFTA separation agreement (protection for EEA EFTA nationals etc. pending a final decision on an application for the new residence status described in Article 17(1));

(g) implementing Article 16(3) of the Swiss citizens' rights agreement (protection for Swiss nationals etc. pending a final decision on an application for the new residence status described in Article 16(1)).

(2) If the Minister considers it appropriate, regulations under subsection (1) relating to the implementation of a provision mentioned in subsection (1)(b), (c) or (d) may be made so as to apply both to—

(a) persons to whom the provision in question applies, and

(b) persons to whom that provision does not apply but who may be granted leave to enter or remain in the United Kingdom by virtue of residence scheme immigration rules (see section 17) and who do not have such leave.

(3) If the Minister considers it appropriate, regulations under subsection (1) relating to the implementation of a provision mentioned in subsection (1)(e), (f) or (g) may be made so as to apply both to—

(a) persons to whom the provision in question applies, and

(b) persons to whom that provision does not apply but who make an application for leave to enter or remain in the United Kingdom by virtue of residence scheme immigration rules.

(4) The power to make regulations under subsection (1) may (among other things) be exercised by modifying any provision made by or under an enactment.

Frontier workers

8.—(1) A Minister of the Crown may by regulations make such provision as the Minister considers appropriate for the purpose of implementing any of the following—
  (a) Articles 24(3) and 25(3) of the withdrawal agreement (rights of employed and self-employed frontier workers) other than as regards rights enjoyed as workers (see section 14(1));
  (b) Articles 23(3) and 24(3) of the EEA EFTA separation agreement (rights of employed and self-employed frontier workers) other than as regards rights enjoyed as workers (see section 14(2));
  (c) Article 20(2) of the Swiss citizens' rights agreement (rights of frontier workers to enter and exit).

(2) A Minister of the Crown may by regulations make such provision as the Minister considers appropriate for the purpose of implementing any of the following—
  (a) Article 26 of the withdrawal agreement (issue of documents);
  (b) Article 25 of the EEA EFTA separation agreement (issue of documents);
  (c) Article 21(1)(a) and (2) of the Swiss citizens' rights agreement (issue of documents).

(3) The power to make regulations under subsection (1) or (2) may (among other things) be exercised by modifying any provision made by or under the Immigration Acts.

Restrictions of rights of entry and residence

9.—(1) A Minister of the Crown may by regulations make such provision as the Minister considers appropriate for the purpose of implementing any of the following—
  (a) Article 20(1), (3) and (4) of the withdrawal agreement (restrictions of the rights of entry and residence);
  (b) Article 19(1), (3) and (4) of the EEA EFTA separation agreement (restrictions of the rights of entry and residence);
  (c) Articles 17(1) and (3) and 20(3) of the Swiss citizens' rights agreement (restrictions of the rights of entry and residence).

(2) If the Minister considers it appropriate, regulations under subsection (1) relating to the implementation of a provision mentioned in subsection (1)(a), (b) or (c) may be made so as to apply both to—
  (a) persons to whom the provision in question applies, and
  (b) persons to whom that provision does not apply but who—
    (i) have entry clearance granted by virtue of relevant entry clearance immigration rules (see section 17),
    (ii) have leave to enter or remain in the United Kingdom granted by virtue of residence scheme immigration rules (see section 17), or

      (iii) otherwise have leave to enter granted after arriving with entry clearance granted by virtue of relevant entry clearance immigration rules.

(3) In subsection (2)(b), references to a person who has entry clearance or leave to enter or remain include references to a person who would have had entry clearance or leave to enter or remain but for—

    (a) the making of a deportation order under section 5(1) of the Immigration Act 1971, or

    (b) the making of any other decision made in connection with restricting the right of the person to enter the United Kingdom.

(4) The power to make regulations under subsection (1) may (among other things) be exercised by modifying any provision made—

    (a) by or under the Immigration Acts, or

    (b) under other primary legislation.

Co-ordination of social security systems

4.055   **13.** (1) An appropriate authority may by regulations make such provision as the authority considers appropriate—

    (a) to implement Title III of Part 2 of the withdrawal agreement (co-ordination of social security systems),

    (b) to supplement the effect of section 7A of the European Union (Withdrawal) Act 2018 in relation to that Title, or

    (c) otherwise for the purposes of dealing with matters arising out of, or related to, that Title (including matters arising by virtue of section 7A of that Act and that Title).

(2) An appropriate authority may by regulations make such provision as the authority considers appropriate—

    (a) to implement Title III of Part 2 of the EEA EFTA separation agreement (co-ordination of social security systems),

    (b) to supplement the effect of section 7B of the European Union (Withdrawal) Act 2018 in relation to that Title, or

    (c) otherwise for the purposes of dealing with matters arising out of, or related to, that Title (including matters arising by virtue of section 7B of that Act and that Title).

(3) An appropriate authority may by regulations make such provision as the authority considers appropriate—

    (a) to implement social security co-ordination provisions of the Swiss citizens' rights agreement,

    (b) to supplement the effect of section 7B of the European Union (Withdrawal) Act 2018 in relation to those provisions, or

    (c) otherwise for the purposes of dealing with matters arising out of, or related to, those provisions (including matters arising by virtue of section 7B of that Act and those provisions).

(4) For the purposes of subsection (3) the following are "social security co-ordination provisions" of the Swiss citizens' rights agreement—

    (a) Part 3 of that agreement (co-ordination of social security systems);

    (b) Article 23(4) of that agreement as regards social security co-ordination.

(5) The power to make regulations under subsection (1), (2) or (3) may (among other things) be exercised by modifying any provision made by or under an enactment.

(6) In this section, 'appropriate authority' means—

(a) a Minister of the Crown,

(b) a devolved authority, or

(c) a Minister of the Crown acting jointly with a devolved authority.

(7) Schedule 1 contains further provision about the power of devolved authorities to make regulations under this section.

Non-discrimination, equal treatment and rights of workers etc.

14. (1) An appropriate authority may by regulations make such provision as the authority considers appropriate for the purpose of implementing any of the following provisions of the withdrawal agreement— 4.056

(a) Article 12 (prohibition of discrimination on grounds of nationality);

(b) Article 23 (right to equal treatment);

(c) Articles 24(1) and 25(1) (rights of workers and the self-employed);

(d) Articles 24(3) and 25(3) (rights of employed or self-employed frontier workers) as regards rights enjoyed as workers.

(2) An appropriate authority may by regulations make such provision as the authority considers appropriate for the purpose of implementing any of the following provisions of the EEA EFTA separation agreement—

(a) Article 11 (prohibition of discrimination on grounds of nationality);

(b) Article 22 (right to equal treatment);

(c) Articles 23(1) and 24(1) (rights of workers and the self-employed);

(d) Articles 23(3) and 24(3) (rights of employed or self-employed frontier workers) as regards rights enjoyed as workers.

(3) An appropriate authority may by regulations make such provision as the authority considers appropriate for the purpose of implementing any of the following provisions of the Swiss citizens' rights agreement—

(a) Article 7 (prohibition of discrimination on grounds of nationality);

(b) Article 18 (right to take up employment etc.);

(c) Article 19 (rights of employed or self-employed persons etc.);

(d) Article 20(1) (rights of frontier workers);

(e) Article 23(1) (rights of persons providing services).

(4) If the appropriate authority considers it appropriate, regulations under subsection (1), (2) or (3) relating to the implementation of a provision mentioned in that subsection, may be made so as to apply both to—

(a) persons to whom the provision in question applies, and

(b) persons to whom that provision does not apply but who may be granted leave to enter or remain in the United Kingdom by virtue of residence scheme immigration rules, whether or not they have been granted such leave (see section 17).

(5) The power to make regulations under subsection (1), (2) or (3) may (among other things) be exercised by modifying any provision made by or under an enactment.

(6) In this section, 'appropriate authority' means—

(a) a Minister of the Crown,

(b) a devolved authority, or

(c) a Minister of the Crown acting jointly with a devolved authority.

(7) Schedule 1 contains further provision about the power of devolved authorities to make regulations under this section.

Independent Monitoring Authority for the Citizens' Rights Agreements

4.057   **15.** (1) A body corporate called the Independent Monitoring Authority for the Citizens' Rights Agreements is established.

(2) In this Part that body is referred to as 'the IMA'.

(3) Schedule 2 contains provision relating to the IMA (including provisions about the IMA's constitution and functions).

Regulations: supplementary

4.058   **16.** (1) In sections 7, 8, 9 and 14—

(a) a power to make provision for the purpose of implementing a provision of the withdrawal agreement includes power to make provision to supplement the effect of section 7A of the European Union (Withdrawal) Act 2018 in relation to that provision of the agreement,

(b) a power to make provision for the purpose of implementing a provision of the EEA EFTA separation agreement includes power to make provision to supplement the effect of section 7B of that Act in relation to that provision of the agreement, and

(c) a power to make provision for the purpose of implementing a provision of the Swiss citizens' rights agreement includes power to make provision to supplement the effect of section 7B of that Act in relation to that provision of the agreement.

(2) The conferral of a power on a Minister of the Crown under section 7, 8, 9 or 11 does not affect the extent of any power of a devolved authority under section 12, 13 or 14 which overlaps with a power under section 7, 8, 9 or 11 by virtue of section 17(4).

(3) Regulations under this Part may not provide for the conferral of functions (including the conferral of a discretion) on, or the delegation of functions to, a person who is not a public authority (but may so provide if the person is a public authority).

(4) In subsection (3), 'public authority' means a person who exercises functions of a public nature.

Interpretation: Part 3

17. (1) In this Part, 'residence scheme immigration rules' means—

(a) Appendix EU to the immigration rules except those rules, or changes to that Appendix, which are identified in the immigration rules as not having effect in connection with the residence scheme that operates in connection with the withdrawal of the United Kingdom from the EU, and

(b) any other immigration rules which are identified in the immigration rules as having effect in connection with the withdrawal of the United Kingdom from the EU.

(2) In this Part, 'relevant entry clearance immigration rules' means any immigration rules which are identified in the immigration rules as having effect in connection with the granting of entry clearance for the purposes of acquiring leave to enter or remain in the United Kingdom by virtue of residence scheme immigration rules.

(3) In this Part, references to having leave to enter or remain in the United Kingdom granted by virtue of residence scheme immigration rules include references to having such leave granted by virtue of those rules before this section comes into force.

(4) In this Part, a reference to a Chapter, Title, Part or other provision of the withdrawal agreement, EEA EFTA separation agreement or Swiss citizens' rights agreement includes a reference to—

(a) any other provision of the agreement in question so far as relating to that Chapter, Title, Part or other provision, and

(b) any provision of EU law which is applied by, or referred to in, that Chapter, Title, Part or other provision (to the extent of the application or reference).

(5) In this Part—

'entry clearance' has the meaning given by section 33(1) of the Immigration Act 1971 (interpretation);

'immigration rules' has the same meaning as in the Immigration Act 1971.

Repeal of unnecessary or spent enactments

GENERAL NOTE

Section 36 repeals a number of provisions of the European Union (Withdrawal) Act 2018 and the European Union (Withdrawal) Act 2019. They are only of historic interest and are not reproduced here.

Parliamentary sovereignty

38. (1) It is recognised that the Parliament of the United Kingdom is sovereign. 4.061

(2) In particular, its sovereignty subsists notwithstanding—

(a) directly applicable or directly effective EU law continuing to be recognised and available in domestic law by virtue of section 1A or 1B of the European Union (Withdrawal) Act 2018 (savings of existing law for the implementation period),

(b) section 7A of that Act (other directly applicable or directly effective aspects of the withdrawal agreement),

(c) section 7B of that Act (deemed direct applicability or direct effect in relation to the EEA EFTA separation agreement and the Swiss citizens' rights agreement), and

(d) section 7C of that Act (interpretation of law relating to the withdrawal agreement (other than the implementation period), the EEA EFTA separation agreement and the Swiss citizens' rights agreement).

(3) Accordingly, nothing in this Act derogates from the sovereignty of the Parliament of the United Kingdom.

Interpretation

4.062   **39.** (1) In this Act—

'devolved authority' means—

(a) the Scottish Ministers,

(b) the Welsh Ministers, or

(c) a Northern Ireland department;

'EEA EFTA separation agreement' means (as modified from time to time in accordance with any provision of it) the Agreement on arrangements between Iceland, the Principality of Liechtenstein, the Kingdom of Norway and the United Kingdom of Great Britain and Northern Ireland following the withdrawal of the United Kingdom from the European Union, the EEA Agreement and other agreements applicable between the United Kingdom and the EEA EFTA States by virtue of the United Kingdom's membership of the European Union;

'enactment' means an enactment whenever passed or made and includes—

(a) an enactment contained in any Order in Council, order, rules, regulations, scheme, warrant, byelaw or other instrument made under an Act of Parliament,

(b) an enactment contained in any Order in Council made in exercise of Her Majesty's Prerogative,

(c) an enactment contained in, or in an instrument made under, an Act of the Scottish Parliament,

(d) an enactment contained in, or in an instrument made under, a Measure or Act of the National Assembly for Wales,

(e) an enactment contained in, or in an instrument made under, Northern Ireland legislation,

(f) an enactment contained in any instrument made by a member of the Scottish Government, the Welsh Ministers, the First Minister for Wales, the Counsel General to the Welsh Government, a Northern Ireland Minister, the First Minister in Northern Ireland, the deputy First Minister in Northern Ireland or a Northern Ireland department in exercise of prerogative or other executive functions of Her Majesty which are exercisable by such a person on behalf of Her Majesty,

(g) an enactment contained in, or in an instrument made under, a Measure of the Church Assembly or of the General Synod of the Church of England, and

(h) any retained direct EU legislation;

'IP completion day' means 31 December 2020 at 11.00 p.m (and see subsections (2) to (5));

'Minister of the Crown' has the same meaning as in the Ministers of the Crown Act 1975 and also includes the Commissioners for Her Majesty's Revenue and Customs;

'modify' includes amend, repeal or revoke (and related expressions are to be read accordingly);

'primary legislation' means—

(a) an Act of Parliament,

(b) an Act of the Scottish Parliament,

(c) a Measure or Act of the National Assembly for Wales, or

(d) Northern Ireland legislation;

'subordinate legislation' means any Order in Council, order, rules, regulations, scheme, warrant, byelaw or other instrument made under any primary legislation;

'Swiss citizens' rights agreement' means (as modified from time to time in accordance with any provision of it) the Agreement signed at Bern on 25 February 2019 between the United Kingdom of Great Britain and Northern Ireland and the Swiss Confederation on citizens' rights following the withdrawal of the United Kingdom from—

(a) the European Union, and

(b) the free movement of persons agreement,

so far as the Agreement operates for the purposes of the case where "specified date" for the purposes of that Agreement has the meaning given in Article 2(b)(ii) of that Agreement;

'withdrawal agreement' means the agreement between the United Kingdom and the EU under Article 50(2) of the Treaty on European Union which sets out the arrangements for the United Kingdom's withdrawal from the EU (as that agreement is modified from time to time in accordance with any provision of it).

(2) In this Act references to before, after or on IP completion day, or to beginning with IP completion day, are to be read as references to before, after or at 11.00 p.m. on 31 December 2020 or (as the case may be) to beginning with 11.00 p.m. on that day.

(3) Subsection (4) applies if, by virtue of any change to EU summertime arrangements, the transition or implementation period provided for by Part 4 of the withdrawal agreement is to end on a day or time which is different from that specified in the definition of *'IP completion day'* in subsection (1).

(4) A Minister of the Crown may by regulations—

(a) amend the definition of "IP completion day" in subsection (1) to ensure that the day and time specified in the definition are the day and time that the transition or implementation period provided for by Part 4 of the withdrawal agreement is to end, and

(b) amend subsection (2) in consequence of any such amendment.

(5) In subsection (3) 'EU summer-time arrangements' means the arrangements provided for by Directive 2000/84/EC of the European Parliament and of the Council of 19 January 2001 on summer-time arrangements.

(6) In this Act any reference to an Article of the Treaty on European Union includes a reference to that Article as applied by Article 106a of the Euratom Treaty.

Regulations

4.063   **40.** Schedule 4 contains provision about regulations under this Act (including provision about procedure).

GENERAL NOTE

In the interests of saving space, Schedule 4 is not reproduced.

Consequential and transitional provision etc.

4.064   **41.** (1) A Minister of the Crown may by regulations make such provision as the Minister considers appropriate in consequence of this Act.

(2) The power to make regulations under subsection (1) may (among other things) be exercised by modifying any provision made by or under an enactment.

(3) In subsection (2) *'enactment'* does not include primary legislation passed or made after IP completion day.

(4) Parts 1 and 2 of Schedule 5 contain minor and consequential provision.

(5) A Minister of the Crown may by regulations make such transitional, transitory or saving provision as the Minister considers appropriate in connection with the coming into force of any provision of this Act (including its operation in connection with exit day or IP completion day).

(6) Part 3 of Schedule 5 contains transitional, transitory and saving provision.

GENERAL NOTE

In the interests of saving space, Schedule 5 is in general not reproduced, but the following provision should be noted:

1. (1) Any provision in subordinate legislation made before exit day under—
  (a) any provision of the European Union (Withdrawal) Act 2018 (or any provision made under any such provision), or
  (b) any other enactment,
which provides, by reference to exit day (however expressed), for all or part of that or any other subordinate legislation to come into force immediately before exit day, on exit day or at any time after exit day is to be read instead as providing for the subordinate legislation or (as the case may be) the part to come into force immediately before IP completion day, on IP completion day or (as the case may be) at the time concerned after IP completion day.

400

(2) Sub-paragraph (1) does not apply so far as it is expressly disapplied by the subordinate legislation that provides as mentioned in that sub-paragraph.

(3) An appropriate authority may by regulations—

(a) provide for sub-paragraph (1) not to apply to any extent in particular cases or descriptions of case, or

(b) make different provision in particular cases or descriptions of case to that made by sub-paragraph (1).

(4) But see paragraph 2 for further provision about the power of a devolved authority acting alone to make regulations under sub-paragraph (3).

(5) No regulations may be made under sub-paragraph (3) after the end of the period of one year beginning with IP completion day.

(6) In this paragraph "appropriate authority" means—

(a) a Minister of the Crown,

(b) a devolved authority, or

(c) a Minister of the Crown acting jointly with a devolved authority.

Extent, commencement and short title

42. (1) Subject to subsections (2) to (5), this Act extends to England 4.065 and Wales, Scotland and Northern Ireland.

(2) Any provision of this Act which amends or repeals an enactment has the same extent as the enactment amended or repealed.

(3) Accordingly, section 1 (but not section 2) also extends to the Isle of Man, the Channel Islands and Gibraltar.

(4) The power in section 36 of the Immigration Act 1971 or (as the case may be) section 60(4) of the UK Borders Act 2007 may be exercised so as to extend (with or without modifications) to the Isle of Man or any of the Channel Islands the modifications made to that Act by section 10 above.

(5) Paragraphs 1 and 2 of Schedule 5, so far as they relate to the modification of any provision in subordinate legislation which extends outside England and Wales, Scotland and Northern Ireland, also extend there.

(6) The following provisions—

(a) sections 3 and 4,

(b) sections 11, 16 and 17,

(c) sections 20, 29 and 31 to 40 (including Schedule 4),

(d) section 41(1) to (3) and (5),

(e) the following provisions of Schedule 5—

    (i) paragraphs 1(3) to (6) and 2,

    (ii) paragraph 3(2) to (8),

    (iii) paragraph 4,

    (iv) paragraphs 5 and 7(a) and (b),

    (v) paragraphs 8 and 12(a) and (b),

    (vi) paragraphs 17, 20, 22, 24, 27 and 31,

    (vii) paragraphs 32, 36(a) and (b) and 37(b) and (c),

    (viii) paragraphs 38, 41(1) and (3)(a), 42 44(1), (2)(a), (d) and (e) and (3), 47(1), (2), (4) and (6) and 50,

    (ix) paragraphs 51 and 56(1) and (7)(b) for the purposes of making regulations under section 8A of, or Part 1A of Schedule 2 to, the European Union (Withdrawal) Act 2018,

(x) paragraphs 52(1) and (3) to (7) and 53(1) to (4), (6), (7)(a), (8)(a) and (9) to (13),

(xi) paragraph 56(1) and (6)(b) to (d), and

(xii) paragraphs 65 to 68,

(and section 41(4) and (6) so far as relating to any provision so far as it falls within any of sub-paragraphs (i) to (xii)), and

(f) this section,

come into force on the day on which this Act is passed.

(7) The provisions of this Act, so far as they are not brought into force by subsection (6), come into force on such day as a Minister of the Crown may by regulations appoint; and different days may be appointed for different purposes.

(8) This Act may be cited as the European Union (Withdrawal Agreement) Act 2020.

GENERAL NOTE

For the issues around the commencement of this Act and the European Union (Withdrawal) Act 2018 and a list of the relevant commencement orders, see the General Note to the 2018 Act, s.25.

p.1082, *European Communities Act 1972*

4.066   Following the repeal of s.1A (1)–(4) of the European Union (Withdrawal) Act 2018 from December 31, 2020, the European Communities Act 1972, already formally repealed, no longer has the preserved life for which the 2018 Act provided.

For the extent to which matters of EU law discussed in the notes to the 1972 Act may have any continuing relevance from December 31, 2020, see the European Union (Withdrawal) Act 2018.

Note the role of s.2(1) of the 1972 Act in defining a category of preserved right under section 4 of the European Union (Withdrawal) Act 2018.

p.1102, *Withdrawal Agreement—Part Two, Citizens' Rights*

4.067   Following the end of the implementation/transition period for the Withdrawal Agreement on December 31, 2020, Part Two is now in force. In general terms it provides for continuing rights to reside for those who exercised rights of free movement before the end of the transition period and their families on a basis which, though not identical to that of Directive 2004/38/EC, has many references to it.

In respect of people within the scope of Part Two, provision is made for ongoing equal treatment and for the continuance of rights under Regulation (EU) No.492/2011.

Title III of Part Two (arts 30–36) makes provision for the ongoing application of Regulations (EC) No.883/2004 and (EC) No.987/2009 to the persons covered by the Title, namely United Kingdom nationals who at the end of the transition period are subject to the legislation of a Member State or who reside in a Member State and are subject to the legislation of the United Kingdom and (in each case) their family members and survivors; and vice versa in respect of Union Citizens. Title III also makes provision for those who, though not falling within the above, have accumulated rights in the United Kingdom and a Member State as the result of previous periods of activity in the Member State.

The United Kingdom has the status of observer in the Administrative Commission, whose decisions listed in Annex I to the Withdrawal Agreement continue to apply.

Art.158 provides the opportunity for courts and tribunals in the United Kingdom to request the CJEU to give a preliminary ruling concerning the interpretation of Part Two in cases which commence at first instance within (in general) 8 years of the transition period. Art.159 provides for the creation of an independent authority in the United Kingdom to monitor the implementation and application of Part Two. The text of arts 158 and 159 follows the text of Part Two below.

Detailed Guidance to staff on the application of Part Two, prepared jointly by the DWP, HMRC and the Department of Health and Social Care may be found at *https://www.gov.uk/government/publications/social-security-arrangements-between-the-uk-and-the-eu-from-january-2021-staff-guide/guidance-relating-to-the-uks-operational-implementation-of-the-social-security-coordination-provisions-of-part-2-of-the-eu-withdrawal-agreement-citi* (accessed December 31, 2020).

For other relevant parts of the Withdrawal Agreement, refer to the main volume, commencing at 3.56.

PART TWO

CITIZENS' RIGHTS

Title I
General Provisions

Article 9

Definitions

For the purposes of this Part, and without prejudice to Title III, the 4.068
following definitions shall apply:

  (a) "family members" means the following persons, irrespective of
      their nationality, who fall within the personal scope provided for in
      Article 10 of this Agreement:
       (i) family members of Union citizens or family members of
           United Kingdom nationals as defined in point (2) of Article
           2 of Directive 2004/38/EC of the European Parliament and
           of the Council;

(ii) persons other than those defined in Article 3(2) of Directive 2004/38/EC whose presence is required by Union citizens or United Kingdom nationals in order not to deprive those Union citizens or United Kingdom nationals of a right of residence granted by this Part;

(b) "frontier workers" means Union citizens or United Kingdom nationals who pursue an economic activity in accordance with Article 45 or 49 TFEU in one or more States in which they do not reside;

(c) "host State" means:

(i) in respect of Union citizens and their family members, the United Kingdom, if they exercised their right of residence there in accordance with Union law before the end of the transition period and continue to reside there thereafter;

(ii) in respect of United Kingdom nationals and their family members, the Member State in which they exercised their right of residence in accordance with Union law before the end of the transition period and in which they continue to reside thereafter;

(d) "State of work" means:

(i) in respect of Union citizens, the United Kingdom, if they pursued an economic activity as frontier workers there before the end of the transition period and continue to do so thereafter;

(ii) in respect of United Kingdom nationals, a Member State in which they pursued an economic activity as frontier workers before the end of the transition period and in which they continue to do so thereafter;

(e) "rights of custody" means rights of custody within the meaning of point (9) of Article 2 of Council Regulation (EC) No.2201/2003, including rights of custody acquired by judgment, by operation of law or by an agreement having legal effect.

Article 10

Personal scope

1. Without prejudice to Title III, this Part shall apply to the following persons:

(a) Union citizens who exercised their right to reside in the United Kingdom in accordance with Union law before the end of the transition period and continue to reside there thereafter;

(b) United Kingdom nationals who exercised their right to reside in a Member State in accordance with Union law before the end of the transition period and continue to reside there thereafter;

(c) Union citizens who exercised their right as frontier workers in the United Kingdom in accordance with Union law before the end of the transition period and continue to do so thereafter;

(d) United Kingdom nationals who exercised their right as frontier workers in one or more Member States in accordance with Union law before the end of the transition period and continue to do so thereafter;

(e) family members of the persons referred to in points (a) to (d), provided that they fulfil one of the following conditions:

   (i) they resided in the host State in accordance with Union law before the end of the transition period and continue to reside there thereafter;

  (ii) they were directly related to a person referred to in points (a) to (d) and resided outside the host State before the end of the transition period, provided that they fulfil the conditions set out in point (2) of Article 2 of Directive 2004/38/EC at the time they seek residence under this Part in order to join the person referred to in points (a) to (d) of this paragraph;

 (iii) they were born to, or legally adopted by, persons referred to in points (a) to (d) after the end of the transition period, whether inside or outside the host State, and fulfil the conditions set out in point (2)(c) of Article 2 of Directive 2004/38/EC at the time they seek residence under this Part in order to join the person referred to in points (a) to (d) of this paragraph and fulfil one of the following conditions:

   –   both parents are persons referred to in points (a) to (d);

   –   one parent is a person referred to in points (a) to (d) and the other is a national of the host State; or

   –   one parent is a person referred to in points (a) to (d) and has sole or joint rights of custody of the child, in accordance with the applicable rules of family law of a Member State or of the United Kingdom, including applicable rules of private international law under which rights of custody established under the law of a third State are recognised in the Member State or in the United Kingdom, in particular as regards the best interests of the child, and without prejudice to the normal operation of such applicable rules of private international law;

(f) family members who resided in the host State in accordance with Articles 12 and 13, Article 16(2) and Articles 17 and 18 of Directive 2004/38/EC before the end of the transition period and continue to reside there thereafter.

2. Persons falling under points (a) and (b) of Article 3(2) of Directive 2004/38/EC whose residence was facilitated by the host State in accordance with its national legislation before the end of the transition period in accordance with Article 3(2) of that Directive shall retain their right of residence in the host State in accordance with this Part, provided that they continue to reside in the host State thereafter. The notion of rights

of custody is to be interpreted in accordance with point (9) of Article 2 of Regulation (EC) No.2201/2003. Therefore, it covers rights of custody acquired by judgment, by operation of law or by an agreement having legal effect.

3. Paragraph 2 shall also apply to persons falling under points (a) and (b) of Article 3(2) of Directive 2004/38/EC who have applied for facilitation of entry and residence before the end of the transition period, and whose residence is being facilitated by the host State in accordance with its national legislation thereafter.

4. Without prejudice to any right to residence which the persons concerned may have in their own right, the host State shall, in accordance with its national legislation and in accordance with point (b) of Article 3(2) of Directive 2004/38/EC, facilitate entry and residence for the partner with whom the person referred to in points (a) to (d) of paragraph 1 of this Article has a durable relationship, duly attested, where that partner resided outside the host State before the end of the transition period, provided that the relationship was durable before the end of the transition period and continues at the time the partner seeks residence under this Part.

5. In the cases referred to in paragraphs 3 and 4, the host State shall undertake an extensive examination of the personal circumstances of the persons concerned and shall justify any denial of entry or residence to such persons.

Article 11

Continuity of residence

Continuity of residence for the purposes of Articles 9 and 10 shall not be affected by absences as referred to in Article 15(2).

The right of permanent residence acquired under Directive 2004/38/EC before the end of the transition period shall not be treated as lost through absence from the host State for a period specified in Article 15(3).

Article 12

Non-discrimination

Within the scope of this Part, and without prejudice to any special provisions contained therein, any discrimination on grounds of nationality within the meaning of the first subparagraph of Article 18 TFEU shall be prohibited in the host State and the State of work in respect of the persons referred to in Article 10 of this Agreement.

TITLE II
RIGHTS AND OBLIGATIONS

CHAPTER 1
RIGHTS RELATED TO RESIDENCE, RESIDENCE DOCUMENTS

Article 13

Residence rights

1. Union citizens and United Kingdom nationals shall have the right   4.069
to reside in the host State under the limitations and conditions as set out
in Articles 21, 45 or 49 TFEU and in Article 6(1), points (a), (b) or (c)
of Article 7(1), Article 7(3), Article 14, Article 16(1) or Article 17(1) of
Directive 2004/38/EC.

2. Family members who are either Union citizens or United Kingdom
nationals shall have the right to reside in the host State as set out in
Article 21 TFEU and in Article 6(1), point (d) of Article 7(1), Article
12(1) or (3), Article 13(1), Article 14, Article 16(1) or Article 17(3) and
(4) of Directive 2004/38/EC, subject to the limitations and conditions
set out in those provisions.

3. Family members who are neither Union citizens nor United Kingdom nationals shall have the right to reside in the host State under
Article 21 TFEU and as set out in Article 6(2), Article 7(2), Article
12(2) or (3), Article 13(2), Article 14, Article 16(2), Article 17(3) or (4)
or Article 18 of Directive 2004/38/EC, subject to the limitations and
conditions set out in those provisions.

4. The host State may not impose any limitations or conditions for
obtaining, retaining or losing residence rights on the persons referred to
in paragraphs 1, 2 and 3, other than those provided for in this Title.
There shall be no discretion in applying the limitations and conditions
provided for in this Title, other than in favour of the person concerned.

Article 14

Right of exit and of entry

1. Union citizens and United Kingdom nationals, their respective
family members, and other persons, who reside in the territory of the
host State in accordance with the conditions set out in this Title shall
have the right to leave the host State and the right to enter it, as set out
in Article 4(1) and the first subparagraph of Article 5(1) of Directive
2004/38/EC, with a valid passport or national identity card in the case of
Union citizens and United Kingdom nationals, and with a valid passport
in the case of their respective family members and other persons who are
not Union citizens or United Kingdom nationals.

Five years after the end of the transition period, the host State may decide no longer to accept national identity cards for the purposes of entry to or exit from its territory if such cards do not include a chip that complies with the applicable International Civil Aviation Organisation standards related to biometric identification.

2. No exit visa, entry visa or equivalent formality shall be required of holders of a valid document issued in accordance with Article 18 or 26.

3. Where the host State requires family members who join the Union citizen or United Kingdom national after the end of the transition period to have an entry visa, the host State shall grant such persons every facility to obtain the necessary visas. Such visas shall be issued free of charge as soon as possible, and on the basis of an accelerated procedure.

Article 15

Right of permanent residence

1. Union citizens and United Kingdom nationals, and their respective family members, who have resided legally in the host State in accordance with Union law for a continuous period of 5 years or for the period specified in Article 17 of Directive 2004/38/EC, shall have the right to reside permanently in the host State under the conditions set out in Articles 16, 17 and 18 of Directive 2004/38/EC. Periods of legal residence or work in accordance with Union law before and after the end of the transition period shall be included in the calculation of the qualifying period necessary for acquisition of the right of permanent residence.

2. Continuity of residence for the purposes of acquisition of the right of permanent residence shall be determined in accordance with Article 16(3) and Article 21 of Directive 2004/38/EC.

3. Once acquired, the right of permanent residence shall be lost only through absence from the host State for a period exceeding 5 consecutive years.

Article 16

Accumulation of periods

Union citizens and United Kingdom nationals, and their respective family members, who before the end of the transition period resided legally in the host State in accordance with the conditions of Article 7 of Directive 2004/38/EC for a period of less than 5 years, shall have the right to acquire the right to reside permanently under the conditions set out in Article 15 of this Agreement once they have completed the necessary periods of residence. Periods of legal residence or work in accordance with Union law before and after the end of the transition period shall be included in the calculation of the qualifying period necessary for acquisition of the right of permanent residence.

Article 17

Status and changes

1. The right of Union citizens and United Kingdom nationals, and their respective family members, to rely directly on this Part shall not be affected when they change status, for example between student, worker, self-employed person and economically inactive person. Persons who, at the end of the transition period, enjoy a right of residence in their capacity as family members of Union citizens or United Kingdom nationals, cannot become persons referred to in points (a) to (d) of Article 10(1).

2. The rights provided for in this Title for the family members who are dependants of Union citizens or United Kingdom nationals before the end of the transition period, shall be maintained even after they cease to be dependants.

Article 18

Issuance of residence documents

1. The host State may require Union citizens or United Kingdom 4.070 nationals, their respective family members and other persons, who reside in its territory in accordance with the conditions set out in this Title, to apply for a new residence status which confers the rights under this Title and a document evidencing such status which may be in a digital form.

Applying for such a residence status shall be subject to the following conditions:

(a) the purpose of the application procedure shall be to verify whether the applicant is entitled to the residence rights set out in this Title. Where that is the case, the applicant shall have a right to be granted the residence status and the document evidencing that status;

(b) the deadline for submitting the application shall not be less than 6 months from the end of the transition period, for persons residing in the host State before the end of the transition period. For persons who have the right to commence residence after the end of the transition period in the host State in accordance with this Title, the deadline for submitting the application shall be 3 months after their arrival or the expiry of the deadline referred to in the first subparagraph, whichever is later.

A certificate of application for the residence status shall be issued immediately;

(c) the deadline for submitting the application referred to in point (b) shall be extended automatically by 1 year where the Union has notified the United Kingdom, or the United Kingdom has notified the Union, that technical problems prevent the host State either from registering the application or from issuing the certificate of application referred to in point (b). The host State shall publish that notification and shall provide appropriate public information for the persons concerned in good time;

(d) where the deadline for submitting the application referred to in point (b) is not respected by the persons concerned, the competent authorities shall assess all the circumstances and reasons for not respecting the deadline and shall allow those persons to submit an application within a reasonable further period of time if there are reasonable grounds for the failure to respect the deadline;

(e) the host State shall ensure that any administrative procedures for applications are smooth, transparent and simple, and that any unnecessary administrative burdens are avoided;

(f) application forms shall be short, simple, user friendly and adapted to the context of this Agreement; applications made by families at the same time shall be considered together;

(g) the document evidencing the status shall be issued free of charge or for a charge not exceeding that imposed on citizens or nationals of the host State for the issuing of similar documents;

(h) persons who, before the end of the transition period, hold a valid permanent residence document issued under Article 19 or 20 of Directive 2004/38/EC or hold a valid domestic immigration document conferring a permanent right to reside in the host State, shall have the right to exchange that document within the period referred to in point (b) of this paragraph for a new residence document upon application after a verification of their identity, a criminality and security check in accordance with point (p) of this paragraph and confirmation of their ongoing residence; such new residence documents shall be issued free of charge;

(i) the identity of the applicants shall be verified through the presentation of a valid passport or national identity card for Union citizens and United Kingdom nationals, and through the presentation of a valid passport for their respective family members and other persons who are not Union citizens or United Kingdom nationals; the acceptance of such identity documents shall not be made conditional upon any criteria other than that of the validity of the document. Where the identity document is retained by the competent authorities of the host State while the application is pending, the host State shall return that document upon application without delay, before the decision on the application has been taken;

(j) supporting documents other than identity documents, such as civil status documents, may be submitted in copy. Originals of supporting documents may be required only in specific cases where there is a reasonable doubt as to the authenticity of the supporting documents submitted;

(k) the host State may only require Union citizens and United Kingdom nationals to present, in addition to the identity documents referred to in point (i) of this paragraph, the following supporting documents as referred to in Article 8(3) of Directive 2004/38/EC:

(i) where they reside in the host State in accordance with point (a) of Article 7(1) of Directive 2004/38/EC as workers or self-employed, a confirmation of engagement from the employer or a certificate of employment, or proof that they are self-employed;

(ii) where they reside in the host State in accordance with point (b) of Article 7(1) of Directive 2004/38/EC as economically inactive persons, evidence that they have sufficient resources for themselves and their family members not to become a burden on the social assistance system of the host State during their period of residence and that they have comprehensive sickness insurance cover in the host State; or

(iii) where they reside in the host State in accordance with point (c) of Article 7(1) of Directive 2004/38/EC as students, proof of enrolment at an establishment accredited or financed by the host State on the basis of its legislation or administrative practice, proof of comprehensive sickness insurance cover, and a declaration or equivalent means of proof, that they have sufficient resources for themselves and their family members not to become a burden on the social assistance system of the host State during their period of residence. The host State may not require such declarations to refer to any specific amount of resources.

With regard to the condition of sufficient resources, Article 8(4) of Directive 2004/38/EC shall apply;

(l) the host State may only require family members who fall under point (e)(i) of Article 10(1) or Article 10(2) or (3) of this Agreement and who reside in the host State in accordance with point (d) of Article 7(1) or Article 7(2) of Directive 2004/38/EC to present, in addition to the identity documents referred to in point (i) of this paragraph, the following supporting documents as referred to in Article 8(5) or 10(2) of Directive 2004/38/EC:

(i) a document attesting to the existence of a family relationship or registered partnership;

(ii) the registration certificate or, in the absence of a registration system, any other proof that the Union citizen or the United Kingdom national with whom they reside actually resides in the host State;

(iii) for direct descendants who are under the age of 21 or who are dependants and dependent direct relatives in the ascending line, and for those of the spouse or registered partner, documentary evidence that the conditions set out in point (c) or (d) of Article 2(2) of Directive 2004/38/EC are fulfilled;

> (iv) for the persons referred to in Article 10(2) or (3) of this Agreement, a document issued by the relevant authority in the host State in accordance with Article 3(2) of Directive 2004/38/EC.

With regard to the condition of sufficient resources as concerns family members who are themselves Union citizens or United Kingdom nationals, Article 8(4) of Directive 2004/38/EC shall apply;

(m) the host State may only require family members who fall under point (e)(ii) of Article 10(1) or Article 10(4) of this Agreement to present, in addition to the identity documents referred to in point (i) of this paragraph, the following supporting documents as referred to in Articles 8(5) and 10(2) of Directive 2004/38/EC:

> (i) a document attesting to the existence of a family relationship or of a registered partnership;
> (ii) the registration certificate or, in the absence of a registration system, any other proof of residence in the host State of the Union citizen or of the United Kingdom nationals whom they are joining in the host State;
> (iii) for spouses or registered partners, a document attesting to the existence of a family relationship or a registered partnership before the end of the transition period;
> (iv) for direct descendants who are under the age of 21 or who are dependants and dependent direct relatives in the ascending line and those of the spouse or registered partner, documentary evidence that they were related to Union citizens or United Kingdom nationals before the end of the transition period and fulfil the conditions set out in point (c) or (d) of Article 2(2) of Directive 2004/38/EC relating to age or dependence;
> (v) for the persons referred to in Article 10(4) of this Agreement, proof that a durable relationship with Union citizens or United Kingdom nationals existed before the end of the transition period and continues to exist thereafter;

(n) for cases other than those set out in points (k), (l) and (m), the host State shall not require applicants to present supporting documents that go beyond what is strictly necessary and proportionate to provide evidence that the conditions relating to the right of residence under this Title have been fulfilled;

(o) the competent authorities of the host State shall help the applicants to prove their eligibility and to avoid any errors or omissions in their applications; they shall give the applicants the opportunity to furnish supplementary evidence and to correct any deficiencies, errors or omissions;

(p) criminality and security checks may be carried out systematically on applicants, with the exclusive aim of verifying whether the restrictions set out in Article 20 of this Agreement may be applicable. For that purpose, applicants may be required to declare past criminal convictions which appear in their criminal record in accordance with the law of the State of conviction at the time of the application. The host State may, if it considers this essential, apply the procedure set out in Article 27(3) of Directive 2004/38/EC with respect to enquiries to other States regarding previous criminal records;

(q) the new residence document shall include a statement that it has been issued in accordance with this Agreement;

(r) the applicant shall have access to judicial and, where appropriate, administrative redress procedures in the host State against any decision refusing to grant the residence status. The redress procedures shall allow for an examination of the legality of the decision, as well as of the facts and circumstances on which the proposed decision is based. Such redress procedures shall ensure that the decision is not disproportionate.

2. During the period referred to in point (b) of paragraph 1 of this Article and its possible one-yearextension under point (c) of that paragraph, all rights provided for in this Part shall be deemed to apply to Union citizens or United Kingdom nationals, their respective family members, and other persons residing in the host State, in accordance with the conditions and subject to the restrictions set out in Article 20.

3. Pending a final decision by the competent authorities on any application referred to in paragraph 1, and pending a final judgment handed down in case of judicial redress sought against any rejection of such application by the competent administrative authorities, all rights provided for in this Part shall be deemed to apply to the applicant, including Article 21 on safeguards and right of appeal, subject to the conditions set out in Article 20(4).

4. Where a host State has chosen not to require Union citizens or United Kingdom nationals, their family members, and other persons, residing in its territory in accordance with the conditions set out in this Title, to apply for the new residence status referred to in paragraph 1 as a condition for legal residence, those eligible for residence rights under this Title shall have the right to receive, in accordance with the conditions set out in Directive 2004/38/EC, a residence document, which may be in a digital form, that includes a statement that it has been issued in accordance with this Agreement.

Article 19

Issuance of residence documents during the transition period

1. During the transition period, a host State may allow applications for a residence status or residence document as referred to in Article 18(1) and (4) to be made voluntarily from the date of entry into force of this Agreement.

4.071

2. Decisions to accept or refuse such applications shall be taken in accordance with Article 18(1) and (4). Decisions under Article 18(1) shall have no effect until after the end of the transition period.

3. If an application under Article 18(1) is accepted before the end of the transition period, the host State may not withdraw the decision granting the residence status before the end of the transition period on any grounds other than those set out in Chapter VI and Article 35 of Directive 2004/38/EC.

4. If an application is refused before the end of the transition period, the applicant may apply again at any time before the expiry of the period set out in point (b) of Article 18(1).

5. Without prejudice to paragraph 4, the redress procedures under point (r) of Article 18(1) shall be available from the date of any decision to refuse an application referred to in paragraph 2 of this Article.

Article 20

Restrictions of the rights of residence and entry

1. The conduct of Union citizens or United Kingdom nationals, their family members, and other persons, who exercise rights under this Title, where that conduct occurred before the end of the transition period, shall be considered in accordance with Chapter VI of Directive 2004/38/EC.

2. The conduct of Union citizens or United Kingdom nationals, their family members, and other persons, who exercise rights under this Title, where that conduct occurred after the end of the transition period, may constitute grounds for restricting the right of residence by the host State or the right of entry in the State of work in accordance with national legislation.

3. The host State or the State of work may adopt the necessary measures to refuse, terminate or withdraw any right conferred by this Title in the case of the abuse of those rights or fraud, as set out in Article 35 of Directive 2004/38/EC. Such measures shall be subject to the procedural safeguards provided for in Article 21 of this Agreement.

4. The host State or the State of work may remove applicants who submitted fraudulent or abusive applications from its territory under the conditions set out in Directive 2004/38/EC, in particular Articles 31 and 35 thereof, even before a final judgment has been handed down in the case of judicial redress sought against any rejection of such an application.

Article 21

Safeguards and right of appeal

The safeguards set out in Article 15 and Chapter VI of Directive 2004/38/EC shall apply in respect of any decision by the host State that restricts residence rights of the persons referred to in Article 10 of this Agreement.

Article 22

Related rights

In accordance with Article 23 of Directive 2004/38/EC, irrespective of nationality, the family members of a Union citizen or United Kingdom national who have the right of residence or the right of permanent residence in the host State or the State of work shall be entitled to take up employment or self-employment there.

Article 23

Equal treatment

1. In accordance with Article 24 of Directive 2004/38/EC, subject to the specific provisions provided for in this Title and Titles I and IV of this Part, all Union citizens or United Kingdom nationals residing on the basis of this Agreement in the territory of the host State shall enjoy equal treatment with the nationals of that State within the scope of this Part. The benefit of this right shall be extended to those family members of Union citizens or United Kingdom nationals who have the right of residence or permanent residence.

2. By way of derogation from paragraph 1, the host State shall not be obliged to confer entitlement to social assistance during periods of residence on the basis of Article 6 or point (b) of Article 14(4) of Directive 2004/38/EC, nor shall it be obliged, prior to a person's acquisition of the right of permanent residence in accordance with Article 15 of this Agreement, to grant maintenance aid for studies, including vocational training, consisting in student grants or student loans to persons other than workers, self-employed persons, persons who retain such status or to members of their families.

CHAPTER 2
RIGHTS OF WORKERS AND SELF-EMPLOYED PERSONS

Article 24

Rights of workers

1. Subject to the limitations set out in Article 45(3) and (4) TFEU, 4.072 workers in the host State and frontier workers in the State or States of work shall enjoy the rights guaranteed by Article 45 TFEU and the rights granted by Regulation (EU) No 492/2011 of the European Parliament and of the Council. These rights include:
   (a) the right not to be discriminated against on grounds of nationality as regards employment, remuneration and other conditions of work and employment;

(b) the right to take up and pursue an activity in accordance with the rules applicable to the nationals of the host State or the State of work;

(c) the right to assistance afforded by the employment offices of the host State or the State of work as offered to own nationals;

(d) the right to equal treatment in respect of conditions of employment and work, in particular as regards remuneration, dismissal and in case of unemployment, reinstatement or re-employment;

(e) the right to social and tax advantages;

(f) collective rights;

(g) the rights and benefits accorded to national workers in matters of housing;

(h) the right for their children to be admitted to the general educational, apprenticeship and vocational training courses under the same conditions as the nationals of the host State or the State of work, if such children are residing in the territory where the worker works.

2. Where a direct descendant of a worker who has ceased to reside in the host State is in education in that State, the primary carer for that descendant shall have the right to reside in that State until the descendant reaches the age of majority, and after the age of majority if that descendant continues to need the presence and care of the primary carer in order to pursue and complete his or her education.

3. Employed frontier workers shall enjoy the right to enter and exit the State of work in accordance with Article 14 of this Agreement and shall retain the rights they enjoyed as workers there, provided they are in one of the circumstances set out in points (a), (b), (c) and (d) of Article 7(3) of Directive 2004/38/EC, even where they do not move their residence to the State of work.

Article 25

Rights of self-employed persons

1. Subject to the limitations set out in Articles 51 and 52 TFEU, self-employed persons in the host State and self-employed frontier workers in the State or States of work shall enjoy the rights guaranteed by Articles 49 and 55 TFEU. These rights include:

(a) the right to take up and pursue activities as self-employed persons and to set up and manage undertakings under the conditions laid down by the host State for its own nationals, as set out in Article 49 TFEU;

(b)he rights as set out in points (c) to (h) of Article 24(1) of this Agreement.

2. Article 24(2) shall apply to direct descendants of self-employed workers.

3. Article 24(3) shall apply to self-employed frontier workers.

Article 26

Issuance of a document identifying frontier workers' rights

The State of work may require Union citizens and United Kingdom nationals who have rights as frontier workers under this Title to apply for a document certifying that they have such rights under this Title. Such Union citizens and United Kingdom nationals shall have the right to be issued with such a document.

CHAPTER 3
PROFESSIONAL QUALIFICATIONS

Arts 27–29 *omitted*   4.073

TITLE III
COORDINATION OF SOCIAL SECURITY SYSTEMS

Article 30

Persons covered

1. This Title shall apply to the following persons:
   (a) Union citizens who are subject to the legislation of the United Kingdom at the end of the transition period, as well as their family members and survivors;
   (b) United Kingdom nationals who are subject to the legislation of a Member State at the end of the transition period, as well as their family members and survivors;
   (c) Union citizens who reside in the United Kingdom and are subject to the legislation of a Member State at the end of the transition period, as well as their family members and survivors;
   (d) United Kingdom nationals who reside in a Member State, and are subject to the legislation of the United Kingdom at the end of the transition period, as well as their family members and survivors;
   (e) persons who do not fall within points (a) to (d) but are:
       (i) Union citizens who pursue an activity as an employed or self-employed person in the United Kingdom at the end of the transition period, and who, based on Title II of Regulation (EC) No 883/2004 of the European Parliament and of the Council, are subject to the legislation of a Member State, as well as their family members and survivors; or
       (ii) United Kingdom nationals who pursue an activity as an employed or self-employed person in one or more Member States at the end of the transition period, and who, based on

Title II of Regulation (EC) No 883/2004, are subject to the legislation of the United Kingdom, as well as their family members and survivors;

(f) stateless persons and refugees, residing in a Member State or in the United Kingdom, who are in one of the situations described in points (a) to (e), as well as their family members and survivors;

(g) nationals of third countries, as well as members of their families and survivors, who are in one of the situations described in points (a) to (e), provided that they fulfil the conditions of Council Regulation (EC) No 859/2003.

2. The persons referred to in paragraph 1 shall be covered for as long as they continue without interruption to be in one of the situations set out in that paragraph involving both a Member State and the United Kingdom at the same time.

3. This Title shall also apply to persons who do not, or who no longer, fall within points (a) to (e) of paragraph 1 of this Article but who fall within Article 10 of this Agreement, as well as their family members and survivors.

4. The persons referred to in paragraph 3 shall be covered for as long as they continue to have a right to reside in the host State under Article 13 of this Agreement, or a right to work in their State of work under Article 24 or 25 of this Agreement.

5. Where this Article refers to family members and survivors, those persons shall be covered by this Title only to the extent that they derive rights and obligations in that capacity under Regulation (EC) No 883/2004.

Article 31

Social security coordination rules

1. The rules and objectives set out in Article 48 TFEU, Regulation (EC) No 883/2004 and Regulation (EC) No 987/2009 of the European Parliament and of the Council shall apply to the persons covered by this Title.

The Union and the United Kingdom shall take due account of the Decisions and Recommendations of the Administrative Commission for the Coordination of Social Security Systems attached to the European Commission, set up under Regulation (EC) No 883/2004 ("Administrative Commission") listed in Part I of Annex I to this Agreement.

2. By way of derogation from Article 9 of this Agreement, for the purposes of this Title, the definitions in Article 1 of Regulation (EC) No 883/2004 shall apply.

3. With regard to nationals of third countries who fulfil the conditions of Regulation (EC) No 859/2003, as well as their family members or survivors within the scope of this Title, the references to Regulation (EC) No 883/2004 and Regulation (EC) No 987/2009 in this Title shall be understood as references to Council Regulation (EEC) No 1408/71

and Council Regulation (EEC) No 574/72 respectively. References to specific provisions of Regulation (EC) No 883/2004 and Regulation (EC) No 987/2009 shall be understood as references to the corresponding provisions of Regulation (EEC) No 1408/71 and Regulation (EEC) No 574/72.

Article 32

Special situations covered

1. The following rules shall apply in the following situations to the extent set out in this Article, insofar as they relate to persons not or no longer covered by Article 30:

(a) the following persons shall be covered by this Title for the purposes of reliance on and aggregation of periods of insurance, employment, self-employment or residence, including rights and obligations deriving from such periods in accordance with Regulation (EC) No 883/2004:

   (i) Union citizens, as well as stateless persons and refugees residing in a Member State and nationals of third countries who fulfil the conditions of Regulation (EC) No 859/2003, who have been subject to the legislation of the United Kingdom before the end of the transition period, as well as their family members and survivors;

   (ii) United Kingdom nationals, as well as stateless persons and refugees residing in the United Kingdom and nationals of third countries who fulfil the conditions of Regulation (EC) No 859/2003, who have been subject to the legislation of a Member State before the end of the transition period, as well as their family members and survivors; for the purposes of the aggregation of periods, periods completed both before and after the end of the transition period shall be taken into account in accordance with Regulation (EC) No 883/2004;

(b) the rules set out in Articles 20 and 27 of Regulation (EC) No 883/2004 shall continue to apply to persons who, before the end of the transition period, had requested authorisation to receive a course of planned health care treatment pursuant to Regulation (EC) No 883/2004, until the end of the treatment. The corresponding reimbursement procedures shall also apply even after the treatment ends. Such persons and the accompanying persons shall enjoy the right to enter and exit the State of treatment in accordance with Article 14, *mutatis mutandis*;

(c) the rules set out in Articles 19 and 27 of Regulation (EC) No 883/2004 shall continue to apply to persons who are covered by Regulation (EC) No 883/2004 and who are on a stay at the end of the transition period in a Member State or the United Kingdom, until the end of their stay. The corresponding reimbursement procedures shall also apply even after the stay or treatment ends;

(d) the rules set out in Articles 67, 68 and 69 of Regulation (EC) No 883/2004 shall continue to apply, for as long as the conditions are fulfilled, to awards of family benefits to which there is entitlement at the end of the transition period for the following persons:

   (i) Union citizens, stateless persons and refugees residing in a Member State as well as nationals of third countries who fulfil the conditions of Regulation (EC) No 859/2003 and reside in a Member State, who are subject to the legislation of a Member State and have family members residing in the United Kingdom at the end of the transition period;

   (ii) United Kingdom nationals, as well as stateless persons and refugees residing in the United Kingdom and nationals of third countries who fulfil the conditions of Regulation (EC) No 859/2003 and reside in the United Kingdom, who are subject to the legislation of the United Kingdom and have family members residing in a Member State at the end of the transition period;

(e) in the situations set out in point (d)(i) and (ii) of this paragraph, for any persons who have rights as family members at the end of the transition period under Regulation (EC) No 883/2004, such as derived rights for sickness benefits in kind, that Regulation and the corresponding provisions of Regulation (EC) No 987/2009 shall continue to apply for as long as the conditions provided therein are fulfilled.

2. The provisions of Chapter 1 of Title III of Regulation (EC) No 883/2004 as regards sickness benefits shall apply to persons receiving benefits under point (a) of paragraph 1 of this Article. This paragraph shall apply *mutatis mutandis* as regards family benefits based on Articles 67, 68 and 69 of Regulation (EC) No 883/2004.

Article 33

Nationals of Iceland, Liechtenstein, Norway and Switzerland

1. The provisions of this Title applicable to Union citizens shall apply to nationals of Iceland, the Principality of Liechtenstein, the Kingdom of Norway, and the Swiss Confederation provided that:

(a) Iceland, the Principality of Liechtenstein, the Kingdom of Norway, and the Swiss Confederation, as applicable, have concluded and apply corresponding agreements with the United Kingdom which apply to Union citizens; and

(b) Iceland, the Principality of Liechtenstein, the Kingdom of Norway, and the Swiss Confederation, as applicable, have concluded and apply corresponding agreements with the Union which apply to United Kingdom nationals.

2. Upon notification from the United Kingdom and from the Union of the date of entry into force of the agreements referred to in paragraph 1 of this Article, the Joint Committee established by Article 164 ("Joint

Committee") shall set the date from which the provisions of this Title shall apply to the nationals of Iceland, the Principality of Liechtenstein, the Kingdom of Norway, and the Swiss Confederation, as applicable.

Article 34

Administrative cooperation

1. By way of derogation from Articles 7 and 128(1), as of the date of   4.074
entry into force of this Agreement, the United Kingdom shall have the
status of observer in the Administrative Commission. It may, where the
items on the agenda relating to this Title concern the United Kingdom,
send a representative, to be present in an advisory capacity, to the
meetings of the Administrative Commission and to the meetings of the
bodies referred to in Articles 73 and 74 of Regulation (EC) No 883/2004
where such items are discussed.

2. By way of derogation from Article 8, the United Kingdom shall take
part in the Electronic Exchange of Social Security Information (EESSI)
and bear the related costs.

Article 35

Reimbursement, recovery and offsetting

The provisions of Regulations (EC) No 883/2004 and (EC) No
987/2009 on reimbursement, recovery and offsetting shall continue to
apply in relation to events, insofar as they relate to persons not covered
by Article 30, that:
  (a) occurred before the end of the transition period; or
  (b) occur after the end of the transition period and relate to persons
       who were covered by Articles 30 or 32 when the event
       occurred.

Article 36

Development of law and adaptations of Union acts

1. Where Regulations (EC) No 883/2004 and (EC) No 987/2009 are
amended or replaced after the end of the transition period, references to
those Regulations in this Agreement shall be understood as referring to
those Regulations as amended or replaced, in accordance with the acts
listed in Part II of Annex I to this Agreement.

The Joint Committee shall revise Part II of Annex I to this Agreement
and align it to any act amending or replacing Regulations (EC) No
883/2004 and (EC) No 987/2009 as soon as such act is adopted by the
Union. To that end, the Union shall, as soon as possible after adoption,

421

inform the United Kingdom within the Joint Committee of any act amending or replacing those Regulations.

2. By way of derogation from the second subparagraph of paragraph 1, the Joint Committee shall assess the effects of an act amending or replacing Regulations (EC) No 883/2004 and (EC) No 987/2009 where that act:

(a) amends or replaces the matters covered by Article 3 of Regulation (EC) No 883/2004; or

(b) makes a cash benefit exportable where that cash benefit was non-exportable under Regulation (EC) No 883/2004 at the end of the transition period, or makes a cash benefit non-exportable, where that cash benefit was exportable at the end of the transition period; or

(c) makes a cash benefit exportable for an unlimited period of time, where that cash benefit was exportable only for a limited period of time under Regulation (EC) No 883/2004 at the end of the transition period, or makes a cash benefit exportable only for a limited period of time, where that cash benefit was exportable for an unlimited period of time under that Regulation at the end of the transition period. In making its assessment, the Joint Committee shall consider in good faith the scale of the changes referred to in the first subparagraph of this paragraph, as well as the importance of the continued good functioning of Regulations (EC) No 883/2004 and (EC) No 987/2009 between the Union and the United Kingdom and the importance of there being a competent State in relation to individuals within the scope of Regulation (EC) No 883/2004.

If the Joint Committee so decides within 6 months from receiving the information given by the Union pursuant to paragraph 1, Part II of Annex I to this Agreement shall not be aligned to the act referred to in the first subparagraph of this paragraph.

For the purposes of this paragraph:

(a) "exportable" means payable under Regulation (EC) No 883/2004 to or in relation to a person residing in a Member State or in the United Kingdom if the institution responsible for providing the benefit is not situated there; "non-exportable" shall be interpreted accordingly; and

(b) "exportable for an unlimited period of time" means exportable for as long as the conditions giving rise to the entitlements are met.

3. Regulations (EC) No 883/2004 and (EC) No 987/2009 shall, for the purposes of this Agreement, be understood as comprising the adaptations listed in Part III of Annex I to this Agreement. As soon as possible after the adoption of any changes in domestic provisions of relevance to Part III of Annex I to this Agreement, the United Kingdom shall inform the Union thereof within the Joint Committee.

4. The Decisions and Recommendations of the Administrative Commission shall, for the purposes of this Agreement, be understood as comprising the decisions and recommendations listed in Part I of Annex I. The Joint Committee shall amend Part I of Annex I to reflect any new

Decision or Recommendation adopted by the Administrative Commission. To that end, as soon as possible after adoption of decisions and recommendations of the Administrative Commission, the Union shall inform the United Kingdom thereof within the Joint Committee. Such amendments shall be made by the Joint Committee on a proposal of the Union or the United Kingdom.

TITLE IV
OTHER PROVISIONS

Article 37

Publicity

The Member States and the United Kingdom shall disseminate informa-   4.075
tion concerning the rights and obligations of persons covered by this Part, in particular by means of awareness—raising campaigns conducted, as appropriate, through national and local media and other means of communication.

Article 38

More favourable provisions

1. This Part shall not affect any laws, regulations or administrative provisions applicable in a host State or a State of work which would be more favourable to the persons concerned. This paragraph shall not apply to Title III.
2. Article 12 and Article 23(1) shall be without prejudice to the Common Travel Area arrangements between the United Kingdom and Ireland as regards more favourable treatment which may result from these arrangements for the persons concerned.

Article 39

Life-long protection

The persons covered by this Part shall enjoy the rights provided for in the relevant Titles of this Part for their lifetime, unless they cease to meet the conditions set out in those Titles.

PART SIX
INSTITUTIONAL AND FINAL PROVISIONS

Article 158

References to the Court of Justice of the European Union concerning Part Two

4.076   1. Where, in a case which commenced at first instance within 8 years from the end of the transition period before a court or tribunal in the United Kingdom, a question is raised concerning the interpretation of Part Two of this Agreement, and where that court or tribunal considers that a decision on that question is necessary to enable it to give judgment in that case, that court or tribunal may request the Court of Justice of the European Union to give a preliminary ruling on that question. However, where the subject matter of the case before the court or tribunal in the United Kingdom is a decision on an application made pursuant to Article 18(1) or (4) or pursuant to Article 19, a request for a preliminary ruling may be made only where the case commenced at first instance within a period of 8 years from the date from which Article 19 applies.

2. The Court of Justice of the European Union shall have jurisdiction to give preliminary rulings on requests pursuant to paragraph 1. The legal effects in the United Kingdom of such preliminary rulings shall be the same as the legal effects of preliminary rulings given pursuant to Article 267 TFEU in the Union and its Member States.

3. In the event that the Joint Committee adopts a decision under Article 132(1), the period of eight years referred to in the second subparagraph of paragraph 1 shall be automatically extended by the corresponding number of months by which the transition period is extended.

Article 159

Monitoring of the implementation and application of Part Two

1. In the United Kingdom, the implementation and application of Part Two shall be monitored by an independent authority (the "Authority") which shall have powers equivalent to those of the European Commission acting under the Treaties to conduct inquiries on its own initiative concerning alleged breaches of Part Two by the administrative authorities of the United Kingdom and to receive complaints from Union citizens and their family members for the purposes of conducting such inquiries. The Authority shall also have the right, following such complaints, to bring a legal action before a competent court or tribunal in the United Kingdom in an appropriate judicial procedure with a view to seeking an adequate remedy.

2. The European Commission and the Authority shall each annually inform the specialised Committee on citizens' rights referred to in point (a) of Article 165(1) on the implementation and application of Part Two in the Union and in the United Kingdom, respectively. The information provided shall, in particular, cover measures taken to implement or comply with Part Two and the number and nature of complaints received.

3. The Joint Committee shall assess, no earlier than 8 years after the end of the transition period, the functioning of the Authority. Following such assessment, it may decide, in good faith, pursuant to point (f) of Article 164(4) and Article 166, that the United Kingdom may abolish the Authority.

ANNEX I
SOCIAL SECURITY COORDINATION

PART I
DECISIONS AND RECOMMENDATIONS OF THE ADMINISTRATIVE
COMMISSION

Applicable legislation (A series):   4.077

— Decision A1 of 12 June 2009 concerning the establishment of a dialogue and conciliation procedure concerning the validity of documents, the determination of the applicable legislation and the provisions of benefits under Regulation (EC) No 883/2004 of the European Parliament and of the Council;

— Decision A2 of 12 June 2009 concerning the interpretation of Article 12 of Regulation (EC) No 883/2004 of the European Parliament and of the Council on the legislation applicable to posted workers and self-employed workers temporarily working outside the competent State;

— Decision A3 of 17 December 2009 concerning the aggregation of uninterrupted posting periods completed under the Council Regulation (EEC) No 1408/71 and Regulation (EC) No 883/2004 of the European Parliament and of the Council.

Electronic Data Exchange (E series):

— Decision E2 of 3 March 2010 concerning the establishment of a change management procedure applying to details of the bodies defined in Article 1 of Regulation (EC) No 883/2004 of the European Parliament and of the Council which are listed in the electronic directory which is an inherent part of EESSI;

— Decision E4 of 13 March 2014 concerning the transitional period as defined in Article 95 of Regulation (EC) No 987/2009 of the European Parliament and of the Council;

— Decision E5 of 16 March 2017 concerning the practical arrangements for the transitional period for the data exchange via electronic means referred to in Article 4 of Regulation (EC) No 987/2009 of the European Parliament and of the Council.

Family benefits (F series):

— Decision F1 of 12 June 2009 concerning the interpretation of Article 68 of Regulation (EC) No 883/2004 of the European Parliament and of the Council relating to priority rules in the event of overlapping of family benefits;
— Decision F2 of 23 June 2015 concerning the exchange of data between institutions for the purpose of granting family benefits.

Horizontal issues (H series):

— Decision H1 of 12 June 2009 concerning the framework for the transition from Council Regulations (EEC) No 1408/71 and (EEC) No 574/72 to Regulations (EC) No 883/2004 and (EC) No 987/2009 of the European Parliament and of the Council and the application of Decisions and Recommendations of the Administrative Commission for the coordination of social security systems;.
— Decision H3 of 15 October 2009 concerning the date to be taken into consideration for determining the rates of conversion referred to in Article 90 of Regulation (EC) No 987/2009 of the European Parliament and of the Council;
— Decision H4 of 22 December 2009 concerning the composition and working methods of the Audit Board of the Administrative Commission for the Coordination of Social Security Systems;
— Decision H5 of 18 March 2010 concerning cooperation on combating fraud and error within the framework of Council Regulation (EC) No 883/2004 and Regulation (EC) No 987/2009 of the European Parliament and of the Council on the coordination of social security systems;
— Decision H6 of 16 December 2010 concerning the application of certain principles regarding the aggregation of periods under Article 6 of Regulation (EC) No 883/2004 on the coordination of social security systems;
— Decision H7 of 25 June 2015 on the revision of Decision H3 concerning the date to be taken into consideration for determining the rates of conversion referred to in Article 90 of Regulation (EC) No 987/2009 of the European Parliament and of the Council on the coordination of social security systems;
— Decision H8 of 17 December 2015 (updated with minor technical clarifications on 9 March 2016) concerning the methods of operation and the composition of the Technical Commission for data processing of the Administrative Commission for the coordination of social security systems;
— Recommendation H1 of 19 June 2013 concerning the *Gottardo* judgment, according to which the advantages enjoyed by a State's

own nationals under a bilateral convention on social security with a non-member country must also be granted to workers who are nationals of other Member States.

Pensions (P series):

— Decision P1 of 12 June 2009 on the interpretation of Articles 50(4), 58 and 87(5) of Regulation (EC) No 883/2004 of the European Parliament and of the Council for the award of invalidity, old-age and survivors' benefits.

Recovery (R series):

— Decision R1 of 20 June 2013 concerning the interpretation of Article 85 of Regulation (EC) No 987/2009.

Sickness (S series):

— Decision S1 of 12 June 2009 concerning the European Health Insurance Card;
— Decision S2 of 12 June 2009 concerning the technical specifications of the European Health Insurance Card;
— Decision S3 of 12 June 2009 defining the benefits covered by Articles 19(1) and 27(1) of Regulation (EC) No 883/2004 of the European Parliament and of the Council and Article 25(A)(3) of Regulation (EC) No 987/2009 of the European Parliament and of the Council;
— Decision S5 of 2 October 2009 on interpretation of the concept of "benefits in kind" as defined in Article 1(va) of Regulation (EC) No 883/2004 of the European Parliament and of the Council in the event of sickness or maternity pursuant to Articles 17, 19, 20, 22, 24(1), 25, 26, 27(1, 3, 4 and 5), 28, 34 and 36(1 and 2) of Regulation (EC) No 883/2004 and on calculation of the amounts to be refunded under Articles 62, 63 and 64 of Regulation (EC) No 987/2009 of the European Parliament and of the Council;
— Decision S6 of 22 December 2009 concerning the registration in the Member State of residence under Article 24 of Regulation (EC) No 987/2009 and the compilation of the inventories provided for in Article 64(4) of Regulation (EC) No 987/2009[2]
— Decision S8 of 15 June 2011 concerning the granting of prostheses, major appliances and other substantial benefits in kind provided for in Article 33 of Regulation (EC) No 883/2004 on the coordination of social security systems;
— Decision S9 of 20 June 2013 concerning refund procedures for the implementation of Articles 35 and 41 of Regulation (EC) No 883/2004;
— Decision S10 of 19 December 2013 concerning the transition from Regulations (EEC) Nos 1408/71 and 574/72 to Regulations (EC) Nos 883/2004 and 987/2009 and the application of reimbursement procedures;
— Recommendation S1 of 15 March 2012 concerning financial aspects of cross-border living organ donations;

427

— Recommendation S2 of 22 October 2013 concerning the entitlement to benefits in kind for insured persons and members of their family during a stay in a third country under a bilateral convention between the competent Member State and the third country.

Unemployment (U series):

— Decision U1 of 12 June 2009 concerning Article 54(3) of Regulation (EC) No 987/2009 of the European Parliament and of the Council relating to increases in unemployment benefit for dependent members of the family;
— Decision U2 of 12 June 2009 concerning the scope of Article 65(2) of Regulation (EC) No 883/2004 of the European Parliament and of the Council on the right to unemployment benefits of wholly unemployed persons other than frontier workers who were resident in the territory of a Member State other than the competent Member State during their last period of employment or self-employment;
— Decision U3 of 12 June 2009 concerning the scope of the concept of "partial unemployment" applicable to the unemployed persons referred to in Article 65(1) of Regulation (EC) No 883/2004 of the European Parliament and of the Council;
— Decision U4 of 13 December 2011 concerning the reimbursement procedures under Article 65(6) and (7) of Regulation (EC) No 883/2004 and Article 70 of Regulation (EC) No 987/2009;
— Recommendation U1 of 12 June 2009 concerning the legislation applicable to unemployed persons engaging in part-time professional or trade activity in a Member State other than the State of residence;
— Recommendation U2 of 12 June 2009 concerning the application of Article 64(1)(a) of Regulation (EC) No 883/2004 of the European Parliament and of the Council to unemployed persons accompanying their spouses or partners pursuing a professional or trade activity in a Member State other than the competent State.

Part II
Acts Referred To

4.078 Regulation (EC) No 883/2004 of the European Parliament and of the Council of 29 April 2004 on the coordination of social security systems, as amended by:
— Regulation (EC) No 988/2009 of the European Parliament and of the Council of 16 September 2009;
— Commission Regulation (EU) No 1244/2010 of 9 December 2010;
— Regulation (EU) No 465/2012 of the European Parliament and of the Council of 22 May 2012;
— Commission Regulation (EU) No 1224/2012 of 18 December 2012;

— Council Regulation (EU) No 517/2013 of 13 May 2013;
— Commission Regulation (EU) No 1372/2013 of 19 December 2013, as amended by Commission Regulation (EU) No 1368/2014 of 17 December 2014;
— Commission Regulation (EU) 2017/492 of 21 March 2017.
Regulation (EC) No 987/2009 of the European Parliament and of the Council of 16 September 2009 laying down the procedure for implementing Regulation (EC) No 883/2004 on the coordination of social security systems, as amended by:
— Commission Regulation (EU) No 1244/2010 of 9 December 2010;
— Regulation (EU) No 465/2012 of the European Parliament and of the Council of 22 May 2012;
— Commission Regulation (EU) No 1224/2012 of 18 December 2012;
— Commission Regulation (EU) No 1372/2013 of 19 December 2013;
— Commission Regulation (EU) No 1368/2014 of 17 December 2014;
— Commission Regulation (EU) 2017/492 of 21 March 2017.

PART III
ADAPTATIONS TO REGULATION (EC) No 883/2004
AND REGULATION (EC) No 987/2009

The provisions of Regulation (EC) No 883/2004 shall, for the purposes of this Agreement, be adapted as follows:
(a) the following shall be added to Annex II:
   "UNITED KINGDOM–GERMANY
   (a) Article 7(5) and (6) of the Convention on social security of 20 April 1960 (legislation applicable to civilians serving in the military forces);
   (b) Article 5(5) and (6) of the Convention on unemployment insurance of 20 April 1960 (legislation applicable to civilians serving in the military forces).
   UNITED KINGDOM–IRELAND
   Article 19(2) of the Agreement of 14 December, 2004 on social security (concerning the transfer and reckoning of certain disability credits).";
(b) the following shall be added to Annex III:
   "UNITED KINGDOM";
      (c) the following shall be added to Annex VI:
   "UNITED KINGDOM
   Employment and Support Allowance (ESA)
   (a) For awards granted before 1 April 2016 ESA is a cash sickness benefit for the initial 91 days (Assessment Phase). From the 92nd day ESA (Main Phase) becomes an invalidity benefit.

(b) For awards granted on or after 1 April 2016 ESA is a cash sickness benefit for the initial 365 days (Assessment Phase). From the 366th day ESA (Support Group) becomes an invalidity benefit.

Great Britain legislation: Part 1 of the Welfare Reform Act 2007.
Northern Ireland legislation: Part 1 of the Welfare Reform Act (Northern Ireland) 2007.";

(d) the following shall be added to Part 1 of Annex VIII:
"UNITED KINGDOM
All applications for retirement pension, state pension pursuant to Part 1 of the Pensions Act 2014, widows' and bereavement benefits, with the exception of those for which during a tax year beginning on or after 6 April 1975:

(i) the party concerned had completed periods of insurance, employment or residence under the legislation of the United Kingdom and another Member State; and one (or more) of the tax years was not considered a qualifying year within the meaning of the legislation of the United Kingdom;

(ii) the periods of insurance completed under the legislation in force in the United Kingdom for the periods prior to 5 July 1948 would be taken into account for the purposes of Article 52(1)(b) of the Regulation by application of the periods of insurance, employment or residence under the legislation of another Member State.

All applications for additional pension pursuant to the Social Security Contributions and Benefits Act 1992, section 44, and the Social Security Contributions and Benefits (Northern Ireland) Act 1992, section 44.";

(e) the following shall be added to Part 2 of Annex VIII:
"UNITED KINGDOM
Graduated retirement benefits paid pursuant to the National Insurance Act 1965, sections 36 and 37, and the National Insurance Act (Northern Ireland) 1966, sections 35 and 36.";

(f) the following shall be added to Annex X:
"UNITED KINGDOM

(a) State Pension Credit (State Pension Credit Act 2002 and State Pension Credit Act (Northern Ireland) 2002);

(b) Income-based allowances for jobseekers (Jobseekers Act 1995 and Jobseekers (Northern Ireland) Order 1995);

(d) Disability Living Allowance mobility component (Social Security Contributions and Benefits Act 1992 and Social Security Contributions and Benefits (Northern Ireland) Act 1992);

(e) Employment and Support Allowance Income-related (Welfare Reform Act 2007 and Welfare Reform Act (Northern Ireland) 2007).";

(g) the following shall be added to Annex XI:

"UNITED KINGDOM

1. Where, in accordance with United Kingdom legislation, a person may be entitled to a retirement pension if:

(a) the contributions of a former spouse are taken into account as if they were that person's own contributions; or

(b) the relevant contribution conditions are satisfied by that person's spouse or former spouse, then provided, in each case, that the spouse or former spouse is or had been exercising an activity as an employed or self-employed person, and had been subject to the legislation of two or more Member States, the provisions of Chapter 5 of Title III of this Regulation shall apply in order to determine entitlement under United Kingdom legislation. In this case, references in the said Chapter 5 to "periods of insurance" shall be construed as references to periods of insurance completed by:

(i) a spouse or former spouse where a claim is made by:
– a married woman, or
– a person whose marriage has terminated otherwise than by the death of the spouse; or

(ii) a former spouse, where a claim is made by:
– a widower who immediately before pensionable age is not entitled to widowed parent's allowance, or
– a widow who immediately before pensionable age is not entitled to widowed mother's allowance, widowed parent's allowance or widow's pension, or who is only entitled to an age-related widow's pension calculated pursuant to Article 52(1)(b) of this Regulation, and for this purpose 'age-related widow's pension' means a widow's pension payable at a reduced rate in accordance with section 39(4) of the Social Security Contributions and Benefits Act 1992.

2. For the purposes of applying Article 6 of this Regulation to the provisions governing entitlement to attendance allowance, carer's allowance and disability living allowance, a period of employment, self-employment or residence completed in the territory of a Member State other than the United Kingdom shall be taken into account insofar as is necessary to satisfy conditions as to required periods of presence in the United Kingdom, prior to the day on which entitlement to the benefit in question first arises.

3. For the purposes of Article 7 of this Regulation, in the case of invalidity, old-age or survivors' cash benefits, pensions for accidents at work or occupational diseases and death grants, any beneficiary under United Kingdom legislation who is staying in the territory of another Member State shall, during that stay, be

considered as if he resided in the territory of that other Member State.

4. Where Article 46 of this Regulation applies, if the person concerned suffers incapacity for work leading to invalidity while subject to the legislation of another Member State, the United Kingdom shall, for the purposes of Section 30A (5) of the Social Security Contributions and Benefits Act 1992, take account of any periods during which the person concerned has received, in respect of that incapacity for work:

    (i) cash sickness benefits or wages or salary in lieu thereof; or

    (ii) benefits within the meaning of Chapters 4 and 5 of Title III of this Regulation granted in respect of the invalidity which followed that incapacity for work, under the legislation of the other Member State, as though they were periods of short-term incapacity benefit paid in accordance with Sections 30A (1)–(4) of the Social Security Contributions and Benefits Act 1992.

In applying this provision, account shall only be taken of periods during which the person would have been incapable of work within the meaning of United Kingdom legislation.

5. (1) For the purpose of calculating an earnings factor in order to determine entitlement to benefits under United Kingdom legislation, for each week of activity as an employed person under the legislation of another Member State, and which commenced during the relevant income tax year within the meaning of United Kingdom legislation, the person concerned shall be deemed to have paid contributions as an employed earner, or have earnings on which contributions have been paid, on the basis of earnings equivalent to two-thirds of that year's upper earnings limit.

(2) For the purposes of Article 52(1)(b)(ii) of this Regulation, where:

    (a) in any income tax year starting on or after 6 April 1975, a person carrying out activity as an employed person has completed periods of insurance, employment or residence exclusively in a Member State other than the United Kingdom, and the application of point 5(1) above results in that year being counted as a qualifying year within the meaning of United Kingdom legislation for the purposes of Article 52(1)(b)(i) of this Regulation, he shall be deemed to have been insured for 52 weeks in that year in that other Member State;

    (b) any income tax year starting on or after 6 April 1975 does not count as a qualifying year within the meaning of United Kingdom legislation for the purposes of Article 52(1)(b)(i) of this Regulation, any periods of insurance, employment or residence completed in that year shall be disregarded.

432

(3) For the purpose of converting an earnings factor into periods of insurance, the earnings factor achieved in the relevant income tax year within the meaning of United Kingdom legislation shall be divided by that year's lower earnings limit. The result shall be expressed as a whole number, any remaining fraction being ignored. The figure so calculated shall be treated as representing the number of weeks of insurance completed under United Kingdom legislation during that year, provided that such figure shall not exceed the number of weeks during which in that year the person was subject to that legislation.".

The provisions of Regulation (EC) No 987/2009 shall, for the purposes of this Agreement, be adapted as follows:

(a) the following shall be added to Annex 1:

"UNITED KINGDOM–BELGIUM

(a) The Exchange of Letters of 4 May and 14 June 1976 regarding Article 105(2) of Regulation (EEC) No 574/72 (waiving of reimbursement of the costs of administrative checks and medical examinations)

(b) The Exchange of Letters of 18 January and 14 March 1977 regarding Article 36(3) of Regulation (EEC) No 1408/71 (arrangement for reimbursement or waiving of reimbursement of the costs of benefits in kind provided under the terms of Chapter 1 of Title III of Regulation (EEC) No 1408/71) as amended by the Exchange of Letters of 4 May and 23 July 1982 (agreement for reimbursement of costs incurred under Article 22(1)(a) of Regulation (EEC) No 1408/71)

UNITED KINGDOM–DENMARK

The Exchange of Letters of 30 March and 19 April 1977 as modified by an Exchange of Letters of 8 November 1989 and of 10 January 1990 on agreement of waiving of reimbursement of the costs of benefits in kind and administrative checks and medical examinations

UNITED KINGDOM–ESTONIA

The Arrangement finalised on 29 March 2006 between the Competent Authorities of the Republic of Estonia and of the United Kingdom under Articles 36(3) and 63(3) of Regulation (EEC) No 1408/71 establishing other methods of reimbursement of the costs of benefits in kind provided under this Regulation by both countries with effect from 1 May 2004

UNITED KINGDOM–IRELAND

The Exchange of Letters of 9 July 1975 regarding Articles 36(3) and 63(3) of Regulation (EEC) No 1408/71 (arrangement for reimbursement or waiving of reimbursement of the costs of benefits in kind provided under the terms of Chapter 1 or 4 of Title III of Regulation (EEC) No 1408/71) and Article 105(2) of Regulation (EEC) No 574/72 (waiving of reimbursement of the costs of administrative checks and medical examinations)

433

UNITED KINGDOM–SPAIN

The Agreement of 18 June 1999 on the reimbursement of costs for benefits in kind granted pursuant to the provisions of Regulations (EEC) No 1408/71 and (EEC) No 574/72

UNITED KINGDOM–FRANCE

(a) The Exchange of Letters of 25 March and 28 April 1997 regarding Article 105(2) of Regulation (EEC) No 574/72 (waiving of reimbursement of the costs of administrative checks and medical examinations)

(b) The Agreement of 8 December 1998 on the specific methods of determining the amounts to be reimbursed for benefits in kind pursuant to Regulations (EEC) No 1408/71 and (EEC) No 574/72

UNITED KINGDOM–ITALY

The Arrangement signed on 15 December 2005 between the Competent Authorities of the Italian Republic and of the United Kingdom under Articles 36(3) and 63(3) of Regulation (EEC) No 1408/71 establishing other methods of reimbursement of the costs of benefits in kind provided under this Regulation by both countries with effect from 1 January 2005

UNITED KINGDOM–LUXEMBOURG

The Exchange of Letters of 18 December 1975 and 20 January 1976 regarding Article 105(2) of Regulation (EEC) No 574/72 (waiving of reimbursement of the costs entailed in administrative checks and medical examinations referred to in Article 105 of Regulation (EEC) No 574/72)

UNITED KINGDOM–HUNGARY

The Arrangement finalised on 1 November 2005 between the Competent Authorities of the Republic of Hungary and of the United Kingdom under Articles 35(3) and 41(2) of Regulation (EEC) No 883/2004 establishing other methods of reimbursement of the costs of benefits in kind provided under that Regulation by both countries with effect from 1 May 2004

UNITED KINGDOM–MALTA

The Arrangement finalised on 17 January 2007 between the Competent Authorities of Malta and of the United Kingdom under Articles 35(3) and 41(2) of Regulation (EEC) No 883/2004 establishing other methods of reimbursement of the costs of benefits in kind provided under that Regulation by both countries with effect from 1 May 2004

UNITED KINGDOM–NETHERLANDS

The second sentence of Article 3 of the Administrative Arrangement of 12 June 1956 on the implementation of the Convention of 11 August 1954

UNITED KINGDOM–PORTUGAL

The Arrangement of 8 June 2004 establishing other methods of reimbursement of the costs of benefits in kind provided by both countries with effect from 1 January 2003

UNITED KINGDOM–FINLAND
The Exchange of Letters 1 and 20 June 1995 concerning Articles 36(3) and 63(3) of Regulation (EEC) No 1408/71 (reimbursement or waiving of reimbursement of the cost of benefits in kind) and Article 105(2) of Regulation (EEC) 574/72 (waiving of reimbursement of the cost of administrative checks and medical examinations)
UNITED KINGDOM–SWEDEN
The Arrangement of 15 April 1997 concerning Article 36(3) and Article 63(3) of Regulation (EEC) No 1408/71 (reimbursement or waiving of reimbursement of the cost of benefits in kind) and Article 105(2) of Regulation (EEC) No 574/72 (waiving of refunds of the costs of administrative checks and medical examinations)";
(b) the following shall be added to Annex 3: "UNITED KINGDOM".

p.1107, *Extracts from the Treaty on European Union*

For the extent to which matters of EU law may have continuing relevance from December 31, 2020, see the European Union (Withdrawal) Act 2018 and the Withdrawal Agreement.　4.079

p.1110, *Treaty on European Union, Article 6—Charter of Fundamental Rights of the European Union*

The Charter does not form part of domestic law from December 31, 2020: see European Union (Withdrawal) Act 2018, s.5(4) (but note s.5(5)).　4.080

p.1113, *Extracts from the Treaty on the Functioning of the European Union*

For the extent to which matters of EU law may have continuing relevance from December 31, 2020, see the European Union (Withdrawal) Act 2018 and the Withdrawal Agreement.　4.081

p.1114, *Article 18 TFEU*

The CJEU held that the existence of the more specific non-discrimination provision in art.24 of Directive 2004/38 did not supplant art.18 TFEU which could accordingly be relied upon where a person's right to reside arose otherwise than under the Directive (in that case via art.10 of Regulation 492/2011): see *Krefeld* (C–181/19) Judgment of October 6, 2020. *Krefeld* was applied, and the vitality of *Martinez Sala, Grzelczyk* and *Trojani* (discussed under art.21 at 3.109–3.110 of the main volume) affirmed, by the Court of Appeal in *R. (Fratila and Tanase) v SSWP* [2020] EWCA Civ 1741, ruling that the legislative provisions preventing those who under domestic law had been given a right to reside based on　4.082

"pre-settled status" from relying on those rights to access means-tested benefits constituted direct discrimination contrary to art.18. Note that on February 22, 2021 the Secretary of State was given permission to appeal against the Court of Appeal's decision.

pp.1124-5, *Article 21 TFEU*

4.083   For the continuing relevance under EU law (where it applies or is otherwise relevant) of *Martinez Sala, Grzelczyk* and *Trojani,* see the discussion of *Krefeld* and of *R(Fratila and Tanase) v SSWP* in the notes to p.1114.

p.1133, *Article 45 TFEU*

4.084   For those outside the scope of Part Two of the Withdrawal Agreement, any ability there might otherwise have been to rely after December 31, 2020 on art.45 via s.4 of the European Union (Withdrawal) Act 2018 is likely to be excluded by the sweeping provision in Immigration and Social Security Co-ordination (EU Withdrawal) Act 2020, s.1 and Sch.1, para 6.

p.1141, *Article 49—Right of Establishment*

4.085   While art.13(1) of the Withdrawal Agreement preserves the ability to rely on art.49 for those within the scope of the Agreement, any ability which might otherwise have existed for others to rely on this Article after December 31, 2020 via s.4 of the European Union (Withdrawal) Act 2018 has been removed by the Freedom of Establishment and Free Movement of Services (EU Exit) Regulations 2019/1401.

p.1142, *Article 56—Services*

4.086   Any ability which might otherwise have existed to rely on this Article after December 31, 2020 via s.4 of the European Union (Withdrawal) Act 2018 has been removed by the Freedom of Establishment and Free Movement of Services (EU Exit) Regulations 2019/1401.

pp.1148-1164, *Charter of Fundamental Rights of the European Union*

4.087   The Charter does not form part of domestic law from December 31, 2020: see European Union (Withdrawal) Act 2018, s.5(4), subject to s.5(5).

p.1164, *Regulation (EU) No.492/2011*

4.088   For those covered by Part Two of the Withdrawal Agreement, art.24 preserves the ability to rely on this Regulation. For others, Immigration and Social Security Co-ordination (EU Withdrawal) Act 2020 Schedule, para.4 (introduced by s.1) provides:

"Retained direct EU legislation
      4(1) Article 1 of the Workers Regulation is omitted.

(2) Articles 2 to 10 of the Workers Regulation cease to apply so far as—

(a) they are inconsistent with any provision made by or under the Immigration Acts (including, and as amended by, this Act), or

(b) they are otherwise capable of affecting the interpretation, application or operation of any such provision.

(3) In this paragraph, "the Workers Regulation" means Regulation (EU) No 492/2011 of the European Parliament and of the Council of 5 April 2011 on freedom of movement for workers within the Union."

p.1176, *Directive 2004/38/EC*

For those outside the scope of Part Two of the Withdrawal Agreement, any ability there might otherwise have been to rely after December 31, 2020 on the Directive via s.4 of the European Union (Withdrawal) Act 2018 is likely to be excluded by the sweeping provision in Immigration and Social Security Co-ordination (EU Withdrawal) Act 2020, s.1 and Schedule 1, para 6. For those within the scope of Part Two, the content of the Part does not entirely mirror, but borrows substantially from, the Directive. As regards the interpretation of Part Two where it adopts provisions from the Directive, note art.4 of the Withdrawal Agreement (at para 3.60 of the main volume) as well as the provisions of domestic law referred to in the General Note linked to p.1061. **4.089**

pp.1202-1203, *Directive 2004/38/EC, art.7—Comprehensive sickness insurance cover*

A reference to the CJEU (C–247/20) has been made by the Appeal Tribunal in Northern Ireland in *VI v HMRC* asking the following questions: **4.089.1**

"Is a child EEA Permanent Resident required to maintain Comprehensive Sickness Insurance in order to maintain a right to reside, as s/he would as a self-sufficient person, pursuant to Regulation 4(1) of the 2016 Regulations?

Is the requirement, pursuant to Regulation 4(3)(b) of The Immigration (European Economic Area) Regulations 2016 (that Comprehensive Sickness Insurance cover in the United Kingdom is only satisfied for a student or self-sufficient person, with regard to Regulation 16(2)(b)(ii) of The Immigration (European Economic Area) Regulations 2016, if such cover extends to both that person and all their relevant family members), illegal under EU law in light of Article 7(1) of Directive 2004/381 and the jurisprudence of the Court of Justice of the European Union in paragraph 70 of Teixeira C–480/08?

Following the decision in paragraph 53 of *Ahmad v Secretary of State for the Home Department* [2014] EWCA Civ 988, are the Common Travel Area reciprocal arrangements in place regarding Health Insurance cover between the United Kingdom and the Republic of Ireland considered 'reciprocal arrangements' and therefore constitute Comprehensive Sickness Insurance for the purposes of Regulation 4(1) of the 2016 Regulations?"

p.1227, *Regulation 883/2004 General Note*

4.090   Following the expiry on December 31, 2020 of the implementation period for the UK's withdrawal from the EU, Regulation 883/2004 has a somewhat complex status. As regards those who fall within the scope of art.30 of the Withdrawal Agreement or within one of the special circumstances addressed in art.32, it continues to apply via art.31. Note should be taken of the modifications for which the Withdrawal Agreement provides, including those in Annex I, Part 2 (although, curiously, most of these were already within the Regulation as it previously stood). The position with regard to the implementing regulation, Regulation 987/2009, is similar. Provisions in the Withdrawal Agreement, which are intended to be directly enforceable, take effect in domestic law via s.7A of the European Union (Withdrawal) Act 2018.

However, Regulation 883/2004 in its own right (i.e. divorced from its underpinning by the Withdrawal Agreement), which would otherwise have constituted "retained direct EU legislation" under section 3 of the 2018 Act is repealed, subject to very limited savings, by the Social Security Co-ordination (Revocation of Retained Direct EU Legislation and Related Amendments) (EU Exit) Regulations 2020/1508. (The same also applies to its predecessor, Regulation 1408/71 and its implementing Regulation 574/72, which are no longer included within the main volumes.) (Equivalent provision is made in relation to devolved benefits in Scotland by Scottish SI 2020/399.)

Those not in a position to rely on the Withdrawal Agreement will in consequence be reliant on the Protocol on Social Security Co-ordination which forms part of the Trade and Co-operation Agreement concluded between the European Union and the United Kingdom on December 24, 2020. It forms part of domestic law by virtue of the European Union (Future Relationship) Act 2020, s.26, the effect of which remains to be explored. SI 2020/1508 also makes amendments to Social Security Administration Act 1992 s.179 to permit an overall reciprocal agreement with the European Union.

Irish nationals will enjoy a special position because of the Common Travel Area and the Convention on Social Security between the UK and Ireland: see *https://www.gov.uk/government/publications/memorandum-of-understanding-between-the-uk-and-ireland-on-the-cta* (accessed December 28, 2020) and the Social Security (Ireland) Order 2019 SI 2019/622 (which has the Convention in its Schedule).

pp.1232-1233, *General Note—application of Regulation 883/04 to Iceland, Liechtenstein, Norway and Switzerland*

4.091   The Citizens Rights' Agreements between the UK and Switzerland and the UK and Iceland, Liechtenstein and Norway are part of domestic law by virtue of European Union (Withdrawal) Act 2018, s.7B. See the General Note to that section for further detail.

p.1253, *Article 4, Equality of Treatment*

Although not itself a case under this provision *R(Fratila and Tanase) v SSWP* [2020] EWCA Civ 1741 illustrates that there is a difference between the indirect discrimination involved in whether a person has a right to reside and the direct discrimination involved in denying them the ability to access benefits relying on a right which they do possess. The case is, however, subject to a pending appeal to the Supreme Court.   **4.092**

p.1329, *Article 72—Tasks of the Administrative Commission—General Note*

Article 36(4) of the Withdrawal Agreement provides a list of the Decisions of the Administrative Commission for the purposes of the Withdrawal Agreement. There is provision for the list to be modified.   **4.093**

p.1343, *Annex II—Provisions of conventions which remain in force and which, where applicable, are restricted to the persons covered thereby*

Annex I of the Withdrawal Agreement purports to add provisions to this Annex which, however, it appears already formed part of the Regulation as amended.   **4.094**

p.1343, *Annex III—Restriction of rights to benefits in kind for members of the family of a frontier worker*

The United Kingdom has been added to Annex III for the purposes of the Withdrawal Agreement by Annex I of the latter.   **4.095**

pp.1344-1346, *Annex VI—Identification of Type A legislation which should be subject to special coordination*

Annex I of the Withdrawal Agreement purports to add provisions to this Annex which, however, it appears already formed part of the Regulation as amended.   **4.096**

pp.1347-1351, *Annex VIII—Cases in which the pro rata calculation shall be waived or shall not apply*

Annex I of the Withdrawal Agreement purports to add provisions to both Part 1 and Part 2 of this Annex which, however, it appears already formed part of the Regulation as amended.   **4.097**

pp.1354-1358, *Annex X—Special non-contributory cash benefits*

Annex I of the Withdrawal Agreement purports to add provisions to this Annex which, however, it appears already formed part of the Regulation as amended.   **4.098**

pp.1358-1360, *Annex XI—Special provisions for the application of the legislation of the Member States*

4.099   Annex I of the Withdrawal Agreement purports to add provisions to this Annex which, however, it appears already formed part of the Regulation as amended.

p.1361, *Regulation 987/2009 General Note*

4.100   Following the expiry on December 31, 2020 of the implementation period for the UK's withdrawal from the EU, Regulation 987/2009, like Regulation 883/2004 which it implements, has a somewhat complex status. As regards those who fall within the scope of art.30 of the Withdrawal Agreement or within one of the special circumstances addressed in art.32, it continues to apply via art.31. Note should be taken of the modifications for which the Withdrawal Agreement provides, including those in Annex I, Part 2 (although, curiously, most of these were already within the Regulation as it previously stood). Provisions in the Withdrawal Agreement, which are intended to be directly enforceable, take effect in domestic law via s.7A of the European Union (Withdrawal) Act 2018.

However, Regulation 987/2009 in its own right (i.e. divorced from its underpinning by the Withdrawal Agreement), which would otherwise have constituted "retained direct EU legislation" under section 3 of the 2018 Act is repealed, subject to very limited savings, by the Social Security Co-ordination (Revocation of Retained Direct EU Legislation and Related Amendments) (EU Exit) Regulations 2020/1508. (The same also applies to the predecessor regulations, Regulation 1408/71 and its implementing Regulation 574/72, which are no longer included within the main volumes.) (Equivalent provision is made in relation to devolved benefits in Scotland by Scottish SI 2020/399.)

Those not in a position to rely on the Withdrawal Agreement will in consequence be reliant on the Protocol on Social Security Co-ordination which forms part of the Trade and Co-operation Agreement concluded between the European Union and the United Kingdom on December 24, 2020. It forms part of domestic law by virtue of the European Union (Future Relationship) Act 2020, s.26, the effect of which remains to be explored.

SI 2020/1508 also makes amendments to Social Security Administration Act 1992 s.179 to permit an overall reciprocal agreement with the European Union.

pp.1431-1433, *Annex 1—Implementing provisions for bilateral agreements remaining in force and new bilateral implementing agreements*

4.101   Annex I of the Withdrawal Agreement purports to add provisions to this Annex most, but not all, of which, however, it appears already formed part of the Regulation as amended.

p.1433, *Annex 3—Member states claiming the reimbursement of the cost of benefits in kind on the basis of fixed amounts*

Annex I of the Withdrawal Agreement purports to add the United Kingdom to this Annex but it appears it already was under the Regulation as previously amended. 4.102

p.1435, *General Note to Regulation 859/2003*

Following the expiry on December 31, 2020 of the implementation period for the UK's withdrawal from the EU, third country nationals fulfilling the conditions of Regulation 859/2003 and members of their families and survivors are entitled to rely on Part Two of the Withdrawal Agreement if they meet the other qualifying conditions for doing so. Apart from that, the Regulation, which would otherwise have constituted "retained direct EU legislation" under European Union (Withdrawal) Act 2018, s.3, is repealed, subject to very limited savings, by the Social Security Co-ordination (Revocation of Retained Direct EU Legislation and Related Amendments) (EU Exit) Regulations 2020/1508. 4.103

p.1441, *Council Directive 79/7/EEC—General Note*

Directly enforceable rights under a Directive will unless excluded by the legislature be capable of being enforced via European Union (Withdrawal) Act 2018, s.4. 4.104

Additionally, art.2 and Annex 1 of the Ireland/Northern Ireland Protocol to the Withdrawal Agreement entrench various provisions against discrimination, of which this Directive is one. The legislation establishing a general principle of parity between the social security systems of Great Britain and Northern Ireland (see Northern Ireland Act 1998, s.87) bolsters the likelihood that the provisions of the Directive will continue to be applied in Great Britain also.

p.1452, *Council Directive 79/7/EEC—Article 7(1)(a)*

The conclusion of the Divisional Court on this point was upheld by the Court of Appeal: [2020] EWCA Civ 1199. 4.105

p.1491, *Human Rights Act 1998, s.21—Interpretation etc*

As regards the status of "retained direct principal EU legislation" and "retained direct minor EU legislation" for the purposes of this Act following the United Kingdom's withdrawal from the European Union, see the European Union (Withdrawal) Act 2018, Sch.8, para.30. 4.106

pp.1519-1520, *National authorities on art.14 read with art.1 of Protocol 1— "Bedroom Tax"*

A challenge by a disabled young adult to being restricted to the one bedroom shared accommodation rate was rejected in *CM v Bradford MDC and SSWP* [2020] UKUT 285. 4.107

p.1522, *National authorities on art.14 read with art.1 of Protocol 1—Bereavement*

4.108   On 28 July 2020, the Minister announced to Parliament the intention to make a remedial order under section 10 of the Human Rights Act 1998 to address the breach of human rights found to have occurred in cases such as *McLaughlin* and *Jackson*. That would in principle be capable of conferring rights retrospectively: see 1998 Act, sch.2, para. 1(1)(b).

p.1524, *National authorities on art.14 read with art.1 of Protocol 1—Bereavement*

4.109   *O'Donnell v Department for Communities* [2020] NICA 36 concerned a claim for bereavement support payment by the husband whose late wife had, throughout her working life (as the court was at pains to emphasise), been unable to work on account of congenital disability and so to satisfy the contribution conditions for the benefit, which required actual payment of a modest level of contributions. The court held that the failure to differentiate between the respective situations of such a person and of a person who, though able to work, had not done so, constituted *Thlimmenos* discrimination and failed the test of justification. The court read wording into the Northern Ireland equivalent of s.30(1)(d) of the Pensions Act 2014 treating the contribution condition as having been met where the deceased was unable to comply with it throughout her working life due to disability. Although the decision does not ultimately turn on it, the case highlights how the Northern Ireland equivalent of what is primary legislation in Great Britain may constitute secondary legislation, being made under the Northern Ireland Act 1998, something which may significantly affect the remedy available under the Human Rights Act.

p.1525, *National authorities on art.14 read with art.1 of Protocol 1—Disability*

4.110   Erratum: the discussion of *JA-K v SSWP* which appears (in error) at the end of 4.131 should appear in 4.130.

In *Re Cox's Judicial Review* [2020] NIQB 53, the High Court of Northern Ireland has held that the requirement that, in order to be eligible for universal credit and personal independence payment automatically and immediately on the ground of terminal illness a person had to demonstrate that their death could reasonably be expected within 6 months, was manifestly without reasonable foundation. Having a terminal illness with uncertain prognosis constituted a "status", the appropriate comparator was someone with a terminal illness who had been expected to die within 6 months but in the event did not and who would continue to benefit from the terminal illness rules and (para.102) no justification existed for the difference in treatment.

A challenge to the rule that when a claimant has received a Loan for Mortgage Interest, it is immediately due and repayable when the property is sold was brought by people with severe disabilities, arguing that applying the rule to them involved *Thlimmenos* discrimination. The challenge failed: *R(Vincent) v SSWP* [2020] EWHC 1976 (Admin).

p.1525, *National authorities on art.14 read with art.1 of Protocol 1—Family issues*

In *R. (on the application of Taylor Moore) v SSWP* [2020] EWHC 2827   4.111
(Admin), Swift J rejected a claim that the difference in how statutory maternity pay and maternity allowance were taken into account for universal credit purposes breached art.14. While the former counted as earned income, attracting the application of a taper, while the latter did not, the difference was held to be justified by a range of practical considerations linked to the universal credit system, prominent among which were the close links between statutory maternity pay and the Real Time Information system used by HMRC and the DWP.

In *SK and LL v SSWP (IS)* [2020] UKUT 145 (AAC) the "first child only" rule in the regulations governing Sure Start Maternity Grant was found to be discriminatory against two categories of claimant.

p.1526, *National authorities on art.14 read with art.1 of Protocol 1—Hospitalisation and other payability issues*

The Upper Tribunal has given permission to appeal to the Court of   4.112
Appeal in *MOC (by MG) v SSWP (DLA)* [2020] UKUT 134 (AAC).

p.1527, *National authorities on art.14 read with art.1 of Protocol 1—Migration, residence*

In *TS v SSWP (DLA); EK v SSWP (DLA)* [2020] UKUT 284   4.113
(AAC), the Upper Tribunal held that the increase in the "Past Presence Test" required for eligibility for disability living allowance from 26 weeks out of 52 to 104 weeks out of 156 breached art.14 in respect of two children who had lived abroad with their families before returning to the United Kingdom. The judge had additional and differing evidence from that which had been before the Upper Tribunal in *FM v SSWP (DLA)* [2017] UKUT 380; [2019] AACR 8, which he declined to follow. The case also contains a lengthy consideration of whether on a statutory appeal the First-tier Tribunal and Upper Tribunal have jurisdiction to consider an alleged breach of the Public Sector Equality Duty in Equality Act 2010, s.149, concluding that they do not.

p.1528, *National authorities on art.14 read with art.1 of Protocol 1—Pensions and pension credit*

On appeal in *Delve and Glynn v SSWP* [2020] EWCA Civ 1199, as   4.114
regards age discrimination, the Court of Appeal distanced itself from the Divisional Court's conclusion regarding the *Ackermann* line of cases but held that the measure was in any event not manifestly without reasonable foundation. As regards indirect discrimination on the ground of gender,

the Court of Appeal, while indicating a degree of difficulty with some aspects of the Divisional Court's expression of its reasoning, concluded that there was no sufficient causal link between the withdrawal of the state pension from women in the age group 60 to 65 and the disadvantage caused to that group.

p.1529, *National authorities on art.14 read with art.1 of Protocol 1— Universal credit*

4.115   For a discussion of the differential treatment of statutory maternity pay and maternity allowance for universal credit purposes, see the *Taylor Moore* case, noted under p.1525.

A challenge to the formulae used for converting weekly housing costs into monthly figures for universal credit purposes, which was capable of creating a limited disadvantage to weekly tenants in some instances, failed in *R (Sheena Caine) v SSWP* [2020] EWHC 2482 (Admin). There were sound administrative aims behind the formulae and the differences to which they might lead were small even in those instances where they did arise.

p.1536, *Human Rights Act 1998, Sch.2*

4.116   The schedule, previously omitted, attains increasing importance in the light of the remedial order announced in respect of bereavement support payment and widowed parent's allowance and that concerning the issues raised by *Reilly and Hewstone v SSWP* [2016] EWCA Civ 413; [2017] AACR 14, now in force as the Jobseekers (Back to Work Schemes) Act 2013 (Remedial) Order 2020 (SI 1085/2020).

SCHEDULE 2
REMEDIAL ORDERS

Orders

4.117   1.(1) A remedial order may—
(a) contain such incidental, supplemental, consequential or transitional provision as the person making it considers appropriate;
(b) be made so as to have effect from a date earlier than that on which it is made;
(c) make provision for the delegation of specific functions;
(d) make different provision for different cases.
(2) The power conferred by sub-paragraph (1)(a) includes—
(a) power to amend primary legislation (including primary legislation other than that which contains the incompatible provision); and
(b) power to amend or revoke subordinate legislation (including subordinate legislation other than that which contains the incompatible provision).
(3) A remedial order may be made so as to have the same extent as the legislation which it affects.
(4) No person is to be guilty of an offence solely as a result of the retrospective effect of a remedial order.

Procedure

2. No remedial order may be made unless—
(a) a draft of the order has been approved by a resolution of each House of Parliament made after the end of the period of 60 days beginning with the day on which the draft was laid; or
(b) it is declared in the order that it appears to the person making it that, because of the urgency of the matter, it is necessary to make the order without a draft being so approved.

Orders laid in draft

3. (1) No draft may be laid under paragraph 2(a) unless—
(a) the person proposing to make the order has laid before Parliament a document which contains a draft of the proposed order and the required information; and
(b) the period of 60 days, beginning with the day on which the document required by this sub-paragraph was laid, has ended.
(2) If representations have been made during that period, the draft laid under paragraph 2(a) must be accompanied by a statement containing—
(a) a summary of the representations; and
(b) if, as a result of the representations, the proposed order has been changed, details of the changes.

Urgent cases

4. (1) If a remedial order ("the original order") is made without being approved in draft, the person making it must lay it before Parliament, accompanied by the required information, after it is made.
(2) If representations have been made during the period of 60 days beginning with the day on which the original order was made, the person making it must (after the end of that period) lay before Parliament a statement containing—
(a) a summary of the representations; and
(b) if, as a result of the representations, he considers it appropriate to make changes to the original order, details of the changes.
(3) If sub-paragraph (2)(b) applies, the person making the statement must—
(a) make a further remedial order replacing the original order; and
(b) lay the replacement order before Parliament.
(4) If, at the end of the period of 120 days beginning with the day on which the original order was made, a resolution has not been passed by each House approving the original or replacement order, the order ceases to have effect (but without that affecting anything previously done under either order or the power to make a fresh remedial order).

Definitions

5. In this Schedule—
"representations" means representations about a remedial order (or proposed remedial order) made to the person making (or proposing to make) it and includes any relevant Parliamentary report or resolution; and

"required information" means—

(a) an explanation of the incompatibility which the order (or proposed order) seeks to remove, including particulars of the relevant declaration, finding or order; and

(b) a statement of the reasons for proceeding under section 10 and for making an order in those terms.

Calculating periods

6. In calculating any period for the purposes of this Schedule, no account is to be taken of any time during which—

(a) Parliament is dissolved or prorogued; or

(b) both Houses are adjourned for more than four days.

[¹**7.** (1) This paragraph applies in relation to—

(a) any remedial order made, and any draft of such an order proposed to be made,—

    (i) by the Scottish Ministers; or

    (ii) within devolved competence (within the meaning of the Scotland Act 1998) by Her Majesty in Council; and

(b) any document or statement to be laid in connection with such an order (or proposed order).

(2) This Schedule has effect in relation to any such order (or proposed order), document or statement subject to the following modifications.

(3) Any reference to Parliament, each House of Parliament or both Houses of Parliament shall be construed as a reference to the Scottish Parliament.

(4) Paragraph 6 does not apply and instead, in calculating any period for the purposes of this Schedule, no account is to be taken of any time during which the Scottish Parliament is dissolved or is in recess for more than four days.]

AMENDMENT

1. The Scotland Act 1998 (Consequential Modifications) Order 2000 (SI 2000/2040) art.2, Sch. Pt I para. 21 (July 27, 2000).

pp.1543-1568, *annotation to Tribunals, Courts and Enforcement Act 2007 s.3 (The First-tier Tribunal and the Upper Tribunal)*

4.118   The principle of open justice was considered in *DVLA v IC (Rule 14 Order)* [2020] UKUT 310 (AAC) (see the supplementary annotation to r.14 of the Tribunal Procedure (First-tier Tribunal) (Social Entitlement Chamber) Rules 2008, below).

Where, in an industrial injuries case, the issue of causation has not been addressed either in medical reports submitted by the claimant nor in the health case professional's report submitted by the Secretary of State, the inquisitorial role of the First-tier Tribunal requires it to investigate the issue itself, either by taking a history from the claimant or by obtaining a medical report on the issue. It may not be possible properly to discharge its function if the claimant has declined to attend a hearing and the failure of the health care professional to consider the issue may make it unfair for the First-tier Tribunal to determine an appeal in the

Appellant's absence unless it has been made clear to the claimant why his or her attendance is important (*MH v SSWP (II)* [2020] UKUT 297 (AAC) at [54], [55] and [57]).

In *BF v SSWP (PIP)* [2019] UKUT 420 (AAC), the Upper Tribunal held that an apparent failure to ensure that there was an interpreter when the claimant attended for assessment by a health care professional, after he had requested an interpreter for that assessment, was a procedural irregularity that rendered the First-tier Tribunal's proceedings irregular when it relied upon the health care professional's report. In *BF v SSWP (PIP)* [2020] UKUT 300 (AAC) a different judge disagreed, on the ground that a medical assessment was an administrative process, rather than a judicial one, and the report was merely evidence, the weight of which was a matter for judicial determination by the First-tier Tribunal. The judge accepted that a failure to use an interpreter where one is required is likely to reduce the value of such evidence, but he held that it was not made inadmissible unless excluded under r.15(2) of the Tribunal Procedure (First-tier Tribunal) (Social Entitlement Chamber) Rules 2008.

Rule 15(2)(b)(iii) (unfairness) might be relevant, but it is suggested that it would generally be simpler to find that no weight at all should be given to the report, or parts of it, if the lack of an interpreter is thought to render it, or parts of it, completely unreliable. In practice, this issue is most likely to arise in a case where a claimant has sufficient English for the health care professional to have thought that the claimant could cope without an interpreter, so some of the conversation may have been understood and there may be parts of the report that are not in dispute and are of assistance to the First-tier Tribunal even if other parts of the report are in dispute and are regarded as unreliable.

Evidence that is confidential to a third party but is relevant to proceedings before the First-tier Tribunal is not inadmissible unless excluded under r.15(2)(b): see *NSP v Stoke-on-Trent CC (HB)* [2020] UKUT 311 (AAC) at [74] to [78], where it was also pointed out that legitimate interests of the third party may require the First-tier Tribunal to make an order under r.14(1) of the 2008 Rules prohibiting publication or disclosure of the evidence.

Proof of the authorisation of surveillance required under the Regulation of Investigatory Powers Act 2000 was considered in *TD v SSWP (PIP)* [2020] UKUT 283 (AAC), where it was suggested that any challenge to the evidence requiring proof of authorisation ought generally to be raised in advance so that the necessary evidence could be produced either before or at the hearing and that, if the Secretary of State wished any part of the evidence to be withheld from the claimant, her representative should be ready to provide a redacted copy of the evidence so that the claimant at least could see that. Any issue over the extent of any redactions could be considered by the First-tier Tribunal under r.14 of the 2008 Rules.

It has recently been confirmed both that the First-tier Tribunal does have jurisdiction to consider arguments based on the doctrine of legitimate expectation, where they are relevant (*Fielder v Harrogate BC*

[2020] UKUT 288 (AAC)) and that it does not have jurisdiction to consider whether there has been a breach of the public sector equality duty in section 149 of the Equality Act 2010 (*TS (by TS) v SSWP (DLA)* [2020] UKUT 284 (AAC)).

In *KT and SH v SSWP (PIP)* [2020] UKUT 252 (AAC), the Upper Tribunal considered in detail the risks posed to claimants with significant hearing impediments who had to remove their hearing aids while showering or bathing and one of the reasons for doing so was to avoid different panels of the First-tier Tribunal from reaching different decisions in different cases on the issue in so far as it arose from factors external to the claimants (at [53(b)]). At [147], the judge said: "I have decided above that there should *not* be room for different First-tier Tribunal panels across the country to make different decisions as to risk based on factors external to claimants." (emphasis in the original). Nonetheless, her findings should presumably strictly be read as persuasive guidance rather than as being binding. Despite the guidance being contentious, counsel appear not to have referred the judge to *MN (Somalia) v Secretary of State for the Home Department* [2014] UKSC 30; [2014] 1 W.L.R. 2064 (mentioned, albeit with the wrong neutral citation number, on p.1561 of the main work), in which it was authoritatively stated that, while the Upper Tribunal is entitled to give persuasive guidance on matters other than matters of law, its decisions on such matters cannot be binding (see the judgment of Lord Carnwath, with whom the other Justices agreed, at [26] to [28]). Rules of precedent apply only to points of law.

In *Secretary of State for the Home Department v Suffolk CC* [2020] EWCA Civ 731; [2020] 3 W.L.R. 742, the Court of Appeal held that, because proceedings before the First-tier Tribunal (Immigration and Asylum Chamber) were adversarial, findings of that tribunal bound only the parties to proceedings before it and so did not bind other parties to proceedings in the family court although they could be taken into account, being accorded such weight as was appropriate having regard to "the precise assessment in which each court or tribunal is involved, the available relevant evidence and any particular rules (evidential or otherwise) that apply". The Court also said—

> "38. It is not even clear that the family court and the FtT (IAC) can be considered to be courts of coordinate jurisdiction. The point has not been fully argued before us and we do not purport to express a concluded view on the question; but, on the face of it, there are significant relevant differences. Whereas the family court is a court of record, the FtT (IAC) is not. The FtT has the features of a court but is quintessentially an independent judicial tribunal which is a specialist administrative law decision maker. The UT is a superior court of record that is able to bind itself and the FtT (IAC) but neither the Family Division of the High Court nor the family court can make a decision that has precedential effect in either the FtT (IAC) or the UT. And, as we have remarked, the FtT (IAC) is adversarial while, when exercising its powers under the [Female Genital Mutilation Act] 2003, the family court is essentially investigatory."

pp.1579-1596, *annotation to Tribunals, Courts and Enforcement Act 2007 s.11 (Right to appeal to Upper Tribunal)*

Although some doubt was expressed in *Panayioutou v Waltham Forest LBC* [2017] EWCA Civ 1624; [2018] Q.B. 1232 as to what was said in *Nipa Begum v Tower Hamlets LBC* [2000] 1 W.L.R. 306 (mentioned in the main work on pp. 1579-80) about the scope of an appeal "on a point of law" in housing cases, the approach in the latter case has been reaffirmed authoritatively by the Court of Appeal in *James v Hertsmere BC* [2020] EWCA Civ 489; [2020] 1 W.L.R. 3606.

4.119

In *SM v SSWP (II)* [2020] UKUT 287 (AAC), the First-tier Tribunal dismissed the claimant's appeal on the ground that she could not be suffering from carpal tunnel syndrome because her condition affected her ring finger and the median nerve, which passes through the carpal tunnel, does not, it said, serve the ring finger. On the claimant's further appeal to the Upper Tribunal, the Secretary of State conceded that the appeal should be allowed because the median nerve does in fact serve the ring finger. The Upper Tribunal considered on what ground it could be said that the First-tier Tribunal had erred in law. Having referred to *E v Secretary of State for the Home Department* [2004] EWCA Civ 49; [2004] Q.B. 1044 and *Ladd v Marshall* [1954] 1 W.L.R. 1489 (both mentioned on pp.1583-1584 of the main work), the judge observed that the *Ladd v Marshall* principles were concerned with the admissibility of evidence in adversarial proceedings, whereas there had been no mention of the median nerve in the evidence before the First-tier Tribunal and the error was entirely that of the First-tier Tribunal, acting inquisitorially with a medical practitioner among its members. He concluded that—

"45. . . . the *Ladd v Marshall* principles do not apply where, in the exercise of an inquisitorial jurisdiction and enabling role—and/or in reliance on the expertise or experience of a specialist member—a tribunal misdirects itself as to an uncontentious and primary fact on which there was no evidence before it.

46. Making such an error is simply one of a number of ways in which a tribunal might fail to exercise its inquisitorial jurisdiction and enabling role correctly. The Upper Tribunal is entitled to raise the issue, and either party to the appeal is entitled to seek to prove that the Tribunal has gone astray, by the same mechanisms—including the provision of relevant additional evidence—as would be the case with any other procedural lapse.

47. By basing its decision in this appeal on the mistaken premise that the Median nerve does not supply the ring finger, the First-tier Tribunal failed to exercise its enabling role correctly. On the contrary, it hindered the proper presentation of the claimant's case by setting up an obstacle of which she was unaware and which had no basis in fact. , , ,"

The same result could perhaps have been reached on the ground that the First-tier Tribunal's decision was perverse (see pp.1581-1582 of the main work).

In *TS (by TS) v SSWP (DLA)* [2020] UKUT 284 (AAC), the Upper Tribunal rejected an argument that *JA-K v SSWP (DLA)* [2017] UKUT 420 (AAC); [2018] 1 W.L.R. 2657 (mentioned on p.1585 of the main work) was wrongly decided and confirmed that "[n]either the First-tier Tribunal nor the Upper Tribunal (when considering a statutory appeal in a social security case) has jurisdiction to rule on whether there has been a breach of the public sector equality duty in section 149 of the Equality Act 2010" in the light of s.113 of that Act. However, in *In re A* [2020] EWCOP 38; [2020] 1 W.L.R. 4008, Hayden J held that, although the Court of Protection could not provide a remedy for a breach of the public sector equality duty, such a breach might nonetheless be relevant when it was considering the exercise of a discretion.

The Chamber President of the Administrative Appeals Chamber of the Upper Tribunal has again emphasised the reluctance of the Upper Tribunal to interfere with case-management decisions of the First-tier Tribunal unless they are clearly unreasonable or the First-tier Tribunal has clearly misdirected itself in law, both judicially (*Crossland v IC* [2020] UKUT 263 (AAC)) and in published guidance for appellants.

Upper Tribunal
(Administrative Appeals Chamber)

Applications for Permission to Appeal to the Upper Tribunal from interim decisions of the First-tier Tribunal

Guidance for Appellants

4.120
1. This guidance has been issued to explain to appellants (particularly litigants in person) the principles governing the determination of applications for permission to appeal to the Upper Tribunal (Administrative Appeals Chamber) from interim decisions of the First-tier Tribunal (FTT). The guidance applies with equal force to applications arising from proceedings in the equivalent devolved tribunals, i.e. the MHRT (Wales) and SENT(W).
2. Interim decisions are those taken by a tribunal during the course of proceedings before it determines (i.e. allows or dismisses) an appeal. They include (but are not limited to) case management decisions.
3. A relatively small number of applications for permission to appeal against interim decisions of the FTT consume a disproportionate amount of the Chamber's judicial, administrative and clerical resources, to the detriment of the many other cases awaiting decision in the Chamber across all its jurisdictions.
4. Parties have a statutory duty to help the FTT and Upper Tribunal to further the overriding objective and to co-operate with the Upper Tribunal generally (rule 2(4) of the Tribunal Procedure

(Upper Tribunal) Rules 2008). This obligation applies to case management rulings as much as to the tribunal's substantive decision. It includes being realistic about the conduct of litigation. As Lord Roskill observed in *Ashmore v Corporation of Lloyd's* [1992] 1 WLR 446 at 448H:

> " . . . it is the trial judge who has control of the proceedings. It is part of his duty to identify the crucial issues and to see they are tried as expeditiously and as inexpensively as possible. It is the duty of the advisers of the parties to assist the trial judge in carrying out his duty. Litigants are not entitled to the uncontrolled use of a trial judge's time. Other litigants await their turn. Litigants are only entitled to so much of the trial judge's time as is necessary for the proper determination of the relevant issues."

5. Appellants are reminded that the Upper Tribunal exercises an error of law jurisdiction under section 11 of the Tribunals, Courts and Enforcement Act 2007. As such, the Upper Tribunal will only grant permission to appeal if there is an arguable error of law on the part of the FTT (the standard categories of error of law are summarised by the Court of Appeal in *R (Iran) v Secretary of State for the Home Department* [2005] EWCA Civ 982 at paragraph [9] (available on Bailii: *https://www.bailii.org/*)) or there is some other good reason for doing so.

6. Although interim rulings are, in principle, subject to appeal to the Upper Tribunal, there is ample authority from the senior courts that appellate courts and tribunals, especially those whose jurisdiction is confined to errors of law, should not seek to 'micro-manage' cases on appeal. The senior courts have also repeatedly warned of the dangers of satellite litigation, which simply has the effect of deferring resolution of the substantive appeal and disrupting the proper case management of both the case in hand and other appeals.

7. Before starting an appeal in the Upper Tribunal against a case management decision, all appellants (whether or not legally represented) should keep in mind that tribunals have a broad discretion in their case management decisions and are best placed to decide how the case should be handled. It is no surprise that supposed errors of law often amount to no more than a difference of opinion over the way that the case is being handled. Indeed, it is usually only when a final decision has been made that it is possible to assess whether the alleged error of law was material to the outcome of the appeal (within the meaning of the test in R (Iran)). The limited circumstances in which permission to appeal is given against such decisions reflect their essential characteristics. That is why it is considered best practice for a tribunal to refuse permission to appeal and to continue with the proceedings rather than give permission or stay the proceedings pending a possible appeal.

8. In some jurisdictions, appellants may apply under the rules for an oral renewal of an application, if the Upper Tribunal has refused permission to appeal on the papers. However, the Upper Tribunal has power, where necessary and appropriate, to strike out applications as having no reasonable prospects of success and without any such hearing (rule 8(3)(c)).

9. Special considerations apply to rulings on recusal in respect of a judge who has been accused of actual or apparent bias. Although as a general rule challenges to interim decisions should be taken as part of an appeal against a final FTT decision, recusal is an important exception as bias should be raised at the earliest available opportunity. The test of apparent bias was set out in *Porter v Magill* [2002] AC 377, namely "whether the fair-minded and informed observer, having considered the facts, would conclude that there was a real possibility that the tribunal was biased." All too often, unparticularised allegations of bias prove on examination to be no more than a disagreement with the ruling the judge has made. It is important for appellants to set out as clearly as possible the way in which bias is said to arise. This will help them to state their case in accordance with the legal test and the Upper Tribunal to decide whether it has any substance. If it does not, the tribunal may refuse permission to appeal or strike out that part of the proceedings under rule 8.

DAME JUDITH FARBEY DBE
CHAMBER PRESIDENT
1 October 2020

The fact that a judge has recused herself does not necessarily undermine findings of fact made by that judge at an earlier stage of the proceedings: see *W (Children: Reopening/Recusal)* [2020] EWCA Civ 1685, where the judge had recused herself administratively because she had discovered that her son was an acquaintance of a party to the proceedings but had not been aware of that connection when she made her findings of fact. The Court also said that, once the judge had decided to withdraw from the case on the basis of recusal, she should have ensured that the parties were formally notified of her reason for withdrawing.

In *HMRC v SSE Generation Ltd* [2021] EWCA Civ 105, the Court of Appeal held the Upper Tribunal to have erred in law in allowing the respondent to argue a point upon which it had been unsuccessful before the First-tier Tribunal but in respect of which it had not obtained permission to appeal, even though the point had been raised in the response to the appeal. This decision is considered in more detail in the supplementary annotation to r.24 of the Tribunal Procedure (Upper Tribunal) Rules 2008, below. It takes a similar approach to that taken by the Upper Tribunal in *SSHD v Smith (appealable decisions; PTA requirements; anonymity)* [2019] UKUT 216 (IAC) (mentioned on p.1595 of the main work), save that, importantly, the Court of Appeal was not referred to r.7(2)(a) of the Tribunal Procedure (Upper Tribunal) Rules 2008 which enables the Upper Tribunal to waive the requirement under r.21(2) to apply to the First-tier Tribunal for permission to appeal before applying to the Upper Tribunal.

pp.1596-1602, *annotation to Tribunals, Courts and Enforcement Act 2007 s.12 (Proceedings on appeal to Upper Tribunal)*

In *TS (by TS) v SSWP (DLA)* [2020] UKUT 284 (AAC) at [171] to [184], it was pointed out that, when considering whether it is appropriate to disapply a provision of subordinate legislation in order to provide a remedy where the legislation, as amended, has been found to be incompatible with the European Convention on Human Rights, it can be important to consider not only whether it would be appropriate to disapply the provision of the amended legislation but also whether it would instead be appropriate to disapply the relevant provision of the amending instrument. 4.120.1

pp.1607-1609, *annotation to Tribunals, Courts and Enforcement Act 2007 s.13(3)-(5) (Right to appeal to Court of Appeal etc.)*

The fact that permission to appeal has been given by the Court of Appeal itself on a particular point is immaterial if it is a new point that the appellant ought not to be allowed to take on the appeal because taking it would be unfair (*Longfret (UK) Ltd v Revenue and Customs Commissioners* [2020] EWCA Civ 569; [2020] 1 W.L.R. 3809, following *Singh v Dass* [2019] EWCA Civ 360 and *Mullarkey v Broad* [2009] EWCA Civ 2). 4.121

In November 2020, the Government launched a six-week consultation on *Proposals for reforms to arrangements for obtaining permission to appeal from the Upper Tribunal to the Court of Appeal.*

p.1623, *annotation to Tribunals, Courts and Enforcement Act 2007 s.23 (Practice directions)*

A Practice Direction cannot override or amend Tribunal Procedure Rules but must, if possible, be interpreted so as to be valid and therefore in a way that is consistent with the Rules (*EB v Dorset Healthcare NHS Trust* [2020] UKUT 362 (AAC), a decision of a three-judge panel). 4.122

p.1638, *annotation to Tribunals, Courts and Enforcement Act 2007 s.29(1) to (3) (Costs or expenses)*

Where a refusal of the Upper Tribunal to give permission to appeal is successfully challenged by way of an application for judicial review and the case is remitted to the Upper Tribunal, the Administrative Court is unable simply to order that the costs of the application for judicial review be treated as costs in the remitted proceedings (and so determined in the light of the outcome of those proceedings) because the Upper Tribunal 4.123

has no jurisdiction to award costs of proceedings in the Administrative Court. However, this jurisdictional problem can be avoided by the Administrative Court transferring the judicial review proceedings to the Upper Tribunal, notwithstanding that the Upper Tribunal is formally the respondent in the proceedings, solely for the purpose of making an order for costs in the judicial review proceedings at the same time as enabling the Upper Tribunal to make an order for costs in the remitted proceedings (*JH (Palestinian Territories) v Secretary of State for the Home Department* [2020] EWCA Civ 919; [2021] 1 WLR 455).

p.1651, *amendment to Tribunals, Courts and Enforcement Act 2007 Sch.5, para.12(2)(b) and (d))*

4.123.1   With effect from April 22, 2014, s.17(5) of, and para.52 of Sch.9 to, the Crime and Courts Act 2013 substituted "the county court" for "a county court" in para.12(2)(b) and (d) of Sch.5 to the 2007 Act.

pp.1663-1668, *annotation to the First-tier Tribunal and Upper Tribunal (Composition of Tribunal) Order 2008 art.2 (Number of members of the First-tier Tribunal)*

4.124   The "Pilot Practice Directions" mentioned in the main work have been replaced by an Amended Pilot Practice Direction (see the note to pp.1874-1875, below).

In *MH v SSWP (II)* [2020] UKUT 297 (AAC), a district tribunal judge had directed that the panel hearing the claimant's appeal should be composed of a judge and two registered medical practitioners, the effect of para.7b of the Practice Statement set out on p.1664-1665 of the main work being that a second registered medical practitioner could be added to the one required by para.5e "where the complexity of the medical issues in the appeal so demands". One of the registered medical practitioners was unable to attend due to illness and the First-tier Tribunal, presided over by the same district judge, proceeded to determine the appeal in the absence of that member and the parties who had both not attended the hearing. On appeal, the Secretary of State conceded that the First-tier Tribunal had erred in proceeding in the absence of one of the members hearing the case without obtaining the consent of the parties as required by paragraph 15(6) of Sch.4 to the Tribunals, Courts and Enforcement Act 2007. However, the judge said—

"49. I prefer not to decide these appeals on that basis because I consider it arguable that, even though the district tribunal judge did not in fact issue another direction under the Practice Statement, he could be treated as having done so if there was no unfairness to the claimant and the reasoning process he would have gone through was precisely the same as the reasoning process he did go through. It would be wrong to issue such a direction merely to circumvent paragraph 15(6), but if, as appears to have been the case here, the district tribunal judge was satisfied, having consulted the registered medical practitioner who was present, that the expertise of a consultant neurologist was not in fact necessary for the proper determination of the appeals, it is difficult to see why there should have been unfairness to the claimant when a claimant has no right in the first place to insist on a second registered medical practitioner or a registered medical practitioner having particular expertise. . . . "

p.1675, *annotation to the Tribunal Procedure (First-tier Tribunal) (Social Entitlement Chamber) Rules 2008 r.1 (Citation, commencement, application and interpretation)*

In *NSP v Stoke-on-Trent CC (HB)* [2020] UKUT 311 (AAC), it was   **4.124.1**
held that, because a decision that there had been an overpayment of housing benefit involved a decision superseding or revising an award made to the claimant, the claimant was a "respondent" to an appeal by the landlord against a decision that the overpayment was recoverable from the landlord, since the question whether there had been an overpayment was necessarily before the First-tier Tribunal and, in most cases, also because an overpayment is recoverable from a claimant as well as, or instead of, the landlord. In that case, there was no evidence that there had been a separate decision terminating or varying the tenant's award. If there had been, that might have affected the analysis, because it is arguable that, as the legislation does not give a landlord a right to intervene in most appeals regarding a claimant's entitlement, he or she has no independent right to argue that there has not in fact been an overpayment if the tenant does not do so and all the local authority is obliged to do to prove the overpayment is to provide a copy of the decision issued to the claimant, but there would still be the point that, usually, an overpayment is recoverable from the claimant whether or not it is also recoverable from the landlord.

p.1678, *amendments to the Tribunal Procedure (First-tier Tribunal) (Social Entitlement Chamber) Rules 2008 r.4 (Delegation to staff)*

With effect from July 21, 2020, r.3(1) and (2) of the Tribunal Proce-   **4.125**
dure (Amendment) Rules 2020 (SI 2020/651) amended r.4(1) and revoked r.4(2). As amended, r.4(1) provides (with the amendments in square brackets)—

"**4.**—(1) Staff appointed under section 40(1) of the 2007 Act (tribunal staff and services) [or section 2(1) of the Courts Act 2003 (court officers, staff and services)] may, [if authorised by] the Senior President of Tribunals [under paragraph 3(3) of Schedule 5 to the 2007 Act], carry out functions of a judicial nature permitted or required to be done by the Tribunal.

These amendments were made in the light of the amendments made to para.3 of Sch.5 to the 2007 Act with effect from April 6, 2020 (see p.1648 of the main work).

p.1691, *annotation to the Tribunal Procedure (First-tier Tribunal) (Social Entitlement Chamber) Rules 2008 r.5A (Coronavirus temporary rule (decisions without a hearing)*

4.125.1   See the *Amended General Pilot Practice Direction: Contingency Arrangements in the First-Tier Tribunal and the Upper Tribunal* and the annotation thereto in the up-dating of pp.1871-1873, below.

pp.1710-1712, *annotation to the Tribunal Procedure (First-tier Tribunal) (Social Entitlement Chamber) Rules 2008 r.14 (Use of documents and information)*

4.125.2   In *TD v SSWP (PIP)* [2020] UKUT 283 (AAC), it was suggested that any challenge to surveillance evidence requiring proof of authorisation under the Regulation of Investigatory Powers Act 2000 ought generally to be raised in advance so that the necessary evidence of authorisation can be produced either before or at the hearing. In that case, the Secretary of State's representative had handed up at the hearing an unredacted copy of the authorisation, marked "For Judge only". It was suggested that, if the Secretary of State wished any part of the evidence to be withheld from the claimant, her representative should be ready to provide a redacted copy so that the claimant at least could see that, and it was held that any issue over the extent of any redactions should be determined by the whole tribunal. No reference was made to the relevant Practice Statement on the composition of tribunals (see pp.1664-1665 of the main work) but, although para.5 of that Practice Statement is made subject to para.10, the latter merely provides that a decision under r.14 "may" be made by a judge alone. It is clearly generally appropriate, as the Upper Tribunal held, for important case-management decisions made at a hearing that are likely to affect the panel's decision to be determined by the whole panel.

In *DVLA v IC (Rule 14 Order)* [2020] UKUT 310 (AAC), the Upper Tribunal held that, as in courts, documents and information which are disclosed in litigation are subject to an implied undertaking that they will not be used other than for the purposes of the litigation concerned. Accordingly, while a litigant can show them to a legal advisor, he or she cannot publish them on the Internet, even for the purpose of soliciting advice, without permission. In the circumstances of the particular case, the Upper Tribunal considered the principle of open justice (see pp.1543 to 1544 of the main work) but nonetheless made an order under the equivalent r.14 of the Tribunal Procedure (Upper Tribunal) Rules 2008, prohibiting the second respondent from publishing the electronic documents and bundles (including the skeleton arguments) provided in accordance with case management directions for the purposes of the proceedings.

pp.1713-1714, *annotation to the Tribunal Procedure (First-tier Tribunal) (Social Entitlement Chamber) Rules 2008 r.15 (Evidence and documents)*

4.125.3   If evidence is relevant, it is not inadmissible just because it is confidential to a third party, and so it can be excluded only under r.15(2)(b)

(*NSP v Stoke-on-Trent CC (HB)* [2020] UKUT 311 (AAC) at [74] to [78]).

p.1740-1751, *annotation to the Tribunal Procedure (First-tier Tribunal) (Social Entitlement Chamber) Rules 2008 r.27 (Decision with or without a hearing)*

See para.4 of the *Amended General Pilot Practice Direction: Contingency Arrangements in the First-Tier Tribunal and the Upper Tribunal* and the annotation thereto in the up-dating of pp.1871-1873, below.   4.126

In *DS v SSWP (ESA)* [2013] UKUT 572 (AAC), it was accepted that there had been a procedural irregularity in the proceedings before the First-tier Tribunal because the claimant's request that an interpreter be provided at his hearing was mislaid by the tribunal's administration and so not considered by a judge. However, it was held that no unfairness had resulted because the claimant had in fact been able to communicate effectively. In reaching that conclusion, the Upper Tribunal did not merely rely upon the First-tier Tribunal having recorded that the claimant had been "able to make himself understood as he attended the medical and the tribunal hearing and gave evidence by himself and had no problems in communicating" but, having made the point that "[o]ne must surely be alive to the possibility that a combination of not wishing to lose face and not wishing to challenge the tribunal's authority might create the impression of good communication skills" and that "[i]t is also possible that some nuances may have been lost", it also considered the detailed record of proceedings and statement of reasons, which enabled it to be satisfied both that the claimant's allegations that the tribunal had misunderstood him had not been made out and that the claimant had understood the questions put to him by the tribunal. In *BF v SSWP (PIP)* [2019] UKUT 420 (AAC) on the other hand, there was not that evidence of an ability to communicate well. The claimant had requested that there be an interpreter for a hearing and it is not clear from the Upper Tribunal's decision whether there had been. In the event, the claimant refused to go in to the hearing room, but there were nonetheless issues before the Upper Tribunal as to whether the health care professional's report was flawed because there had not been an interpreter and whether there had been adequate communication between the claimant and the clerk to the tribunal. The judge pointed out that the claimant had used an interpreter for an NHS consultation and said that "it was not for the First-tier Tribunal to substitute its own judgment of how fluent and confident the appellant was in English for the purposes of legal proceedings".

There is not necessarily a conflict between the decisions. It is material that the claimant's appeal was opposed in *DS*, but supported in *BF*, and, more importantly, that there was clear evidence as to the claimant's ability to communicate effectively in *DS*, but apparently not in *BF*. Both judges, were alert to the danger of too readily assuming from an ability to speak and understand some English that a claimant is sufficiently fluent to be able to participate properly in tribunal proceedings. In principle, a judge ought to be able to decide whether a person can, or did, have a fair hearing without an interpreter, but needs an evidential basis for deciding that.

In *Kirkham v IC (Record of Proceedings)* [2020] UKUT 336 (AAC), Mr Kirkham asked the First-tier Tribunal to provide both a transcript of a hearing and the judge's notes. He was eventually provided with a transcript, but the judge refused to provide a copy of her notes, relying on *R. (McIntyre) v Parole Board* [2013] EWHC 1969 (Admin), in which the Administrative Court drew a clear distinction between a record of proceedings and other notes made by a judge. The Upper Tribunal refused Mr Kirkham permission to appeal, rejecting arguments that *McIntyre* was wrongly decided or did not apply to tribunals.

p.1752, *annotation to the Tribunal Procedure (First-tier Tribunal) (Social Entitlement Chamber) Rules 2008 r.29 (Notice of hearings)*

4.126.1   As the terms of para.(1) make clear, the requirement to give 14 days' notice applies where the time of a hearing is changed, just as much as it applies to a change of date. In *MB v SSWP (PIP)* [2020] UKUT 296 (AAC), the claimant received a telephone message on her answer phone on the evening before her hearing, telling her that the time had been changed from 2 pm to 10 am. She had been intending to be accompanied to the hearing by her sister, but because of the late change of time her sister had been unable to change her work schedule. The claimant could nonetheless have waived the right to notice, but the Upper Tribunal said that "the FtT would have to take great care to ensure that a claimant, who may have felt they had little option but to attend, was giving genuine and informed consent" and was not satisfied that it had done so.

p.1757, *amendment to the Tribunal Procedure (First-tier Tribunal) (Social Entitlement Chamber) Rules 2008 r.30A (coronavirus temporary rule (recording of remote hearings))*

4.127   With effect from July 21, 2020, r.3(1) and (3) of the Tribunal Procedure (Amendment) Rules 2020 (SI 2020/651) amended r.30A by inserting after para.(3)—

> "(4) On the application of any person, any recording made pursuant to a direction under paragraph (1) is to be accessed with the consent of the Tribunal in such manner as the Tribunal may direct."

The inserted paragraph expires on the same day as the rest of r.30A (see r.1(2) of the amending Rules), which does not appear entirely desirable unless a saving can be read into it.

pp.1758-1760, *annotation to the Tribunal Procedure (First-tier Tribunal) (Social Entitlement Chamber) Rules 2008 r.31 (Hearings in a party's absence)*

4.127.1   It may be a relevant consideration when deciding whether to proceed in a claimant's absence that a health care professional has failed to ask relevant questions so that the First-tier Tribunal needs to do so—see *MH v SSWP (II)* [2020] UKUT 297 (AAC) at [55]. In that case, the First-tier Tribunal gave as one reason for proceeding in the claimant's absence that "this was an appeal where the Tribunal has specifically directed that it should proceed by way of an oral hearing where the claimant might attend for the purposes of being examined and in order that the Tribunal might obtain a detailed medical and work history" but the Upper Tribunal could find no indication that the claimant had been told that that was why an oral hearing had been directed.

In *GL v Elysium Healthcare Hospital* [2020] UKUT 308 (AAC), the patient was self-isolating during the Covid–19 pandemic, within a flat that he shared with another patient. He was allowed to participate in the hearing before the First-tier Tribunal by telephone but he declined to do so because he was anxious about being overheard by his flatmate. The First-tier Tribunal refused an application for an adjournment and decided to proceed in his absence on the ground that "in the current difficult climate the hearing was fair and the patient had been given the opportunity to participate and it was largely due to his anxiety that he was unable to do so." The Upper Tribunal allowed the patient's appeal because the First-tier Tribunal had not adequately considered either whether his fear about being overheard was reasonable or whether his anxiety was genuine. It had also erred because it had approached the question of an adjournment on the basis that the patient's concern was the mode of hearing, rather than the possibility of being overheard. That the hearing was by telephone was merely part of the context.

pp.1778-1781, *annotation to the Tribunal Procedure (First-tier Tribunal) (Social Entitlement Chamber) Rules 2008 r.37 (Setting aside a decision which disposes of proceedings)*

Even where a tribunal has proceeded in the absence of a party after 4.127.2 a judge has refused an application for postponement or adjournment, it is permissible to set the decision aside under r.37. In *Family Channel Ltd v Fatima* [2020] EWCA Civ 824; [2020] 1 W.L.R. 5104, decided under the equivalent provision in C.P.R. r.39.3(3), it was held that that provision justified "a less draconian approach" than was required on an application for an adjournment so that it did not matter that the medical evidence on the setting-aside application was much the same as it had been on the application for adjournment. However, it is arguable that both the C.P.R. provision and r.37 merely require that the issue of fairness be reconsidered afresh on a setting-aside application, with the benefit of hindsight and perhaps a better appreciation of all the circumstances. Either approach supports the point made in *KO v SSWP (ESA)* [2013] UKUT 544 (AAC) that a decision to proceed in the absence of a party needs to be kept under review throughout the hearing (see the annotation to r.27 on p.1760 of the main work).

pp.1783-1784, *annotation to the Tribunal Procedure (First-tier Tribunal) (Social Entitlement Chamber) Rules 2008 r.38(7) (Application for permission to appeal)*

4.127.3   Notwithstanding what had apparently happened in *SB v SSWP (PIP)* [2020] UKUT 198 (AAC) (mentioned on p.1784 of the main work), in *HMRC v AD (CHB)* [2020] UKUT 353 (AAC) the Upper Tribunal was prepared to presume that HMRC's application to the First-tier Tribunal for permission to appeal had been considered by a judge—perhaps, due to the Covid–19 pandemic, he did not have access to the First-tier Tribunal's file to check whether that was so—but he said that a copy of the judge's determination should have been sent to the parties.

p.1796, *amendments to the Tribunal Procedure (Upper Tribunal) Rules 2008 r.1(3) (Citation, commencement, application and interpretation)*

4.128   With effect from July 21, 2020, r.5(1) and (2) of the Tribunal Proce- dure (Amendment) Rules 2020 (SI 2020/651) omitted the definition of "fast-track case" and amended the definition of "immigration case". The definition of "immigration case" was further amended with effect from 11.00pm on December 31, 2020 by the Immigration and Social Security Co-ordination (EU Withdrawal) Act 2020 (Consequential, Saving, Transitional and Transitory Provisions) (EU Exit) Regulations 2020 (SI 2020/1309). The amendments do not have any relevance to social security cases and so they are not set out here.

p.1802, *amendments to the Tribunal Procedure (Upper Tribunal) Rules 2008 r.4 (Delegation to staff)*

4.129   With effect from July 21, 2020, r.5(1) and (3) of the Tribunal Proce- dure (Amendment) Rules 2020 (SI 2020/651) amended r.4(1) and omitted r.4(2). As amended, r.4(1) provides (with the amendments in square brackets)—

"**4.**—(1) Staff appointed under section 40(1) of the 2007 Act (tribunal staff and services) [or section 2(1) of the Courts Act 2003 (court officers, staff and services)] may, [if authorised by] the Senior Presi- dent of Tribunals [under paragraph 3(3) of Schedule 5 to the 2007 Act], carry out functions of a judicial nature permitted or required to be done by the Tribunal.

These amendments are made in the light of the amendments made to para.3 of Sch.5 to the 2007 Act with effect from April 6, 2020 (see p.1648 of the main work).

p.1803, *amendment to the Tribunal Procedure (Upper Tribunal) Rules 2008 r.5 (Case management powers)*

4.130   With effect from July 21, 2020, r.5(1) and (4) of the Tribunal Proce- dure (Amendment) Rules 2020 (SI 2020/651) revoked r.5(4).

pp.1810-1811, *annotation to Tribunal Procedure (Upper Tribunal) Rules 2008 r.8 (Striking out a party's case)*

In *SSWP v LK (RP)* [2019] UKUT 421 (AAC) at [53] to [60], the Upper Tribunal accepted that r.8(3)(c) did not confer a power to strike out a reference under r.26 on the ground that it had no reasonable prospect of success.   4.131

Applications for permission to appeal and for permission to apply for judicial review were struck out without oral hearings in *Crossland v IC* [2020] UKUT 263 (AAC) and *Crossland v IC* [2020] UKUT 264 (AAC), the former being a decision of the Chamber President of the Administrative Appeals Chamber of the Upper Tribunal. In both cases, the Applicant was seeking permission to appeal against case-management decisions of the First-tier Tribunal and the judges emphasised the limited circumstances in which the Upper Tribunal would interfere with interlocutory decisions of the First-tier Tribunal and considered that the applications for permission to appeal had no merit.

pp.1814-1816, *annotation to the Tribunal Procedure (Upper Tribunal) Rules 2008 r.10 (Orders for costs)*

See the supplementary annotation to s.29 of the Tribunals, Courts and Enforcement Act 2007, above.   4.131.1

p.1822, *annotation to the Tribunal Procedure (Upper Tribunal) Rules 2008 r.14 (Use of documents and information)*

See the supplementary annotation to r.14 of the Tribunal Procedure (First-tier Tribunal) (Social Entitlement Chamber) Rules 2008, above.   4.131.2

p.1829, *amendment to the Tribunal Procedure (Upper Tribunal) Rules 2008 r.21 (Application to the Upper Tribunal for permission to appeal)*

With effect from July 21, 2020, r.5(1) and (6) of the Tribunal Procedure (Amendment) Rules 2020 (SI 2020/651) substituted r.21(3)(aa). That sub-paragraph does not have any relevance to social security cases and so the new version is not set out here.   4.132

p.1834, *annotation to the Tribunal Procedure (Upper Tribunal) Rules 2008 r.22((3) to (5) (Decision in relation to permission to appeal)*

See the supplementary annotation to r.8, above.   4.133

p.1837, *amendments to the Tribunal Procedure (Upper Tribunal) Rules 2008 r.24 (Response to the notice of appeal)*

With effect from July 21, 2020, r.5(1) and (8) of the Tribunal Procedure (Amendment) Rules 2020 (SI 2020/651) omitted r.24(2)(aa) and inserted "or" at the end of r.24(2)(ab).   4.134

pp.1838-1839, *annotation to the Tribunal Procedure (Upper Tribunal) Rules 2008 r.24 (Response to the notice of appeal)*

4.134.1   In *HMRC v SSE Generation Ltd* [2021] EWCA Civ 105, the Court of Appeal held the Upper Tribunal to have erred in law in allowing the respondent to argue a point upon which it had been unsuccessful before the First-tier Tribunal but in respect of which it had not obtained permission to appeal although it had raised it in the response to the appeal and the Upper Tribunal had been satisfied that there was no unfairness to HMRC.

There are two important elements in the Court of Appeal's reasoning. First, it accepted a concession by leading counsel for the respondent as to the Upper Tribunal's power to give permission to appeal. Secondly, it took a narrow approach to r.24(3)(e), upon which the respondent had relied and which requires a response to state "the grounds on which the respondent relies, including (in the case of an appeal against the decision of another tribunal)any grounds on which the respondent was unsuccessful in the proceedings which are the subject of the appeal, but intends to rely in the appeal". Rose LJ (with whom David Richards and Popplewell LJJ agreed) said at [77]—

> "SSE did not seek permission to appeal from the FTT and Mr Peacock accepts that they could not have sought permission from the Upper Tribunal without first having made an unsuccessful application to the FTT.I agree with HMRC's submission that rule 24(3)(f) [sic] cannot obviate the need for permission set out in section 11 TCEA. The grounds referred to there are the grounds on which the party relies in its character as a respondent to appeal. Certainly if the respondent succeeded on an issue before the FTT because the FTT accepted one of a number of arguments while rejecting other arguments for the same result, the respondent can raise those unsuccessful arguments if its success is challenged on appeal by the opposing party. But the respondent cannot raise an issue which it lost before the FTT unless it obtains permission to appeal for itself."

The respondent's concession that the Upper Tribunal could not have given permission to appeal because there had been no application to the First-tier Tribunal was based on r.21(2), but it overlooks the Upper Tribunal's power to waive the requirement imposed by r.21(2) under r.7(2)(a). The respondent had instead submitted that HMRC's concern that a broad interpretation of r.24(3)(e) would entitle a respondent to re-run every issue on which it lost before the FTT without the filter of the permission stage could be met through the Upper Tribunal's case management powers under r.5, as applied in accordance with the overriding objective in r.2.

The court acknowledged the practical difficulties facing respondents —although it may only have had in mind legally-represented parties in tax cases and not also unrepresented parties in social security cases—and noted that C.P.R. r.52.13 allows a respondent to an appeal in the courts to seek permission to appeal within a response to an appeal. It also referred to the "venerable principle" that the task of the First-tier Tribunal and the Upper Tribunal is to arrive at the collection of the correct amount of tax (see *Investec Asset Finance plc v HMRC* [2020] EWCA Civ 579 at [60] and [100]). However, in the light of the respondent's concession that the Upper Tribunal could not give permission to appeal, it considered itself driven, as a matter of statutory construction, to the conclusion it reached.

In the absence of the concession, it might perhaps have reached a different decision, given the Upper Tribunal's clear finding that there was no unfairness to HMRC in allowing the respondent's argument to be advanced before it. It is noteworthy that, in *SSHD v Smith (appealable decisions; PTA requirements; anonymity : Belgium)* [2019] UKUT 216 (IAC), where the Upper Tribunal reached a similar conclusion to the Court of Appeal's, the Upper Tribunal expressly referred to the possibility of waiver under r.7(2) although, in the immigration and asylum context, it did not envisage the Upper Tribunal being sympathetic where a person "could and should" have applied to the First-tier Tribunal. Rule 7(2)(a) would enable the Upper Tribunal to achieve the same effect as can be achieved by an appellate court under C.P.R. r.52.13 and it presumably remains open to the Upper Tribunal to rely on that provision on the basis that the Court of Appeal's decision was reached without its attention having been drawn to it. In the light of the Court's decision, it may be necessary for it expressly to do so, unless and until the 2008 Rules are amended.

p.1839, *amendment to the Tribunal Procedure (Upper Tribunal) Rules 2008 r.25 (Appellant's reply)*

With effect from July 21, 2020, r.5(1) and (9) of the Tribunal Procedure (Amendment) Rules 2020 (SI 2020/651) substituted r.25(2A). That paragraph does not have any relevance to social security cases and so the new version is not set out here.   4.135

p.1840, *annotation to the Tribunal Procedure (Upper Tribunal) Rules 2008 r.26 (References under the Forfeiture Act 1982)*

As to the duty to make a reference under this rule, see *SSWP v LK (RP)* [2019] UKUT 421 (AAC) discussed in the annotation to s.4 of the Forfeiture Act 1982 above.   4.136

p.1852, *amendments to the Tribunal Procedure (Upper Tribunal) Rules 2008 r.36 (Notice of hearings)*

With effect from July 21, 2020, r.5(1) and (10) of the Tribunal Procedure (Amendment) Rules 2020 (SI 2020/651) amended r.36(2) by inserting "and" at the end of sub-para.(a) and omitting sub-para.(aa) and the words "in any case other than a fast-track case" in sub-para.(b).   4.137

p.1855, *amendment to the Tribunal Procedure (Upper Tribunal) Rules 2008 r.37A (coronavirus temporary rule (recording of remote hearings))*

4.138   With effect from July 21, 2020, r.5(1) and (11) of the Tribunal Procedure (Amendment) Rules 2020 (SI 2020/651) amended r.37A by inserting after para.(3)—

"(4) On the application of any person, any recording made pursuant to a direction under paragraph (1) is to be accessed with the consent of the Tribunal in such manner as the Tribunal may direct."

The inserted paragraph expires on the same day as the rest of r.37A (see r.1(2) of the amending Rules), which does not appear entirely desirable unless a saving can be read into it.

pp.1871-1873, *replacement of Pilot Practice Direction: Covid–19: Contingency Arrangements in the First-tier Tribunal and the Upper Tribunal*

4.139   This Practice Direction expired on 18 September 2020 and has effectively been replaced by a new Practice Direction.

Amended General Pilot Practice Direction:

Contingency Arrangements in the First-tier Tribunal and the Upper Tribunal

Background

1. On 19 March 2020, Sir Ernest Ryder, Senior President of Tribunals, issued a Pilot Practice Direction setting out how the First-tier Tribunal and Upper Tribunal might adjust their ways of working during the Covid–19 pandemic, to limit the spread of the virus and manage their workloads appropriately. Paragraphs 10 and 11 of that Practice Direction were amended on 23 June 2020. The Practice Direction, as amended, is due to expire on 18 September 2020.

2. Having reviewed the Practice Direction, I have decided to extend it to 18 March 2021, amend paragraph 5 and 10, remove the previous paragraph 11 and add a new paragraph 7A. For ease of reference, the full text of the Practice Direction as now amended, is set out below. The Practice Direction may be reviewed again prior to its expiry should it become inappropriate or unnecessary, and may be revoked at any time. The Lord Chancellor has approved the amendments in accordance with s23 Tribunals, Courts and Enforcement Act 2007.

Scope

3. This Practice Direction applies to all appeals and applications in the First-tier Tribunal and the Upper Tribunal, save for paragraph 10, which applies solely to the First-tier Tribunal Property Chamber.

Decisions on the papers without a hearing

4. Where a Chamber's procedure rules allow decisions to be made without a hearing, decisions should usually be made in this way, provided this is in accordance with the overriding objective, the parties' ECHR rights and the Chamber's procedure rules about notice and consent.

Triage

5. In many tribunal jurisdictions, a hearing is required unless a temporary rule inserted into their procedure rules by the Tribunal Procedure (Coronavirus) (Amendment) Rules 2020 applies, or the parties consent to a determination on the papers. To deal more efficiently with cases in which a hearing would otherwise be required and a successful outcome for the applicant or appellant is highly likely, Chamber Presidents may decide to follow the following scheme to 'triage' appeals and applications for some or all of their jurisdictions where paper determinations are possible with the parties' consent:

(a) Where the parties have not already consented to a determination without a hearing, the tribunal may assess a case on the papers.

(b) If the tribunal considers it could decide the matter without a hearing, it will provide a provisional decision to the parties.

(c) The parties will then be asked whether they consent to the tribunal making a binding decision on the papers that is in the same terms as the provisional decision.

(d) If one or both of the parties confirm that they require a hearing, a hearing will be listed (which may be conducted remotely).

(e) If the parties consent to a paper determination (or do not object, if there is a provision in the Chamber's rules that allows for non-objection), the tribunal will issue a final decision in the same form as the provisional decision, unless:

(i) it considers that it made an error in relation to the provisional decision; or

(ii) the circumstances have materially changed since the provisional decision was made.

(f) If paragraph 5.(e)(i) or (ii) above applies, the tribunal shall either provide the parties with a revised provisional decision and follow paragraph 5.(c) onwards in respect of the new provisional decision, or list a hearing. In either case, the tribunal will explain to the parties why it decided not to issue the first provisional decision.

Hearings

Paragraphs 6-9 apply where a tribunal decides in a particular case that a hearing is necessary.

465

Remote hearings

6. Where it is reasonably practicable and in accordance with the overriding objective to hear the case remotely (that is in any way that is not face-to-face, but which complies with the definition of 'hearing' in the relevant Chamber's procedure rules), it should be heard remotely.

7. For the avoidance of doubt, where a tribunal decides that a hearing will take place remotely, references in the Chamber's procedure rules to a 'hearing' will apply to that remote hearing and references in the Chamber's procedure rules to a party's entitlement to attend a hearing shall be such participation as may be directed.

Hybrid Hearings

17A. Where a tribunal decides to conduct a 'hybrid' hearing (i.e. a hearing where there are participants attending the hearing in a physical courtroom and participants attending the same hearing remotely), the places from which participants attend the hearing shall, for the duration of the hearing, be deemed an extension of the courtroom.

Hearings in a party's absence

8. Where a party fails to attend a hearing without an application made in advance to adjourn or postpone the hearing, and the relevant Chamber's procedure rules allow the tribunal to continue with the proceedings in the party's absence, the hearing may proceed on that basis provided this is in accordance with the overriding objective.

9. Where a party fails to attend a hearing without an application made in advance to adjourn or postpone it, a request by that party to set aside a decision made in their absence will not usually be granted if the decision fully upholds or allows their appeal or application.

Inspections

10.—*Omitted.*

General

11. Insofar as compatible with the efficient administration of justice, the tribunals will take into account the impact of the Covid–19 pandemic when considering applications for the extension of time for compliance with directions and the postponement of hearings.

The Rt. Hon. Sir Keith Lindblom
Vice President of Tribunals and Acting Senior President of Tribunals
14 September 2020

It was recorded in *R. (Joint Council for the Welfare of Immigrants) v President of the Upper Tribunal (Immigration and Asylum Chamber)* [2020] EWHC 3103 (Admin) at [3.7] that an earlier challenge to para.4 of the predecessor Practice Direction had failed because the proviso draws attention to the proper considerations to be taken into account in deciding whether to decide a case without a hearing. However, in the *JCWI* case itself, it was held that the Chamber President had given unlawful guidance to judges in his Chamber in a Practice Guidance Note because it had effectively stated, without any such proviso, that cases should normally be decided without a hearing.

pp.1874-1875, *replacement of Pilot Practice Direction: Covid–19: Panel Composition in the First-tier Tribunal and the Upper Tribunal*

This Practice Direction, and the supplementary Practice Direction dated 26 March 2020, expired in September 2020 and have effectively been replaced by a new Practice Direction. 4.140

Amended Pilot Practice Direction:

Panel Composition in the First-tier Tribunal and the Upper Tribunal

Background

1. The Senior President of Tribunals is responsible for determining panel composition by virtue of an order made by the Lord Chancellor under section 145(1) of, and paragraph 15 of Schedule 4 of, the Tribunals, Courts and Enforcement Act 2007.
2. On 19 March 2020, Sir Ernest Ryder, Senior President of Tribunals, issued a Pilot Practice Direction setting out how the First-tier Tribunal and Upper Tribunal might adjust their ways of working in relation to panel composition during the Covid–19 pandemic, to limit the spread of the virus and manage their workloads appropriately.
3. Having reviewed that Practice Direction, I have decided to extend it to 18 March 2021, amend paragraph 6, incorporate into it an amendment to paragraph 7 that was previously effected by a separate Practice Direction, and add a new paragraph 9. For ease of reference, the full text of the Practice Direction as now amended, is set out below. The Practice Direction may be reviewed again prior to its expiry should it become inappropriate or unnecessary, and may be revoked at any time. The Lord Chancellor has approved the amendments in accordance with s23 Tribunals, Courts and Enforcement Act 2007.

Scope

4. This Practice Direction applies to all appeals and applications within the First-tier and Upper Tribunal, except in mental health

cases as defined in rule 1(3) of the Tribunal Procedure (First-tier Tribunal) (Health, Education and Social Care Chamber) Rules 2008, and save that paragraph 9 applies only to the War Pensions and Armed Forces Compensation Chamber.

Number of members who will decide cases

5. The Composition Statements previously issued in respect of each of the Chambers of the First-tier Tribunal and Upper Tribunal (including such pilot composition statements as already exist) will remain in force, and composition will ordinarily be determined in accordance with those statements ('the Standard Composition Arrangements').

6. However, while this Pilot Practice Direction remains in force, the following provisions will also apply to all decisions (whether on preliminary issues, or those that determine proceedings):
   a. If a salaried judge considers that a case could not proceed, or would be subject to unacceptable delay, if the Standard Composition Arrangements were applied, that judge may decide that the case shall be heard by a judge alone, or by panel consisting of fewer or different members
   b. When making a decision under paragraph 6.a., salaried judges must have regard to the urgency within which a case needs to be determined and the need to ensure the case is dealt with in accordance with the overriding objective.
   c. Where a salaried judge decides to alter the composition requirements in accordance with paragraph 6.a., that salaried judge may determine which members will deal with the case, and can select salaried or fee paid members.

7. For the purposes of paragraph 6 above, a 'salaried judge' is:
   a. A salaried, or former salaried, judge of the relevant Chamber; or
   b. A salaried, or former salaried, judge assigned to the relevant Chamber; or,
   c. A salaried surveyor member of Upper Tribunal Lands Chamber.

Involvement of Non-Legal Members not on a panel

8. If the composition arrangements for a case are altered from what they would have been under the Standard Composition Arrangements, the tribunal may seek the advice of one or more non-legal members to assist with its decision-making, provided the advice is recorded and disclosed to the parties.

War Pensions and Armed Forces Compensation Chamber

9. While this Practice Direction remains in force, the Standard Composition Arrangements for the War Pensions and Armed Forces Compensation Chamber will be amended so that a case which is decided without a hearing pursuant to rule 5A or rule 25 of The Tribunal Procedure (First-tier Tribunal) (War Pensions

and Armed Forces Compensation Chamber) Rules 2008 may be determined by a panel consisting of a judge and either one or two members.

The Rt. Hon. Sir Keith Lindblom
Vice President of Tribunals and Acting Senior President of Tribunals
14 September 2020

pp.1879-1883, *amendments to the Social Security (Scotland) Act 2018—Contents*

Sections 28, 81 and 82 and Sch.2 were omitted from Volume I of the main work and are in Part I of this Supplement instead. 4.141

Sections 10 and 35 been brought into force but are omitted from this work.

Sections 30, 31, 36, 79 and 80 and Schs. 4, 5 and 10 have been brought into force and are in Part I of this Supplement.

Sections 68 and 98 have been repealed or revoked (see the supplementary annotations to those sections, below).

Sections 75 and 76 have been renumbered as sections 84A and 84B, but remain omitted from this work. The title of Chapter 6 of Part 2 has accordingly been shortened to "OFFENCES"

Sections 80A and 87A have been inserted but are omitted from this work.

Sections 85A and 85B have also been inserted and are in the supplementary annotation to p.1902, below.

p.1884, *coming into force of Social Security (Scotland) Act 2018 s.10*

Section 10 has been brought into force but is omitted from this work. 4.142

p.1886, *coming into force of Social Security (Scotland) Act 2018 ss.28, 30, 31, 35 and 36*

Sections 28, 30, 31 and 36 have been brought into force and are in Part I of this Supplement. Section 35 has also been brought into force but is omitted from this work. 4.143

p.1889, *annotation to Social Security (Scotland) Act 2018 s.41 (Right to request re-determination)*

The period prescribed under reg.9(1) of the Winter Heating Assistance for Children and Young People (Scotland) Regulations 2020 (see Part I of this Supplement) is 42 days. 4.144

Note that the Carer's Assistance (Young Carer Grants) (Scotland) Regulations 2019 were omitted from Volume 1 of the main work and are in Part I of this Supplement instead.

p.1890, *annotation to Social Security (Scotland) Act 2018 s.43 (Duty to re-determine)*

4.145   The period prescribed under reg.9(1) of the Winter Heating Assistance for Children and Young People (Scotland) Regulations 2020 (see Part I of this Supplement) is also 16 days.

Note that the Carer's Assistance (Young Carer Grants) (Scotland) Regulations 2019 were omitted from Volume 1 of the main work and are in Part I of this Supplement instead.

p.1894, *annotation to Social Security (Scotland) Act 2018 s.52 (Determination without application)*

4.146   See also reg.5 of the Winter Heating Assistance for Children and Young People (Scotland) Regulations 2020 (see Part I of this Supplement) is also 16 days.

Note that the Carer's Assistance (Young Carer Grants) (Scotland) Regulations 2019 were omitted from Volume 1 of the main work and are in Part I of this Supplement instead.

p.1901, *repeal of Social Security (Scotland) Act 2018 s.68 (First-tier Tribunal's jurisdiction)*

4.147   With effect from November 11, 2020, s.14 of the Social Security Administration and Tribunal Membership (Scotland) Act 2020 repealed s.68 of the 2018 Act and inserted s.87A in its place. The new section is to broadly similar effect but is omitted from this work as no regulations have yet been made under it.

p.1902, *various amendments etc. to the Social Security (Scotland) Act 2018*

4.148   Sections 79 and 80 came into force on May 1, 2020 and are in Part I of this Supplement.

In relation to ss. 81 and 82, the reference in the main work to Volume II should have been to Volume I but the provisions were omitted from that volume and are in Part I of this Supplement instead.

With effect from November 11, 2020, s.5 of the Social Security Administration and Tribunal Membership (Scotland) Act 2020 amended the title of Chapter 6 of Pt.2 of the 2018 Act. It is now simply "OFFENCES". That is because s.5 of the 2020 Act also moved ss. 75 and 76 to Pt.4 and renumbered them as ss. 84A and 84B. With effect from the same date, ss. 4 and 14 of the 2020 Act inserted, respectively, ss. 80A and 87A into the 2018 Act. Those provisions are omitted from this work.

Also with effect from November 11, 2020, s.1 of the 2020 Act inserted s.85A into the 2018 Act. With effect from December 23, 2020, s.2(4) of the 2020 Act inserted s.85B into the 2018 Act. Sections 85A and 85B provide—

"Appointees

Appointment of person to act on behalf of child

85A.—(1) The Scottish Ministers may appoint a person (an "appointee") to act on behalf of a child in connection with the determination of the child's entitlement to assistance under section 24 or regulations under section 79.

(2) An appointment under subsection (1) may, if the Scottish Ministers consider it appropriate, include an appointment of the person to receive such assistance on the child's behalf.

(3) The Scottish Ministers may only appoint an appointee if it appears to them that there is no person who—

(a) has authority to act on behalf of the child,

(b) resides with, and has care of, the child, and

(c) is willing, and practicably able, to act on the child's behalf in relation to the matter mentioned in subsection (1).

(4) An individual who is under 16 years may not be appointed as an appointee.

(5) Where an appointee is appointed under subsection (1) to act on behalf of a child—

(a) the appointee can do anything that a person with authority (however arising) to act on behalf of the child in relation to the determination of the child's entitlement to assistance could do in connection with the determination of the child's entitlement to assistance (including making an application for assistance),

(b) the Scottish Ministers may request that the appointee provide them with information that the Ministers may otherwise request under section 54 or (as the case may be) the regulations under section 79 (and in the case of section 54, subsections (2) and (3) of that section apply to that request as they apply to a request made to the child),

(c) any information that would be given to the child under or by virtue of Part 2 or (as the case may be) the regulations, must be given to the appointee instead.

(6) The Scottish Ministers may terminate an appointment under subsection (1) at any time.

(7) In this section, "child" means an individual who is under 16 years.".

Appointment of person to act in other circumstances

85B.—(1) The Scottish Ministers may appoint a person (an "appointee") to act on behalf of an individual in connection with the determination of the individual's entitlement to assistance under section 24 or regulations under section 79.

(2) An appointment under subsection (1) may, if the Scottish Ministers consider it appropriate, include an appointment of the person to receive such assistance on the individual's behalf.

(3) The Scottish Ministers may only appoint an appointee if—

(a) the individual is 16 years or over and the conditions in subsection (4) are met, or

(b) it appears to them that subsection (6) or (7) applies.

(4) The conditions are—

(a) the individual indicates (in such form as the Scottish Ministers require) that the individual agrees to the appointment, and

(b) an appropriate person certifies (in such form as the Scottish Ministers require) that in the person's opinion—

    (i) the individual is not incapable within the meaning of the Adults with Incapacity (Scotland) Act 2000,

    (ii) the individual understands the effect of the appointment,

    (iii) the individual has not been subject to any undue influence in agreeing to the appointment, and

    (iv) the person proposed to be appointed is suitable to act as the individual's appointee.

(5) The Scottish Ministers are to make regulations defining "appropriate person" for the purposes of subsection (4)(b).

(6) This subsection applies if—

(a) the individual is deceased, and

(b) there is no executor appointed on the individual's estate.

(7) This subsection applies if, in relation to the matter mentioned in subsection (1)—

(a) the individual is incapable within the meaning of the Adults with Incapacity (Scotland) Act 2000,

(b) there is no guardian acting or appointed under that Act,

(c) the individual's estate is not being administered by a judicial factor, and

(d) there is no other person who has authority to act on behalf of the individual and is willing to do so.

(8) An individual who is under 16 years may not be appointed as an appointee.

(9) Where an appointee is appointed under subsection (1) to act on behalf of an individual—

(a) the appointee can do anything that a relevant individual could do in connection with the determination of the individual's entitlement to assistance (including making an application for assistance),

(b) the Scottish Ministers may request that the appointee provide them with information that the Ministers may otherwise request under section 54 or (as the case may be) the regulations under section 79 (and in the case of section 54, subsections (2) and (3) of that section apply to that request as they apply to a request made to the individual),

(c) any information that would be given to the individual under or by virtue of Part 2 or (as the case may be) the regulations, must be given to the appointee instead.

(10) In subsection (9)(a), "relevant individual" means—

(a) in the case of an appointment by virtue of subsection (3)(a), the individual in relation to whom the appointment is made,

(b) in the case of an appointment by virtue of subsection (6), an executor appointed on the individual's estate,

(c) in the case of an appointment by virtue of subsection (7), a person with authority (however arising) to act on behalf of the individual in relation to the determination of the individual's entitlement to assistance.

(11) The Scottish Ministers may terminate an appointment under subsection (1) at any time.

(12) The Scottish Ministers must—

(a) terminate an appointment made by virtue of subsection (3)(a) if the individual withdraws agreement to it,

(b) consider whether to terminate an appointment made by virtue of subsection (3)(a) if requested to do so by anyone who appears to the Ministers to have an interest in the welfare or financial affairs of the individual.

(13) The Scottish Ministers must consider whether to terminate an appointment made by virtue of subsection (6) if requested to do so by anyone who appears to the Ministers to have an interest in the financial affairs of the individual.

(14) The Scottish Ministers must consider whether to make an appointment by virtue of subsection (7), or to terminate such an appointment, if requested to do so by—

(a) the individual, or

(b) anyone else who appears to the Ministers to—

    (i) have authority to act on behalf of the individual, or

    (ii) have an interest in the welfare or financial affairs of the individual.

(15) Subsection (16) applies where the Scottish Ministers are deciding whether to make an appointment by virtue of subsection (7) or to terminate such an appointment.

(16) In making the decision, the Scottish Ministers must, insofar as practicable, have regard to—

(a) the wishes and feelings of the individual, and

(b) the views of anyone else who appears to the Ministers to have an interest in the welfare or financial affairs of the individual."

Note that s.85B has been brought into force only in so far as is necessary to allow appointments to be made by the Scottish Ministers in connection with the determination of an individual's entitlement to assistance under regulations made under s.79 in circumstances where the condition in s.85B(3)(b) is met (Social Security Administration and Tribunal Membership (Scotland) Act 2020 (Commencement No.1) Regulations 2020 (SSI 2020/422) reg.3).

p.1903, *amendment to Social Security (Scotland) Act 2018 s.96 (Regulation—making powers)*

With effect from November 11, 2020, s.5(1) and (8) of the Social Security Administration and Tribunal Membership (Scotland) Act 2020 amended s.96(2) by repealing "75," and inserting "84A," after "82,". With effect from the same date, s.14(1) and (4) of the 2020 Act amended s.96(2) of the 2018 Act by repealing "68," and inserting ", 87A" after "86".   4.149

p.1904, *revocation and coming into force of provisions of the Social Security (Scotland) Act 2018*

4.150   With effect from September 11, 2019, reg.5 of the Social Security (Scotland) Act 2018 (Commencement No.5, Revocation and Saving Provision) Regulations 2019 (SSI 2019/269) revoked s.98 of the 2018 Act (temporary disapplication of further procedure for regulations about assistance).

Schedules 4, 5 and 10 to the 2018 Act have come into force and are in Part I of this Supplement.

p.1908, *annotation to Tribunals (Scotland) Act 2014 s.1 (Establishment of the Tribunals)*

4.151   Lord Woolman has replaced Lady Smith as President of Tribunals.

p.1909, *annotation to the Tribunals (Scotland) Act 2014 s.43 (Review of decisions)*

4.151.1   In *Aberdeen CC v LS* [2021] UT 1 at [29], the Upper Tribunal was critical of the lengthy procedure adopted by the Health and Education Chamber of the First-tier Tribunal when considering applications for review and for permission to appeal brought on the same point of law. The judicial member, Lady Poole (a former judge of the UK Upper Tribunal), said that there was no reason why the same legal member could not have dealt with both applications at the same time and she also suggested that the approach taken in *R (RB) v First-tier Tribunal* [2010] UKUT 160 (AAC); [2010] AACR 41 in relation to reviews under s.9 of the Tribunals, Courts and Enforcement Act 2007 was equally applicable in Scottish tribunals, even though there are differences between the two systems. She said—

> "Given the availability of an appeal on a point of law, in my opinion, a review is unlikely to be in the interests of justice within Rule 11 of the FtT Rules [relating to the Housing and Education Chamber] if what is being challenged is merely an arguable point of law. Set aside powers on a review under Section 44(1)(b) of the 2014 Act in my view cover situations in which there has been a clear error of law, which may encompass some material errors in fact. Review is primarily intended for cases where a decision is plainly wrong, so avoiding the need for an appeal that would inevitably succeed. This might happen, for example, if a binding legal authority or provision has been overlooked. It should be relatively obvious where this type of error exists, with the result that a review need not be an unduly time-consuming exercise. Review is not intended to usurp the function of the UTS to determine appeals on contentious points of law."

p.1910, *annotation to the Tribunals (Scotland) Act 2014 s.44 (Actions on review)*

4.151.2   In *Skoll v Humanes* [2020] UT 36, the Upper Tribunal held that it was not competent to consider a reference under s.44(2)(b) because the

Housing and Property Chamber of the First-tier Tribunal had failed to set aside its decision under s.44(1)(b) before making the reference. The rules applicable in the Housing and Property Chamber do not limit the grounds of review to points of law (unlike r.35(1) of the rules applicable in the Social Security Chamber), but it was still necessary for the First-tier Tribunal to find that its decision had been wrong if it was to set it aside. Merely describing its consideration of a point of law as "incomplete and in places irrelevant" did not amount to a finding that the decision had been wrong. The Upper Tribunal remitted the case to the First-tier Tribunal and extended the claimant's time for applying to the First-tier Tribunal for permission to appeal. The latter direction appears to have been necessary because the Housing and Property Chamber rules do not provide for an application for review to be treated also as an application for permission to appeal (unlike r.36 of the rules applicable in the Social Security Chamber).

p.1911, *annotation to the Tribunals (Scotland) Act 2014 s.46 (Actions on review)*

For the meaning of "a point of law", see *Murray Group Holdings Ltd v Revenue and Customs Commissioners* [2015] CSIH 77; 2016 S.C. 201 at [42] and [43], set out on pp. 1580-1583 of the main work. See also the detailed discussion in *Garrett v Your Place Property Management Limited* [2020] UT 34 at [20] to [23]. In an earlier determination in the latter case, it was held that the test of "arguability" in s.46(4) is "a relatively low hurdle" for an applicant to overcome (*Garrett v Your Place Property Management Limited* [2020] UT 32 at [4]). Permission to appeal will not generally be given unless the point of law is not only arguable but also material in the sense that it might have made a difference to the outcome (*Mansfield v Thomson* [2020] UT 14 at [7]; *Aberdeenshire Council v SS* [2020] UT 25 at [16] to [19]).   **4.151.3**

p.1924, *amendment to the First-tier Tribunal for Scotland Social Security Chamber (Procedure) Regulations 2018 reg.2 (Application of the Rules set out in the schedule)*

With effect from December 24, 2020, reg.5(1) and (2) of the First-tier Tribunal for Scotland Social Security Chamber and Upper Tribunal for Scotland (Allocation of Functions, Procedure and Composition) (Miscellaneous Amendments) Regulations 2020 (SSI 2020/476) amended reg.2 of the 2018 Regulations by substituting for the words from "the Social Security (Scotland) Act 2018" to the end, the words—   **4.152**

"—

    (a) the Social Security (Scotland) Act 2018;

    (b) regulations made under the Social Security (Scotland) Act 2018; or

    (c) the Carer's Allowance Supplement and Young Carer Grants (Residence Requirements and Procedural Provisions) (EU Exit) (Scotland) Regulations 2020.".

pp.1924-1926, *amendments to the schedule of the First-tier Tribunal for Scotland Social Security Chamber (Procedure) Regulations 2018 r.1 (Interpretation)*

4.153   With effect from November 9, 2020, reg.3(1) and (2) of the First-tier Tribunal for Scotland Social Security Chamber (Procedure and Composition) Amendment Regulations 2020 (SSI 2020/353) amended r.1 by inserting a definition of "the 2020 Regulations" and substituting new definitions for "the prescribed time period" and "process decision" as follows—

"the 2020 Regulations" means the Scottish Child Payment Regulations 2020,",

"the prescribed time period" means—

(a) in relation to re-determination of entitlement to assistance under Chapter 2 of Part 2 of the 2018 Act, the period prescribed by the Scottish Ministers by virtue of section 43(5) of the 2018 Act;

(b) in relation to re-determination of entitlement to assistance under the 2020 Regulations, the period provided for in paragraph 14(2) of the schedule of the 2020 Regulations.

"process decision" means—

(a) in relation to an appeal under section 61 of the 2018 Act, a decision made under section 38, 41(3) or 42 of that Act;

(b) in relation to an appeal under paragraph 23 of the schedule of the 2020 Regulations, a decision made under paragraph 1(4), 14(5) or 15(2)(b) of the schedule of those Regulations.

With effect from December 24, 2020, reg.5(1) and (3)(a) of the First-tier Tribunal for Scotland Social Security Chamber and Upper Tribunal for Scotland (Allocation of Functions, Procedure and Composition) (Miscellaneous Amendments) Regulations 2020 (SSI 2020/476) amended r.1 by inserting a definition of "the Carer's Allowance Supplement Regulations" and by amending the recently substituted definitions of "the prescribed time period" and "process decision". The new definition is—

"the Carer's Allowance Supplement Regulations" means the Carer's Allowance Supplement and Young Carer Grants (Residence Requirements and Procedural Provisions (EU Exit) (Scotland) Regulations 2020;

In the definition of "the prescribed time period", after sub-paragraph (b) there is inserted—

"(c) in relation to re-determination of entitlement to a carer's allowance supplement, the period provided for in paragraph 6(2) of schedule 2 of the Carer's Allowance Supplement Regulations."

In the definition of "process decision" after sub-paragraph (b) there is inserted—

"(c) in relation to an appeal under paragraph 13 of schedule 2 of the

Carer's Allowance Supplement Regulations, a decision made under paragraph 1(5), 4(6) or 5(2)(b) of schedule 2 of those Regulations."

p.1929, *annotation to the schedule of the First-tier Tribunal for Scotland Social Security Chamber (Procedure) Regulations 2018 r.4 (Case management powers)*

The First-tier Tribunal should not direct that there be a separate 4.153.1 hearing to consider an issue as a preliminary issue if that would cause undue delay (*Aberdeen CC v LS* [2021] UT 1 at [29.1]).

p.1932, *annotation to the schedule of the First-tier Tribunal for Scotland Social Security Chamber (Procedure) Regulations 2018 r.9 (Representatives)*

In *Roberts v Hacking and Paterson* [2020] UT 30, the respondent had 4.153.2 challenged the applicant's mother's right to represent him before the First-tier Tribunal because no formal intimation had been made. The First-tier Tribunal had repelled that preliminary plea on the ground that, not only was it was evident from the application and subsequent correspondence that the applicant's mother was representing her son, but also there was evidence that the respondent had previously corresponded with her on behalf of the applicant. Thus, the First-tier Tribunal, having regard to the overriding objective, had taken the view that the fact that the applicant's mother had been acting as her son's representative was evidence that he had appointed her to do so. However, when she applied to the First-tier Tribunal for permission to appeal, describing herself as the applicant, the First-tier Tribunal rejected the application on the ground that she was not a party. The Upper Tribunal considered that the First-tier Tribunal should have taken the same approach as it had taken in the substantive proceedings and, having regard to the requirement in the overriding objective to avoid unnecessary formality, should have treated her as making the application as agent for a disclosed principal who was a party.

pp.1935–1936, *amendments to the schedule of the First-tier Tribunal for Scotland Social Security Chamber (Procedure) Regulations 2018 r.20 (notice of appeal to the First-tier Tribunal against a determination of entitlement to assistance of a type provided for in Part 2 of the 2018 Act)*

With effect from November 9, 2020, reg.3(1) and (3) of the First-tier 4.154 Tribunal for Scotland Social Security Chamber (Procedure and Composition) Amendment Regulations 2020 (SSI 2020/353) amended r.20 by amending para.(8)(b)—inserting after the words "the prescribed time period" the words "and the determination under section 37 is being appealed"—and substituting new paras. (5)(g), (9) and (10) as follows—

"(g) where the notice of appeal is received after the end of the period of 31 days beginning with whichever is the later of—
  (i) the day on which the appellant is informed of a determination made under section 43 of the 2018 Act; or
  (ii) the day on which the appellant is informed of the right to appeal against the determination made under section 37 of the Act,

the reasons why the notice of appeal was not submitted sooner.",

"(9) Where [a] notice of appeal is received by the Scottish Ministers after the end of the period of 31 days beginning with the later of the days specified in paragraph (4)—
  (a) if the notice of appeal is received before the end of the period of one year beginning with the day on which the appellant is informed of a determination made under section 43 of the 2018 Act or, as the case may be, of the right to appeal against the determination made under section 37 of the Act, the First-tier Tribunal may give permission for the appeal to proceed, but only if satisfied that there was a good reason for the notice of appeal not having been sent or delivered to the Scottish Ministers sooner; or
  (b) if the notice of appeal is received after the end of the period of one year beginning with the day on which the appellant is informed of a determination made under section 43 of the 2018 Act or, as the case may be, of the right to appeal against the determination made under section 37 of the Act, the First-tier Tribunal must refuse to consider the notice of appeal.

(10) The Scottish Ministers must forward a notice of appeal to the First-tier Tribunal even if one of the following situations applies—
  (a) the notice of appeal is received after the end of the period of 31 days beginning with the later of the days specified in paragraph (4), but less than one year after that day; or
  (b) the notice of appeal is received one year or more after the later of the days specified in paragraph (4).".

The word in square brackets at the beginning of para.(9) was inserted by reg.5(1) and (3)(b) of the First-tier Tribunal for Scotland Social Security Chamber and Upper Tribunal for Scotland (Allocation of Functions, Procedure and Composition) (Miscellaneous Amendments) Regulations 2020 (SSI 2020/476) with effect from December 24, 2020.

p.1936, *insertion of rr.20A and 20B into the Schedule of the First-tier Tribunal for Scotland Social Security Chamber (Procedure) Regulations 2018*

4.155   With effect from November 9, 2020, reg.3(1) and (4) of the First-tier Tribunal for Scotland Social Security Chamber (Procedure and Composition) Amendment Regulations 2020 (SSI 2020/353) inserted r.20A as follows—

"Notice of appeal to the First-tier Tribunal against a determination of entitlement to a Scottish child payment

20A.—(1) This rule applies where an individual brings an appeal under paragraph 19 of the schedule of the 2020 Regulations against a determination by the Scottish Ministers of the appellant's entitlement to a Scottish child payment.

(2) Where in this rule, and in rule 21 (response of the decision maker to a notice of appeal against a determination of entitlement) in so far is it applies to the Scottish child payment, reference is made to a "notice of appeal", this means the form provided by the Scottish Ministers under paragraph 17(1)(b) (or as the case may be paragraph 18(1)(b)) of the schedule of the 2020 Regulations on notifying of the outcome of a re-determination of entitlement, or of a failure to re-determine entitlement within the prescribed time period.

(3) An individual must start proceedings by submitting the notice of appeal to the Scottish Ministers along with any documents which have not so far been provided to Ministers that the appellant wishes them to submit to the First-tier Tribunal in support of the appeal.

(4) Except as provided for in paragraph (10), a notice of appeal must be received by the Scottish Ministers before the end of the period of 31 days beginning with whichever is the later of the day on which the appellant—

(a) is informed of a determination made under paragraph 16 of the schedule of the 2020 Regulations following a request for a re-determination; or

(b) is informed of the appellant's right to appeal against the determination made under paragraph 3 of the schedule of the 2020 Regulations as a result of the failure of the Scottish Ministers to re-determine entitlement within the prescribed time period.

(5) The notice of appeal must state—

(a) the name and address of the appellant;

(b) the name and address of the appellant's representative (if any);

(c) a postal or email address where documents for the appellant may be sent or delivered;

(d) the determination being challenged;

(e) the reasons for bringing the appeal; and

(f) where the notice of appeal is received after the end of the period of 31 days beginning with whichever is the later of—

(i) the day on which the appellant is informed of a determination made under paragraph 16; or

(ii) the day on which the appellant is informed of the right to appeal against the determination made under paragraph 3, but less than one year after that day,

the reasons why the notice of appeal was not sent or delivered to the Scottish Ministers sooner.

(6) A notice of appeal and any accompanying documents may be sent by pre-paid post, by fax, or by electronic communication to such address as may be specified for receipt by the Scottish Ministers.

(7) The Scottish Ministers must forward to the First-tier Tribunal any notice of appeal and accompanying documents submitted to them, regardless of whether the requirements set out in paragraph (5) are met, or the extent to which they are met, and inform the appellant when this has been done.

(8) At the same time as forwarding the notice of appeal and any documents under paragraph (7), the Scottish Ministers must send—

(a) a copy of any application for a Scottish child payment that has been made by the appellant under paragraph 1(1) of the schedule of the 2020 Regulations in respect of the child to whom the determination of entitlement which is being appealed relates;

(b) a copy of—

(i) the determination issued under paragraph 16 of the schedule of the 2020 Regulations following a request that entitlement be re-determined; or

(ii) the determination issued under paragraph 3 of the schedule of the 2020 Regulations, where there has been a failure to re-determine entitlement within the prescribed time period and the determination under paragraph 3 is being appealed; and

(c) a copy of any written record of the decision under challenge.

(9) Where [a] notice of appeal is received by the Scottish Ministers after the end of the period of 31 days beginning with the later of the days specified in paragraph (4)—

(a) if the notice of appeal is received before the end of the period of one year beginning with the day on which the appellant is informed of a determination made under paragraph 16 of the schedule of the 2020 Regulations or, as the case may be, of the right to appeal against the determination made under paragraph 3, the First-tier Tribunal may give permission for the appeal to proceed, but only if satisfied that there was a good reason for the notice of appeal not having been sent or delivered to the Scottish Ministers sooner; or

(b) if the notice of appeal is received after the end of the period of one year beginning with the day on which the appellant is informed of a determination made under paragraph 16 or, as the case may be, of the right to appeal against the determination made under paragraph 3, the First-tier Tribunal must refuse to consider the notice of appeal.

(10) The Scottish Ministers must forward a notice of appeal to the First-tier Tribunal even if one of the following situations applies—

(a) the notice of appeal is received after the end of the period of 31 days beginning with the later of the days specified in paragraph (4) but less than one year after that day; or

(b) the notice of appeal is received one year or more after the later of the days specified in paragraph (4).".

The word in square brackets at the beginning of r.20A(9) was inserted by reg.5(1) and (3)(b) of the First-tier Tribunal for Scotland Social Security Chamber and Upper Tribunal for Scotland (Allocation of Functions,

Procedure and Composition) (Miscellaneous Amendments) Regulations 2020 (SSI 2020/476) with effect from December 24, 2020.

With effect from December 24, 2020, reg.5(1) and (3)(c) of SSI 2020/476 inserted r.20B as follows—

"Notice of appeal to the First-tier Tribunal against a determination of entitlement to a carer's allowance supplement

20B.—(1) This rule applies where an individual brings an appeal under paragraph 9 of schedule 2 of the Carer's Allowance Supplement Regulations against a determination by the Scottish Ministers of the appellant's entitlement to a carer's allowance supplement.

(2) Where in this rule, and in rule 21 (response of the decision maker to a notice of appeal against a determination of entitlement) in so far as it applies to carer's allowance supplement, reference is made to a "notice of appeal", this means the form provided by the Scottish Ministers under paragraph 7(1)(b) (or as the case may be paragraph 8(1)(b)) of schedule 2 of the Carer's Allowance Supplement Regulations on notifying of the outcome of a re-determination of entitlement, or of a failure to re-determine entitlement within the prescribed time period.

(3) An individual must start proceedings by submitting the notice of appeal to the Scottish Ministers along with any documents which have not so far been provided to Ministers that the appellant wishes them to submit to the First-tier Tribunal in support of the appeal.

(4) Except as provided for in paragraph (10), a notice of appeal must be received by the Scottish Ministers before the end of the period of 31 days beginning with whichever is the later of the day on which the appellant—

(a) is informed of a determination made under paragraph 6 of schedule 2 of the Carer's Allowance Supplement Regulations following a request for a re-determination; or

(b) is informed of the appellant's right to appeal against the determination made under regulation 5 (determination of EEA resident's entitlement to a carer's allowance supplement) of the Carer's Allowance Supplement Regulations as a result of the failure of the Scottish Ministers to re-determine entitlement within the prescribed time period.

(5) The notice of appeal must state—

(a) the name and address of the appellant;

(b) the name and address of the appellant's representative (if any);

(c) a postal or email address where documents for the appellant may be sent or delivered;

(d) the determination being challenged;

(e) the reasons for bringing the appeal; and

(f) where the notice of appeal is received after the end of the period of 31 days beginning with whichever is the later of—

(i) the day on which the appellant is informed of a determination made under paragraph 6 of schedule 2 of the Carer's Allowance Supplement Regulations; or

(ii) the day on which the appellant is informed of the right to appeal against the determination made under regulation 5 of the Carer's Allowance Supplement Regulations, but less than one year after that day,

the reasons why the notice of appeal was not sent or delivered to the Scottish Ministers sooner.

(6) A notice of appeal and any accompanying documents may be sent by pre-paid post, by fax, or by electronic communication to such address as may be specified for receipt by the Scottish Ministers.

(7) The Scottish Ministers must forward to the First-tier Tribunal any notice of appeal and accompanying documents submitted to them, regardless of whether the requirements set out in paragraph (5) are met, or the extent to which they are met, and inform the appellant when this has been done.

(8) At the same time as forwarding the notice of appeal and any documents under paragraph (7), the Scottish Ministers must send—

(a) a copy of any application for a carer's allowance supplement that has been made by the appellant under regulation 5 of the Carer's Allowance Supplement Regulations;

(b) a copy of—

(i) the determination issued under paragraph 6 of schedule 2 of the Carer's Allowance Supplement Regulations following a request that entitlement be re-determined; or

(ii) the determination issued under regulation 5 of the Carer's Allowance Supplement Regulations, where there has been a failure to re-determine entitlement within the prescribed time period and the determination under regulation 5 is being appealed; and

(c) a copy of any written record of the decision under challenge.

(9) Where a notice of appeal is received by the Scottish Ministers after the end of the period of 31 days beginning with the later of the days specified in paragraph (4)—

(a) if the notice of appeal is received before the end of the period of one year beginning with the day on which the appellant is informed of a determination made under paragraph 6 of schedule 2 of the Carer's Allowance Supplement Regulations or, as the case may be, of the right to appeal against the determination made under regulation 5 of the Carer's Allowance Supplement Regulations, the First-tier Tribunal may give permission for the appeal to proceed, but only if satisfied that there was a good reason for the notice of appeal not having been sent or delivered to the Scottish Ministers sooner; or

(b) if the notice of appeal is received after the end of the period of one year beginning with the day on which the appellant is informed of a determination made under paragraph 6 of schedule 2 or, as the case may be, of the right to appeal against the determination made under regulation 5, the First-tier Tribunal must refuse to consider the notice of appeal.

(10) The Scottish Ministers must forward a notice of appeal to the First-tier Tribunal even if one of the following situations applies—

(a) the notice of appeal is received after the end of the period of 31 days beginning with the later of the days specified in paragraph (4) but less than one year after that day; or

(b) the notice of appeal is received one year or more after the later of the days specified in paragraph (4).",

p.1936, *amendments to the schedule of the First-tier Tribunal for Scotland Social Security Chamber (Procedure) Regulations 2018 r.21(1) and (2) (response of the decision maker to a notice of appeal against a determination of entitlement)*

With effect from November 9, 2020, reg.3(1) and (5) of the First-tier Tribunal for Scotland Social Security Chamber (Procedure and Composition) Amendment Regulations 2020 (SSI 2020/353) briefly amended r.21 by inserting after the words in parenthesis in each of para.(1) and para.(2) the words "or rule 20A (notice of appeal to the First-tier Tribunal against a determination of entitlement to a Scottish child payment)". **4.156**

However, with effect from December 24, 2020, reg.5(1) and (3)(d) of the First-tier Tribunal for Scotland Social Security Chamber and Upper Tribunal for Scotland (Allocation of Functions, Procedure and Composition) (Miscellaneous Amendments) Regulations 2020 (SSI 2020/476) substituted new paras. (1) and (2) as follows—

"(1) The First-tier Tribunal must notify each party in writing when a notice of appeal submitted under any of the following provisions has been accepted as containing sufficient information to be valid—

(a) rule 20 (notice of appeal to the First-tier Tribunal against a determination of entitlement to assistance of a type provided for in Part 2 of the 2018 Act);

(b) rule 20A (notice of appeal to the First-tier Tribunal against a determination of entitlement to a Scottish child payment); or

(c) rule 20B (notice of appeal to the First-tier Tribunal against a determination of entitlement to a carer's allowance supplement).

(2) The decision maker must send or deliver to the First-tier Tribunal a response to any notice of appeal submitted under rule 20, 20A or 20B before the expiry of the period of 31 days beginning with the day on which the decision maker received notification from the First-tier Tribunal that the notice of appeal had been accepted as containing sufficient information to be valid.".

p.1937, *amendments to the schedule of the First-tier Tribunal for Scotland Social Security Chamber (Procedure) Regulations 2018 r.22(1) (notice of appeal against a process decision)*

4.157   With effect from November 9, 2020, reg.3(1) and (6) of the First-tier Tribunal for Scotland Social Security Chamber (Procedure and Composition) Amendment Regulations 2020 (SSI 2020/353) briefly amended r.22(1) by inserting "or paragraph 23 of the schedule of the 2020 Regulations" after the words "2018 Act".

However, with effect from December 24, 2020, reg.5(1) and (3)(e) of the First-tier Tribunal for Scotland Social Security Chamber and Upper Tribunal for Scotland (Allocation of Functions, Procedure and Composition) (Miscellaneous Amendments) Regulations 2020 (SSI 2020/476) substituted a new para.(1) as follows—

"(1) This rule applies where an individual brings an appeal under any of the following provisions against a process decision—
  (a) section 61 of the 2018 Act;
  (b) paragraph 23 of the schedule of the 2020 Regulations; or
  (c) paragraph 13 of schedule 2 of the Carer's Allowance Supplement Regulations.".

p.1939, *annotation to the schedule of the First-tier Tribunal for Scotland Social Security Chamber (Procedure) Regulations 2018 r.26 (Public and private hearings)*

4.157.1   In *Hamilton v Glasgow Housing Association Limited* [2020] UT 37, the appellant apparently had mental health difficulties and interrupted proceedings at a hearing before the Housing and Property Chamber of the First-tier Tribunal on numerous occasions. The First-tier Tribunal found that he "had endeavoured to control himself but was unable to do so." Rather than excluding him from the hearing under a provision equivalent to r.26(4), the First-tier Tribunal barred him from presenting submissions or presenting arguments or questioning witnesses in person, at that or any future hearings, and then adjourned to allow him to obtain representation, which he was unable to do. The Upper Tribunal allowed his appeal against that decision, holding that it could not be assumed that a person could obtain representation and that the First-tier Tribunal had not had adequate regard either to the overriding objective or the possibility of taking other action. For instance, consideration had not been given to whether regular short breaks to enable the appellant to recover his equilibrium might have been appropriate or whether a supporter (see r.10 of these Rules) might have been obtained.

p.1942, *annotation to the schedule of the First-tier Tribunal for Scotland Social Security Chamber (Procedure) Regulations 2018 r.34 (First-tier Tribunal's consideration of application for permission to appeal against its decision)*

4.157.2   It was pointed out in *Aberdeen CC v LS* [2021] UT 1 at [29.4] that, like r.34, the equivalent provision in the rules applicable in the Housing and Education Chamber does not require reasons to be provided where permission to appeal is granted and it was suggested that, when granting permission, it may not be necessary for the First-tier Tribunal to say much more than that grounds of appeal in respect of which permission has been granted are arguable (see s.46(4) of the Tribunals (Scotland) Act 2014), thus saving judicial time and avoiding both unnecessary delay and any impression of pre-judgement of issues to be decided in the substantive hearing of the appeal. However, it is good practice for the First-tier Tribunal to make clear that the issue of arguability has been addressed (*Zukowski v Charles White Limited* [2020] UT 26 at [19]).

p.1944, *amendment to the Upper Tribunal for Scotland (Social Security Rules of Procedure) Regulations 2018 reg.3 (application of Rules in schedule)*

With effect from December 24, 2020, reg.3 of the First-tier Tribunal **4.158** for Scotland Social Security Chamber and Upper Tribunal for Scotland (Allocation of Functions, Procedure and Composition) (Miscellaneous Amendments) Regulations 2020 (SSI 2020/476) amended reg.3 of the 2018 Regulations by substituting for the words "the 2018 Act or by regulations made under that Act" the words—

"__

(a) the 2018 Act;
(b) regulations made under the 2018 Act; or
(c) the Carer's Allowance Supplement and Young Carer Grants (Residence Requirements and Procedural Provisions) (EU Exit) (Scotland) Regulations 2020.".

p.1949, *annotation to the schedule of the Upper Tribunal for Scotland (Social Security Rules of Procedure) 2018 r.3 (Application for permission to appeal against a decision of the First-tier Tribunal)*

In *Zahorowicz v Pawlowska* [2020] UT 19, the Upper Tribunal clearly **4.158.1** doubted the value of the right to apply for reconsideration in r.3(7) of the rules applicable in cases other than social security cases, which is equivalent to para.(6) of this rule. The judicial member said –

"It may be desirable to review the function of rule 3(7), as the hearing amounted to no more than a further discussion of the explanation already set out in the original decision to refuse leave."

The equivalent right to apply for reconsideration of a refusal of permission to appeal to the UK Upper Tribunal (r.22(3) to (5) of the Tribunal Procedure (Upper Tribunal) Rules 2008, set out on p.1832 of the main work) does not apply in social security cases.

p.1961, *amendment to the First-tier Tribunal for Scotland (Allocation of Functions to the Social Security Chamber) Regulations 2018 reg.3(2) (allocation of social security functions to the Social Security Chamber)*

With effect from December 24, 2020, reg.2 of the First-tier Tribunal **4.159** for Scotland Social Security Chamber and Upper Tribunal for Scotland

(Allocation of Functions, Procedure and Composition) (Miscellaneous Amendments) Regulations 2020 (SSI 2020/476) substituted a new reg.3(2) as follows—

"(2) The social security functions of the First-tier Tribunal are the functions conferred on the Tribunal by—
  (a) the 2018 Act;
  (b) regulations made under the 2018 Act; and
  (c) the Carer's Allowance Supplement and Young Carer Grants (Residence Requirements and Procedural Provisions) (EU Exit) (Scotland) Regulations 2020.".

PART V

UPDATING MATERIAL
VOLUME IV

TAX CREDITS AND HMRC-ADMINISTERED SOCIAL SECURITY BENEFITS

Commentary by

Ian Hooker

Edward Mitchell

Nick Wikeley

p.285, *annotation to the Income Tax (Earnings and Pensions) Act 2003*
s.210 (Exemption of minor benefits)

A further exemption is provided for by the Income Tax (Exemption of   5.001
Minor Benefits) (Coronavirus) Regulations 2020 (SI 2020/1293).

p.303, *amendment to the Income Tax (Earnings and Pensions) Act 2003*
s.655 (Structure of Part 10)

Section 655 is amended by the insertion in subs.(2) of "section 13 of   5.002
FA 2020 (power to exempt social security benefits from income tax)"
after the entry for "section 44 of FA 2016".

p.314, *amendment to the Income Tax (earnings and Pensions) Act 2003*
s.677 (UK social security benefits wholly exempt from tax: Table B)

Section 677(1) is amended by the insertion in Table B-Part 1 of the   5.003
following entry after that for council tax benefit:

Disability assistance for children   SS(S)A 2018, ss.24 and 31
and young people

p.315, *amendment to the Income Tax (earnings and Pensions) Act 2003*
s.677 (UK social security benefits wholly exempt from tax: Table B)

Section 677(1) is amended by the insertion in Table B-Part 1 of the   5.004
following entry after that for industrial injuries benefit:

Job start   ETA 1973, s.2

p.316, *amendment to the Income Tax (earnings and Pensions) Act 2003*
s.677 (UK social security benefits wholly exempt from tax: Table B)

Section 677(1) is amended by the insertion in Table B-Part 2 of the   5.005
following entry after that for payment under a council tax reduction
scheme: Wales:

Scottish child payment   SS(S)A 2018, s.79

p.533, *annotation to the Welfare Reform Act 2012 (Commencement*
No.23) Order 2015 (SI 2015/634) art.7 (Transitional provision: claims
for . . . a tax credit)

In *W v HMRC* (TC) [2020] UKUT 239 (AAC) Upper Tribunal   5.006
Judge Mitchell held that the exception in Article 7(6) was not satisfied
where a person whose original award was as a member of a couple
subsequently claimed a tax credit as a single person:

"11 . . . After the introductory injunction ("paragraph (1) does not
apply to a claim for a tax credit"), Article 7(6) contains two compo-
nents whose purpose is to identify the class of individuals benefit from
that injunction:

    (a) the first component identifies a wide class comprised of two groups: (i) a person who has or had an award of a tax credit; and (ii) persons who have or had an award of tax credit;

    (b) the second component narrows down that wide class. In doing so, it maintains, and operates on, the distinction drawn by the first component between sole and joint claimants, as is shown by it use of the referential pronouns 'that' and 'those'. For a person within group (i) under what I have described as the first component, 'that person' must make a claim for tax credit for the next tax year to avoid being filtered out of article 7(6). For persons within group (ii), 'those persons' must make a claim.

12.. A person in Mr W's position, that is a person residing in a UC 'Full Service Area' who jointly claimed a tax credit in the previous tax year, will only benefit from article 7(6) if he re-claims together with the previous year's partner."

p.535, *annotation to the Welfare Reform Act 2012 (Commencement No.29) Order 2017 (SI 2017/664) art.14 (Modification of the No 23 Order: claims for housing benefit, income support or a tax credit)*

5.007   As Upper Tribunal Judge Mitchell observed in *W v HMRC* (TC) [2020] UKUT 239 (AAC), "the complex UC/tax credits transitional legislation is hardly accessible to a specialist legal representative let alone a lay person".

p.558, *amendment to the Universal Credit (Transitional Provisions) Regulations 2014 (SI 2014/1230) reg.13 (Appeals etc relating to certain existing benefits)*

5.008   With effect from July 22, 2020, reg.4 of the Universal Credit (Managed Migration Pilot and Miscellaneous Amendments) Regulations 2019 (SI 2019/1152) amended reg.13 by inserting the words "46 or 47" at the end of para.(3).

p.566, *amendment to the Universal Credit (Transitional Provisions) Regulations 2014 (SI 2014/1230) reg.46 (Termination of existing benefits if no claim before the deadline)*

5.009   With effect from July 22, 2020, reg.4 of the Universal Credit (Managed Migration Pilot and Miscellaneous Amendments) Regulations 2019 (SI 2019/1152) amended reg.46 by inserting the following words after "housing benefit" in para.(1)(a):

"income support, income-based jobseeker's allowance or income-related employment and support allowance"

p.566, *amendment to the Universal Credit (Transitional Provisions) Regulations 2014 (SI 2014/1230) reg.46 (Termination of existing benefits if no claim before the deadline)*

5.010   With effect from July 22, 2020, reg.4 of the Universal Credit (Managed Migration Pilot and Miscellaneous Amendments) Regulations

2019 (SI 2019/1152) amended reg.46 by substituting "a tax credit" for "any other existing benefit" in para.(1)(b).

p.566, *amendment to the Universal Credit (Transitional Provisions) Regulations 2014 (SI 2014/1230) reg.47 (Notified persons who claim as a different benefit unit)*

With effect from July 22, 2020, reg.4 of the Universal Credit (Man-   5.011
aged Migration Pilot and Miscellaneous Amendments) Regulations 2019 (SI 2019/1152) amended reg.47 by inserting the following words after "housing benefit" in para.(2)(a):

"income support, income-based jobseeker's allowance or income-related employment and support allowance,"

p.566, *amendment to the Universal Credit (Transitional Provisions) Regulations 2014 (SI 2014/1230) reg.47 (Notified persons who claim as a different benefit unit)*

With effect from July 22, 2020, reg.4 of the Universal Credit (Man-   5.012
aged Migration Pilot and Miscellaneous Amendments) Regulations 2019 (SI 2019/1152) amended reg.47 by substituting "a tax credit" for "any other existing benefit" in para.(2)(b).

p.577, *revocation of the Universal Credit (Transitional Provisions) Regulations 2014 (SI 2014/1230) reg.59 (Minimum income floor not to apply for first 12 months)*

With effect from September 23, 2020, reg.6 of the Universal Credit   5.013
(Managed Migration Pilot and Miscellaneous Amendments) Regulations 2019 (SI 2019/1152) revoked reg.59.

pp.585-587, *amendment to the Working Tax Credit (Entitlement and Maximum Rate) Regulations 2002 (SI 2002/2005) reg.2 (Interpretation)*

With effect from May 23, 2020, reg.2(2) of the Tax Credits (Coro-   5.014
navirus, Miscellaneous Amendments) Regulations 2020 (SI 2020/534) amended reg.2(1) by inserting at the appropriate places the following new definitions—
""coronavirus" means severe acute respiratory syndrome coronavirus 2;
    "Coronavirus Job Retention Scheme" means the scheme of that name established under the direction given by the Chancellor of the Exchequer under section 76 of the Coronavirus Act 2020 on 15th April 2020 (as that Scheme has effect from time to time);
    "coronavirus-impacted worker" has the meaning given by regulation 7E(3); and
    "furloughed employee under the Coronavirus Job Retention Scheme" means a person who is within paragraph 6.1 of the Schedule to the direction given by the Chancellor of the Exchequer under section 76 of the Coronavirus Act 2020;".

With effect from September 25, 2020, reg.3(2) of the Tax Credits (Coronavirus, Miscellaneous Amendments) (No.2) Regulations 2020 (SI 2020/941) amended the above definition of "furloughed employee under the Coronavirus Job Retention Scheme" by inserting the phrase "or a person who is within paragraph 10.1 of the Schedule to the further direction given by the Chancellor under section 76 of that Act on 25th June 2020" after "Coronavirus Act 2020".

p.588, *annotation to the Working Tax Credit (Entitlement and Maximum Rate) Regulations 2002 (SI 2002/2005) reg.2 (Interpretation)*

5.015   The direction given by the Chancellor of the Exchequer on 15 April 2020, as referred to in the definition of "Coronavirus Job Retention Scheme", and the Chancellor's direction of 25 June 2020, as referred to in the definition of "furloughed employee under the Coronavirus Job Creation Scheme", are available at *http://www.gov.uk/government/publications/treasury-direction-made-under-sections-71-and-76-of-the-coronavirus-act-2020.*

p.593, *amendment to the Working Tax Credit (Entitlement and Maximum Rate) Regulations 2002 (SI 2002/2005) reg.4(1A) (Entitlement to basic element of Working Tax Credit: qualifying remunerative work)*

5.016   With effect from May 23, 2020, reg.2(3)(a) of the Tax Credits (Coronavirus, Miscellaneous Amendments) Regulations 2020 (SI 2020/534) amended reg.4(1A) by inserting after sub-para.(d) the following new sub-paragraph—

"(da) regulation 7E applies—
    (i) where a person, or in the case of a joint claim, one or both persons, reduces the hours worked, including a reduction to nil, to the extent that that person, or those persons, no longer satisfy the Second condition in paragraph (1);
    (ii) any reduction in hours is as a consequence of coronavirus; and
    (iii) any reduction in hours is temporary;".

p.595, *amendment to the Working Tax Credit (Entitlement and Maximum Rate) Regulations 2002 (SI 2002/2005) reg.4(4) (Entitlement to basic element of Working Tax Credit: qualifying remunerative work)*

5.017   With effect from May 23, 2020, reg.2(3)(b) of the Tax Credits (Coronavirus, Miscellaneous Amendments) Regulations 2020 (SI 2020/534) amended reg.4(4) by omitting the "and" at the end of sub-para.(a); inserting "and" after the comma at the end of sub-para.(b); and inserting after sub-para.(b) the following new sub-paragraph—

"(c) any period of absence from work due to taking emergency volunteering leave under Schedule 7 to the Coronavirus Act 2020,".

p.606, *amendment to the Working Tax Credit (Entitlement and Maximum Rate) Regulations 2002 (SI 2002/2005) reg.7D (Ceasing to undertake work or working for less than 16, 24 or 30 hours per week)*

With effect from May 23, 2020, reg.2(4) of the Tax Credits (Coro-   5.018
navirus, Miscellaneous Amendments) Regulations 2020 (SI 2020/534)
amended reg.7D by inserting after para.(2) the following new paragraph—

"(3) This regulation does not apply to a person who is either—
  (a) a furloughed employee under the Coronavirus Job Retention
      Scheme; or
  (b) a coronavirus-impacted worker.".

p.606, *amendment to the Working Tax Credit (Entitlement and Maximum Rate) Regulations 2002 (SI 2002/2005) insertion of new reg.7E (Alteration in hours worked due to coronavirus)*

With effect from May 23, 2020, reg.2(5) of the Tax Credits (Coro-   5.019
navirus, Miscellaneous Amendments) Regulations 2020 (SI 2020/534)
inserted after reg.7D a new regulation 7E as follows—

"Alteration in hours worked due to coronavirus

7E.—(1) For the purposes of the conditions of entitlement in this
Part, a person to whom paragraph (2) applies is treated as being
engaged in qualifying remunerative work during the period that that
person is either—
  (a) a furloughed employee under the Coronavirus Job Retention
      Scheme; or
  (b) a coronavirus-impacted worker.
(2) This paragraph applies to—
  (a) a person, whether or not a member of a couple, who is a
      furloughed employee under the Coronavirus Job Retention
      Scheme;
  (b) a person (A), whether or not a member of a couple, who was
      engaged in qualifying remunerative work for no less than 16
      hours per week—
      (i) who starts to work less than 16 hours per week and that
          reduction in hours is due to coronavirus;
      (ii) who is notified by A's employer that A is not required to
          work any hours due to coronavirus, but A's employer has
          not made any application under the Coronavirus Job
          Retention Scheme in respect of A; or
      (iii) who is unable to work as a consequence of shielding;
  (c) a person (B), whether or not a member of a couple, who
      satisfies paragraph (c) of the first variation or paragraph (b) of
      the second variation of the Second condition in regulation 4(1)
      (qualifying remunerative work) and who is engaged in qualify-
      ing remunerative work for not less than 30 hours per week—
      (i) who starts to work less than 30 hours per week and that
          reduction in hours is due to coronavirus;

    (ii) who is notified by B's employer that P is not required to work any hours due to coronavirus, but B's employer has not made any application under the Coronavirus Job Retention Scheme in respect of B; or

    (iii) who is unable to work as a consequence of shielding; or

(d) one or both members of a couple who satisfy paragraph (a) of the third variation of the Second condition in regulation 4(1) and who are engaged in qualifying remunerative work—

    (i) who reduce their hours (including a reduction to nil) so that they no longer meet the condition that one member of the couple works no less than 16 hours per week and the aggregate number of hours for which the couple are engaged in qualifying remunerative work is not less than 24 hours per week and any reduction in hours worked is as a consequence of coronavirus; or

    (ii) who are unable to work as a consequence of shielding.

(3) For the purposes of this regulation, a person is a coronavirus-impacted worker if that person is—

(a) an employed person who is within paragraph (2)(b), (c) or (d); or

(b) a self-employed person who is within paragraph (2)(b)(i) or (iii), paragraph (2)(c)(i) or (iii) or paragraph (2)(d).

(4) Where paragraph (2)(a) applies, at the date at which a person (P) ceases to be a furloughed employee under the Coronavirus Job Retention Scheme if—

(a) during the period of eight weeks beginning with the date on which P ceases to be a furloughed employee under that Scheme, the hours that P works do not satisfy the variation in the Second condition of regulation 4(1) which P satisfied immediately before P was furloughed under that Scheme, but it is P's intention that at the end of that period P will satisfy that variation—

    (i) where P does satisfy that variation at the end of that eight-week period, P will be treated as meeting the conditions of entitlement for the purposes of this Part; and

    (ii) where P does not satisfy that variation at the end of that eight-week period, for the purposes of the conditions of entitlement for the purposes of this Part, P will be treated as being engaged in qualifying remunerative work for the four-week period which begins immediately after the end of that eight-week period;

(b) at any time during the period of eight weeks beginning with the date on which P ceases to be a furloughed employee under that Scheme—

    (i) the hours that P works are permanently reduced so that P is not able to satisfy the variation in the Second condition of regulation 4(1) which P satisfied immediately before P became a furloughed employee under that Scheme; or

    (ii) P ceases to undertake work,

for the purposes of the conditions of entitlement in this Part, P will be treated as being engaged in qualifying remunerative work for the four-week period which begins immediately after the reduction in hours or the cessation of employment;

(c) P does not undertake work, for the purposes of the conditions of entitlement in this Part, P will be treated as being engaged in qualifying remunerative work for the four-week period which begins immediately after P ceases to be a furloughed employee under that Scheme; or

(d) there is a permanent reduction in the hours that P works such that P is unable to satisfy the variation in the Second condition of regulation 4(1) which P satisfied immediately before P became a furloughed employee under that Scheme, for the purposes of the conditions of entitlement for this Part, P will be treated as being engaged in qualifying remunerative work for the four-week period which begins immediately after P ceases to be a furloughed employee under that Scheme.

(5) For the purposes of paragraph (4) a person ceases to be a furloughed employee under the Coronavirus Job Retention Scheme when that Scheme no longer applies in respect of that person.

(6) Where paragraph (2)(b), (c) or (d) applies, at the date where a person (P) ceases to be a coronavirus-impacted worker, if—

(a) during the period of eight weeks beginning with the date on which P ceases to be a coronavirus-impacted worker, the hours that P works do not satisfy the variation in the Second condition of regulation 4(1) which P satisfied immediately before P became a coronavirus-impacted worker, but it is P's intention that at the end of that period P will satisfy that variation—

   (i) where P does satisfy that variation at the end of that eight-week period, for the purposes of the conditions of entitlement in this Part, P will be treated as being engaged in qualifying remunerative work during that eight-week period; and

   (ii) where P does not satisfy that variation at the end of that eight-week period, for the purposes of the conditions of entitlement in this Part, P will be treated as being engaged in qualifying remunerative work for the four-week period which begins immediately after the end of that eight-week period;

(b) at any time during the period of eight weeks beginning with the date on which P ceases to be a coronavirus-impacted worker—

   (i) the hours that P works are permanently reduced so that P is not able to satisfy the variation in the Second condition of regulation 4(1) that P satisfied immediately before P became a coronavirus-impacted worker; or

   (ii) P ceases to undertake work,

for the purposes of the conditions of entitlement in this Part, P will be treated as being engaged in qualifying remunerative work for the four-week period which begins immediately after the reduction in hours or after P ceases to work; or

(c) P does not undertake work, for the purposes of the conditions of entitlement in this Part, P will be treated as being engaged in qualifying remunerative work for the four-week period which begins immediately after P ceases to be a coronavirus-impacted worker;

(d) there is a permanent reduction in the hours that P works such that is unable to satisfy the variation in the Second condition of regulation 4(1) which P satisfied immediately before P became a coronavirus-impacted worker, for the purposes of the conditions of entitlement in this Part, P will be treated as being engaged in qualifying remunerative work for the four-week period which begins immediately after P ceases to be a coronavirus-impacted worker.

(7) For the purposes of paragraph (6) if—

(a) a person is within paragraph (2)(b)(i) or (ii), paragraph (2)(c)(i) or (ii) or paragraph (2)(d)(i), that person ceases to be a coronavirus-impacted worker on the day that the Coronavirus Job Retention Scheme ceases; and

(b) a person is within paragraph (2)(b)(iii), paragraph (2)(c)(iii) or paragraph (2)(d)(ii), that person ceases to be a coronavirus-impacted worker the day after the day on which the period for which that person was shielding ends.

(8) In this regulation a person (P) is shielding, or required to shield, if P, or another person living in the same household as P, has been notified by the National Health Service, their specialist or their general practitioner that they are clinically extremely vulnerable due to coronavirus.".

DEFINITIONS

"coronavirus" —see reg.2.
"coronavirus Job Retention Scheme"—see reg.2.
"couple"—see reg.2.
"furloughed employee under the Coronavirus Job Retention Scheme"—see reg.2.
"qualifying remunerative work"—see reg.4.

GENERAL NOTE

5.020   This regulation modifies reg.4's qualifying remunerative work requirements for the intended benefit of claimants whose working hours have been reduced, whose work has ceased, or who have been furloughed, due to coronavirus. In a range of circumstances, claimants whose work has been so affected by coronavirus are treated as if they continued to meet reg.4's qualifying remunerative work requirements.

Employees who have been furloughed are to be treated as engaged in qualifying remunerative work during the period of furlough (reg.7E(1)(a)). Any employee who ceases to be furloughed is treated as being in qualifying remunerative work for the next four weeks whether or not the claimant in fact satisfies reg.4's requirements as to what constitutes qualifying remunerative work (reg.7E(4A)). The same applies to claimants who cease to be one of the other types of coronavirus-impacted worker provided for in reg.7E(2) (reg.7E(6A)).

Persons who used to be engaged in qualifying remunerative work for not less than 16 hours per week, but are no longer so engaged due to coronavirus, are treated as if they were if any of the circumstances in reg.7E(2)(b) apply, for example where their hours of work are reduced to less than 16 hours per week due to coronavirus or they are unable to work as a consequence of shielding (as defined in reg.7E(8)). Similar deeming provisions apply to employees who, within four weeks of ceasing to be furloughed, accept a new job offer whose hours of work are then reduced, or who are not required to work at all, due to coronavirus (reg.7E(2)(aa)) as well as to claimants who, following a statutory absence as provided for by regs 5 and 6, no longer work for at least 16 hours per week (reg.7E(2)(e)). Provision is also made for claimants who, due to coronavirus, longer work for not less than 30 hours per week, which is relevant to, for example, claimants who are not responsible for a qualifying child or young person (reg.7E(2)(c)).

Note that reg.7E(2)'s deeming provisions apply to both employed claimants and, in the case of the self-employed, those whose hours of work reduce due to coronavirus or as a consequence of shielding (see reg.7E(3)(b)). **5.021**

Regulation 7E also provides for a type of entitlement run-on intended to benefit claimants who, upon ceasing to be furloughed, do not initially work sufficient hours each week to satisfy reg.4's requirements as to what constitutes qualifying remunerative work. If, by the end of the period of eight weeks after a claimant ceased to be furloughed, the claimant satisfies reg.4's weekly hours of work requirements, the claimant is treated as satisfying the working tax credit conditions of entitlement (reg.7E(4)(a)(i)). If, by the end of that eight-week period, a claimant person does not satisfy reg.4's requirements, the claimant is nevertheless treated as being in qualifying remunerative work for the next four weeks (reg.7E(4)(a)(ii)).

Where, during the period of eight weeks following cessation of furloughing, a claimant's hours of work are permanently reduced so that the claimant no longer satisfies the previously-met weekly hours of work requirement under reg.4, or the person ceases to work, the claimant is treated as engaged in qualifying remunerative work for the four week period following the reduction or cessation (reg.7E(4)(b)). Similar provision is made for claimants who do not return to work after furlough (reg.7E(4)(c)).

Similar provision to that made for claimants who cease to be furloughed is made for other claimants, including self-employed claimants, whose weekly hours of work reduce or come to an end after they cease to be 'coronavirus-impacted workers' (reg.7E(6)).

p.613, *amendment to the Working Tax Credit (Entitlement and Maximum Rate) Regulations 2002 (SI 2002/2005) reg.10 (30 hour element)*

With effect from May 23, 2020, reg.2(6) of the Tax Credits (Coronavirus, Miscellaneous Amendments) Regulations 2020 (SI 2020/534) amended reg.10 by inserting ", except where paragraph (4) applies" in para.(1) after "per week" but before the full stop and by inserting at the end— **5.022**

"(4) This paragraph applies where—
  (a) the claimant or, where it is a joint claim, one of the claimants is, or both of the claimants are, impacted by coronavirus;

(b) during the period of the Coronavirus Job Retention Scheme, the claimant undertakes work for no more than 29 hours per week; and

(c) immediately before the date on which the claimant became impacted, the maximum rate did not include a 30 hours element.

(5) In this regulation a person is impacted by coronavirus if that person is—

(a) a furloughed employee under the Coronavirus Job Retention Scheme; or

(b) a coronavirus-impacted worker.".

pp.641–643, *amendment to the Tax Credits (Definition and Calculation of Income) Regulations 2002 (SI 2002/2006) reg.2 (Interpretation)*

5.023   With effect from May 23, 2020, reg.3(2) of the Tax Credits (Coronavirus, Miscellaneous Amendments) Regulations 2020 (SI 2020/534) amended reg.2(2) by inserting in the appropriate places the following new definitions—

""coronavirus" means severe acute respiratory syndrome coronavirus 2;"

""coronavirus support scheme" means—

(a) any scheme in relation to which HMRC have functions by virtue of a direction made under section 76 of the Coronavirus Act 2020 (HMRC functions);

(b) the scheme known as the Small Business Grant Fund established in response to coronavirus;

(c) any scheme established in the tax year 2020-2021 in response to coronavirus to support the fishing industry;

(d) the scheme known as the Retail, Hospitality and Leisure Grant Fund established in response to coronavirus;

(e) the scheme known as the Newly Self-Employed Hardship Fund established by the Scottish Ministers in the tax year 2020-2021 in response to coronavirus; and

(f) any other support scheme established in the tax year 2020-2021 in response to coronavirus;"

""Scottish Ministers" has the meaning given by section 44(2) of the Scotland Act 1998.".

p.647, *annotation to the Tax Credits (Definition and Calculation of Income) Regulations 2002 (SI 2002/2006) reg.3 (Calculation of income of claimant)*

5.024   In *JQ v HMRC (TC)* [2020] UKUT 340 (AAC) Upper Tribunal Judge Jones dismissed the claimant's appeal against a decision of the First-tier Tribunal that he was not entitled to offset against his tax credits income an asserted property loss relief provided for by s.120(1) of the Income Tax 2007. Section 120(1) provides that a person may make a claim for property loss relief against general income where a loss "has a

498

capital allowances connection". In deciding that the First-tier Tribunal's decision involved no error on a point of law, Judge Jones relied on the apparently undisputed evidence before the First-tier Tribunal that the claimant had not, as s.120(1) anticipates and s.3 of the Capital Allowances Act 2001 requires, made any claim in a tax return for property loss relief to be offset against an income tax liability for the relevant tax year. In any event, on that evidence, the First-tier Tribunal was bound to find that the claimant was not in fact carrying on an overseas property business during the relevant tax year. The evidence was that, during the tax year, the claimant received no income from his overseas property. The claimant's overseas property was in the nature of an investment rather than a business. Moreover, there was no evidence that the claimant incurred expenditure on plant or machinery. Section 123 of the 2007 Act defines a loss "with a capital connection" and, in doing so, expressly excludes structures and buildings allowances under Part 2A of the Capital Allowances Act 2001, so that this claimant would have needed to establish that his claimed loss involved expenditure on plant or machinery. However, there was no evidence that the claimant incurred expenditure on plant and machinery for his overseas property business during the relevant tax year.

pp.661-662, *amendments to the Tax Credits (Definition and Calculation of Income) Regulations 2002 (SI 2002/2006) reg.6 (Trading income)*

With effect from May 23, 2020, reg.3(3) of the Tax Credits (Coronavirus, Miscellaneous Amendments) Regulations 2020 (SI 2020/534) substituted a new reg.6 (trading income) as follows—

5.025

"Trading Income

5.026

6.—(1) The claimant's trading income is—
  (a) the amount of the claimant's taxable profits for the tax year from—
      (i) any trade carried on in the United Kingdom or elsewhere; and
      (ii) any profession or vocation the income from which does not fall under any other provisions of these Regulations; and
  (b) any grant or any sum paid to the claimant under a coronavirus support scheme, except any payment made under the Coronavirus Job Retention Scheme in respect of an employee,
except where the claimant is a partner in the trade, profession or vocation in which case paragraph (2) applies.
  (2) Where the claimant is a partner in a trade, profession or vocation, the claimant's trading income is—
  (a) the taxable profits for the tax year arising from the claimant's share of the partnership's trading or professional income; and
  (b) any grant or any sum paid to the claimant under a coronavirus support scheme, except any payment made under the Coronavirus Job Retention Scheme in respect of an employee.
  (3) In this regulation—

(a) "taxable profits" has the same meaning as it has in Part 2 of ITTOIA but disregarding the relevant benefit amount in section 23E (tax treatment of relevant benefits) and Chapter 16 of that Part (averaging profits of farmers and creative artists); and

(b) "Coronavirus Job Retention Scheme" means the scheme of that name established under the direction given by the Chancellor of the Exchequer under section 76 of the Coronavirus Act 2020 on 15th April 2020 (as that Scheme has effect from time to time)."

However, with effect from September 25, 2020, reg.2(2) of the Tax Credits (Coronavirus, Miscellaneous Amendments) (No.2) Regulations 2020 (SI 2020/941) substituted a new reg.6 as follows—

"Trading income

6. The claimant's ("C") trading income is—
(a) the amount of C's taxable profits for the tax year arising from—
(i) any trade carried on in the United Kingdom or elsewhere;
(ii) any profession or vocation the income from which does not fall under any other provision of these Regulations; or
(b) the amount of C's taxable profits for the year arising from C's share of the partnership trading or professional income where C is a partner in a trade, profession or vocation.
In this regulation "taxable profits" has the same meaning as it has in Part 2 of ITTOIA, but disregarding the relevant benefit amount in section 23E (tax treatment of relevant benefits) and Chapter 16 of that Part (averaging profits of farmers and creative artists)."

p.662, *annotation to the Tax Credits (Definition and Calculation of Income) Regulations 2002 (SI 2002/2006) reg.6 (Trading income)*

5.027   While the current text of reg.6 was substituted by SI 2020/941, it is now in materially the same form as its pre-May 23, 2020, version. Between May 23, 2020 and September 24, 2020, reg.6 was amended by SI 2020/534 to take account of certain coronavirus support scheme payments. Those amendments were removed by SI 2020/941 so that reg.6 reverted, in material respects, to its earlier form.

p.684, *amendment to the Tax Credits (Definition and Calculation of Income) Regulations 2002 (SI 2002/2006) reg.18 (Miscellaneous income)*

5.028   With effect from May 23, 2020, reg.3(4) of the Tax Credits (Coronavirus, Miscellaneous Amendments) Regulations 2020 (SI 2020/534) substituted a new reg.18 (miscellaneous income) as follows—

"Miscellaneous Income

18. In these Regulations "miscellaneous income" means income which does not fall within any other provision of these Regulations, and which is either—
(a) subject to income tax under Part 5 of ITTOIA; or
(b) a payment under, or in connection with, a coronavirus support scheme."

p.684, *amendment to the Tax Credits (Definition and Calculation of Income) Regulations 2002 (SI 2002/2006) reg.19 (General disregards in the calculation of income)*

With effect from May 23, 2020, reg.3(5)(a) of the Tax Credits (Coronavirus, Miscellaneous Amendments) Regulations 2020 (SI 2020/534) omitted from para.(2) the definition of "Scottish Ministers".   5.029

p.689, *amendments to the Tax Credits (Definition and Calculation of Income) Regulations 2002 (SI 2002/2006) reg.19 (General disregards in the calculation of income), Table 6 (Sums disregarded in the calculation of income)*

With effect from May 23, 2020, reg.3(5)(b) of the Tax Credits (Coronavirus, Miscellaneous Amendments) Regulations 2020 (SI 2020/534) inserted in Table 6 (sums disregarded in the calculation of income) after entry 33 the following new entries—   5.030

"**34.** A payment, whether in cash or by way of a voucher, in lieu of free school meals.
35. A payment in connection with emergency volunteering leave under Schedule 7 to the Coronavirus Act 2020.
36. A payment made under the scheme known as the NHS and Social Care Coronavirus Life Assurance Scheme 2020.".

However, with effect from September 25, 2020, reg.2(3) of the Tax Credits (Coronavirus, Miscellaneous Amendments) (No.2) Regulations 2020 (SI 2020/941) omitted entry 36 and inserted after entry 35 the following new entry—

"**37.** Any payment made under the scheme known as the NHS Test and Trace Self-Isolation Payment Scheme established on 1st September 2020 in respect of England or under any similar scheme established in respect of Wales, Scotland or Northern Ireland.".

p.744, *amendment to the Tax Credits (Income Thresholds and Determination of Rates) Regulations 2002 (SI 2002/2008)*

With effect from December 31, 2020, at 11.00pm, reg.5 of the Tax Credits and Child Trust Funds (Amendment) (EU Exit) Regulations 2019 (SI 2019/713) inserted the following regulation after reg.8 of the 2002 Regulations: 5.031

"[1 Cases where there is a reciprocal agreement

8A.—(1) This regulation applies where the United Kingdom is competent to pay family benefits in accordance with Article 39 of the Reciprocal Agreement with Ireland but where Ireland has primary competence for payment of those benefits.

(2) Where this regulation applies, child tax credit shall be paid at the rate according to the calculation set out in paragraph (4) of Article 39 of the Reciprocal Agreement with Ireland.

(3) Child tax credit shall be paid on a provisional basis where—

(a) Article 39(5) of the Reciprocal Agreement with Ireland applies;

(b) the United Kingdom is Party B in the circumstances set out under Article 40(1)(b) of the Reciprocal Agreement with Ireland; or

(c) the United Kingdom does not agree that it has primary competence for payment of family benefits where the child resides or the children reside in the United Kingdom and Article 63(2) of the Reciprocal Agreement with Ireland applies.

(4) In this regulation—

(a) "family benefits" has the meaning as set out in Article 3(1)(x) of the Reciprocal Agreement with Ireland; and

(b) "the Reciprocal Agreement with Ireland" means the Convention on Social Security between the Government of the United Kingdom of Great Britain and Northern Ireland and the Government of Ireland signed at Dublin on 1st February 2019.]

AMENDMENT

1. The Tax Credits and Child Trust Funds (Amendment) (EU Exit) Regulations 2019 (SI 2019/713) reg.5 (31 December 2020, at 11.00pm: see the definition of 'IP completion day' in s.39(1) of the European Union (Withdrawal Agreement) Act 2020).

DEFINITIONS

The Convention on Social Security between the Government of the United Kingdom and Northern Ireland and the Government of Ireland, as referred to in the definition of "the Reciprocal Agreement with Ireland" is scheduled to, and given effect in UK law by Article 2(1) of, the Social Security (Ireland) Order 2019 (SI 2019/622)). The Convention took effect on December 31, 2020.

GENERAL NOTE

5.032   The relevant parts of the Reciprocal Agreement with Ireland, reference to which is necessary to understand regulation 8A, are set out below:

"ARTICLE 1

Definitions

(1) For the purposes of this Convention the following definitions apply, except where the context otherwise requires:

. . . "competence", in relation to a Party, means responsibility for payment of a particular benefit under the legislation it applies to a person who:

     (i) is insured in that Party in relation to a benefit of that type, at the time of their claim for it; or . . .

     (ii) would be entitled to such benefit if they (or a member of their family or survivor, where relevant) resided in that Party,

and the word "competent" shall be construed accordingly;

. . . "insured" means, in relation to a person,

     (i) under the legislation of the United Kingdom, that they have the right to a type of benefit set out in Article 3(1), taking into account the provisions of this Convention . . .

ARTICLE 3

Scope of legislation

(1) This Convention shall apply:

    (a) in relation to the United Kingdom, to . . . the Tax Credits Act 2002 . . . and the subordinate legislation made under those Acts . . . as they relate . . . to:

     (x) the following family benefits:

      . . . Child Tax Credit . . .

ARTICLE 7

Waiving of residence rules

Unless otherwise provided by this Convention, benefits payable to a person or a member of their family under the legislation of a Party, or by a Party under this Convention, shall not be subject to any reduction, amendment, suspension, withdrawal or confiscation on account of the fact that such a person or a member of their family resides in the other Party.

ARTICLE 9

General provisions

(1) A person shall be subject to the legislation of a single Party which shall be determined in accordance with this Part.

(2) A person receiving a benefit from one Party because or as a consequence of their activity as an employed or self-employed person shall be considered to be pursuing that activity in that Party.

. . .

(4) Subject to Articles 10 to 13:

(a) a person pursuing an activity as an employed or self-employed person in one Party shall be subject to the legislation of that Party;

. . .

(d) any other person to whom sub-paragraphs (a) to (d) do not apply shall be subject to the legislation of the Party in which they reside, without prejudice to other provisions of this Convention guaranteeing them benefits under the legislation of the other Party.

ARTICLE 38

Responsibility for payment of family benefits

(1) A person, other than a pensioner, shall be entitled to family benefits in accordance with the legislation applied by a Party where it is competent for the payment of such benefits, including for any members of the family residing in the other Party, as if they were residing in the former Party . . .

ARTICLE 39

Priority rules where both Parties' legislation applies

(1) Priority rules in this Article apply to determine which Party pays family benefits where during the same period and for the same family members a person (including a pensioner) is entitled to such benefits under the legislation of both Parties.

(2) Where such benefits are payable by both Parties on a different basis, the order of priority shall be decided on the basis of rights:

(a) a vailable on the basis of an activity as an employed or self-employed person;

(b) available on the basis of receipt of a pension; and

(c) obtained on the basis of residence.

(3) Where such benefits arc payable by both Parties on the same basis, the order of priority shall be decided by reference to the following criteria:

(a) in the case of rights available on the basis of an activity as an employed or self-employed person, the Party of residence of the child or children in respect of whom benefits are paid;

(b) in the case of rights available on the basis of receipt of pensions, the Party of residence of the child or children in respect of whom benefits are paid;

(c) in the case of rights available on the basis of residence, the Party of residence of the child or children in respect of whom benefits are paid.

(4) Where such benefits are payable by both Parties, they shall be paid by the Party having priority in accordance with paragraphs (I) to (3) (the Party with priority), and the following rules shall apply:

(a) entitlement to family benefits under the legislation applying to the other Party shall be suspended up to the amount provided by the Party with priority and a differential supplement shall, if necessary, be provided by the other Party for the sum which exceeds this amount;

(b) but where entitlement to family benefits is based on residence only, and whichever Party has priority, no differential supplement is payable for a child or children residing in the other Party.

(5) Where the order of priority cannot be established on the basis of the child or children's place of residence in accordance with paragraphs (3)(a) and (b), the Party whose legislation provides for the higher level of benefits (Party A) shall pay the full amount of such benefits on a provisional basis. The payment shall be made taking into account any children not residing in Party A. Party A shall then be reimbursed by the other Party (Party B) half the sum it has paid up to the limit of the amount provided for in the legislation of Party B.

(6) Where a claim is made to the Party whose legislation is applicable but not by priority right in accordance with paragraphs (1) to (3) (Party A):

(a) the relevant authority of Party A shall send the claim, without delay, to the relevant authority of the other Party (Party B), inform the person concerned and, without prejudice to Article 63(1), provide, if necessary, the differential supplement mentioned in paragraph (4);

(b) the relevant authority of Party B will deal with this claim as though it had been submitted to it in the first instance, and the date on which the claim was submitted to the relevant authority of Party A shall be treated as the date on which it was received by Party B.

ARTICLE 40

Provisional award of family benefits

(1) Where family benefits are payable by both Parties, but no decision has been made on how the priority rules in Articles 39(1) to (3) apply to a particular claim, the following rules shall apply:
. . .

(b) if Party A decides that the other Party (Party B) is competent to pay such benefits, it will forward the application without delay to the relevant authority of Party B and inform the person concerned; . . .

505

ARTICLE 63

Provisional application of legislation and provisional granting of benefits

. . .

(2) Where there is a difference of views between the Parties as to which is competent for payment of a benefit to a person who has made a claim, they shall he entitled, on a provisional basis, to such benefits under the legislation of their Party of residence."

p.747, *amendments to the Tax Credits (Claims and Notifications) Regulations 2002 (SI 2002/2014) reg.2 (Interpretation)*

5.033   With effect from May 23, 2020, reg.4(2) of the Tax Credits (Coronavirus, Miscellaneous Amendments) Regulations 2020 (SI 2020/534) amended reg.2 by inserting the following new definitions in the appropriate places after the definitions of "the Contributions and Benefits Act" and "couple" respectively—

""Coronavirus Job Retention Scheme" means the scheme of that name established under the direction given by the Chancellor of the Exchequer on 15th April 2020 (as that Scheme has effect from time to time);";
""critical worker" means a worker in a critical sector listed—
    (a) in England in the version of the document entitled "Guidance for schools, childcare providers, colleagues, local authorities in England on maintaining educational provision" published by the Cabinet Office and the Department for Education on 14th May 2020;
    (b) in Scotland in the document entitled "Coronavirus (COVID-19): school and early learning closures— guidance about key workers and vulnerable children" published on 31st March 2020;
    (c) in Wales in the version of the document entitled "Coronavirus key (critical) workers" published on 18th May 2020; and
    (d) in Northern Ireland in the document entitled "General Guidance on COVID-19 for schools;"

With effect from the same date the same amending regulations substituted "for Her Majesty's Revenue and Customs" for "of Inland Revenue" in the definition of "the Board".

p.747, *amendment to the Tax Credits (Claims and Notifications) Regulations 2002 (SI 2002/2014) reg.2 (Interpretation)*

5.034   With effect from December 31, 2020, at 11.00pm, reg.3(a) of the Tax Credits and Child Trust Funds (Amendment) (EU Exit) Regulations 2019 (SI 2019/713) amended the definition of "relevant authority" in reg.2(1) by omitting "or" at the end of paragraph (b) of the definition, inserting "or" at the end of paragraph (c), and inserting the following wording after paragraph (c):

"(d) the Department of Employment Affairs and Social Protection in Ireland, in connection with a claim to a child tax credit made pursuant to Part IV Section 4 of the Convention on Social Security between the Government of the United Kingdom of Great Britain and Northern Ireland and the Government of Ireland signed at Dublin on 1st February 2019;"

p.748, *annotation to the Tax Credits (Claims and Notifications) Regulations 2002 (SI 2002/2014) reg.2 (Interpretation)*

The direction given by the Chancellor of the Exchequer on April 15, 2020, as referred to in the definition of "Coronavirus Job Retention Scheme", as referred to in the definition of "furloughed employee under the Coronavirus Job Creation Scheme", is available at *http://www.gov.uk/government/publications/treasury-direction-made-under-sections-71-and-76-of-the-coronavirus-act-2020.* 5.035

p.767, *amendment to the Tax Credits (Claims and Notifications) Regulations 2002 (SI 2002/2014) reg.21 (Requirement to notify changes of circumstances which may decrease rate)*

With effect from May 23, 2020, reg.4(3) of the Tax Credits (Coronavirus, Miscellaneous Amendments) Regulations 2020 (SI 2020/534) amended reg.21 so as to insert after para.(3) the following new paragraph— 5.036

"(4) Where the claimant is a critical worker, this paragraph does not apply for the period beginning on 23rd May 2020 and ending on the date on which the Coronavirus Job Retention Scheme ends, but regulation 21A applies during that period."

p.769, *amendment to the Tax Credits (Claims and Notifications) Regulations 2002 (SI 2002/2014) new reg.21A inserted (Coronavirus— date of notification—cases where change of circumstances which may decrease the rate at which a person is, or persons are, entitled to a tax credit or mean that entitlement to that tax credit ceases)*

With effect from May 23, 2020, reg.4(4) of the Tax Credits (Coronavirus, Miscellaneous Amendments) Regulations 2020 (SI 2020/534) inserted after reg.21 the following new regulation 21A— 5.037

"Coronavirus—date of notification—cases where change of circumstances which may decrease the rate at which a person is, or persons are, entitled to a tax credit or mean that entitlement to that tax credit ceases

21A.—(1) This regulation only applies—
   (a) for the period beginning on 23rd May 2020 and ending on the date on which the Coronavirus Job Retention Scheme ends; and

(b) if the claimant is a critical worker during that period.

(2) Where this regulation applies, the claimant must give notification within the time prescribed by paragraph (3) if there is a change of circumstances of the description prescribed by paragraph (2) of regulation 21 (requirement to notify changes of circumstances which may decrease the rate etc.) which may decrease the rate at which that person is entitled to that tax credit or means that that person ceases to be entitled to that tax credit.

(3) The time prescribed by this paragraph is the period of three months beginning on the date on which the change of circumstances occurs."

p.769, *amendment to the Tax Credits (Claims and Notifications) Regulations 2002 (SI 2002/2014) reg.25 (Date of notification—cases where a change of circumstances which may increase the maximum rate)*

5.038   With effect from May 23, 2020, reg.4(5) of the Tax Credits (Coronavirus, Miscellaneous Amendments) Regulations 2020 (SI 2020/534) amended reg.25 so as to insert after para.(3) the following new paragraph—

"(4) Where the claimant is a critical worker, this regulation does not apply for the period beginning on 23rd May 2020 and ending on the date on which the Coronavirus Job Retention Scheme ends, but regulation 25A applies during that period."

p.771, *annotation to the Tax Credits (Claims and Notifications) Regulations 2002 (SI 2002/2014) reg.25 (Date of notification—cases where a change of circumstances which may increase the maximum rate)*

5.039   The first sentence of the General Note is altered to add the italicised words below:

Where a change in circumstances leads to an increase in the claimant's entitlement to tax credits, the change can only be backdated for up to one month before the date of notification (*unless the claimant is a critical worker who satisfies the requirements of regulation 25A*).

p.771, *amendment to the Tax Credits (Claims and Notifications) Regulations 2002 (SI 2002/2014) new reg.25A inserted (Coronavirus— date of notification—cases where change of circumstances may increase the maximum rate)*

5.040   With effect from May 23, 2020, reg.4(6) of the Tax Credits (Coronavirus, Miscellaneous Amendments) Regulations 2020 (SI 2020/534) inserted after reg.25 the following new regulation 25A—

"Coronavirus—date of notification—cases where change of circumstances may increase the maximum rate

25A.—(1) This regulation only applies—
    (a) for the period beginning on 23rd May 2020 and ending on the

508

date on which the Coronavirus Job Retention Scheme ends; and

(b) if the claimant is a critical worker during that period.

(2) Where—

(a) this regulation applies; and

(b) a notification of change of circumstances which may increase the maximum rate at which a critical worker may be entitled to a tax credit is given in the circumstances prescribed by paragraph (2) of regulation 25 (date of notification—cases where change of circumstances which may increase the maximum rate),

that notification is to be treated as having been given on the date prescribed by paragraph (3).

(3) The date prescribed by this paragraph is—

(a) the date falling three months before the notification date; or

(b) if later, the date of the change of circumstances."

p.772, *amendment to the Tax Credits (Claims and Notifications) Regulations 2002 (SI 2002/2014) reg.26 (Date of notification—disability element and severe disability element of working tax credit)*

With effect from May 23, 2020, reg.4(7) of the Tax Credits (Coronavirus, Miscellaneous Amendments) Regulations 2020 (SI 2020/534) amended reg.26 so as to insert after para.(3) the following new paragraph— **5.041**

"(4) Where the claimant is a critical worker, this regulation does not apply for the period beginning on 23rd May 2020 and ending on the date on which the Coronavirus Job Retention Scheme ends, but regulation 26B applies during that period."

p.772, *amendment to the Tax Credits (Claims and Notifications) Regulations 2002 (SI 2002/2014) reg.26A (Date of notification—disability element where child is disabled or severely disabled)*

With effect from May 23, 2020, reg.4(8) of the Tax Credits (Coronavirus, Miscellaneous Amendments) Regulations 2020 (SI 2020/534) amended reg.26 so as to insert after para.(4) the following new paragraph— **5.042**

"(5) Where the claimant is a critical worker, this regulation does not apply for the period beginning on 23rd May 2020 and ending on the date on which the Coronavirus Job Retention Scheme ends, but regulation 26B applies during that period."

p.773, *amendment to the Tax Credits (Claims and Notifications) Regulations 2002 (SI 2002/2014) new reg.26B inserted (Coronavirus—date of notification of disability)*

With effect from May 23, 2020, reg.4(9) of the Tax Credits (Coronavirus, Miscellaneous Amendments) Regulations 2020 (SI 2020/534) inserted after reg.26A the following new regulation 26B— **5.043**

"Coronavirus—date of notification of disability

26B.—(1) This regulation only applies—

(a) for the period beginning on 23rd May 2020 and ending on the date on which the Coronavirus Job Retention Scheme ends; and

(b) if the claimant is a critical worker during that period.

(2) Where—

(a) this regulation applies; and

(b) a notification of a change of circumstances which may increase the maximum rate at which a critical worker may be entitled to working tax credit is given in the circumstances prescribed by paragraph (4),

the notification is to be treated as having been given on the date prescribed by paragraph (5).

(3) Where—

(a) this regulation applies; and

(b) a notification of a change of circumstances which may increase the maximum rate at which a critical worker may be entitled to child tax credit is given in the circumstances prescribed by paragraph (6),

the notification is to be treated as having been given on the date prescribed by paragraph (7).

(4) The circumstances prescribed by this paragraph are where—

(a) a notification is given of a change of circumstances in respect of a claim to working tax credit, which results in the Board making an award of the disability element or the severe disability element of working tax credit (or both of them) in favour of a person or persons; and

(b) the notification date is within three months of the date that a claim for any of the benefits referred to in regulations 9(2) to (8) or 17(2) of the Working Tax Credit Regulations is determined in favour of those persons (or one of them).

(5) The date prescribed by this paragraph is the latest of the following—

(a) the first date in respect of which the benefit claimed was payable;

(b) the date falling three months before the claim for the benefit was made;

(c) the date the claim for working tax credit was made (or treated as made under regulations 7 (time limits for claims) and 7A (time limit for claims—the Childcare Payments Act 2014));

(d) for the purposes of the disability element only, the first date that the person or persons satisfied the conditions of entitlement for the disability element.

(6) The change of circumstances prescribed by this paragraph are where—

(a) a notification is given of a change of circumstances in respect of a claim to child tax credit which results in the Board making an award of the disability element of that tax credit in favour of a person or persons, in respect of a child where that child is disabled or severely disabled; and

(b) the notification date is within three months of the date that a claim for a disability benefit, personal independence payment or armed forces independence payment in respect of the child is determined in favour of those persons (or one of them).

(7) The date prescribed by this paragraph is the latest of the following—

(a) the first date in respect of which the disability benefit, the personal independence payment or the armed forces independence payment was payable;

(b) the date falling three months before the claim for a disability benefit, personal independence payment or armed forces independence payment was made;

(c) the date the claim for child tax credit was made (or treated as made under regulations 7 and 7A).

(8) In this regulation "disability benefit" has the meaning given by regulation 26A(4)."

p.807, *amendment to the Tax Credits (Immigration) Regulations 2003 (SI 2003/653) reg.3 (Exclusion of person subject to immigration control from entitlement to tax credits)*

With effect from January 1, 2021, reg.4(2) of the Social Security, Child Benefit and Child Tax Credit (Amendment) (EU Exit) Regulations 2020 (SI 2020/1505) amended Case 5 by substituting for the text after "he is" until the end of the Case the following— 5.044

"a person who is lawfully working in the United Kingdom and—

(a) who—

(i) made a claim before 1st January 2021; and

(ii) is a national of a State with which the European Union had, before 1st January 2021, concluded an agreement under Article 217 of the Treaty on the Functioning of the European Union providing in the field of social security for the equal treatment of workers who are nationals of the signatory State and their families; or

(b) who is a national of a State with which the United Kingdom has concluded an agreement which replaces, in whole or in part, an agreement under Article 217 of the Treaty on the Functioning of the European Union which either—

(i) makes provision in the field of social security for the equal treatment of workers who are nationals of the State with which the agreement has been concluded and their families, or

(ii) makes provision for receipt of family allowances by members of a worker's family who are legally resident in the United Kingdom.".

p.809, *annotation to the Tax Credits (Immigration) Regulations 2003 (SI 2003/653) reg.3 (Exclusion of persons subject to immigration control from entitlement to tax credits)*

5.045   The following sentence of the General Note is omitted: "The exception in Case 5 is adapted from para.2 of Pt II of the Schedule to the 2000 Regulations, which deals with exceptions from the preclusionary rule in respect of certain non-contributory benefits."

p.809, *annotation to the Tax Credits (Immigration) Regulations 2003 (SI 2003/653) reg.3 (Exclusion of persons subject to immigration control from entitlement to tax credits)*

5.046   Case 5 was amended in consequence of the United Kingdom's withdrawal from the European Union. Previously Case 5 referred to a person working lawfully in the United Kingdom who was a national of a State party to a Community Agreement for the equal treatment, in the field of social security, of workers and their families. The current Case 5 draws a distinction between those who claim before January 1, 2021 and those who claim subsequently.

  Those who claim before January 1, 2021 must be lawfully working in the UK and a national of a State that was party to an equal treatment agreement made with the European Union under Art.217 of the Treaty on the Functioning of the European Union.

  For those claiming on or after January 1, 2021, the claimant must be a national of State with which the UK has entered into an equal treatment agreement, meeting a condition in (b)(i) or (ii) of Case 5, in place of an agreement under Art.217. This may include the Convention on Social Security between the Government of the United Kingdom and Northern Ireland and the Government of Ireland, of February 1, 2019, given effect in UK law by art.2 of the Social Security (Ireland) Order 2019 (SI 2019/622), which came into force on December 31, 2020. For details of that Convention, which covers child tax credit, see the note to regulation 8A of the Child Tax Credit Regulations 2002 above in this volume.

pp.813-814, *amendments to the Tax Credits (Residence) Regulations 2003 (SI 2003/654) reg.3 (Circumstances in which a person is treated as not being in the United Kingdom)*

5.047   With effect from December 31, 2020, at 11.00pm, reg.14(2)(a)-(c) of the Immigration (Citizens' Rights etc.) (EU Exit) Regulations 2020 (SI 2020/1372) amended reg.3(5) by inserting "(P)" after "person" and omitting "he" in para.(5) and at the beginning of para.(5)(a) inserting "P" and substituting "and one of sub-paragraphs (b), (c) or (d) applies;" for "; and". The same amening regulations substitute the following new sub-paragraphs for para.(5)(b):

  "(b) P does not have a right to reside in the United Kingdom;
  (c) P has a right to reside under paragraph (1) of regulation 16 of the Immigration (European Economic Area) Regulations 2016, but

only in a case where the right exists under that regulation because P satisfies the criteria in paragraph (5) of that regulation; or

(d) P would fall within sub-paragraph (b) or (c) but for the fact that P has limited leave to enter, or remain in, the United Kingdom under the Immigration Act 1971 by virtue of—

  (i) Appendix EU to the immigration rules; or

  (ii) having arrived in the United Kingdom with an entry clearance that was granted under Appendix EU (Family Permit) to the immigration rules made under section 3(2) of that Act.".

p.814, *amendments to the Tax Credits (Residence) Regulations 2003 (SI 2003/654) reg.3 (Circumstances in which a person is treated as not being in the United Kingdom) insertion of new paras (5A) and (5B)*

With effect from December 31, 2020, at 11.00pm, reg.5(2)(a) of the Social Security, Child Benefit and Child Tax Credit (Amendment) (EU Exit) Regulations 2020 (SI 2020/1505) amended reg.3 by substituting a new para.(5A) as follows— **5.048**

"(5A) Paragraph (5)(c) does not apply to a person who is lawfully working in the United Kingdom—

(a) who—

  (i) made a claim for child tax credit before 1st January 2021, and

  (ii) is a national of a State with which the European Union had, before 1st January 2021, concluded an agreement under Article 217 of the Treaty on the Functioning of the European Union providing in the field of social security for the equal treatment of workers who are nationals of the signatory State and their families; or

(b) who is a national of a State with which the United Kingdom has concluded an agreement which replaces, in whole or in part, an EU Agreement which has ceased to apply in the United Kingdom."

With effect from August 24, 2020, reg.3(2)(a) of the Child Benefit and Child Tax Credit (Persons of Northern Ireland) (Amendment) Regulations 2020 (SI 2020/672) inserted after para.(5A) the following new paragraph—

"(5B) Paragraph (5)(b)(iii) does not apply to a person who—

(a) has limited leave to enter, or remain in, the United Kingdom under the Immigration Act 1971 which has been granted by virtue of Appendix EU to the Immigration Rules;

(b) has been granted such leave in reliance of being a family member of a relevant person of Northern Ireland in accordance with those Rules; and

(c) would have a right to reside under the Immigration (European Economic Area) Regulations 2016 if the relevant person of

Northern Ireland were an EEA national within the meaning of regulation 2 of those Regulations."

With effect from December 31, 2020, reg.14(2)(d)-(e) of the Immigration (Citizens' Rights etc.) (EU Exit) Regulations 2020 (SI 2020/1505) amended para.(5A) by substituting "(5)(c)" for "(5)(b)(ii)" and substituting "(5)(d)(i)" for "(5)(b)(iii)" in para.(5B).

p.814, *amendments to the Tax Credits (Residence) Regulations 2003 (SI 2003/654) reg.3(7) (Circumstances in which a person is treated as not being in the United Kingdom)*

5.049 With effect from December 31, 2020, reg.61(2) of the Immigration and Social Security Co-ordination (EU Withdrawal) Act 2020 (Consequential, Saving, Transitional and Transitory Provisions) (EU Exit) Regulations 2020 (SI 2020/1309) amended reg.3(7) by substituting ", (i) or (o)" for "or (i)" in sub-para.(e) and substituting for sub-para.(i) the following—

"(i) is not a national of an EEA State and would be a worker or self-employed person in the United Kingdom for the purposes of the Immigration (European Economic Area) Regulations 2016 if that person—
    (i) were a national of an EEA State; and
    (ii) a "member of the post-transition period group" within the meaning of paragraph 1 of Schedule 4 to the Immigration and Social Security Co-ordination (EU Withdrawal) Act 2020 (Consequential, Saving, Transitional and Transitory Provisions (EU Exit) Regulations 2020;".

The same amending regulations inserted after sub-para.(n), but before the full stop, the following new sub-paragraph—

"(o) is a national of an EEA State and would satisfy the criteria in sub-paragraph (b) or (c) if they were a "member of the post-transition period group" within the meaning of paragraph 1 of Schedule 4 to the Immigration and Social Security Co-ordination (EU Withdrawal) Act 2020 (Consequential, Saving, Transitional and Transitory Provisions (EU Exit) Regulations 2020".

p.815, *amendment to the Tax Credits (Residence) Regulations 2003 (SI 2003/654) reg.3 (Circumstances in which a person is treated as not being in the United Kingdom)*

5.050 With effect from December 31, 2020, at 11.00pm, reg.9 of the Tax Credits and Child Trust Funds (Amendment) (EU Exit) Regulations 2019 (SI 2019/713) inserted the following paragraphs after paragraph (7) of reg.3:

"(7A) A person ("P") who is within Part IV Section 4 of the Reciprocal Agreement with Ireland will be treated as being ordinarily resident in the United Kingdom where P makes a claim for child tax credit if—

(a) P resides in Ireland; and

(b) P is in a relevant situation.

(7B) Both members of a couple ("A and B") who are within Part IV Section 4 of the Reciprocal Agreement with Ireland will be treated as being ordinarily resident in the United Kingdom where they make a joint claim for child tax credit tax if—

(a) either —

   (i) A or B is resident in Ireland; or

   (ii) both A and B are resident in Ireland; and

(b) either—

   (i) A or B is in a relevant situation; or

   (ii) both A and B are in a relevant situation and it does not matter if A and B are not in the same relevant situation.

(7C) For the purposes of paragraphs (7A) and (7B), a person is in a "relevant situation" if that person is—

(a) an employed person as defined in Article 1 of the Reciprocal Agreement with Ireland and subject to the legislation of the United Kingdom in accordance with Part II of that Agreement;

(b) a self-employed person as defined in Article 1 of the Reciprocal Agreement with Ireland and subject to the legislation of the United Kingdom in accordance with Part II of that Agreement;

(c) receiving a contributory benefit from the United Kingdom in accordance with Article 9(2) of the Reciprocal Agreement with Ireland;

(d) receiving a state pension from the United Kingdom within the meaning of Article 3(1)(a)(v) of the Reciprocal Agreement with Ireland; or

(e) receiving a survivor's benefit from the United Kingdom within the meaning of Article 3(1)(a)(vi) of the Reciprocal Agreement with Ireland.

(7D) For the purposes of paragraphs (7A) to (7C), "the Reciprocal Agreement with Ireland" means the Convention on Social Security between the Government of the United Kingdom of Great Britain and Northern Ireland and the Government of Ireland signed at Dublin on 1st February 2019."

p.815, *amendment to the Tax Credits (Residence) Regulations 2003 (SI 2003/654) reg.3(8) (Circumstances in which a person is treated as not being in the United Kingdom)*

With effect from August 24, 2020, reg.3(2)(b) of the Child Benefit and Child Tax Credit (Persons of Northern Ireland) (Amendment) Regulations 2020 (SI 2020/672) substituted "For the purposes of paragraph (7)(e)" for "In this regulation" in para.(8). 5.051

p.815, *amendment to the Tax Credits (Residence) Regulations 2003 (SI 2003/654) reg.3 (Circumstances in which a person is treated as not being in the United Kingdom), insertion of new paras.(11) and (12)*

5.052 With effect from August 24, 2020, reg.3(2)(b) of the Child Benefit and Child Tax Credit (Persons of Northern Ireland) (Amendment) Regulations 2020 (SI 2020/672) inserted after para.(10) the following new paragraph—

"(11) In this regulation, "relevant person of Northern Ireland" means a person who—

    (a) is—
        (i) a British citizen; or
        (ii) an Irish citizen; or
        (iii) a British citizen and an Irish citizen; and
    (b) was born in Northern Ireland and, at the time of that person's birth, at least one of their parents was—
        (i) a British citizen;
        (ii) an Irish citizen; or
        (iii) a British citizen and an Irish citizen; or
        (iv) otherwise entitled to reside in Northern Ireland without any restriction on their period of residence."

With effect from December 31, 2020, reg.61(2) of the Immigration and Social Security Co-ordination (EU Withdrawal) Act 2020 (Consequential, Saving, Transitional and Transitory Provisions) (EU Exit) Regulations 2020 (SI 2020/1309) amended reg.3 by inserting after para.(11) the following new paragraph:

"(12) In this regulation references to the Immigration (European Economic Area) Regulations 2016 are to be read with Schedule 4 to the Immigration and Social Security Co-ordination (EU Withdrawal) Act 2020(Consequential, Saving, Transitional and Transitory Provisions) Regulations 2020.".

With effect from January 1, 2021, reg.5(2)(b) of the Social Security, Child Benefit and Child Tax Credit (Amendment) (EU Exit) Regulations 2020 (SI 2020/1505) inserted a new para.(13) (originally a second para.(12), but rectified by a correction published on January 7, 2021):

"(13) In this regulation "EU Agreement" means—

    (a) an Association Agreement concluded under Article 217 of the Treaty on the Functioning of the European Union which makes provision in the field of social security for equal treatment for workers who are nationals of the State with which the agreement has been concluded and their families, or
    (b) a Stabilisation and Association Agreement concluded under Article 217 of the Treaty on the Functioning of the European Union which makes provision for receipt of family allowances for members of a worker's family who are legally resident in the United Kingdom.".

p.818, *annotation to the Tax Credits (Residence) Regulations 2003 (SI 2003/654) reg.3 (Circumstances in which a person is treated as not being in the United Kingdom)*

In the first paragraph, the first sentence is substituted by the following: 5.053
"HMRC guidance document *HMRC6* (which replaced the code of guidance *IR20*) sets out how HMRC deal with disputed issues of ordinary residence for tax purposes."

p.818, *annotation to the Tax Credits (Residence) Regulations 2003 (SI 2003/654) reg.3 (Circumstances in which a person is treated as not being in the United Kingdom)*

In the first paragraph, for the words from "The working practice is to 5.054
treat someone as resident . . . " to the end of the paragraph, there is substituted the following:

"However, *HMRC6*, at 2.2, states that HMRC will take a person to be resident in the UK for tax purposes if present here for at least 183 days of a tax year. For a person present for fewer than 183 days, *HMRC6* says the question whether the person is resident in the UK for tax purposes will "depend on how often and how long you are here, the purpose and pattern of your presence and your connections to the UK". In determining whether a person is *ordinarily* resident in the UK for tax purposes, *HMRC6* at 3.2, states that the following requirements must be met: a person's presence in the UK must have a settled purpose; their presence must form "part of the regular and habitual mode of your life for the time being"; and the person must have come to the UK voluntarily. While *HMRC6* may well influence HMRC's ordinary residence determinations in tax credits cases, it should be noted that it is concerned with residency questions for the purposes of tax liability. In tax credits cases, HMRC's Tax Credits Manual provides that, in determining ordinary residence for tax credits purposes, officials should use the guidance in TCM0128100, which states that the issue is whether "residence here has been adopted voluntarily for settled purposes as part of the regular order of their life for the time being". In contrast to *HMRC6*, which expects a person to have 'come to the UK' voluntarily, TCM0128100 states that "a customer who is in the UK as a result of their deportation, expulsion or other removal by compulsion of law from another country should automatically be treated as ordinarily residing in the UK"."

p.818, *annotation to the Tax Credits (Residence) Regulations 2003 (SI 2003/654) reg.3 (Circumstances in which a person is treated as not being in the United Kingdom)*

In the paragraph beginning "*(2) When someone arrives* . . . ", for the 5.055
sentence beginning "The position of the worker . . . " there is substituted:

"The position of the worker whose work here may not last that period but who has rights under EU law, the EU-UK Withdrawal Agreements or the 2020 Convention on Social Security entered into between the Government of the United Kingdom and Northern Ireland and the Government of Ireland is protected by reg.3(4)-(5B)."

p.819, *annotation to the Tax Credits (Residence) Regulations 2003 (SI 2003/654) reg.3 (Circumstances in which a person is treated as not being in the United Kingdom)*

5.056   In the paragraph beginning "*(3) When someone has strong links . . .*", at the end of the sentence beginning "Unlike regs 5 and 6 below . . . ", there is inserted: "(with the limited exception of reg.3(7B))".

p.819, *annotation to the Tax Credits (Residence) Regulations 2003 (SI 2003/654) reg.3 (Circumstances in which a person is treated as not being in the United Kingdom)*

5.057   The paragraph beginning "The Treasury published a consultative with the 2003 Budget . . . " is omitted.

p.819, *annotation to the Tax Credits (Residence) Regulations 2003 (SI 2003/654) reg.3 (Circumstances in which a person is treated as not being in the United Kingdom)*

5.058   The second paragraph is omitted.

p.819, *annotation to the Tax Credits (Residence) Regulations 2003 (SI 2003/654) reg.3 (Circumstances in which a person is treated as not being in the United Kingdom)*

5.059   The cross-heading to 2.485 is changed to "Paragraphs (4) to (5B)", and for the first sentence of the first paragraph of 2.485 there is substituted: "Paragraphs (4) to (4C) provide a test for working tax credit, while paragraphs (5) to (5B) provides a test for child tax credit".

p.819, *annotation to the Tax Credits (Residence) Regulations 2003 (SI 2003/654) reg.3 (Circumstances in which a person is treated as not being in the United Kingdom)*

5.060   At the end of the second paragraph of 2.485 there is inserted:

"Paragraphs (4A) to (4C) were added as from the date on which the UK ceased to be subject to the law of the European Union (December 31, 2020). They deem certain Irish citizens and UK nationals, who reside in Ireland, to be ordinarily resident in the UK, for working tax credit purposes, without needing to demonstrate that they are exercising rights as a worker or have the right to reside in the UK. The most obvious cases falling within paragraphs (4A) to (4C) are those of Irish resident-citizens who work in Northern Ireland and British nationals who reside in the Republic of Ireland but work in Northern Ireland."

p.819, *annotation to the Tax Credits (Residence) Regulations 2003 (SI 2003/654) reg.3 (Circumstances in which a person is treated as not being in the United Kingdom)*

For the paragraph beginning "The paragraph therefore now introduces . . . " there is substituted the following: 5.061

Paragraphs (5) to (5B) operate as follows:
- para.(5) retains, in material respects, its pre-Brexit wording so that it disentitles a child tax credit claimant (through deeming him/her not to be in the UK) where s/he either has no right to reside in the UK ((5)(b)) or whose right to reside is, briefly, a derivative right to reside attained through the claimant being the primary carer of a British citizen ((5)(c));
- para.(5A) disapplies para.(5)(c) where a person lawfully working in the UK is a national of a State with which the European Union has concluded an equal treatment agreement under Art.217 of the Treaty on the Functioning of the European Union but only in the case of child tax credits claims made before January 1, 2021. Paragraph (5A) also disapplies paragraph (5)(c), but without limiting its application to claims for child tax credit made before January 1, 2021, in respect of nationals of States with whom the UK has entered into an agreement in place of an agreement under Art.217, which may include the February 2019 Social Security Convention entered into between the Government of the United Kingdom and Northern Ireland and the Government of Ireland (for details of that Convention see the notes to the Child Tax Credit Regulations 2002 above in this volume);
- para.(5B) contains a further disapplication of para.(5)(c) but is limited in its application to certain family members of a relevant person of Northern Ireland.

p.819, *annotation to the Tax Credits (Residence) Regulations 2003 (SI 2003/654) reg.3 (Circumstances in which a person is treated as not being in the United Kingdom)*

The final paragraph of 2.485 is omitted.   5.062

p.819, *annotation to the Tax Credits (Residence) Regulations 2003 (SI 2003/654) reg.3 (Circumstances in which a person is treated as not being in the United Kingdom)*

At the end of 2.486, there is inserted: 5.063

"Paragraphs (6) and (7)

Paragraph (6) enacts the general rule that a person must have been living in the UK for 3 month before claiming child tax credit. A range of exceptions to the general rule are provided for by para.(7).

Paragraphs (7A) to (7D)

These paragraphs deem certain claimants residing in Ireland to be ordinarily resident in the UK, for child tax credit purposes, and its presumed purpose is to meet the UK Government's obligations under the February 2019 Social Security Convention agreed with the Government of Ireland. The Convention took effect on December 31, 2020.

p.855, *amendment to the Child Benefit (General) Regulations 2006 (SI 2006/223) reg.1 (Citation, commencement and interpretation)*

5.064   With effect from August 24, 2020, reg.2(2) of the Child Benefit and Child Tax Credit (Persons of Northern Ireland) (Amendment) Regulations 2020 (SI 2020/672) amended reg.1 by inserting after the definition of "relevant education" the following new definition—

""relevant person of Northern Ireland" means a person who—
    (a) is—
        (i) a British citizen; or
        (ii) an Irish citizen; or
        (iii) a British citizen and an Irish citizen; and
    (b) was born in Northern Ireland and, at the time of that person's birth, at least one of their parents was—
    (i) a British citizen; or
    (ii) an Irish citizen; or
    (iii) a British citizen and an Irish citizen; or
    (iv) otherwise entitled to reside in Northern Ireland without any restriction on their period of residence;".

p.855, *amendment to Child Benefit (General) Regulations 2006 (SI 2006/223) reg.1 (Citation, amendment and interpretation)*

5.065   With effect from December 31, 2020, reg.66(2) of the Immigration and Social Security Co-ordination (EU Withdrawal) Act 2020 (Consequential, Saving, Transitional and Transitory Provisions) (EU Exit) Regulations 2020 (SI 2020/1309) amended reg.1 by inserting after para. (3) the following:

"(3A) In these Regulations references to the Immigration (European Economic Area) Regulations 2016 are to be read with Schedule 4 to the Immigration and Social Security Co-ordination (EU Withdrawal) Act 2020(Consequential, Saving, Transitional and Transitory Provisions) Regulations 2020."

p.870, *amendment to Child Benefit (General) Regulations 2006 (SI 2006/223) reg.23 (Circumstances in which person treated as not being in Great Britain)*

With effect from August 24, 2020, reg.2(3) of the Child Benefit and Child Tax Credit (Persons of Northern Ireland) (Amendment) Regulations 2020 (SI 2020/672) amended reg.23 as follows: **5.066**

(a) after paragraph (4A) insert—
 "(4B) Paragraph (4)(c) does not apply to a person who—
   (a) has limited leave to enter, or remain in, the United Kingdom under the Immigration Act 1971 which has been granted by virtue of Appendix EU to the Immigration Rules;
   (b) has been granted such leave in reliance of being a family member of a relevant person of Northern Ireland in accordance with those Rules; and
   (c) would have a right to reside under the Immigration (European Economic Area) Regulations 2016 if the relevant person of Northern Ireland were an EEA national within the meaning of regulation 2 of those Regulations;" and
(b) in paragraph (7), for "In this regulation" substitute "For the purposes of paragraph (6)(e)".

p.870, *amendment to Child Benefit (General) Regulations 2006 (SI 2006/223) reg.23 (Circumstances in which person treated as not being in Great Britain)*

With effect from December 31, 2020, reg.22(2) of the Immigration (Citizens' Rights etc.) (EU Exit) Regulations 2020 (SI 2020/1372) amended reg.23 as follows: **5.067**

(a) in paragraph (4), in sub-paragraph (c), for "Appendix EU to the immigration rules" substitute—
 "(i) Appendix EU to the immigration rules; or
 (ii) having arrived in the United Kingdom with an entry clearance that was granted under Appendix EU (Family Permit) to the immigration rules.";
(b) in paragraph (4B), after "Paragraph (4)(c)" insert "(i)".

p.871, *amendment to Child Benefit (General) Regulations 2006 (SI 2006/223) reg.23 (Circumstances in which person treated as not being in Great Britain)*

With effect from December 31, 2020, reg.66(3) of the Immigration and Social Security Co-ordination (EU Withdrawal) Act 2020 (Consequential, Saving, Transitional and Transitory Provisions) (EU Exit) Regulations 2020 (SI 2020/1309) amended reg.23(6) as follows: **5.068**

(a) in sub-paragraph (e), for "or (i)" substitute ", (i) or (o)";

(b) for sub-paragraph (i) substitute—

"(i) is not a national of an EEA State and would be a worker or self-employed person in the United Kingdom for the purposes of the Immigration (European Economic Area) Regulations 2016 if that person—

(i) were a national of an EEA State; and

(ii) a "member of the post-transition period group" within the meaning of paragraph 1 of Schedule 4 to the Immigration and Social Security Co-ordination (EU Withdrawal) Act 2020 (Consequential, Saving, Transitional and Transitory Provisions (EU Exit) Regulations 2020;";

(c) after sub-paragraph (n), but before the full stop, insert—

"(o) is a national of an EEA State and would satisfy the criteria in sub-paragraph (b) or (c) if they were a "member of the post-transition period group" within the meaning of paragraph 1 of Schedule 4 to the Immigration and Social Security Co-ordination (EU Withdrawal) Act 2020 (Consequential, Saving, Transitional and Transitory Provisions (EU Exit) Regulations 2020".

GENERAL NOTE

5.069   Note that there are saving provisions that apply to these amendments in Sch.4 para.3(o) of the amending regulations. The saving provisions apply to a "member of the post-transition period group" as that is defined in para.1(b) of the Schedule.

p.875, *amendment to Child Benefit (General) Regulations 2006 (SI 2006/223) reg.27 (Circumstances in which person treated as not being in Northern Ireland)*

5.070   With effect from August 24, 2020, reg.2(4) of the Child Benefit and Child Tax Credit (Persons of Northern Ireland) (Amendment) Regulations 2020 (SI 2020/672) amended reg.27 as follows:

(a) after paragraph (3A) insert—

"(3B) Paragraph (3)(c) does not apply to a person who—

(a) has limited leave to enter, or remain in, the United Kingdom under the Immigration Act 1971 which has been granted by virtue of Appendix EU to the Immigration Rules;

(b) has been granted such leave in reliance of being a family member of a relevant person of Northern Ireland in accordance with those Rules; and

(c) would have a right to reside under the Immigration (European Economic Area) Regulations 2016 if the relevant person of Northern Ireland were an EEA national within the meaning of regulation 2 of those Regulations."; and

(b) in paragraph (6), for "In this regulation" substitute "For the purposes of paragraph (5)(e)".

p.875, *amendment to Child Benefit (General) Regulations 2006 (SI 2006/223) reg.27 (Circumstances in which person treated as not being in Northern Ireland)*

With effect from December 31, 2020, reg.66(4) of the Immigration 5.071 and Social Security Co-ordination (EU Withdrawal) Act 2020 (Consequential, Saving, Transitional and Transitory Provisions) (EU Exit) Regulations 2020 (SI 2020/1309) amended reg.27(5) as follows:

(a) in sub-paragraph (e), for "or (i)" substitute ", (i) or (o)";
(b) for sub-paragraph (i) substitute—
   "(i) is not a national of an EEA State and would be a worker or self-employed person in the United Kingdom for the purposes of the Immigration (European Economic Area) Regulations 2016 if that person—
      (i) were a national of an EEA State; and
      (ii) a "member of the post-transition period group" within the meaning of fell within paragraph 1 of Schedule 4 to the Immigration and Social Security Co-Ordination (EU Withdrawal) Act 2020 (Consequential, Saving, Transitional and Transitory Provisions (EU Exit) Regulations 2020;"; and
(c) after sub-paragraph (n), but before the full stop, insert—
   "(o) is a national of an EEA State and would satisfy the criteria in sub-paragraphs (b) or (c) if they were a "member of the post-transition period group" within the meaning of paragraph 1 of Schedule 4 to the Immigration and Social Security Co-Ordination (EU Withdrawal) Act 2020 (Consequential, Saving, Transitional and Transitory Provisions (EU Exit) Regulations 2020".

GENERAL NOTE

Note that there are saving provisions that apply to these amendments in Sch.4 5.072 para.3(o) of the amending regulations. The saving provisions apply to a "member of the post-transition period group" as that is defined in para.1(b) of the Schedule.

p.875, *amendment to Child Benefit (General) Regulations 2006 (SI 2006/223) reg.27 (Circumstances in which person treated as not being in Northern Ireland)*

With effect from December 31, 2020, reg.22(3) of the Immigration 5.073 (Citizens' Rights etc.) (EU Exit) Regulations 2020 (SI 2020/1372) amended reg.27 as follows:

(a) in paragraph (3), in sub-paragraph (c), for "Appendix EU to the immigration rules" substitute—
   "(i) Appendix EU to the immigration rules; or
   (ii) having arrived in the United Kingdom with an entry clearance that was granted under Appendix EU (Family Permit) to the immigration rules.";

(b) in paragraph (3B), after "Paragraph (3)(c)" insert "(i)".

pp.900-901, *amendment to the Statutory Sick Pay (General) Regulations 1982 (SI 1982/894) reg.2(1) (Persons deemed incapable of work)*

5.074   With effect from July 6, 2020, reg.2(2)(c) of the Statutory Sick Pay (Coronavirus) (Suspension of Waiting Days and General Amendment) (No.2) Regulations 2020 (SI 2020/681) amended reg.2(1) so as to insert a new category of person incapable of work as sub-paragraph (d) as follows:

"(d) he is—
(i) shielding himself in such a manner as to prevent infection or contamination with coronavirus in accordance with Schedule 2; and
(ii) by reason of that shielding is unable to work."

With effect from the same date, regulation 2(2)(a) and (b) of the same amending regulations made the necessary consequential amendments to reg.2(1), namely omitting "or" at the end of sub-para.(b) and in sub-para.(c) substituting "Schedule 1" for "the Schedule" in head (i) and inserting "r" at the end.

p.901, *amendment to the Statutory Sick Pay (General) Regulations 1982 (SI 1982/894) reg.2(4) (Persons deemed incapable of work)*

5.075   With effect from July 6, 2020, reg.2(3) of the Statutory Sick Pay (Coronavirus) (Suspension of Waiting Days and General Amendment) (No.2) Regulations 2020 (SI 2020/681) amended reg.2(4) so as to insert "and (d) and Schedules 1 and 2" after "paragraph (1)(c)".

pp.922-923, *amendment to the Statutory Sick Pay (General) Regulations 1982 (SI 1982/894) Sch. (Isolation due to Coronavirus)*

5.076   As a result of a series of further amendments, and from various dates as noted below, the Schedule to the SSP Regulations has been re-numbered as Schedule 1 and amended so that it reads as follows:

[¹SCHEDULE [⁴1]   Regulation 2(1)

ISOLATION DUE TO CORONAVIRUS

1. A person is isolating himself from other people in such a manner as to prevent infection or contamination with coronavirus in accordance with this Schedule if he is doing so pursuant to paragraphs 2 to [² [⁵[⁶5G]]].
2. The person has symptoms of coronavirus, however mild, and is staying at home for [⁵[⁷ 11]] days, beginning with the day ("day 1") the symptoms started [⁴or, if earlier, until the end of the isolation period].
3. The person lives with someone [⁴, or is in an extended household or a linked household with someone,] who is isolating himself in accordance with paragraph 2, and that person is staying at home for [⁷11] days, beginning with day 1 [⁴or, if earlier, until the end of the isolation period].

4. The person is staying at home under paragraph 3 and develops the symptoms of coronavirus, however mild, and is staying at home for [⁵[⁷11]] days, beginning with the day the symptoms started [⁴or, if earlier, until the end of the isolation period].

5. Where the person is staying at home pursuant to paragraph 4, paragraph 3 no longer applies to that person.

[²5A. [⁴ . . .]]

[³5B. The person—

(a) has been advised by a relevant notification that he has had contact with a person who at the time of the contact was infected with coronavirus, and

[⁵(b) is staying at home until the date specified in a relevant notification.]]

[⁵[⁷5C. The person (P1) has tested positive for coronavirus and is staying at home—

(a) for—

    (i) the period specified in a relevant notification which informs P1 that they have tested positive for coronavirus;

    (ii) where no period is specified within a relevant notification, and the Health Protection Regulations (England) apply, the period beginning with the day on which P1 first had the symptoms of coronavirus or, if earlier, the day on which P1 was given the coronavirus test which returned a positive result, and ending on the day on which P1 ceases to be required to self-isolate pursuant to regulations 2 and 3 of the Health Protection Regulations (England);

    (iii) where no period is specified within a relevant notification, and the Health Protection Regulations (Wales) apply, the period beginning with the day on which P1 first had the symptoms of coronavirus or, if earlier, the day on which P1 was given the coronavirus test which returned a positive result, and ending on the day on which P1 ceases to be required to isolate pursuant to Chapter 1 of Part 4 of the Health Protection Regulations (Wales); or

    (iv) in any other circumstances, 11 days beginning with the day on which P1 first had the symptoms of coronavirus or, if earlier, the day on which P1 was given the coronavirus test which returned a positive result; or

(b) if P1 still has symptoms of coronavirus at the end of the period mentioned in paragraph (a)(i), (ii), (iii) or (iv) (as the case may be), until P1 no longer has those symptoms.]]

[⁵5D. Where P is staying at home pursuant to paragraph 5C, paragraphs 2, 4 and 5B no longer apply.]

[⁵[⁷5E. The person (P2) lives with, or is in an extended household or a linked household with, a person (S) who has tested positive for coronavirus and P2 is staying at home for—

(a) the period specified in a relevant notification which—

    (i) informs P2 that they have had close contact with a person who has tested positive for coronavirus; or

    (ii) informs S that they have tested positive for coronavirus;

(b) where no period is specified within a relevant notification and—

    (i) the Health Protection Regulations (England) apply, the period beginning with the day on which S first had the symptoms of coronavirus or, if earlier, the day on which S was given the coronavirus test which returned a positive result, and ending on the day on which P2 ceases to be required to self-isolate pursuant to regulations 2 and 3 of the Health Protection Regulations (England); or

    (ii) the Health Protection Regulations (Wales) apply, the period beginning with the day on which S first had the symptoms of coronavirus or, if earlier, the day on which S was given the coronavirus test which returned a positive result, and ending on the day on which P2 ceases to be required to isolate pursuant to Chapter 1 of Part 4 of the Health Protection Regulations (Wales); or

(c) in any other circumstances, 11 days beginning with the day on which S first had the symptoms of coronavirus or, if earlier, the day on which S was given the coronavirus test which returned a positive result."]]

[⁵5F. Where S is staying at home pursuant to paragraph 5E, paragraphs 2 to 5B no longer apply.]

[⁶5G. The person—

(a) has received a pre-surgery notification;

(b) has been advised to stay at home for a period of up to 14 days before the date on which the person is to be admitted to hospital for the purpose of undergoing the procedure referred to in the pre-surgery notification; and

(c) is staying at home in accordance with that advice.]

6. In this Schedule—

"Chief Medical Officer" means—

(a) the Chief Medical Officer of the Department of Health and Social Care; and

(b) the Officer with corresponding functions in relation to Scotland and Wales;

"Deputy Chief Medical Officer" is to be construed by reference to the definition of "Chief Medical Officer"; [² . . .]

[⁴"extended household"—

(a) in relation to households in Scotland, has the meaning given in regulation 10 of the Health Protection (Coronavirus) (Restrictions) (Scotland) Regulations 2020;

(b) in relation to households in Wales, means two households in relation to which the adults in those households have agreed to be treated as a single household in accordance with public health guidance;]

[⁷ "the Health Protection Regulations (England)" means the Health Protection (Coronavirus, Restrictions) (Self-Isolation) (England) Regulations 2020;

"the Health Protection Regulations (Wales)" means the Health Protection (Coronavirus Restrictions (No.4) (Wales) Regulations 2020;]

[⁴"isolation period" means the period ending on the day on which a relevant notification is received advising that the person with the symptoms of coronavirus is not in fact infected or contaminated with coronavirus;]

[⁴"linked household" in relation to households in England, has the meaning given in regulation 7A of the Health Protection (Coronavirus, Restrictions) (England) Regulations 2020;]

[⁶"pre-surgery notification" means a notification in writing, advising a person that they are to undergo a surgical or other hospital procedure, which is sent by or on behalf of—

(a) any person or body who may issue a relevant notification; or

(b) a registered medical practitioner;]

[² [⁴ "public health guidance"] means guidance, as amended from time to time, issued by—

(a) Public Health England;

(b) the Scottish Ministers; or

(c) Public Health Wales National Health Service Trust; [³ . . .]]

[³ "relevant notification" means a notification [⁷given orally (either in person or by telephone) or in writing [⁷ . . .] to, or in respect of, a person by—

(a) the Department of Health and Social Care;

(b) Public Health England;

(c) Public Health Wales National Health Service Trust;

(d) the Common Services Agency for the Scottish Health Service;

(e) a person employed or engaged for the purposes of the health service (within the meaning of section 275 of the National Health Service Act 2006 or section 108 of the National Health Service (Scotland) Act 1978);

(f) any other person employed or engaged by a Government Department or other public authority in communicable disease surveillance; [⁷ . . .]]

[⁷(g) Scottish Ministers;

(h) Welsh Ministers; and]

"symptoms of coronavirus" means the recent onset of —

(a) a continuous cough;

(b) a high temperature;

(c) both a continuous cough and a high temperature; or

(d) any other symptoms of coronavirus as may be specified by the Chief Medical Officer or one of the Deputy Chief Medical Officers in guidance as amended from time to time.]

AMENDMENTS

1. Statutory Sick Pay (Coronavirus) (Suspension of Waiting Days and General Amendment) Regulations 2020 (SI 2020/374) reg.3(4) and Sch. (March 28, 2020).

2. Statutory Sick Pay (General) (Coronavirus Amendment) (No.3) Regulations 2020 (SI 2020/427) reg.2 (April 16,2020).

3. Statutory Sick Pay (General) (Coronavirus Amendment) (No.4) Regulations 2020 (SI 2020/539), reg.2 (May 28,2020).

4. Statutory Sick Pay (Coronavirus) (Suspension of Waiting Days and General Amendment) (No.2) Regulations 2020 (SI 2020/681), reg.2(4)-2(9) (July 6, 2020).

5. Statutory Sick Pay (General) (Coronavirus Amendment) (No.5) Regulations 2020 (SI 2020/829), reg.2 (August 5, 2020).

6. Statutory Sick Pay (General) (Coronavirus Amendment) (No.6) Regulations 2020 (SI 2020/892), reg.2 (August 26, 2020).

7. Statutory Sick Pay (General) (Coronavirus Amendment) (No.7) Regulations 2020 (SI 2020/1638), reg.2 (December 24, 2020).

DEFINITIONS

"Chief Medical Officer"—para.(6).
"day 1"—para.(2).
"Deputy Chief Medical Officer"—para.(6).
"extended household"—para.(6).
"isolation period"—para.(6).
"linked household"—para.(6).
"pre-surgery notification"—para.(6).
"public health guidance"—para.(6).
"relevant notification"—para.(6).
"symptoms of coronavirus"—para.(6).

pp.923–924, *annotation to the Statutory Sick Pay (General) Regulations 1982 (SI 1982/1349) Sch. (Isolation due to Coronavirus)*

The final paragraph to the General Note on p.924 should be deleted 5.077 and replaced by the following text:

The third set of amendments were made by the Statutory Sick Pay (Coronavirus) (Suspension of Waiting Days and General Amendment) (No.2) Regulations 2020 (SI 2020/681) with effect from July 6, 2020. These amendments were intended to clarify eligibility of the shielding group for SSP. They provided that where a person self-isolates for less than 7 or 14 days because they or a member of their household (or extended household in Scotland, or linked household in England and Wales) receives a negative test result for coronavirus, they do not have to serve waiting days for the days in self-isolation. They also provided that a person who has formed an extended household or a linked household and is self-isolating because a member of that other household has symptoms of coronavirus may be eligible for SSP.

The fourth set of amendments were made by the Statutory Sick Pay (General) (Coronavirus Amendment) (No.5) Regulations 2020 (SI 2020/829) with effect from August 5, 2020. They extend eligibility for SSP to cover people where they are self-isolating for a minimum of 10 days (previously seven days) in line with Public Health England guidance published on July 30, 2020.

The fifth set of amendments were made by the Statutory Sick Pay (General) (Coronavirus Amendment) (No.6) Regulations 2020 (SI 2020/892) with effect from August 26, 2020. They extended SSP eligibility to people self-isolating for up to 14 days prior to admittance to hospital for planned or elective surgery. Revised NICE guidelines published on July 27, 2020 set out guidance for healthcare professionals on Covid-19 and arranging planned care in hospitals. Clinicians may recommend that a patient self-isolate for a period prior to their surgery, based on a number of individual and clinical risk factors. Patients may be advised to self-isolate for 3 days prior to being admitted into hospital, while those patients who are deemed at higher risk may be advised to self-isolate for 14 days prior.

The seventh set of amendments were made by the Statutory Sick Pay (General) (Coronavirus Amendment) (No.6) Regulations 2020 (SI 2020/892) and came into force on August 26, 2020. They provide that a person is entitled to statutory sick pay if they (a) have been notified that they are to undergo a surgical or other hospital procedure; (b) have been advised to stay at home for a period of up to 14 days before admission to hospital for that procedure; and (c) stay at home following that advice.

The eighth set of amendments were made by the Statutory Sick Pay (General) (Coronavirus Amendment) (No.7) Regulations 2020 (SI 2020/1638) and were effective from December 24, 2020. These reflect changes to the self-isolation requirements where a person has symptoms of coronavirus, tests positive for coronavirus or is a household contact of a person who has coronavirus.

The net result is that reg.2 (as amended) provides that individuals may be eligible for SSP if they are unable to work because they are staying at home and self-isolating in accordance with guidance because:

a.   They have symptoms of coronavirus;
b.   They live with, or are in a linked or extended household with, someone who has symptoms;
c.   They have been informed that they have had contact with a person who was, at the time of the contact, infected with coronavirus;
d.   They are shielding in accordance with public health guidance;
e.   They have tested positive for coronavirus;
f.   They live with someone who has tested positive for coronavirus;
g.   They have been advised that they should self-isolate for up to 14 days prior to a planned or elective surgical or other hospital procedure.

p.940, *amendment to the Statutory Sick Pay (Coronavirus) (Suspension of Waiting Days and General Amendment) Regulations 2020 (SI 2020/374) reg.2 (Suspension of waiting days)*

5.078   With effect from July 6, 2020, reg.3 of the Statutory Sick Pay (Coronavirus) (Suspension of Waiting Days and General Amendment) (No.2)

Regulations 2020 (SI 2020/681) amended reg.2 so that it reads (and as correctly formatted) as follows:

"Suspension of waiting days

2.—(1) Section 155(1) (limitations on entitlement) of the Social Security Contributions and Benefits Act 1992 ("the 1992 Act") does not apply in relation to an employee where— (a) that employee's period of incapacity for work is related to coronavirus; and (b) the first day of incapacity for work in that period arose on or after 13th March 2020.

(2) Paragraph (1) applies in relation to a day of incapacity for work that falls on or after 13th March 2020.

(3) In this regulation—

(a) "period of incapacity for work" has the meaning given by section 152 of the 1992 Act; and

(b) a period of incapacity for work is related to coronavirus if the employee is—

(i) incapable by reason of infection or contamination with coronavirus, or

(ii) deemed, in accordance with regulation 2(1)(c) [¹or (d)] of the Statutory Sick Pay (General) Regulations 1982, to be incapable by reason of coronavirus, of doing work which the employee can reasonably be expected to do under the employee's contract of service.

(4) The reference to regulation 2(1)(c) [¹or (d)] in paragraph (3)(b) above is a reference to the regulation which was in force on the first day of incapacity for work in question."

pp.941-942, *annotation to the Statutory Sick Pay (Coronavirus) (Funding of Employers' Liabilities) Regulations 2020 (SI 2020/512)*
General Note

The amendments made by the Statutory Sick Pay (Coronavirus) (Funding of Employers' Liabilities) (Amendment) Regulations (SI 2020/1030) with effect from October 15, 2020 fall into three categories. First, they reflect further changes made by the European Commission to the provision of State aid to small and medium-sized enterprises (SMEs) in difficulty (a SME is a business with fewer than 250 employees and either turnover below €50m or balance sheet total below €43m) (see reg.4). Second, they ensure that SSP can be reclaimed by employers in line with the changes made by the DWP to extend eligibility to receive coronavirus related SSP.In particular, they ensure that employers can claim for coronavirus related SSP for those employees who were required to shield and formed part of an extended or linked household and are therefore eligible for SSP in accordance with the amendments made by the Statutory Sick Pay (Coronavirus) (Suspension of Waiting Days and General Amendment) (No.2) Regulations 2020 (SI 2020/681) with effect from July 6, 2020 (see reg.5). Third, they change the notification mechanism for employers who realise they have mistakenly overstated the amount of a previous claim (see reg.9).

5.079

p.943, *amendment to the Statutory Sick Pay (Coronavirus) (Funding of Employers' Liabilities) Regulations 2020 (SI 2020/512) reg.4 (Meaning of eligible employer)*

5.080   With effect from October 15, 2020 (but note that the amendments have effect in relation to any day of incapacity for work which falls on or after June 29, 2020), reg.3(2) of the Statutory Sick Pay (Coronavirus) (Funding of Employers' Liabilities) (Amendment) Regulations (SI 2020/1030) amended reg.4(2) so as to substitute a new para.(2) as follows:

> "(2) An employer is "in difficulty" if—
> (a) in the case of an employer who is not an SME, it is reasonable to assume that the employer would be regarded as an undertaking in difficulty under Article 2(18) of the General Block Exemption Regulation; or
> (b) in the case of an employer who is an SME, it is reasonable to assume that the employer would be regarded as an undertaking in difficulty under Article 2(18)(c) of the General Block Exemption Regulation, as if the words after "collective insolvency proceedings", in the first place it appears, to the end were omitted, or under Article 2(18)(d) of the General Block Exemption Regulation."

p.944, *amendment to the Statutory Sick Pay (Coronavirus) (Funding of Employers' Liabilities) Regulations 2020 (SI 2020/512) reg.4 (Meaning of eligible employer)*

5.081   With effect from October 15, 2020 (but note that the amendments have effect in relation to any day of incapacity for work which falls on or after June 29, 2020), reg.3(3) of the Statutory Sick Pay (Coronavirus) (Funding of Employers' Liabilities) (Amendment) Regulations (SI 2020/1030) amended reg.4(5) so as to add the following new definitions:

> ""General Block Exemption Regulation" means Commission Regulation (EU) No.651/2014 of 17 June 2014 declaring certain categories of aid compatible with the internal market in application of Articles 107 and 108 of the Treaty;
> "SME" means an employer who is within the category of micro, small and medium-sized enterprises in paragraph 1 of Annex 1 of the General Block Exemption Regulation."

p.944, *amendment to the Statutory Sick Pay (Coronavirus) (Funding of Employers' Liabilities) Regulations 2020 (SI 2020/512) reg.5 (When an employee's incapacity for work is related to coronavirus)*

5.082   With effect from October 15, 2020 (but note that the amendment has effect in relation to any day of incapacity for work which falls on or after July 6, 2020), reg.4 of the Statutory Sick Pay (Coronavirus) (Funding of Employers' Liabilities) (Amendment) Regulations (SI 2020/1030) amended reg.5(1)(b) so as to insert "or (d)" after "regulation 2(1)(c)"

p.945, *amendment to the Statutory Sick Pay (Coronavirus) (Funding of Employers' Liabilities) Regulations 2020 (SI 2020/512) reg.6 (Making a claim)*

With effect from October 15, 2020, reg.5(1) of the Statutory Sick Pay (Coronavirus) (Funding of Employers' Liabilities) (Amendment) Regulations (SI 2020/1030) amended reg.6(5) so as to insert "or regulation 9(2)"after "paragraph (6)".   5.083

pp.946-947, *amendment to the Statutory Sick Pay (Coronavirus) (Funding of Employers' Liabilities) Regulations 2020 (SI 2020/512) reg.9 (Correcting a claim when the amount has been mistakenly overstated)*

With effect from October 15, 2020, reg.5(2)-(8) of the Statutory Sick Pay (Coronavirus) (Funding of Employers' Liabilities) (Amendment) Regulations (SI 2020/1030) amended reg.9 so as to read as follows: 5.084

"Correcting a claim when the amount has been mistakenly overstated

9.—(1) Where an employer—
  (a) becomes aware that the employer mistakenly overstated the amount in a claim (the "original claim"); and
  (b) has received payment from HMRC in respect of the original claim,
the employer must correct the error in accordance with this regulation.

[1(2) The next claim that the employer makes under regulation 6 (the "next claim") must be made in the manner provided for in paragraph (8) and in it the employer must specify the amount by which the original claim was overstated.]

(3) The amount by which the original claim was overstated must be repaid to HMRC by the employer by way of set-off against the amount stated in the next claim, up to a maximum of the amount stated in the next claim.

(4) Where the amount by which the original claim was overstated exceeds the maximum amount required to be set off in accordance with paragraph (3), the employer must repay the excess to HMRC within the period of 30 days beginning on the day on which the next claim is made.

(5) Where an employer does not make another claim under regulation 6 within the period of 60 days beginning with the day on which the original claim was made, the employer must notify HMRC of the overstatement in accordance with paragraphs (6) to (8) [1 . . .].

(6) [1The employer must provide the following information to HMRC]—
  (a) the employer PAYE reference number for the PAYE scheme to which the original claim related;
  (b) the amount by which the original claim was overstated; and
  (c) the beginning and end dates of the period of time to which the original claim related.

531

[¹(7) The employer must declare to HMRC that the information provided under paragraph (6) is true and accurate.]

[¹(8) An employer who makes a next claim referred to in paragraph (2), a declaration under paragraph (7) or who provides information under paragraph (6) must do so by telephone or in writing, as determined by HMRC in its discretion and notified to the employer.]

(9) The employer must repay to HMRC the amount [¹referred to in paragraph (6)(b)] within the period of 30 days beginning on the day on which [¹the employer provides the information under paragraph (6) and the declaration under paragraph (7)]."

p.1306, *amendment to the Childcare Payments (Eligibility) Regulations 2015 (SI 2015/448) reg.15 (Income not to exceed a certain level)*

5.085　With effect from July 21, 2020, regs 2 and 3(a) of the Childcare Payments (Coronavirus and Miscellaneous Amendments) Regulations 2020 (SI 2020/656) amended reg.15 so as to insert after para.(1) the following new paragraphs—

"(1A) A person who is a critical worker—
    (a) who does not expect their adjusted net income for the tax year 6th April 2020 to 5th April 2021 to exceed £150,000;
    (b) who, in the absence of the coronavirus outbreak, would not expect their adjusted net income for that tax year to exceed £100,000; and
    (c) who satisfies the condition in paragraph (1B),
is treated as meeting the condition of eligibility in section 10.

(1B) The condition is that, where the critical worker's income exceeds £100,000, that excess must be mainly attributable to earnings from work undertaken directly or indirectly as a result of the incidence or transmission of coronavirus."

p.1306, *amendment to the Childcare Payments (Eligibility) Regulations 2015 (SI 2015/448) reg.15(4) (Income not to exceed a certain level)*

5.086　With effect from July 21, 2020, regs. 2 and 3(b) of the Childcare Payments (Coronavirus and Miscellaneous Amendments) Regulations 2020 (SI 2020/656) amended reg.15(4) so as to inert in para.(4) before the definition of "hypothetical adjusted net income" the following new definitions—

""coronavirus" means severe acute respiratory syndrome coronavirus 2 (SARS-CoV-2);

"critical worker" means a worker in any part of the United Kingdom in a critical sector listed in the document entitled "Critical workers who can access schools or educational settings" in the version published by the Cabinet Office and the Department for Education on 16 June 2020.;"

p.1320, *amendment to the Childcare Payments Regulations 2015 (SI 2015/522) new reg.16A inserted (Payments that may be made from childcare accounts)*

With effect from July 21, 2020, regs 4 and 5 of the Childcare Payments (Coronavirus and Miscellaneous Amendments) Regulations 2020 (SI 2020/656) inserted after reg.16 (variation of relevant maximum: infrastructure failure) the following new regulation—   5.087

"Payments that may be made from childcare accounts

16A.—(1) A payment is treated as a permitted payment where it includes a reasonable fee payable to an intermediary.

(2) For the purposes of paragraph (1), where there is more than one intermediary in the payment chain the total of all fees must be reasonable.

(3) In this regulation "intermediary" means a supplier of an electronic payment system which allows persons to make payments into that system for the ultimate purpose of making payments to qualifying childcare providers."

pp.1333–1334, *substitution of the HMRC Charter*

With effect from November 5, 2020, the HMRC Charter is substituted by the following: 5.088

"1. About the HMRC Charter

The HMRC Charter is a legal requirement under the Finance Act 2009. The legislation states that the Charter 'must include standards of behaviour and values to which Her Majesty's Revenue and Customs will aspire when dealing with people in the exercise of their functions'.

HMRC is committed to improving its customer experience and the HMRC Charter defines the service and standard of behaviour that customers should expect when interacting with us. The Charter is supported by further principles of support for customers who need extra help [*see https://www.gov.uk/government/publications/hmrc-charter/ hmrcs-principles-of-support-for-customers-who-need-extra-help*].

2. The HMRC Charter

Working with you to get tax right

HMRC is here to collect the tax that pays for the UK's public services.

We'll help you meet your tax responsibilities and make sure you get any benefits, tax credits, refunds or other support you can claim. However, we will take firm action against the small minority who bend or break the law.

Our standards

Getting things right

We'll give you accurate, consistent and clear information. This will help you meet your obligations, and understand your rights and what you can claim. When we ask for information, we rely on you to give us full, accurate and timely answers. If you disagree with us, we'll tell you about options available to you and work with you to reach an appropriate outcome quickly and simply.

Making things easy

We'll provide services that are designed around what you need to do, and are accessible, easy and quick to use, minimising the cost to you.

Being responsive

When you get in touch with us, we'll make sure that the people you deal with have the right level of expertise. We'll answer your questions and resolve things first time, or as quickly as we can. We'll also explain what happens next and when you can expect a response from us. If we make a mistake, we'll put it right as soon as possible. If you're not satisfied with the service you've received, we'll explain how you can make a complaint.

Treating you fairly

We'll work within the law to make sure everyone pays the right amount of tax and gets their benefits and other entitlements. We'll assume you're telling the truth, unless we've good reason to think you're not.

Being aware of your personal situation

We'll listen to your worries and answer any questions clearly and concisely. We'll be mindful of your wider personal situation, and will give you extra support if you need it.

Recognising that someone can represent you

We'll respect your wish to have someone else deal with us on your behalf, such as an accountant, friend or a relative. We'll only deal with them if you have authorised them to represent you. To protect you, HMRC works with professional bodies to set the standard expected of professional agents who support you to meet your tax obligations. We can refuse to work with professional agents who fail to adhere to this standard.

Keeping your data secure

We'll protect information we hold about you and treat it as private and confidential. We'll always use that information fairly and lawfully.

Mutual respect

We take any threats, intimidation or harassment very seriously and will take appropriate action against any behaviour of this type. We'll always treat you in line with our values of respect, professionalism and integrity. Our employees are people too and we expect you to treat them in the same way.

3. Feedback

HMRC undertakes to identify and keep under review how the Charter standards apply in all aspects of its work.

HMRC welcomes any feedback about your interactions with them and how they have performed against the Charter. You can email HMRC.Charter@hmrc.gov.uk. A summary of feedback received will be included in the regular reviews of performance conducted by HMRC's Customer Experience Committee.

4. If you are not happy with a decision or the service you have received

If you do not feel the service you've received has met the standards of the Charter you can make a complaint. HMRC will deal with it quickly and fairly. Please make sure you mention the Charter in your complaint and explain which aspects of the Charter you feel HMRC has not met.

If you disagree with a tax decision you can:
- ask for a statutory review of the decision
- appeal to the independent tax tribunal
- do both

A statutory review is undertaken by an impartial review officer in HMRC who was not involved in the original decision and acts as a fresh pair of eyes. A statutory review is quicker and more cost-effective than appealing directly to the tribunal. If you are still not satisfied following the review you can then appeal to the tribunal. Approximately three-quarters of disagreements are settled at review and do not need to go to tribunal.

Find out what to do if you disagree with a tax decision. If you received a decision letter from HMRC, that will also have instructions about what to do.

5. How we monitor and report on performance against the Charter

Performance against the Charter is monitored by specific service standards, customer surveys and other data, linked to wider HMRC performance measures. We have published the latest set of indicators and data.

HMRC's Customer Experience Committee oversees performance against the Charter—find out more about the Customer Experience Committee.

The committee provides a report each year, assessing HMRC's performance against the Charter, and includes progress and priorities for further improvement.

From December 2020 the committee will also conduct reviews of performance at its quarterly meeting. These quarterly reviews are also informed by feedback from the Adjudicator (who sits on the committee) and from a group of tax professionals, who will also meet quarterly with HMRC to provide their perspectives on HMRC's performance against the Charter.

6. More information about HMRC

Find out how to contact HMRC.
Learn more about our:

- role and responsibilities [*see https://www.gov.uk/government/ organisations/hm-revenue-customs/about*]
- governance and how we're organised [*see https://www.gov.uk/ government/organisations/hm-revenue-customs/about/our-governance*]

Read our:

- annual reports and accounts [*see https://www.gov.uk/government/collections/hmrcs-annual-report-and-accounts*]
- Personal Information Charter [*see https://www.gov.uk/government/organisations/hm-revenue-customs/about/personal-information-charter*]
- consultations [*see https://www.gov.uk/search/policy-papers-and-consultations?content_store_document_type%5B%5D=open_consultations&content_store_document_type%5B%5D=closed_consultations&organisations%5B%5D=hm-revenue-customs*]

p.1334, *annotation to the HMRC Charter*

5.089   For the second paragraph of 11.16 there is substituted:

"The above version of the HMRC Charter has been in force since 5 November 2020. While the Charter itself commits HMRC to provide "accurate, consistent and clear information", regrettably it provides inaccurate information about rights of appeal insofar as tax credits decisions are concerned. In tax credits cases, the right of appeal lies not to "the independent tax tribunal" but to the Social Entitlement Chamber of the First-tier Tribunal."

pp.1335-1339, *amendment to Leaflet WTC7—Tax Credits Penalties—What Happens at the End of a Tax Credits Check*

5.090   With effect from 6 April 2020, Leaflet WTC7 is amended as follows:

11.17—in the title "6 April 2020" is substituted for "23 April 2018"
11.17—for the second paragraph there is substituted:

"Read this factsheet if we charged you a penalty after checking your tax credits claim. It tells you:
— what's likely to happen next
— what you can do if we charge you a penalty
— how to ask for a reconsideration if you disagree with the penalty."

11.19—For the second paragraph (beginning "We can also charge you . . . ") there is substituted:
"We can also charge you a penalty of up to £300 if you've failed to give us information or tell us about certain changes of circumstances within one month of it happening."

11.20—For the first sentence of the first paragraph there is substituted "Deliberate error is where you gave the wrong information on purpose."

11.20—in the first bullet point, for "claiming for a fictitious child or children" there is substituted "claiming for children that do not exist"

11.20—for the third bullet point there is substituted "claiming for childcare costs above what is actually paid£

11.20—for the fifth bullet point there is substituted
"giving us wrong information about working hours, such as:
— claiming to be working when you're not
— claiming to be working over 16 or 30 hours when you do not
— couples with children, who claim to be working a combined total of 24 hours when you do not work those hours, have not done so recently and have no intention of doing so"

11.20—for the eighth bullet point there is substituted "claiming to be entitled to the disability element when you're not"

11.20—for the ninth bullet point there is substituted "telling us your income was less than it actually was"

11.22—for 11.22 there is substituted:
"Penalty amounts
A maximum penalty of £300 may be charged if you do not:
* notify us of a change of circumstances within one month of it happening
* declare circumstances or income when requested during an annual review
* comply with a request for information—we have to ask an independent tribunal to impose this penalty

If any of these failures continue, we may charge a penalty of up to £60 a day.

For a deliberate and wrong declaration when reporting any other information, the penalty levels for a:
* first wrong declaration is 30% of the amount you've over-claimed (up to a maximum of £3,000)
* second wrong declaration is 50% of the amount you've over-claimed (up to a maximum of £3,000)
* third or subsequent wrong declaration is 100% of the amount you've over-claimed (up to a maximum of £3,000)

If you do not understand our explanation of the penalty, you can ask us to put it in writing so that you can get independent advice."

11.23—for the final paragraph there is substituted:

"We'll tell you:

- the maximum amount that we can charge
- the penalty amount that we propose to charge and why

We're always willing to discuss with you the amount of the penalty and the reasons for it."

11.24—for the heading, line 1 and the following three bullet points, there is substituted:

"Payment arrangements

We'll discuss arrangements for paying:

- any overpaid tax credits
- the penalty
- any interest due"

11.25—At the beginning, the following new paragraph is inserted:

"We may decide to reduce or stop your current tax credits payments based on the information we hold."

11.25—the second paragraph is deleted

11.27—for 11.27 there is substituted:

"If we cannot change our decision, you can appeal to an independent tribunal. You'll find details about this in our Mandatory Reconsideration Notice."

11.30 and 11.31—omitted

11.31—At the end insert "The above version of WTC7 has been in force since 6 April 2020."

pp.1135-1137, *amendment to HMRC Code of Practice 26—What Happens If We've Paid You Too Much Tax Credits*

5.091   With effect from 6 April 2020, HMRC Code of Practice 26 is amended as follows:

11.32—in the title for "6 April 2018" there is substituted "6 April 2020".

11.32—Second paragraph, for ", delete "if we decided to charge interest" there is substituted "interest we decided to charge".

11.32—At the end there is inserted:

"If you make a claim for Universal Credit (UC) and your mandatory reconsideration or appeal is successful, we will only be able to pay you tax credits up to the day before you made your claim for UC. This is because UC is replacing tax credits and if you make a claim to UC, tax credits must stop, even if you are not entitled to UC. For information go to www.gov.uk/how-tax-credits-affect-other-benefits"

11.33—first paragraph, for "pages 8 to12" there is substituted "pages 4 to 12".

11.33—first paragraph, for "[see 10.36 to 10.42 below]" there is substituted "[see 11.38 to 11.60 below]".

11.33—for the second paragraph (including its three bullet points), there is substituted:

"Contact us (read page 17) [see 11.72 below] if:
- you do not agree that you've been overpaid
- you're unsure about disputing the decision to recover an overpayment
- you're unsure whether to ask for a mandatory reconsideration against the decision that caused the overpayment"

11.34—paragraph beginning "If you claim Universal Credit . . . ", for "may end your tax credits" there is substituted "we'll end your tax credits".

11.35—for the third bullet point there is substituted "your income in 2019 to 2020 is more than £2,500 higher than it was in 2018 to 2019".

11.35—after 11.35 there is inserted:

"Managing your tax credits

To understand how to manage your tax credits to get the money you're entitled to, watch our short YouTube video. Go to www.gov.uk/tax-credits-webinars-videos"

11.36—for the final paragraph there is substituted:

"If a change of circumstances means you've already received more than we estimate for your full year award, your tax credits payments will normally stop. If this leaves you without enough to live on, tell us and we may consider making further payments.

Each case is assessed on an individual basis. If a change of circumstances means you have not received more than we estimated for your full year award, your tax credits payments will continue at a reduced rate (read page 15, 'Financial hardship' [see 11.67 below])."

11.37—in the paragraph beginning "Your claim will legally end . . . ", the second sentence is omitted.

11.37—in the final paragraph, the second and third sentences are deleted.

11.37—at the end there is inserted:

"If you've made a new tax credits claim we may consider reducing the amount that you have to pay back. We'll work out how much you would have been paid in your new claim if you'd told us about the change on time and take that amount off your overpayment.

Tax credits are being replaced for most people.

Go to www.gov.uk/claim-tax-credits for information on who can still claim.

You may be able to claim Universal Credit if you're of working age, or Pension Credit if you're of pension credit age.

For more information on claiming:
- Universal Credit, go to www.gov.uk/universal-credit
- Pension Credit, go to www.gov.uk/pension-credit"

11.40—after second bullet point, a new bullet point is inserted:

"let us know as soon as possible if you do not get an award notice within 30 days of telling us about a change in circumstance"

11.40—in the paragraph beginning "We'll send you a corrected . . . ", the second sentence is omitted.

11.40—for the paragraph beginning "If you had difficult personal . . . " there is substituted:

"If you have difficult personal circumstances that mean you cannot check your award notice or bank payments, for example, a member of your family has been seriously ill, let us know if anything is missing or incomplete as soon as possible. Also tell is the reason why you're reporting this late."

11.44—for the final paragraph there is substituted:

"Whenever you tell us about a mistake, we'll not collect an overpayment that may build up if we do not correct our mistake from this time."

11.50—for the final paragraph there is substituted:

"If you're not able to manage your own tax affairs, handle money or understand or complete forms, you can get another person to act on your behalf. We call these people appointees."

11.51—for the second bullet point there is substituted "you, if you need help in dealing with your tax affairs".

11.54—in the first paragraph, for the second sentence there is substituted:

"You cannot dispute overpayments from previous awards where it's been more than 3 months since you received your final decision notice."

11.54—in the third paragraph, for the first sentence there is substituted:

"If you were able to reclaim tax credits and received payments, we'll tell you if we're recovering historic debts from your ongoing award."

11.56—for the final paragraph there is substituted:

"If a dispute is found in your favour, we'll send you a revised award notice and refund any amount that has already been recovered."

11.57—in the second paragraph, for the first sentence there is substituted:

"We incorrectly told you that you were not entitled to the disability element and decided not to make the change you reported.

11.57—in the second paragraph, for the penultimate sentence there is substituted "You contacted us and asked about our original decision in 2013."

11.58—for the paragraph beginning "Once we've decided whether . . . " (including its two bullet points) there is substituted:

"After we've checked that we've met our responsibilities and you've met yours, we'll decide if you must pay back:
  • an overpayment
  • all or only part of an overpayment"

11.61—paragraph beginning "If you want help understanding . . . ", for "[10.53 below]" there is substituted "[11.70 below]".

11.61—In the Table, for the heading of the right-hand column there is substituted "The most we'll take back from your award"

11.62—11.62 is substituted by:

"We'll ask you to make a direct payment to us, if:

- you're no longer entitled to tax credits
- your tax credits award ends—this can happen if there's a change in your household, for example, you were in a couple and now you're single"

11.66—11.66 is substituted by:

"If you claim Universal Credit we may transfer your tax credits debts to the DWP or the DfC so they can recover it from your Universal Credit payments unless they tell you otherwise. Where we've previously agreed a payment plan with you, this will stop and the method and/or rate of recovery made by DWP or DfC may differ from HMRC's. If this is going to happen we'll write to you with more details. For more information go to www.gov.uk/tax-credits-overpayments"

11.66—at the end there is inserted:

"If you no longer claim tax credits and have an outstanding debt
If you're no longer claiming tax credits and have an outstanding overpayment or penalty, we may transfer these to the DWP or the DfC for them to recover."

11.68—for first paragraph (including bullet points) there is substituted:

"Phone the Payment Helpline on 0345 302 1429 if you cannot pay for your essential living expenses such as your rent, gas or electricity and:

- you're paying back an overpayment directly
- we've asked you to pay back an overpayment

We'll ask you about your circumstances in more detail to determine if we can adjust your payments. You'll be asked for more information regarding your income and living costs. Once we have this information we aim to make a decision within 2 working days."

11.68—in the paragraph beginning "If we've reduced your ongoing payments . . . " the second sentence is omitted.

11.68—for the paragraph beginning "Whether you are repaying . . . " there is substituted:

"Whether you're repaying your overpayment through a reduction in your tax credits payments or through a direct payment, we may offer you an option for extending the period of time over which you pay back the overpayment. We can do this by reducing the amount we recover each month. However, this means it'll take you longer to pay off the overpayment."

11.69—in the paragraph beginning "When you have reached an agreement . . . ", for the first sentence there is substituted:

"When you've reached an agreement with your ex-partner, you should both phone the Payment Helpline on 0345 302 1429 to arrange repaying the overpayment."

11.69—for the paragraph beginning with "If you and your partner . . ." and the two following paragraphs, there is substituted:

"You must tell us within one month if you and your partner separate. Your joint tax credits claim will end. To find out if you can make a new tax credits claim, go to www.gov.uk/claim-tax-credits

If you're able to make a new claim after a separation, we cannot reduce your payments from your new claim to collect back an overpayment that you had with your previous partner.

You must pay this overpayment back directly by ringing the Payment Helpline.

However, if you get back together with your ex-partner and are able to claim again, we may reduce your payments to recover the overpayment."

11.71—for third bullet point there is substituted:

"Next Generation Text (NGT) relay (if you cannot hear or speak on the phone) 18001-0345-300-3900"

11.72—the words from "You can . . . " to "address below" are omitted.

11.72—at the end there is inserted:

"Help and support

To understand how to manage your tax credits to get the money you're entitled to, watch our short YouTube video. Go to www.gov.uk/tax-credits-webinars-videos"

11.73—for "www.gov.uk/complain-to-hm-revenue-and-customs." there is substituted "www.gov.uk/complain-about-hmrc"

11.74—the following is inserted after 11.74:

GENERAL NOTE

5.092   The above version of Code of Practice 26 has been in force since 6 April 2020.

PART VI

UPDATING MATERIAL
VOLUME V

UNIVERSAL CREDIT

Commentary by

John Mesher

Richard Poynter

Nick Wikeley

p.42, *amendment to the Immigration and Asylum Act 1999 s.115(9) (Exclusion from benefits—definition of "A person subject to immigration control")*

With effect from December 31, 2020 at 11.00 pm, reg.12 of the   **6.001** Immigration and Social Security Co-ordination (EU Withdrawal) Act 2020 (Consequential, Saving, Transitional and Transitory Provisions) (EU Exit) Regulations 2020 (SI 2020/1309) amended subs.(9) by omitting the words ""who is not a national of an EEA State and".

p.70, *annotations to the Welfare Reform Act 2012 s.15 (Work-focused interview requirement)*

JB v SSWP (UC) [2018] UKUT 360 (AAC) was endorsed and   **6.002** applied in *KG v SSWP (UC)* [2020] UKUT 307 (AAC). Before the Upper Tribunal the Secretary of State accepted that the available evidence did not show that the claimant had been properly notified of the requirement to take part in the particular interview with his work coach, so that no sanction could be applied under s.27. The documents were ambiguous as to whether the telephone interview was under s.15 or s.23 (connected requirements) and what issues the claimant was told were to be investigated, and left it unclear whether he had been adequately informed of the consequences of non-compliance.

p.87, *annotations to the Welfare Reform Act 2012 s.23 (Connected requirements)*

JB v SSWP (UC) [2018] UKUT 360 (AAC) (see the notes to ss.14   **6.003** and 15 in the main volume) was endorsed and applied in *KG v SSWP (UC)* [2020] UKUT 307 (AAC). Before the Upper Tribunal the Secretary of State accepted that the available evidence did not show that the claimant had been properly notified of the requirement to take part in the particular telephone interview with his work coach, so that no sanction could be applied under s.27. The documents were ambiguous whether the interview was under s.15 (work-focused interview requirement) or s.23 and what issues the claimant was told were to be investigated, and left it unclear whether he had been adequately informed of the consequences of non-compliance.

p.90, *annotations to the Welfare Reform Act 2012 s.24 (Imposition of requirements)*

JB v SSWP (UC) [2018] UKUT 360 (AAC) (see the notes to ss.14   **6.004** and 15 in the main volume) was endorsed and applied in *KG v SSWP (UC)* [2020] UKUT 307 (AAC). Before the Upper Tribunal the Secretary of State accepted that the available evidence did not show that the claimant had been properly notified of the requirement to take part in the particular telephone interview with his work coach, so that no sanction could be applied under s.27. The documents were ambiguous whether the interview was under s.15 (work-focused interview require-ment) or s.23 (connected requirements) and what issues the claimant was told were to be investigated, and left it unclear whether he had been adequately informed of the consequences of non-compliance.

p.149, *amendment to the Universal Credit Regulations 2013 (SI 2013/376) reg.2 (Interpretation—definition of "EEA Regulations")*

6.005   With effect from December 31, 2020 at 11.00 pm, reg.75 of the Immigration and Social Security Co-ordination (EU Withdrawal) Act 2020 (Consequential, Saving, Transitional and Transitory Provisions) (EU Exit) Regulations 2020 (SI 2020/1309) amended the definition of "EEA Regulations" by inserting the following at the end:

"and references to the EEA Regulations are to be read with Schedule 4 to the Immigration and Social Security Co-ordination (EU With-drawal) Act 2020(Consequential, Saving, Transitional and Transitory Provisions) Regulations 2020."

By reg.83, of and paras 2 and 3(w) of Sch.4 to the Immigration and Social Security Co-ordination (EU Withdrawal) Act 2020 (Consequen-tial, Saving, Transitional and Transitory Provisions) Regulations 2020 (SI 2020/1309), the provisions of the Immigration (European Economic Area) Regulations 2016 that are specified in para.(4) of that Schedule continue to have effect in relation to a "member of the post-transition period group" (i.e., to those who have "pre-settled status") as if they had not been revoked, but subject to the modifications set out in para.(4): see further the Noter-up to the 2016 Regulations below.

p.151, *modification of the Universal Credit Regulations 2013 (SI 2013/376) reg.2 (Interpretation)*

6.006   With effect from November 12, 2020, the final sentence under the heading, *Modification,* should read:

"By reg.6 of SI 2020/409, as amended by reg.2 of the Social Security (Coronavirus) (Prisoners) Amendment Regulations 2020 (SI 2020/1156), the modification will expire at the end of May 12, 2021."

pp.165-166, *amendment to the Universal Credit Regulations 2013 (SI 2013/376) reg.9 (Persons treated as not being in Great Britain)*

6.007   As a result of a series of further amendments, and from various dates as noted below, reg.70 has been amended so that it reads as follows:

Persons treated as not being in Great Britain

9.—(1) For the purposes of determining whether a person meets the basic condition to be in Great Britain, except where a person falls within paragraph (4), a person is to be treated as not being in Great

Britain if the person is not habitually resident in the United Kingdom, the Channel Islands, the Isle of Man or the Republic of Ireland.

(2) A person must not be treated as habitually resident in the United Kingdom, the Channel Islands, the Isle of Man or the Republic of Ireland unless the person has a right to reside in one of those places.

(3) For the purposes of paragraph (2), a right to reside does not include a right which exists by virtue of, or in accordance with—

(a)   regulation 13 of the EEA Regulations [⁵];

(aa) regulation 14 of the EEA Regulations, but only in cases where the right exists under that regulation because the person is–

  (i) a qualified person for the purposes of regulation 6(1) of those Regulations as a jobseeker; or

  (ii) a family member (within the meaning of regulation 7 of those Regulations) of such a jobseeker;

(b)   regulation 16 of the EEA Regulations, but only in cases where the right exists under that regulation because the person satisfies the criteria in regulation 16(5) of those Regulations or [⁵]; or

(c)   a person having been granted limited leave to enter, or remain in, the United Kingdom under the Immigration Act 1971 by virtue of—

  (i) Appendix EU to the immigration rules made under section 3(2) of that Act; [⁶]

  (ii) being a person with a Zambrano right to reside as defined in Annex 1 of Appendix EU to the immigration rules made under section 3(2) of that Act [⁶; or

  (iii) having arrived in the United Kingdom with an entry clearance that was granted under Appendix EU (Family Permit) to the immigration rules made under section 3(2) of that Act.]

[⁴ (3A) Paragraph (3)(c)(i) does not apply to a person who—

(a)   has a right to reside granted by virtue of being a family member of a relevant person of Northern Ireland; and

(b)   would have a right to reside under the EEA Regulations if the relevant person of Northern Ireland were an EEA national, provided that the right to reside does not fall within paragraph (3)(a) or (b);]

(4) A person falls within this paragraph if the person is—

(a)   a qualified person for the purposes of regulation 6 of the EEA Regulations as a worker or a self-employed person;

(b)   a family member of a person referred to in subparagraph (a) [⁴ . . .];

(c)   a person who has a right to reside permanently in the United Kingdom by virtue of regulation 15(1)(c), (d) or (e) of the EEA Regulations;

[⁴(ca) a family member of a relevant person of Northern Ireland, with a right to reside which falls within paragraph (3)(c)(i), provided that the relevant person of Northern Ireland falls within paragraph (4)(a), or would do so but for the fact that they are not an EEA national;]

[⁵(cb) a frontier worker within the meaning of regulation 3 of the Citizens' Rights (Frontier Workers) (EU Exit) Regulations 2020;

(cc) a family member of a person referred to in sub-paragraph (cb), who has been granted limited leave to enter, or remain in, the United Kingdom by virtue of Appendix EU to the immigration rules made under section 3(2) of the Immigration Act 1971;]

(d) a refugee within the definition in Article 1 of the Convention relating to the Status of Refugees done at Geneva on 28th July 1951, as extended by Article 1(2) of the Protocol relating to the Status of Refugees done at New York on 31st January 1967;

(e) a person who has been granted, or who is deemed to have been granted, leave outside the rules made under section 3(2) of the Immigration Act 1971 where that leave is—

(i) discretionary leave to enter or remain in the United Kingdom,

(ii) leave to remain under the Destitution Domestic Violence concession, or

(iii) leave deemed to have been granted by virtue of regulation 3 of the Displaced Persons (Temporary Protection) Regulations 2005;

(f) a person who has humanitarian protection granted under those rules; or

(g) a person who is not a person subject to immigration control within the meaning of section 115(9) of the Immigration and Asylum Act 1999 and who is in the United Kingdom as a result of their deportation, expulsion or other removal by compulsion of law from another country to the United Kingdom.

[⁴(5) In this regulation—

"EEA national" has the meaning given in regulation 2(1) of the EEA Regulations;

"family member" has the meaning given in regulation 7(1)(a), (b) or (c) of the EEA Regulations, except that regulation 7(4) of the EEA Regulations does not apply for the purposes of paragraphs (3A) and (4)(ca);

"relevant person of Northern Ireland" has the meaning given in Annex 1 of Appendix EU to the immigration rules made under section 3(2) of the Immigration Act 1971.]

AMENDMENTS

4. Social Security (Income-Related Benefits) (Persons of Northern Ireland - Family Members) (Amendment) Regulations 2020 (SI 2020/683) reg.8 (August 24, 2020).

5. Immigration and Social Security Co-ordination (EU Withdrawal) Act 2020 (Consequential, Saving, Transitional and Transitory Provisions) (EU Exit) Regulations 2020 (SI 2020/1309) reg.75 (December 31, 2020 at 11.00 pm).

6. Immigration (Citizens' Rights etc.) (EU Exit) Regulations 2020 (SI 2020/1372) reg.25 (December 31, 2020 immediately after 11.00 pm).

MODIFICATIONS

By reg.83 of and paras 2 and 3(w) of Sch.4 to SI 2020/1309, the provisions of the Immigration (European Economic Area) Regulations 2016 that are specified in para.(4) of that Schedule continue to have effect in relation to a "member of the post-transition period group" (*i.e.*, to those who have "pre-settled status") as if they had not been revoked, but subject to the modifications set out in para.(4): see further the *Noter-up* to the 2016 Regulations below.

p.169, *amendment to the Universal Credit Regulations 2013 (SI 2013/376) reg.11 (Temporary absence from Great Britain)*

With effect from December 31, 2020 at 11.00 pm, reg.4 of, and para. 11 of the Schedule to, the Social Security (Amendment) (EU Exit) Regulations 2019 (SI 2019/128) amended the definition of "prescribed area" in para.(5) by omitting the words "(other than the United Kingdom)".   6.008

pp.172-173, *amendments to the Universal Credit Regulations 2013 (SI 2013/376) reg.14 (Exceptions to the requirement not to be receiving education)*

With effect from August 5, 2020, reg.2 of the Universal Credit (Exceptions to the Requirement not to be receiving education) (Amendment) Regulations 2020 (SI 2020/827) amended reg.14 so that it reads as follows: 6.009

"Exceptions to the requirement not to be receiving education

14.—[(1)] A person does not have to meet the basic condition in s.4(1)(d) of the Act (not receiving education) if—
  (a) the person—
     (i) is undertaking a full- time course of study or training which is not a course of advanced education,
     (ii) is under the age of 21, or is 21 and reached that age whilst undertaking the course, and
     (iii) is without parental support (as defined in regulation 8(3));
  [(b) the person is entitled to attendance allowance, disability living allowance or personal independence payment and it has been determined—
     (i) that the person has limited capability for work or limited capability for work and work-related activity on the basis of an assessment under Part 5 of these Regulations or Part 4 or 5 of the ESA Regulations;
     (ii) that the person is to be treated as having limited capability for work under Schedule 8 or limited capability for work and work-related activity under Schedule 9;

(iii) that the person is to be treated as having limited capability for work or limited capability for work and work-related activity under regulation 19(2)(b) or (4)(b) of the Universal Credit (Transitional Provisions) Regulations 2014,

and that determination was made on or before the date of claim to universal credit, where the person is receiving education on the date the claim is made, or the date on which the person starts receiving education, where the person starts receiving education after the date of claim to universal credit;]

(c) the person is responsible for a child or a qualifying young person;

(d) the person is a single person and a foster parent with whom a child is placed;

(e) the person is a member of a couple, both of whom are receiving education, and the other member is—

(i) responsible for a child or qualifying young person, or

(ii) a foster parent with whom a child is placed; or

(f) the person—

(i) has reached the qualifying age for state pension credit, and

(ii) is a member of a couple the other member of which has not reached that age.

[(2) Where regulation 9(6)(a) or 9(10) of the Universal Credit, Personal Independence Payment, Jobseeker's Allowance and Employment and Support Allowance (Claims and Payments) Regulations 2013 (award of universal credit without a claim) applies to a person who is receiving education, paragraph (1)(b) is to be read as if each reference to "date of claim" was a reference to "date of award".]

The amendments appear to be a response to the litigation in *R (Kauser and JL) v Secretary of State for Work and Pensions* CO/987/2020, in which the High Court (Fordham J) subsequently issued a declaration that, under the previous law the Secretary of State had breached reg.14(b) when read with regs 38 and 39(1)(a), in failing to determine whether the Claimants had limited capability for work; and failing to conduct a Work Capability Assessment *before* deciding the Claimants' entitlement to Universal Credit. The order making the regulation is available at *https:// www.rightsnet.org.uk/pdfs/CO_987_2020.pdf* on Rightsnet.

p.190, *annotation to the Universal Credit Regulations 2013 (SI 2013/376) reg.24 (Child element)*

6.010   A legal challenge to the two-child limit as it applies to CTC was rejected by the Court of Appeal (Patten, Leggatt and Nicola Davies LJJ) in *R. (SC, CB) v Secretary of State for Work and Pensions and others* [2019] EWCA Civ 615, (upholding the decision of the High Court (Ouseley J) in [2018] EWHC 864 (Admin)). The claimants had argued, first, that the limit was incompatible with their Convention Rights to respect for their private and family lives (*i.e.*, under Art.8) and to marry and to found a family (Art.12); and, second, that the limit discriminated against

550

them unlawfully contrary to Article 14 taken together with Art.8 and Article 1 of the First Protocol. An appeal to the Supreme Court (Case ID: UKSC 2019/0135) was heard on October 20-22, 2020. At the time of going to press, judgment is awaited.

p.222, *annotation to the Universal Credit Regulations 2013 (SI 2013/376) reg.46 (What is included in capital?)*

MS v DfC (JSA) [2020] NICom 42 holds that where a tribunal is not **6.011** satisfied by a claimant's assertion that they have disposed of money, so that the amount remains part of their actual capital, it is not necessary for the tribunal to make a positive finding of fact about where the money was held. Submissions to the contrary were based on a misreading of remarks in *DMcC v DSD (IS)* [2012] NICom 326.

pp.262-263, *annotations to the Universal Credit Regulations 2013 (SI 2013/376) reg.54 (Calculation of earned income—general principles)*

See the entry for pp.293-4 for the new form of reg.61 substituted with **6.012** effect from November 16, 2020, and its relationship with the decision of the Court of Appeal in *Secretary of State for Work and Pensions v Johnson* [2020] EWCA Civ 778; [2020] P.T.S.R. 1872.

The Court of Appeal has given the Secretary of State permission to appeal against the Administrative Court's decision on claimants who are paid four-weekly in *R. (on the application of Pantellerisco) v Secretary of State for Work and Pensions* [2020] EWHC 1944 (Admin); [2020] P.T.S.R. 2289. The hearing is currently listed to float on June 15 or 16, 2021.

pp.282-284, *annotations to the Universal Credit Regulations 2013 (SI 2013/376) reg.57 (Self-employed earnings—coronavirus payments)*

A third tranche of SEISS payments in respect of the three months **6.013** from November 2020 to January 2021 has been made available for application (see the Self-employed Income Support Scheme Grant Extension 3 Direction signed on November 21, 2020). The payment will meet 80% of qualifying trading profits, capped at £7,500 for the three months. The previous tranche in respect of the three months from August to October 2020 met only 70% of qualifying trading profits capped at £6,750 (see the Self-employed Income Support Scheme Extension Direction signed on July 1, 2020). Since both of the extension schemes operate by way of modification of the original scheme, they are all encompassed in the definition in reg.2(3) of SI 2020/522 (see Part I of this Supplement), so that grants under all of them fall within the rule in reg.2(1)(a) and come in as receipts in Step 1 of the calculation of self-employed earnings. A fourth tranche for the period from February to April 2021 has been announced.

The Coronavirus Job Retention Scheme has been extended to cover the period from November 2020 to the end of April 2021 with the level of reimbursement for hours not worked being 80% of usual salary (see the Coronavirus Act 2020 Functions of Her Majesty's Revenue and Customs (Coronavirus Job Retention Scheme) Direction signed on November 12, 2020 and the announcement of December 17, 2020 with the Direction signed on January 25, 2021). The previous extension, mentioned in the main volume, was authorised by the Direction signed on June 25, 2020.

pp.293-294, *amendment to the Universal Credit Regulations 2013 (SI 2013/376) reg.61 (Information for calculating earned income—real time information etc.)*

6.014   With effect from November 16, 2020, reg.2 of the Universal Credit (Earned Income) Amendment Regulations 2020 (SI 2020/1138) substituted the following for reg.61:

"Information for calculating earned income - real time information etc.

61.—(1) Unless paragraph (2) applies, a person must provide such information for the purposes of calculating their earned income at such times as the Secretary of State may require.

Real time information

(2) Where a person is, or has been, engaged in an employment in respect of which their employer is a Real Time Information employer—

   (a) the amount of the person's employed earnings from that employment for each assessment period is to be based on the information reported to HMRC under the PAYE Regulations and received by the Secretary of State from HMRC in that assessment period; and

   (b) for an assessment period in which no information is received from HMRC, the amount of employed earnings in relation to that employment is to be taken to be nil.

Exceptions to use of Real Time Information

(3) Paragraph (2) does not apply where—

   (a) in relation to a particular employment the Secretary of State considers that the employer is unlikely to report information to HMRC in a sufficiently accurate or timely manner;

   (b) it appears to the Secretary of State that the amount of a payment reported to HMRC is incorrect, or fails to reflect the definition of employed earnings in regulation 55 (employed earnings), in some material respect; or

   (c) no information is received from HMRC in an assessment period and the Secretary of State considers that this is likely to be because of a failure to report information (which includes the failure of a computer system operated by HMRC, the employer or any other person).

(4) Where paragraph (2) does not apply by virtue of any of the exceptions in paragraph (3) the [Secretary] of State must determine the amount of employed earnings for the assessment period in question (or, where the exception in paragraph (3)(a) applies, for each assessment period in which the person is engaged in that employment) in accordance with regulation 55 (employed earnings) using such information or evidence as the Secretary of State thinks fit.

Reallocation of reported payments

(5) Where it appears to the Secretary of State that a payment of employed earnings has been reported late, or otherwise reported in the wrong assessment period, the Secretary of State may determine that the payment is to be treated as employed earnings in the assessment period in which it was received.

(6) Where a person is engaged in an employment where they are paid on a regular monthly basis and more than one payment in relation to that employment is reported in the same assessment period, the Secretary of State may, for the purposes of maintaining a regular pattern, determine that one of those payments is to be treated as employed earnings in respect of a different assessment period.

Consequential adjustments

(7) Where the Secretary of State makes a determination under any of paragraphs (4) to (6), the Secretary of State may make such other adjustment to the calculation of the person's employed earnings as may be necessary to avoid duplication or to maintain a regular payment pattern.

(8) In this regulation "Real Time Information Employer" has the meaning in regulation 2A(1) of the PAYE Regulations."

The explanatory memorandum recites that in *Secretary of State for Work and Pensions v Johnson* [2020] EWCA Civ 778; [2020] P.T.S.R. 1872 the Court of Appeal decided that the lack of adjustment in the drafting of regs 54 and 61 for those who have two calendar monthly salary payments taken into account in one assessment period due to a "non-banking day salary shift" was not rational and continues:

"7.4 These regulations therefore provide a solution to that Judgment. The policy intent is to ensure that ordinarily no more than one set of calendar monthly salary payments from a single employer are taken into account in each assessment period. This will also enable certain claimants to benefit from any applicable work allowance in each assessment period. This change in regulations will allow DWP to reallocate a payment reported via real time information (RTI) to a different assessment period, either because it was reported in the wrong assessment period, or (in the case of monthly paid employee) it is necessary to maintain a regular payment cycle. This issue applies to less than 1% of the people who are working and receiving Universal Credit."

The new reg.61, in effect from November 16, 2020, has thus been presented as if it were not just "a solution", but the complete solution to the irrationality identified by the Court of Appeal and necessarily operative only prospectively from that date. That assumption also seems to underlie the DWP's presentation to the Social Security Advisory Committee on October 7, 2020 (SSAC Minutes October 2020), following which the SSAC agreed not to take the proposed regulations on formal reference. Such an assumption fails to grapple with the consequences of the terms of the declaration agreed by the parties (set out in the notes to reg.54 at p.261 of the main volume), which declares the earned income calculation method in the regulations to be irrational and unlawful as applied to the monthly paid employees identified. The main consequence, as argued in the main volume, is that neither the four *Johnson* claimants nor any others who are able to bring an effective challenge to any past decisions can have that unlawful method applied to them. That appears consistent with the approach of Rose LJ in para.108 of *Johnson*, where she said that the claimants' argument of discrimination under the ECHR did not arise for consideration because of the success of their case on irrationality. It is submitted that the judge, and thus the Court, could only have taken that view if she thought that the four *Johnson* claimants had, by that success, achieved all that they could have achieved by success in the discrimination argument. Since the judicial reviews were directed against the decisions made in particular assessment periods in 2017 or 2018, the Court must by necessary implication from that part of its judgment have accepted that those decisions had to be re-made without applying the method of calculation found to be unlawful, even though the apparent mismatch between the nature of irrationality accepted and that result was unaddressed in the judgments. A mere redrafting of the regulations with effect from a subsequent date does not achieve that result. Thus the argument made in the main volume stands, that *Johnson* means that the earned income calculation method in the pre-November 16, 2020 form of the regulations has been unlawful from the outset.

6.015 However, as from November 16, 2020 (probably in relation to assessment periods beginning on or after that date: see para.32 of Sch.1 to the Decisions and Appeals Regulations 2013 for the rule on supersessions where there is an existing award) the new form of reg.61 must be applied (subject to arguments that other categories of claimant might succeed in irrationality or discrimination arguments, e.g. *R. (Pantellerisco) v Secretary of State for Work and Pensions* [2020] EWHC 1944 (Admin); [2020] P.T.S.R. 2289 on claimants paid four-weekly, discussed in the notes to reg.54 in the main volume and see the entry for pp.262-263 above). The main difference from the previous form of reg.61 is in the substitution of the new paras (5) to (7), giving various discretionary powers, for the previous para.(5) and in the omission of the previous para.(6) (see detailed discussion below). There have also been several changes to the drafting of paras (1) to (4), some of which are merely cosmetic or clarificatory, such as the helpful introduction of some sub-headings, but some of which potentially introduce changes of substance. The integration of the changes into the structure of reg.61 has not been entirely coherent. The administrative guidance in Memo ADM 27/20 does little more than paraphrase the terms of the regulation.

Note that the new powers in reg.61 are not restricted to cases where the work allowance is in play, as it was for the four *Johnson* claimants. The discretions may thus sometimes be very difficult to exercise, especially where claimants would be better off overall (apart from difficulties caused by fluctuations in total income) by having two monthly payments taken into account in the same assessment period and none in another period.

The new paras (1) and (2) are in substance the same as the previous paras (1) and (2), except that the rules are said to be "in respect of" particular assessment periods rather than "for" them. There has thus been no change to the unequivocal rule in para.(2)(b) that the amount of employed earnings "is to be taken to be nil" for any assessment period in which no information is received from HMRC. However, it would appear that, in order to allow the new provision to bite on the mischief identified in the explanatory memorandum, para.(2) must be read as subject to paras (5) to (7) as well as to the exceptions expressly made in para.(3).

The new para.(3), establishing three exceptions from the para.(2) rules, is made non-discretionary. Then the first exception in the new sub-para.(a) is in substance the same as in the previous sub-para.(a) with some rejigging of language. The second exception in the new sub-para.(b) is the replacement of the previous sub-para.(b)(ii), but with significant changes. The exception now only applies if the *amount* of a payment reported to HMRC is incorrect or fails to reflect the definition of employed earnings in reg.55. Previously, the reference was to the *information* received from HMRC. It was argued in the main volume that if an employer reported a payment as made on the actual date it was made instead of the date specified in HMRC guidance/instructions (i.e. the usual pay day) the information received from HMRC was incorrect in a material effect, so that a departure from the para.(2) rules was authorised. That argument seems no longer to hold if the amount of the payment reported is correct (but see new para.(5) below). The new sub-para.(c) is in substance the same as the previous sub-para.(b)(i), again with some slight rejigging of language.

The new para.(4) is in substance the same as the previous para.(4), **6.016** although set out differently and now expressly restricted to cases where para.(3) has been applied. Note that it only requires the determination of the amount of any employed earnings for the assessment period(s) in question in accordance with reg.55, which is about what payments count as employed earnings. But the use of whatever information or evidence is thought fit is also still authorised and in addition the general power in the new para.(7) to make "other" adjustments necessary for avoiding duplication or maintaining a regular payment pattern applies to para.(4). Thus it is not entirely clear whether para.(4) gives an open-ended power in para.(3) cases (free of the conditions in paras (5) and (6)) to calculate the amount of employed earnings in relation to any assessment period, including the reallocation of payments to a different assessment period than that prescribed under the para.(2) rules or under reg.54, or whether such a process requires the invocation of para.(5) or (6). It looks as though the intention was that paras (5) and (6) should apply whenever their conditions are met, so that para.(4) would be subject to those provisions, but there is a doubt whether that intention has been achieved.

The new para.(5) is the first major departure from the previous structure, although it seems to have limited effect. It gives the Secretary of State (and thus a tribunal on appeal) discretion, where a payment has been reported late or in the wrong assessment period, to treat the payment as employed earnings in the assessment period in which it was received. In the context, "reported" must mean reported to HMRC under the RTI system. Paragraph (5) applies whatever the usual pay interval; it is not restricted to those, like the *Johnson* claimants, who are paid monthly. However, it cannot solve the systemic problem identified in *Pantellerisco* (above) for those paid four-weekly of there inevitably being one assessment period each year containing two usual pay-days. Claimants in that position must therefore still rely on the irrationality argument in *Pantellersico* or on discrimination under the ECHR.

The power given by para.(5) is limited to treating a payment as part of employed earnings in the assessment period in which it was received. Paragraph (5) does not in itself authorise any more extensive reallocation. For instance, take a claimant with an assessment period running from the 28th of one month to the 27th of the next, who is usually paid on the 28th of the month and is paid their December salary on December 23. If the employer, say because office systems were down over the period, did not report the payment through the RTI system until January 3, that would appear to fall within the "late report" category. But para.(5) would only allow the payment to be allocated to the assessment period including December 23, i.e. the same assessment period to which the payment received as usual on November 28 would have been allocated. For the payment to be allocated to the assessment period beginning on December 28, to avoid the *Johnson* irrationality, there would apparently have to be recourse to para.(6), with its limitation to those paid on a regular monthly basis. But the operation of para.(5) brings in the general power to make any "other adjustments" in new para.(7), which might open up the possibility of reallocation to an assessment period other than that of receipt and of application to claimants paid otherwise than monthly. But what then would have been the point of the restriction in effect in para.(5)?

Presumably, para.(5) is not made expressly subject to para.(6) because both provisions are discretionary, thus allowing the Secretary of State and tribunals to apply whichever is more appropriate, as the justice of the case requires. But para.(6) only applies to claimants who are paid on a regular monthly basis, not to claimants paid at any other intervals. Although para.(2)(b), requiring the taking of employed earnings to be nil in respect of any assessment period in which no information is received by the DWP from HMRC, has not been made subject to paras (5) to (7), that result must presumably follow in order to allow those provisions to operate (see above).

It is no doubt easy enough to identify when a report to HMRC is made 6.017
late, but what is meant by a report being made "in the wrong assessment
period" remains obscure. Presumably, it covers only an assessment
period other than that in which the report ought to have been made in
accordance with HMRC guidance/instructions, rather than wrongness
in any wider sense. But if the report is made after the "right" assessment
period, the case would appear already to be covered by the lateness
provision. Possibly, there could be some independent operation if the
report was made *before* the "right" assessment period, but there would
still be the limitation as to the date to which the payment can be
allocated, subject to the possible application of para.(7). There is no
guidance as to the meaning of "the wrong assessment period" or example of the application of the rule in Memo ADM 27/20.

The new para.(6) is the main provision designed to deal with the
problem identified by the Court of Appeal in *Johnson*. It is restricted to
employees paid on a regular monthly (calendar monthly: Interpretation
Act 1978, Sch.1) basis. That formula, including the word "basis", must
entail that the scope is not restricted to those usually paid on the same
day each month, so long as their pay is calculated per month and they are
paid a month at a time. Then, if more than one payment is reported (to
HMRC) in any one assessment period, the Secretary of State and a
tribunal on appeal may, for the purposes of maintaining a regular pattern, allocate one (but only one) of those payments to a different assessment period, either earlier or later. The discretion, particularly in
conjunction with the general power in new para.(7) to make any other
adjustments, is fairly open, so long as a purpose (main purpose?) is to
maintain a regular pattern (of allocation of monthly payments).
Although para.(2)(b), requiring the taking of employed earnings to be nil
in respect of any assessment period in which no information is received
by the DWP from HMRC, has not been made subject to paras (5) and
(6), that result must presumably follow in order to allow those provisions
to operate (see above).

See the note to para.(5) above for an example of how para.(6) might
be applied. Note that it is not necessary for a report to have been made
to HMRC on any wrong date or that there has been a "non-banking day
salary shift" in the strictest sense. All that is necessary is that more than
one payment has been reported for a monthly-paid claimant in the same
assessment period. If the pattern of usual payment on the last working
day of the month produces that result, reporting on the two usual pay-
days will have been in accordance with HMRC guidance/instructions
and there will not have been a "shift" in the sense of a departure from the
usual pay-day, but para.(6) can be applied. It might just be that payments other than monthly salary could trigger the potential application
of para.(6), for instance if a claimant received a bonus or a reimbursement of non-allowable expenses on a different date from the usual
monthly pay-day. But in such a case, there would be no need to exercise
the discretion to reallocate such a payment.

The effect of the power in the new para.(7) to make other adjustments
in the calculation of employed earnings has been discussed in the notes
to paras (4)–(6) above.

The previous para.(6), apparently giving a power where decisions are made under reg.41(3) of the Decisions and Appeals Regulations 2013, arguably unnecessarily, has not been reproduced in the new form of reg.61, but a footnote to the preamble to SI 2020/1138 does refer to reg.41(1) and to s.159D(1)(b)(vi) of the SSAA 1992. See the main volume for extensive discussion of those provisions and for how they should not be allowed to stand in the way of a right of appeal.

The SSAC, despite considering the new regulation to be sufficiently helpful to claimants that a formal reference of the proposal was not necessary, remained "concerned that the new arrangements will be overly reliant on claimants to notify the Department when they have received two monthly payments in a single assessment period and that as a result a significant number could still fail to benefit from a work allowance every month as they should" (letter of October 23, 2020 from the Chair to the Secretary of State). Therefore, they recommended that the Department should closely monitor the impact of the change. The DWP had accepted that their manual process would depend on claimants coming forward with information, but said that it intended to ask employed claimants about the interval at which they are paid at the start of the claim, so as to flag up cases that might encounter problems in the future.

pp.301-308, *annotation to the Universal Credit Regulations 2013 (SI 2013/376) reg.62 (Minimum income floor: temporary coronavirus provisions)*

6.018   With effect from November 12, 2020, the new reg.10(2A) of the Social Security (Coronavirus) (Further Measures) Regulations 2020 (SI 2020/371), as inserted by reg.2 of the Social Security (Coronavirus) (Further Measures) (Amendment) and Miscellaneous Amendment Regulations 2020 (SI 2020/1201), made April 30, 2021 the date of expiry of the effect of reg.2 of SI 2020/371.

p.308, *amendment to the Universal Credit Regulations 2013 (SI 2013/376) reg.63(1)(a) (Start-up period)*

6.019   With effect from September 26, 2020, reg.6(1) of the Universal Credit (Managed Migration Pilot and Miscellaneous Amendments) Regulations 2019 (SI 2019/1152) substituted the following for sub-para.(a) of reg.63(1):

"(a) regulation 62 (minimum income floor) has not previously applied to the claimant in relation to the trade, profession or vocation which is currently the claimant's main employment (whether in relation to the current award or a previous award); and"

This amendment makes an important change to the operation of the minimum income floor (MIF) for all claimants, whether migrated naturally or under the managed process or not. It removes the condition for being excepted from the application of the MIF under the start-up period rule that the claimant had begun to carry on the self-employment that is the main employment within the 12 months preceding the assessment period in which the MIF would otherwise have started to apply. The new condition, in addition to reg.63(1)(b), is that the MIF has not previously applied to the claimant in relation to the current self-employment. See the entry for p.309 for the provisions for managed migration claimants that have also been removed from the same date as redundant

p.309, *annotation to the Universal Credit Regulations 2013 (SI 2013/376) reg.63 (Start-up period)*

With effect from September 26, 2020, reg.6(2) of the Universal Credit (Managed Migration Pilot and Miscellaneous Amendments) Regulations 2019 (SI 2019/1152) revoked reg.59 of the Transitional Provisions Regulations, which had applied a special rule (not to apply reg.63(1)(a)) to those who claimed universal credit under "natural migration", as discussed in the main volume. That special rule has become unnecessary as a result of the introduction of a new form of reg.63(1)(a) applying to all claimants with effect from the same date (see the entry for p.308). Note also that that amendment has rendered some of the discussion in the notes redundant. 6.020

With effect from November 12, 2020, the new reg.10(2A) of the Social Security (Coronavirus) (Further Measures) Regulations 2020 (SI 2020/371), as inserted by reg.2 of the Social Security (Coronavirus) (Further Measures) (Amendment) and Miscellaneous Amendment Regulations 2020 (SI 2020/1201), made April 30, 2021 the date of expiry of the effect of reg.2 of SI 2020/371 (mentioned in the temporary coronavirus provisions section).

pp.310-314, *annotation to the Universal Credit Regulations 2013 (SI 2013/376) reg.64 (Meaning of "gainful self-employment": temporary coronavirus provisions)*

With effect from November 12, 2020, the new reg.10(2A) of the Social Security (Coronavirus) (Further Measures) Regulations 2020 (SI 2020/371), as inserted by reg.2 of the Social Security (Coronavirus) (Further Measures) (Amendment) and Miscellaneous Amendment Regulations 2020 (SI 2020/1201), made April 30, 2021 the date of expiry of the effect of reg.2 of SI 2020/371. 6.021

pp.316-320, *annotations to the Universal Credit Regulations 2013 (SI 2013/376) reg.66 (What is included in unearned income?)*

With effect from May 29, 2020, reg.26(1)(a) of the Victims' Payments Regulations 2020 (SI 2020/103) provides that a victims' payment or a lump sum under those Regulations is to be disregarded as income. 6.022

The £500 payment, administered by local authorities, to be made to those in England entitled to a qualifying income-related benefit (including universal credit) who are required by NHS Test and Trace on or after September 28, 2020 (down to at least March 31) to self-isolate for 14 (or 10) days, are unable to work from home and will lose income from employment or self-employment as a result has not been listed in reg.66 and so cannot be taken into account as unearned income. Nor has the discretionary payment available to those not entitled to a qualifying benefit been listed. Nor have payments under the very similar, but not identical, schemes available in Wales, Scotland and Northern Ireland. The position is different for "legacy" benefits.

The intention was also expressed when the English scheme was first put forward that the £500 payments were not to be taken into account as capital. The eligibility condition of loss of income indicates that the payments are in their nature income receipts rather than capital receipts, being compensation for the loss of the income that would otherwise have been received. But there is nothing in the legislation to prevent any amount remaining out of the £500 at the end of the required days of self-isolation (or possibly at the end of the assessment period containing the last of those days) from counting as capital under the usual principles.

In *R. (on the application of Moore) v Secretary of State for Work and Pensions* [2020] EWHC 2827 (Admin), Swift J, while finding two of the grounds of judicial review arguable, rejected the case for the claimants against the inclusion of maternity allowance in the list of social security benefits to count as unearned income, although statutory maternity pay counts as earned income with the advantage of the 63% taper and the work allowance. An application for permission to appeal has been made to the Court of Appeal.

pp.321-322, *amendments to the Universal Credit Regulations 2013 (SI 2013/376) reg.68 (Persons treated as having student income)*

6.023   With effect from July 15, 2020, reg.8(3) of the Social Security (Income and Capital) (Miscellaneous Amendments) Regulations 2020 (SI 2020/618) omitted the words "master's degree" in all places in paras (1), (2) and (5) and substituted the following for the definition of "postgraduate master's degree loan" in para.(7):

> ""postgraduate loan" means a loan to a student undertaking a post-graduate master's degree course or a postgraduate doctoral degree course pursuant to regulations made under section 22 of the Teaching and Higher Education Act 1998;"

p.323, *amendments to the Universal Credit Regulations 2013 (SI 2013/376) reg.69(1A) and (2) and heading (Calculation of student income—student loans and postgraduate master's degree loans)*

6.024   With effect from July 15, 2020, reg.8(4) of the Social Security (Income and Capital) (Miscellaneous Amendments) Regulations 2020 (SI 2020/618) omitted the words "master's degree" in paras (aa) and (b) of Step 1.

p.325, *amendments to the Universal Credit Regulations 2013 (SI 2013/376) reg.71 (Calculation of student income—amount for an assessment period)*

With effect from July 15, 2020, reg.8(5) of the Social Security (Income and Capital) (Miscellaneous Amendments) Regulations 2020 (SI 2020/618) omitted the words "master's degree" in all places.   6.025

p.331, *amendments to the Universal Credit Regulations 2013 (SI 2013/376) reg.76 (Special schemes for compensation)*

With effect from July 15, 2020, reg.8(5) of the Social Security (Income and Capital) (Miscellaneous Amendments) Regulations 2020 (SI 2020/618) omitted the word "or" at the end of head (v) of para.(1)(a) and inserted the following after head (v):   6.026

"(vi) the fire at Grenfell Tower on 14th June 2017; or"

It also inserted the following after para.(1):

"(1A) This regulation also applies where a person receives a payment from—
  (a) the National Emergencies Trust, registered charity number 1182809;
  (b) the Child Migrants Trust, registered charity number 1171479, under the scheme for former British child migrants; or
  (c) the Royal Borough of Kensington and Chelsea or a registered charity where the payment is made because that person was affected by the fire at Grenfell Tower on 14th June 2017 or is the personal representative of such a person."

p.349, *amendments to the Universal Credit Regulations 2013 (SI 2013/376) reg.89(4) and (5) (Claimants subject to no work-related requirements)*

With effect from July 15, 2020, reg.8(6) of the Social Security (Income and Capital) (Miscellaneous Amendments) Regulations 2020 (SI 2020/618) omitted the words "master's degree" in both places.   6.027

pp.352-353, *annotations to the Universal Credit Regulations 2013 (SI 2013/376) reg.90 (Claimants subject to no work-related requirements—the earnings thresholds)*

Note the effect of reg.6(1A)(a) in rounding down reg.90 calculations to the nearest pound.   6.028

pp.371-372, *annotations to the Universal Credit Regulations 2013 (SI 2013/376) reg.99(3) and temporary coronavirus provisions (Circumstances in which requirements must not be imposed)*

With effect from November 12, 2020, the period of operation of the modification to the definition of "prisoner" in reg.2 (not reg.2(3)) has   6.029

been extended to May 12, 2021 by reg.2 of the Social Security (Coronavirus) (Prisoners) Amendment Regulations 2020 (SI 2020/1156).

pp.376–378, *annotations to the Universal Credit Regulations 2013 (SI 2013/376) reg.99(6) and (6A) (Circumstances in which requirements must not be imposed—the administrative earnings threshold)*

6.030   Note the effect of reg.6(1A)(b) in rounding down reg.99(6) calculations to the nearest pound.

pp.436–437, *commentary to the Universal Credit Regulations 2013 (SI 2013/376) Sch.4, para.7 (Housing costs element for renters—relevant payments calculated monthly)*

6.031   A legal challenge to the "conversion ratio" (*i.e.*, 52/12) used to calculate the monthly housing costs of renters who pay weekly, two-weekly and four-weekly was rejected by the High Court (Julian Knowles J) in *R. (on the application of Caine) v Secretary of State for Work and Pensions* [2020] EWHC 2482 (Admin).

p.458, *amendment to the Universal Credit Regulations 2013 (SI 2013/376) Sch.10 (Capital to be disregarded)*

6.032   The text of para.22 (Scottish funeral expense assistance) should be corrected by adding the words "within the past 12 months" between "given" and "in accordance".

With effect from November 9, 2020, art.8 of the Social Security (Scotland) Act 2018 (Young Carer Grants, Short-Term Assistance and Winter Heating Assistance) (Consequential Provision and Modifications) Order 2020 (SI 2020/989) inserted the following after para.22:

> "**23.** Any assistance given within the past 52 weeks in accordance with the Carer's Assistance (Young Carer Grants) (Scotland) Regulations 2019."

Under the specified regulations (SSI 2019/324, in operation from October 21, 2019), young carer grants of (from April 2020) £305.10, limited to one a year, are payable in Scotland to carers aged 16 to 18 who care for at least 16 hours a week over a 13-week period for a person who normally receives a disability benefit (see Part I of this Supplement). The 52-week limitation is absent from the equivalent provisions for "legacy" benefits. There appears to have been a gap during which grants were not disregarded as capital. Young carer grants are not listed as unearned income in reg.66.

With effect from the same date art.21 of the same Order inserted the following after para.23:

> "**24.** Any winter heating assistance given within the past 52 weeks in accordance with regulations made under section 30 of the Social Security (Scotland) Act 2018."

The relevant regulations are the Winter Heating Assistance for Children and Young People (Scotland) Regulations 2020 (SSI 2020/352, in operation from November 9, 2020) (see Part I of this Supplement), which initially provide an automatic annual grant in November 2020 to a family of £200 for each child entitled to the highest rate of the care component of DLA in the week of September 21–27, 2020. The 52-week limitation is absent from the equivalent provisions for "legacy" benefits.

Note that there has been no amendment equivalent to those made to Sch.10 to the Income Support Regulations, Sch.7 to the JSA Regulations 1996 and Sch.8 to the ESA Regulations 2008 by SI 2020/482 to disregard as capital payments of arrears of Scottish child payments under the Scottish Child Payments Regulations 2020 (SSI 2020/351). But such payments would already be covered by the disregard in para.18(1)(c).

p.459, *annotation to the Universal Credit Regulations 2013 (SI 2013/376) Sch.10 (Capital to be disregarded)*

With effect from May 29, 2020, reg.26(1)(a) of the Victims' Payments **6.033** Regulations 2020 (SI 2020/103) (see Part I of this Supplement) provides that a victims' payment or a lump sum under those Regulations is to be disregarded as capital.

With effect from July 15, 2020, reg.10C of the Universal Credit (Transitional Provisions) Regulations 2014 (SI 2014/1230), as inserted by reg.9 of the Social Security (Income and Capital) (Miscellaneous Amendments) Regulations 2020 (SI 2020/618) (see the entry for p.578 below) provides for the disregard as capital for 12 months from the date of receipt of certain compensatory payments for delay or failure to carry out an assessment for old style contributory ESA, with additional conditions and a potential extension for payments of £5,000 or more.

There has been no legislation to disregard as capital the £500 payments, administered by local authorities, to be made to those who are entitled to a qualifying income-related benefit (including universal credit) who are required by NHS Test and Trace on or after September 28, 2020 (down to at least March 31) to self-isolate for 14 (or 10) days, are unable to work from home and will lose income from employment or self-employment as a result (see the entry for pp.316-20 for further details). It is suggested there that the payment is in the nature of income, but if that is wrong it cannot be disregarded as capital, nor can any amount of the payment left over at the end of the isolation period.

p.467, *annotation to the Universal Credit Regulations 2013 (SI 2013/376) Sch.10, para.13 (Capital to be disregarded: proceeds of sale of former home received within past six months (or longer if reasonable) to be used for purchase of new home)*

In *EAM v SSWP (UC)* [2020] UKUT 247 (AAC), Judge Poynter has **6.034** declined to follow *R(IS) 7/01* and the other decisions referred to there as being inconsistent with the principle conclusively confirmed in *In re B*

(Children) [2008] UKHL 35, [2009] A.C. 11 that there is only one civil standard of proof and that is proof that the fact in issue more probably occurred than not. His view was that to apply a test under para.13 in terms of any kind of certainty was to place a higher burden on the claimant than the balance of probabilities. Although he agreed with the proposition in *R(IS) 7/01* that a mere genuine intention to use the sum to purchase a new home is not enough, he continued in para.33 that the phrase "is to be used for the purchase of premises" is about "what in all the circumstances of the case (including the claimant's intentions) is likely to happen in practice. Then he said in para.34 that to the extent that the *R(IS) 7/01* test requires a claimant to prove any fact to any standard other than the balance of probabilities he declined to follow that decision.

There are at least two problems in applying *EAM*. One is that it was not necessary to the decision for the judge to reach a definite conclusion on the correctness of *R(IS) 7/01*. On the facts as found by the First-tier Tribunal, the remaining amount attributable to the proceeds of sale of the claimant's home (£37,000) was not enough to buy a new home for her and her partner, so that they would need a mortgage, which on the balance of probabilities they would be unable to secure because of the level of their indebtedness. Accordingly, although the tribunal had been inconsistent on the nature of the test and had seemed to apply a test of practical certainty in concluding that the sum was not to be disregarded, its decision was not set aside because the same result would have followed if Judge Poynter's suggested test had been used. That undermines the basis for not following a reported decision that might otherwise have existed if a First-tier Tribunal or the Secretary of State considered Judge Poynter's reasoning, especially as supported by House of Lords' authority, to be persuasive.

The second problem is that the judge's reasoning appears dubious. There is a slight uncertainty about whether the disagreement with *R(IS) 7/01* extends only to the burden of proving facts necessary to the application of the legislative test or whether it extends also to the burden of showing that that test is met in all the circumstances as established by findings of fact. On balance, the latter seems to be intended. But then the result in accordance with para.33 is that the test to be applied is whether it is more likely than not that the sum will be used for the purchase of premises. Such a test appears, as a matter of the ordinary use of language, to be significantly different from and less restrictive than the legislative test in terms of "is to be used". Arguably, Judge Poynter's approach conflates the nature of the burden of proving that the legislative test is met with the true meaning of that test.

Unless and until *EAM* is taken to the Court of Appeal or there is some further decision clarifying the issue (which may well take some years), tribunals may wish to hedge their bets by applying both approaches in the alternative, but only if properly satisfied that the outcome would be the same whichever was applied. If not so satisfied, a choice will have to be made as to whether the reasoning in *EAM* is sufficiently persuasive to be preferred to the approach approved in *R(IS) 7/01*.

p.469, *annotation to the Universal Credit Regulations 2013 (SI 2013/376) Sch.10, para.22 (Capital to be disregarded: Scottish funeral expense assistance)*

The note in the main volume is incorrect in stating that there is no   6.034.1
limit in this disregard as to the past period in which the payment was
received. The limit is 12 months from the date the assistance was
given.

p.542, *amendment to the Loans for Mortgage Interest Regulations 2017 (SI 2017/725) Sch.4 (Direct payments to qualifying lenders)*

With effect from August 2, 2020, reg.2 of the Loans for Mortgage   6.035
Interest (Transaction Fee) (Amendment) Regulations 2020 (SI
2020/666) amended Sch.4 by omitting para.6 (Fees payable by qualifying lenders).

p.549, *amendments to the Social Security (Coronavirus) (Further Measures) Regulations 2020 (SI 2020/371) reg.10 (Expiry)*

With effect from November 12, 2020, reg.2 of the Social Security   6.036
(Coronavirus) (Further Measures) (Amendment) and Miscellaneous
Amendment Regulations 2020 (SI 2020/1201) amended reg.10 by substituting "6 and 7" for "2, 6, 7, 8 and 9" in para.(2) and inserting the
following after para.(2):

"(2A) Regulation 2 ceases to have effect on 30th April 2021.
(2B) Regulations 8 and 9 cease to have effect on 12th May 2021."

pp.555-557, *amendments to the Universal Credit (Transitional Provisions) Regulations 2014 (SI 2014/1230) reg.2 (Interpretation)*

With effect from November 25, 2020, reg.6(2) of the Universal   6.037
Credit (Persons who have attained state pension credit qualifying age)
(Amendment) Regulations 2020 (SI 2020/655) amended reg.2(1) by
inserting at the appropriate places the following definitions—

""the 2006 (SPC) Regulations" means the Housing Benefit (Persons
who have attained the qualifying age for state pension credit) Regulations 2006;";
""the Decisions and Appeals Regulations" means the Universal
Credit, Personal Independence Payment, Jobseeker's Allowance and
Employment and Support Allowance (Decisions and Appeals) Regulations 2013;";
""qualifying age for state pension credit" has the meaning given by
section 1(6) of the State Pension Credit Act 2002;"; and
""state pension credit" means state pension credit under the State
Pension Credit Act 2002;".

p.560, *annotation to the Universal Credit (Transitional Provisions) Regulations 2014 (SI 2014/1230) reg.4A (Restriction on claims for universal credit by persons entitled to a severe disability premium)*

6.038   Regulation 4A is due to be repealed by reg. 7 of the Universal Credit (Managed Migration Pilot and Miscellaneous Amendments) Regulations 2019 (SI 2019/1152) with effect from January 27, 2021.

p.564, *amendments to the Universal Credit (Transitional Provisions) Regulations 2014 (SI 2014/1230) reg.5 (Exclusion of entitlement to certain benefits)*

6.039   With effect from July 22, 2020, reg.4(2) of the Universal Credit (Managed Migration Pilot and Miscellaneous Amendments) Regulations 2019 (SI 2019/1152) substituted for sub-para.(a) the following—

"(a)   to housing benefit in respect of specified accommodation or temporary accommodation;

(ab)   to housing benefit or income support where regulation 8(2A), 46(1) or 47(2) applies; or".

With effect from November 25, 2020, reg.6(3) of the Universal Credit (Persons who have attained state pension credit qualifying age) (Amendment) Regulations 2020 (SI 2020/655) amended reg.5(1) by omitting "under the State Pension Credit Act 2002" in sub-para.(d). The same amending regulations made the following amendments to reg.5(2):

(i)   in sub-para.(a), omit "or" at the end;

(ii)   in sub-para.(b)(ii), insert "or (c)" after "regulation 7(5)(b)" and at the end omit "or";

(iii)   at the end of sub-para.(b)(iii) insert—
"; or

(iv)   state pension credit, where an award to which the new claimant partner is entitled terminates after the first date of entitlement to universal credit; or

(c)   during the last assessment period for universal credit, where the claimant reaches the qualifying age for state pension credit and paragraph 26 of Schedule 1 to the Decisions and Appeals Regulations applies, to housing benefit or state pension credit from the date the claimant reaches that age".

pp.567–568, *amendment to the Universal Credit (Transitional Provisions) Regulations 2014 (SI 2014/1230) reg.6 (Exclusion of claims for certain benefits)*

6.040   With effect from November 25, 2020, reg.6(4) of the Universal Credit (Persons who have attained state pension credit qualifying age) (Amendment) Regulations 2020 (SI 2020/655) amended reg.6 (4)(b) by substituting "the 2006 (SPC) Regulations" for "the Housing Benefit

(Persons who have attained the qualifying age for state pension credit) Regulations 2006 ("the 2006 (SPC) Regulations")" and by inserting after para.(8) the following new paragraph—

"(8A) A universal credit claimant is not precluded from making a claim for housing benefit under the 2006 (SPC) Regulations during the last assessment period for universal credit, where the claimant reaches the qualifying age for state pension credit and paragraph 26 of Schedule 1 to the Decisions and Appeals Regulations applies, in respect of entitlement arising from the date the claimant reaches that age.".

p.571, *amendment to the Universal Credit (Transitional Provisions) Regulations 2014 (SI 2014/1230) reg.7 (Termination of awards of certain existing benefits: new claimant partners)*

With effect from November 25, 2020, reg.6(5) of the Universal Credit 6.041 (Persons who have attained state pension credit qualifying age) (Amendment) Regulations 2020 (SI 2020/655) amended reg.7(5) by omitting "or" at the end of sub-para.(a) and inserting at the end of sub-para.(b)—

"; or
(c) the new claimant partner has reached the qualifying age for state pension credit and the award is made in accordance with the 2006 (SPC) Regulations".

p.572, *amendment to the Universal Credit (Transitional Provisions) Regulations 2014 (SI 2014/1230) reg.8 (Termination of awards of certain existing benefits: other claimants)*

With effect from July 22, 2020, reg.4(3) of the Universal Credit 6.042 (Managed Migration Pilot and Miscellaneous Amendments) Regulations 2019 (SI 2019/1152) amended reg.8 by omitting "income support or" in para.(2) and, in para.(2A), omitting the words "income support or" where they appear before "a tax credit" and inserting them instead before " housing benefit ".

p.575, *amendment to the Universal Credit (Transitional Provisions) Regulations 2014 (SI 2014/1230) by insertion of new reg.8B (Effect on universal credit award of two week run-on of income support, income-based jobseeker's allowance and income-related employment and support allowance)*

With effect from July 22, 2020, reg.4(4) of the Universal Credit 6.043 (Managed Migration Pilot and Miscellaneous Amendments) Regulations 2019 (SI 2019/1152) inserted after reg.8A the following new regulation:

"Effect on universal credit award of two week run-on of income support, income-based jobseeker's allowance and income-related employment and support allowance

8B. In a case where an award of income support, income-based jobseeker's allowance or income-related employment and support allowance is to continue for two weeks after the commencement of an award of universal credit by virtue of regulation 8(2A), 46(1) or 47(2) or by virtue of regulation 5 (two week run-on of income-based job-seeker's allowance and income-related employment and support allowance: day appointed for abolition) of the Universal Credit (Managed Migration Pilot and Miscellaneous Amendments) Regulations 2019—

   (a) regulation 79 of the Universal Credit Regulations applies as if the benefit in question was not included in the list of welfare benefits in section 96(10) of the Act (benefit cap); and

   (b) in a case where the claimant has become entitled to an award of new style JSA or new style ESA on the termination of an award of income-based jobseeker's allowance or income-related employment and support allowance, the claimant is to be treated, for the purposes of regulation 73 of the Universal Credit Regulations (unearned income calculated monthly), as if they had been entitled to that award of new style JSA or new style ESA from the first day of the award of universal credit.".

p.576, *amendment to the Universal Credit (Transitional Provisions) Regulations 2014 (SI 2014/1230) reg.10 (Treatment of overpayments)*

6.044   With effect from November 25, 2020, reg.6(6) of the Universal Credit (Persons who have attained state pension credit qualifying age) (Amendment) Regulations 2020 (SI 2020/655) amended reg.10(3)(c) by substituting "the 2006 (SPC) Regulations" for "the Housing Benefit (Persons who have attained the qualifying age for state pension credit) Regulations 2006".

p.578, *amendment to the Universal Credit (Transitional Provisions) Regulations 2014 (SI 2014/1230) by insertion of new reg.10C (Compensatory payment disregarded as capital)*

6.045   With effect from July 15, 2020, reg.9 of the Social Security (Income and Capital) (Miscellaneous Amendments) Regulations 2020 (SI 2020/618) inserted after reg.10B the following new regulation—

Compensatory payment disregarded as capital

10C.—(1) This regulation applies in relation to the calculation of an award of universal credit where—

   (a) the claimant has received a payment made to rectify, or to compensate for, an error made by an officer of the Department for Work and Pensions which was not caused or materially

568

contributed to by any person outside the Department and which prevented or delayed an assessment of the claimant's entitlement to contributory employment and support allowance; and

(b) the payment is received before the first date on which, by virtue of section 33 of the Act (abolition of benefits), no claimant is entitled to an existing benefit.

(2) Where this regulation applies and the amount of the payment is less than £5,000, the payment is to be disregarded from the calculation of the claimant's capital for 12 months from the date of receipt of the payment.

(3) Where—

(a) this regulation applies;

(b) the amount of the payment is £5,000 or more; and

(c) the conditions set out in regulation 10A(1)(a) and (c) are met,

the payment is to be disregarded from the calculation of the claimant's capital for 12 months from the date of receipt of the payment, or until the termination of the current award (if later).

p.582, *amendment to the Universal Credit (Transitional Provisions) Regulations 2014 (SI 2014/1230) reg.13 (Appeals etc relating to certain existing benefits)*

With effect from July 22, 2020, reg.4(7) of the Universal Credit 6.046 (Managed Migration Pilot and Miscellaneous Amendments) Regulations 2019 (SI 2019/1152) amended reg.13(3) by inserting ", 46 or 47" after "regulation 8".

p.620, *amendment to the Universal Credit (Transitional Provisions) Regulations 2014 (SI 2014/1230) reg.46 (Termination of existing benefits if no claim before the deadline)*

With effect from July 22, 2020, reg.4(5) of the Universal Credit 6.047 (Managed Migration Pilot and Miscellaneous Amendments) Regulations 2019 (SI 2019/1152) amended reg.46(1)(a) by inserting "income support, income-based jobseeker's allowance or income-related employment and support allowance," after "housing benefit" and substituting "a tax credit" for "any other existing benefit" in sub-para.(1)(b).

p.621, *amendment to the Universal Credit (Transitional Provisions) Regulations 2014 (SI 2014/1230) reg.47 (Notified persons who claim as a different benefit unit)*

With effect from July 22, 2020, reg.4(6) of the Universal Credit 6.048 (Managed Migration Pilot and Miscellaneous Amendments) Regulations 2019 (SI 2019/1152) amended reg.47(2)(a) by inserting "income support, income-based jobseeker's allowance or income-related employment and support allowance," after "housing benefit" and substituting "a tax credit" for "any other existing benefit" in sub-para.(2)(b).

p.633, *repeal of the Universal Credit (Transitional Provisions) Regulations 2014 (SI 2014/1230) reg.59 (Minimum income floor not to apply for first 12 months)*

6.049   With effect from September 23, 2020, reg.6(2) of the Universal Credit (Managed Migration Pilot and Miscellaneous Amendments) Regulations 2019 (SI 2019/1152) repealed reg.59.

p.783, *amendment to the Welfare Reform Act 2012 (Commencement No. 31 and Savings and Transitional Provisions and Commencement No.21 and 23 and Transitional and Transitory Provisions (Amendment)) Order 2019 (SI 2019/37) art.2 (Interpretation)*

6.050   With effect from November 25, 2020, reg.7(2) of the Universal Credit (Persons who have attained state pension credit qualifying age) (Amendment) Regulations 2020 (SI 2020/655) amended art.2(1) by inserting at the appropriate place—

""assessment period", in relation to universal credit entitlement, has the same meaning as in regulation 21 of the Universal Credit Regulations 2013;".

The same amending regulations substituted for sub-para.(1A)(b) the following—

"(b) in article 7(3), in relation to references to persons being treated as a couple in accordance with article 7(2)(a)(ii), where it has the meaning referred to in article 7(2)(a)(ii)".

p.785, *amendment to the Welfare Reform Act 2012 (Commencement No.31 and Savings and Transitional Provisions and Commencement No.21 and 23 and Transitional and Transitory Provisions (Amendment)) Order 2019 (SI 2019/37) art.7 (transitional provision: application of the rules in universal credit for treatment of couples and polygamous marriages)*

6.051   With effect from November 25, 2020, reg.7(3) of the Universal Credit (Persons who have attained state pension credit qualifying age) (Amendment) Regulations 2020 (SI 2020/655) amended art.7 by inserting "to housing benefit" after "application" in the heading and substituting for paras (1) to (3) the following—

"(1) Paragraph (3) applies where a person ("P"), who has attained the qualifying age, would otherwise not be entitled to either state pension credit or universal credit, because—
    (a) but for that paragraph, P would be a member of the same household as a partner who has not attained the qualifying age and therefore a member of a mixed-age couple, who—
        (i) is prevented from claiming housing benefit under article 6 of the No. 21 Order or article 7 of the No. 23 Order; or
        (ii) has an award of housing benefit terminated under article 6; and

(b) P is neither entitled to universal credit jointly with that partner, nor entitled to universal credit as a single person, in one of the cases set out in paragraph (2).

(2) The cases are where P is not entitled to universal credit because P has attained the qualifying age and—

    (a) any of the following paragraphs of regulation 3 of the Universal Credit Regulations 2013 (couples) applies, and in the case of paragraph (ii) below, one of the following circumstances applies—

        (i) paragraph (3) (treatment of certain couples—universal credit may only be claimed as a single person);

        (ii) paragraph (4) (treatment of polygamous marriages), so that P is not entitled to universal credit because P may only claim universal credit either as one of two parties to a polygamous marriage to be treated as a couple and the other party has also attained the qualifying age, or as a remaining party to such a marriage to be treated as single;

        (iii) paragraph (6) (absence from the household—universal credit may only be claimed as a single person); or

    (b) P lost joint entitlement to universal credit as part of a mixed-age couple due to one of the following changes of circumstances taking effect from a date (namely the first day of the universal credit assessment period in which the change occurred) that is earlier than when, but for paragraph (3), the same change would take effect for the purposes of housing benefit, those changes being where—

        (i) P and their partner are no longer a couple;

        (ii) P is party to a marriage that is no longer polygamous and P's remaining spouse has attained the qualifying age.

(3) Where this paragraph applies—

    (a) P and their partner who are to be treated as a non-polygamous couple in accordance with paragraph (2)(a)(ii), or who are no longer parties to a polygamous marriage in accordance with paragraph (2)(b)(ii), are to be treated as members of the same household as each other but not of that of any party (or parties) with whom they are not part of a couple in accordance with those provisions and one of them may claim or remain entitled to housing benefit as part of that couple; or

    (b) P who is to be treated as single in accordance with paragraph (2)(a)(i) to (iii), or is single in accordance with paragraph (2)(b)(i), is to be treated as though P is not a member of the same household as any party (or parties) with whom P is not part of a couple in accordance with those provisions and may claim or remain entitled to housing benefit as a single person,

where paragraph (2)(a) applies, with effect from the date on which the relevant paragraph of regulation 3 of the Universal Credit Regulations 2013 first applies to C, or, where paragraph (2)(b) applies, with effect from the date referred to in paragraph (2)(b) on which C lost universal credit entitlement.".

p.830, *commentary to the Universal Credit, Personal Independence Payment, Jobseeker's Allowance and Employment and Support Allowance (Claims and Payments) Regulations 2013 (SI 2013/380) reg.26 (Time within which a claim for universal credit is to be made)*

6.052   In *CP v SSWP (UC)* [2020] UKUT 309 (AAC), the Upper Tribunal (Judge Jacobs) accepted an important concession by the Secretary of State about the interpretation of para.3(aa) (see under the heading, *Modification*, on p.829 of the main work). The claimants had been claiming HB from South Ribble Council until September 24, 2018 when they moved to Preston, which was a full/digital service area. It appears that they then made a claim for HB to Preston City Council and only claimed universal credit once that authority had written to them explaining that they needed to do so. As a result, the universal credit claim was not made until October 22, 2018. At first, the Secretary of State refused to extend time for claiming universal credit from September 24 to October 22 and that decision was upheld by the First-tier Tribunal. On appeal to the Upper Tribunal, however, the Secretary of State's representative made the following submission:

"The key question, in my submission, is whether the administration of the appellant's *housing benefit* allows the time for claiming universal credit to be extended by way of regulation 26(3)(aa). In my submission, it does. Strictly speaking, the appellant's move from the area of one local authority to another involved the ending of the old award and the making of a new claim. On a narrow view, it might be argued that the appellant was entitled to housing benefit under the award *by South Ribble Council,* and therefore one must ask whether there was a delay in notification of *that* award, and whether any such delay made it reasonable for the couple not to have claimed universal credit earlier than it did. However, I submit that the language and purpose of regulation 26(3)(aa) allow a broader view to be taken. In my submission, the function of regulation 26(3)(aa) is to provide relief for claimants who have only belatedly discovered that the benefit they have been receiving has been replaced by universal credit, and therefore have been left unable to satisfy the usual requirement that a claim for universal claim be made on the very day that one wishes to claim from (regulation 26(1)). In view of this, in the instant case, I submit that, for the purposes of regulation 26(3)(aa), the 'notification of expiry of entitlement' to housing benefit should be taken to be the letter *from Preston County Council* that spelled out that the old mechanism for re-establishing entitlement to housing benefit in a new borough by way of a new claim to the new council was no longer available (and hence a claim for universal credit had to be made instead). *This* notification was sent after the claimant's last day of entitlement to housing benefit . I submit, therefore, that regulation 26(3)(aa) is satisfied. I further submit that regulation 26(2)(b) is also met. The couple could not reasonably be expected to claim universal credit until the appellant had been made aware that he could no longer claim housing benefit, and they did not unreasonably delay his [*sic*] claim for universal credit once they became aware of their position. Accordingly, the time for claiming from 24 September 2018 can be extended down to 22 October 2018, which was when the claim was made ."

Accepting that concession, Judge Jacobs allowed the appeal to the Upper Tribunal and extended the time for the claimants to claim universal credit to October 22, 2018.

p.833, *amendment to the Universal Credit, Personal Independence Payment, Jobseeker's Allowance and Employment and Support Allowance (Claims and Payments) Regulations 2013 (SI 2013/380) reg.32A (Reclaims of universal credit after nil award due to earnings)*

With effect from May 21, 2020, reg.3 of the Universal Credit (Coronavirus) (Self-employed Claimants and Reclaims) (Amendment) Regulations 2020 (SI 2020/522) inserted a new reg.32A immediately before reg.33 as follows:

6.053

"Reclaims of universal credit after nil award due to earnings

32A.—(1) This regulation applies where—
   (a) a claim is made for universal credit, but no award is made because the condition in section 5(1)(b) or 5(2)(b) of the 2012 Act (condition that the claimant's income, or joint claimants' combined income is such that the amount payable would not be less than the prescribed minimum) is not met; or
   (b) entitlement to an award of universal credit ceases because that condition is not met.

(2) The Secretary of State may, subject to any conditions the Secretary of State considers appropriate, treat the claimant (or joint claimants) as making a claim on the first day of each subsequent month, up to a maximum of 5, that would have been an assessment period if an award had been made or, as the case may be, if the award had continued."

pp.836-837, *amendment to the Universal Credit, Personal Independence Payment, Jobseeker's Allowance and Employment and Support Allowance (Claims and Payments) Regulations 2013 (SI 2013/380) reg.38 (Evidence and information in connection with an award)*

With effect from July 13, 2020, reg.3 of the Universal Credit (Miscellaneous Amendments) Regulations 2020 (SI 2020/611) amended reg.38 by substituting the words "apart from paragraphs (7) and (9)" for the words "apart from paragraph (7)" in para.(1), and inserting a new para.(9) immediately after para.(8) as follows:

6.054

"(9) A landlord, in a case where a claimant's award of universal credit includes an amount in respect of housing costs or where the award may be revised or superseded to include such an amount, must supply such information or evidence in connection with the award, or any question arising out of it, as the Secretary of State may require, and must do so within one month of being required to do so or such longer period as the Secretary of State considers reasonable."

pp.837–838, *amendment to the Universal Credit, Personal Independence Payment, Jobseeker's Allowance and Employment and Support Allowance (Claims and Payments) Regulations 2013 (SI 2013/380) reg.40 (Information to be provided to rent officers)*

6.055   With effect from July 13, 2020, reg.3 of the Universal Credit (Miscellaneous Amendments) Regulations 2020 (SI 2020/611) amended para.(5) by substituting the words "regulations 37 and 38" for the words "regulation 37".

pp.842–843, *amendment to the Universal Credit, Personal Independence Payment, Jobseeker's Allowance and Employment and Support Allowance (Claims and Payments) Regulations 2013 (SI 2013/380) reg.47 (Payment of universal credit)*

6.056   With effect from November 25, 2020, reg.4 of the Universal Credit (Persons who have attained state pension credit qualifying age) (Amendment) Regulations 2020 (SI 2020/655) amended reg.47 by omitting para.(7).

p.844, *commentary to the Universal Credit, Personal Independence Payment, Jobseeker's Allowance and Employment and Support Allowance (Claims and Payments) Regulations 2013 (SI 2013/380) reg.47 (Payment of universal credit)*

6.057   Following the revocation of para.(7) with effect from November 25, 2020, a superseding decision made in consequence of person reaching the qualifying age for SPC now takes effect on the first day of the assessment period following that in which that change of circumstances occurs or is expected to occur: see para.26 of Sch.1 to the Universal Credit, Personal Independence Payment, Jobseeker's Allowance and Employment and Support Allowance (Decisions and Appeals) Regulations 2013 as substituted with effect from that date (below).

p.905, *amendment to the Universal Credit, Personal Independence Payment, Jobseeker's Allowance and Employment and Support Allowance (Decisions and Appeals) Regulations 2013 (SI 2013/381) Sch.1 (Effective dates for superseding decisions made on the ground of a change of circumstances)*

6.058   With effect from November 25, 2020, reg.5 of the Universal Credit (Persons who have attained state pension credit qualifying age) (Amendment) Regulations 2020 (SI 2020/655) amended Sch.1 by substituting the following for para.26:

"26. Where, in any assessment period, a claimant reaches the qualifying age for state pension credit under the State Pension Credit Act 2002, where claiming as a single person or as a member of a couple to whom regulation 3(2)(a) of the Universal Credit Regulations applies, a superseding decision made in consequence of the person reaching that age takes effect on the first day of the assessment period following that in which the change of circumstances occurs or is expected to occur."

p.913, *commentary to the Social Security (Immigration and Asylum) Consequential Amendments Regulations 2000 (SI 2000/636) (General Note—the Implementation Period)*

As predicted in the main volume, the Implementation Period ended on December 31, 2020 at 11.00 pm. Subject to the exceptions that are explained in the noter-up to General Note to the Immigration (European Economic Area) Regulations 2016 (see below), the free movement rights of EEA nationals in relation to the UK came to an end. **6.059**

At the same time, reg.12 of the Immigration and Social Security Co-ordination (EU Withdrawal) Act 2020 (Consequential, Saving, Transitional and Transitory Provisions) (EU Exit) Regulations 2020 (SI 2020/1309) amended the definition of "person subject to immigration control" in s.115(9) of the Immigration and Asylum Act 1999 with the effect that EEA nationals are no longer automatically excluded from that definition.

As a result, and subject to the exceptions referred to above, EEA nationals are in the same position as other nationals of non-CTA states for the purposes of entitlement to social security benefits. Those who have indefinite leave to remain (including settled status under the EU Settlement scheme) will not be persons subject to immigration control and will therefore be entitled to any benefits for which they satisfy the conditions of entitlement (including the residence conditions). Those who do not have indefinite leave to remain will be persons subject to immigration control and will therefore be excluded from entitlement to benefit under s.115(1) unless they fall within the categories specified in reg.2 and Sch. (as amended) or, exceptionally, are former asylum seekers with the benefit of the transitional provision established by reg.12.

p.919, *commentary to the Social Security (Immigration and Asylum) Consequential Amendments Regulations 2000 (SI 2000/636) (General Note—Spouses and family members of EEA nationals)*

In *SSWP v AS (CA)* [2021] UKUT 24 (AAC), the Upper Tribunal (Judge Ward) followed the decision of the Deputy Commissioner in *CDLA/708/2007* rather than the decision of the Chief Commissioner of Northern Ireland in *JFP v DSD (DLA)* [2012] NI Com 267. However, para.1 of Pt.II of the Schedule was revoked with effect from December 31, 2020 at 11.00 pm, by reg. 57 of the Immigration and Social Security Co-ordination (EU Withdrawal) Act 2020 (Consequential, Saving, Transitional and Transitory Provisions) (EU Exit) Regulations 2020 (SI 2020/1309), so the issue will no longer arise in the future. **6.060**

p.920, *commentary to the Social Security (Immigration and Asylum) Consequential Amendments Regulations 2000 (SI 2000/636) (General Note—EEA reciprocal arrangements)*

6.061 Para.2 of Pt.II of the Schedule was amended with effect from December 31, 2020 at 11.00 pm and then again, with effect from January 1, 2021, an hour later. The combined effect of the amendments is to remove the benefit of that provision from nationals of States with which the European Union has concluded a reciprocal agreement under Art.217 of the Treaty on the Functioning of the European Union, but to confer that benefit on nationals of any State with which the UK concludes an agreement that replaces an Art.217 agreement in whole or in part.

By the new paragraph (3A) of reg.2, a national of a State in the latter category is not excluded from entitlement to child benefit if the replacement agreement "makes provision for receipt of family allowances for members of their family who are legally resident in the United Kingdom".

pp.922–923, *amendment to the Social Security (Immigration and Asylum) Consequential Amendments Regulations 2000 (SI 2000/636), reg.2 (Persons not excluded from specified benefits under section 115 of the Immigration and Asylum Act 1999)*

6.062 With effect from January 1, 2021, reg.2(1) and (2) of the Social Security, Child Benefit and Child Tax Credit (Amendment) (EU Exit) Regulations 2020 amended reg.2 by substituting the words "paragraphs 2 and 3" for the words "paragraphs 2, 3 and 4" in para.(1A) and inserting the following immediately after para.(3):

> "(3A) For the purposes of entitlement to child benefit under the Contributions and Benefits Act, a person who is a national of a State with which the United Kingdom has concluded an agreement which replaces, in whole or in part, an agreement under Article 217 of the Treaty on the Functioning of the European Union which makes provision for receipt of family allowances for members of their family who are legally resident in the United Kingdom, is a person to whom section 115 of the Act does not apply."

p.926, *amendment to the Social Security (Immigration and Asylum) Consequential Amendments Regulations 2000 (SI 2000/636) Sch., Pt II (Persons not excluded from certain benefits under Section 115 of the Immigration and Asylum Act 1999)*

6.063 With effect from December 31, 2020 at 11.00 pm, reg. 57 of the Immigration and Social Security Co-ordination (EU Withdrawal) Act 2020 (Consequential, Saving, Transitional and Transitory Provisions) (EU Exit) Regulations 2020 (SI 2020/1309) omitted para.1 of Pt II of the Schedule.

With effect from December 31, 2020 at 11.00 pm, reg.2 of the Social Security, Child Benefit and Child Tax Credit (Amendment) (EU Exit)

Regulations 2019 (SI 2019/1431) substituted the following for para.2 of Pt II of the Schedule:

"**2.** A person who is lawfully working in Great Britain and is a national of a State with which—

(a) the European Union has concluded an agreement under Article 217 of the Treaty on the Functioning of the European Union (an "EU Agreement") providing, in the field of social security, for the equal treatment of workers who are nationals of the signatory State and their families; or

(b) the United Kingdom has concluded an agreement which replaces in whole or in part an EU Agreement in sub-paragraph (a) which has ceased to apply to, and in, the United Kingdom, providing, in the field of social security, for the equal treatment of workers who are nationals of the signatory State and their families."

With effect from January 1, 2021, reg.2(1) and (3) of the Social Security, Child Benefit and Child Tax Credit (Amendment) (EU Exit) Regulations 2020 further amended para.2 of Pt II of the Schedule to read as follows:

"**2.** A person who is lawfully working in Great Britain and is a national of a State with which—

(a) [. . .]

(b) the United Kingdom has concluded an agreement which replaces in whole or in part [an agreement under Article 217 of the Treaty on the Functioning of the European Union] which has ceased to apply to, and in, the United Kingdom, providing, in the field of social security, for the equal treatment of workers who are nationals of the signatory State and their families."

pp.950–952, *commentary to the Immigration (European Economic Area) Regulations 2016 (SI 2016/1052) (General Note—the United Kingdom's withdrawal from the European Union)*

As predicted in the main volume, the Implementation Period ended   6.064
on December 31, 2020 at 11.00 pm. As a result, ss.1A and 1B of the European Union Withdrawal Act 2018 ("the Withdrawal Act"), which are noted in the main work, expired and (subject to what is said below about the Withdrawal Agreement itself) EU law ceased to have effect in the UK except to the extent that it had been retained as part of UK domestic law by sections 2-7 of the Withdrawal Act and subordinate legislation made under that Act.

Similarly, the subordinate legislation which had not come into effect by virtue of s.41(4) of, and Sch.5 para.(1) and (2) to, the European Union (Withdrawal Agreement) Act 2020—including the Statutory Instruments listed on p.952 of the main volume—came into effect when the Implementation Period ended. Where relevant, their provisions have been included in the Noter-up.

The consequence for the right to reside test is that, with four exceptions, the free movement rights of EEA nationals in relation to the UK have come to an end. The rights of EEA nationals under UK immigration law have become the same as those of nationals of other states that are not in the Common Travel Area ("CTA"). Any non-CTA national who does not have either indefinite leave to enter or remain (including settled status under the EU settlement scheme), or limited leave to enter or remain that does not fall within s.115(9)(b)–(d) of the Immigration and Asylum Act 1999, is likely to be a "person subject to immigration control" and excluded from entitlement to benefit by s.115(1) unless one of the exceptions in the amended Social Security (Immigration and Asylum) Consequential Amendments Regulations 2000 (SI 2000/636), applies.

The three exceptions referred to above are as follows:

1. *Nationals of the Common Travel Area*

The Channel Islands and the Isle of Man were never part of the EU or EEA and the rights of Island nationals in the CTA remain unchanged. The Republic of Ireland continues to be part of the CTA and the rights of Irish citizens have been confirmed by s.3ZA which was inserted into the Immigration Act 1971 by s.2(2) of Immigration and Social Security Co-ordination (EU Withdrawal) Act 2020 immediately after 11.00 pm on December 31, 2020. That section provides that "[a]n Irish citizen does not require leave to enter or remain in the United Kingdom, unless" an order restricting that right has been made under paras (2)-(4).

2. *EEA nationals and their family members with "pre-settled" status*

EU nationals who wish to continue to live in the UK after the end of the implementation period are required to apply under the EU Settlement Scheme in Appendix EU to the Immigration Rules. Applicants who can satisfy the Home Office that they meet the criteria in paras EU11 or EU12 of the Appendix, and that they should not be refused on grounds of suitability (paras EU15 and EU16), are given indefinite leave to remain (also known in this context as "settled status"). Those who have been granted settled status have a right to reside in the UK that counts for the purposes of all income-related benefits. Applicants who do not qualify for settled status will be given limited leave to remain for five years (also known as "pre-settled status") if they meet the criteria in para.EU14. Those with pre-settled status may apply for settled status as soon as they meet the criteria in paras EU11 or EU12.

For those with pre-settled status—technically those who are "members of the post-transition period group" as defined by reg.1(2) of SI 2020/1309—parts of the 2016 Regulations are continued in force (often subject to modifications) by the Immigration and Social Security Co-ordination (EU Withdrawal) Act 2020 (Consequential, Saving, Transitional and Transitory Provisions) (EU Exit) Regulations 2020 (SI 2020/1309) (see *New Legislation,* above). Those savings and modifications are referenced in the Noter-up to the affected regulations (below).

The provisions of social security law that establish the right to reside test (other than reg.9 of the Universal Credit Regulations 2013, but see the Noter-up to that provision) have been amended to state that references in those Regulations to the 2016 Regulations "are to be read with Schedule 4 to the Immigration and Social Security Co-ordination (EU Withdrawal) Act 2020 (Consequential, Saving, Transitional and Transitory Provisions) Regulations 2020". The effect is that those with pre-settled status who have a right to reside under the saved and modified 2016 regulations that counts for the purpose of the benefit in question continue to satisfy the right to reside test. So, for example, a person with pre-settled status who retains worker status while temporarily incapable of work is potentially entitled to universal credit.

But what of those whose *only* right to reside derives from their pre-settled status? As noted in the commentary to reg.9 of the Universal Credit Regulations 2013 on p.166 of the main volume, in *R. (on the application of Fratila and Tanase) v Secretary of State for Work and Pensions* [2020] EWHC 998 (Admin), the High Court (Swift J) upheld the validity of reg.9(3)(c)(i) (which excludes such people from entitlement) in the face of a submission that it discriminated unlawfully on the grounds of nationality contrary to art.18 TFEU. However, in *Fratila and Tanase v Secretary of State for Work and Pensions* [2020] EWCA Civ 1741 the Court of Appeal, by a majority (McCombe and Moylan LJJ, Dingemans LJ dissenting), reversed that decision. The majority held that the exclusion from benefit of those whose only right of residence was their pre-settled status amounted to unlawful discrimination on the grounds of nationality contrary to Art.18 TFEU. On February 22, 2021 the Secretary of State was given permission to appeal against the Court of Appeal's decision. If the Supreme Court upholds the majority in the Court of Appeal, it will also be necessary to consider the extent to which the decision continues to apply following the end of the Implementation Period.

3. EEA nationals and their family members who have yet to apply under the EU Settlement Scheme or whose applications have yet to be determined.

The position of those who are eligible to apply under the EU Scheme but who have not yet done so, or who have done so but are waiting for a decision, is governed by the Citizens' Rights (Application Deadline and Temporary Protection) (EU Exit) Regulations 2020 (SI 2020/1209) (see *New Legislation*, above).

Those regulations establish two periods, a "grace period" for applying under the EU Scheme that expires on June 30, 2021, and a "relevant period" which, for those who have made a timeous application, begins immediately after the grace period and lasts until the application is finally determined. During the grace period, parts of the 2016 Regulations continue in effect, usually in a modified form, as they apply to a "relevant person" (as defined in reg.3(6)). During the relevant period, they apply, again usually in a modified form, to a person who has made an in-time application (as defined in reg.4(6), and immediately before IP completion day, was either lawfully resident in the United Kingdom by virtue of the EEA Regulations 2016, or had a right of permanent residence in the United Kingdom under those Regulations: see reg.4(2). Those savings and modifications are referenced in the Noter-up to the affected regulations (below).

4. *Those with directly effective rights under the Withdrawal Agreement*

Section 7A of the Withdrawal Act (inserted by s.5 of the Withdrawal Agreement Act) gives direct effect to those rights "created by" or "arising under" the Withdrawal Agreement "as in accordance with the withdrawal agreement are without further enactment to be given legal effect or used in the United Kingdom". Furthermore, by section 7A(3),"[e]very enactment (including an enactment contained in this Act) is to be read and has effect subject to those directly effective rights. If therefore, SI 2020/1209 or SI 2020/1309 have not implemented the Withdrawal Agreement in a way that gives full effect to those rights, an EEA National may be able to derive rights of residence directly from the Citizens Rights provisions in Part 2 of the Withdrawal Agreement itself. The existence, and extent, of any such rights will be established by case law.

Finally, a note of caution. The savings and modifications of the 2016 Regulations noted below are those that apply *for the purposes of access to benefits*. Different regulations may have been saved—and differently modified—for other purposes. It is unsafe to rely on what follows in order, for example, to ascertain which parts of those Regulations have been saved, and how they have been modified, for the purposes of making an application for an EEA Family Permit under reg.12 or any of the Residence Documentation specified in Pt.3.

Further, it must be remembered that what follows is a list of *exceptions*. If a provision of the 2016 Regulations that is reproduced in the main volume is not mentioned below that is because, at least for the purposes of access to benefits, it has been revoked without any savings.

pp.965-968, *saving and modification of the Immigration (European Economic Area) Regulations 2016 (SI 2016/1052) reg.2 (General interpretation)*

6.065   For those with pre-settled status, reg.2 is saved for the purposes of the right to reside test by reg.83 of, and Sch.4, paras 2, 3 and 4(a) of Immigration and Social Security Co-ordination (EU Withdrawal) Act 2020 (Consequential, Saving, Transitional and Transitory Provisions) (EU Exit) Regulations 2020 (SI 2020/1309) and modified as set out in para.4(a): see *New Legislation*, above.

For those without settled or pre-settled status, reg.2 is saved for the purposes of the right to reside test by regs 3(2), 4(3) and 5(a) of the Citizens' Rights (Application Deadline and Temporary Protection) (EU Exit) Regulations 2020 (SI 2020/1209) and modified as set out in reg.5(a): see *New Legislation*, above.

p.970, *saving and modification of the Immigration (European Economic Area) Regulations 2016 (SI 2016/1052) reg.3 (Continuity of residence)*

For those with pre-settled status, reg.3 is saved for the purposes of the   6.066
right to reside test by reg.83 of, and Sch.4, paras 2, 3 and 4(b) of
Immigration and Social Security Co-ordination (EU Withdrawal) Act
2020 (Consequential, Saving, Transitional and Transitory Provisions)
(EU Exit) Regulations 2020 (SI 2020/1309) and modified as set out in
para.4(b): see *New Legislation,* above.

For those without settled or pre-settled status, reg.3 is saved in an
unmodified form for the purposes of the right to reside test by regs 3(2),
4(3) and 5(b) of the Citizens' Rights (Application Deadline and Temporary Protection) (EU Exit) Regulations 2020 (SI 2020/1209).

pp.971-973, *saving and modification of the Immigration (European Economic Area) Regulations 2016 (SI 2016/1052) reg.4 ("Worker", "self-employed person", "self-sufficient person" and "student")*

For those with pre-settled status, reg.4 is saved for the purposes of the   6.067
right to reside test by reg.83 of, and Sch.4, paras 2, 3 and 4(c) of
Immigration and Social Security Co-ordination (EU Withdrawal) Act
2020 (Consequential, Saving, Transitional and Transitory Provisions)
(EU Exit) Regulations 2020 (SI 2020/1309) and modified as set out in
para.4(c): see *New Legislation,* above.

For those without settled or pre-settled status, reg.4 is saved for the
purposes of the right to reside test by regs 3(2), 4(3) and 5(c) of the
Citizens' Rights (Application Deadline and Temporary Protection) (EU
Exit) Regulations 2020 (SI 2020/1209) and modified as set out in
reg.5(c): see *New Legislation,* above.

pp.981-982, *commentary to the Immigration (European Economic Area) Regulations 2016 (SI 2016/1052) reg.4 ("Worker", "self-employed person", "self-sufficient person" and "student"—self-employed persons—comprehensive sickness insurance)*

In *VI v Commissioners for Her Majesty's Revenue and Customs,* an appeal   6.068
tribunal in Northern Ireland has referred the following questions to the
CJEU for a preliminary ruling:

"Is a child EEA Permanent Resident required to maintain Comprehensive Sickness Insurance in order to maintain a right to reside, as
s/he would as a self-sufficient person, pursuant to Regulation 4(1) of
the 2016 Regulations?
Is the requirement, pursuant to Regulation 4(3)(b) of The Immigration (European Economic Area)Regulations 2016 (that Comprehensive Sickness Insurance cover in the United Kingdom is only satisfied
fora student or self-sufficient person, with regard to Regulation
16(2)(b)(ii) of The Immigration (European Economic Area) Regulations 2016, if such cover extends to both that person and all their
relevant family members), illegal under EU law in light of Article 7(1)

of Directive 2004/38 and the jurisprudence of the Court of Justice of the European Union in paragraph 70 of Teixeira C-480/08?

Following the decision in paragraph 53 of *Ahmad v. Secretary of State for the Home Department* [2014]EWCA Civ 988, are the Common Travel Area reciprocal arrangements in place regarding Health Insurance cover between the United Kingdom and the Republic of Ireland considered 'reciprocal arrangements' and therefore constitute Comprehensive Sickness Insurance for the purposes of Regulation 4(1) of the 2016 Regulations?"

The reference has been assigned the Case No. C-247/20. At the time of going to press, no date has been fixed for the issue of the Advocate General's opinion.

p.983, *saving of the Immigration (European Economic Area) Regulations 2016 (SI 2016/1052) reg.5 ("Worker or self-employed person who has ceased activity")*

6.069   For those with pre-settled status, reg.5 is saved in an unmodified form for the purposes of the right to reside test by reg.83 of, and Sch.4, paras 2, 3 and 4(d) of Immigration and Social Security Co-ordination (EU Withdrawal) Act 2020 (Consequential, Saving, Transitional and Transitory Provisions) (EU Exit) Regulations 2020 (SI 2020/1309).

For those without settled or pre-settled status, reg.5 is saved in an unmodified form for the purposes of the right to reside test by regs 3(2), 4(3) and 5(d) of the Citizens' Rights (Application Deadline and Temporary Protection) (EU Exit) Regulations 2020 (SI 2020/1209).

pp.985–987, *saving and modification of the Immigration (European Economic Area) Regulations 2016 (SI 2016/1052) reg.6 (Qualified person)*

6.070   For those with pre-settled status, reg.6 is saved for the purposes of the right to reside test by reg.83 of, and Sch.4, paras 2, 3 and 4(e) of Immigration and Social Security Co-ordination (EU Withdrawal) Act 2020 (Consequential, Saving, Transitional and Transitory Provisions) (EU Exit) Regulations 2020 (SI 2020/1309) and modified as set out in para.4(e): see *New Legislation,* above.

For those without settled or pre-settled status, reg.6 is saved for the purposes of the right to reside test by regs 3(2), 4(3) and 5(e) of the Citizens' Rights (Application Deadline and Temporary Protection) (EU Exit) Regulations 2020 (SI 2020/1209) and modified as set out in reg.5(e): see *New Legislation,* above.

p.1004, *saving of the Immigration (European Economic Area) Regulations 2016 (SI 2016/1052) reg.7 ("Family member")*

6.071   For those with pre-settled status, reg.7 is saved in an unmodified form for the purposes of the right to reside test by reg.83 of, and Sch.4, paras 2, 3 and 4(f) of Immigration and Social Security Co-ordination (EU

Withdrawal) Act 2020 (Consequential, Saving, Transitional and Transitory Provisions) (EU Exit) Regulations 2020 (SI 2020/1309).

For those without settled or pre-settled status, reg.7 is saved in an unmodified form for the purposes of the right to reside test by regs 3(2), 4(3) and 5(f) of the Citizens' Rights (Application Deadline and Temporary Protection) (EU Exit) Regulations 2020 (SI 2020/1209).

pp.1008–1009, *saving and modification of the Immigration (European Economic Area) Regulations 2016 (SI 2016/1052) reg.8 ("Extended family member")*

For those with pre-settled status, reg.8 is saved for the purposes of the   **6.072** right to reside test by reg.83 of, and Sch.4, paras 2, 3 and 4(g) of Immigration and Social Security Co-ordination (EU Withdrawal) Act 2020 (Consequential, Saving, Transitional and Transitory Provisions) (EU Exit) Regulations 2020 (SI 2020/1309) and modified as set out in para.4(g): see *New Legislation*, above.

For those without settled or pre-settled status, reg.8 is saved for the purposes of the right to reside test by regs 3(2), 4(3) and 5(g) of the Citizens' Rights (Application Deadline and Temporary Protection) (EU Exit) Regulations 2020 (SI 2020/1209) and modified as set out in reg.5(e): see *New Legislation*, above.

pp.1013–1014, *saving and modification of the Immigration (European Economic Area) Regulations 2016 (SI 2016/1052) reg.9 (Family members and extended family members of British citizens)*

For those with pre-settled status, reg.9 is saved for the purposes of the   **6.073** right to reside test by reg.83 of, and Sch.4, paras 2, 3 and 4(h) of Immigration and Social Security Co-ordination (EU Withdrawal) Act 2020 (Consequential, Saving, Transitional and Transitory Provisions) (EU Exit) Regulations 2020 (SI 2020/1309) and modified as set out in para.4(h): see *New Legislation*, above.

For those without settled or pre-settled status, reg.9 is saved for the purposes of the right to reside test by regs 3(2), 4(3) and 5(h) of the Citizens' Rights (Application Deadline and Temporary Protection) (EU Exit) Regulations 2020 (SI 2020/1209) and modified as set out in reg.5(h): see *New Legislation*, above.

p.1018, *saving of the Immigration (European Economic Area) Regulations 2016 (SI 2016/1052) reg.9A (Dual national: national of an EEA State who acquires British citizenship)*

For those with pre-settled status, reg.9A is saved in an unmodified   **6.074** form for the purposes of the right to reside test by reg.83 of, and Sch.4, paras 2, 3 and 4(i) of Immigration and Social Security Co-ordination (EU Withdrawal) Act 2020 (Consequential, Saving, Transitional and Transitory Provisions) (EU Exit) Regulations 2020 (SI 2020/1309).

For those without settled or pre-settled status, reg.9A is saved in an unmodified form for the purposes of the right to reside test by regs 3(2),

4(3) and 5(i) of the Citizens' Rights (Application Deadline and Temporary Protection) (EU Exit) Regulations 2020 (SI 2020/1209).

pp.1019–1020, *saving and modification of the Immigration (European Economic Area) Regulations 2016 (SI 2016/1052) reg.10 ("Family member who has retained the right of residence")*

6.075 For those with pre-settled status, reg.10 is saved for the purposes of the right to reside test by reg.83 of, and Sch.4, paras 2, 3 and 4(j) of Immigration and Social Security Co-ordination (EU Withdrawal) Act 2020 (Consequential, Saving, Transitional and Transitory Provisions) (EU Exit) Regulations 2020 (SI 2020/1309) and modified as set out in para.4(j): see *New Legislation*, above.

For those without settled or pre-settled status, reg.10 is saved for the purposes of the right to reside test by regs 3(2), 4(3) and 5(j) of the Citizens' Rights (Application Deadline and Temporary Protection) (EU Exit) Regulations 2020 (SI 2020/1209) and modified as set out in reg.5(j): see *New Legislation*, above.

pp.1022–1023, *saving and modification of the Immigration (European Economic Area) Regulations 2016 (SI 2016/1052) reg.11 (Right of admission to the United Kingdom)*

6.076 For those without settled or pre-settled status, reg.11 is saved for the purposes of the right to reside test by regs 3(2), 4(3) and 6(a) of he Citizens' Rights (Application Deadline and Temporary Protection) (EU Exit) Regulations 2020 (SI 2020/1209) and modified as set out in reg.6(a): see *New Legislation*, above.

pp.1024–1025, *saving and modification of the Immigration (European Economic Area) Regulations 2016 (SI 2016/1052) reg.12 (Issue of EEA family permit)*

6.077 For those without settled or pre-settled status, reg.12 is saved for the purposes of the right to reside test by regs 3(2), 4(3) and 6(b) of the Citizens' Rights (Application Deadline and Temporary Protection) (EU Exit) Regulations 2020 (SI 2020/1209) and modified as set out in reg.6(b): see *New Legislation*, above.

pp.1025–1026, *saving and modification of the Immigration (European Economic Area) Regulations 2016 (SI 2016/1052) reg.13 (Initial right of residence)*

6.078 For those with pre-settled status, reg.13 is saved for the purposes of the right to reside test by reg.83 of, and Sch.4, paras 2, 3 and 4(k) of Immigration and Social Security Co-ordination (EU Withdrawal) Act 2020 (Consequential, Saving, Transitional and Transitory Provisions) (EU Exit) Regulations 2020 (SI 2020/1309) and modified as set out in para.4(k): see *New Legislation*, above.

For those without settled or pre-settled status, reg.13 is saved for the purposes of the right to reside test by regs 3(2), 4(3) and 6(c) of the Citizens' Rights (Application Deadline and Temporary Protection) (EU Exit) Regulations 2020 (SI 2020/1209) and modified as set out in reg.6(c): see *New Legislation,* above.

pp.1026-1027, *saving and modification of the Immigration (European Economic Area) Regulations 2016 (SI 2016/1052) reg.14 (Extended right of residence)*

For those with pre-settled status, reg.14 is saved for the purposes of 6.079
the right to reside test by reg.83 of, and Sch.4, paras 2, 3 and 4(l) of Immigration and Social Security Co-ordination (EU Withdrawal) Act 2020 (Consequential, Saving, Transitional and Transitory Provisions) (EU Exit) Regulations 2020 (SI 2020/1309) and modified as set out in para.4(l): see *New Legislation,* above.

For those without settled or pre-settled status, reg.14 is saved for the purposes of the right to reside test by regs 3(2), 4(3) and 6(d) of the Citizens' Rights (Application Deadline and Temporary Protection) (EU Exit) Regulations 2020 (SI 2020/1209) and modified as set out in reg.6(d): see *New Legislation,* above.

pp.1027-1028, *saving and modification of the Immigration (European Economic Area) Regulations 2016 (SI 2016/1052) reg.15 (Right of permanent residence)*

For those with pre-settled status, reg.15 is saved for the purposes of 6.080
the right to reside test by reg.83 of, and Sch.4, paras 2, 3 and 4(m) of Immigration and Social Security Co-ordination (EU Withdrawal) Act 2020 (Consequential, Saving, Transitional and Transitory Provisions) (EU Exit) Regulations 2020 (SI 2020/1309) and modified as set out in para.4(m): see *New Legislation,* above.

For those without settled or pre-settled status, reg.15 is saved for the purposes of the right to reside test by regs 3(2), 4(3) and 6(e) of the Citizens' Rights (Application Deadline and Temporary Protection) (EU Exit) Regulations 2020 (SI 2020/1209) and modified as set out in reg.6(e): see *New Legislation,* above.

p.1037, *commentary to the Immigration (European Economic Area) Regulations 2016 (SI 2016/1052) reg.15 (Right of permanent residence—A8 and A2 nationals—Prefeta)*

The decision of the CJEU in *Rafal Prefeta v Secretary of State for Work* 6.081
and Pensions (Case C-618/165) has been reported as [2019] AACR 6.

pp.1038-1039, *saving and modification of the Immigration (European Economic Area) Regulations 2016 (SI 2016/1052) reg.16 (Derivative right to reside)*

For those with pre-settled status, reg.16 is saved for the purposes of 6.082
the right to reside test by reg.83 of, and Sch.4, paras 2, 3 and 4(n) of

Immigration and Social Security Co-ordination (EU Withdrawal) Act 2020 (Consequential, Saving, Transitional and Transitory Provisions) (EU Exit) Regulations 2020 (SI 2020/1309) and modified as set out in para.4(n): see *New Legislation*, above.

For those without settled or pre-settled status, reg.16 is saved for the purposes of the right to reside test by regs 3(2), 4(3) and 6(f) of the Citizens' Rights (Application Deadline and Temporary Protection) (EU Exit) Regulations 2020 (SI 2020/1209) and modified as set out in reg.6(f): see *New Legislation*, above.

pp.1047–1048, *saving and modification of the Immigration (European Economic Area) Regulations 2016 (SI 2016/1052) reg.21 (Procedure for applications for documentation under this Part and regulation 12)*

6.083   For those without settled or pre-settled status, reg.21 is saved for the purposes of the right to reside test by regs 3(2), 4(3) and 6(g) of the Citizens' Rights (Application Deadline and Temporary Protection) (EU Exit) Regulations 2020 (SI 2020/1209) and modified as set out in reg.6(g): see *New Legislation*, above.

pp.1048–1049, *saving and modification of the Immigration (European Economic Area) Regulations 2016 (SI 2016/1052) reg.22 (Verification of a right of residence)*

6.084   For those without settled or pre-settled status, reg.22 is saved for the purposes of the right to reside test by regs 3(2), 4(3) and 6(h) of the Citizens' Rights (Application Deadline and Temporary Protection) (EU Exit) Regulations 2020 (SI 2020/1209) and modified as set out in reg.6(h): see *New Legislation*, above.

p.1049, *saving of the Immigration (European Economic Area) Regulations 2016 (SI 2016/1052) reg.43 (Effect on other legislation)*

6.085   For those without settled or pre-settled status, reg.43 is saved in an unmodified form for the purposes of the right to reside test by regs 3(2), 4(3) and 10(a) of the Citizens' Rights (Application Deadline and Temporary Protection) (EU Exit) Regulations 2020 (SI 2020/1209).

p.1050, *saving of the Immigration (European Economic Area) Regulations 2016 (SI 2016/1052) reg.45 (Revocations, savings, transitory and transitional provisions and consequential modifications)*

6.086   For those without settled or pre-settled status, reg.43 is saved in an unmodified form for the purposes of the right to reside test by regs 3(2), 4(3) and 10(b) of the Citizens' Rights (Application Deadline and Temporary Protection) (EU Exit) Regulations 2020 (SI 2020/1209), except in so far as it relates to Pt.1 of Sch.4 of the 2016 Regulations.

pp.1050–1051, *saving and modification of the Immigration (European Economic Area) Regulations 2016 (SI 2016/1052) Sch.3 (Effect on other legislation)*

For those without settled or pre-settled status, Sch.3 is saved for the   6.087
purposes of the right to reside test by regs 3(2), 4(3) and 10(c) of the Citizens' Rights (Application Deadline and Temporary Protection) (EU Exit) Regulations 2020 (SI 2020/1209) and modified as set out in reg.10(c): see *New Legislation,* above.

pp.1051–1052, *saving and modification of the Immigration (European Economic Area) Regulations 2016 (SI 2016/1052) Sch.4, Pt.2 (Savings and modifications)*

For those without settled or pre-settled status, Sch.4. Pt.2 is saved in   6.088
an unmodified form for the purposes of the right to reside test by regs 3(2), 4(3) and 10(d) of the Citizens' Rights (Application Deadline and Temporary Protection) (EU Exit) Regulations 2020 (SI 2020/1209).

PART VII

FORTHCOMING CHANGES AND UP-RATING OF BENEFITS

FORTHCOMING CHANGES

Universal Credit

The Universal Credit (Transitional Provisions) (Claimants previously   7.001
entitled to a severe disability premium) Amendment Regulations 2021
(SI 2021/4) came into force on January 27, 2021 and substituted a new
Sch.2 to the Universal Credit (Transitional Provisions) Regulations
2014 (SI 2014/1230) (claimants previously entitled to a severe disability
premium: transitional payments). The so-called Severe Disability Premium (SDP) gateway, which prevented people in receipt of the SDP in
legacy benefits from making a new claim to Universal Credit was
removed as from January 27, 2021, meaning that from this date this
group of people will be able to make new claims to Universal Credit.
Previous SDP claimants are eligible to be considered for a transitional
SDP element to help with the financial transition to the new benefit and
the new Schedule 2 provides the criteria for such payments.

The Universal Credit (Work-Related Requirements) In Work Pilot
Scheme (Extension) Order 2021 (SI 2021/147) further extends the
period for which the pilot scheme established under the Universal
Credit (Work-Related Requirements) In Work Pilot Scheme and
Amendment Regulations 2015 (SI 2015/89) has effect from February
19, 2021 for a further period of twelve months to February 18, 2022.
The 2015 Regulations established the pilot scheme under section 41
of the Welfare Reform Act 2012 for the purpose of testing the imposition of work-related requirements on Universal Credit claimants in
paid work (where those requirements would otherwise be suspended
by virtue of regulation 99(6) of the Universal Credit Regulations 2013
(SI 2013/376)).

The Loans for Mortgage Interest Regulations 2017

Regulation 2 of the Loans for Mortgage Interest (Amendment) Reg-   7.002
ulations 2021 (SI 2021/131), in force from March 15, 2021, amends the
Loans for Mortgage Interest Regulations 2017 (SI 2017/725) to provide
that a claimant will not be required to repay their support for mortgage
interest loan on sale of the relevant accommodation, if they meet specified conditions, and clarifies that claimants who have fled the accommodation for which they receive support for mortgage interest loan
payments due to fear of violence in the home will be able to continue
receiving loan payments for that accommodation for a specified period of
time.

Tax Credits

7.003   The Tax Credits Reviews and Appeals (Amendment) Order 2021 (SI 2021/44), which came into force on January 15, 2021, inserted a new s.21C into the Tax Credit Act 2002. This enables HMRC to review tax credits awards and apply disability elements to tax years which have already been finalised in the case of claimants who notify HMRC of their entitlement to qualifying disability benefits within the period set out in regs 26 and 26A of the Tax Credits (Claims and Notifications) Regulations 2002 (SI 2002/2014).

NEW BENEFIT RATES FROM APRIL 2021

NEW BENEFIT RATES FROM APRIL 2021

(Benefits covered in Volume I)

	April 2020	April 2021
	£ pw	£ pw
Disability benefits		
Attendance allowance		
higher rate	89.15	89.60
lower rate	59.70	60.00
Disability living allowance		
care component		
highest rate	89.15	89.60
middle rate	59.70	60.00
lowest rate	23.60	23.70
mobility component		
higher rate	62.25	62.55
lower rate	23.60	23.70
Personal independence payment		
daily living component		
enhanced rate	89.15	89.60
standard rate	59.70	60.00
mobility component		
enhanced rate	62.25	62.55
standard rate	23.60	23.70
Carer's allowance	67.25	67.60
Maternity benefits		
Maternity allowance		
standard rate	151.20	151.97

593

New Benefit Rates from April 2021

	April 2020 £ pw	April 2021 £ pw
Bereavement benefits and retirement pensions		
Widowed parent's allowance or widowed mother's allowance	121.95	122.55
Widow's pension		
standard rate	121.95	122.55
Retirement pension		
Category A or Category B (higher)	134.25	137.60
Category B (lower), Category C or Category D	80.45	82.45
New state pension	175.20	179.60
Dependency increases		
Child	11.35[1]	11.35[1]
Industrial injuries benefits		
Disablement benefit		
100%	182.00	182.90
90%	163.80	164.61
80%	145.60	145.32
70%	127.40	126.03
60%	109.20	109.74
50%	91.00	91.45
40%	72.80	73.16
30%	54.60	54.87
20%	36.40	36.58
unemployability supplement		
basic rate	112.55	113.10
increase for adult dependant	67.25	67.60
increase for child dependant	11.35[1]	11.35[1]
increase for early incapacity—higher rate	23.30	23.40
increase for early incapacity—middle rate	14.90	14.00
increase for early incapacity—lower rate	7.45	7.50
constant attendance allowance		
exceptional rate	145.60	146.40
intermediate rate	109.20	109.80
normal maximum rate	72.80	73.20
part-time rate	36.40	36.60

Note 1. These sums payable in respect of children are reduced if payable in respect of the only, elder or eldest child for whom child benefit is being paid (see reg.8 of the Social Security (Overlapping Benefits) Regulations 1979 on p.631 of Vol.1 of the main work).

	April 2020	April 2021
	£ pw	£ pw
exceptionally severe disablement allowance	72.80	73.20
reduced earnings allowance—*maximum rate*	72.80	73.16
retirement allowance—*maximum rate*	18.20	18.29

Death benefit
	April 2020	April 2021
widow's pension (higher rate) or widower's pension	134.25	137.60
widow's pension (lower rate)	40.28	41.28

Employment and support allowance

Contributory or "new-style" personal rates

	April 2020	April 2021
assessment phase—*aged under 25*	58.90	59.20
aged 25 or over	74.35	74.70
main phase	74.35	74.70

Components
	April 2020	April 2021
work-related activity	29.55	29.70
support	39.20	39.40

Income-related personal allowances
	April 2020	April 2021
single person—*aged under 25*	58.90	59.20
aged 25 or over	73.35	74.70
lone parent—*aged under 18*	58.90	59.20
aged 18 or over	74.35	74.70
couple—*both aged under 18*	58.90	59.20
both aged under 18, with a child	89.00	89.45
both aged under 18, (main phase)	74.35	59.20
both aged under 18, with a child (main phase)	116.80	117.40
one aged under 18, one aged 18 or over	116.80	117.40
both aged 18 or over	116.80	117.40

Premiums
	April 2020	April 2021
pensioner—*single person with no component*	99.40	102.40
couple with no component	148.40	152.90
enhanced disability—*single person*	17.10	17.20
couple	24.50	24.60
severe disability—*single person*	66.95	67.30
couple (one qualifies)	66.95	67.30
couple (both qualify)	133.90	134.60
carer	37.50	37.70

NEW BENEFIT RATES FROM APRIL 2021

(Benefits covered in Volume II)

	April 2020	April 2021
	£ pw	£ pw
Contribution-based and "new-style" jobseeker's allowance		
personal rates—*aged under 25*	58.90	59.20
aged 25 or over	74.35	74.70
Income support and income-based jobseeker's allowance		
personal allowances		
single person—*aged under 25*	58.90	59.20
aged 25 or over	74.35	74.80
lone parent—*aged under 18*	58.90	59.20
aged 18 or over	74.35	74.70
couple—*both aged under 18*	58.90	59.20
both aged under 18, with a child	89.00	89.45
one aged under 18, one aged under 25	58.90	59.20
one aged under 18, one aged 25 or over	74.35	74.70
both aged 18 or over	116.80	117.40
child	68.27	68.60
premiums		
family—*ordinary*	17.60	17.65
lone parent	17.60	17.65
pensioner—*single person (JSA only)*	99.40	102.40
couple	148.40	152.90
disability—*single person*	34.95	35.10
couple	49.80	50.05
enhanced disability—*single person*	17.10	17.20
couple	24.50	24.60
disabled child	26.60	26.67
severe disability—*single person*	66.95	67.30
couple (one qualifies)	66.95	67.30
couple (both qualify)	133.90	134.60
disabled child	65.52	65.94
carer	37.50	37.70

New Benefit Rates from April 2021

	April 2020 £ pw	April 2021 £ pw
Pension credit		
Standard minimum guarantee		
single person	173.75	177.10
couple	265.20	270.30
Additional amount for severe disability		
single person	66.95	67.30
couple (one qualifies)	66.95	67.30
couple (both qualify)	133.90	134.60
Additional amount for carers	37.50	37.70
Savings credit threshold		
single person	150.47	153.70
couple	239.17	244.12
Maximum savings credit		
single person	13.97	14.04
couple	15.62	15.71

NEW TAX CREDIT AND BENEFIT RATES 2021–2022

(Benefits covered in Volume IV)

	2020–21 £ pw	2021–22 £ pw
Benefits in respect of children		
Child benefit		
only, elder or eldest child (couple)	21.05	21.15
each subsequent child	13.95	14.00
Guardian's allowance	17.90	18.00
Employer-paid benefits		
Standard rates		
Statutory sick pay	95.85	96.35
Statutory maternity pay, Statutory paternity pay	151.20	151.97
Statutory shared parental pay	151.20	151.97
Statutory adoption pay	151.20	151.97
Income threshold	120.00	120.00

	2020–21 £ pa	2021–22 £ pa
Working tax credit		
Basic element	3,040[1]	2,005[1]
Couple and lone parent element	2,045	2,060
30 hour element	825	830
Disabled worker element	3,220	3,240
Severe disability element	1,390	1,400
Child care element		
maximum eligible cost for one child	*175 pw*	*175 pw*
maximum eligible cost for two or more children	*300 pw*	*300 pw*
per cent of eligible costs covered	*70%*	*70%*
Child tax credit		
Family element	545	545
Child element	2,830	2,845
Disabled child element	3,415	3,435
Severely disabled child element	4,800	4,825
Tax credit income thresholds		
Income threshold	6,530	6,565
Income threshold for those entitled to child tax credit only	16,385	16,480

Note 1. The 2020-21 figure for the basic element includes the £20 pw uplift provided for by s.77 of the Coronavirus Act 2020. In the Budget on March 3, 2021, it was announced that "a one-off payment of £500 to eligible Working Tax Credit claimants across the UK, to provide continued extra support over the next six months", would be made in place of the uplift.

NEW UNIVERSAL CREDIT RATES FROM APRIL 2021

(Benefits covered in Volume V)

	April 2020 £ pm	April 2021 £ pm
Standard allowances		
Single claimant—*aged under 25*	342.72[1]	257.33[1]
aged 25 or over	409.89[1]	324.84[1]
Joint claimant—*both aged under 25*	488.50[1]	403.93[1]
one or both aged 25 or over	594.09[1]	509.91[1]
Child element—*first child*	281.25	282.50
second/ subsequent child	235.83	237.08
Disabled child addition—*lower rate*	128.35	128.89
higher rate	340.29	402.41
Limited Capability for Work element	128.25	128.89
Limited Capability for Work and Work-Related Activity element	341.92	343.63
Carer element	162.92	163.73
Childcare element—*maximum for one child*	646.35	646.35
maximum for two or more children	1,108.04	1,108.04
Non-dependants' housing cost contributions	75.15	75.53
Work allowances		
Higher work allowance (no housing element)		
one or more children	512.00	515.00
limited capability for work	512.00	515.00
Lower work allowance		
one or more children	292.00	293.00
limited capability for work	292.00	293.00

Note 1. The 2020-21 figures for the single claimant and joint claimant standard allowances include the £20 pw uplift provided for by reg.3 of the Social Security (Coronavirus) (Further Measures) Regulations 2020 (SI 2020/371). In the Budget on March 3, 2021, it was announced that the uplift would be continued until the end of September 2021, which would increase each of the relevant 2020-21 figures by £86.67 pm until then.